FIGHTING FITT

Chris Ryder

THE BREHON PRESS
BELFAST

First published 2006 by The Brehon Press Ltd
1A Bryson Street, Belfast BT5 4ES, Northern Ireland

ISBN: 1 905474 11 3

Design: December Publications
Printed and bound by J.H. Haynes & Co Ltd, Sparkford

CONTENTS

For Richard Ford

AUTHOR'S NOTE

ONE DAY IN 1983, soon after he was elevated to the peerage, I was walking the opulent corridors of the House of Lords with Gerry Fitt when one of the policemen on guard duty stopped him to say there was an urgent message at the central lobby. At the next archway, another policeman advised that a messenger was roaming the corridors looking for him. 'Tell him I'm on my way to the Terrace Bar,' said Gerry.

Soon afterwards, as we were savouring the first gin of the day, the courier tracked him down and proffered a large, embossed envelope. 'My Lord,' he said deferentially as he handed it over. Gerry was meanwhile fumbling in his inside pocket from where he produced a scrap of paper. 'Can you look after that for me?' he said, pressing it into the messenger's hand.

'Certainly, My Lord.'

After the messenger had left, Gerry opened the envelope. I watched, expecting a great missive of state to tumble out, but all he extracted was a bundle of grubby banknotes and a handful of coins – his previous day's winnings on the horses, he explained. The scrap of paper was his follow-up bet for that day. This was the real Gerry Fitt, a man who never lost the common touch even when striding the most gilded corridors of power.

On that particular occasion I was with Gerry to discuss the writing of his autobiography. Not long before, Andre Deutsch, the celebrated London publisher, had given us lunch in his Dickensian offices in Bloomsbury and agreed terms for the book. It was a long and liquid affair, with Gerry holding court in his customary manner and reducing everyone to tears of laughter with his wit and stories.

Over the next few months, drawing on the contents of several long, unstructured interviews with Gerry and a body of other primary source material, such as my long acquaintance with him, my own observations of his life and times as a *Sunday Times* journalist, the Westminster and Stormont Hansards, newspaper cuttings and broadcast transcripts, I produced the first draft of a manuscript. The idea was that Gerry would read it and provide much more input to complete the book.

He didn't read it too closely himself, but his wife, Ann, did and was unimpressed. She thought there were so many 'I's' and 'me's' in the book that people in Belfast would think he had a big head. She was not persuaded that, as an autobiography, a first-person account of his life and times was unavoidable. In any case, she also took exception to some of the views he expressed about his contemporaries. It was not them she wished to spare, but their wives and children. As with everything else in his life, Ann's attitude was decisive and the book project was quietly abandoned. Thereafter it became the elephant in the room every time Gerry and I met – large as life, but rarely mentioned.

At that point I had known Gerry for the best part of twenty years, and for the next twenty there would be periodic promises from him to revive the book, re-visit the draft and do the necessary work to complete it. All came to nothing. So, recognising his great significance as one of the pivotal figures of modern Irish history, I quietly compiled a dossier of the stories with which he regaled his friends and his political recollections so that a biography could ultimately be published, most probably after his death.

The task was all the more important because Gerry was a man of conviction, not one of letters or great scholarship. He was an instinctive politician who spoke from the heart and off-the-cuff. Nothing was ever written down by him, save for a few scrawled notes on the back of an envelope or the margin of a newspaper, which were quickly discarded. There are few letters, no private papers and not much else of a personal archive by which to judge him.

This book is therefore aimed at putting on permanent record the life and times of one of the most colourful and notable politicians ever to parade the British and Irish political stages before the first-hand material on which it is based becomes eroded by time, and to provide an informed account for future historians to examine. It is also intended to be a tribute to a remarkable life of distinctive achievement, vision and extraordinary personal courage in the face of political intransigence, violence and terrorism.

I make no apology for my admiration of Gerry Fitt. Together with Paddy Devlin he was one of my closest friends and I learnt much from them both about political pragmatism, generosity, tolerance, reconciliation and bravery – qualities that are sadly all too scarce in the gene pool from which we draw our political representatives in Northern Ireland.

From my standpoint, this book is therefore not a rigorously critical or entirely objective account of Gerry Fitt's career, but I have nevertheless endeavoured to ensure that, while it is an affectionate one, it is also balanced and informative. It is primarily based on the draft autobiography, augmented by other material that is sourced throughout the text, notably the official records of the times. In gaining access to them, I must record my thanks for the assistance of the staff at the National Archives in London and Dublin and at the Public Record Office in

Belfast, especially David Huddleston, and I acknowledge material reproduced from the records they hold.

In putting together the account of Gerry's journeys as a merchant seaman during the Second World War I found a series of websites chronicling the composition and fate of hundreds of convoys to be most useful. I thank the enthusiasts who compiled them.

Walter Macauley, the former librarian at the *Belfast Telegraph*, now enjoying a well-earned retirement, not only assisted me in researching the original autobiography but helped me update it for this book, assistance for which I am most grateful.

My gratitude is also due to Austin Currie, Eugene McEldowney, Mick Skelton, Berkley Farr and Pat Devlin of the Lecale Historical Society, Lieutenant-Colonel Robin Bullock-Webster OBE, Regimental Adjudant of the Irish Guards, Danny Walsh, John Carmichael, Priscilla Baines and Mary Cummings for their help in unravelling various aspects of my subject's life.

Many other people have helped me with this task and I apologise to anyone whose name I have omitted. I wish to thank them for all for their assistance and to stress that, much as I appreciate their help, the comments I make and the conclusions I draw are entirely mine, except where specifically attributed to others.

Most of the images in the picture section were supplied by the Fitt family and the *Irish News*. Along with the publisher, I acknowledge the copyright and permissions granted to use text and illustrations in this book. Every effort had been made to trace and acknowledge copyright owners.

Brendan Anderson and Damian Keenan at Brehon Press are offered my appreciation in gargantuan measure for taking on publication of the book, and I thank Rachel Pierce for the insightful and efficient way in which she has edited the manuscript.

Above all I must acknowledge the co-operation of the 'Miss Fitts' – Eileen, Patsy, Betty and Geraldine – and thank them for sharing memories of their father and mother with me. Apart from Gerry's death in August 2005, they suffered a second great loss when their sister, Joan, died suddenly a mere two months later. I also appreciate the assistance of other members of Gerry's family circle.

Finally, I must thank my wife, Genny, for all her support, encouragement and tolerance. She is as much a tower of strength for me as Ann was for Gerry. As ever my children, Michelle, Paul, Declan and Edward, my son-in-law Colin, and grandchildren Ciara and Erin, took an abiding interest in the progress of 'the book'. I thank them for their encouragement.

Chris Ryder
Belfast
October 2006

CHAPTER ONE

AN EXTRAORDINARY ACT OF COMPASSION

LORD GERRY FITT CLAIMED – in *Who's Who* and the other standard reference books – that he was born on 9 April 1926. By his own account, he came into the world at the Jubilee, the maternity wing of the Belfast City Hospital, and was the third child in a family of six. The people he declared as his parents were George Fitt, a cigarette machine operator in Gallaher's tobacco factory in York Street, and his wife, the former Mary Ann Murphy, who was employed in domestic service. Earlier in his career, he often said he was born at home in Walbeck Street in the Dock constituency of Belfast. Neither version of his origins is entirely accurate, however, and both stories conceal a far more interesting and extraordinary ancestry, the privacy of which he guarded carefully through his long, eventful and very public life.

Although the official ledgers of the Northern Ireland Registrar-General faithfully record the Fitt-Murphy marriage at St Joseph's Catholic Church in Princes Dock Street, Belfast, on 11 August 1921 and the subsequent births of Elizabeth (Betty), George, Aloysius, Rita and Teresa between 1922 and 1931, they reveal no trace whatsoever of a Gerald, or indeed a Gerard (as he more usually described himself), Fitt, being born to them in 1926, or any other year. In fact, he could not have been born at the Jubilee, as he said, because, according to the *Ulster Medical Journal*, that maternity unit was not built until almost a decade later, in 1935. The entire medical establishment was not designated as the Belfast City Hospital until some time after 1939, during the Second World War. There is thus no record of his birth at either of these institutions.

The long-concealed fact is that Gerry Fitt – who was to become a Belfast councillor, MP at Stormont and Westminster, a peer of the realm and one of the pivotal figures in modern Irish history – was, officially at least, never born at all. What has never before been revealed is that he was actually born in the Infirmary of the Belfast Workhouse on 8 April 1926. His natural mother, who was unmarried, then christened him Gerald and he was baptised into the Catholic

Church, but they were quickly separated – whether willingly or not is unknown – and he was boarded out to the Fitt family, who later adopted him and reared him as their own. He took their surname and he, and later his wife and five daughters, unreservedly accepted the Fitts as his real family until his death in 2005.

During his lifetime, Fitt never revealed the truth about his origins – not even to his own daughters. By the social and moral standards of the times, both illegitimacy and dependence on the Workhouse were deeply ingrained stigmas, and even though any vestige of shame has long since been eradicated, for a man of Fitt's generation the topic remained sensitive and was always carefully avoided. Eileen, Fitt's second eldest daughter, remembers the day of her fiftieth birthday when her father brought her to the House of Lords for a celebratory drink:

> There had always been confusion about his birthday, whether it was the eighth or ninth of April and vague, passing references to the fact that he had been adopted as a baby. I asked him to tell me about it, but he refused. He said it wasn't important.

Fitt remained equally tight-lipped with his closest acquaintances, none of whom was ever told that he was adopted. Apart from the Fitt family members, the only person who fully shared his secret was his beloved wife, Ann, who also took the details to her grave. Despite this secrecy, it has been possible to assemble some facts about Fitt's origins from surviving official records.

According to the Northern Ireland Registrar-General's records, a single woman gave birth to a boy at 51 Lisburn Road, Belfast on 9 April 1926. Her name was Rose Martin and her occupation was given as 'servant'. The birth of a male infant was registered officially three days afterwards by James Mahood, described as the occupier of that address. The baby was not given the dignity of a name. The mother's age was not recorded, and her address was declared as 40 Chatham Street – then a sidestreet of spartan, terraced houses off Hooker Street, in the Crumlin Road area of the city. In the Belfast Street Directory of 1926 the resident of that address is listed as Mrs Magee. The location where Fitt was born, however – 51 Lisburn Road – was at that time one of the best-known and most notorious addresses in Belfast because it was the Union Workhouse and the man who registered the infant's birth was the Master of that austere and grim institution.

By the terms of the Poor Law Act 1838, every district in Ireland was required to establish a Board of Guardians, usually elected and funded by the ratepayers, to provide a Workhouse where the infirm and destitute could be looked after. They took a miserly approach to their task and in Belfast what meagre resources were available were dispensed by the thirty-four members of the Board of Guardians, who met every Tuesday at noon in the Union Workhouse 'to transact business connected with the institution and the dispensaries of the [Poor Law] union'. The Belfast Workhouse had opened in January 1841 with provision for 1,000 inmates, and was extended regularly thereafter to accommodate twice that number. Living conditions were harsh. The interior stone walls were whitewashed and the inmates slept on straw palliasses laid side by side on long wooden platforms. Applicants for admission, or for the grocery chits and rudimentary medicines provided for the non-resident needy and sick, were interrogated ruthlessly about their predicament, the questions based on the assumption that they were idle and feckless and out to exploit the good ratepayers of Belfast. Prosperous Protestants all, the Poor Law Guardians were also decidedly sectarian in their outlook. In the early 1900s, one of them, Mrs Lily Coleman, was notorious for frequently humiliating Catholic fathers with large families by remarking that there was 'no poverty under the blankets'.

The Workhouse registers record that Rose Martin, a single woman aged 30, and a Catholic, was admitted on 13 March 1926 at an advanced stage of pregnancy. In the first week of April, when she gave birth there were 2,453 inmates including 157 'lunatics, idiots and epileptics' and sixty-eight children, an equal number of girls and boys. The average cost of looking after each of them was 6s – 11d. During that particular week, eighteen inmates died and six other mothers gave birth. Indeed at that time the Guardians were concerned about the number of unmarried mothers who came to them for help. According to the Workhouse records, which survive at the Public Record Office in Belfast, there were an average of fifty women and their illegitimate children in residence at any time during the early 1900s. A contemporary report states that:

> Belfast is peculiarly situated with regard to this matter owing to the fact that there are a considerable number of young girls from the adjoining counties, employed as servants, factory and wareroom workers in the city, whose parents are in the country and with whom almost invariably the girls refuse to communicate when they are obliged to seek shelter in the workhouse for confinement or after confinement. These girls very often come into the Workhouse in the dead of night; apparently they don't want anyone to know where they are going.

Robert Wilson, the Master, recorded how he made it a rule to receive these young girls: 'One respectable girl from whom I had an application told me, after I had decided to admit her, that it was just as well I had done so, for had she been turned away she would have thrown herself into the river.' These pregnant women were sometimes boarded out for a time at the Guardians' expense, but when their children were due they were admitted to the Workhouse Infirmary, where they customarily gave birth with the assistance of a nurse and usually without the benefit of drugs, unless a doctor was called to deal with complications.

Within days of his birth, Rose Martin's baby was christened Gerald and baptised in the Infirmary by Fr J B Murray, a curate of the parish of St Brigid. He recorded the baptism in the register at the parochial house in nearby Derryvolgie Avenue naming Nurse Keenan as the child's sponsor. The name of the father was not recorded; no address or other details were entered for the mother.

However, the records reveal that shortly after his birth, Gerald Martin was taken from his natural mother and 'boarded out' to the Fitt family, a procedure that corresponds to what is known as fostering today. Rose Martin remained in the Workhouse for some time afterwards before being discharged on 12 August 1926.

Fitt's sensitivity about his origins prompted a lifelong cover-up. In 1936, when he was aged ten, he was confirmed at St Patrick's Church in Donegall Street, taking the name 'Joseph' to mark the reception of the sacrament, as was the custom. When he married Ann in 1947, he did not, as was customary, declare the name of his father for either the religious or civil registration of the union, because he most likely never knew it. Although his Christian name was recorded as 'Gerald' at baptism, by 1942 he was using the name 'Gerard' as his forename, which he did for the rest of his days, but the official 'Gerald' still appeared on his marriage certificate. He never fully explained his past to his family. His daughters recall some vague talk of his mother being from Cavan. (The only Rose Martin recorded in the all-Ireland birth registers for 1896 is listed as being born at Midleton, which is in Co. Cork.) They believe that his natural mother may have reclaimed him as an infant for a brief period, but that he failed to settle with her and was soon returned to his adoptive parents. Some forty years later, when Rose Martin reportedly attempted to make contact with her son again after he became an MP at Westminster, he refused to see her and for the rest of his life he refused to acknowledge her existence.

There were, though, some people in Belfast who were apparently aware of the true circumstances of Fitt's personal history. Mary Cummings, a close friend of the family for some forty years, remembers a man coming into her bakery and grocery shop on the Antrim Road soon after Fitt's 1966 election as a Westminster MP. The visitor told her that 'Fitt came from the wrong side of the blanket' and although she wondered why he had said this, she dismissed the remark as being without foundation. A few years later, in 1969, at the height of the civil disorder, an illegal pirate radio station operating from the Protestant Shankill Road area repeatedly played 'Nobody's Child' and dedicated the song to Fitt, who was MP for the area. Fitt complained angrily to the British authorities and requested that the army jam the station's transmissions. Given what is now known about his background, it is likely that his anger may well have stemmed from personal reasons rather than the political ones he gave at the time.

Whatever the truth of the situation, the Fitts were able to adopt the unwanted infant without difficulty because Northern Ireland did not introduce laws to prevent unofficial adoptions until 1931. Rescuing the infant from what would undoubtedly have been a tough life in institutions and taking him into their care was an extraordinary act of compassion and generosity by George and Mary Ann Fitt. They both came from impoverished, working-class backgrounds, lived in grinding penury and had to work extremely hard for the pittance they earned.

George Fitt was born in 1899, the son of a shipyard driller of the same name who lived at Donore Street. A year before George's birth, his father married Elizabeth McShane, a domestic servant and daughter of John McShane, a labourer, at St Patrick's Catholic church in Donegall Street. In August 1921 George Fitt married Mary Ann, the daughter of joiner John Murphy, who resided at 52 Marine Street in the shadow of Belfast's busy docks and shipyards. After their wedding at St Joseph's – known as the 'Chapel on the Quays' to the thousands of 'Sailortown' Catholics who lived in the densely packed rows of terraced streets surrounding it, the young couple moved in with George's widowed mother Elizabeth, into a small terrace house at 1 Walbeck Street, off the Antrim Road, in the New Lodge area just north of the city centre. The tiny house had no bathroom or running hot water and the toilet was outside in the backyard. George and Mary Ann's first child, Elizabeth (Betty), was born in 1922 followed by a son, George Patrick, in 1924. Two years later, they adopted Rose Martin's son. Thereafter, Gerald Martin was known as Gerry Fitt. For him, these people were his true family, 'Mum and Dad', and he remained devoted to them for the rest of his life. Accordingly, he erased all details of his natural mother from his life, as a result of which there are gaps that simply can't be explained: how his birth mother came to be in Belfast in the early 1920s, where she came from. These and other details about his real parents remain a mystery. In the end, no one can be sure if Fitt himself ever knew who his real father was.

Belfast in the early 1920s was a city divided by sectarianism and fear. On 7 June 1921 King George V opened the Northern Ireland Parliament and soon afterwards the Anglo-Irish Treaty confirmed the partition of Ireland. By the time of Fitt's birth in 1926, when the Duke of Abercorn was governor of Northern Ireland, Sir James Craig was Prime Minister and Alderman W.G. Turner lord mayor of Belfast, memories of the sectarian pogroms and widespread murder that attended partition were still raw and vivid. During these disturbances, Mary Ann's family had been driven from their comfortable house on the Limestone Road by an armed mob. They were fortunate to be able to arrange an exchange with a Protestant family that was evicted from Marine Street in the predominantly Catholic docks area.

In those days the only thing Belfast's Catholics and Protestants had in common was extreme poverty. Conditions were no better in the densely populated working-class Protestant areas than they were in the Catholic streets; penury and sickness were not discriminating. In the early 1920s, Fitt's adoptive grandfather and uncle, both skilled joiners, his aunt and a baby cousin all died within one week during an influenza epidemic. George Fitt was lucky to have a job and a wage coming in, however paltry, not least because very few Catholics worked in Gallaher's tobacco factory in York Street. In 1926 unemployment in Northern Ireland was at 23.3% – twice what it was in Britain – and assistance for the poor and unemployed was not as generous or well-organised as it is today. Looking back to the divisive social and political situation into which he was born, Fitt recalled:

> In this atmosphere you quickly got a feeling of being part of a tribe. We believed that the Protestants had things better than us, that they got all the jobs. From our street you could see the gantries of the Belfast shipyards where we were told only Protestants worked. The sense of division surfaced in our play. I remember turning a skipping-rope chanting rhyme to the tune of 'If you're Irish, come into the parlour'. It went: 'If your name is Timothy or Pat, you won't get a job in the shipyard, with a Catholic name like that.'

The Fitts were a devout Catholic family and observing the rituals of their faith was paramount. Every night they recited the rosary together, a litany of 'Our Fathers' and 'Hail Marys' divided into five decades and counted on rosary beads: 'It was the practice that my granny, whom we lived with, would slip out to the scullery after the fourth decade and put on the kettle for tea afterwards. One night the rosary ended in a shambles when she stood on my chilblains, causing me to roar with pain.' Every Sunday they all went to Mass at St Patrick's Church, Donegall Street, dressed up in Sunday-best outfits run up their mother, who was 'a wizard with the sewing machine'. As he got older, young Fitt often broke away from them after church and walked through the quiet city to the Queen's Bridge, where he would watch the cross-channel steamers tied up along Donegall Quay. Already he was dreaming of going to sea.

The rituals of Catholicism were important to families like the Fitts, as were the manifestations of Protestantism for their neighbours. Every July, or the 'mad month' as Fitt quickly learned to call it, sectarian feeling in the city reached a peak when the Orange Order marchers took to the streets. The climax came on 'The Twelfth' when the Order celebrated the victory of Protestant King William of Orange over the Catholic King James at the Battle of the Boyne in 1690. Fitt remembered a particular year when the service in St Patrick's was almost drowned out by the noise of Orange bandsmen, who halted outside thumping their drums louder and louder: 'When we came out of church, there was an air of tension, of something about to happen, then the bricks and stones began to fly.' One of his most vivid memories is of July 1932, the year of the Eucharistic Congress in Belfast:

> Our area was decorated with papal flags and yellow-and-white bunting, the papal colours. There were makeshift altars in most streets and people had taken statues of the Blessed Virgin Mary and the Sacred Heart from their homes to decorate them. It all must have cost a pretty penny and some sacrifice by the neighbours, for money was not plentiful. However, there was a tremendous feeling of community and solidarity and the Catholic colours contrasted starkly with the red, white and blue in the Protestant areas. I never remember the Catholic areas being decorated like that again.

Another 'Twelfth' significantly coloured his attitude to the forces of law and order. The Orange lodges and their bands walked across Belfast to the 'field' in the south of the city, where they assembled and heard political speeches. One Twelfth morning Gerry went to watch them:

> I had not been there very long when a big B-Special gave me a slap on the ear and chased me away round the corner into the Catholic area, from where I could only hear the bands. This confirmed the feeling of division I had begun to sense. This was their day. An ascendant tribe was on the march. The way the B-Special chased me widened the gulf further for me. The police, the Royal Ulster Constabulary and the B-men, as the exclusively Protestant special constabulary was known, were 'their' police, not 'ours'. Some Catholics were so terrified of them they used to cross the street to avoid them.

The same lines of division dominated education as Catholics and Protestants attended separate, segregated schools. Fitt started his education at the Star of the Sea Convent primary school on Hallidays Road, which catered only for Catholics. Nevertheless, getting home every afternoon, although it was only a short distance, meant running the gauntlet of bigger, Protestant boys from neighbouring schools, and there weren't many days free of fisticuffs between the rival pupils.

By the time Fitt started school his father had been forced to leave his job in Gallaher's – expelled along with the few other Catholic employees, during one of the periodic bouts of sectarian disturbances. He was fortunate to obtain a new job quickly, this time supervising a gang of Belfast Corporation workmen. But one day, in 1932, a heavy paving-stone fell on him and broke his foot. The injury turned gangrenous but his fear of doctors, nurses and surgical instruments meant he would not allow them to amputate the foot to save his life. After a lengthy illness, complicated by tuberculosis, he died on 8 September 1934 in The Abbey, a sanatorium at Whiteabbey on the north-east fringe of Belfast. He was just thirty-four years old.

> I vividly remember the night his coffin was brought to St Patrick's to lie before the altar. Next day he had a big, respectable funeral because of his trade union links and membership of the local Labour party. My brothers and I felt very well-to-do in the seats of honour we had in the procession of horses and carriages along Carrick Hill and up the Falls Road to Milltown Cemetery.

Fitt often asked himself if his father had been foolish. 'With one leg he would not have been able to work or look after us. I do not know. The reality of the situation however was that my mother, who had already struggled for two years without wages, was left with six of us to feed and rear with no breadwinner.'

Mary Ann Fitt started working full-time as a domestic help in 'the big houses' further up the Antrim Road, earning about two shillings a day. 'I can vividly recall her arriving home exhausted from doing big washings and other chores and then setting about looking after us. Although there was poverty in our house, I can never remember being hungry.' The family lived on basics like porridge, stew, potatoes, tea, bread and margarine, with no sweets, buns or puddings, except at Christmas time. Billy John Stewart, a Protestant from Donore Street who had been a friend of George's, kept greyhounds and exercised them every day over Cave Hill. He always came back from these trips with hares for the family. Those succulent meals were lapped up in the Fitt household, where the meat was stewed, roasted, boiled, jugged or in soup, even for Christmas dinner. Another culinary benefactor was Scotty Logan, a fish-seller. Friday was his busiest day because Catholics were forbidden to eat meat that day. 'If his big, wooden box of Ardglass herrings had not been sold by Monday, I used to drag it down to our house and we would have a big tuck-in,' recalled Gerry.

Mary Ann couldn't keep the whole family on her own so to help the ever-tight family budget, Gerry managed to get a job in Cooper's grocery shop in Dawson Street. Every morning at 7.30am he did deliveries for two hours before going to school, first on foot, then later on a bicycle when he had learned to ride one. He also worked for Cooper's most evenings, from 8.00pm until as late as 11.00pm earning about half-a-crown a week (two shillings and sixpence in old money; $12^{1}/2$p today). There were bonuses, however. Early on a Sunday morning he would deliver the milk. In those days, before the advent of the milk bottle or carton, people who could afford what was called 'sweet milk' put a container on the window-ledge the night before. Fitt's job was to go door-to-door, filling these containers with a half-pint measure from a two-gallon can:

> Now working-class families like us would never have sweet milk. We poured sticky, condensed milk into our tea so the taste of this fresh, sweet milk was something of a novelty for me. I therefore 'bulled' my can with a pint of water before leaving the shop and, taking further advantage of the owner, who lay in late on Sundays, I would fill my pockets with Peek Frean wafers by rifling the biscuit tins in the shop. Then halfway round my deliveries I would find a quiet spot and have my weekly feast.

His feast was marred by just one thing: conscience. The devout Catholic values being drummed into him at home and at school and the fact that, at eight years of age, he had made his First Confession and Holy Communion, led the young Fitt to eventually feel guilty about what he was doing. He duly decided he had better own up next time he went to confession:

> But when I told Father Bradley at St Patrick's what I was doing with the milk, I got the distinct impression that he was not all that seriously perturbed by my sin. He asked me lots of questions about how much milk was in the large can and how much water I put in. Indeed, I think at one point he was indirectly warning me not to get too greedy and get caught.

Torn between the priest's leniency, his conscience and the obvious pleasures of his

Sunday breakfast, Fitt hit upon what he innocently took to be a compromise:

> St Patrick's was a big parish, with six priests, all of whom had their own
> confession box around the sides of church. So I decided to go to a different
> priest each week. But the plot misfired very quickly when Father Bradley
> took over the box of another priest who was away. 'I thought you told me
> you were going to stop that,' he said sharply upon hearing the now-familiar
> declaration of guilt. For the rest of my life, I had a picture in my mind of
> the priests sipping their port around a blazing fire after Saturday night
> confessions. 'Have you had wee Fitt yet?' asks one. 'Oh, the wee boy
> watering the milk,' says another and they all laughed heartily.

The fact that he was earning money and contributing to the household was very
important: 'It made me feel very grown up, the man of the family,' he would say
later. However, the pressures on his hard-pressed mother, working full-time and
trying to look after six children single-handedly, inevitably meant Fitt had a great
deal of unsupervised freedom and, naturally enough, he often got into mischief.
School had few attractions for him, especially as his fellow pupils called him 'speccy
four-eyes' and other such names because he wore glasses on account of a 'buckle'
or 'turn' in his left eye. According to Fitt, this condition developed when he was a
baby: 'I was lying asleep in my pram during a visit to a farm owned by relatives in
Maghera and I woke up to find a donkey braying at me. Frightened silly, I began
to cry, went into convulsions and my eye turned.' (There is some, unproven
suspicion that this traumatic incident may actually have taken place during the
short period when he was returned to his natural mother. According to vague
allusions Fitt made to his daughters at various times, after this incident he kept
crying and asking to go back to 'mine's own mammy', meaning Mary Ann Fitt.)

By his own account, Gerry spent more time 'mitching' from school than he did
in the classroom:

> After my early morning stint at the grocery shop, I would make a great
> pretence of collecting my schoolbag and going off to class. Instead I would
> head for Alexandra Park, hide my bag in the bushes and play. If anyone
> tackled me about not being at school, I fibbed, 'My wee sister has got scarlet
> fever and I'm not allowed to go.'

One day, however, fearing contagion a park-keeper expressed serious reservations
about his presence and Fitt had to run away to avoid being frog-marched either
home or to school. Of course, before long he was inevitably found out after
somebody stole his schoolbag from its hiding place and he was forced to confess
the loss of the expensive books inside. The result was a transfer to St Patrick's
School, beside St Patrick's Church, in Donegall Street. Twelve-year-old Gerry and
his younger brother, Aloysius, were enrolled there on 28 February 1938. The
school was run by the Christian Brothers, who had a reputation for a high
standard of education achieved, it was said, by 'hammering' the lessons into their

pupils by cane and strap. The new school, like the old one, was an uninteresting, uphill struggle for Fitt, who found the Irish language as incomprehensible as all the other subjects he was required to study. Unfortunately, and contrary to the printed instructions for keeping the school register, his teachers documented only the sparsest details about his time at the school. There is no daily record of his attendances or absences. All that was recorded was that he had achieved Standard IV by June 1938 and Standard V by June 1939. There is no formal record of when he left school, or what he was going to do thereafter.

If his mother hoped the Brothers would academically inspire or motivate her son, she was to be disappointed. About the same time as he joined St Patrick's he founded 'RABCA' – the Royal Avenue Butt Collectors Association. On dry nights, he and his friends would scour the streets of the city centre for cigarette ends – butts, they called them – which were diligently collected and the dregs recycled into one new cigarette. It was the root of an addiction that would see him smoke his way through eighty cigarettes a day for many years.

Another act of boyhood mischief had far more serious consequences. His mother was forever warning him not to play in a nearby factory yard. One Sunday afternoon, defying her yet again, he was walking across a glass roof when he tumbled through it and fell 30ft, landing in the back of a lorry. Nursing a badly cut thigh, he pulled himself out of the lorry, climbed a wall and made his way to the Mater Hospital, half-a-mile away. The doctors diagnosed a ruptured artery and muscle injuries and for a time it was feared he would never walk again, as repeated operations to repair the damage failed. He did recover but the episode left a lasting scar on his inner left thigh, which was later recorded as a distinguishing mark on his various official identity documents when he joined the Merchant Navy. Fitt always maintained that the real hero of his recovery was his mother, who went against advice to put him into a home so she could look after him herself. 'She fought the idea like a Trojan, despite her financial difficulties,' he recalled. By this stage, the family was in financial dire straits. As was a common enough occurrence at the time, Mary Ann was behind with the rent and when the arrears reached £5, a court summons was delivered.

> She couldn't afford to take the time off work so Betty, my older sister, who was then about thirteen, was kept off school for the day to attend in her place, but Betty was bewildered by the complexity of the courts and found the right one just in time to hear the magistrate issue a decree giving us a month to get out of the house. It was served on my mother later that day by a court officer. So by the time I had recovered and left hospital, we had moved to a large, cheaper house on the Crumlin Road where we lived in two rooms, sharing the cooking and washing facilities with the other tenants.

The ever-industrious Fitt found another job as soon as he was able, this time selling the *Belfast Telegraph*. Apart from touring the pubs and hopping on and off the trams, one of the places he used sell the papers was outside the Lyceum picture house on the New Lodge Road. This was in a mainly Protestant area and there was a big fellow called Bickerstaff who used to get very angry at this cheeky Catholic diving in among the crowds to sell his papers. One night Bickerstaff caught Fitt waiting for the cinema crowd to emerge and challenged him to a fight. They adjourned down a back street but, as soon as Fitt set his bundle of papers down on the ground, he was hit 'an unmerciful thump on the nose' by his assailant, who then ran off: 'I was left with my nose bleeding profusely over my stock of papers, so with a handkerchief in one hand and the best of the papers turned inside out to hide the bloodstains, I tried to cut my losses and get rid of them.'

The night the Second World War was declared, on 3 September 1939, was his most successful as a paperboy:

> I sold ten dozen copies, more than three times the normal. I had a bike then and I remember riding through the heavy rain, with the papers under my cape, shouting: 'War declared.' I was quite excited, not least because I had made a right few bob. But an old man quickly punctured my mood. 'There'll be a lot of people dead before this lot is over,' he said. 'I know, I was in the last one.'

Around this time and just before Fitt was due to leave school, one of the Christian Brothers sent for his mother and told her that her son was very good at English and, indeed, had an unusual command of words for his age. He offered to enrol him in St Mary's, a more advanced school. Despite his mother's encouragement, Fitt just wanted out of school as quickly as possible and when he was old enough to go to sea: 'I think she was secretly pleased that I wanted to leave because she could be doing with the few shillings I would earn. So I finished school and began my first proper job soon afterwards as a six shilling a week message boy for a firm in East Belfast.'

Belfast's industrial engineering base was quickly geared up to assist the war effort, especially by making ships and aircraft, but the Second World War did not hit the city in earnest until Easter weekend 1941, when over 1,000 people died in air raids aimed principally at the shipyards, which were playing a crucial role in equipping the British Royal Navy:

> That weekend I recall watching about 200 volunteers from the Irish Republic march from the Great Northern Railway in Great Victoria Street, where the Europa hotel now stands, to the lodging house in Carrick Hill, used for down-and-outs. They were billeted there for a night before being shipped to England for training and then to war. Later in the evening I shouted, 'Invasion, there's a paratrooper,' as I watched a parachute float earthwards. I was brought to my senses by an air raid warden who shouted to everyone to get down. It was in fact a landmine, which devastated Marshall's Buildings in Donegall Street, opposite St Patrick's. Nobody was

badly hurt by that but we were all showered with debris and the place shook. Up around the corner there was blind panic at Carrick House after the explosion. In those days the inmates were locked in at night and when I reached there they were tearing at the window grilles to get out. I directed many terrified young fellows, with broad southern brogues, back to the station and they abandoned their plans to go to war. Over the next few days rescuers clawed through the rubble of whole streets and I watched as two young children, who had been saved by a crashing beam from being buried, were taken out alive.

The Fitts were then living at 66 York Street, on the fringe of the vulnerable docks and harbour area, and with their house too badly damaged to be habitable and the fear of being caught in further raids, they joined the massive exodus of people from the city. They eventually ended up in a disused farmhouse owned by John Hutton at Taughlea, Bell's Hill, in the townland of Dunnanelly, some 30 miles from Belfast. There they forged an affectionate link with the place that would last for Fitt's lifetime. Although born and bred in the city, Mary Ann Fitt took to rural life 'like a demon possessed', as he later described it, and was soon rearing goats and hens.

By then Fitt had moved from the message boy's job to being a soap boy in Billy Esler's barber shop in Donegall Street. Dressed in a smart white coat, his job was to sweep up the hair cuttings from the floor, run the basins full of hot water and soap-up the customers waiting to be shaved with Billy's cut-throat razor, which he sharpened constantly on a leather hanging by the door. Thanks to tips from the customers, wealthy lawyers, businessmen and the like, he was usually able to double his basic weekly wage of six shillings.

One morning in March 1942, just a month short of his sixteenth birthday, he was staring idly out the window as he soaped up a man for shaving when he noticed his older brother, George, beckoning him to come outside. 'Come on quick, Gerry,' he said. 'I've got you a job as a fireman on a ship.'

> I could hardly believe my ears. I went back into the shop, put an extra layer of soap on the man waiting for a shave, hung up my white coat and said I was slipping out to the bookmakers down the street. Then I came out the door and ran all the way to the York Dock.

His idol was Davy Nelson, one of his neighbours at 12 Walbeck Street, who was in the Royal Navy. From an early age, Gerry had seen him walking along the street, resplendent in his bell-bottomed trousers and naval uniform and he was hugely impressed by this display. 'From the age of eight I had really wanted to go to sea. When I was mitching school, from Alexandra Park, I could see Belfast Lough and I used to longingly watch the ships manoeuvring up and down between the lines of marker buoys on their way to and from the open sea over the horizon, and that horizon was always like a magnet pulling me towards it.' Now he was on his way.

'Hallo, son. How are you doing?' asked the chief engineer as he went on board the *Theems*, a captured German coaster bound for Salford at the inland end of the Manchester Ship Canal.

'I had never met an Englishman before and I was surprised how friendly he was,' remembered Gerry.

'What age are you?' asked the engineer.

'Seventeen,' Gerry lied, drawing himself up to his fullest height. 'After a funny look, which showed he did not really believe me, he nodded assent. I was accepted. George and my brother-in-law, Abe Mohamed, a seaman who had married my sister, Betty, took me below to show me my duties and bunk.' Soon afterwards, the ship slipped her moorings and chugged out into Belfast Lough:

> I sat on the deck, watching for the first time the receding skyline of my native Belfast. I felt as if I was escaping into the real world from a mental and physical ghetto. My excitement and elation were beyond measure. I looked over the side into the sea and was surprised to find the water was green, not deep blue, as I had expected.

During the voyage, George and Abe explained how they had secured the vacancy for him. On previous trips they had harassed the third fireman, pouring cold water over him in the stoke hole and making it quite clear they wanted him to leave. 'I did not care. I was as happy as could be helping them shovel coal into the boilers.' Some hours out of Belfast a message from the Captain announced that he had just received a communication warning that there was a German submarine in the vicinity. Gerry remembers:

> We put on our lifejackets and suddenly the sobering reality of war had intruded. I felt very vulnerable sitting on the deck of that coaster in the middle of the Irish Sea thinking that somewhere under the waves the captain of a U-boat might be looking at us through his periscope preparing to fire a torpedo. I could not help thinking of the difference between the peaceful bustle in the barber shop and the stark threat of sinking. I remembered too the man I sold the paper to on the first night of the war and what he had said about people dying.

In the event, nothing happened. The ship soon reached the comparative safety of the Salford docks:

> I was enjoying myself again, chain-smoking from a tin of unrationed Woodbine cigarettes. When I stepped ashore, my first footing outside Ireland, I felt really grown-up, one of the boys. I walked across with George and Abe to the Black Bull and confidently downed my first pint of English beer. I quickly re-ordered and was only halfway through the second when I collapsed, dead drunk.

CHAPTER TWO

MURMANSK COCKTAILS

FOR THE NEXT FEW MONTHS life was 'fine and fulfilling', as Fitt later put it, plying between Belfast and Salford with cargoes of coal and earning the magnificent sum of £24-10s a month. But eventually the *Theems* went into dry dock and he had to return to Belfast and apply for a discharge book. There the dream ended. It was discovered that he had falsely declared himself to be a year older than he actually was and as seventeen was the minimum age for working in the stoke hole 'the only way I could stay at sea was to take a position as a junior cabin boy and a substantial drop in wages'. But the sea was truly in his blood now and in 1943 he signed on for his first deep-sea trip aboard the *Empire Chapman,* an 8,194-tonne Ocean Class tanker, built by Harland and Wolff in Belfast and launched in 1942. It was one of hundreds of merchant ships with the '*Empire*' prefix which had been hastily commissioned by the Ministry of War Transport after the outbreak of hostilities in 1939 as part of the effort to increase merchant tonnage and the capacity to run desperately needed raw materials into the United Kingdom. Winston Churchill had declared on 27 January 1942, 'But for the Merchant Navy, who bring us the food and munitions of war, Britain would be in a parlous state and indeed, without them, the Army, Navy and Air Force could not operate.' Later that year, Allied Merchant Navy shipping losses were estimated at 1,664 merchant ships, totalling 7,790,697 gross registered tonnes – a peak that exceeded recorded losses for any other year during the Second World War. The majority of these losses were in the Atlantic Ocean, where German submarines, the notorious *Unterseeboots* or U-boats, sank 1,006 Allied ships, mainly British.

This was the bloody conflict in which the young Gerry Fitt now became involved. Many of the ships lost were sister vessels of the *Empire Chapman* (renamed the *British Commando* after the war). By the time, Fitt signed on for a trip to South America, the ship had already made several hazardous Atlantic crossings. These trips, which could take as long as fourteen days in each direction, were undertaken in convoys, containing as many as eighty heavily laden ships spread out over a five-mile radius. For security reasons, the ship's name was not painted on the hull but instead put on two hinged Convoy Boards, mounted on either side of the bridge, which could be displayed in port but folded over at sea. Each convoy was surrounded and escorted by a heavily armed flotilla of Royal Navy corvettes, which circled back and forth alongside the cargo ships, 'like sheepdogs guarding a flock', as Fitt described it. The outside ships trailed large protective nets alongside to help prevent torpedoes smashing into their hulls. The main defence against the prowling U-boats were the high-explosive depth charges which were ejected into the water from launchers, or 'throwers' as they were known, at the stern of the corvettes. These warships, and many of the merchant vessels, were also equipped with deck and anti-aircraft guns to deal with attacks from the surface of the sea or air. When 'action stations' was called, the merchant seamen, including Fitt, pulled on lifejackets and tin helmets to man the guns.

After his stint on the *Empire Chapman*, Fitt's first transatlantic trip took him to Montreal aboard a ship called the *Parkhaven*. During the voyage the convoy was attacked by a 'wolf-pack' of German submarines and, as Fitt recalled it, the escort corvettes sallied around the convoy perimeter, dropping barrages of depth charges. Deep down in the ship's coal bunkers and boiler room, Fitt and the other crewmen could see nothing of the exchanges:

> When the ship was shaken from stern to bow by the bangs there was no way of knowing if it was our depth charges or one of their torpedoes. After every bang there were agonising seconds when we looked anxiously at the plates fearing they would burst open signifying a hit.

During one such barrage, Fitt came down from the bunker, where he had been shovelling coal, to make tea for the firemen down in the stoke hole.

> As I was pouring it, my rosary beads fell out of my pocket and one of the firemen, who was very friendly to me despite being a Belfast Protestant, lifted them and waved them around asking: 'What are they?'
>
> 'You know very well,' I replied making a grab for them, but the fireman avoided me and continued waving the beads around.
>
> 'Do you think if a tin-fish [torpedo] came in here, these would save you?' he asked.
>
> 'No, but they might stop one,' I said.
>
> 'Go on up there and fill that bunker,' he said, putting the beads in his pocket.
>
> 'What about my beads?' I said to him.
>
> 'Go on. Fill the bunker,' insisted the fireman.

When Fitt retold the story in later life he would say: 'I went off thinking that for a Protestant, he wasn't all that much of a disbeliever.' Like many other seamen who experienced such fraught days at sea, Fitt developed a great sense of superstition, and for the rest of his life he carried a battered little purse, in what he always called 'my arse pocket', containing the collection of relics, coins, religious medals and other good luck tokens he accumulated over the years. In July 1944 Fitt joined the *Drina*, a 9,789-tonne Royal Mail Lines refrigerated cargo carrier, which had been launched on 30 December 1943 and just recently delivered to its owners:

> I remember us putting into Lisbon in neutral Portugal. Before going ashore we were lectured about security and secrecy and advised on the bars to avoid because German spies frequented them, plying sailors with drink to get information about convoy movements. Well, once ashore they were the very bars the seamen made for. The prospect of free drink was irresistible, even if it was Hitler ultimately buying it, for the lads thought that, even drunk, they were too cute to let anything slip that would be of value to the enemy.

On Christmas Eve 1944 he was off again into another danger zone, this time to Greenock, near Glasgow, to join a ship, the *Nacella*, a 12,196-tonne fuel tanker, in one of the convoys forming up to go to Russia – unarguably the most gruelling and dangerous of the Merchant Navy's wartime assignments. Apart from the menace of the U-boats and extensive minefields, the ships had to traverse some of the most inhospitable waters in the world strewn with icebergs and subject to extremes of weather. It was a bitterly cold, windy night when Fitt and Bertie Girvan, the son of a Ballyclare publican, who had signed on with him, clambered aboard the blacked-out vessel and there was no sign of life: 'We went up and down the dark deck shouting greetings, looking for the crew quarters and trying doors, but all were locked and there was no response. Finally, at a locked door marked "Cook", a small man dressed in chef's clothing opened up. "What's all the shouting about? Do you think we're all deaf?" he asked.'

Fitt recognised at once that the man was pretty drunk and they followed him inside where he lifted a Black and White Scotch whisky bottle down from the shelf behind him as they dropped their kit-bags on the floor. 'Have a drink,' he said hospitably, pouring two bumper measures into half-pint tumblers. Fitt nudged Girvan and winked, signalling it might not be too bad a trip after all. Fitt raised his glass. 'Happy Christmas,' he said before taking a big swig, but as the liquid went into his mouth, it took his breath away. 'I felt it burn down through my chest and into my stomach. It was a fair few moments before I could ask, "What's that?" "Cargo," replied the cook nonchalantly.'

Fitt explained: 'That was in fact my introduction to "Murmansk cocktails". I found out later it was the done thing on the Russia-bound fuel tankers to siphon off some "cargo", i.e. high-octane petrol, when the ship was being loaded or unloaded. Doctored with brown sugar, it looked just like the real thing.' For years afterwards, Fitt attributed the onset of his receding hairline to the effect of these 'fiery cocktails'.

In the days after Fitt and Girvan joined the ship it travelled up the west coast of Scotland to a rendezvous on the northernmost coast at Loch Ewe, where it met with thirty-seven other merchantmen in what was designated Convoy JW 63. This shipment to Russia included not only the fuel aboard the *Nacella* and other tankers but hundreds of lorries, tanks and armoured personnel carriers, as well as other materials of war for the Russian Red Army. The completed convoy finally moved out towards the Arctic Sea on 30 December, escorted by six destroyers and three corvettes. Two days later a cruiser, an aircraft carrier and six more British destroyers joined the flotilla. Also deployed with them were two Canadian warships, and one from Norway.

Under what was an unusually heavy level of protection, the entire convoy reached the Kola inlet safely on 8 January 1945, from where the ships put into either Archangel or Murmansk to be offloaded. While in port, the crewmen were allowed ashore, where they were entertained at Intourist seamens' missions by hostesses who spoke fluent English and doled out a drink ration of three large vodkas from earthenware jugs. Unknown to their hostesses, the seamen were topping up the vodka with their own 'cargo', smuggled ashore in considerable quantity in anything that was spill-proof. 'The Russians must have thought we were poor drinkers who couldn't hold our drink because every night, thanks to our top-ups, we ended up very drunk, singing John McCormack songs at the tops of our voices as we staggered back to our ship,' laughed Fitt.

The American ships on the other hand were dry, except for beer, so the American sailors were pining for a real drink. Fitt and his colleagues obliged by bartering quantities of their 'brew' for high quality, warm underwear, dungarees, pullovers, shirts and other clothing that was rationed at home but easily available to the Americans. There was a salutary reminder of how dangerous it was to drink the 'cargo' however. On the day they were leaving for home, Fitt was on deck watching the convoy form up when his skipper told him that a burial at sea was taking place: 'I watched as, off our starboard deck, the body of a young US sailor was committed to the icy water. It was literally a sobering moment for we heard that he had died from a heart attack after drinking a bottle of adulterated petrol.'

In all, Fitt completed five trips on those dangerous convoys to Russia. In spite of the thick Arctic clothing, balaclavas, gloves and anoraks they wore, the crewmen still suffered from the intense cold: 'I remember one young fellow whose hand was frozen to the rail.' The work was hard and dirty on those coal-burning ships. As a fireman/trimmer, Fitt worked either in the intense heat from the boilers or on the dirty blackness of the bunker, shovelling coal by the light of a paraffin lamp.

Overnight on 16/17 February 1945, the *Nacella* was one of thirty-three ships mustered in the Kola inlet to begin another hazardous return journey to the Clyde. Ahead of the convoy were two Royal Navy warships – the *Alnwick Castle* and the *Lark* – as well as several aircraft conducting an air-sea hunt for U-boats lurking in the path of the convoy. It proved to be an eventful twenty-four hours. Soon after the operation started, the ships detected and attacked *U425*, devastating the submarine and its entire crew. Not long afterwards, however, *Lark* was torpedoed and crippled by *U968*, although her crew survived. The same submarine then attacked one of the merchantmen, the American-registered *Thomas Scott*. The ship was in ballast but carrying forty refugee passengers, as well as its crew. The Americans ensured all crew and evacuees got safely into lifeboats, and they were all rescued by a British destroyer before the ship sank. That afternoon, with the convoy pressing on, Fitt was off-duty and standing idly on deck, staring across the water at neighbouring ships while waiting for a kettle to boil. 'Suddenly there was a blinding flash. It was one of our escorting ships. It took a direct hit.' The casualty this time was HMS *Bluebell*, a 925-tonne corvette that had been in service since 1940. The torpedo came from *U711*, and from the eighty-six sailors on board there was only one survivor.

Over the next few days bad weather eased the threat of submarine or air attack, but the hurricane-force winds damaged several ships and caused the convoy to break its formation. After another few days, when the weather had eased, a force of twenty-five Junkers torpedo-bombers attacked, but none of the ships was hit although they did manage to strike one straggling US vessel, the 7,177-tonne *Henry Bacon*, and it went down. Sixty-four survivors were rescued, but the captain and some twenty crew, including many of the gunners, were lost. The ship, which was named after the American architect who designed many monuments, including Washington's Lincoln Memorial, was the last Allied casualty of the war.

Serving on the tankers, which Fitt did several times, was regarded as the most hazardous assignment:

> The theory was that empty, with only air in the tanks, you were a less valuable target, so you were given an outside position in the convoy. This of course made the ship more vulnerable to surprise attack by submarine. Alternatively, loaded up with oil or petrol, although in a more favourable inside position, if you were hit, the ship just exploded in a fireball leaving little chance of survival or rescue.

In May 1945, when the end of the war was declared, Girvan and Fitt were in New York: 'We had gone ashore one night in Philadelphia and got back to the docks only in time to watch the *Nacella* sailing away without us. We stayed in the United States for three months, escaping imprisonment as illegal immigrants, through the good offices of the British Consul.' During their unplanned sojourn in New York they lived at The Battery, a seamen's hostel near Staten Island. There was a hospital nearby called The Bellevue and from time to time, when they let it be known their blood bank had run dry, there was a stampede of seamen to its doors, attracted by the $5 they paid for every pint:

> I still have doubts about the value the hospital got for its money given the

amount some of the donors drank. However, selling my blood became a useful source of revenue at that time, although I once overdid it, fainting in the street after donating my third pint in a week. Girvan and I also earned a few easy dollars in the Irish pubs at Columbus Circle, where we were handsomely tipped and provided with ample free drink for rendering maudlin Irish songs.

By September, when VJ day was celebrated, Fitt was back home in Belfast: 'People had been horrified by the two A-bombs, but when the Japanese surrendered the city erupted. Crowds at the City Hall cheered and sang so loudly they drowned the hoots of the ship sirens in the harbour.' By the end of the year, peace had engendered a new sense of hope and liberation and Fitt, now almost twenty years of age, took stock of his life and tried to come to terms with the bewildering images of conflict and human degradation he had encountered and the differing political and social ideologies used to explain or condemn them:

> I never seriously thought of dying when I was at sea but realised just how many nasty scrapes I had been in and how fortunate I was to have survived. On a trip from Naples to Leghorn, near Pisa, where I had seen the famous leaning tower, we missed a live mine by yards after it was spotted by another tanker. My experiences of conflict had by then convinced me of the futility of war – the pointlessness of young men like me trying to kill identical young men on the other side. My lifelong opposition to war or violence as a way of settling problems was rooted then.

Fitt had also developed an aversion to what he had come to regard as the sterility of nationalism and class structures:

> In the aftermath of the liberation of Europe, I saw rock-bottom human degradation. I had been amazed when people in Naples pleaded with me for soap when I thought their need for food would be paramount. In Hamburg I watched the widows of German soldiers barter their starving bodies for food. The grinding poverty I witnessed in Jamaica is still a vivid memory. The police were keeping the beggars and scavengers away from the dock gates and the ships but their need was so desperate many of them were walking a mile or so down the road and then swimming back to reach the ships on the waterside. They carried tins which they attached to ropes we dropped over the side. We filled them up with whatever food we could find, often an almighty mess of potatoes, soup, jelly and custard. The swimmers then floated to the shore lying on their backs with the tin carefully balanced on their chest. I was so affected by what I saw in Jamaica I even gave my own food away.

The war had inevitably brought personal loss too. Many of the young men he had served with did not survive, among them George, his adopted brother, who was killed in action in France with the Irish Guards soon after D-Day in 1944.

George Fitt enlisted on 7 June 1943 at the regimental depot in Caterham,

Surrey, from where he was posted to the training battalion the following October. On 6 December 1943, while at home in Belfast on leave, the nineteen-year-old soldier married Mary Henry at the Registrars Office in Belfast. The witnesses were his brother-in-law, Mohamed Hussein (Betty's husband), and his sister, Rita. The bride gave her address as 'c/o the Royal Victoria Hospital' in Belfast. It was a bizarre union: Mary was not his girlfriend and was pregnant by another man. In due course she gave birth to a mixed-race infant, and later settled in Liverpool.

Some months later, on 13 March 1944, George Fitt completed his training and was posted to the 3rd Battalion of the Irish Guards, by then preparing for the widely expected invasion of continental Europe, the final push of the Second World War intended to liberate the Nazi-occupied countries and finally defeat Adolf Hitler.

According to the regimental war diary for 1944, Guardsman Fitt and his colleagues were still in Eastbourne on D-Day, 6 June 1944, when the massive invasion force landed on the heavily defended beaches of north-west France. 'Today comes the news that we have waited for,' the watch-keeper recorded. 'From now on we are on our toes to move, but no order has been given.' It was to be another ten days before the order came through, directing them to set out for the marshalling area at Wanstead in Essex at 4.00am on 16 June. From there, the regiments' vehicles were moved to Tilbury in the port of London, where they were loaded on to the freighter *Samphill*. A day later, the 'marching party', or the 'poor bloody infantry' including the young Belfastman, embarked on the 1929-vintage, 11,951-tonne former Union Castle passenger liner, *Llangibby Castle*, which had been converted into a wartime troopship. The weather at sea was so bad it prevented them transferring to a landing craft for two days. 'We got our feet wet, somewhat to everyone's annoyance,' the battalion diarist recorded. After landing, the unit marched to an assembly area north of Creully, before moving on to Bayeux.

Some days later, on 29 June, the Irish Guards had their first contact with the enemy when a reconnaissance party encountered mortar fire while scouting a railway bridge with doubled sentries on the line between Bretteville-sur-Odon and Verson. They were not thrown into the full heat of battle until 3 August, when they were given orders to capture the village of Montchamp, 'an enemy strongpoint', according to the war diary.

'We had quite an exciting night advancing along the road between St Charles de Percy and Montchamp,' the war diary records but the advance initially was halted by 'German Spandau [machine gun] posts' ... 'well backed-up by two troops of [Coldstream Guards] tanks and, after three efforts, they overcame the opposition and a combat group ... passed through to deepen the penetration by 300 metres ... with very slight losses.'

By dawn on 4 August the Irish Guards infantrymen were holding a position astride the road to the west of Courteil and coming under sustained and heavy shelling. At the same time, their forward companies were exchanging small-arms fire with enemy soldiers dug in not more than 100 yards in front of them. 'Casualties suffered during the day were four ORs [Other Ranks] killed and 16 ORs wounded and were mainly caused by shelling and mortar fire,' the diary records.

Among those four OR casualties was Guardsman 272384 George Fitt. The regimental records contain the testimony of Guardsman Patrick O'Brien, who was in the same section as Fitt:

> We were going down a country lane. I was carrying the Bren gun at the front of the section when the Sergeant halted us and told Guardsman Fitt to take over the Bren. We took it in turns. He was number one on the gun and I was number two. Five minutes later we were all told to get down. Guardsman Fitt was given a target to fire at, but they fired first. He was killed instantly.

In due course George Fitt was buried at the St Charles de Percy military cemetery. Teresa Fitt, his sister, remembers seeing him off for the last time and that she was in a field at Bell's Hill in Co. Down, cutting flax, when the news came through of his death. Gerry had not seen much of George since they had sailed together on the *Theems*. The last time they met was one day on the Queen's Bridge in Belfast, when George had told him he was volunteering to join the army.

Although he did not realise it at the time, the various strands of Gerry Fitt's life had begun to weave together and the opinions and values that would later inform his political philosophy were beginning to be shaped. The first hint of his interest in politics came at the age of eight when there was an election meeting one evening at the junction of Walbeck and Dawson streets. The speaker was standing in the back of a pony and trap, his voice booming out across the crowd, who were clapping and cheering loudly. There were no loudhailers in those days, so a strong voice was absolutely vital to rouse the crowd. Fitt later found out that the speaker was Harry Midgley – a man who broke all the rules of Northern Ireland's sectarian politics. A Protestant and trade unionist, in 1921 he had opposed the partition of Ireland. In 1933 he became the MP for Dock, but lost five years later when his views on the Spanish Civil War clashed with mainstream Catholic opinion. According to the lurid stories circulating around Belfast at the time, Franco's men were going to rout the republicans, who were raping nuns and beheading priests. Midgley later became MP for Willowfield, fighting and winning the seat under three different party labels before finally joining the Unionist party. When he died in 1957 he was a Unionist Cabinet minister at Stormont. Fitt remembered Midgley:

> But as far as I was concerned then, in 1933, it was the charisma of politics, the roar of the approving crowd, rather than the essence or substance that impressed and attracted me. During that election I followed Midgley

around for days, drinking in the atmosphere of the poll and getting into trouble at home for disappearing until late at night.

At the barber's shop where he worked Fitt's interest in the more glamorous side of politics was stimulated by one of the regular customers, TJ Campbell, a distinguished barrister and editor of the nationalist morning newspaper, the *Irish News*. The paper's offices were just a few doors away and Campbell came in most mornings to be shaved. 'As I soaped him up I would quiz him about politics and politicians, for he was also a member of the senate, the upper house at Stormont. I must have tried his patience many times for he usually got a mouthful of soap trying to answer me,' Fitt recalled.

As a paperboy, Fitt often kept a copy of the *Belfast Telegraph* for himself and his mother frequently had to come into his bedroom late at night to take the paper from him and tell him to sleep. This, too, fostered his interest in local politics, although Fitt himself always attributed his first real interest in the substance of politics to his extensive reading at sea during the war:

> This quest for knowledge led to my first challenge of authority. A junior engineer I was sailing with talked about a very good book he had been reading, *For Whom The Bell Tolls* by Ernest Hemingway. I asked him to lend it to me when he was finished, but he replied that would not be possible. It was a book from the officers' library. Now this distinction was based on the supposition that ordinary crewmen would be content with reading Cowboys and Indians or whatever trash was available.
>
> As the union rule book I always carried in my hip pocket did not cover the situation, I decided to confront the chief mate. But when I asked him if I could borrow a book from the officers' library he gave me a withering look as if I was mad. Never in his experience, it was clear, had a callow young seaman ever made such an outrageous request. I stood my ground, pointing out that the books were supplied by either the Flying Angel Missions or the Catholic Seamens' Mission, and they should be interchangeable. I pointed out too that, in my opinion, neither organisation would approve of such a ridiculous class system. He told me to get off the officers' deck as fast as possible or he would log me, which could lead to a fine. Incongruously the convoy was under attack as I was making my point and I smiled at how the class system had remained firm under simultaneous attack by me and the Germans. I resolved to wait, knowing that when we reached our destination, New York, the contents of the library would be changed over.

When the ship docked, Fitt was among the first off and immediately went to see the padre at the Flying Angel. He listened sympathetically to the passionate young man, accepted his case and made representations to the officers on board. On the way home, Fitt asked for and obtained as many books as he wanted. 'At sea my interest in English also developed and I became an avid hunter for new words. I used to eagerly scan every edition of *Readers Digest* for the "Increase your word power" feature. I was quite pleased therefore when I came home and my mother remarked on all the big words in my vocabulary. "Jawbreakers," she called them.'

The war also forced Fitt to think about and research Irish history. He was struck by the bitter reaction of some of his fellow crewmen whenever they encountered brightly lit, neutral Irish ships – in stark contrast to the total black-out and camouflage paint that was standard for the Merchant Navy. He found the contradictions of the various Irish positions on the war difficult to understand and to explain:

> In Naples, after the liberation, a NAAFI [Navy, Army and Air Force Institute which provided recreational facilities] had been set up in the ruins of a seventeenth-century palace. One night, while having a drink there, I met members of a Northern Ireland regiment. Most of them, like myself, were from the North and there were quite a few Catholics. But one of the sergeants was a Dubliner and after a few drinks he began to eulogise De Valera for keeping the South out of the war. Everybody thought this was very strange, even funny, coming from a brave soldier who had fought his way from the Libyan desert halfway across north Africa into Italy. No one has summed up the contradictory role of the Irishman at war better than WB Yeats who wrote: 'Those that I fight I do not hate, those that I guard I do not love.'

What Fitt understood as 'Irish nationalism' held few attractions for him:

> I felt it was more urgent to tackle the poverty and hardship afflicting the world. My lifelong commitment to socialism began then. I was deeply affected by the inequality all around the world. I couldn't see why those at the top of the heap, who had more than enough food money and things for their own needs, could not give the excess to those at the bottom who had virtually nothing.

At the time of the 1945 post-war general election, Fitt was still a year too young to vote, but claimed he would have voted Labour: 'I told that to a BBC interviewer who was recording impressions in New York and the interview was broadcast back home. Unknown to me at the time, it was the first of literally hundreds of broadcasts I would ultimately make.'

While these experiences and impressions were moulding Fitt's political character, this period in his life was also marked by another significant encounter. One day in 1946 he travelled to London with Bertie Girvan to pick up a ship. On the packed cross-channel ferry from Belfast they met a crowd of girls and spent the night in a sing-song. One of the girls was from Castlederg, Co. Tyrone, and when they all reached London, Fitt asked her for a date. Nothing came of it, however, because for he left quickly for New Zealand, but she introduced him to one of her friends, Ann Doherty, a tailor's daughter from Castlederg, and he was entranced. Some months later, in February 1947, when he had returned from the voyage, he rang Ann Doherty in London:

> I could only recall her first name but I knew she was working as a
> telephonist at the Ladies Imperial Carlton Club at Hyde Park Corner and I
> soon tracked her down. Although she was suffering from flu, she agreed to
> meet me at the local tube station. I turned up well-armed to impress her
> with a big box of chocolates and three pairs of nylons, which were real prizes
> in those austere days of rationing and ration books. We went to a cinema at
> Piccadilly Circus and saw James Mason in *Odd Man Out* but I ran out of
> cigarettes and by the time the film was over I was dying for a smoke. It was
> impossible to buy cigarettes without ration coupons and I had none so we
> went into an amusement arcade where there was a darts game with
> cigarettes as prizes. But my need for a smoke affected my nerves and the
> harder I tried to win a prize, the worse my score was. Ann then decided to
> have a go and in no time at all she had won ten Players Weights. I
> recognised something special in her after that and began to entertain
> thoughts of marrying her.

It proved to be a whirlwind romance. After that first date he returned to Belfast
and Ann followed for a holiday a month later. There they had a long talk about
their dreams and hopes for the future. Fitt told her he would like to settle in
London, join the Labour party, then at the height of its post-war popularity, and
perhaps become a politician. He told her of the books that had inspired him and
what he had seen of the world. After talking everything over, they decided to get
married and make their lives together in Belfast. Then he went back to sea for
another trip and Ann returned to London. When he returned again, Ann gave up
her job and they wed in St Joseph's Church, Crossgar, Co. Down on 5 November
1947. For a time, between voyages, they lived at Bell's Hill, but when they got the
chance of a rented room at Ship Street, they moved back to Belfast and settled in
the electoral constituency of Dock.

CHAPTER THREE

SPLIT THE UNIONIST VOTE

DURING HIS EARLY MARRIED LIFE, Fitt continued to work as a merchant seaman voyaging regularly from Belfast. By now he was deeply interested in politics and taking an avid interest in current events both at home and in the countries to which his travels brought him. His mother and sisters kept him up-to-date by posting copies of the *Irish News* and *Northern Whig* out to him. He also took an interest in what was going on in the various far-flung countries where he docked. In Jamaica, for instance, he enjoyed a discussion with the secretary-general of the Caribbean Communist party, and it was in Australia where he made what he always maintained was his first public political speech:

> One of the Sydney stevedores asked me to speak about Ireland at a lunchtime protest meeting to get support for a strike because Robert Menzies, the Prime Minister, would not allow a Chinese delegation into the country. I remember the cold feeling of the microphone as I took it but the sight of the audience of tough stevedores and dockers, 'wharfies' they are called, soon inspired me to passionate oratory about the perils of capitalism and the reactionary attitudes of the Australian government. I spoke for nearly an hour but just as I was reaching my crescendo about the tragedies of Ireland I spotted a familiar face in the crowd, the chief engineer of my ship. I was caught red-handed for, instead of haranguing the 'wharfies', I was supposed to be greasing the ships' winches. On the basis that attack is the best form of defence I singled him out and denounced him as a lackey of the capitalist classes of ship-owners paying low wages for slave labour. Although the episode cost me a fine of £1.10 shillings for my absence I reckoned I had got my money's worth with the satisfaction of a standing ovation from the audience and the blast I had at the chief.

At this point in his life, and from a standpoint well beyond the physical and mental ghettoes of his native Belfast, Fitt was relating and comparing the situations he encountered to those prevailing in his home port. His aversion to what he called 'sterile nationalism' and his opposition to 'the unionist ruling class' increased markedly, and he came to believe both were, in fact, standing in the way of tackling and solving the most pressing political problems: the grinding unemployment, squalor and poverty in the slums, the lack of opportunity to progress and the gross limitations of the education system. Within his deepening socialist viewpoint, he became committed to the concept of a strong, vigorous, non-sectarian labour movement as the only way to break the unionists' crippling political stranglehold. Fitt's principal political inspiration and influence was James Connolly, whose life and times he had been studying since 1938, ever since a friend gave him a 'penny pamphlet' of his writings. 'Connolly inspired me to become a politician and throughout my political career motivated me more than anything else.' But while Connolly's dream of national unity and social freedom died with him when he was executed for his part in the failed 1916 Rising in Dublin, it became the cornerstone of Fitt's political beliefs.

Post-partition the unionists set about snuffing out the fledgling labour movement in the North. They knew the emergence of a working-class organisation engaged in conventional class politics would split their support and undermine the monopoly they needed to stay in power. Above all, they feared the emergence of a non-sectarian workers party would pose even greater dangers to their hegemony in the North with the strong possibility that it would make common cause with its counterparts in the South, thereby seriously compromising the partition settlement. In an attempt to encourage and prolong the established class divisions, the unionist hierarchy encouraged the labouring classes into the Orange Order and permitted some workers groups to flourish within the ambit of the Unionist party. The split was also reinforced in a more effective way by ensuring that it was Protestant workers, not Catholics, who got the jobs in the shipbuilding, heavy engineering and rope-making industries which were then the bedrock of what passed for prosperity in Northern Ireland.

A small labour movement struggled persistently against this tribal, divisive sectarianism, but it too finally succumbed to division in 1949. One faction eventually became the Northern Ireland Labour party and enjoyed a modicum of support for its 'labour policies under partition' approach. Meanwhile the second faction, the Irish nationalist-labour grouping, split further into a series of small local party groups, each dominated by a single, strong personality such as Jack Beattie and Harry Diamond. The Dock Irish Labour party, which would eventually become Fitt's political power base, emerged from a clash between these two labour giants of the day.

The split was instigated during the summer of 1951, after Tommy Watson, councillor for Smithfield Ward in Belfast, resigned his seat and emigrated to Australia. Beattie and Diamond both put forward nominees for the vacancy and a bitter argument ensued between them. It became so bad that, in the end,

Diamond resigned his seat in another ward to fight Beattie face-to-face in Smithfield Ward. The battle that followed between these two stalwarts of the labour movement was acrimonious and angry, but in the end Diamond managed only 312 votes and was easily beaten by Beattie, who polled 1,402. After the election, Diamond was expelled from the labour movement along with a number of branches that had supported him. Among them was Dock, where the small cadre of labour activists still loyal to him promptly renamed themselves the Dock Irish Labour party.

By now Fitt was actively involved on the political fringe. He had steered a middle course through the Beattie – Diamond clash, but privately he favoured Beattie, who ranked alongside Connolly as his political hero. Fitt's desire for a role, if not a career, in politics was now the dominant preoccupation in his life. When Clement Attlee, the Labour Prime Minister of Britain, called a general election in October 1951, Fitt volunteered to work for Beattie, who was hoping to retake the West Belfast seat in the Westminster parliament. A year earlier Beattie had been beaten decisively by the Rev Godfrey McManaway, a Church of Ireland clergyman who peddled the same brand of Pope-bashing politics that would later propel Ian Paisley to power. However, after McManaway had taken his seat at Westminster, the validity of his election was challenged and the Privy Council ruled that he was indeed ineligible under the 1801 Disqualification of Clergy Act, which prevented churchmen of the Anglican communion from sitting in the Commons, and which was held to include the Church of Ireland. At the ensuing by-election in November 1950 Beattie lost again, but by only 913 votes, which meant this time out he had a decent chance of winning if his election workers could get the full vote.

As one of Beattie's election workers, Fitt was appointed captain of a polling station – 'my first real political office'. Another member of the team was Billy Napier, who would later become Fitt's 'Siamese twin' in politics, and the mainstay of his subsequent election campaigns.

> But of all the elections we fought together, I doubt if we ever had to work as hard as we did in 1951. We worked like Trojans, especially on polling day itself, and then, after the booths were closed, Billy and I went to the City Hall to await the result. The voting was so close that a recount was called. In all we had to wait through five recounts before Beattie was finally declared the victor by a margin of only twenty-five votes. A remark by a Unionist speaker at an eve of poll rally was generally regarded as being decisive in tilting the balance in our favour. Ending his speech he had said: 'God Save the King, to hell with the Pope', a remark which moved sufficient moderate Protestants not to vote.

Beattie and his supporters had to leave City Hall through an angry, Protestant crowd but when they got to their own election headquarters at Leeson Street, on the Falls Road, a large, jubilant crowd had gathered to welcome them. There, with tears of joy coursing down his cheeks, Fitt announced the result through a loudhailer: 'It was the first, sweet, addictive taste of political success. I made up my mind that night it would be mine too, one day!'

As soon as the excitement of the election had died down, however, Fitt headed back to sea, but in May 1952 he was home again and his political friends in the Dock party were preparing to fight local council elections. According to the electoral register there was a unionist majority, so it was a hopelessly uneven contest. The local government franchise at that time heavily favoured the unionists because limited companies had votes – one for each £10 of their valuation up to a maximum of six votes. As all the mills, wood-yards, warehouses and tobacco factories in the ward were Protestant-owned and predominantly unionist the Dock candidates were 'beat before we started', as the Belfast vernacular has it. As it turned out, the Northern Ireland Labour party decided to contest the seat and the 300 or so votes they denied the unionist candidate was enough to elect Murty Morgan and Mickey Fearon, chairman of the Dock Irish Labour party, onto the city council. It was an historic victory in the area – the first time the unionist deadlock had been broken. Fitt learned two valuable lessons from that fight: the value of a split unionist vote; and the importance of maintaining the register to ensure that every eligible voter was listed as entitled to vote.

The fact that Fitt was analysing so carefully the methodology of the contest underlined what was still a publicly undeclared ambition: to get elected. This commitment to politics was now so strong, he decided the time had come to stay ashore. Armed with a glowing reference from Councillor Murty Morgan, he applied for and obtained a job as a stoker in the Belfast Corporation gasworks, which then stood at the edge of the Markets area, in Cromac Street. Few Catholics were employed there, as was the case in most public agencies, and Fitt always believed it was his wartime service that clinched the job for him:

> There was a fair bit of initial interest at a 'taig' [Catholic] getting the job, but after a bit of political talk, which was more banter than argument, I made a lot of friends. It was a dirty, filthy job, shovelling mountains of coke, with a now-recognised risk of cancer, and it proved a long-held belief of mine that the working-class Protestant was no better off than his Catholic counterpart, despite all the unionist promises of preferential treatment for them.

Fitt was very unsettled, however, and with no alternative employment prospects he wrote to ask for his old job back aboard the *Somerset*. He rejoined the ship at Victoria Docks on 12 May 1950 and returned to sea, this time on a voyage to Australia. Two weeks earlier, Ann had safely delivered their first child, Joan, and soon afterwards moved from Ship Street to a post-war, prefabricated bungalow at

Beechmount, on the Falls Road where the rent was 13s. 9d. per week. Fitt was no more settled by his return to sea and, 'pining for politics', left the *Somerset* on 19 September 1953. His discharge book was stamped 'very good' for both conduct and ability, as it had been for every trip he made. This time, though, the salt water had been flushed out of his veins for good: his seagoing career was over and he had his mind made up to become a politician.

His return was timely. Basil Brooke, the long-serving Stormont Prime Minister and later ennobled as Lord Brookeborough, had called an election to the Northern Ireland Parliament for October 1953 and Murty Morgan was nominated to fight Tommy Cole, the sitting Unionist member. Brooke appeared to campaign for him on Cole's behalf, brandishing a sword he said had been used by King William at the Battle of the Boyne. The surprise victory at the council election had proven the Unionist party was not invincible, and the Dock Labour party scented victory. The Unionists were clearly fearful because they nobbled one of their opponents, offering him money if he took active steps to sabotage the campaign and ensure that Morgan lost. The individual concerned approached Fitt, offering to cut him in on the reward, but 'shocked by his treachery', Fitt exposed him to the rest of the party and found himself appointed election agent in his stead.

In those days, when television was still in its infancy, election campaigns were fought on the streets. The candidates made their case and attacked their opponents at street-corner meetings and used door-to-door canvassing to consolidate support. When the campaigning started, Cole toured the constituency on a gaily decorated lorry accompanied by a band. The DLP had no funds to match that level of razzmatazz, so Fitt and his team were forced to wait until Harry McGreevy came home from his coal round in the evening so they could borrow his lorry for their own electioneering. Fitt remembered:

> But there was coal dust everywhere and by the time we climbed up and down off the lorry and clung onto each other as it was going round the corners of the wee narrow streets, we looked more like *The Black and White Minstrel Show* than a political party. It was always worse when it rained and one wet night outside the Seamens' Mission in Corporation Street, seeing Murty Morgan covered in coal dust and wet through, I said to him: 'You're some candidate. You look more like Al Jolson.'

A month before polling day, Fitt's team discovered the names of sixteen deceased people who had applied successfully for postal votes, and there were suspicions about some other names. It was Fitt's first experience of the dark side of electioneering, something at which the unionist election machine excelled. Undeterred, the team fought on and were amply rewarded when Morgan won the seat by a comfortable 179 votes. Fitt was ecstatic: 'It was a most satisfying victory, but it fired me with renewed determination that one day I would be elected myself.'

Now that it had an MP at Stormont the party began to take itself more seriously and elected office bearers, but there were so few members that everyone got a title. 'All officers, no privates,' said Fitt. They were also chronically short of funds, and set out to raise money to fight future elections by organising a raffle and an excursion by bus to the seaside. For weeks they toured the Catholic areas of Belfast selling tickets, promising fantastic prizes – 'A brace of ducks, a phrase one of us had seen in a book, attracted a lot of interest,' recalled Fitt – but despite their best efforts they could muster only half-a-busload of old ladies and children for a windy day at a seaside resort. While they wandered round, the party officers spent the afternoon blowing the few shillings they had on a few pints of beer and slow horses. Fitt had already learned that in publicity terms the facts should not interfere with a good story, and upon his return to Belfast he called in to give the *Irish News* a glowing report about the memorable excursion. Next morning he was pleased to read that the annual excursion of the Dock Irish Labour party, so ably organised by vice-chairman Gerard Fitt, had been an immense success. 'It was the first time I had got my name into print. But the excursion had raised no funds. The party was still as broke as ever.'

Fitt was broke, too, as he had been unable to land a steady job since returning home. Thanks to Jimmy Regan, a leading activist in the party and an official of the Musicians Union, Fitt had secured work several evenings a week as a bouncer at the Phoenix Ballroom in North Queen Street. It was a rough, tough assignment. When the pubs closed at 10.00pm, drunken lads came staggering across to meet the all-too-sober girls, who had arrived earlier and were by then lined up in rows along one side of the dance hall, waiting to be paired off. Fitt's job was to stop the worst of the drunkards getting inside, but as part of the night's enjoyment was to fight with the bouncers, the police, or each other, Fitt inevitably got and gave many black eyes.

The next electoral opportunity for the Dock Labour Party came in March 1954, when they nominated Jimmy Regan to fight for a post as one of the city's Water Commissioners. According to Fitt:

> Water was not even mentioned during the campaign, which was fought on the traditional anti-unionist platform with all the fervour and ferocity of an American presidential contest. I was again the agent and the candidate's address outlined the party's policy as 'the twin ideals of national unity and social freedom' and the party's aim as 'the elimination of the unionist party from all aspects of representation in Dock'. We were bitterly disappointed when Jimmy lost by 97 votes.

Fitt took the lead in analysing the reasons for their disappointment, and quickly concluded that they had to work harder at the register to ensure all their potential supporters were listed and entitled to vote. The defence of their first council victory was looming in May 1955, and with ambition still burning in his heart,

Fitt took it upon himself to do much of the necessary work. He began to study the rules regarding eligibility to vote and discovered that many Catholic businessmen neglected their right to company votes. When the omission was pointed out to them, many were happy to let Fitt do the paperwork and pledged him their support. With a little prompting from him, others, like publicans and bookmakers, actually set up limited companies so they could get votes. Fitt persuaded them it was a good move by pointing out that if they had sympathetic councillors, they could have a say in how issues affecting them were decided, especially the level of rates.

In those days many young married couples lived with their parents or other relatives, or in rented lodgings because of the shortage of money and houses. These married lodgers – and there were quite a few in the Dock ward – were entitled to vote, but very few were on the electoral list. Fitt spent hours and walked miles going from door-to-door ensuring that married lodgers had rent books, so they could claim their vote, and that everybody eligible in each house was on the roll. Fitt was still jobless and living very much from hand-to-mouth and the kindly Peter Kelly, who ran a fish and chip shop in North Queen Street, was so worried about him tramping around in the wet with holes in his shoes that he offered him a free supper every time he saw him.

All the hard work was soon recognised, however. When nominations for the 1955 council elections came round, Fitt was selected as the candidate for what was his first election fight. His elation was short-lived. When the nominations closed, the Northern Ireland Labour party had not put forward a candidate to split the Protestant vote, so the unionist majority prevailed. Fitt now had Ann and three children to provide for – Joan, Eileen (born 1951) and Patsy (born 1953) – so he was forced to put his political activities on the backburner and search for a job. Someone told him an insurance round with the City of Glasgow Friendly Society was up for grabs and he got a start there. Apart from the commission on the routine collection, there was another ten shillings bonus to be earned – a veritable fortune to him then – if he could reduce the £40 arrears on the book. For a time he thought he had it made:

> I rode around the Falls and Glen roads on my bicycle doing my collections.
> I had a big thick overcoat in those days, with a large inside pocket, and there
> was always plenty of money in it. For the first time in years, when I wanted
> cigarettes I would buy twenty whenever the notion took me. When the
> cycling made me thirsty I popped into one of the many pubs for a big pint
> or two of thirst-quenching Ulster Brewery – 'UB beer' we called it.

During his ever-more frequent visits to the pubs, he noticed the afternoon shuttle between the bar and the always-adjacent bookmakers. The unemployed passed their afternoons in a cycle of rising and falling expectancy, depending on whether or not their horses were winning. If not, they went home sober at six for their tea and an evening before a rented black-and-white television. If they were, it would be pints all round until the winnings ran out:

> Well, before long I, too, got hooked into the sure things and tips from the crush that were the heroin of these men. Sometimes I won, more often I lost, but then there was always the chance of getting it back with the next day's insurance money. I never really accepted that all this money in my pocket belonged to somebody else.

Before long, inevitably, he was unable to fulfil his payment to the insurance company at the end of the week and finding it impossible to give Ann housekeeping. To postpone the day of reckoning he resorted to moneylenders, who charged five shillings a week for the loan of £1. If the borrower was unable to pay the original £1, he paid the five shillings interest, and so on. Soon he had exhausted all lines of credit and was in serious debt to the insurance company and a succession of potentially dangerous moneylenders. Ann came to the rescue when he finally confessed his plight:

> She contacted her brother who was then working in Scotland on a scheme to drive a tunnel for a hydro-electric power station in Perthshire. He got me a job driving a tractor, earning £15 for an eighty-four hour week. My debts in Belfast were almost £200, although they seemed like millions to me then, and it took me ten months to earn enough to send back to Ann in Belfast to pay them off.

During the time he spent in Perthshire, his political ambitions were further fired by three influential books – Robert Tressell's *The Ragged Trousered Philanthropists*, Howard Spring's *Fame is the Spur* and Nye Bevan's *In Place of Fear* – and he could hardly wait to fight another election. But when he got back to Belfast in 1957, there was the more urgent need to earn a living to support his wife and family. Enthused by a flamboyant newspaper advertisement asking if anyone wanted to earn £20 a week, he presented himself at a room above a pub. He learned that this magic salary could be earned by trudging from door to door selling from a large, brown suitcase. When he opened the case there were brushes inside for every conceivable human need – nail, tooth, boot, clothes, floor and car. The deal was 20% commission on everything sold. Fitt signed up, collected his case of stock and headed home to Beechmount Bungalows, where he announced to Ann his intention of starting his new job early the following morning with calls around the area. His high hopes were promptly shattered by her reaction: 'Round here? The neighbours will laugh at you.'

Heeding her advice, early next morning he dragged the bulky, heavy suitcase on two bus journeys to the Skankill Road, the heart of Protestant Belfast, where he reasoned nobody would know him. He made an encouraging start. At the very first door he knocked, he talked his way along the hall and into the living room, where he got the case open on the table, ready to start his spiel about the various implements on offer. The prospect was a busy housewife with a gaggle of toddlers crawling around. Every time Fitt began to persuade her of a brush's brilliance he was interrupted by one or other of the kids wanting a piece of bread and jam, or needing to go to the toilet. Before long they began climbing up around the table and delving into the case and as fast as he took the brushes out for inspection, they would grab them:

> After a few minutes of this I realised there was little chance of a sale and my thoughts turned urgently to getting all my stock of brushes back and into the case. By now the kids were all over the place with their sticky, jammy fingers and my brushes. When one climbed up on my back it was the final straw. I shook the kid off and gave it a slap. The woman yelled and I grabbed my case, what brushes I could and ran off along the street with her shouts of anger ringing all over the place. I jumped on a passing bus, returned and handed in my case, having decided that was one career where I was unlikely to make a clean sweep.

Soon afterwards, he followed up another advertisement, this time offering the equally bleak prospect of selling encyclopaedias door-to-door. This employer, who also paid commission instead of wages, had a much more scientific approach to selling though and on Fitt's first day he was given Dale Carnegie's book to study: *How to Win Friends and Influence People*. The next step was to report for a selling lesson, where he was taught how to target prospects from the Belfast Street Directory, which listed householders and their trades, occupations or professions. The ideal prospect was a skilled man, such as a civil servant, plumber or electrician, who would in all likelihood be earning a reasonable wage. The modus operandi was to call in the morning, when only the wife was at home, citing as an introduction an unnamed mutual friend. The main objective was to find out what children were in the house, when the wage-earner would be in, his name and any other intimate details that would help build a speedy rapport on the return call. After a lengthy briefing along these lines, Fitt was told to report back at 6.30pm when the chief and the most successful salesman would take him out on a number of follow-up calls.

Their first stop was at a house in Gilnahirk, East Belfast. On the bus journey out there, Fitt was stunned to realise that this super salesman had the most pronounced stammer he had ever heard:

> When we made the call it took him, what seemed to me, like five minutes just to say 'hallo'. When we got settled down inside, offered the rapport-building cigarettes to husband and wife, as we were instructed, and began explaining the clear advantage it would be to his children if he bought this ten-volume encyclopaedia for the paltry sum of £17, I could not credit how this man was so successful. I was forced to the unkind conclusion that people bought the books to be rid of him or that they felt sorry for him.

Fitt decided to give the job a try and over several months made a number of successful sales, earning a princely £3 a time: 'I like to think I contributed to the education and entertainment of some kids by persuading their parents to buy, but sometimes there were setbacks when my enthusiastic selling became the subject of second thoughts by the customers and they cancelled.'

Although earning a living was his principal preoccupation, Fitt was still politically active and his ambition for elected office as sharp as ever. When a vacancy arose on the Belfast City Council in the Falls Ward, he was easily persuaded to go forward by neighbours in Beechmount. His opponent, in a straight fight, was Paddy Devlin, standing as an Irish Labour party nominee. During the war, Devlin, who was then active in the IRA, had been interned without trial for three years in Belfast prison but after the war had renounced violence and become an Irish Labour party member. Fitt had no money, and on nomination day met a moneylender outside City Hall to borrow his £25 election deposit. As a newcomer to the Falls, with little local support and a shoestring party organisation, largely imported from Dock, Fitt was at a considerable disadvantage to Devlin, who was backed by the big guns in the trade union and labour movement, including Jack Beattie. Fitt's campaign headquarters was the bungalow at Beechmount and Ann, who was pregnant again, 'performed miracles in the middle of a bread strike', making tea and sandwiches around the clock for his helpers.

The poll was a disaster for Fitt, as on a total register of nearly 20,000, fewer than 1,000 people turned out to vote and he was defeated 600 to 400, allowing Paddy Devlin, later a close political colleague, to become a councillor. Within hours, however, the election disappointment was overshadowed by a far more personal tragedy: the baby he and Ann were expecting was born prematurely in the Royal Victoria Hospital and died after just seven hours. Before her death she was baptised and christened Linda. Billy Napier's brother was a carpenter and he made a tiny wooden coffin, no bigger than a shoebox. In the hospital morgue, Fitt placed a picture of her sisters with the tiny body and then, 'with a heavy heart and tears in my eyes, I carried the brown paper-wrapped parcel on the bus to Milltown Cemetery, where Linda was buried in the communal grave for premature babies. For a time Ann and I were inconsolable. Politics hardly seemed to matter.'

Life, as always, went on and when another Stormont election was called for March 1958 and Murty Morgan announced that he was stepping down, Fitt secured the nomination quite easily. He was eager to win given that success would mean much more than the fulfilment of his own political ambition. It would also provide financial security for at least the next five years, the life of the parliament, as an MP's salary and allowances were more than £15 a week. More immediately, the most pressing problem for the impoverished Fitt was how to raise the considerable sum of £150 for the deposit all candidates had to lodge. The problem was solved when a young nephew, who had recently been awarded £400 as compensation for an industrial accident, agreed to lend him the money.

At 4.00pm on 7 March, the day before nominations closed, Fitt was walking along York Street when he heard the blast of a horn and a car he recognised pulled up beside him. The driver was a florist he knew well as a member of the Dock party, and he motioned Fitt into the car and introduced him to the passenger, a well-known Belfast solicitor. After initial pleasantries, it was suggested Fitt should stand down as the candidate in favour of the solicitor. In return, he would give Fitt the equivalent of a year's parliamentary salary and let him act as his election agent.

> This crude offer angered me and I refused. They tried pleading with me. I was unemployed, Ann was pregnant again and suffering from asthma. The money would come in useful. When I refused again they became abusive. I was a nobody, with no education. This man was an eminent solicitor, he had an MA degree, a man of substance. They showed me his nomination papers, signed already by two priests from the Dock area. I refused again and again as the conversation became more heated and nasty. I was threatened with the IRA; gunmen would change my mind. Finally I shouted I would fight, got out of the car and angrily slammed the door.

Fitt headed straight off to find Billy Napier, who was acting as his election agent, and together they rounded up the Dock party committee for an urgent meeting. From the initial tone of the conversation, it was pretty clear some nobbling had been going on, but after the air had been cleared the party reaffirmed Fitt's unanimous nomination. Next morning at the Belfast City Hall, after the nominations closed, there was a fracas between Fitt and the solicitor. He had already been nominated for Belfast Central, but had been advised to muscle in on Dock, as his chances there were thought to be better and now he tried to get Fitt to promise not to reveal his inducement. Another solicitor, to whom Fitt told the story, sent him at once to make an affidavit and, after it had been duly sworn and witnessed, advised him to head for York Road police station to lodge an official complaint. Halfway there, however, Fitt decided against taking the matter further.

Fitt and Napier now faced the prospect of fighting the election with no funding and very limited resources. In one novel propaganda exercise, which only cost them the price of a few felt pencils, they toured all forty-one pubs in the Dock constituency and inscribed the walls of the Gents in each with a variety of pro-Fitt slogans: 'If you're fit to vote, vote for Fitt'; 'Fitt is fit for Dock'; 'Fighting Fitt'. But when the slogan 'Fitt for Dock' appeared in white paint on a wall in North Queen Street, his opponents quickly amended it to 'Fitt for nothing'.

On the eve of polling day, Fitt held his last rally at the Walbeck Street/Dawson Street corner, the precise spot where Harry Midgley had triggered his first serious interest in politics. His buoyant optimism about his prospects was shattered early the next morning when polling day dawned with heavy rain that was forecast to continue all day. A further complication was the coincidence of the men's mission at St Patrick's, an annual event when preachers from the Church's commandos – the Jesuits or Carmelites – were brought in to each parish for a week to preach hell-fire and brimstone and keep the faithful and backsliders on the road to heavenly salvation.

The polls were due to close at 9.00pm and the hour-long evening service at 7.30pm would make significant inroads into the time the men would have to vote after coming home from work. About 5.00 in the afternoon, Fitt suggested to Napier that he should go to Sally O'Neill, the moneylender, in Great Georges Street, and borrow £20 to pay for taxis to ferry people to vote later in the day. Napier talked him out of it. Later in the evening, after the count in the City Hall showed Fitt had lost by 262 votes, the two of them, wet, bedraggled and disappointed, argued fiercely about the pros and cons of that decision and whether it had cost Fitt the election.

During the campaign his fifth child, another daughter, was born and this time both mother and baby were in fine form. Pre-occupied with the election, however, Fitt did not appear at the hospital to see them until the morning after the count. Understandably Ann was quite annoyed by his neglect and made her point. During her pregnancy, he had expressed his dislike of royal names such as James, George, Edward: 'When she gave me the birth certificate I saw she had ignored my opinion. The new baby had been called Elizabeth Marie Louise, the names of an English and French queen.'

Fitt remained as determined as ever to get into politics and, with city council elections due the following May, he again began the task of trudging from door to door to work up the local government register:

> Everyone who knew me thought I was a headcase. Most thought that having fought the good fight and lost I should throw it in. Party colleagues calculated that having lost the parliamentary election, half fair, they argued because of the one-man, one-vote system, compared with the antiquated local government system with company votes, there was no way I could win, so I had no volunteers to stand with me.

One evening a few weeks before the poll, Fitt was dozing on the sofa in his mother's house in York Street when her insurance man called, as he did every week, to collect her premium. His name was Hughie Hawks and as Fitt emerged from his slumber, Hawks said, 'Too bad about the election.'

'Oh, thanks very much,' replied Fitt as Hawks launched into a diatribe about the unionists, in particular, and politicians in general.

'If only I was a councillor...' said Hawks, but Fitt never heard the end of his statement because he had just realised that Hughie, good Shankill Road Protestant that he was, could well be the key to beating the unionists and securing the seat. The first lesson of Dock politics flashed back into his head – split the unionist vote.

'Do you fancy a drink Hughie?' Fitt asked nonchalantly.

As they walked along York Street to the Organ Bar, Fitt was already calculating the effect Hughie's intervention would have. Now all that was needed was for Hughie to be sufficiently enthused to agree to stand. Before they left the bar that night, a fast-talking Fitt had convinced him to do so, subject to his wife's approval. Next morning, bright and early, Fitt called on her at their Silvio Street home to do some more fast-talking. There followed what the superstitious old sailor in Gerry Fitt always regarded as another critical stroke of luck. Gar Cunningham, a gas meter inspector, with a great facility for raising money, was grandly known as the 'Director of Election Finance' for Dock Labour party. One day during the campaign Fitt and Cunningham called on a jeweller in Smithfield called Bobby Gunning. Cunningham told him what a great fellow Fitt was and how badly they needed money to fight the coming election. Gunning pulled open the drawer of his till and said he had a lot of children and very little money, but to take what was there. All too aware of what it was like to be short of money, Fitt took just half-a-crown (2/6d) 'for luck'.

When the nominations closed, Fitt and a New Lodge Road publican called James O'Kane were standing for the Dock Irish Labour party. There were three Unionist candidates and Hughie Hawks, on a independent unionist ticket, just as Fitt had planned. At the last moment Fitt almost lost the friendship of Billy Napier, who decided he wanted to stand as well, and Fitt had a job persuading him not to upset the carefully planned strategy.

As soon as the campaigning got under way, Fitt launched a series of attacks on Hawks, describing him as the worst kind of unionist bigot and more. His supporters weighed in on similar lines. All these attacks, Fitt calculated, meant he was going up in the estimation of the Protestant voters although, at one point, when his victim heard of them, Fitt had to placate him and his wife by saying that while he could not endorse him in public, he was most certainly doing so on the doorsteps.

Fitt's strategy worked out beautifully. When the votes were counted, Hawks had mopped up some 400 Protestant votes and Fitt was elected by a majority of twenty-seven. His running mate, O'Kane, got in by ten votes after a recount. After all the disappointments, Fitt could hardly believe that he had made it to councillor. He always attributed his success to the twin effects of Hughie Hawks' split vote and Bobby Gunning's lucky half-crown, which he kept as a talisman for the rest of his life.

CHAPTER FOUR

NOBODY TURNED AWAY

BY ANY STANDARDS OF ARCHITECTURE Belfast's City Hall is an impressive building. Opened in 1906, its green dome and ornate grey masonry dominate the heart of the city centre, in spite of the towering glass and concrete skyscrapers thrown up nearby in the affluent 1960s. Inside it is just as gracious, with marble floors, skilfully floodlit murals, elaborate staircases and rooms panelled in the finest woods. It is also, inevitably, an historic building. In September 1912 thousands of Ulster Protestants converged on City Hall to sign the Covenant – many in their own blood – protesting at the British government's proposal to grant home rule to Ireland. Their dramatic gesture and the subsequent threat of armed resistance was crucial in securing partition and in 1921 City Hall was chosen for the inaugural meeting of the new parliament, and King George V performed the State opening, processing by carriage from the docks through streets crowded with cheering unionists.

It may have appeared a moment of defiant triumph, but partition and its accompanying sectarian violence divided the island of Ireland and consolidated the sectarian divisions between the two distinct communities in the thriving city of Belfast. As a result, instead of being a magnificent reflection of the achievements of a then world-renowned industrial city and its citizens, City Hall became an enduring symbol of the city's deep rifts and, unfortunately, the people who governed there worked not to heal but to perpetuate them. The boundaries of the fifty-two council seats were arranged so there were only eight safe seats for Catholics, with maybe one or two marginal if the votes split the right way. Thus there was always an overwhelming unionist majority. So to Catholics City Hall became 'theirs'; to Protestants, 'ours'. In reality both sides were exploited as the controlling caucus of unionist councillors, dominated by wealthy merchants, businessmen, developers and estate agents, treated its elegant rooms like a private club – it cost £1-10s-0 a year to join the coffee set in the Members' Room – and carved up the affairs of the city to their own considerable advantage. More decisions were actually taken there than were ever taken in the council chamber, and the majority were unashamedly sectarian. Planning decisions favoured those in the right Orange or Masonic lodge; houses were awarded on contacts, loyalty and religion, never according to need; civic spending in non-Catholic areas received priority; jobs were not awarded on merit, they were given to sympathisers. The whole operation, like its parliamentary big brother at Stormont, was designed to protect unionist ascendancy, to keep the Protestant working class in their place and to maintain the status of Catholics as inferior citizens.

Before ever entering its doors, Fitt considered the workings of City Hall to be an offence to the many people experiencing poverty and hardship in Catholic and Protestant working-class areas, a conviction that was to be the pole star of his entire political career. His election gave him a foothold in this corrupt system, but he realised quickly that it would require a far more extensive power-base to undermine City Hall's sectarianism and convert it into a vehicle for social justice and equality for the people he represented. As he assumed his unpaid public duties, he was determined to build that power-base by becoming what he called 'the champion of the ordinary working man'.

So, by the time he entered City Hall in 1958, Fitt had already articulated a clear political philosophy and devised a strategy to implement it:

> I recognised that partition was not the immediate issue. Adapting the teaching of James Connolly, I determined to try and bring about working class unity as a prerequisite of tackling the campaign for the united Ireland. I knew that many working class Protestants would not see that their best interests might lie in a united Ireland, and that many would violently disagree with me, but I never allowed their unionist views to prevent me from helping them with their everyday problems.

Since 1952, long before his election success, when Fitt first trudged the streets canvassing votes and contesting elections, he had also been conducting another vital part of his political apprenticeship: learning how to help and advise people with problems. This was particularly relevant in Belfast, as continues to be the case today, because the local public representative is the first port of call for the majority of constituents. This aspect of Fitt's public life had its origins in the dole queue at the Labour Exchange in Corporation Street, which was widely known as 'the Broo' (a corruption of 'Bureau'). After signing on each week, claimants might be called upstairs to the 'glasshouse' to discuss their benefit entitlement. Many on the dole were illiterate and therefore at a disadvantage and they began to consult Fitt about their treatment and rights. In order to be able to advise them properly, he started reading up the various national insurance acts, translating the legal jargon and building an understanding of the various complex regulations. Before long he had become the classic dole queue lawyer and accompanied people to the various tribunals dealing with their claims and appeals.

Word spread quickly, and Fitt's services were increasingly in demand. As he had done at sea, he held no great respect for authority and therefore refused to be intimidated by the officials who could hand out, or deny, money from the public purse. Indeed, Fitt was often appalled by their insensitivity and in turn could be tough and abrasive with them on behalf of the people he was helping, who were far less confident and articulate than himself.

Over the years, Fitt was asked to take up many strange and funny cases and he demonstrated considerable psychological insight, guile and ingenuity in the various strategies he devised to pursue them. When he was asked to represent a man who was accused of over-claiming benefits by not declaring his bounty payments for Territorial Army duty, Fitt judged the best way to make light of his position before the tribunal was to play on the political sympathies of the members, drawn as usual from a panel of what he said were 'mainly unionist-minded worthies'. So he explained, straight-faced, how the extra money had been earned on guard duty against the possibility of IRA attacks. The soldier was unable to report this to his counter-clerk because, rightly or wrongly, he suspected him of IRA sympathies and he did not want to disclose his military connection. As Fitt correctly anticipated, playing on unionist paranoia about the IRA won the day, but not every member of the tribunal had been fooled: as he left the room, one of the members winked knowingly at Fitt.

Sometimes Fitt resorted to a bit of stage-managing to maximise a case. One unfortunate man, with no eyebrows or eyelashes, was contesting a ruling that he was fit for work. Fitt pre-arranged that, as soon as he began to speak on his behalf, his client should take off his glasses and began to fidget, cough and stare wildly all round the room. The man performed on cue and went on to stamp the floor, loosen his tie and pull the buttons off his coat. As the members of the tribunal looked over at him with growing consternation, Fitt asked to consult with his client and then informed the chairman he would have to go outside as he was feeling ill. This was agreed to with much haste and once the man had left the room, Fitt adopted a highly reverential tone. As the tribunal could see, the poor man was obviously seriously ill and clearly unfit for work. When he came back into the room, he was treated with great consideration and Fitt won the case.

After one tribunal triumph, all adjourned to Tommy McCluskey's pub in North Queen Street for celebratory drinks. The man whom Fitt had helped proclaimed to all and sundry that Fitt had put up a show like Perry Mason – the flamboyant American lawyer who was the hero of a television series in which he never lost any of his cases. The nickname stuck, and from then on Fitt was widely acclaimed as the Perry Mason of the tribunals.

Generally speaking, Fitt concluded that the tribunals were fair, but he found

a coldness, indeed, callousness on the part of many of the officials operating the system. Their attitude all too often smacked of doing you a favour instead of providing a facility to which you were entitled. They often patronised their clients or humiliated them like the former Poor Law Guardians had done. Many of them were regimented into queues and kept hanging around needlessly as a form of power-mongering and, as with everything else in Northern Ireland, there was an element of sectarianism. Many were sent day after day for jobs to firms well known for employing only Protestants. Some spent hours walking, because they could not afford the bus fare, to have their cards inevitably marked 'unsuitable'. Whatever few jobs were allocated through the 'Broo' never came to Catholics. In the 'Placing Section', where no Catholic was ever allowed to work, the jobs were handed on from Protestant to Protestant. This sort of blatant discriminatory treatment therefore alienated Catholics further and directly contributed to the higher rate of unemployment among Catholics.

Fitt's willingness to take on any cause and fight it did not always result in victory, however, and he learned some important lessons from his failures. One such case was that of a group of people living in a dingy tenement in Lepper Street. They came to him to complain about their landlord, who was charging them exorbitant rents. Fitt advised them not to pay any more, for which refusal they were prosecuted and brought to court. Obviously they had no money for a solicitor, so Fitt went with them to act as their advocate:

I was called into the witness box and questioned by an aggressive young solicitor. Was I a merchant seaman? How long was I a councillor? What did I know about housing? What right had I to get involved? The encounter was very hostile. I argued back equally aggressively. The next witness, a sanitary inspector from the Belfast Corporation, did my case no good at all refusing to condemn the property. By the lunch adjournment, recognising it was not going well and concerned about these old ladies sitting mystified in the court, wrapped up in their shawls, I was very angry. Brushing past the inspector on the way out of court I attacked him with abusive language and said he should care more about the places some people had to live. As soon as the court resumed I was called before the magistrate, threatened with arrest for contempt of court and warned strongly not to interfere with the witnesses.

Fitt's election to the council meant a dramatic increase in the number of people coming to him for help at one of his regular morning surgeries in City Hall: 'My office was a window sill in one of the corridors and my filing cabinet was my jacket pockets, which were invariably bulging with notes and documents.' By word-of-mouth recommendation his workload mounted steadily. On an average morning he would see around thirty people: 'Many of my clients started off apologising for not being Catholics or supporters of mine, but I tried as hard to help them and solve their problems as any one brought by a Catholic.' Harry Castles, then a young reporter, remembers people clustering around the door of the committee

room or the council chamber, waiting for a meeting to finish so they could talk to
Fitt about their problems:

> He was the only man they wanted to talk to and I saw many Protestant
> people ignoring their own councillors and waiting, in what were sometime
> long queues, because they had total faith in him and knew that he would
> go in fighting to assist them.

It was true that Fitt often went out of his way to solve a problem for a Protestant
person, which enhanced his credentials as a working-class representative who
could get things done. It also carved out what would be his enduring reputation
as a truly non-sectarian politician, one who was prepared to help anyone in trouble
on basic humanitarian grounds. As demand for his services grew, people also
began to besiege his home when they could not track him down elsewhere. His
daughter Eileen remembers that 'nobody was ever turned away and nobody was
asked where they came from'.

In the meantime, life was hard for Ann and the children. She later expressed
regret that she could not afford to give her children the Christmas treats she would
have liked. The only money coming into the house was unemployment benefit, or
occasionally his meagre wages when he managed to find work – for a time he had
a part-time job as a clerk at the Labour Exchange. Money for bus fares was a
luxury, so most mornings Fitt walked from Beechmount to City Hall, sucking
baking soda to relieve a constantly painful stomach ulcer. What kept him going
during these times was his ambition to become an MP at Stormont, which would
pay him a salary to do the work he loved.

By far the most common and pressing problem he had to deal with during this
period was the lack of adequate housing. Belfast had a large number of late
nineteenth-century terraced houses, with no bathrooms, hot water or plumbed
toilets. All were badly in need of repair and modernisation, and many fit only for
demolition. The crisis was compounded by the number of young families living
with their parents, or in unsanitary and overcrowded rented accommodation. If
they chose to rent, they faced callous exploitation by private landlords, who
unscrupulously charged up to £3 a week for a single, dingy room.

There was inevitably a lengthy waiting list for modern housing, with at least
8,000 families listed, more than half of them with an income of less than £8 a
week to feed, clothe and rear a family. Despite the obvious and critical need for
better accommodation, little modernisation work was being carried out and very
few new houses were being built and when any became available, they were
generally allocated to Protestants. In the late 1950s, Belfast Corporation embarked
on its first schemes to replace the slums with fashionable tower-blocks of flats and
high-rise maisonettes and devised an allocation system awarding points for family
size, the lack of basic facilities in existing accommodation and the state of the

family's health. Fitt believed this points scheme was completely weighted against working-class people because it took into account their ability to pay the higher rents being demanded for the new properties. He was well aware that the families on the lowest wages and living in sub-standard accommodation at rents of between seven and ten shillings a week were going to find it hard to satisfy the Council they could afford to pay the projected rents of £1.5s – £1.15s a week. Even if they could do so, they immediately faced another problem in that the new houses were to be run solely on electricity, which would set them back another £1.10s a week, compared with the eleven shillings a week they were currently paying for a bag of coal.

For Fitt, however, the most unsatisfactory element in the points system was that it was designed to discriminate against larger families with several children, usually Catholics, because it only allotted points for up to three children. This meant a skilled tradesman with a small family stood a better chance of getting a house than a poorly paid labourer with a large family, whose need was plainly more acute. As far as Fitt was concerned, this underlined the hard fact that the Council was more interested in revenue than tackling human hardship.

He took up the cause and suggested the planned rents were too high, the means test unfair and the all-electric policy unwise. For once, he received some unionist support in the form of Alderman Tommy Henderson. When he heard there was to be only one electric fire per house, he demanded to know 'how a working man coming into the house completely drenched ever hoped to get his clothes dry?' Henderson was one of the few unionist councillors who had any idea of the realities of life for ordinary working people but he was regarded with derision by his unionist contemporaries, who mocked him for famously talking about the evil 'testicles' of the IRA rather than its 'tentacles'.

On 1 May 1959, after it was revealed that twenty-eight new houses at Springfield Parade, in the west of the city, had all been allocated to Protestant families, there was a row at the monthly meeting of the council, the debate running along the sterile sectarian lines that had become a seam running through every issue the council handled. One Catholic councillor claimed that his co-religionists were being regarded not as second-class, but third-class citizens. Another accused the council of operating policies of apartheid on South African lines by allocating houses on the basis of segregation of the two communities. This brought the retort, from a haughty woman unionist councillor, that thousands of pounds of ratepayers' money went to provide the separate education system on which Catholics insisted. It was, she contended, the Catholics who wanted apartheid policies.

The housing issue was debated at the council meeting on 4 August 1959. Fitt began what was the first major campaign of his political life by insisting that he was not out to attack any political party or official in the Estates Department, which handled housing allocations. Instead, he wanted change because the system was outmoded and inefficient. He argued that the worst feature of the points system was that need was overruled by ability to pay, quoting specific examples of Catholic families to back his claim. However, he stressed that he was not fighting the question from either a Catholic or Protestant standpoint. He concluded with the proposal that allocations be handled by a committee consisting of six councillors, four unionist and two non-unionist, and the relevant department officials.

There were no constructive replies to his arguments. Alderman Sir Cecil McKee, a former Lord Mayor, claimed that if Fitt's proposal were adopted, Catholics would get all the houses. He said they were already receiving more generous treatment than Protestants, quoting a scheme at Turf Lodge where all 1,000 homes under construction were earmarked for Catholic families. 'Needless to say,' Fitt remarked, 'my motion was overwhelmed twenty-eight to eight.'

The irreconcilable strands of Northern Ireland's divided society were neatly illustrated by the newspaper headlines on the story the following morning. 'Points system discriminates against Catholic families' reported the Catholic *Irish News*. 'RCs treated better than Protestants,' said the Protestant *News Letter*. Both communities were told what they wanted to hear.

About this time Belfast Corporation was building nine new flats in a modern block at Annadale Street in the Dock ward. Fitt visited the estates superintendent to discuss allocation and, after a lot of argument, it was agreed that five of the flats would go to Protestant families and four to Catholics, one of which would be Fitt's own family.

> I was delighted for two reasons. It was the fairest allocation of new homes anyone could remember and I was delighted to be getting back to my roots, as it were, for the new flats were only a few hundred yards from Walbeck Street.

However, when he told the good news to some of his closest friends in the Dock party, they were horrified. They would not accept he got the flat fairly, on the grounds that he had a young family and Ann was suffering from poor health; her regular asthma attacks were aggravated by the condensation-soaked bungalow at Beechmount and she had been in hospital several times.

> Do not take it, I was advised for I could not survive the inevitable allegations that I had got preferential treatment. Some of my friends even wanted me to resign my council seat. There was a party meeting called to consider the matter but I stood my ground and accepted the flat. My conscience was clear. I knew I had not pulled strings and I realised that our need was just. We moved in.

It did not take long for people to find out where he had moved and the tide of people looking for his assistance continued morning, noon and night: 'The family spent more time in the bedrooms and kitchen than they did in the living room, where I interviewed the callers.'

In time, Fitt found out that the unfairness in housing allocation was matched by the unfairness of job allocation. Belfast Corporation electoral area was divided into fifteen wards, only three of which – Falls, Central and Dock – were sufficiently populated with Catholics to guarantee the return of non-unionist councillors. This structure was reflected in the make-up of the council committees, which comprised a member from each ward. On every vote the minority was guaranteed to be out-ranked by at least 12 to 3, which meant no decision could be approved without unionist agreement, and this monopoly was ruthlessly exploited in relation to the allocation of council jobs.

Some months after Fitt's election in 1958, it fell to the transport committee – which operated the city's bus services – to appoint a new claims inspector. Fitt thought it a foregone conclusion that the current deputy would be appointed: he had been in the job for twenty-three years and was by far the best qualified candidate. Although the deputy warned him that he would be overlooked because he was a Catholic, Fitt lobbied his cause with the other councillors. When it came to the vote, however, another man was promoted, even though he was much more inexperienced. Fitt was intensely frustrated: 'Up to that, I thought I was going to change the whole workings of the Corporation and get jobs and houses for everybody but after that I could see there was no chance of a Catholic getting a job in the Corporation.'

Despite the odds being stacked heavily against him, Fitt refused to give up the fight and, whenever necessary, fought hard on behalf of Catholic applicants:

> One of the most frustrating committees was the police committee which was responsible, among many other things, for appointing the lower grades of administrative officers ... There would always be two or three Catholics on a shortlist of six or seven for every job, but no matter how well qualified they were, or the length of service they had, they were never appointed or promoted. During the years I was on that committee there was never one [Catholic] appointed and the unionists used to sneer and jeer and you would argue and argue, but nothing doing. You could never beat them on the vote. This was the first time that I experienced such real, calculated discrimination.

In October 1961, Fitt was again at the centre of a job allocation controversy. When a post became vacant at the city surveyor's department, he lobbied for a Belfastman, already employed by the Corporation, to be appointed, but as the party caucus had decided on a Scotsman, his lobbying was unsuccessful. In January 1962, when the police committee divided on the question of the most suitable candidate for the position of chief officer of the Belfast fire brigade, Fitt, naturally, became very interested in exploiting the impasse. After interviewing thirty-three applicants, the councillors were torn between appointing the deputy, a Belfastman, or the deputy fire chief of Exeter. Fitt favoured the local man for it seemed to him that, their qualifications being equal, the local candidate should get preference. The final decision was to be taken at a meeting in February, and when Fitt heard on the City Hall grapevine that the outcome would depend on the casting vote of the chairman, he resolved to meddle.

On the morning of the meeting he established that one of the councillors involved, 'a crusty bigot with Paisleyite leanings' as he described him, was in the Members' Room. Fitt crossed the lobby to the public telephone behind the porter's box and telephoned the councillor. The man answered and, without divulging his identity, Fitt asked him if he realised that the Exeter man was a Catholic. Fitt returned to the Members' Room a little later and was pleased to find that the councillors had risen to the bait and there was much scurrying around between them and the committee officials, who had been ordered to ascertain whether the anonymous information was correct.

In the event the committee appointed the man from Exeter by seven votes to six, but when the appointment came before the full council for ratification Fitt proposed that it be referred back for further consideration. The Belfastman had local knowledge, he argued, and his promotion would open the way for those below him. Belfast was five times the size of Exeter, therefore a more experienced man was needed. He also complained that too many Englishmen came over with the 'gift of the gab' and an Oxford accent and blinded the committees with science, thereby securing jobs at the expense of local candidates. Again, and as he expected, his proposal was overwhelmingly defeated, but nonetheless he was quietly pleased to have so thoroughly irritated the unionists.

Whenever criticism of things British was voiced, or questions of patriotism arose regarding whether allegiance was owed to London or to Dublin, the unionists invariably reacted angrily:

> What always annoyed me in those situations, was the mandatory unionist shout that I only enjoyed my right to free speech because brave, Protestant Ulstermen had fought and died for it in two world wars. Similarly, the way they hijacked the wearing of poppies and the annual remembrance ceremonies always rankled. As a result, the poppy itself had even come to be regarded by Catholics as a symbol of unionism.

Fitt believed that his own naval service and the death of his brother, George, and other friends in the war gave him an equally valid right to mark Remembrance Sunday, and he resented the way extremist Paisley adherents sought to exclude Catholics from the occasion. Once, when Paisley was chiding him, Fitt asked what he was doing during the war year. 'Studying religion,' came the reply. 'Well, I was serving at sea so that you could study in peace.'

Although Fitt's personal beliefs on this matter were very clear, as a councillor for a Catholic area he simply could not afford to be seen wearing a poppy, much to his regret. Instead, each November, as the poppies went on sale in the run-up to Remembrance Sunday, he would seek out Eric Gallagher, a Methodist clergyman who sold poppies along Donegall Place: 'I put a few bob in the collecting box but told him to keep the poppy. He invariably gave me a wry grin and I'm sure he shared my feelings about the way the true meaning of the poppy was so abused for narrow political ends.'

Early in 1961 Fitt began to plan the party's defence of the two council seats in Dock. Given their record of service to the electorate he was pretty confident they could win again, and he hoped his various campaigns and his growing reputation for working for people's rights regardless of religion would be valued by the working-class people of the city who would thus give him their votes. Before the campaign could be fought, however, he had another battle on his hands. A campaign of personal harassment had been initiated by his opponents.

One evening, about ten minutes before six o'clock, a man in a trilby hat and white raincoat came to the door. 'Are you Councillor Fitt? Can I speak to you?' he asked.

'Yes, come on in,' said Fit, thinking it was yet another constituent with a problem. 'But would you mind waiting a few minutes until the news is over?' he asked, looking over his shoulder at the second-hand, black-and-white television.

'No,' replied the caller, settling himself on the sofa.

They sat in attentive silence for fifteen minutes or so before Fitt leaned over, turned down the sound and said, 'Well, what can I do for you?'

'I'm from the Post Office. Can I see your television licence, please?'

'Hang on,' said Fitt, dashing out to the kitchen, from where he despatched his two eldest daughters to warn the neighbours to turn off their televisions. He was sure that, like him, they had no TV licences. Then he went back to face the man, who was quite reasonable and said he would take no action if Fitt obtained a licence the next day. Before he left he disclosed there had been a complaint and he had been sent out to check up on it. Fitt was sure this was no random visit. Somebody had set up the inspection to harass him.

Soon afterwards, when he routinely reported to the dole to sign on, he was promptly sent upstairs to the dreaded 'glasshouse'. There he was told that as he had been unemployed for a long time and had no prospect of permanent employment, his classification as a clerk was being changed. From now on he would be listed as a labourer because there were plenty of vacancies in that occupation. Fitt protested that he had been a merchant seaman, encyclopaedia and insurance salesman, a stoker and a clerk, but never a labourer. He queried whether they could make his part-time post as a temporary clerk a permanent position to solve the problem, and was told pointedly that they could change his classification if they so wished, and without any right of appeal.

Fitt stormed angrily from the labour exchange and, for once in dire need of advice himself, sought out Harry Diamond, the Stormont MP. He promptly tabled a question to Ivan Neill, then Minister of Labour. When the question was answered three days later, Fitt was in the gallery listening. Yes, it was possible to change the classification of a long-term unemployed person, Neill confirmed, looking up directly at Fitt and convincing him, beyond all doubt, of his suspicions: 'If I was out of the way, tied up with a full-time labouring job, I would not have the time to pursue constituency cases but more significantly for Alderman Billy Oliver and the Unionist party I would not be around to fight the election.'

When Fitt signed on the following week he was indeed sent for a job as a labourer with the McAlpine construction firm, which at the time was building the stretch of the M1 motorway near Dungannon. Danny Walsh, a friend who ran a scrapyard, agreed to drive Fitt out to the site office and helped him prepare for the interview. He recalls:

> I made sure he was dressed as smartly as possible and his shoes were cleaned up. I told him to raise as many difficulties as possible so he asked what assistance there was to get him to the site in the mornings, was it possible to get a sub [advance] on his pay and whether they provided protective gloves as his hands were very soft. When he came out of the hut he was grinning from ear to ear and he showed me where they had marked his dole card as 'not suitable'.

If Fitt had not gone to the interview or had turned down the job offer, his benefits would have been discontinued. The following week he faced yet another problem. This time he was given a form instructing him to turn up next morning, at 8.00am, at the Belfast Corporation Yard in Cliftonpark Avenue where he would begin work digging up the New Lodge Road for a sewer. The works were right in the middle of the main road through the Dock ward, which convinced him more than ever that it was part of a deliberate plot to humiliate him.

Fitt told the dole clerk that, as an elected Belfast city councillor, he was prohibited, by Act of Parliament, from working for the Belfast Corporation. This presented an unforeseen dilemma and, after much toing and froing by various officials, he was given a note in a sealed envelope with instructions to take it to the Town Clerk at City Hall, wait for the reply and return to the Labour Exchange. Bursting with fury at this stage, Fitt demanded to know what was in the note. The counter clerk replied that he must do as he was told and not ask questions. At that, Fitt lost his temper and threatened him.

'That'll get you a month in jail,' sneered the clerk.

Finally, barely able to contain himself, Fitt tore open the envelope and read the typed note: 'The bearer is signing the unemployment register and is in receipt of benefit totalling £7.5s a week. He advises he cannot be employed as a labourer by Belfast Corporation. Please confirm.' He tore up the letter and walked out. A few hours later he returned and demanded his cards, thus effectively signing off the register and severing his entitlement to unemployment benefit.

Danny Walsh came to his rescue by attesting that he was 'employing' Fitt as a clerk. Walsh generously slipped him some money from time to time as well, but in reality Fitt was still as jobless as ever and now considerably worse-off, with no regular money coming in at all. Some time later, though, he managed to get his benefits reinstated when a sympathetic clerk removed his file from the dole office, brought it to him and said that if he made a fresh claim, there would be no evidence to disqualify him. For Fitt, that was one of the lowest times in his life:

> This was a very difficult period for me. To survive I was forced to borrow from friends and relatives and live on whatever odd jobs I could get. Everybody urged me to wise up, settle down and forget the political rat race, where they could see no future for me. They pleaded with me to find a job. But now I was so embittered, I would not listen. I was obsessed only with retaining my council seat and I was sure if I could hold on there would be a general election for Stormont soon after that. If I could win that, I calculated my problems would be solved because I would have an MP's salary.

Despite his own plight, he continued to focus on defending the council seats and dealing with the daily workload of problems brought to him. One day, approached by an impoverished woman with several children who had been denied all benefits, he slipped her £1 he had borrowed earlier from his mother to meet the needs of his own family. Later, when he arrived home to Ann empty-handed, she went 'ballistic', as she later described it. This was the low-point of their relationship and she was far from enthusiastic about his ongoing obsession with full-time, unpaid politics. Two days before nominations closed he was dealt another blow when Jim O'Kane refused to defend his seat because he believed there would not be a split unionist vote and that he therefore could not win. Fitt was totally dispirited by this unexpected turn of events because he had been depending on O'Kane, a prosperous publican, to put up the money for their election deposits. Later that day, Fitt wandered into City Hall, where a group of Catholic councillors – known by the unionists as the 'Pope's brass band' – were having a meeting. Afterwards, they took Fitt over to the International Hotel at the back gate of the City Hall and in the basement bar he poured out his troubles to one of them. 'Look,' the man replied, 'up in Andersonstown there's a fellow called Jimmy Gallagher. He's originally from Dock and thinks the world of you. He'd make a good councillor. Give him a ring and see if he'll stand.'

Fitt knew of Gallagher, although they had never met, but he rang him from the hotel and he came down almost immediately for a talk. After listening to Fitt's proposition, Gallagher agreed to go forward for nomination and to put up deposits for both of them, but he made one important stipulation: he would not undertake public speaking. It made things difficult, but they overcame it by having him share the platform with Fitt at the various public meetings. Fitt assured the potential electors: 'The fact that this worthy candidate is not long-winded like myself is no indication of his great ability to represent the people of Dock. It is in the committees of Belfast Corporation, where it is needed, that his voice will ring out loud and clear.'

As the campaign was drawing to a close, Billy Napier, a plasterer who was Fitt's most faithful ally, suggested they needed to do something to stimulate publicity, but with no funds available this was a tall order. Undeterred, Fitt came up with a plan. He got his sister, Betty, to parcel up an empty box to look really impressive and then persuaded George Craig, a one-eyed photographer and one of Belfast's most likeable characters, to go to an empty dance hall and photograph it being presented to Mickey Ferran, the chairman, to mark his long association with the Dock Irish Labour party. Next day, there they were in the *Irish News*, presenting Mickey with the gift-wrapped empty box, pretending for all the world as if they were all at a crowded celebration.

A few days later the votes were counted and Fitt's effort and determination were well rewarded. He topped the poll by more than 500 votes, and Gallagher was also elected. What pleased him most was that the size of the majority proved he had broken the sectarian barrier and attracted Protestant support. He hoped this would be an appreciating asset in future elections. With a renewed three-year term on the council and a mandate like that, Fitt was also more confident than ever that it was the springboard from which he could win the parliamentary seat. Given his parlous financial state of affairs, the sooner the election was called, the better for him. Lord Brookeborough, the Prime Minister, did not oblige for another year, however, eventually fixing polling day for 31 May 1962. The intervening year was the most difficult of all: 'My closest friends and family were still at me constantly to give up and find a job. I ignored them, sure in my own mind at what I was doing, but things were tight. I had no money, no cigarettes and nothing to buy a drink.'

Instead he spent all his time tramping the streets of Dock, canvassing the electorate, working up the register and dealing with the deluge of problems that swept over him at home and in City Hall. Come polling day, his great efforts paid off handsomely: he polled 3,288 votes in a straight fight with his long-standing unionist opponent, Billy Oliver, and was comfortably elected with a 507 majority. It was the only defeat for the unionists in the city and Fitt was overjoyed.

Next morning, flushed with victory but still penniless, he went down to City Hall: 'All I had in my pockets was an empty matchbox and three halfpence.' A group of women who had worked for him during the election pursued him there, looking for the 'few bob' he had promised in return for their help. He sought refuge in the Members' Room where, literally under siege, he was thrown an unexpected lifeline by a retired army major called Ronnie Bunting, who was chairman of the Northern Ireland Ratepayers Association. After accepting Bunting's congratulations, Fitt poured out his heart about his terrible financial plight. The Major's face lit up.

'Look, you're an MP now,' he said. 'Come with me to the Ulster Bank in Donegall Place. Say "no" to everything, but when I put the pressure on, agree with me in the end,' he instructed Fitt as they walked out of City Hall.

At the bank, Bunting gave some nonsense of an excuse for needing to see the manager, then introduced Fitt to him as the new MP for Dock. Before long, he skilfully turned the conversation to Fitt's banking arrangements and soon Fitt was under pressure from both of them to open an account. As arranged, Fitt refused, then finally agreed, signed on the dotted line and lodged Bunting's own fiver, slipped to him earlier, to open his first bank account. Within minutes, Fitt walked out with the first cheque book he had ever owned. On the way back to City Hall, Bunting told him what a 'post-dater' was and they went to see Tom McGrattan, the friendly manager of the International Hotel. He agreed to give Fitt £40 against a post-dated cheque. Fitt returned to City Hall with a bundle of ten shillings and £1 notes, paid off his helpers and returned Bunting's fiver. After a few celebratory drinks back at the hotel, he went home to Ann and the children with boxes of chocolates for them and his new cheque book in his pocket.

CHAPTER FIVE

GET THE DIRT ON FITT

A FEW MORNINGS AFTER THE ELECTION, Jimmy Gallagher cornered Fitt in a City Hall corridor and whispered an invitation to join the Knights of Columbanus. Now that he was an MP, Gallagher told him, it would be a good move for Catholics and for him. Fitt was astonished that throughout their close association Gallagher had never before admitted his membership, or even mentioned the organisation. He replied that if he could not join as a councillor, he was not going to join as an MP. Fitt was aware that membership could transform personal fortunes, but he regarded the Catholic Knights of Columbanus with as much disdain as the exclusively Protestant Orange Order and Freemasons and he wanted no part of the dubious influence-peddling he saw as characterising their activities. Nonetheless, he was impressed by the social life of the members: 'I remember many times sympathising with acquaintances who were nursing hangovers acquired at their secret get-togethers.'

Such mundane matters were far from Fitt's mind though when he turned up at Stormont for the first time as an MP, to be signed in and duly sworn. The Greek classical-style parliament building sits on the side of the Castlereagh Hills, with panoramic views across the city of Belfast. Approached along a sloping, tree-lined driveway, no detail of its construction or the layout of its environs was neglected by James Craig, Lord Craigavon, the first Prime Minister of Northern Ireland. It was cast in the mould of the cherished mother of parliaments at Westminster, with identical conventions and rules and officials in court dress and a wigged Speaker, but there the resemblance ended. Thanks to British disinterest in Northern Ireland affairs after partition, the unionists had free rein to run, in Craig's own words, 'a Protestant parliament and Protestant state'. Accordingly, the building's decor gave full expression to the unionist passion for flags, uniforms, ceremony and false grandeur.

Lord Craigavon and his cohorts took considerable steps to maintain control of

Northern Ireland from Stormont. The border was drawn to ensure a Protestant majority and constituency boundaries delineated to keep Catholics in a minority. The practice of gerrymandering ensured there was always an overwhelming unionist majority among the fifty-two members of the Stormont commons. All the Prime Ministers and Cabinet ministers were unionists and up until the parliament was finally prorogued in 1972, every single administration in its fifty-one-year lifespan was exclusively unionist. There was an upper house too, the senate, with twenty-four members elected by the commons and two additional seats reserved for the Lord Mayor of Belfast and Mayor of Londonderry/Derry (hereafter 'Derry'). So that their grip on this powerful edifice could be maintained, the Unionist party itself took good care to preserve its support among the grassroots electorate. Membership was confined to Protestants.

Indeed, a virulent anti-Catholic attitude had permeated the private, political and professional lives of the unionists since the foundation of the state. One example illustrates the sectarianism: Dawson Bates, the first Minister of Home Affairs, would not allow his typing to be done by a Catholic and refused to use the telephone when a Catholic was appointed to operate the switchboard. However, the man who sat in the Prime Minister's chair when Fitt arrived at Stormont was Lord Brookeborough, a 'huntin', shootin', fishin'' landowner of great wealth who had made the definitive remarks on the unionist philosophy some years earlier. At a 12 July rally in 1933 he confessed that he had not a Roman Catholic about his own place – an extensive estate in Fermanagh – and appealed to 'loyalists', 'to employ good Protestant lads and lassies'. Returning to the subject a year later, Brookeborough stated publicly that 99 per cent of Catholics were 'disloyal' to the Northern Ireland state and he warned employers that if they did not act properly, by employing Protestants, 'before we know where we are we shall find ourselves in the minority instead of the majority'. When he was invited in Parliament to disown Brookeborough's definition of the role of Catholics in the state, Lord Craigavon refused to do so because 'there is not one of my colleagues who does not agree with him'. The grievances Fitt articulated about the status of Catholics were therefore far from imagined. He later said wryly, 'As I stepped into the unionist den at Stormont, I knew how Daniel felt.'

Before Fitt could tangle with the unionist lions, however, he learned a valuable political lesson from an unexpected source:

> As I had frequently been watching debates from the public gallery as part of serving my political apprenticeship, the personalities, protocol and procedure were familiar to me. So, unawed by them, I was bursting to make my maiden speech. The speaker had taken me to the side on my arrival and told me when I wanted to speak to stand up. Whoever is in the chair will then call you, for that was the convention, I was told. A maiden speaker always gets priority, he is expected to be non-controversial and supposed to

suffer no interruptions. So when the business commenced I proudly took my seat on the backbench and waited my moment. When I eventually stood up, so too did Harry Diamond. The Speaker called him. Astonished I went round to the Chair. He was most apologetic. 'Sorry,' he said, 'the rules appear to have been broken, but this situation has never happened before. He insisted on being called before you. Although it is an unwritten convention, nothing could be done.' Angrily I resumed my seat and as Diamond droned on about matters of our common concern, I mentally crossed out long sections of my planned oration and thought of the headlines he had hijacked in the well-read and influential evening paper. My effort would come too late for it. I realised then not to expect favours from anyone, not least those with an identity of interest. In the cut-throat rivalry of politics at this level, I had learnt the hard way.

As at City Hall, Fitt quickly became disillusioned with the machinations of Stormont. Some years later, in evidence to the Cameron Commission, he described his 'terrible frustration'.

> As soon as you would get up to ask for an enquiry into some particular issue, all the unionist members would walk out and you would be left talking to a single member on the government benches and when you met them in the corridors they would actually jeer at you. If they didn't walk out, they would make rude remarks or shout or sneer and you knew you were wasting your time in Stormont.'

In spite of these obstacles, Fitt managed to carve out a most unlikely, but enduring friendship with a man born into one of the most distinguished unionist families in the country: Phelim O'Neill, later Lord Rathcavan. Eton-educated O'Neill was a cousin of Terence O'Neill, who succeeded Brookeborough as Prime Minister. Tall, dishevelled, charming and utterly self-confident, with all the mannerisms and eccentricities of the born aristocrat, Phelim O'Neill was far from the typical, 'big house' unionist. He had an independent mind, radical opinions and liberal views, and liked to describe himself as a left-wing conservative. He was also fearless, forthright and frank in expressing his opinions, often to the point of indiscretion. Fitt first met O'Neill soon after his election to Stormont thanks to their shared taste for gin and tonic with no ice or lemon. 'Fitt, let's have a drink,' O'Neill would boom at him across the members' bar in Stormont from which point their friendship developed rapidly.

One day they were having a drink in the bar when the division bells rang and everyone rushed out to vote. When O'Neill remained seated, Fitt asked him if he was not going to vote. 'No,' he replied firmly, 'I don't happen to agree with the government. It's very unwise to bring in so many bills, which only cause more division. I say, Fitt, let's get a taxi and go downtown for a drink. We'll go to my club.' A car was called and they headed into town.

Fitt had never been inside the Ulster Club and his arrival in that bastion of the unionist Establishment, in the company of the eccentric O'Neill, caused some consternation. After a few G&Ts there, in what was plainly a whole new world to Fitt, he persuaded O'Neill to pay a visit to some of his favourite haunts. They headed up to the New Lodge Road where they supped a few more in Jim O'Kane's Starry Plough, before traveling, via the bookies for a flutter, to Tommy McCluskey's pub on Harding Street. By all accounts O'Neill enjoyed the outing very much and in the taxi on the way back to Stormont he said: 'You know, Fitt, one half of the world doesn't know how the other half lives.'

By then O'Neill was locked in battle with the uncompromising unionism and the unshakeable bigotry he so despised. Not long before he had been drummed out of the Orange Order for attending a Catholic service during a civic week in Ballymoney. It was a source of great amusement to him that the local Orange Hall, where he was such a reviled figure, was built on his land. True to character, he did not bother to disguise his contempt for his tormentors. 'Talking to some of one's constituents is as rewarding as addressing one's pigs in their sty,' he told Fitt. On another occasion, when they were gazing out over a field from a window in Lizard Manor, his beloved north Antrim farm, he pointed to a group of bullocks huddled under a tree: 'You know, Fitt, there's more intelligence among them than you'll find among the entire Cabinet.'

Such interludes were rare, however, and failed to disguise the unremitting hostility and aggravation Fitt faced as he persisted in raising his concerns and issues in both Stormont and City Hall. At the end of June, Robert Lowry, then a bright, highflying lawyer and later Lord Chief Justice of Northern Ireland and an eminent Law Lord, presented the conclusions of his twelve-month inquiry into allegations of corruption among unionists in Belfast City Hall. Lowry had been called in after the first whiff of scandal emerged in January 1960, when Fitt was tipped off that a private buyer had outbid Belfast Corporation for land earmarked for housing. The buyer turned out to be a cabinet minister, and even his unionist colleagues disapproved of his behaviour as it was one of them who had leaked the story. Once he had bought the land, he then leased it for private house-building to another company connected to a Belfast legal firm, whose principals were prominent unionists: one was Mayor of a town near Belfast, the other a member of the Stormont Senate. There were many allegations and denials of wrongdoing during public debates at Stormont and at City Hall, but despite the rumours flying at the time, no evidence of illegality was found. The ethics of what had transpired were questionable, though, and there the matter rested for a time.

Then, in early 1961, someone sent anonymous documents to the Minister for Local Government, which alleged that some unionist members of the city council had participated in debates and proceedings of the council in which they had an undeclared pecuniary interest, while others were using knowledge acquired from council business to feather their own nests. It was at this point that the government called in Lowry to publicly sift the allegations and rumours, with powers to compel witnesses to appear before the inquiry and to produce books, notes and documents deemed relevant. Behind the scenes there were intense and bitter recriminations as angry unionists tried to discover who had rocked the boat. So unscrupulous did their behaviour become that a 116-year-old act was quoted in an effort to gag Fitt from speaking in Council about proposed rent increases. The argument ran that as he was a council tenant, he thereby had a pecuniary interest and should not speak or vote on the question of increasing rents for council tenants.

> I ignored the gag to howls of unionist fury and sure enough found myself summoned to Lowry's hearings. The whole affair was now so controversial and attracting so much publicity I had to fend off a queue of ambitious young barristers offering to represent me for free, so valuable an advertisement had the hearings become, but I decided to represent myself. I told Lowry I had no wish to defy the law but I could not deny myself the right to speak for the people I represent. I explained that many of those people were poor and had made representations to me, their elected representative, about being unable to afford the proposed rent increases and I would be failing to represent their views properly by not participating in the debate. The position was actually a higher form of idiocy. The pressure to raise rents was caused by a £79,000 deficit on the housing account but the alternative was to wipe the deficit out by increasing the rates. The vote would then involve members with the pecuniary interest of ratepayers. I told Lowry that the logical extension of this would prevent me from participating in scrutiny of the bus, gas and electricity services, because as a consumer I had a pecuniary interest in all three. I might as well resign from the council and let officials run it without scrutiny.

Lowry eventually accepted the thrust of Fitt's argument and the rightness of his motives and dismissed the complaint against him. On Fitt's part, he was convinced the episode was a unionist red herring, designed to distract or conceal 'all the dirty goings-on that were coming into the spotlight'.

Although he did not prove any criminal behaviour, Lowry found that councillors with business interests in everything from the supply of wines and spirits to crockery had sat through, and sometimes participated in, committee and council meetings without declaring their interest, as a result of which the council had subsequently purchased their wares or approved contracts that were beneficial to them. The central figure in the allegations was Sir Cecil McKee, an estate agent and former Lord Mayor of Belfast. During his ten-year tenure on the Improvement Committee about fifty of his own planning applications had been determined and Lowry, who held that McKee was a 'most unreliable witness' whose evidence he had treated with 'considerable reserve', found that he had specifically influenced one redevelopment scheme in the city in which he owned property. Another prominent unionist councillor, who was involved in an application to run petrol stations, had, according to Lowry, come 'close to acting inconsistently with his duties as a councillor'.

The following November, when the report was debated at Stormont, William Morgan, the Minister for Local Government, said he would be bringing in legislation to ensure councillors declared any interests, refrained from discussing or voting on such matters and withdrew from the meeting. During that debate Fitt was involved in a bit of unionist-baiting. For the first time in his political career he invoked parliamentary privilege to name the solicitor Fred Tughan as the anonymous whistle-blower who had sparked the whole thing off. Tughan never denied this claim. About this same time, Fitt seriously annoyed the unionists in City Hall by opposing the spending of £240 on repairing the robes worn by the aldermen and councillors. 'Archaic and mediaeval symbols,' he called them.

Television was fast becoming a growing influence on politics, as well as all other walks of life and, thanks to his high-profile activities, Fitt was becoming ever more widely recognised wherever he went. His reputation as a politician who was genuinely interested in people and could get things done was spreading far and wide by word-of-mouth, and people flocked to see him in greater numbers than ever. His weekdays had settled into a routine of City Hall in the morning and Stormont in the afternoon, with some days spent at the tribunals trying to prevent benefits being halted or reduced for the sick and the unemployed. Fitt recalled once sitting next to Harry Diamond on a bus to Stormont and remarking to him what a busy week it would be, with seventeen tribunal cases over the next few days: 'He was genuinely shocked that I undertook such work, saying that MPs should not. I said that was the sort of help people who came to me needed and I was going to carry on the same way.'

The problems Fitt was encountering were as varied as ever. One particularly common complaint involved the extortionate interest rates levied by moneylenders, which led people into owing more than they had borrowed in the first place – a situation Fitt knew only too well from his own hard times. One night a man from Portadown came to him in near desperation, saying he was in the grip of a moneylender. Fitt handed him his phone, instructed him to ring the moneylender and explain that, as he had a wife and children to support, he could not pay anything that week. As expected, the moneylender launched into a tirade, threatening dire consequences if the £200 debt were not paid. Fitt took the phone, listened to this rant for a few moments, then stated who he was and told the lender he would get no more money. He warned that if there was any trouble at all, he would personally raise the matter in parliament and report it to the police. Fitt settled many such cases in the same way and went on to introduce a bill at Stormont proposing comprehensive regulation of the activities of moneylenders. His bill was eventually passed with almost unprecedented unanimous all-party support.

One of the busiest committees at City Hall was education, and its workload included the onerous duty of appointing teachers to the many city-run schools. A number of Protestant clergymen had been co-opted onto the committee for this task, which involved interviewing the applicants and identifying the most suitable candidate in each case. (The Catholic schools operated independently and appointed their own staff because they were jointly financed by the Church and government.) There was invariably a lot of lobbying for vacancies by teachers, and consequent horse-trading between the rival churchmen and councillors, who would promise support for one appointment if they received it in return for their preferred candidate. Fitt recalled how he sat on the committee over a period of several weeks and watched a young, well-qualified woman interviewed for job after job and fail to be selected. One day he trailed her after the meeting and said, 'What is wrong with you, love, they never give you a job?' After talking to her a while he discovered the problem: 'The poor girl was a Seventh-day Adventist ... I was relieved to find it was not only Catholics who suffered religious discrimination.'

Fitt's move to Stormont brought him into close contact with the trade union movement for the first time, an institution that was, unusually, organised on all-Ireland lines through the Irish Congress of Trades Unions (ICTU). Soon after his election to Stormont, he was invited by the shop stewards at Short Brothers and Harland to join a deputation to London to see the Minister of Aviation. The aircraft-making firm had played a key role in the war, but had declined steadily ever since, and the deputation's aim was to persuade the minister to put work their way to head off redundancies, possibly even closure.

By Belfast standards, Fitt was well travelled, having been around the world with the Merchant Navy. The short, 500-mile journey to London, which he had made many times during his seagoing days, should therefore have been simplicity itself, but when he received the itinerary from committee member Andy Holmes, however, he realised it involved flying from Aldergrove to London Heathrow on a Vickers Vanguard, a mode of travel Fitt had never used before and did not fancy one little bit:

> I began by manufacturing excuses about visiting non-existent relatives in London and going the night before, by rail and sea. Andy Holmes saw through me like a pane of glass and would not hear of it. So, after much persuasion and even taunting, I found myself, uneasily, checking in at the airport on the appointed morning for my first ever aeroplane flight.

As the party waited to board the aircraft, an increasingly nervous Fitt spotted a 'buy yourself insurance' machine. He ran over and anxiously stuffed in a large quantity of coins:

> If this precarious contraption crashes, I thought, at least Ann and the kids

will have as much to live on as if I had won the jackpot on the pools. As we were called forward to board I spotted, to my intense relief, two clergymen, one a priest, the other a minister from the Churches Industrial Council. So I jostled my way into a seat between them, hopeful that in the event of a crash I would go safely to heaven with both Protestant and Catholic blessings.

After that queasy maiden voyage, Fitt became a frequent, albeit reluctant, flier; he always quipped that he was a better Catholic at 29,000 feet. He made a second trip to London in July that year, to take part in a rally at Trafalgar Square calling for the release of Irish political prisoners. Earlier, in February 1962, the IRA had issued a major policy statement calling off 'the campaign of resistance to British occupation'. The movement said it had dumped all its arms and withdrawn all its volunteers. It had done so because of a distinct lack of grassroots support. Although broadly sympathetic to the concept of a united Ireland, the majority of Northern Ireland's Catholics realised they were better off in the North and benefiting from the British welfare state, which gave them a far higher standard of living than they could have expected in the South. In the North, benefits were paid at exactly the same rate as they were throughout Britain. This was the primary consideration in Fitt's Belfast heartland, where the IRA effort had failed significantly to trigger a popular rising. Although the violence had ended, there were still twenty-nine people in prison, interned without trial, including the brother of James O'Kane, Fitt's former council colleague, and the London rally was to call for their release.

Soon after Christmas 1962, Fitt visited Belfast prison to meet these remaining internees and he then contacted Brian Faulkner, the minister of home affairs, to find out whether he could obtain early release for them. It was Fitt and Faulkner's first close encounter and it sowed the seeds of a mutual respect and trust that would flourish in the years ahead. Fitt described Faulkner as 'a stern, tough politician, unafraid of controversy. He talked in an educated Ulster accent, slightly out of the side of his mouth, but he shot straight from the hip.' At that time, Fitt specifically asked Faulkner to release O'Kane. Faulkner called Fitt back to a second meeting the following week, and was at his desk rifling through the file as Fitt sat down. Faulkner asked him if he could give an undertaking that the prisoner would not resume involvement in IRA activity upon release. Fitt immediately stood up to leave: 'No, I couldn't give you any undertaking. All I'm doing is putting forward a case.' He headed for the door.

'Come back, sit down,' Faulkner said. 'If you had said you could give me such a guarantee, I wouldn't have believed you. All the other representations have been like that. In fact, yours is the only honest one. I've looked at the case. I think I can do something. A nod should be as good as a wink to a blind horse.'

Early next morning, Fitt saw a newspaper placard announcing that three men had been released, one of them being the man on whose behalf he had lobbied Faulkner. Jim O'Kane insisted he come to the Starry Plough to join the celebrations:

> I felt out of place. The 'freedom fighters' were no advertisement for manhood. One was small and balding, the others lanky country fellows. They had little to say for themselves, nothing politically constructive. It was an impression that stuck. That was the moment I realised the IRA was not, and never would be, the instrument of the reunification of Ireland because of their personal and political impotence.

On 23 March 1963 Lord Brookeborough resigned on health grounds after twenty years as Prime Minister. Although the final years of his regime were marked by a growing disenchantment with his stagnant style of government, fulsome tributes were paid to him in the Stormont commons, something Fitt found abhorrent as he regarded the aging Brookeborough as the last of Europe's great dictators. He said all they had in common was a duodenal ulcer. Fitt was astonished that he and his wife, Cynthia, were reputed to have directed that the first motorway in Northern Ireland should be routed east – west, from Belfast to Dungannon, to speed them on their weekend away to the country estates in Fermanagh they loved so much. There was no public leadership battle. Captain Terence O'Neill, who had served as finance minister for the previous seven years, 'emerged' as Brookeborough's successor. His principal opponent, Brian Faulkner, was pipped at the post. O'Neill, ex-Eton and the Guards and a member of the landed classes, was an eminently sincere man but had little charisma and a less-than-flamboyant public personality. Fitt always wondered why Brookeborough had backed him instead of the far more dynamic Faulkner:

> I think O'Neill may have been preferable because Faulkner was a sort of 'Johnny come lately' in unionist terms, whose wealth, position and influence had been earned rather than inherited. For me the mystery remains, particularly as Faulkner's charming and able wife, Lucy [now Lady Faulkner] had for many years been Brookeborough's private secretary. I think Brookeborough made two grievous mistakes, given his strong position. In not preparing the climate for change, both within his party and among the population, he eventually unleashed the most ferocious sectarian lions like Paisley. By entrusting the regime to a well meaning but ineffectual successor he condemned the place to its subsequent misery. If he had had the vision and the courage, he would have ensured the succession for Faulkner, despite his hardline image a modern politician, able, pragmatic, visionary. When Faulkner got his chance it was too late.

The advent of O'Neill heralded, in the fashionable phrase of the time, the 'winds of change'. In actual fact, little gusts of change were already in the air. In 1960 the Down county gaelic football team had won the Sam Maguire Cup, and Belfast

Corporation was prevailed upon to honour the team with a civic reception. It was an unprecedented gesture and many Catholics appreciated it as a symbol of change and long-overdue inclusivity. In 1963 Pope John XXIII died and, despite the raucous protests of Paisleyites, the flag on City Hall was lowered to half-mast as a mark of respect. These simple, courageous gestures convinced many sections of Catholic opinion that reform was possible, fairness achieveable and reconciliation attainable. Indeed, among all but the most extreme republican and nationalist fringe, the question of a united Ireland was downgraded to an aspiration that would be kept alive, but put on the long finger indefinitely. Fitt detected and shared this feeling and was prepared to co-operate with liberal unionism to create a fairer and equal society in Northern Ireland.

Before even twelve months of the O'Neill premiership had passed, however, it was clear that support for the new liberal brand of unionism was far from unanimous. In a bold move to foster constructive community relations, O'Neill instigated a series of civic weeks throughout Northern Ireland but when he was photographed shaking hands with nuns the entire unionist establishment trembled with fury.

Fitt gave a speech at Stormont in October 1963 that summed up for O'Neill the mindset of the Catholic community: 'Something should be done to show my co-religionists that if they do extend the hand of friendship it will be taken in the spirit in which it was given.' He went on to urge the unionist government to reach out to the people he represented, the unemployed, the working class, the men with big families who suffered directly from the discrimination in Belfast. Fitt said nothing had been done in recent times to bridge the deep divisions, which had to be healed before there could be any real prosperity. He encouraged the government to take positive steps to improve relations with the trades unions, in particular, and their political opponents in general, so that real progress could be made. Privately, he realised his demands were already doomed; O'Neill was unable to deliver because of the unyielding hardliners within his party.

O'Neill's premiership spurred the hitherto dormant Northern Ireland Labour party into renewed action. After the split in the all-Ireland Labour movement, the NILP had enjoyed some success in unionist areas, using an incongruous mixture of socialist policies and 'Kick the Pope' bands to persuade voters that they were 'sound' on the constitutional link with Britain. They got four party members into the Stormont Parliament; Fitt irreverently called them 'Matthew, Mark, Luke and John' because they all had lay preacher backgrounds. For many years these 'Protestant socialists' had operated an unwritten truce with the Catholic labour groupings, such as Fitt's Dock Irish Labour party, but sensing change they announced in April 1963 that in future they would challenge Fitt and Harry Diamond on their own ground. The NILP believed the time was ripe to bring socialists together on a non-sectarian ticket.

The NILP's new initiative prompted a political merger between Fitt and Diamond. When they returned to Stormont after the summer recess in October 1963, they declared themselves members of the newly formed Republican Labour party. The nature of this amalgamation was aptly portrayed by one local journalist: 'Two one-man parties merged to become one two-man party.' Initially, there was some acrimony between Fitt's Dock supporters and Diamond's cadre on the Falls Road, but eventually both sets of activists recognised the wisdom of the merger and the winding up of the Dock Irish Labour party although Fitt and his people had some deep reservations about the use of the term 'republican' in the party title.

Despite this reservation, Fitt recognised that if they were to beat off the NILP challenge, they could do so more effectively on a basis of strength and unity. Moreover, he had high hopes that if O'Neill could overcome his opponents and deliver the overdue reforms he had promised, there would be a need for a formal opposition at Stormont, a role that nationalists had hitherto always declined. The same year another new party emerged. The National Democratic Party (NDP) was set up by a group of middle-class Catholic people, mainly teachers. A year of significant political change ended with another interesting move when Eddie McAteer, a Derry tax consultant, became leader of the Nationalist party, a group Fitt disdained as 'green Tories', who mainly represented the Catholic rural areas outside Belfast.

Within just twelve months all of these contenders were given ample chance to prove their worth at the polls. The first contest took place in May 1964, when Fitt consolidated his power-base in the Dock ward by getting re-elected to City Hall, this time alongside Tommy Fitzpatrick, a docker, and Jimmy McMenamin, a publican. Their campaigning priority on the council was to ensure that families living in the slums in the Dock area were rehoused in redeveloped dwellings there and not moved miles away to new suburban estates. However, the most significant poll took place towards the end of the year, when Sir Alec Douglas-Home, who had taken over from Harold Macmillan as British Prime Minister, called a general election for October. In Northern Ireland it proved to be a landmark event.

Harry Diamond was nominated for the West Belfast seat and the usual tough fight was inevitable when three other candidates were nominated: James Kilfedder, a unionist barrister; Billy Boyd, NILP; and Liam McMillan, standing as a republican, meaning the IRA, which, having forsaken its traditional militancy, had come under the influence of Marxism and was becoming involved in agitation over social and economic issues.

McMillan, a tough activist who was known as the 'wee man', established his election headquarters at a shop on Divis Street, where a tricolour was displayed in the window. Strictly speaking, the display was illegal because it contravened the Flags and Emblems Act, but, working on the principle that tricolours on display in Catholic areas offended no one, the police pragmatically turned a blind eye.

The RUC had anyway been opposed to the legislation introduced to ban the tricolour and protect the display of the union flag. Back in 1953, when it was being drafted, the Inspector-General Sir Richard Pim wrote a lengthy objection to the Ministry of Home Affairs:

> Speaking not as Inspector-General but simply as a loyal Ulsterman, the idea of singling out the union flag for special mention in an Act of Parliament does not appeal to me. I feel it would be liable to create, particularly in the minds of those outside the province, the entirely erroneous impression that the union flag cannot be flown in Northern Ireland except under the protection of an Act of Parliament and that the police are at present powerless to deal with any interference with it. I think also that such an Act would provide all those opposed to the government of Northern Ireland with a powerful propaganda weapon.

Inside the ministry, Pim's objection was analysed carefully and a senior official provided a commentary for George B Hanna, the Minister of Home Affairs. Demonstrating how the civil service always adopted a unionist standpoint, the most noteworthy and caustic comment read:

> It is politically impossible to defend any suggestion that a man may not fly the flag of the country on his own property whenever he wants to. If the other side are not disposed to exercise that amount of tolerance, the penal clauses of the Act will provide the means of teaching them to do so.

Fitt also objected to the proposed Act. If the union flag could fly in Protestant areas, where it was cherished, he could not see why other flags could not be flown elsewhere. But someone sympathetic to the Rev Ian Paisley, who had been earning public notoriety for his anti-Catholic activities, informed him about the flag on open display in McMillan's window. On the night of Sunday, 27 September, at his weekly 'gospel' meeting, Paisley told his packed congregation about the 'outrage' being committed on Divis Street and threatened to remove the flag himself if the authorities did not do so within forty-eight hours. Barely twenty-four hours later a team of policemen stormed the republican election premises and seized the tricolour. Crowds who had gathered to see Paisley fulfilling his threat rioted on that and several successive nights. The tricolour was replaced in the window on the fourth night and, once more, police, armed with pickaxe handles and wearing steel helmets, removed it, provoking the worst trouble on the streets for over forty years.

The way the situation was handled greatly offended the entire Catholic community and was an early exhibition of weakness by the O'Neill government which undoubtedly encouraged Paisley into an ever more confrontational posture. Fitt watched as the police broke into the republican election offices:

> My blood was boiling. By not standing up to Paisley and his threats, the

> government and the police stoked up more trouble for themselves [in the]
> future and confirmed fears among all Catholics, even those with no time
> whatsoever for the IRA, that despite his conciliatory talk, O'Neill and the
> unionists were as repressive as ever.

In the event, the unionists won the West Belfast seat. The tricolour was carried at
a republican march the following Sunday and there was no interference from any
quarter. But deep down in the embers, the sparks of sectarian conflict began to
glow again.

At this time three people came into Fitt's life who would play a crucial role in
future events: Paddy Wilson, Paddy Kennedy and Austin Currie. Wilson had
stood against Fitt in the city council elections in Dock in May 1964 and came
bottom of the poll. The following Sunday he met Fitt after the twelve o'clock Mass
at St Patrick's and asked to talk. With his small son, Paul, in tow, they went to a
little café where Wilson, the youngest of seven children from a well-known family
in the Sailortown area, said he did not feel at home in the NILP. Fitt quickly
agreed that he should join the Republican Labour party.

Paddy Kennedy came from a well-known Belfast family who ran a large milk
delivery business. He first met Fitt at a party meeting, where Harry Diamond
introduced them. Fitt was immediately intrigued when Diamond said, 'This is
Paddy Kennedy, BA.' He recalled, 'I was surprised Diamond was so impressed. It
was as if having a fellow with a university degree about the place somehow raised
the tone of the party.'

The third acquaintance was Austin Currie, another graduate from Queen's
University. He came from Dungannon and was elected to Stormont in 1964 at a
by-election. Although Currie was a member of the Nationalist party, Fitt took to
him and they became close political colleagues and even closer friends.

All three shared Fitt's reformist tendencies, but before the year ended they were
again reminded of the great obstacles in their way on both sides of the Irish border.
It was an unfortunate feature of Irish politics in general that political standpoints
were completely identical to religious allegiance. In the south of Ireland, where its
adherents were the overwhelming majority, the Catholic Church enjoyed a special
position and the state's legislation, its administrative practices and everyday life
totally reflected Catholic values and standards. The Angelus bell, for instance,
called the faithful to prayer not only from every church in the land but also over
the airwaves from the state-run radio and television station, Radio Telefís Éireann.

Similarly, Belfast had long refused to open its recreation facilities on a Sunday,
the one day in the week families could enjoy themselves together. The
fundamentalist Protestant lobby was so strong and influential that in some places
the workmen actually chained the swings up on a Saturday lest the Sabbath be
infringed by children climbing a park or playground fence. Against this
background, achieving reform was a particularly tough proposition. In November

1964, when this particular issue was put to a roll-call vote in council, the gallery was packed with Paisleyites and other sabbatarian bigots. The atmosphere was electric as the councillors stood, one by one, and shouted 'For' or 'Against'. The move was defeated by just one vote, that of the NILP's Billy Boyd, the man whose blend of socialism and Orangeism had secured him a place in parliament. But the vote finished him with his own party, divided as it then was between progressives and evangelicals. The newer members saw it as identifying them with the worst elements of fundamentalist religion, unionism and bigotry. It also extinguished whatever lingering respect there might have been for the NILP on the Catholic minority side and dashed any hope that one day, in line with Connolly's aspiration, which Fitt shared, the working class might unite across the sectarian divide and the Irish border.

After the vote there was scuffling outside the council chamber and Fitt – already the number-one hate figure for many in the crowd – was subjected to jostling and punches. One of his supporters, Joe 'Smoothing Iron' McGrath – so named for once beating up a rival with an iron bar – clobbered some of the Paisleyites on Fitt's behalf, causing Paisley to seek the intervention of a nearby policeman.

'Arrest that man,' he demanded, pointing at McGrath.

'What man? I saw nothing,' insisted the officer.

'What is your name?' shouted Paisley. The officer replied politely, giving his name. 'Well, it's no wonder you saw nothing with a Roman Catholic name like that,' bellowed a furious Paisley.

Fit did not win all of his battles, however. Early in 1964, two months after the assassination of John F Kennedy in Dallas, Fitt proposed that the name of the main road running through the newly built Turf Lodge housing estate should be re-named John F Kennedy Road. This was not a welcome proposal because the Irish-American Kennedy dynasty was as unpopular with the unionists as it was popular with nationalists. Predictably, the housing committee rejected Fitt's suggestion and ruled that the road would remain Monagh Road, a name taken from the town land which it bisected.

One Friday afternoon, though, Fitt was able to prove that unionist intransigence could be overcome. Leaving City Hall, he spotted workmen loading the municipal red carpet into a van. One of them told him that next morning, at a North Belfast church, the son of one of the city fathers was being married and the carpet was being borrowed to add an extra gloss to the occasion. Fitt had been having some difficulty with this particular councillor over a planning application for an extension to a Catholic-owned pub in the Dock ward, a matter that had been protracted more than was usual. Sensing an opportunity for a breakthrough, Fitt turned up outside the church at the appointed hour the following morning and watched the bride and groom arrive. 'Good morning, Alderman,' he said to his colleague, to make sure he knew of his presence. Next Monday morning, when the planning matter was scheduled to be discussed yet again, on the way into the committee room Fitt said to his colleague, 'Nice to see you got a good day for the wedding, and didn't the carpet look well.' When they reached the relevant item on the agenda, it was clear the man had been sufficiently embarrassed and the planning approval was given without further dissent.

On the morning of 9 December, as the eventful year of 1964 drew to a close, Fitt had a pretty routine day planned: an appearance before a local tribunal in the morning, then an afternoon at Stormont where he planned to speak in a debate on the National Insurance Bill. As he was on his feet at the despatch box, he felt unwell and managed to exclaim, 'Mr Speaker, I feel ill' before he tumbled to the floor. 'Suddenly it felt again like being on the catwalk of a swaying tanker; then I saw hundreds of colours and collapsed,' he recalled. Ian McClure, an eminent surgeon who sat as Unionist MP for Queen's University, rushed to attend him as he was carried from the chamber. McClure diagnosed a bleeding ulcer and arranged for an ambulance to rush Fitt to the Royal Victoria Hospital. His own reputation for helping people in distress was obviously well-known to the ambulance attendant. On the journey through the city, he told Fitt about his employers and how they often ignored the 42-hour week he was supposed to work. As Fitt was being wheeled into the casualty department, the ambulance man pressed a note into his hand asking him to get in touch later, when he was recovered.

The hospital doctors confirmed McClure's diagnosis and prescribed a massive blood transfusion. By the time Ann got to the hospital, he was safely installed in bed and they were able to reassure her of his complete recovery. Over the next few days he had a stream of visitors from both sides of the political divide and so many flowers that the doctors imposed a ban on any more.

> After a few days I felt my old self again. 'Nurse, can you tell me if the blood they gave me was Protestant or Catholic?' I asked. 'Why do you ask?' said the surprised girl. 'I think it must be Protestant blood myself. I feel like singing "The Sash My Father Wore".'

He was discharged on 21 December and at home with Ann and their five daughters – the youngest, Geraldine, had been born in 1963 – for the last Christmas they would spend in the council flat at Annadale Street. One morning early in the new year as she made her way to school, Betty, their eldest daughter, spotted an open back door and went in to look around an empty, vandalised house. She fell for it instantly and dragged Ann and Gerry round for an inspection. It was a big terrace house, with a basement and enough bedrooms upstairs for the whole family to spread out. Fitt was keen to buy it because he believed that, with his parliamentary salary, he should vacate the council flat so it could be re-allocated to a family more needy than themselves. So, with a loan secured from the bank, the windows covered with curtains made by Ann and following some plastering and other work carried out by Billy Napier, on 12 July 1965, after the Orangemen and bands had passed by, the family moved their possessions the hundred yards or so from the flat to the new house at 85 Antrim Road. Although they could not have foreseen it, the Fitt family were to live through momentous times there.

Back on 14 January 1965, at almost the same moment as Betty found the new house, O'Neill pulled the boldest stroke of his career when he received Sean Lemass, the Prime Minister of the Irish Republic, at Stormont Castle. It was the first time the political heads of the divided country had met since the brief and abortive contacts between James Craig and Michael Collins forty years earlier. A month later, in February, O'Neill reciprocated the gesture by making an equally historic and ground-breaking visit to Dublin.

After so much disappointment that O'Neill's commitment to reform had not been matched with action, Fitt could only applaud his courage. He interpreted the meetings as a clear sign that, regardless of the vigorous Paisleyite mobs who plagued his every move, and regardless of his constant critics within the Unionist party, O'Neill was striking out for new, higher ground. However, as the visits created yet more uncertainty in the minds of O'Neill's opponents, it also strengthened their hostility. O'Neill's assurances that improved relations and economic co-operation with the South would not threaten the constitutional link with Britain were simply not enough for the diehards. Instead of seeing the *rapprochement* as a hopeful sign of a peaceful future, they chose to interpret it as the thin end of the wedge, a ploy to draw them into an all-Ireland state. Fitt was frustrated by the development because the renewed debate over who was for or against the border once more threatened to obscure the far more important issue of achieving equal rights for the working class, Catholic and Protestant:

> I firmly believe that if there had been an organised opposition formed at that time, a coalition of the NILP, nationalists and ourselves, that we could have collectively exerted enough pressure to save Terence O'Neill from the hardline bigots thwarting his desire for reform and plotting all the time to undermine him.

In October 1965, battered by disloyalty and debilitated by constant plots to overthrow him, O'Neill chose an unexpected way to boost his precarious position by calling an election two years early to appeal directly to the electorate over the heads of his divided parliamentary party, which was predominantly hostile to him. For Fitt and his young family, basking in the security of a steady wage, the risk of losing his seat had potentially calamitous personal consequences. He was in the bank the day after polling was announced when the manager called him in for a chat. The conversation showed he was worried about Fitt's ability to repay the recently advanced loan on 85 Antrim Road. 'Tell me about your chances,' he enquired politely.

'Well, I have to be honest,' replied Fitt. 'Nobody has ever held the Dock seat twice in succession,' and he recited the history of the constituency's voting record. As the bank manager showed him to the door, he whispered that if a few cars on polling day would help, he would send them along. Fitt nodded his agreement, sure the offer had more to do with his continued ability to repay the loan than with any sympathy for his political philosophy.

Fitt defied history and retained the Dock seat with a more than doubled majority over his old opponent Billy Oliver, up from 507 to 1,310. It was the highest majority ever achieved in the seat. Harry Midgley, the man on the pony and trap who had been Fitt's earliest political inspiration, had achieved only a 1,208 majority with Catholic and Protestant support. Of all the political records he ever established, this was the one Fitt cherished the most and the bars in the constituency were the scene of great celebrations, which lasted for a couple of days.

The election was a Pyrrhic victory for O'Neill, as he was still surrounded by his hardline opponents. But less than a month after the discouraging result he showed that he was not to be cowed in his efforts to bring about reconciliation when he ventured across the border again. This time it was to visit Patrick Gormley, one of the nationalist MPs at Stormont, who had been injured in a car crash and was recovering in hospital. It was a doubly significant gesture: crossing the border again and visiting a non-Unionist MP.

Unyielding unionism surfaced again in February 1966 when the time came to name a new bridge across the Lagan, the river that courses through the centre of Belfast. The building of the new bridge was a great event in the city's history and when the council invited suggestions from the public about what it should be called, shoals of letters flowed into City Hall. The bookmakers got in on the act too, laying odds on the favourite suggestions: Carson Bridge, after Lord Carson, the architect of partition; or the Somme Bridge, after the thousands of Ulstermen who died there in the First World War. The final choice of name was to be made at a meeting of the Improvement Committee of the council on Tuesday, 15 February, but Fitt learned the actual decision was taken the previous Friday at a caucus meeting of the Unionist party in City Hall. Next morning, one of those present telephoned him and said, 'Gerry, get a few bob on. It's to be Carson.' Fitt gathered up £10 and later that day, as it would not have been prudent to be seen placing the bet himself, sent a friend to do so. The odds on Carson were 6/4.

On Tuesday morning, hours before the committee meeting, the *Belfast News Letter* carried the story that it was to be named Carson Bridge, but also reported some rumblings among the unionists that it ought to be named after Queen Elizabeth, who was to perform the official opening that summer. This suggestion was credible enough for the Governor's secretary at Hillsborough to telephone the

Town Clerk to urge that the Queen should not be embarrassed by being involved in a political controversy. City Hall was buzzing with tension as the committee gathered and there were television cameras present. Fitt exercised his right as a councillor to attend the committee meeting, although as he was not a member he therefore had no vote.

The agenda had the usual dull starters before the main course. It was agreed to drill bore-holes to determine water levels on a new ring road. Then, as if it was spontaneous and not pre-arranged, it was proposed and seconded that the new bridge should be called after Lord Carson, and there were glowing references to his role as the founding father of Ulster. But Sir Cecil McKee threw a spanner into the carefully planned works. Since the Lowry report he had become a maverick unionist and Fitt listened incredulously as this veteran of secret decisions in a thousand smoke-filled caucus rooms challenged the proposal and suggested the bridge should be named after the Queen. Fitt moved liked lightning from his seat and crouched beside McKee, 'Propose that, propose that,' he said, ' and I'll get you a seconder.' He then moved around the table to where his party colleague and full committee member Tommy Fitzpatrick was sitting. 'Second that, Tommy. Second that,' Fitt urged him. He did so, but most reluctantly, thinking Fitt must have taken leave of his senses.

The plot had come to Fitt in a flash, as McKee was speaking. As an amendment, the naming of the bridge would have to be voted on first and, just as he had calculated, the atmosphere in the room changed suddenly when the implication dawned on the unionists that they could not vote against the Queen. For once their much-vaunted loyalty was on the line.

Mrs Hilda Wilson was the first to react. She came from Blackpool, she said, and Ulster was her adopted country and she could not vote against the Queen. Another member, recently knighted, said he would not want to be adversely on the record in such a vote. 'It would be unthinkable to vote against Her Majesty,' said another. The Town Clerk, mindful of the earlier telephone call from the Queen's representative in Northern Ireland, moved to harvest the new consensus. Without resort to a vote, the minutes record to this day that it was decided unanimously to name the new river crossing, the Queen Elizabeth Bridge.

After the meeting Fitt had to face an extremely nervous Tommy Fitzpatrick. His surprise intervention had made him the centre of media attention and he wanted Fitt to handle the consequences. Never short of words to promote his causes, Fitt made the point that the new name was less offensive to Catholics than that proposed originally, and that it was something of a coup to have upset the unionists' well-laid plans. Catholic public reaction over the following days backed up Fitt and he was pleased enough with the debacle he had created for the unionists to write off his £10 bet as being well worth the loss.

Belfast's backstreet poets always amused Fitt with their ingenious parodies of pop songs and rhymes. The bridge row inspired one of them, a man associated with the extreme Ulster Protestant Action organisation, to compose a piece of doggerel that was duplicated and circulated widely around Dock as a piece of black propaganda to discredit him:

> We republicans are worried
> and don't know what to do
> For Gerry Fitt has told us
> that we are British too.
> 'A nation once again,' he squeals
> when he's looking for our vote
> but now for his convenience
> we're supposed to turn our coat.
> For he is now determined
> to pay homage to the Queen
> and forget about ould Ireland
> and the wearing of the green.
> He's used our faithful people
> to further his own cause.
> He'd sell our true religion
> to uphold those foreign laws.

The spectre of a British general election had been constantly in the background since the Wilson government took power in 1964 with a single-figure majority. Early in 1966, as the likelihood of an early election increased, Fitt's thoughts began to turn to what would happen in West Belfast. For some time his sights had been set firmly on winning the seat, and he judged that the time had at last come for him to try to do so.

The constituency – one of twelve Northern Ireland Westminster divisions created after partition – had stayed in unionist hands until 1943 when Jack Beattie, a Protestant shipyard worker representing the NILP, won it with a 5,510 majority. He successfully defended it in the 1945 general election, fighting as Independent Labour, albeit with a majority cut to 4,058. After that Beattie changed his political designation to Federation of Labour (Ireland) and then Irish Labour, but lost the seat in 1950 to the Rev Godfrey McManaway by a margin of 3,378 votes. Beattie's alignment with anti-partition labour groupings played into the hands of his opponent, a Church of Ireland rector, whose virulent sectarian preaching and politicking had already carried him into the Stormont parliament. When he got to Westminster, however, McManaway's eligibility to sit was challenged under the terms of the 1801 Clergy Disqualification Act, which disbarred those of the Anglican communion from serving as MPs. In October 1950 the Privy Council ruled that he was indeed ineligible, and the West Belfast seat was declared vacant and a by-election called for the following month. Beattie fought again but lost by 913 votes to Thomas Teevan, a young lawyer. In the 1951 general election Beattie came back to defeat Teevan and regain the seat, with a majority of just twenty-five votes. Four years later, in another general election and his final contest, he lost it again to Unionist candidate Patricia McLaughlin, who won an 18,141 majority. McLaughlin successfully defended the seat in 1959 before standing down in 1964, at which time another Unionist, James Kilfedder, won it with a 6,659 majority.

One of the defeated candidates in that contest was Harry Diamond, who had stood as Republican Labour. Fitt and Paddy Kennedy went to his house to persuade him to run again, but they encountered great reluctance. In fact, quoting figures and statistics about the profile of the voters, Diamond tried to convince them the seat was unwinnable due to an unassailable unionist majority. With Diamond thus ruled out, the way was clear for Fitt to promote his own candidacy and, undeterred by Diamond's calculations, he continued to debate his chances with Kennedy. Both agreed the seat was winnable if the Catholic vote was not split. They were absolutely convinced that the critical factor that had allowed the unionists to retain the seat for the past decade had been the intervention of Sinn Féin and labour candidates. If that could be changed, the battle lines would be significantly redrawn in their favour.

But before they could resort to any lobbying or plotting, the issue was forced one Monday in mid-February 1966 when Fitt received a telephone call from John Wallace, political correspondent for the *Belfast Telegraph*. He had just received a statement from the NDP announcing its intention to fight the seat. The statement implied that, as they were first in the field, everybody else should stay out and give them a clear run. Fitt was no fan of the party, which he regarded as a breakaway element from the 'green Tory' nationalists he despised:

> The NDP was full of schoolteachers, solicitors, shopkeepers, mostly professional men. They were great theorists and believed that you could sit night after night and draw up a policy and go out and tell the working class people that this was a policy they had to adopt.

So, 'off the top of my head', Fitt dictated a grandiose statement to Wallace stating that at a packed EGM the previous night, the Republican Labour party had unanimously decided that he would be the candidate for West Belfast at the forthcoming general election. 'I am proud and honoured to carry the banner of James Connolly into this historic constituency', he declared.

When the story appeared in the paper that afternoon, there was the predictably stormy reaction from the NDP, which again called for a united nationalist front and insisted it would be putting forward the sole candidate. In the meantime, the effects of his duodenal ulcer had caused Fitt to collapse again at Stormont, forcing a return to hospital for more treatment. Most importantly, however, the Republican Labour party did actually meet in the party rooms at 34 Berry Street and officially backed his self-nomination. Diamond seemed very resentful, talking pessimistically about the unfavourable arithmetic and the lack of campaign funds, but sixteen of the seventeen people present endorsed Fitt's candidature enthusiastically.

At the end of February Cardinal William Conway, the recently appointed Primate of All-Ireland, made a very significant statement that called on the Catholic community to play its full part in public affairs. It set the seal on the new atmosphere of the O'Neill era and the slowly developing relations with Dublin and convinced Fitt that his efforts to achieve social and economic fairness within the structures of the Northern Ireland state was being endorsed as the right one:

> I recognised that if I could win West Belfast the proper forum to pursue those aims was Westminster, forcing the British government to take an interest in the North, but most importantly, to back up Terence O'Neill whose courageous and enlightened approach to necessary reform was being obstructed by his hard-line opponents.

All this time, Fitt was networking extensively behind the scenes, lining up support for his candidature from the trade union movement and other likely sources. On 2 March, three days after Harold Wilson officially called the long-anticipated election, the NDP nominated Joseph Lavery, an unknown, thirty-six-year-old schoolteacher, to stand in West Belfast. When Fitt heard the news he criticised the NDP for foisting the onerous responsibility of a high-pressure contest onto a young teacher with absolutely no experience of political life.

The first good news about the contest came on 7 March when the NILP, which had polled 12,571 votes in 1964, announced it would not be putting forward a candidate. The deep divisions in the party between the progressives and the evangelicals had dictated their move – not a desire to give Fitt a clear run. The question of whether there should be one anti-unionist candidate and who it should be was by now dominating the letter columns of the Belfast papers and exercising the vocabularies of the political writers. Fitt toured the pubs where the opinion-formers drank, pressing his cause. At Jimmy Keaveney's Duke of York bar, he lobbied for support among the eclectic cabal of politicians, trades unions lawyers, writers, artists and journalists, including the political commentators from the *News Letter*, which was published nearby. Up the street and around the corner he imbibed with the writers from the *Belfast Telegraph* and the *Irish News*, who frequented Frank McGlade's Old Vic lounge. All the glad-handing produced results and regular statements of support for him were published in the papers. Even more encouragingly, on the grapevine he heard the NDP was beginning to crack under the pressure.

Three days after the NILP withdrawal, a Nationalist party senator, Patrick McGill, stated bluntly that Lavery should withdraw and give Fitt a clear run. Although the party officially disowned his opinion, Austin Currie did not and weighed in behind Fitt, followed quickly by all but one of his parliamentary colleagues, Eddie McAteer, the party leader. The NDP then changed tack, arguing that an agreed nationalist candidate should be selected jointly by the NDP and the Republican Labour party. Fitt was having none of it. He persuaded Harry Diamond to come out publicly in his favour and the following Sunday, after a meeting of the NDP executive, their candidate was withdrawn. On 21 March, Fitt handed in his deposit and the nomination papers signed by his proposer, Mrs Mary Ann Fitt, and his seconder and election agent, Stephen McKearney. Nobody else nominated. At last, therefore, it was to be the straight fight with James Kilfedder, the sitting Unionist MP, that Fitt had worked so hard to arrange.

The West Belfast Westminster seat covered four Stormont constituencies: St Anne's, Central, Falls and Woodvale. It included Belfast city centre and a densely populated swathe of streets bounded by Sandy Row, the Lisburn Road, the Falls area and the Shankill Road. The arithmetic of a straight fight was highly encouraging for Fitt. Although there was a 4,700 majority of Protestants in the 67,588 electorate, he believed it was possible to win sufficient of the 12,000 labour votes from the previous election to overcome this because of his well-established reputation as a champion of working-class people, regardless of their religion. From the outset he was confident that Kilfedder's 1964 majority of 6,659 was not impregnable; he had not forgotten the night in 1951 when West Belfast had been won by Jack Beattie in a straight fight.

In those days, fighting an election in Northern Ireland bore little resemblance to the way the hustings were conducted elsewhere in the United Kingdom. It was often said that in Northern Ireland the Resurrection is not considered a miracle because there every graveyard is empty on polling day, when the dead vote in their droves. As Fitt often said, however, if everybody who afterwards claimed to have voted for him had actually done so, his majorities would be numbered in many thousands instead of many hundreds.

The principal electoral controversy was undoubtedly the practice of personation, or vote-stealing. Every election in Fitt's early political career was marked by complaints from constituents who turned up at the nominated polling station only to find their vote had been taken. Fitt was always uneasy about responding in kind, but he knew that the contests were so closely run that failure to do so would not only cost him seats but probably the election itself. At the 1966 election he therefore deployed, for the first time, what was to become the best personation-spotting team in the business: his five daughters. They were promptly dubbed 'The Missfitts' by the press. Their routine task was to check the death notices in the newspapers everyday and on the electoral register mark every deceased constituent with a red dot. In the year before the 1966 election, they recorded details of 411 Protestants who had died and these were distributed to the team of workers installed in St Mary's Hall to run Fitt's campaign.

Like all enterprises, the election industry had developed its own jargon. 'Pluggers' were people who personated somebody else to steal their vote. 'Markers' were people placed in each polling station to tick off the votes claimed and try to get a lead on 'pluggers' for the other side. A 'flying squad' was a team of 'pluggers' touring around polling stations to steal votes. Northern Ireland election folklore is rich with stories of jumble sales being patronised by candidates in the run-up to a campaign, and of quick clothing changes on buses as 'pluggers' went about their work on election days. There is also the infamous story of the woman who made repeated visits to a polling station to vote in different names, each time wearing a different set of clothes. However, she was crippled by bunions and could not disguise her specially adapted shoes. At one election, after having voted several times already, the policeman on duty intercepted her and told her sternly, 'I know from your feet that you've already had more than your fair share of votes, so no more,' as he steered her out the door. Fitt remembered these times well:

> It was always alleged that I had a room in my house full of old clothes and priests and nuns vestments, kept for use in elections but that was never true. I could not, though, put my hand on my heart and say that every vote ever cast for me was a straight one. I made one distinction. If somebody came up during a campaign and said, "There is my mother's vote, she is sick', taking that vote, in my opinion, although illegal, is not immoral. But it is clearly wrong to steal votes from someone who may not have had any intention of supporting you. Thus I never organised vote stealing but did not scruple at maximising my legitimate vote. The important thing however was that the candidate, who could ultimately be unseated, was never party to this. The agent always handled things. He was expendable. His fine could always be paid. The result was not at stake. But this creates a vicious circle and candidates of every hue have to steal back votes to keep the balance. I always much preferred the direct methods of getting the vote out. Ever since the wet day when Billy Napier had talked me out of borrowing money for taxis in the 1958 election, I had become almost neurotic about losing by one vote so that every polling day afternoon I would go around with a loudhailer urging people out. 'Every vote counts. Your vote might win the election.'

After nominations had closed and the campaign got under way, Fitt received an offer of help from a group of Shankill Road men that he initially feared was a unionist 'dirty trick'. They signed their letter to him, 'Yours for the working class.' In spite of his reservations, he invited them to meet him and one evening they all spent a long time in his house talking. At least one Fitt recognised as a communist, but after a while he accepted their integrity and they agreed to work for him in an unusual way: as spies in the Unionist camp. He asked them to attend Unionist party meetings, listen to their campaign plans and keep him fully informed. In the end, he learned that some of them were being paid for their help by both sides, but in terms of intelligence from the other camp, they proved invaluable to Fitt.

One of the titbits they passed on was an innovative Unionist plot to equip their 'pluggers' with pioneer pins, the badges of a Catholic abstinence organisation. As a result, Fitt's own polling station workers were alerted and the plot was strangled before it started.

Kilfedder believed that if he could draw Fitt into a controversy about the constitutional position of Northern Ireland, then the statements Fitt would be forced to make would alienate his potential Protestant supporters. Again, Fitt was tipped off by his spies and gained much valuable publicity by disowning a bogus poster planned by the Unionists – 'Vote Republican - Vote Fitt' – before the ink was even dry. Whether in newspaper interviews, on public platforms or on the doorsteps, Fitt focused on the social and economic issues, assuring people that he would fight for the enlightened social welfare policies promised by the Labour government to be implemented in Northern Ireland. The Unionists, he pointed out, had been tardy about importing the British welfare state and had even voted against some social welfare measures already provided in Britain.

His election literature featured an endorsement drawing on a remark passed by Brian Faulkner on a television programme after Fitt's 1965 Stormont victory. With Faulkner's agreement, the leaflet stated: 'Gerry Fitt deserved to win. He is one of the hardest workers that has ever been in parliament. He gets his support because of the work he does.' It was an extraordinary situation for such a prominent Unionist figure as Faulkner to endorse a candidate fighting his own party and it demonstrated the close personal bond that had already developed between the two men.

As polling day approached, Fitt's spies told him that a previously unheard of, shadowy organisation called Ulster Protestant Action was planning to threaten or physically harm any personation agents he sent into the six polling stations in Protestant areas. In the past, anti-unionist candidates had never bothered, or more likely never dared, to put anyone in to protect their interests because of the unspoken threat of intimidation. But as the spine of Fitt's election strategy was to win the support of Protestant voters and with about 2,000 vital votes at stake, he decided it was essential that his agents go in, at the very least to discourage Unionist vote-stealing. On the eve of the election, as he was finalising plans for the operation and trying to recruit some burly dockers for the purpose, he was told that a man who had promised to do the job for him had already been threatened by Ulster Protestant Action. As a result, many potential agents backed off, a fact that his spies told him was gloated over by the hierarchy of the Unionist party. One Fitt worker who did not flinch when asked to go the Sandy Row polling station was a young Catholic from the Ardoyne district of north Belfast, then studying at Queen's University. Eugene McEldowney, who would later gain distinction as an *Irish Times* journalist and crime novelist, remembers:

At the time, stealing of votes was widespread and the Northern Ireland constituencies regularly recorded the highest turn-out of voters in the UK. Turn-outs of over 90% were not uncommon. This is what gave rise to the slogan: Vote Early and Vote Often. To discourage vote stealing, each candidate was entitled to put a personation agent into the polling stations. His job was to challenge voters if he suspected that they weren't the person whose vote they were claiming. In West Belfast, personation agents were rarely used. In fact they may not have been used since the state was founded in 1921. Partly this was due to fear of going into enemy territory. There was also a belief that since personation was practiced by both sides, it cancelled itself out. But Gerry was taking no chances. He decided to put personation agents into all the polling stations in West Belfast. I volunteered to act as a personation agent for Gerry. I attended a meeting in a room in Divis Street and was allocated Hurst Street school in Sandy Row. I was given an electoral register with all the dead voters marked in red. Where Gerry got this information I do not know but I was told if anybody turned up to claim these people's votes, I was to challenge them. The morning of the election at 8.30am, I crossed the Boyne Bridge and descended into Sandy Row. The place was deserted. I turned up at Hurst St school wearing a blue and green rosette which were Gerry's colours. I will never forget the looks of astonishment on the Unionist officials' faces when I told them I was Gerry's personation agent. They couldn't believe that Gerry had pulled a stroke like this. Immediately, they were on the phone ringing around the other polling stations only to find that Fitt personation agents had gone into all the polling stations in the constituency. I think we managed to limit vote-stealing in that election. At least no dead voters turned up at Hurst St while I was there and I didn't have to challenge anybody. I did witness one interesting incident. In those days if you were illiterate or infirm you could declare your vote and it was recorded for you. An old man came into Hurst St school and said he wanted to declare his vote. The two personation agents were called together to witness it.

'Who do you want to vote for?' the man was asked.

'The Labour man,' he said.

'You have to give us his name.'

'Ah ... Mr ... Mr ...'

He scratched his head while we both waited anxiously to see if he could remember.

'... Mr Fitt,' he said at last. And I had the great satisfaction of putting an X against Gerry's name on the ballot paper and dropping it into the box.

Early on polling day, Fitt was alerted to the personation of some eighty voters at a number of polling stations, including Malvern Street in the heart of the Shankill. Jimmy McKearney, a bus conductor, had volunteered to go there on Fitt's behalf, a brave gesture in itself, as he in an even braver gesture had challenged a person trying to claim one of the votes that was red-dotted. In all, three arrests were made for personation and the people involved were subsequently fined.

By far the most bizarre happening of the day was what has become known as 'the nuns story'. One of Fitt's election headquarters, festooned with a Starry Plough/Connolly flag, was in the Hibernian Hall on the Falls Road. On the morning of polling day the nuns from the Mater Hospital on Crumlin Road, whose votes were to be cast at a polling station in a Protestant area, rang the election office and asked for transport as they could not have walked into that area. After sending a car for them, on what he always insisted (with a wink) was an impulse, Fitt rang round the newspapers and television organisations to advise them of the nuns' imminent arrival. Thus, when the sisters were hissed and booed as they exited the polling station, everyone saw the incident on the evening news. Fitt believed this had a tremendous impact on Catholic voters and was responsible for a late surge to the polls.

That election in fact marked the beginning of the end of the old campaigning style, with its street-corner meetings and oratory. Instead, the police forced the candidates into detours away from so-called flash-points and even banned them from some mixed areas. For the first time the real political shin-kicking was done on television and, to a lesser extent, in the columns of the local newspapers, a pattern that has since evolved to the point where street campaigning is now a thing of the past. Ironically, it was also the first campaign for which Fitt had a band – an answer to the envy he had always harboured of the unionists' marching bands. 'Of all the election expenses incurred,' he always said, 'the cheque I most enjoyed writing was that for the £12-10s paid to the John F Kennedy Band.'

The count took place at the Clarence Place Hall, not far from City Hall, and even before the sealed boxes had arrived from the various polling stations there was a strong police presence and crowds had gathered outside, singing and waving Union Jacks. It was impossible to judge the result until the very end of the count when an official whispered the figures and Fitt learned he was in, with a majority of 2,011. The returning officer made the declaration live on national television as the stunned Unionists looked on: 'Fitt, Gerard, Republican Labour, 26,292. Kilfedder, James, Unionist, 24,281.'

As Fitt was being interviewed afterwards, some of the Unionists tried to embarrass him. One walked over and said loudly, 'Gerry, when are you going to pay me? I plugged loads of votes for you.' Others began singing the British national anthem, 'God Save the Queen', but Fitt and his friends stood their ground in silent dignity, determined not to let themselves down at the moment of victory by succumbing to the provocation. Outside the doors the crowd, initially shocked into silence by the result, found its voice again and began chanting choruses of abuse. The police surrounded Fitt and escorted him out of the hall. They headed to City Hall, but in the middle of his triumphant progress a friendly official pulled him to the side of the excited crowd and said he had overheard a conversation between two prominent unionists. He had heard one, already an MP at Westminster, urge the other, a unionist MP at Stormont, to 'get the dirt on Fitt and we'll finish him off in London'.

CHAPTER SIX

THEY'RE VOTING FOR FITTSIE DOWN SANDY ROW WAY

FITT'S VICTORY FRACTURED the ten year Unionist monopoly of the twelve Northern Ireland seats in London, and they were understandably furious. When they finally left City Hall, Fitt and his jubilant supporters again needed the help of the police to push their way out safely through the jeering crowds. Later, as he made the traditional victory speech to his election workers on the Falls Road, Fitt said his thoughts were harking back eleven years, to the night of Jack Beattie's victory, and he told them how deeply he savoured this moment of success. Next, he headed for the *Irish News* offices in Donegall Street, where the printers and drivers gathered to congratulate him before heading out across Northern Ireland to deliver the freshly printed copies of the paper with the news of his great victory. In the reporters' room upstairs, he was delighted to learn that the results pouring in from across the United Kingdom indicated there would be another Labour government in London, this time with an increased majority:

> I knew they would be much more likely than the Conservatives to tackle the problems in what had been graphically described by the *Sunday Times* as 'John Bull's political slum'. The Conservatives were natural allies of the unionists.

When he eventually got home to Ann and his daughters and had time to reflect on what the victory meant, he realised that despite the appalling bigotry that was manifest during the campaign, there were signs of compromise and change: 'The size of my majority indicated that a significant number of Protestants had rejected the flag-waving and slogan-shouting and thought about the issues which I had plugged away at.' Within days, Fitt's victory was immortalised on record by a group called The Kinsfolk, which topped the local pop charts for the next six weeks. 'They're Voting For Fittsie Down Sandy Row Way' was written and sung by Eugene McEldowney and recounted the events of that sweet victory:

> Come gather round boys now and give me an ear
> And I'll sing you a song that will fill you with cheer.
> For this daring story has not been told yet
> It concerns our own hero, the bold Gerry Fitt.
>
> Tooreye yay, tooreye yay.
> They're voting for Fittsie down Sandy Row way.
>
> Nineteen sixty-six being the year of renown,
> An election was coming in old Belfast town,
> But the boys in the west, they were still in great doubt
> For to find the right man to put Kilfedder out.
>
> Fifteen years had passed since the seat had been lost
> And many's the heart with sad grief had been tossed,
> But one man remained who could win it back yet
> The people's own champion, the bold Gerry Fitt.
>
> Now Gerry was a stalwart, from the Docklands he came
> And over the years he'd been rising in fame.
> He followed brave Connolly, a hero indeed,
> And he fought for all workers wherever in need.
>
> When Fittsie came over he said, 'Gentlemen,
> I stand by old Ireland but I'll tell you again,
> If you come from the Shankill, the Row or the Falls,
> When I go to Westminster I'll fight for you all.
>
> 'I'll fight for you all and I'll tell you for why:
> If you want to succeed, all together must try,
> I want to see bigotry laid down the drain
> And Ireland a nation amongst nations again.'
>
> The day it came round and the fight it was fast
> But Gerry's supporters were true to the last.
> From the Whiterock and the Loney and Sandy Row too,
> The votes for bold Fittsie came all piling through.
>
> They took them for counting in the big City Hall
> And they say, in the silence, you could hear a pin fall.
> Then up spake the Lord Mayor from where he did sit,
> 'You have got a new MP – his name's Gerry Fitt!'

Elsewhere in Belfast the unionist candidates retained their seats but saw their majorities clipped substantially by Labour. In East Belfast the unionist majority was slashed by two-thirds, from more than 9,000 to just over 3,000. However, any wishful thinking about breaking the political mould was soon shattered by reality when, next morning, Fitt had to explain patiently to Robin Day why the sectarian facts of life in Belfast prohibited him from going to the shipyard to be interviewed on the gantries. That day was hectic, with non-stop telephone calls from well-wishers and a flood of telegrams. Journalists bombarded him with questions: Would he take the Labour whip at Westminster? Where would he sit? How could he successfully combine the duties of his triple mandate, as a city councillor, Stormont MP and Westminster MP? How much time would he spend at Westminster?

There were also angry confrontations with unionists, televised to the nation, as his opponents tried to refute his charges about dirty work during the campaign. Fitt waved the evening paper at the cameras to show that three people had been charged with personation. He revealed that he knew the full details of the dirty campaign against him, as reported by the men who had volunteered as double agents. The unionists had never faced this kind of media attention and they found it acutely embarrassing. Fitt sensed that this was the start of a new political era:

> I believed that the need for a tide of reform, correctly sensed by Prime Minister Terence O'Neill was beginning to roll, despite the efforts of the hardliners in the Unionist party. All through these interviews I hammered home the message that I was going to Westminster to demand the same rights and benefits for my constituents as the citizens of Manchester or Birmingham.

Austin Currie believes that, within the political conditions prevailing at the time, when one-party rule had been in existence for some forty years and the Unionists employed discrimination and gerrymandering to consolidate and maintain it, Fitt identified correctly 'the Achilles' heel of unionism' as the basis for his coming work at Westminster:

> The weakness was not their opposition to a united Ireland but their professed loyalty and commitment to British standards while refusing those same standards to those they ruled over. Gerry's simple demand ... for the same rights for his constituents in Belfast as were enjoyed by British citizens in Birmingham, had unanswerable logic. His ability to seize every opportunity to embarrass Unionists, his capacity to highlight the intransigence of the Unionist government and a personality which enabled him to win friends and influence people ... were the critical factors.

Just how sensitive the Unionists were about Fitt's election victory became clear a few days after the count. About 3.00am his confidante from the earlier mêlée in City Hall rang from a call box, clearly more than a little inebriated. 'Gerry, Gerry,' he said urgently, 'do you know a woman called Kitty O'Shea? Well watch out. I've heard the Unionists talk about setting you up with her.' Next morning Fitt headed into City Hall and found his friend, as he had expected, nursing a massive hangover. 'Come on for a cure,' he said, encouraging him in the direction of the International Hotel. There he listened patiently as his contact mulled over reasons for the telephone call.

'Look,' he said again, 'do you know a woman called Kitty O'Shea?'

'No,' Fitt replied, managing to keep a straight face. 'But I recognise the name.'

'Well you better watch out then, for she's going to turn up and set you up,' he said.

'What do you mean? Where did you hear this? Who is she?' asked Fitt.

'Look, Gerry, you know I'm a Freemason and I'm not really supposed to talk about it, but last night I was at a "do" in the hall on the Crumlin Road, by the prison, and there were a load of Unionists there, including some members of parliament. Well, I saw them all standing together, laughing and talking, obviously plotting, for I overheard your name. So I moved in to earwig on them to see what they were at. Someone mentioned Kitty O'Shea and they said when they found her, they would use her to fix you good and proper. They all laughed.'

Fitt left his friend without enlightening him about the relevant episode in Irish history that explained the reference, but if the Unionists did actually think he was another Charles Stewart Parnell, it showed not only the depths they would plumb to discredit him but also how badly they had misjudged him. Nevertheless, when he arrived at the Commons to take his seat a few days later, amidst the whirl of introductions, including to Prime Minister Harold Wilson, he was casting a wary eye over every female he met. A few nights later, while drinking in the Strangers Bar at the House of Commons in London, his alarm bells rang loudly when a very pretty girl with a Northern Ireland accent, and 'the shortest miniskirt I had ever seen', joined the company and said how pleased she was by his victory and how much she had wanted to meet him. Fitt recalled:

> Now there are people in Northern Ireland who claim to be able to spot Catholics and Protestants just by looking at them. Some say that Catholics' eyes are closer together than Protestants' and that is how they can tell. Some people even claim they can tell your religion by the way you pronounce the letter 'h'. But I fell back on more trusted methods to find out about this girl. 'Where do you come from? What school did you go to? How long have you been over here? Where do you work? Who do you know?' I probed in quick succession. The more I found out about her, the more I became convinced this was Kitty O'Shea come to entrap me. She was obviously a Protestant, of unionist background if not views, and she was certainly pretty and personable enough to tempt. When she had had a few vodkas and I was emboldened by a few gins, I put it to her that she was Kitty O'Shea. I knew by her look of surprise I had got it badly wrong. She worked at Westminster for many years after that and we have laughed about it often since.

According to Percy Dymond, the veteran London correspondent of the *Belfast*

Telegraph, Fitt was the sixty-third MP elected for Northern Ireland since partition and the sixty-first to attend and take his seat; two Sinn Féiners had previously abstained. At the time it was the practice for new members to bide their time before making their maiden speech, and it was also expected that the sentiments expressed on such occasions would be non-controversial. Fitt ignored both protocols and, barely two weeks after being elected, stood up to make his maiden speech at 7.00pm on 15 April during a debate on education and technology. The heartfelt speech was an outpouring of all the feelings of grievance and frustration that had accumulated in his mind over the previous years. It was a measure of the importance he attributed to the occasion that, instead of speaking off-the-cuff from a few notes scribbled on the back of an envelope, as he usually did, he had a carefully compiled script, written with the assistance of the experienced MPs associated with the Campaign for Democracy in Ulster, who were totally conversant with the situation in Northern Ireland.

During the thirty-one-minute address Fitt outlined his own political standpoint and the themes and issues he would later pursue in much greater detail. Typically, however, he strayed from the text as the delivered version contains a certain amount of rambling and repeated, unstructured sentiments expressed with some emotion. Indeed, at one point, he even said: 'I feel that I do not need a script to put forward the case for democracy in Northern Ireland. One can only speak from the heart and I defy contradiction of the charges which I have levelled this afternoon.' His emotion was also evident when he said he understood the tradition to be uncontroversial 'but I cannot make this speech without being controversial … because I am speaking with all the honesty and sincerity at my command'.

Outlining his political standpoint, he stated that he was not an Irish republican, as had been widely claimed, and that his presence in the House disproved it because a republican would not recognise British authority in any part of Ireland and would therefore refuse to take a seat. He went on to 'marvel at the normality which exists in British politics' and contrasted the recent election in Britain, which was fought on the different economic policies and philosophies of the various parties, with what had happened in Northern Ireland. There, Fitt said, his telephone was tapped constantly during the course of the contest, his agents were threatened with physical assault if they attempted to stand by the ballot box to prevent his opponents from personating votes and he had to have the police protect him from a bigoted, sectarian mob when he was declared the victor:

> This is something which people in Britain cannot understand and it is something on which I intend to educate the British people. I make an appeal to each and every one of those members in this house to ensure that we in Northern Ireland are afforded the same opportunity to fight elections on the economic issues involved and that we will be free from all threats of physical violence.

He attacked the Government of Ireland Act 1920 and called for it to be amended because 'the changing social conditions over the past fifty years' and 'the way every concept of British democracy is being flouted in Northern Ireland' had rendered it completely unworkable. In support of this statement, he explained that the democratic principle of 'one man, one vote' operated only in respect of the twelve Westminster constituencies, and that for other elections in Northern Ireland 'we have an anti-democratic electoral system' that would not be tolerated in any other freedom-loving country. Of the eleven Unionist members, only one, Robin Chichester-Clark, MP for Derry, was present in the chamber as Fitt was speaking. Turning to him, Fitt said:

> ... if he believes in the policies which have been pursued in Northern Ireland and disagrees with my charges, to prove it by supporting me in asking the Government for an inquiry into the Government of Ireland Act. I am willing to stand or fall by that decision. I would ask, I would insist, that the members of the tribunal which would hold this inquiry be taken from both sides of the House, not from this side alone. I would accept any honourable member from any side of the House and I am sure that that inquiry would find that what is happening in Northern Ireland today can no longer be tolerated.

He went on to explain how in Northern Ireland housing needs were being manipulated for partisan electoral purposes:

> The town of Dungannon, in County Tyrone, is run by a Unionist-dominated council. It has a small majority of 400 or 500 on the electoral register, but this ensures that it is elected at successive elections. But there are 2,000 people looking for homes in Dungannon – 2,000 young married couples who have no homes of their own. The Unionist council has met repeatedly. It has held meetings and adjourned meetings. It realises that the vast majority of these 2,000 people are anti-unionist, so it says to itself, 'If we build these people homes, we will also be giving them the vote, and they will vote against us. We will be out.' This is happening not only in Dungannon but all over Northern Ireland. I have no hesitation in predicting that now that I have the honour to represent West Belfast, within the next two or three years further council estates will be built in my constituency, and the houses will be given to government supporters with the intention of unseating me. The first aim of the Northern Ireland Unionist party is to perpetuate its own existence there. Let there be no mistake about that.

Committing himself as a socialist to support the Labour government, Fitt said he was speaking for many progressively minded people not only in West Belfast but all across Northern Ireland by voicing 'disapproval of the present undemocratic system and the election laws which now exist in Northern Ireland. The people there are British subjects and are entitled to the same rights and privileges as are possessed by any other persons living in these islands.' In addressing these remarks to the House, he continued:

> I am appealing to every Member who believes in democracy. I am not asking for preferential treatment, or making an outlandish request on behalf of my constituency; I am asking for exactly what British constituents have. As a member of the Stormont parliament I have spoken on many occasions in this vein. It was very frustrating to realise that the house there, with fifty-two Members, had forty Members of the government party. No matter what plea was made I realised that it would not get anywhere. I realised that when it came to the vote on any subject which I supported, 40 Unionists would go into the lobby to vote against it and to deny any semblance of democracy. I hope that I shall not suffer any of that type of frustration in this house.

Ranging ever more widely across the political spectrum, he mentioned the ongoing difficulties in Vietnam and Rhodesia:

> In Rhodesia, there is an exact parallel to what happened in Ireland in 1912, since when a minority has tried to subjugate a majority. How ridiculous this parliament must look on the stage of world affairs when one views the parliament and this country expending their energy and their treasure on trying to bring about in Rhodesia a state of affairs which would ensure the political and human rights of the black Rhodesians, when, at the same time – either through ignorance or through sheer cowardice – we are not prepared to ensure the rights of our own British subjects in Northern Ireland. The problem at home must be settled before we seek to settle problems abroad.

Another Northern Ireland problem, he noted, was the recent decision to use money from the pockets of the British taxpayers, 'the Lancashire lassie and the Yorkshire yokel', to build a new university at Coleraine, 'a unionist-dominated area, inhabited by government supporters' rather than in 'poor, sad, tragic, gerrymandered Londonderry':

> It has become known as a city where the women work in the shirt factories and the men stay at home. In Londonderry, Catholics and Protestants banded together to have the university sited there. They realised that it would be an injection of lifeblood into Londonderry, that, in the first place, it would do away with the unemployment and that people would be employed. They realised that, as building progressed and students began to attend, it would bring life into Londonderry, which is slowly dying of decay. But this consideration was never accepted by the powers that be in Northern Ireland, even though the money was being found by the British taxpayer. The only consideration which activated the minds of the unionist powers in Northern Ireland was that two-thirds of the population of Londonderry were Catholics. They would not put the university in Londonderry because there were too many Catholics there.

Fitt described the negatives of daily life in Northern Ireland. Discrimination there was an everyday occurrence, he said, and people were being denied jobs solely because of their religion. Industrial developments were sited in unionist areas because 'the government of Northern Ireland take the view that if they give one of their supporters a job they will have his vote for all time and so perpetuate their own reign in Northern Ireland.' Pledging 'to oppose unionism in Northern Ireland until my dying day', Fitt told the house that since winning the West Belfast election he had received 468 telegrams, 700 letters and 1,000 telephone calls from people of all political and religious viewpoints, who saw the result as 'a breakthrough for political wisdom in Northern Ireland, a day of reckoning for the Unionist party':

> Unionist representatives have been coming here for so often that they believe now that they rule by divine right. One of the unionist members of this house actually opened his election address with the words: 'I am sorry that this election has been forced on me at great expense by the intervention of a Liberal candidate.' Disgraceful! How 'disgraceful' that anyone should dare to oppose him. That is why there is such a serious inquest going on now in Northern Ireland. They cannot believe that 3,000 Protestants voted for me. However, there is no more proud representative in this House today than I. I realise that Protestants and Catholics have supported me and that it is with their voice that I speak. I am a socialist. I will defend and support this government with everything at my command, but, having done that, I ask for the support of the government and of every honourable member in doing away with the situation that exists in Northern Ireland today.

It was another tradition at Westminster that a new member received fulsome praise for his maiden effort and it fell to Sir Douglas Glover, Conservative MP for Ormskirk, to reply. As Fitt sat down, Glover said:

> It is a special pleasure for me to follow the new member for Belfast West because in this House, whatever we may think about the arguments put forward, we like people who speak with sincerity and with fire in their bellies; people who hold a cause dear and have come to this House to put that cause forward. If the honourable member considers that his speech was non-controversial, I am sure that we must all look forward with great excitement to the first occasion when he feels that he is not inhibited by the conventions of the House. It is quite obvious that in the honourable member for Belfast West we have a man who feels very sincerely about the things for which he has fought. He has a descriptive turn of phrase, and the House will look forward with great interest to hearing him whenever he feels pressed to speak.

Next morning, the *Irish News* in Belfast reported his words alongside an adulatory report of the Fitt speech. Of course, opinion was divided across Northern Ireland, as Sir Douglas quickly discovered. A week later he bumped into Fitt outside one of the members' toilets. 'Oh, Mr Fitt,' he said, opening his briefcase, 'I have something to show you.' He took out about twenty letters. 'Look at these,' he said, incredulous. 'I can see you were not exaggerating in what you said.' Sir Douglas had received the same sort of vicious hate letters that descended on Fitt in every post. 'I'm very inclined to believe you now,' said the genteel Sir Douglas. 'Dreadful, dreadful.'

The Unionist reaction to the speech was one of anger and there was a heated exchange about the misconduct of elections during an eight-minute confrontation on ITN between Fitt and Captain Lawrence Orr. One of the charges Fitt had made in parliament, and repeated on television, was that unionist supporters in the Post Office had unofficially and illegally tapped his telephone during the election campaign. 'I would be foolish if I expected the Northern Ireland government to admit that there is telephone tapping,' he said. Orr was visibly angry at this allegation and retorted it was without a 'vestige of truth'. Fitt's claim was further denied in an official press release from Stormont on 28 April: 'The Northern Ireland government stated today that no department, force, or service under its control either taps or had entered into any arrangement for tapping telephones in Northern Ireland.' The denial was carefully worded and was probably accurate as far it went, but it did not answer Fitt's allegation that his phone had been tapped by unionist sympathisers.

At Stormont there was an hour-long discussion of 'that speech', as it was now called. Brian McConnell, the minister for home affairs, said it was wrong to magnify election incidents into wholesale intimidation throughout the country. Fitt stuck firmly to his charges, insisting, 'I can substantiate every one'. The Unionist MPs began firing statements to the Belfast newspapers arguing that the Speaker should give them the right of reply, but at Westminster most kept their heads down.

Two weeks later Fitt followed up his electrifying speech by putting down his first question for the Prime Minister. It was answered during question time on 26 May with good news and bad news, as it were. The good news was a clear signal from Wilson that he was going to put renewed pressure on the O'Neill government to bring forward reforms. 'I think that the right thing would be for my right honourable friend the Home Secretary and myself to have informal talks with the Prime Minister of Northern Ireland to see whether some of the difficulties which all of us recognise exist might be overcome in an informal way,' he told the House. (At this time Northern Ireland's affairs were the responsibility of the General Department at the Home Office, where they ranked in importance and priority with the control of London taxis.) The bad news was that the 'convention' at Westminster was to be invoked to prevent Fitt, together with an increasing band of sympathetic Labour backbenchers, from raising and discussing matters deemed to be the responsibility of the Stormont government. Of course these matters, including housing, employment and local government, were the issues Fitt most wanted Westminster to hear about and discuss.

The parliamentary guidelines were spelled out by the Speaker that day when he prohibited all discussion beyond the question of asking for an inquiry into the working of the Government of Ireland Act. Any attempt to query the interpretation of Section 75, which outlined the transferred responsibilities of the Stormont administration, was rebuffed. Fitt and other MPs were referred to the longstanding practice, as outlined in Erskine May, the bible of parliamentary procedure, and were even given a page number to consult by Mr Speaker. One of the British MPs, Manny Shinwell, said, 'Mr Speaker ... if Ulster members come here and interfere in our affairs, cannot we do likewise?' Breaking this convention now became Fitt's first priority. If he could not find a way round it, he would be prevented from raising the most potent of his concerns about the conduct of government in Northern Ireland. After seeking advice from more experienced parliamentarians, he was encouraged to keep challenging it and to use every opportunity the parliamentary proceedings afforded. It was a convention, not a statute, he was told, and therefore could be overturned by the Speaker if Fitt could demonstrate its irrelevance convincingly. Given the catalogue of injustice he had compiled, Fitt was confident that ultimately he could persuade the parliamentary authorities to agree with him.

Fitt's arrival at Westminster had, in fact, discomforted the Unionists far more than he could ever have imagined: from the outset they realised he was more than capable of causing them considerable trouble and their anxieties about his likely activities went far beyond seeking to compromise him with a 'Kitty O'Shea'. For years beforehand the Unionist parliamentary party, bolstered by almost total Westminster disinterest, had sheltered behind the 'convention' and had used its position to promote Northern Ireland's interests as narrowly as it suited them. The Home Secretary of the day was the minister primarily responsible for what was usually referred to as 'the province', but within the Home Office it was an issue of little importance. From time to time, however, the Unionist MPs were able to exploit their connection with the Conservative party to lobby at the highest level for some or other matter, especially when that party was in power. One such initiative, however, nearly fostered an unwelcome governmental interest in events in Belfast.

The episode began on 9 July 1963 when two MPs, Robert Grosvenor and Robin Chichester-Clark, had a meeting with Prime Minister Harold Macmillan in his room at the House of Commons. Grosvenor, the MP for Fermanagh-South Tyrone and heir to the title Duke of Westminster (which he would inherit on his brother's death in 1967), advised the Prime Minister that 'it had not been made known that a Miss Pike was giving the Home Secretary assistance on Northern Ireland matters because people were very reactionary in Northern Ireland and thought that a woman could only do a second-rate job'. The two MPs went on to press Macmillan to appoint an additional parliamentary secretary (junior minister) at the Home Office with a particular responsibility for Northern Ireland affairs. Macmillan said he did not think that would be appropriate, but intimated he had no objection to making known that one of the existing ministers would devote most of his time to the subject. What the Unionists had not bargained for was the implication of a minute dictated to the Home Secretary, Henry Brooke, the next day:

> Would it not be a good idea if the Prime Minister of Northern Ireland could be persuaded to come over here with a few of his colleagues for regular meetings with you and ministers from appropriate departments. I know that this idea has been considered in the past and objected to on the grounds that it hints at some crisis or that hopes are raised which are bound to be disappointed. But if it were announced that these meetings were to become a matter of routine, say every quarter, and if you announced the date of the first a good way ahead, surely these difficulties could be overcome. If you were to make these meetings a social occasion as well, a luncheon together or something of that sort, so much the better.

A week later, on 18 July, Brooke replied to Macmillan having consulted Captain Terence O'Neill, who had become the Prime Minister only a few months earlier, on 25 March. The Home Secretary indicated that O'Neill was as strongly opposed to the idea as his predecessor: 'Any meeting between Northern Ireland ministers and United Kingdom ministers is, as he points out, very small beer to the London newspapers, but it is major news for the papers in Northern Ireland.' O'Neill believed, that 'there would be no means of preventing the Northern Ireland ministers from building up such meetings into an important event which would be anticipated with eager expectation, to be followed by disappointment recorded in every Belfast newspaper if there was not some piece of really good news for Northern Ireland to be announced at the end of the meeting'. Brooke's minute continued:

> Were Northern Ireland not dominated by its heavy rate of unemployment, this might be avoided; but unemployment looms so large in the Northern Ireland political scene and there is such a longing for pieces of good news to relieve it, that he fears that the papers are bound to comment, adversely whenever an occasion which might produce good news passes without the good news eventuating.

Brooke went on to point out that some months earlier he had adopted the practice of sitting in whenever a Northern Ireland minister came to London for a discussion with any UK minister on a matter of importance. 'This is a valuable advance, and I think it is working well; it is welcomed by the Northern Ireland Ministers,' he reported. Meanwhile, he concluded, the Home Office, in conjunction with the Northern Ireland government, was reviewing the arrangements in place for liaison at official level: 'With full mutual approval we think we may be able to make good progress here, even though regular meetings at ministerial level may continue to be unacceptable to the Northern Ireland Cabinet.'

Some months later, in October 1963, Harold Macmillan was diagnosed as suffering from prostate cancer and resigned as Prime Minister. He was replaced soon afterwards by Lord Home of the Hirsel, who promptly renounced his hereditary title, fought a by-election for a safe Scottish seat and became Prime Minister as Sir Alec Douglas Home. To the relief of unionists, there was no substantive change to the Belfast – London consultation conduit and Home continued the arrangement for periodic meetings with the Unionists, meeting with O'Neill in November 1963 and the Unionist MPs on 18 December.

In a letter to Downing Street on 9 December, Grosvenor had given notice that the Unionist MPs wished to discuss: the activities of the IRA; a proposed aircraft carrier for the Royal Navy; and the need for new industries for Northern Ireland. Over the next few days background briefing documents were prepared for Home and Henry Brooke, who had remained in post as Home Secretary, in preparation for the meeting.

Although O'Neill had raised intelligence warnings during his talk with Home regarding a possible resumption of IRA activities, his security advisers in Belfast had since reassessed the threat and informed London that it was not necessary to make immediate representations to Dublin for tough action, as had been requested. A report from the Special Branch at Scotland Yard concluded that while there were 200 activists capable of causing violence, they were inhibited by a lack of money and an internal reorganisation. The fact that the MPs now wanted to pursue the matter further caused some consternation among officials. The Prime Minister was advised to give assurances that there would be strong representations to Dublin should violence erupt, but also to encourage the MPs not to go public on the fact that this topic had been addressed during their meeting. On the other issues, they were told that the Harland and Wolff shipyard would likely be allowed to tender to build the new aircraft carrier when the development work on the project was complete. They were reminded that the recent creation of over 5,000 jobs was evidence that the industrial incentives on offer, which were higher than elsewhere in the UK, were working in Northern Ireland.

During the year it was in office, the Home administration allowed the well-established lines of communication between Stormont and Whitehall to remain unchanged and, as had been the case for many years, there was no serious questioning of the state of affairs in Northern Ireland. All that changed, however, when Harold Wilson, leader of the Labour party, first came to power after a general election in October 1964. For Wilson, the situation in Northern Ireland was one of his primary concerns, and there were rumours that he would appoint a Minister for Northern Ireland. The issue was propelled up the Labour agenda by a group of young left-wing MPs, some of Irish stock, others with large numbers of Irish constituents. Their interest in the matter was greatly influenced by the all-powerful trades unions, which were pledged to help their members in Northern Ireland. Their most powerful ammunition though came from Patricia McCluskey, a local councillor in Dungannon, Co. Tyrone, and the wife of a doctor in that predominantly Catholic town.

In 1963, when the Unionist-controlled council refused to rehouse a group of Catholics from overcrowded houses to more modern accommodation, McCluskey had formed a Homeless Citizens League and led a successful campaign of demonstrations and sit-ins. In 1964, along with her husband Con and a group of fellow Catholics, she founded the Campaign for Social Justice (CSJ) and a wide circle of people throughout the British Isles received their thoroughly researched pamphlets, which listed for the first time and in incontrovertible detail the whole damning indictment of unionist misrule. On 2 July the same year McCluskey travelled to London, where she addressed the inaugural meeting of the Campaign for Democracy in Ulster (CDU) in the House of Commons. The president of the CDU was Lord Fenner Brockway, a renowned pacifist, and its chairman was Paul Rose, a Manchester Labour MP and the real driving force behind the organisation. Among the sixty-three sponsors from across the entire spectrum of the Labour party were Shirley Williams, Eric Heffer, Roy Hattersley, Michael Foot, Stan Orme, Paul Rose, Kevin McNamara and the celebrated Methodist preacher Lord Soper.

Brockway defined the ground upon which the CDU would fight: 'It is not for us to raise the issue of the border. The Irish people themselves will solve the border problem in time.' Instead the CDU had as its objective the setting up of a full, impartial government enquiry into the administration of Northern Ireland and into the allegations of discrimination in housing and employment. It called for electoral law to be brought into line with the rest of the UK and for a fairer re-drawing of electoral boundaries. Finally, it called for the Race Relations Act to include Northern Ireland, with special amendments to outlaw religious discrimination and incitement.

This flurry of activity regarding Northern Ireland meant that when Gerry Fitt arrived at Westminster after the British general election of 1966, he stepped onto thoroughly prepared ground and, given his political credentials and origins in the battlefield area, it was quite natural that he was quickly appraised of the modalities of parliament and pushed to the head of the campaign. Austin Currie had introduced Fitt to the McCluskeys and he made exceedingly good use of their material whenever the opportunity arose at Westminster.

Following his maiden speech and the subsequent response from Wilson, Fitt had to wait until 27 May 1966 for another suitable opening. Paul Rose tried to open up the demand for the Race Relations Act to be applied to Northern Ireland, but the Speaker immediately silenced him, forcing Fitt to back off, too. Nonetheless, a proper discussion on Northern Ireland became possible during July and August when parliament debated the Consolidated Fund Bill. At such debates it was open to a member to raise any topic regarding the spending of money, a tradition that can be a useful parliamentary vehicle to circumvent the normal rules. Although Fitt's attempts to get this Bill amended were unsuccessful, they did serve his purpose because they were listed on the order paper and written about in the newspapers, fulfilling his desire to get Northern Ireland issues on the public political agenda. Undeterred by various setbacks and recognising that he would have to play a long game, Fitt exhaustively explored every conceivable way in which to draw attention to his cause. His persistence finally paid off when he managed to get a debate scheduled for 8 August and was not dented by the fact that it was 4.50am the next morning before the item was reached. When he was called to speak, with Austin Currie watching from the gallery, he could not resist chiding the Unionists: 'I am delighted to see some of my honourable friends from Northern Ireland in the House because if I had not been elected for Belfast West [last March], they would be at home in their beds.'

His main focus was Section 75 of the Government of Ireland Act and he complained that if he were to abide by the 'illogical' convention, 'all I would be able to discuss during this debate would be defence, foreign affairs, income tax and the post office.' The deputy speaker was notably unsympathetic, however: 'My predecessors in this chair have ruled repeatedly that matters within the competence of the Northern Ireland government, and therefore matters for which Her Majesty's ministers in this House are not responsible, are not subjects for debate in this House.' Several Labour members weighed in behind Fitt, raising twenty-one points of order. Michael McGuire, an Irishman and MP for Ince, called it 'a barmy convention that ... allows me to discuss Timbuctoo, Rhodesia, Peru or the Argentine, but forbids me to discuss matters of vital interest to my constituents.' William Hamling followed: 'Does not my honourable friend agree that it is even more barmy that an Irish member can discuss the grievances of constituents in West Woolwich, but cannot discuss the grievances of his constituency of Belfast West?' Alice Bacon, replying on behalf of the Home Secretary, delivered a complete restatement of the position: that while it was open to the government to overrule the Stormont administration, it was not their present intention.

Privately, Fitt was very satisfied. A few days earlier, when he was in the tea room with some colleagues, Harold Wilson had joined them. After the usual small talk, Fitt raised Section 75 and described his difficulties in getting parliamentary questions about matters in Northern Ireland past the Table Office:

> [Wilson] looked me straight in the eye and told me to forget about the convention. The section gave the House full authority over all persons,

places and things in Northern Ireland. He told me it was also my authority
when trying to talk about my own constituency. I knew from the party
grapevine that he was well disposed to reform in Ulster but with Rhodesia,
the economy and all his other difficulties he could not give it a high priority.
I accepted that sympathetically for I knew that within days he was actually
seeing O'Neill for the third time to push him harder along the reform path.

Back in Belfast, the most vocal and determined opposition to O'Neill and his aims
continued to come from the Rev Ian Paisley, who was campaigning noisily with
the blunt slogan, 'O'Neill must go'. His activities were causing widespread tension
and unrest. For example, when Paisley heard that a march to commemorate the
fiftieth anniversary of the 1916 Rising was to take place in West Belfast along a
route that would cause no provocation, he attacked O'Neill for refusing to ban it.
As he was to do so often in the future, he then stoked up further tension by
announcing a counter-demonstration. (It is worth recalling that at this time, as a
gesture of goodwill, the Wilson government returned to Dublin the green flag
bearing the words 'Irish Republic' that had flown above the GPO in Dublin
during the Rising.)

At the beginning of June the General Assembly of the Presbyterian Church
took place in Belfast. Paisley had theological differences with the church and so
established his own, breakaway Free Presbyterian Church, styling himself as
Moderator. He and his followers planned to protest outside the meeting in
Fisherwick Place, and provocatively decided to march through the sensitive
Cromac Square area on their way, provoking violent clashes with local Catholics.
When they eventually reached their destination, Paisley mounted such a rowdy
demonstration, barracking the dignitaries so boisterously from outside the
Assembly, that the wife of the governor, Lord Erskine, became ill. On 15 June
O'Neill condemned the incident at Stormont in no uncertain terms:

> They called themselves loyalists but to what were they loyal? To the Queen,
> whose personal representative they revile? To the United Kingdom, in
> which their fellow citizens view their conduct with a mixture of ridicule and
> contempt? To their Protestantism, many of whose leaders they have
> personally abused? ... To those of us who remember the thirties, the pattern
> is horribly familiar. The contempt for established authority; the crude and
> unthinking intolerance; the emphasis upon monster processions and rallies;
> the appeal to a perverted form of patriotism; each and every one of these
> things has its parallel in the rise of the Nazis to power.

During the same Stormont debate, Fitt contented himself with a more
conventional denigration of Paisley:

> The only sensible thing was to have him certified as a person insane. There
> could be no doubt in any persons' mind that Mr Paisley was insane and an
> absolute lunatic.

Tension in Belfast remained high that summer, with regular sectarian incidents. The brutal murder of a Catholic barman led O'Neill to outlaw the Ulster Volunteer Force (UVF), a Protestant terror organisation. When the Queen visited Belfast that July, a concrete block was dropped on her car from a building under construction in the city centre. Against this turbulent background, O'Neill and Wilson lunched at Downing Street on 5 August. The day before, Fitt had written to Wilson to outline the familiar causes of what he described as 'seething discontent'.

Due to the opposition within his own party, O'Neill persuaded Wilson to allow him a period of consolidation before pressing on with reforms. Wilson agreed because he was persuaded of O'Neill's good faith. Barely a month after that meeting the extent of the opposition to O'Neill became evident. Desmond Boal, a Unionist MP and able lawyer, attempted to overthrow O'Neill in a party coup encouraged by Brian Faulkner and Harry West. O'Neill saw them off by confronting them, but it was clear the rift was widening. The dissidents, he said, did not want just a new Prime Minister but new policies. However, the real threat came from Paisley, who spent part of the summer in prison having chosen to make a martyr of himself rather than pay a fine for his part in the disorder outside the Presbyterian Assembly. Publicly, O'Neill had attempted to link Paisley with the UVF and talked of a drift towards 'Nazism and fascism'. Fitt's own view was that O'Neill had made his worst mistake in 1964, over the tricolour at Divis Street: 'Once the evil genie had been let out of the lamp, it could not be returned to it. Although I understood and privately sympathised with O'Neill's difficulties, I could see no alternative to pressing on relentlessly with my own campaign.'

Accordingly, after the summer recess Paul Rose and Fitt continued to exploit every loophole they could find in a renewed attempt to break the convention regarding debates on Northern Ireland in the Commons. For the first time Fitt feared the situation might spin out of control. Despite the paranoia exhibited regularly by the unionists, the IRA was dormant and was concentrating on social and economic agitation, but it was always possible that the ongoing activities of the UVF could spur them to become active again. Fitt believed that the safest way to manage the pent-up sense of injustice among Catholics was to move, however slowly, towards major reforms, thus neutralising the influence of the extremists on both sides. He was angry when an opportunity to demonstrate good intent was missed in October. The British government proposed the appointment of a parliamentary commissioner, or Ombudsman, to investigate complaints of maladministration by official and public bodies and Fitt obtained more than 100 signatures on a motion urging the extension of the commissioner's powers to include Northern Ireland. In the end, the government opted to stick firmly to its policy of giving O'Neill time.

Such frustrations notwithstanding, as 1966 drew to a close Fitt could look back

on it as a watershed year. There was his great personal achievement of following
Joe Devlin and Jack Beattie to Westminster as the MP for West Belfast. As a result
of his work thereafter, Northern Ireland's problems had received more
parliamentary attention in six months than in the previous forty years:

> I had shaken the complacency of the Westminster unionists to the point
> where they had been put under orders not to debate with me on radio,
> television or in any other forum. I had done a pretty extensive tour of
> universities and other opinion-forming bodies distributing the McCluskey
> literature. I therefore approached 1967 as a year when tangible progress
> could and had to be made but I was aware that many Catholics were still in
> despair or disappointed that nothing concrete had emerged from the
> Wilson – O'Neill summits.

Exploiting his high standing with the Labour government, at the beginning of
January 1967 Fitt persuaded Michael Stewart, the Minister for Economic Affairs,
to receive a deputation from Northern Ireland to discuss industrial development
matters. The meeting was set for 1.00pm on Friday, 3 February. Innocuous as it
seemed, the arrangement provoked strong reactions both within Whitehall and
between London and Belfast. When news of the meeting reached the Home
Office and then Stormont, there was an intensely hostile reaction. On 30 January
a senior Home Office official telephoned his protest to another at the Department
of Economic Affairs, then followed it up with a minute demanding that a Home
Office minister should sit in:

> Mr Gerry Fitt is a Republican Labour MP who is said to be not slow to
> draw attention to the political implications of whatever subject he is
> handling. This makes it more desirable that our handling of Mr Fitt and his
> delegation should be done in close conjunction with the Home Secretary or
> someone representing him.

Meanwhile, the telephone lines between Stormont Castle and Whitehall were
buzzing as Northern Ireland officials passed on the O'Neill government's concern
at the local, political implications of Fitt's move. Their fear was that it would
appear Fitt and his team were the first to put proposals to the British government
about the need for economic assistance. To counter this they demanded that, prior
to receiving Fitt, the London government should make some announcement to
the effect that the Northern Ireland government had already made specific
proposals, which were still under consideration. 'Whether United Kingdom
ministers would feel it justified to go this far, in order to avoid political
embarrassment to the Northern Ireland administration, is a question on which
officials of an economic department are hardly competent to advise,' wrote one
official. The demand was thus shifted to the Home Office for its views and, in the
event, the officials there contented themselves with having a junior minister
present at the meeting, although a stern letter later followed reminding the

economic ministry of the need to observe the constitutional proprieties and to fully consult the Home Secretary in advance regarding Northern Ireland matters.

The meeting was rearranged and took place on 6 February at 3.00pm, but the economic background to it was dispiriting. Although unemployment had fallen slightly between 1964 and 1966, from 6.6% to 6.2%, there were still 31,200 people out of work, many of them living in economic blackspots like Newry, Derry and Strabane, predominatly Catholic towns where one in five men was unemployed. Those who had jobs were only marginally better off as average weekly wages in Northern Ireland amounted to £16-16 shillings – compared with a UK average of £20-5 shillings. What most worried the trade unions and local political leaders was the prevailing uncertainty in the economy, especially about the future of the publicly owned Harland and Wolff shipyard and the nearby Short Brothers and Harland aircraft works, both of which were among the largest local employers. There were also fears that forthcoming cuts would deprive Northern Ireland of a substantial amount of high value work in support of the armed services.

Fitt began the meeting by introducing the eleven members of his deputation to the three ministers and seven officials seated alongside them. His team included the most senior trade union officials in Northern Ireland, four Stormont MPs (including both nationalists and one from the NILP), as well as a Church of Ireland clergyman representing the Churches Industrial Council. By agreement, Andy Barr, chairman of the Northern Ireland Committee of the ICTU, kicked off the discussion. He said the economic outlook was disastrous because of the additional unemployment that would flow from the government's credit squeeze and income freeze. There were men in Northern Ireland who went through their entire life without ever holding a job. He made a plea for orders for the aircraft factory, support for the shipyard, investment in a new steel manufacturing mill and a guarantee that other government-sponsored work would continue, if not expand. Others supported his case for special emergency measures and warned – all too accurately, as it turned out – that in the special circumstances of Northern Ireland, weakness of the economy might pose a threat to public law and order.

In his response, Stewart was non-committal. He could not provide a certificate of health for Northern Ireland's future, he declared, before going on to paint a picture of what he called 'the favourable long-term prospects'. The most tangible thing he offered was agreement to consider a trip to Northern Ireland to meet the Economic Council and study the situation at first-hand.

The last words on the episode were uttered a few days later by an official at the Department of Economic Affairs. He had obtained an assessment from the Ministry of Technology that there was an extremely doubtful economic case to be made for a £6 million dry dock in Belfast with the capacity for constructing 500,000-tonne tankers, a project the deputation had promoted. As a result, the official recommended no follow-up by Stewart: 'Since there is nothing that he could say which they would be glad to hear, I suggest that we take no further action other than bear in mind the information [that has been provided to us] lest the threatened re-appearance of Mr Fitt's deputation should, unhappily, come to pass.'

In Belfast, the most reactionary elements in the Unionist party, now allied closely with Paisley, were leaning on O'Neill and stalling fundamental reforms in the hope that Wilson would eventually be deposed and a more sympathetic Conservative government would sweep everything back under the carpet. Fitt emphasised this worry at a major conference on Ireland organised by the Connolly Association on 25 February in London. He repeated again that all he wanted was normal British standards in Northern Ireland and warned that a 'crunch' was coming. From his acute understanding of Irish history, he knew well it could have violent implications, so he chose his words with care:

> As an Irish socialist, I do not want to see one Irishman shooting another Irishman. I do not believe that will solve the Irish question. But some say that the partition of Ireland has existed now for forty-seven years, that it is useless to try to talk to a British government, that they will not listen, that they themselves created the problem and they are unwilling to take any steps to solve it, and I have been told time and time again that the only answer to the partition of Ireland lies in the hands of Irishmen themselves and it can only be re-united by force. I would sincerely hope that the day will never come when we, once again, have to take to the gun in Ireland.
>
> ... Some people may say that they are prepared to let Terence O'Neill walk over them in bedroom slippers because Paisley would walk over them in hob-nailed boots. I am not prepared to let anyone walk over me or my constituents.'

A short time later, Paisley and Fitt became embroiled in a direct confrontation. Paisley had recently formed the Ulster Constitution Defence Committee (UCDC) and on 13 February 1966 he added to his growing portfolio of protest by publishing the first edition of the *Protestant Telegraph* a vehicle for his strong views and bizarre anti-Catholic tales. 'The truth shall set you free' was its masthead slogan, but the sort of truths printed were biased at best, complete poppycock at worst. One edition ran an article headlined, 'The Common Market exposed as the Pope's power game', and the rest of the page was devoted to an account of how US President Johnson had prayed with nuns because he was worried about doing the right thing in Vietnam. Sex scandals in the Vatican and lurid tales about nuns and priests taking part in orgies were also recurring favourites.

The edition of the *Protestant Telegraph* published on 1 April 1966, carried the bold headline: 'Arrest Fenian Fitt. Why does Ulster's rebel leader go free?' The story was a mish-mash of half-truths and untruths about alleged Sinn Féin oaths, claiming they included such clauses as 'the employment of any means [to unite

Ireland] will be blessed by our earthly fathers the priests, thrice blessed by his Holiness the Pope.' The article, which was clearly intended to stoke up ill-feeling and hostility among Protestants, went on to attack Fitt's plans for a fact-finding visit to the province by a group of Labour MPs and said that he, 'an arch-traitor', had 'gone to Westminster for permission to mount mayhem in Northern Ireland'.

The following Tuesday, 4 April, Fitt raised the matter in the Commons as a potential 'breach of privilege' and the following day the Speaker formally referred the *Protestant Telegraph* article for consideration by the committee of privileges. Richard Crossman, leader of the house, chaired the three meetings of the committee which addressed the matter. The Conservatives on the committee wanted to dismiss the article as a piece of scurrilous abuse. Their man, Edward Heath, then leader of the opposition, was determined to deny Paisley notoriety because he suspected, given his recent record, that Paisley would not apologise and would welcome the martyrdom of imprisonment. Crossman and Attorney-General Sir Elwyn Jones were agreed it was a gross breach of privilege and a gross contempt of the House and decided to draft a form of words that would deny Paisley his martyrdom, but would condemn unequivocally the *prima facie* breach of privilege. On Monday, 24 April they duly reported back, but the full committee did not like the draft. Jo Grimond, leader of the Liberal party, argued that the breach could not be laughed off. In the end, however, Crossman got his way, which he described as being 'to avoid [the breach] being noticed and if noticed, being forced to a debate'. Fitt welcomed the finding in his favour and recognised the benefit of denying Paisley further publicity, but he also realised that, sooner or later, failure to effectively curb Paisley was bound to lead to real trouble.

Despite the real impact he was making at Westminster, Fitt was becoming frustrated that progress on achieving the key root and branch reforms needed in Northern Ireland was so painfully slow. Stan Orme and Paul Rose, who represented Manchester seats, and Dr Maurice Miller, a Glasgow MP, all members of the now 100-strong CDU, also wanted to see real evidence of improved conditions and greater social justice in Northern Ireland. On Friday, 14 April, ignoring Paisley's attempts to discourage them, they arrived in Belfast on a fact-finding visit. Their first engagement was a news conference, held at the International Hotel in Donegall Square South, where Stan Orme said that when O'Neill went to meet Wilson exuding sweet reasonableness, he was falsely presenting a liberal image, an impression, he claimed, many Labour backbenchers shared.

Fitt led the party to Coalisland, Dungannon and then to Strabane, where nearly 3,000 turned out to see them even though they were hours behind schedule and did not reach the town until very late at night. From what they were told by groups of local councillors and activists, such as the McCluskeys and trades unionists, the English MPs were convinced there must be far more urgency

applied to the much-discussed reform programme in order to make a real
difference on the ground. In Derry they heard similar stories and also learned of
the continued deep resentment and bitterness at the decision to locate the new
university in the middle of Protestant Coleraine. Local unionists declined an
invitation to meet the MPs because 'Protestant people resented such a meeting
being called on a Sunday'.

Fitt was delighted by the impact of the visit. It attracted enthusiastic and
attentive crowds to the public meetings and brought together all the various
factions working towards reform. Most importantly, it gave him three well-
informed allies at Westminster to keep the pressure on. 'But for the first time,' he
said, 'I began to see that all this might not be enough and that reform might have
to be fought for outside the confines of Westminster and Stormont.'

While he was campaigning at Westminster, Fitt was also still attending to his
other responsibilities at Stormont and City Hall. There was more constituency
work than ever; Ann had become superbly proficient at getting in touch with
government offices when urgent cases cropped up in his absence. His five
daughters did their bit too, taking messages from the non-stop telephone calls and
making tea for the people queuing up to see Ann or Fitt in the front sitting room,
which had been set aside for that purpose. The family lived mainly in the extensive
basement, where there was a large kitchen and a lounge. By their previous
standards, they were now reasonably prosperous: Fitt's two elected positions and
allowances meant he was earning around £5,000 a year, and the austere days of
post-dated cheques and unemployment benefit had, thankfully, passed. Ann had
turned the once-derelict shell of 85 Antrim Road into a 'wee palace', as they say
in Belfast, painting and decorating every room, and she used her excellent dress-
making skills to turn out clothes for her daughters.

In politics, however, the recurring round of elections are a constant reminder
that it is a precarious business with no job security. In May 1966 Fitt had to return
to Dock to fight the local government elections once again. This time Republican
Labour was on the crest of a wave so there was no difficulty finding candidates or
deposits. Fitt was comfortably elected as Alderman for Dock, giving him a six-year
tenure of office in City Hall. Peter Kelly was also elected, and he made his
memorable and enthusiastic victory speech from the window above his chip shop,
speaking with as much passion as the Pope from his window above St Peter's
Square in Rome, according to Fitt.

A month or so later, on a night in June, Fitt had just arrived back from London
when Ann told him there was an advertisement in the *Irish News* for a speech he
was apparently to make at a victory rally for the Glasgow football team Celtic,
which had just won the European Cup. (In Belfast, Rangers, reputedly a
Protestant team, and Celtic, reputedly a Catholic team, are supported as
fanatically as they are in Glasgow.) Fitt had no knowledge of such an invitation,

but ever the political opportunist he decided to go along and see what was happening. As he crossed over into the Falls Road in a taxi, the crowd spotted him, pulled him out of the car and propelled him through the throng to the platform, where he was pushed up alongside the legendary Charlie Tully, a Belfastman who was idolised as a former Celtic player. 'Gerry, Gerry, we beat them,' shouted a Belfast woman with a shawl and a loud voice. Fitt recalled:

> I am afraid I got carried away with the emotion and excitement. 'Yes, we did it again. We've beaten them in football and we've beaten them in politics and we'll beat them in any field they dare confront us,' I said. It was really a lot of oratorical excitement, but the next thing I knew there it was, all over the *Irish News* next morning in cold print. That speech started a hell of a row, largely because it was the first foot I had put wrong and it did allow the waiting Unionists to get at me. I was accused of sectarianism and bringing politics into sport and disowned by the Celtic supporters club. The *Belfast Telegraph* leader writers thundered at me and the letter columns overflowed. I tried to apologise my way out of it, without real success. It was the first serious mistake I had made in public life and I always bitterly regretted it.

At first glance a parliamentary discussion on the Bermuda Constitution Bill, on 19 June 1966, was a most unpromising forum for Fitt to continue his assault on the convention. However, he had been made aware of a famous parliamentary precedent when the Parnellite MP, Tim Healy, had once talked for three-quarters of an hour about Uganda before finishing with the words, 'Mr Speaker, did I say Uganda throughout my speech? I really meant to say Ireland.' Fitt was determined to emulate him, but the Speaker was also aware of the precedent and he listened with ears pricked after calling him to speak. 'I believe that the House is being asked to endorse a vicious gerrymander in the oldest parliament in the commonwealth,' he started. 'It is a parliament which has been in existence since 1620. I know that in Northern Ireland some people believe that the world began in 1690, but the Bermuda parliament had been in existence since 1620. In my maiden speech in this house – ' He was interrupted.

'Order,' cried the Speaker.

'I will not continue on those lines, Mr Speaker,' said Fitt.

'Parnell learnt the rules of the house by breaking all of them in turn. The honourable member must keep in order,' replied the Speaker.

> Thank you very much, Mr Speaker. I am drawing this parallel because we already have experience of the discontent which can arise from the existence of gerrymandering. I am making a plea to my honourable friend, the Minister of State, to ensure that the same thing does not happen in Bermuda. I do not wish to see exist in Bermuda the trouble, discontent, division and schisms which exist in my homeland.

Fitt managed to continue in the same vein for thirty-five minutes, and without another admonition from the Speaker. The speech attracted a lot of attention and demonstrated beautifully how to flout the parliamentary convention by not discussing the abuses in Northern Ireland directly. Fitt was not comforted by this 'success', however. His satisfaction at using skilful tactics to score points in the gentlemanly, remote atmosphere of the Commons was beginning to fade, to be replaced by gnawing frustration: 'I was beginning to feel that I could go on beating my head against the wall indefinitely, without result.' His exasperation was evident in a landmark speech he made at a rally in Trafalgar Square on 19 June 1967:

> If the position deteriorated, who could blame the minority for taking other means to bring social justice into Northern Ireland? If constitutional methods fail, the people of Northern Ireland, who are at present the victims of this oppression, are quite entitled to take what means they can to end it. I should hope the day would never arise when Irishmen would find it necessary to shoot brother Irishmen. I sincerely hope I shall never live to see that day.

In a speech given to the Orange Order at Cloughmills, Co. Antrim, Terence O'Neill accused Fitt of inciting violence as a means of obtaining social justice. A few days later Fitt hit back at an Irish Labour party meeting in Newry:

> If the Northern Ireland government continues its present policies of discrimination, gerrymander and social injustice, some members of the minority might, in desperation, resort to extreme methods. I believe this is a risk which exists in the unhealthy political atmosphere of Northern Ireland and which persists in the absence of any tangible evidence of bridge-building activities by the Prime Minister about which he talks so much and does so little.

In his 'Ulster letter from London' in the *Belfast Telegraph*, summing up recent events at the end of July prior to the long summer recess, Percy Dymond wrote that one of the most exciting parliamentary sessions of the post-war period was coming to an end:

> Stimulated by the presence of Mr Gerry Fitt, the subject of Northern Ireland affairs has ever been out of sight for long. There have been motions, an abundance of questions and no lack of speeches on Ulster though a formal Northern Ireland debate has yet to come.

Dymond's assessment of Fitt's barnstorming impact explains why the Westminster Unionists had launched a much more sinister operation to discredit him in parliament – even before his Trafalgar Square speech. On 9 June 1967, Stratton Mills, an urbane Belfast solicitor and MP for North Belfast, wrote a note on House of Commons notepaper to Harold Black, secretary to the Northern Ireland Cabinet at Stormont:

> In relation to the forthcoming debate on Northern Ireland, I am very

anxious to use the opportunity to present Fitt in his true light – in the nicest possible way. I am wondering if you have any useful quotations showing him allied with those sections of the community who wish to keep relations at boiling point. Incidentally, has he ever condemned the IRA? I think this could be quite a useful exercise for the benefit of some of the more reasonable Labour MPs.

Upon receiving the letter, Black decided to contact the RUC to see if they could provide any suitable information. In response, a bundle of photocopied newspaper cuttings, accompanied by a sheet of headed notepaper with the typed inscription, 'With the compliments of the Inspector-General', reached Black's office on 15 June. Later the same day, he replied to Mills:

I have been looking at the question posed in your letter of 9th June and I am not sure that I can offer much help. I have gone through such cuttings as we have of GF's utterances and can in fact find very little that would support criticism of his actions in a way that would be likely to appeal to the Labour backbench; certainly many of his utterances can be condemned as objectionable from the Unionist point of view, but considered from his own political standpoint and from that of his supporters at Westminster it is hard to see that he has gone very far wrong. It may be that I have not got enough cuttings! On the question of the IRA, all I can find is that on the 24 June, 1966, he was reported in the *News Letter* as saying 'Ireland cannot be united by the use of force', which in a way is a sort of oblique rejection of the IRA. I enclose the cutting dealing with this. I think he has been fairly assiduous in attending regularly the Easter Rising Parade to Milltown Cemetery which, as you know, is sponsored by the IRA and Sinn Féin. I also enclose a cutting covering the speech which he made during the Belfast celebration of Glasgow Celtic's European Cup win; the reference here to beating 'our opponents in politics, sport and every other field' was much criticised here and it may be that something could be made of the attempt to import politics into the sports arena.

Black concluded his letter by adding that Jim Bailie, secretary of the Unionist party, had also sent a collection of cuttings to Robin Chichester-Clark and 'possibly these will be more useful than those I have looked through'. At a later time, before the letter was posted, he added a PS: 'Since writing the above I have succeeded in extracting from another source a cutting bearing on the point you raised about the IRA … it does, as you see, indicate a change in attitude from that which he was adopting on 24 June 1966, as referred to above.'

Following Fitt's hard-hitting speech at Trafalgar Square, Black took it upon himself to send the cuttings to Mills in case he had missed them. The MP replied on 23 June, thanking him: 'I am storing away this information [regarding GF] for use in the Ulster debate if the Speaker gives me a chance to deliver it before ruling me out of order.'

By any standards this was an extraordinary episode in which Black, supposedly an impartial senior civil servant and not a paid party official, and Albert Kennedy, the most senior police officer in the province, conspired with an MP to find material to discredit another elected MP whose political views were in conflict with their own. As such, it spoke volumes about the abuse of unchallenged unionist power and the collective arrogance of senior public servants. As far as Fitt was concerned, by this stage the gloves were off. He was now convinced that O'Neill, whatever the purity of his personal motives, could not carry his party and that his main preoccupation was keeping at bay the two challengers, Faulkner and William Craig. Early in September the Unionist party in West Belfast ditched the defeated James Kilfedder from the West Belfast seat in favour of the solicitor Brian McRoberts, despite the fact that parliament still had some four years to run. It was yet another indication of just how stung the Unionists were by the steady national prominence Fitt was building.

At Westminster there was a quickening interest in the Northern Ireland situation when politics resumed again after the summer break. Fitt detected growing impatience among the Labour rank and file at O'Neill's government's slowness to act, and it was his intention to marshal this discontent at the party conference in Scarborough in October and translate it into a firm pledge by the party leadership to act decisively to pressurise the tardy Unionists. In the event, the conference was dominated by the Vietnam war, the question of joining the Common Market and unemployment – neither Harold Wilson nor Roy Jenkins mentioned Northern Ireland in their keynote speeches. The motion on discrimination in the province was not reached, and instead remitted to the National Executive. The only real interest was displayed at the fringe meeting organised by the National Council for Civil Liberties. Paul Rose summed up their shared feelings of frustration when he stated afterwards: 'If the Catholics in Northern Ireland were black and this was happening 2,000 miles away, people would take more notice of the situation.'

Fitt came away from Scarborough feeling very depressed. He feared that the problem was being allowed to drift by a preoccupied Labour government. On 25 October he again pleaded in the Commons for attention to be focused on Northern Ireland affairs: 'If that does not happen, I predict that there will be trouble.' At Scarborough, he had been deeply impressed by Anthony Lester's talk on the Race Relations Act and his prediction that racial troubles seen in America, such as the Chicago riots, could be repeated in Britain. Fitt firmly believed the situation in Northern Ireland was even more volatile. Indeed, he had begun to fear that the rising hopelessness in the Catholic community would lead to direct action. He told the Commons: 'When people feel that there can be no redress of their wrongs in a constitutional way by drawing attention to the existing situation, they would be quite entitled and it would be morally valid for them to do something to rectify their position.' In November 1967, he expanded this point at a meeting in Newry, where he talked of making Derry Council unworkable by direct action:

> The opposition members could grab the mace and throw it into the Foyle or take similar action which would bring them before the courts. Then they could present their case and have it brought to the notice of the people across the water by the press and television.

That month, in a bid to deflect their ever more strident criticism, Terence O'Neill attacked Fitt and Austin Currie. Calling Fitt a 'paste-board politician dazzled by his own eloquence', he denounced him as 'the man who seems to believe that myth can be converted into truth by constant repetition'. Stopping just short of accusing the pair of incitement to violence, he said they were 'playing with fire':

> They know as well as I do that the peace of this country has not all times been secure and that there are always people ready – with the slightest encouragement – to take the shortcut to political power by way of violence. I want them and all the people of Northern Ireland to understand that Ulster's government will be decided by votes, not threats.

Currie and Fitt responded immediately, accusing O'Neill of trying to muzzle the political spokesmen of the minority. Currie claimed the Prime Minister was perpetrating a massive confidence trick, 'promises and platitudes but no action', and called him the 'stuntman of a generation'. The attack angered Fitt more than usual because behind the scenes, he was heavily involved in private lobbying to foil yet another Unionist abuse of power:

> One night while I was in a club, having a drink, a senior Catholic lawyer approached me. He said there was a vacancy for a judge and that Ambrose McGonigal, a Catholic QC with a distinguished war record, was to be passed over in favour of a unionist sympathiser. He listed for me the heavily Protestant bias in court appointments. I raised the matter in London with Edward Gardiner, the Lord Chancellor, and Sir Elwyn Jones, the Attorney-General. They called for the papers from Belfast, the first time ever a Stormont appointment had been queried in London. I had several meetings about the case and was told that while the law officers regarded McGonigal as well qualified, there was considerable pressure from Belfast over the vacancy. In the end I was approached by a man from the Lord Chancellor's office who said they had found a way out of the problem. Two judges were to be appointed: McGonigal and another Protestant QC, Edward Jones.

The debate on the Justice Bill in November provided Fitt with a chance to raise the matter in public. Stratton Mills, a solicitor and MP, admitted that of the six judges appointed between 1954 and 1967, three had been Unionist members of parliament. Fitt took this as full justification for his charge that legal appointments had a 'decided political slant'. The Unionist MPs, especially those with legal backgrounds, were clearly uncomfortable that the spotlight was being turned so intensively on the issue and, under pressure in the Stormont commons, William Craig betrayed his own prejudice when he said there must be 'social and educational reasons for the fact that only five out of the fourteen members of the inner bar were Catholics'. With the support of the Law Society, James McSparran, the senior Catholic member of the bar, more than adequately answered Craig in a letter to local newspapers. McSparran disclosed that although six of the Crown prosecutors (barristers taking state briefs) were Catholics, their total fees and earnings in an average year would not equal those of one of the Protestant Crown prosecutors.

On the first day of 1968, in an article for the *Irish News*, Fitt summed up the year just concluded as one of missed opportunity: 'It turned out, by the year's end, that words, promises and gestures were about all the Unionists had to offer. Of any genuine step towards reform there was not a sign.' He knew instinctively that 1968 would be the year of the 'crunch', that the endless prevarication in Belfast and London would have to come to some sort of conclusion. His own patience was exhausted, but he was not at all discouraged and still committed to campaigning. The year had been designated Human Rights Year, so when he travelled to Oxford to take part in a discussion, he decided to highlight the iniquities of the Civil Authorities (Special Powers) Act (Northern Ireland) 1922.

The Special Powers Act, as it was more widely known, infringed twenty-two of the thirty articles in the European Convention for the Protection of Human Right and Fundamental Freedoms. It empowered the government of Northern Ireland to suspend any of the basic civil liberties at will, whether *habeas corpus* or freedom of the press. Citizens could be arrested at the whim of a police officer and interned indefinitely, with trial by order of the Minister of Home Affairs. Widespread searches of people and property, curfews, movement restrictions, road closures, mandatory answering of police questions, outlawing of organisations, films, books, papers, meetings, parades, even the inspection of bank accounts were all permitted. In fact, in truly Dickensian fashion, flogging was prescribed as one of the penalties for infringing the Act. It was not an emergency feature of Northern Ireland legislation, it was a permanent feature, and as such was used frequently to ban parades and demonstrations. The Act was a catch-all: one regulation permitted the Minister of Home Affairs to declare offences retrospectively should something come to light not specifically covered by the Act.

May brought further evidence of the ugliness simmering just below the surface when O'Neill was pelted with stones, eggs and flour by Paisleyites while attending a Unionist meeting in the Shankill area of Belfast. His official car was removed to prevent it being burned and he had to be smuggled out of the hall in a police patrol car after being hit in the eye by one of the missiles. Despite the rising tension, Paul Rose and other MPs from the CDU got no more than a sympathetic hearing from Jim Callaghan, Roy Jenkins' successor at the home office, when they met him to discuss the matter. They wanted and needed resolute commitment to reforms, but it was the same old story: prevarication and a softly, softly approach. Meanwhile, a course of events was underway that would, at last, bring the simmering crisis to a head. One afternoon in June 1968, at the member's bar in Stormont, Nat Minford, a Unionist MP, signed discreetly to Fitt that he wished to talk to him. They both headed outside to the Gents where Minford told Fitt of something that was to have lasting significance in Irish history. According to Fitt, Minford said, 'We are having a terrible row with those bastards in Dungannon Rural Council.' He told him that Emily Beattie, a nineteen-year-old single woman Protestant, had been allocated a council house in the Co. Tyrone village of Caledon by the local unionist-controlled council. Minford said the Cabinet and party were very sensitive about the matter, but could do nothing with their hard men in the area. He was sure that once it became known, there would be 'hell to pay', but he had been told very firmly to mind his own business as the allocation of houses was up to the local council. Minford suggested Austin Currie should take the matter up as it fell within his Stormont constituency.

Fitt immediately recognised the immense propaganda value in the situation. Beattie, who was engaged to be married, was by no stretch of even the most bigoted imagination in urgent need of accommodation. He was also intrigued by the fact that Beattie was employed as a secretary by the Armagh solicitor Brian McRoberts, also solicitor to the council concerned and his potential opponent for the West Belfast seat. He rushed off to find Currie, who was already well aware of the situation in Caledon. In his autobiography, *All Hell Will Break Loose*, Currie recalls that when he heard about the allocation he knew he could have waited for years and not found a better example of unfair housing allocation: 'There was no way the allocation could be justified. It was time to go for broke.'

Currie raised the matter in Stormont on 19 June when the MP for the area, John Taylor, his contemporary at Queen's University, defended the allocation vigorously, provoking an uproar. Currie was so incensed he was eventually ordered from the chamber by the Speaker, whereupon he threw his papers across the floor in frustration as he left. What had angered him so much was that this was not an isolated incident in Caledon, where there were 269 families on the housing list. For some time previously he had been fighting the cases of several Catholic families who were living in appalling conditions. Despite his best efforts, the local council persisted in allocating houses to Protestant families whose need was far less acute. When the Catholic families protested by squatting in two new houses before they were completed, the council cut off the water. When informed this created a health hazard, the council took legal action to evict them. One family was removed forcefully and the house they had been occupying was allocated to Beattie.

The morning after his untimely exit from Stormont, Currie resorted to direct action and moved into the house himself. As he did so, his wife Anita telephoned Fitt to tell him what Currie was doing. After a few hours, Beattie and her brother, a serving police officer, arrived to evict Currie. He left peacefully, but the incident was recorded by a cadre of press and television cameramen and that night made the national television news in Britain. Although Fitt and Currie could not have realised it then, the Caledon affair proved to be the spark that ignited the Troubles.

The emphasis now shifted back to Westminster, where the Labour MP Ben Whitaker had tabled a question for the Prime Minister querying which Northern Irish matters he would answer questions about. Whitaker's move was inspired by Fitt's continued clashes with the Table Office over the scope of the 'convention' and it was timed deliberately for 11 July so that it would dominate the Belfast papers on the Twelfth. Fitt achieved his objective by getting a headline-grabbing answer from Wilson in a supplementary:

> It is certainly the case that he [Fitt] has been very active, since he entered this house, in raising the problems of human rights and discrimination in Northern Ireland. The Prime Minister and his colleagues know we cannot continue indefinitely with the present situation. Something has to be done.

Fitt believed the Prime Minister had paid him a personal compliment because he had heard on the party grapevine that his patience was exhausted. As he had hoped, the Unionists rose to the bait, with Captain Lawrence Orr responding:

> We will resist any attempt at interference with the last breath in our bodies. Wilson has been given a warning about Ulster's future. Anyone who interferes with the just prerogative of the government of Northern Ireland does so at his peril.

Fitt could hardly believe the foolhardy arrogance of the reply and was sure the crunch was now imminent:

> I had campaigned through constitutional channels for reform, endlessly, patiently and unsuccessfully. I had warned what refusal would entail. I had gone out of my way to divorce these demands from my aspirations for a united Ireland to make them acceptable to liberal unionists and Protestants. Yet all I got was 'no surrender'. There was an incredible mood for change sweeping the world in 1968 and I sensed Northern Ireland could not be immune from it. It had been further fuelled by the spring riots in Paris, the assassinations of Martin Luther King and later, Robert Kennedy, especially, with that families' strong Irish association and popularity.

On Sunday, 21 July, in the wake of the Caledon affair, Fitt reflected these sentiments while speaking at a Connolly commemoration rally in Derry and felt quite justified in saying that he had gained absolutely nothing from talking at Westminster and Stormont:

> The day for talking has gone. The day for action has arrived. If

constitutional methods do not bring social justice, if they do not bring democracy to Northern Ireland, then I am quite prepared to go outside constitutional methods.

In line with this defiant thinking, Austin Currie began to plan a four-mile protest march from Coalisland to Dungannon to draw greater attention to the Caledon injustice and the wider demands for reform. Through the McCluskeys, the Northern Ireland Civil Rights Association (NICRA) became involved in the event. Late on the Friday night before the march, which was set for 24 August, Currie and the other organisers were served with police notices banning the march from its planned destination in Market Square, in the centre of Dungannon. The police had acted at the very last minute despite several weeks' advance notice of the march, creating the impression that they had bowed to pressure from local unionists and the Paisley-led Ulster Protestant Volunteers, who had announced a simultaneous counter-demonstration.

In the event, the civil rights march set off from Coalisland on a fine, sunny afternoon with more than 4,000 in its ranks. When the marchers reached the Quarry Lane/Thomas Street junction in Dungannon, they found a double cordon of three tenders and some 200 police drawn up to prevent them reaching the square. Behind the police, about 1,500 jeering Protestants had gathered. As speeches to the civil rights supporters began, a few youths affiliated to the militant Young Socialists tried to break through the police line and were vigorously batoned back. As he later told the Scarman Tribunal, Fitt was horrified when he saw 'a fully-grown policeman with a blackthorn stick in his hand beating up a young girl who was one of the demonstrators'. Fitt recalled, 'It made my blood run cold and I made a few derogatory remarks [about the police] which have been hurled back at me ever since. Then somebody grabbed the microphone from the speaker and handed it to me saying, "For God's sake, try to stop them".' He related the events that followed to the Cameron Commission:

> Now I had read a book many years ago by Gustav le Baum and I think the book was called *How To Control A Crowd*. My own wife and four children were standing there and I didn't want them to be injured. I saw a lot of people, young people, standing there and the police lorry was there and somewhere up the road they had a water cannon and I knew there was absolutely no chance of getting through that barrier. I realised this and, all of a sudden, I remembered this book on how to control a crowd, take them with you so far, get them to agree and bring them back and that was when I said – I remember the words I said – 'Tonight when I saw what was happening to the city of Prague in Czechoslovakia, which has just been invaded, where the ordinary people are fighting to establish their individuality and national freedom, how such different is the mentality which tries to prevent these feelings, the Russians in Prague, the RUC in Dungannon and the RUC are just as bad as the bastards in Prague.' That is

what I said and I stand over that. I feel quite honestly that this is exactly the same mentality. Then I went on to say, 'If there weren't women and children in this crowd, I would lead you through,' which got me a big cheer, but I put in the qualification – 'what is the use of risking innocent women and children?' – and immediately that cooled them down; they had sufficient faith in me and I had taken them so far and brought them back. I stopped the confrontation in Dungannon that night.

NICRA chairman Betty Sinclair then took control of the situation and appealed for restraint. The sporadic stoning and placard-throwing at the police died down and for two hours the meeting at the cordon continued. Austin Currie and Fitt both spoke. 'A fire has been lit tonight which will not go out until civil rights have been established,' Fitt said. The meeting ended with the huge crowd singing 'We Shall Overcome', the song that had become the anthem of the US civil rights marchers, and it was sung with such passion and gusto that it drowned out the sound of 'The Sash My Father Wore' and 'God Save the Queen' coming from the Protestants.

Afterwards, in the McCluskeys' house, the organisers excitedly discussed what they could do to build on the success. During the next few days the newspapers covered the march extensively and the issues it raised, and Fitt also sought and obtained a ten-minute meeting with Harold Wilson during which he said Wilson showed 'great interest' in what Fitt told him. (The Cameron Commission, which investigated and later reported on the early disorders, criticised Fitt for irresponsible abuse of the police. He always contended that he was entitled to challenge them: 'An impartial police force would have protected our right to carry out our lawfully notified march and would have cleared and protected our route.')

The Monday after the demonstration, parliament was recalled in London to discuss the Russian invasion of Czechoslovakia. Fitt seized the opportunity to draw wider attention to what had happened in Dungannon, tabling a motion deploring the tactics of the RUC and the ban and obtaining more than sixty signatures within a few hours:

> I remember saying to Stan Newens how normal it was in London to see the police escorting marchers, both for and against Vietnam, Biafra, Rhodesia, South Africa, every cause under the sun. Knowing that a major anti-Vietnam war demonstration was being planned, I suggested having a march simultaneously in London and Londonderry, which would illustrate the shortcomings and partiality of the RUC.

Stan Newens took up the idea and promptly booked Trafalgar Square for 20 October for a demonstration about Northern Ireland. Fitt spent 'a fortune' drinking with parliamentary journalists at Westminster in an attempt to interest them in the Northern Ireland situation, because the Dungannon march had failed to attract any national publicity. A few days later, when George Clark of *The Times* stopped Fitt in the Westminster lobby, Fitt declined to talk to him: 'You're not interested in what is happening.' But Clark persisted in talking and, to Fitt's great surprise, wrote an article that was published the next morning.

Back in Belfast, Fitt spoke to Currie and others about the plan for a simultaneous demonstration, predicting that it would be a watershed march. However, this time there was no consensus among the disparate and rival groups which had come together at Dungannon: some wanted the march to be in Newry; others argued for Dungannon again and insisted on asserting right of access to the square. NICRA, which prided itself on being non-political and non-sectarian, was bitterly resentful that its members had been treated in a sectarian fashion by the police and confined to the Catholic quarter of Dungannon. Fitt pressed for Derry because it was a potent historical symbol to the unionists and also a microcosm of the ills and evils of modern Northern Ireland which he was so fervently trying to highlight.

In due course, Joe Sherrard, one of Fitt's Republican Labour members who was also on the NICRA executive, secured agreement to hold a march in Derry on 5 October. The date was chosen because it suited the Labour MPs from Westminster whom Fitt had already lined up to act as an observer of what he confidently expected to be 'further police brutality'. This assessment was based on an earlier discussion in Fitt's Antrim Road home with Aidan Corrigan, chairman of NICRA, and Hugh McAteer, a veteran IRA activist. As there were very few non-Catholics living within the old walls of the city, Fitt reckoned the unionist government would not be able to find a reason for banning a march from that area, but McAteer was pessimistic: 'We've tried this for years. The police will beat you into the ground.'

The decision to go ahead with the march was confirmed at a meeting of the interested parties on 31 August. NICRA would sponsor the march, but the actual organisation would be carried out by an *ad hoc* committee called 'the 5 October Group'. They lodged the necessary notification with the police to walk from Waterside railway station, across the Craigavon Bridge and into the Diamond, a route normally processed by Protestant marchers who regarded the old city as a sacred citadel of their combined faith and politics, or, as Fitt more colourfully put it, 'Derry is so steeped in unionist mythology that they couldn't afford to let the enemy traverse their hallowed territory.'

Fitt's ongoing efforts to interest the Fleet Street papers in what was happening suddenly took a decidedly more promising turn. After a couple of days at Westminster, he reached Antrim Road about 10.30am on 2 September after an early flight from London. On the hallstand he found a letter from Mary Holland of *The Observer*: 'Dear Mr Fitt, I have been thinking of doing an article on Northern Ireland and would very much like to meet you.' Fitt said afterwards, 'This was the most wonderful breakthrough that I had ever had – Mary Holland of *The Observer* wanting to know what was happening in Northern Ireland.' He telephoned Holland immediately and, rather than wait until she returned from Sheffield the following week, he arranged to see her that very same evening at the Irish Club in London at 7.00pm. 'I shouted to Ann for a clean shirt and socks and flew straight back to London with a briefcase full of literature about gerrymandering, discrimination and unionist misrule.'

Fitt's stories and material made such an impression on the young reporter that she immediately telephoned David Astor, her editor, who agreed she should abandon her planned assignment in Sheffield and instead return to Belfast with Fitt. Over the next few days he escorted her to Caledon and other places to talk face-to-face with people in desperate circumstances, who were in dire need of jobs and houses. The tour ended in Derry, where Holland was introduced to Eamon McCann and Ivan Cooper and the coming march and its implications were outlined to her.

The march was now only days away, so Fitt left Holland to write up her article and headed off to the Labour party conference in Blackpool, where he was to speak at a meeting of the CDU. In what the *Irish News* categorised as a rousing speech, Fitt repeated what had become an all-too-familiar mantra:

> I do not consider I am making any outlandish requests. All I am asking for is that the same rights and privileges which are enjoyed by the people in Doncaster, should be afforded to the people of Dungannon and Derry. That the same electoral system which is enjoyed by the people of Birmingham should also be made available to the people of Belfast. That the office of the Parliamentary Commissioner should be extended to cover Northern Ireland; and that the Race Relations Act, suitably amended to take account of religious discrimination, should be applied to the Six Counties.

Earlier that day, amidst threats of counter-demonstrations by opponents of the civil rights campaign, Bill Craig, the hardline Home Affairs minister, had banned all marches in Derry city, just as Fitt had expected. Later that night, after the conference meeting, he was standing with Paddy Devlin in the basement of his Blackpool hotel feeding coins into a telephone box to find out if a meeting in Derry had decided that the march would go ahead, in defiance of the government ban. When this was confirmed to him, he set about drumming up interest among Labour MPs at the conference, with a view to recruiting a number of them to act as independent observers. 'I want them to witness what can happen in what is allegedly an integral part of the UK,' he told the *Irish News*. During his tour of the conference hotel bars, he also encouraged the political correspondents of the BBC and ITN to make sure they had cameras there to record what he now anticipated would be a violent confrontation with the police. 'Craig will tell them to lay into us and give us a good beating so that we will not come back again,' he predicted.

First thing on Saturday morning, the appointed day of the march, Fitt was at Aldergrove airport to collect Russell Kerr, Anne Kerr and John Ryan, the three MPs who had agreed to observe the events, plus Mary Holland and her photographer. During the journey to Derry they stopped at Dungiven for refreshments and met Kevin Agnew, a local solicitor and founder member of the Civil Rights executive. Fitt became very angry when Agnew started what he termed 'a lot of republican talk. I told him this was nothing to do with the unity of the country, we were trying to establish natural justice. I didn't want him antagonising the MPs because they were certainly not interested in republicanism that day.' Later that afternoon the marchers formed up at the Waterside railway station, as planned, and began to walk along Duke Street towards Craigavon Bridge, the crossing-point to the city centre. Fitt remembered it in detail:

> I was in the front rank, flanked either side by Ivan Cooper, Austin Currie and Eddie McAteer. In front of us the police had rushed a couple of tenders into position to block the narrow street and some of them were grouped in front of it. We marched on slowly ignoring the police loudhailer warnings about the illegality of the march.

There was no set plan, and Fitt always insisted that from the outset he was clear in his own mind that there would be no attempt to break through the police line or to offer any violence to the police. As he looked around at the three independent MP observers and the cluster of television cameras, he felt he had already achieved what he had set out to do by focusing unprecedented attention on the protest:

> I expected that we would end up sitting down at the barrier, as we had done in Dungannon. As we came within in a few yards of the police, who had drawn their batons, there was suddenly a big surge from behind and we were propelled forward. A sergeant grabbed me and pulled my coat down over my shoulders to prevent me raising my arms. Two other policemen held me as I was batoned twice on the head. A stinging pins-and-needles feeling followed and I could feel the blood coursing down my neck onto my shirt. As I fell to my knees I was roughly grabbed and thrown into a police van. I said to one of the policemen they had been a bit free with their batons. 'You were trying to kick us,' he replied. I said nobody would believe that. Catch yourself on. At the police station I was shown into a room with a filthy washbasin and told to clean up. But I was not interested in that. I wanted the outside world to see the blood, which was still flowing strongly down my face. The police were confused about what to do with me and eventually I was driven to Altnagelvin hospital where my wound was stitched, but the police would not let them put a bandage around my head in case it provoked the crowds who had gathered.

After his arrest more people were batoned by the police before Betty Sinclair was able to get up on a chair and hold a meeting for the 2,000 marchers. An hour later, however, after the speeches had concluded, the police sprang a trap and moved in from two sides with batons and water cannon, dousing and assaulting people indiscriminately. At the hospital, Fitt watched the results: a procession of people, many of them young students, were carried in for treatment after being subject to police attacks. Many were in shock and weeping freely. It was the same story back at the police station, where he met Ann, who had left her sick bed to join the march. By the time he was released from police custody seventy marchers had been injured, most with head wounds.

Fitt gave a succession of television and radio interviews, still wearing his blood-stained shirt, which he preserved, unwashed, for the rest of his life. 'I knew it had been a watershed, that the smouldering embers ignited by Caledon had now flared up.' The unionists did not recognise it then, but that was the beginning of the end of their half-century of hegemony. Back in Belfast that evening, as soon as one call ended Fitt's telephone rang again – Fleet Street had suddenly discovered the Northern Ireland story in a big way. As he nursed his sore head with its three stitches, even the hard-campaigning Fitt could not have foreseen the enormity of the course of events that he had helped trigger off.

CHAPTER SEVEN

PUBLIC ENEMY NUMBER ONE

THE WORST WEEKEND OF VIOLENCE for forty years followed the march. Nearly 100 people were injured by steel-helmeted, baton-wielding police officers. The Irish papers naturally made big news of the clash, but the most important feature for Fitt was the long-overdue interest of the influential national British newspapers, particularly the *Times* and *Guardian*, which both carried extensive front-page reports, pictures and leaders. The *Guardian* suggested a Royal Commission might be the best way to expedite the process of change. The *Times* called for an inquiry and likened Bill Craig to the notorious Mayor Daley of Chicago for his handling of the situation.

The Unionists were badly shaken as the full implications of what had happened began to sink in. Within days, immediately upon his return from Rhodesia, Wilson summoned Terence O'Neill to London to account for the incident. Back in Northern Ireland, Craig was giving his version of police behaviour, insisting they had not used their batons until attacked by marchers with placard poles, and even then had stuck to the guidelines of baton drill, hitting marchers about the legs to minimise injury. O'Neill also claimed Fitt had been hit by a placard wielded by one of the demonstrators. Apart from his very obvious head wound to contradict them, Fitt had obtained some 8mm film, shot by Tom Hughes, a constituent, which showed clearly what had taken place: Fitt was singled out and assaulted as soon as the front rank of marchers reached the police cordon. Several people even gave him the name of the police sergeant who had pulled his jacket down and pinioned his arms.

Labour MPs John Ryan, Russell Kerr and Anne Kerr, who had been in the thick of the police activity, were very critical of what they had seen and made a damning report to the Home Secretary, James Callaghan, the Whitehall minister nominally responsible for matters in Northern Ireland. Anne Kerr, who had recently witnessed the activities of Mayor Daley's Chicago police at first-hand, had been so incensed in Derry that – foreshadowing the *Guardian* editorial – she had shouted, 'Chicago, Chicago', at the RUC. John Ryan also reported that women and children had been beaten by the police.

Clearly feeling that defence was the best form of attack, the Unionist government initiated another of its perennial but groundless IRA scares. Craig stated that the IRA had turned communist and infiltrated the civil rights movement. The police, he claimed, had photographed known IRA men among the marchers and he named one of them as Cathal Goulding. Soon afterwards, however, Goulding rang various newspapers to protest, insisting he was having his car mended at a garage near Dublin when the march was taking place.

The unprecedented intensity of the press, radio and television coverage really hurt the unionists. The dawning age of television meant the incriminating pictures were satellited around the world within hours, resulting in a vast amount of international attention. Interest in the USA was particularly high and Fitt did several broadcasts for US news channels explaining why and how the trouble had erupted. Journalists flocked into Belfast and queued for interviews in the hallway and on the stairs of the Fitts' home, their waiting punctuated by cups of tea distributed by the Fitt family females.

The scale of outside interest in the situation was underlined when David Frost, the biggest name in television current affairs at the time, flew into Belfast to present his nationally networked programme live from the cramped, spartan studio at UTV. Predictably enough, the programme degenerated into a shouting match after, as had been rehearsed, Fitt began to draw on a blackboard to illustrate the way the electoral boundaries in Derry were gerrymandered. When the cameras swung onto him and he produced a stick of chalk, there were noisy shouts of 'Fix' from the extreme loyalists present. Undeterred, Fitt demonstrated how the Catholic majority was denied political control.

The city was divided into three wards: North, South and Waterside. South had a Catholic majority of 12,000, while the other two wards had small Unionist majorities of 1,500 in North and 1,700 in Waterside. This meant the Unionists were able to secure twelve council seats out of twenty, which in turn ensured that the elected representatives of the one-third Unionist minority population controlled local government affairs. Research into the activities of the council in Derry had revealed that every department head was a Protestant. In fact, no Catholic worked in the Guildhall, the council offices, or meeting place. In all, those centres employed 145 Protestant workers and only thirty-two Catholics. The Council's record of housing allocation and construction was equally scandalous. In 1963, for instance, it had built just thirty-three houses when 211 applications had been lodged, nearly all from Catholics. In 1965 ninety families were still living in 'Nissen Huts', twenty years after they had been vacated by the US Army at the end of the Second World War. Needless to say, the inhabitants of the huts were all Catholics. Fitt concluded his demonstration by saying that the same sorry situation was repeated in virtually every town in the province. In fact, discrimination in Northern Ireland was so endemic that a priest had been blackballed by a golf club purely on sectarian grounds and a newspaper advertisement seeking a new home for a stray dog had bluntly specified that it must be a Protestant home.

The turbulent programme caused raised eyebrows throughout Britain, but the real trouble did not start until it had gone off the air. An angry Protestant crowd gathered outside and surrounded the building and Frost had to wait in the studios for several hours until it had dispersed. Fitt was now firmly regarded as their 'public enemy number one' and it took a strong police presence to escort him safely from the building through a side-door. Fitt's raised public profile and uncompromising statements meant the 'hate' letters became a feature of every postal delivery and his family laughed as he read out the lengthy tirades of abuse over breakfast. One of the more extreme examples arrived in a thick envelope that contained virtually an entire writing pad with just three words – 'Fuck you, Fitt' – spelled out in large black letters, one on each page. The *Guardian* commented that Fitt had overtaken the Pope as the most hated man in Ulster.

But the best indication that his message was at long last getting through to where it mattered most came from Harold Wilson himself during exchanges in the Commons on 22 October. In answer to a supplementary from Paul Rose, Wilson paid tribute to what O'Neill had done and went on to say: 'But I don't think anyone in this house is satisfied with what has been done and, in particular, the feeling that he is being blackmailed by thugs, who are putting pressure on him, is something this house cannot accept.' Captain Lawrence Orr then waded in with a eulogy to the RUC, describing it as 'probably the best and finest police force in the world' and deplored the 'mischief-making questions'. Wilson replied:

> Those who have tabled them have as great sincerity in this matter as you. Without in any way seeking to trespass on the ground covered by the Government of Ireland Act, I say to you that you are entitled to your view. Up to now perhaps we have had to rely on statements of yours and others on these matters ... since then we have had British television.

It was the most stinging rebuke Fitt had ever heard addressed to a Unionist and for the first time he felt there just might be some positive action taken to right the many wrongs in Northern Ireland. This was precisely the position Fitt and his allies had worked to achieve. For him, meaningful reform within Northern Ireland was the only issue:

> The civil rights movement had attracted support right across the political divide, including from liberal and moderate Protestants, who all wanted a better state of affairs in Northern Ireland. That is why I was so angry both at the Unionist's IRA smear and at the opportunist intervention of Jack

Lynch, the Irish Prime Minister who tried to put Irish unity on the agenda. Both were taking attention off the real issue – the crying need for social justice in Northern Ireland.

In the week after the march Taoiseach Jack Lynch twice spoke about the root cause of the problem being the 'partition of our country against the wishes of the overwhelming majority of the Irish people'. Fitt was furious because he knew such sentiments played into the hands of the unionists and endangered the great changes he was convinced the civil rights movement was poised to deliver. In order to avoid any doubt about the situation, and also to avoid alienating the many contacts and allies he had made in Westminster, Fitt took the opportunity to put the record straight when he spoke in the Commons on 4 November:

> The present situation is in no way aimed at the achievement of an Irish Republic. The question of partition does not enter into the demand for civil rights. As one who lives in Northern Ireland, I have already clearly shown the House where my social allegiance lies. I hope that I shall live to see the day when we have a socialist republic in Ireland. That situation can come about only by the will of the Irish people, both north and south of the border. I believe the Prime Minister of the Irish Republic last week made a statement which should not have been made in connection with the present circumstances.

The non-sectarian basis of the civil rights movement was illustrated dramatically at Queen's University, where many students who had attended the banned march, in the days afterwards, picketed Craig's home in Belfast, staged a peaceful sit-down outside City Hall and, during a series of almost non-stop debates in the University, formed the People's Democracy. Undoubtedly the students were inspired in part by the Paris Spring, but what they represented in local terms was noteworthy because they drew their strength right across the campus, from the full student population, which was 75% Protestant and 25% Catholic. Fitt believed that if the brightest and most able young people of the day, the rulers of tomorrow, could overcome their native sectarianism and work together, it augured well for the future.

In answer to Wilson's earlier summons, O'Neill arrived in London on 4 November, accompanied by Faulkner and Craig, the principal pretenders to his leadership. After the meeting the Prime Minister said that if O'Neill were deposed by extremists, it would lead the British government to review its entire relationship with Northern Ireland. On 22 November, however, it became clear that Wilson had pressurised them heavily on reforms. After a Stormont Cabinet meeting that day a five-point plan was announced: fairer housing allocation would be introduced through a new points system based on need; an Ombudsman would be appointed to tackle complaints of discrimination; the Special Powers Act would be reviewed; the company vote in local elections would be replaced by 'one man, one vote'; and the notorious Londonderry Council was to be wound up and replaced by a Development Commission, the brief for which would be to revitalise the social and economic wasteland the Unionists had allowed the city to become. The plan represented virtually a clean sweep of the changes Fitt and his allies had been demanding for years, and he regarded the announcement as a total vindication of all that he had done. The changes were not welcomed by the uncompromising elements of the Unionist Establishment, however, and after the 5 October clashes they had organised counter-marches at every event planned by the civil rights campaign. Many passed off peacefully, but others culminated in confrontations, minor skirmishes and stone-throwing. Whenever the police were caught between the two sides, the RUC invariably seemed to favour the Protestants, often standing with their backs to them and facing the Catholics directly. It was this perception of the RUC as the 'armed-wing' of the Unionist party that contributed significantly to the worsening of events.

Early one evening in mid-November 1968, Fitt was having a cup of tea with Paddy Wilson when two policemen came to the door of his home. Ann lied and said he was out, asking them to return at 8.00pm. Sensing he was to be prosecuted for taking part in the banned Derry march, Fitt rang McGlade's Old Vic lounge, the haunt of local journalists which had now been over-run by the Fleet Street pack. So, by 8.00pm, before the police returned, a good number of cameramen, photographers and reporters had been dragged away from their evening cocktails and were hidden in nearby doorways and gardens. As soon as the RUC officers arrived, bearing their summonses to Fitt, they were bathed in a flood of television lights and flashbulbs as they handed them over.

One Sunday morning, at this time, Ronnie Bunting rang to tell Fitt that while he had been laid up in hospital, recovering from a heart attack, he had been visited by the Rev Ian Paisley. He confided that he had been at death's door until 'the Doctor', as he called Paisley, had talked to him and he was now a disciple. He was keen for Fitt to talk to Paisley because he believed he, too, would then see things differently. Fitt could hardly believe that Bunting, who had shared many platforms with him, had completed such a political somersault and was identifying himself with the most violent extremes of unionism but it was in that role, soon afterwards, that he was central to events when they took a decidedly ugly turn in Armagh on 30 November.

In order to foil a civil rights march planned for that afternoon, Paisley and Bunting, along with carloads of their cudgel-carrying supporters, invaded the town centre the night before and were allowed to roam without police interference. Later in the day, when the 5,000 civil rights marchers came into confrontation with these loyalists, inevitably there was violence and for the first time there were casualties among the newsmen – those blamed by the Paisleyites for giving such bad publicity to Northern Ireland. The ugly clashes at Armagh heightened the political crisis, opening wide the rift already destabilising O'Neill's Cabinet. In a bid to consolidate his position, O'Neill took the unprecedented step of making a prime ministerial broadcast on television on Monday 9 December. Throughout the small towns and villages, in pubs and homes, people clustered around television sets to hear O'Neill's last plea for sanity: 'Ulster is at a crossroads. What kind of Ulster do you want?'

The answer was not long coming. The middle ground rallied around and over the next few days he received 150,000 letters and telegrams of support. But the hardliners, with Craig at their head, stepped up their defiance. The next night, in Belfast, Craig said that O'Neill was allowing the British government to 'blackmail' the Northern Ireland government and that a strong Unionist party would not tolerate it. Less than twelve hours later, an emboldened O'Neill sacked Craig and appointed a new Minister of Home Affairs.

By this stage, Fitt's home life had become completely dominated by his political life. The family's house at 85 Antrim Road became the target for nightly attacks, which would become a permanent feature of life, although the IRA sympathisers who abused them most in the end were of an opposing political persuasion from the loyalists who began the process. At first Fitt and Ann were philosophical about the harassment. The clatter of stones and bottles hitting the house, usually aimed by passing drunks, became commonplace and they would lie awake in bed late at night, laughing at the slurred insults that frequently accompanied the various missiles.

One Saturday night in December 1968, when Fitt was away, Ann and her daughters were watching a late-night television movie in the basement when they were disturbed by the now-routine sound of a bottle shattering one of the front windows upstairs. Patsy recalls seeing the shadows of people as she looked up towards the front steps of the house, before she fainted. Ann stepped over her and grabbed the phone to call the police. Meanwhile, Eileen and Joan raced upstairs to the front door and opened it just in time to see four men running away. The two girls followed the men along the main road towards Carlisle Circus. When the culprits went into a side-street, Joan followed from a distance, keeping them in sight, while Eileen flagged down the arriving police patrol and pointed them in the right direction. Joan then identified the culprits and watched as they were taken into custody. Later, when sentencing the loyalist bottle-thrower to a month in prison, the magistrate, Gerald Lynn, complimented Joan, then aged eighteen, on her courage, which led to a full report of her bravery in the *Daily Mirror* complete with a pin-up picture.

Although they were in most respects a typically close Belfast family, life in the Fitt household was, of course, far from normal because of the incessant stream of callers and telephone calls and the constant threat of violence.

Fitt always pointed out that in England an MP was a legislator first, whereas in Northern Ireland he was a social worker first. He spent three to four days a week in London, sometimes making two round trips if something important was going on at City Hall or Stormont. On the mornings he was at home, one of his daughters would be sent out to pick up twenty cigarettes, a pint of milk and the local papers and he would enjoy a lie-in, reading the papers from cover to cover, smoking and swigging milk to calm the constant discomfort of his ulcer. When he wanted something, he rattled the buttons on the bedside phone, causing a tinkling which could be heard in the kitchen, and Ann or one of his daughters would be expected to fulfil his demand. He would also scrutinise the horse racing lists as no day was complete without a few bets. After that he would go out and about, dropping into City Hall, Stormont and one or more of a whole network of pubs he used. Invariably, he would not come home until late, usually by taxi, or sometimes dropped off by someone with a car because he had, of course, never learned to drive. Ann, who was as dedicated to him as he was to her, acted as secretary, housekeeper and cook to ensure all his needs were met. He never had to wash a dish, or polish his own shoes. He could not even change a plug. Ann dealt with all that kind of thing, making curtains, painting rooms and even picking the suits, co-ordinated shirts and ties he wore and which many people admired. In other words, the entire family revolved completely around Fitt and the many demands on his time and energy.

There was, for instance, no such thing as regular mealtimes in the house. Eileen and Patsy recall that the frying pan was constantly on the cooker as Fitt would arrive in, with one acquaintance or another, and demand 'tea and some grub'. More often sandwiches were served and the family ran an account at Mary Cummings' shop and home bakery, a few doors away, which in those pre-supermarket days was used to maintain supplies of such basic items as bread, tea and cooked ham and to replenish them at short notice when an unexpected influx of visitors arrived. Mary Cummings recalls that Fitt would always send one of his daughters to clear the bill on the eve of every election, in case he lost and his income ceased. Ann did most of the catering, but occasionally Fitt would make a big pot of stew, which was a particular favourite. The food he most enjoyed though was steamed, smoked brown fish, followed closely by other seafood, such as jellied eels, potted herrings, mussels, prawns or lobster. On Sundays, when Fitt was at home, he attended Mass at St Patrick's, followed by a traditional family lunch. The timing of the meal was always uncertain, his daughters remember, because 'what should have been a ten-minute walk home used to take an eternity because people would stop him outside the church and every step of the way home, for a yarn or with a problem,' said Eileen.

Fitt had always harboured secret ambitions to be a ship's captain or a virtuoso violinist. The former notion had, of course, been abandoned years earlier when he entered politics, but Ann and he had shared musical instincts and, playing by ear, they occasionally led family sing-songs on the piano in their basement living room. Fitt also played the accordion, or 'melodeon' as he preferred to call it, and the mouth organ, which he often carried with him and produced when drinking sessions had reached a suitably maudlin level for singing to start.

Although he had devoured books when at sea, a daily bundle of newspapers was now his main reading matter and he would frequently rip out articles that interested him and file them in envelopes in his office. They were often shown to other people, but he rarely consulted them again;. an excellent memory enabled him to store and recall whatever information he needed to make his various public and parliamentary orations. With the advent of the pocket-sized cassette tape-recorder he began to make recordings of himself every time he appeared on radio or television, and even to record other events in which he participated, such as conferences. This habit endured for the rest of his life and over the years he accumulated hundreds of 'tapes' charting key aspects of his life and times, although they contain only modest amounts of commentary, analysis, justification or reaction to the events through which he lived. The only television programmes he ever watched were news bulletins and current affairs documentaries. He was disinterested in virtually everything except politics. Indeed, he listed full-time politics as his recreation in *Who's Who*.

Fitt was a proud and affectionate father, but took little interest in his daughters' activities or education. Eileen says he never once attended a single event at any of their schools, such as a parents' evening. Patsy recalls that he obtained her 11-plus results a day early thanks to one of his contacts, but she thinks he was more interested in sparing her the anxiety of waiting for the postman than appreciative of her achievement in passing. Eileen remembers that when she wanted to attend Trinity College in Dublin, the first of the family to go to university, she had to complete all the formalities herself. 'It was as if he had a blind spot for education because he never enjoyed school himself,' she said. All of them remember him as an emotional and often romantic man although it is true he was what would now be termed a chauvinist, or politically incorrect, but that was because he was a product of his time. He was though attentive to the women in his life, frequently bringing home or sending Ann flowers and arriving with bars or boxes of chocolates for his daughters, and always Frys Chocolate Cream, her favourite, for Ann. Another regular treat was a trip to an Italian, family-run café at Carlisle Circus for ice-creams. The only respite from all the hubbub came during July and August, when Fitt rented accommodation, either at Cushendall, Cushendun in the Glens of Antrim or in Donegal, and the entire family would decamp for a well-earned break.

There was one other resident at 85 Antrim Road who deserves mention: a mongrel dog called Mickey. Known as a 'Heinz' dog because of the '57 varieties' in his uncertain pedigree, Mickey was found and brought home by Joan while just a pup. He was a much cherished pet, but as nobody ever found the time to take him for a walk, Mickey found out for himself that if he hopped onto one of the buses passing by the Fitts' door, the park at the former Waterworks was only a couple of stops away. Mickey soon became known to the drivers and conductors on the route, and they ensured he got off at the right stop on his way home. Mickey also had an aversion to uniforms and when a police officer or the like would visit, the dog had to be contained in one of the rooms to allay the barrage of barking he put up to demonstrate his hostility. Other visitors were greeted with friendly sniffing and tail-wagging, as was Fitt's fellow MP, Clement Freud, when he visited. The family were bemused when the doleful Freud, who at the time was co-starring, with a bloodhound called Henry, in a series of television advertisements for dog food, insisted the dog be put outside. They were further bemused when Freud, who enjoyed some repute as a discerning gourmet, complimented Ann Fitt on the excellence of her home-baked cakes. She didn't have the heart to tell him they came from a Mr Kipling box, hastily fetched from Mary Cummings' shop upon his arrival.

In a signed article for the *Irish News* written at the end of 1967, Fitt paid fulsome tribute to his family:

> Sometimes it has been rather difficult to keep up with my three representative seats – Belfast Corporation, Stormont and Westminster. On numerous occasions I have in fact attended City Hall in the morning, Stormont in the afternoon and back to Westminster on the same day. But I was elected to do just this and I have no other interest outside of politics. I have indeed been blessed with a very understanding wife and family.

Towards the end of an eventful 1968, the groundswell of support stimulated by O'Neill's 'Crossroads' broadcast continued apace right through the Christmas period. One of the Dublin newspapers declared him its 'Man of the Year'. As his own contribution to the benevolent atmosphere, Fitt announced a 'Christmas truce', promising to become the 'quiet man of Ulster politics' for a period to test O'Neill's sincerity and give him another chance to get the declared reform programme up and running at last but a cadre of hotheads quickly rushed in to fill the vacuum.

On New Year's morning, 1 January 1969, a sorrowing Fitt watched from his window as a bedraggled bunch of forty Queen's University students, all members of the People's Democracy, marched along the Antrim Road on their way to Derry. Fitt had strongly opposed the march as an exercise in 'coat-trailing' and he feared it would cause trouble as it passed through Protestant areas. In Fitt's view, the students were being led by 'a nest of revolutionaries more interested in confrontation than civil rights'.

As Fitt anticipated, the march did lead to confrontation after confrontation on the road to Derry – the most serious when it walked into a carefully laid ambush by masked loyalists at Burntollet, on the final lap of the journey to Derry. Ann later sympathised with one of the marchers, Michael Farrell (later an author and journalist), when she saw his injuries, but he told her he was delighted they had been beaten up because it would bring sharp media focus onto what was happening in Northern Ireland. The students' decision to break ranks caused the 'broad church' that had hitherto characterised the civil rights movement to crumble, and all Fitt's political instincts warned him the results could only be tragic and the descent from confrontation to the more serious violence Fitt feared was not long in coming.

To enforce restrictions along the route of a civil rights march in the predominantly Catholic town of Newry on Saturday, 11 January, the RUC parked a line of personnel tenders along Merchants Quay, in the town centre. During the afternoon a confrontation developed at this cordon and a group of marchers began throwing stones at the police vehicles before setting light to them and pushing several of the vehicles into the nearby canal. Fitt believed these 'rioters', as he did not hesitate to describe them, had no justification for attacking the police. In his judgement, the situation was quite unlike that in Derry, where defenceless, peaceful marchers were set upon by the police.

> I watched the violence with a sinking feeling in the pit of my stomach. I should have said what I actually thought, that it was in fact the end of the civil rights campaign.

Those police tenders took with them into the murky waters of the Newry canal the last hopes for a peaceful introduction of a fair society and helped unleash the violent forces that were to convulse both Ireland and Britain for well over three decades.

Despite the disastrous events on the streets in recent months, O'Neill's Cabinet ministers remained solidly hardline and unyielding when it came to implementing the reform programme. They believed that 'firm government' through the exercise of police power and more stringent security measures would suppress the disorder. At first, and in spite of pressure from Whitehall to implement the reforms, O'Neill did not dissent from this collective view, but he became increasingly convinced that it was in fact both a short-sighted and doomed strategy, one which risked the complete alienation of the substantial Catholic minority. At that point their principal demand, as Fitt well understood, was for critical reforms to give them equal rights and treatment, not a united Ireland. For all but a tiny, fanatical republican cadre, a united Ireland was nothing more than a cherished aspiration.

In mid-January, the Protestant leaders of the Irish Council of Churches (ICC) wrote a letter outlining the need for 'a judicial public inquiry into all the events and decisions which surround the present controversy'. This prompted O'Neill to inject a more pragmatic note into his Cabinet's policy. In a prophetic memorandum to his ministers on 14 January, O'Neill wrote:

> As things stand it is all too widely accepted throughout the United Kingdom that a sectarian government, directing a partisan police force, is confronting a movement of idealists. As I see it, stubborn political resistance to a change which is in any case inevitable is causing Northern Ireland immense damage… our loss of prestige, authority and standing since October 5th has already been catastrophic, and in my view, the most cold-blooded appraisal of the situation shows that in resisting this molehill of reform we are allowing a mountain to fall upon us.

In view of this, O'Neill recommended an independent and wide-ranging public inquiry should be established, as suggested, and universal suffrage in local government should also be established, to meet the primary civil rights demand for 'one-man, one vote'. Brian Faulkner, the highly ambitious and uncompromising minister of commerce, led the resistance to these proposals, warning that they

> … would be regarded as an abdication by the government of responsibilities which were properly its own …a commission could too easily develop into a fundamental far-reaching and potentially highly embarrassing inquest into every aspect of Northern Ireland's affairs.

A majority of ministers supported O'Neill, however, and his range of measures – setting up the inquiry, pledging to ban provocative demonstrations and extending the Public Order Act and police powers – but their hand was not strengthened when Wilson said that O'Neill had only gone 'some way' to doing what the British government expected. Within days Faulkner resigned, followed closely by William Morgan, Minister of Health and Social Services. On 3 February 1969 twelve Unionist MPs met at Portadown and called for O'Neill's resignation. Once again appealing over their heads, O'Neill said that what they wanted was not a change of leadership but a change of policy and he called a general election for 24 February in the vainglorious hope that the ordinary people, on both sides, would break the traditional political mould and give him the decisive mandate he needed.

When nominations for the election closed, 119 candidates were fighting for 45 of the 52 seats. There was little cross-community co-operation. The Unionists split into pro- and anti-O'Neill camps, while on the nationalist side the new personalities thrown up by the civil rights campaign entered the political contest for the first time, all fighting an acrimonious election conducted in bitterly cold weather. The Republican Labour party put forward five candidates: Harry Diamond stood in Falls, Paddy Kennedy in Central, Jim O'Kane in North Derry, Fitt in Dock and Gerry 'Bugsy' O'Hare in Larkfield. Fitt always regretted that he did not support Paddy Wilson for Central: 'If I had done so, in the trying days ahead I would have had a trusted ally rather than the Trojan Horse Paddy Kennedy turned out to be.' Mary Cummings, the local shopkeeper, remembers that during this watershed election campaign one of the priests preaching at St Patrick's emphasised how important it was for democracy that people turned out to vote. 'I will not tell you who to support,' he said, 'just vote as you see fit.'

The Dock contest in this 1969 Stormont election was particularly important for Fitt as he knew that, due to redevelopment, it was the last time it would be fought on the old boundaries. Therefore, when the votes were counted on 25 February, he was doubly satisfied with his 1,310 majority because it exceeded comfortably the 1,208 majority of his hero, Harry Midgley. In the event, Harry Diamond lost his Falls seat to Paddy Devlin of the NILP, a well-known trade unionist who had been prominent in the civil rights struggle, but Paddy Kennedy's election was some compensation for Republican Labour.

For O'Neill, on the other hand, the election results were disastrous. In his first run at gaining elected office, Paisley, who stood against the Prime Minister in his own Bannside constituency, polled a discomforting 6,331 votes to O'Neill's 7,745. Elsewhere the results showed a clear emergence of support for Paisley. Although the Unionist parliamentary party immediately endorsed O'Neill as their leader, it was abundantly clear that it was now only a matter of time before he would be forced to resign.

After the election Fitt went to the USA, where there was strong interest in the civil rights cause, especially among the more liberal elements of the Irish-American community, who had helped campaign for an end to second-class treatment for 'blacks', or 'negroes' as they were then universally described. For the American audience Fitt drew similarities with the plight of Catholics at home in order to enlist their support for his cause. Speaking to newsmen in Los Angeles, he compared the unionist government with those in the southern states and also to the apartheid regime in South Africa, saying: 'Catholics in Northern Ireland are treated worse than Negroes.'

The two-week long trip – his first abroad since his days as a seaman – got under way in March, the month of St Patrick, when Irish-American fervour for the 'auld sod' is at its peak. 'Even the beer is green and the street markings are overpainted with one of its forty shades,' Fitt commented in a call home. The frantic schedule, arranged jointly by Al McAloon, an Irish-American psychiatry professor, and an organisation called ERIN (Equal Rights in Northern Ireland), took him back and forth from coast to coast. Accompanied by Roddy Connolly, the son of James, he met with Senator Edward Kennedy, addressed the state legislature in Boston, Massachusetts, and spoke in high schools, universities and hotels in New York, Chicago, San Francisco, Rhode Island and Washington. On St Patrick's Day he was guest of honour at the top table of the banquet of the Friendly Sons of St Patrick in Los Angeles, at which he was most interested to meet former vice-president Hubert Humphrey but disconcerted by the applause afforded to a black-bashing, Irish-American police chief. Altogether, Fitt made forty-seven major speeches, appeared on seventeen television and twenty radio programmes, some of them coast to coast, putting forward his views about Northern Ireland society and the slowness of reform. In Los Angeles he was welcomed by a kilted pipe band, 'a limousine the size of some of the houses back in Dock constituency' and police motorcycle outriders. Fitt later summed up his reaction to the trip:

> The people there were highly appreciative of the clusters of shamrock I had brought with me from Ireland. I did not take too well to the Irish-Americans and their embarrassing razzamatazz on my first close encounter with them as a politician. I was amazed at the maudlin, tear jerking speeches, even by priests in mass, and I found some of their organisations too right wing and well-heeled for my socialist taste. Generally I noticed how they were motivated more by hatred of Britain than love of Ireland and I can see how later they so easily became a soft touch for dollars for guns to kill British soldiers.

Upon his return to Westminster, Robin Chichester-Clark sought to capitalise on the fact that Fitt had travelled on an Irish passport:

> He must now realise that he cannot go on any longer presenting himself to the British people as a straight-forward socialist. It seems a little odd that somebody who purports to insist on British standards of behaviour finds it necessary and convenient to travel abroad on a non-British passport.

In reply, Fitt retorted that his decision to travel on an Irish passport was a deliberate ploy to upset the unionists. The truth was far more prosaic, however. Due to the circumstances of his birth and informal adoption into the Fitt family, which occurred before formal adoption laws were in existence, Fitt had great difficulty in producing paperwork necessary to satisfy all the requirements for obtaining a passport. In the end, the Department of Foreign Affairs in Dublin facilitated him and provided an Irish passport.

All the time he was away in the States, Ann kept him updated on a developing situation at home that was to have far-reaching political consequences. George Forrest, an O'Neill-supporting Westminster MP for Mid-Ulster, who in 1967 had been hauled off a Twelfth of July Orange platform and kicked unconscious, never regained his full health and died in December 1968. A by-election for the vacant Mid-Ulster seat was fixed for 17 April and Forrest's widow, Anna, emerged as the unionist candidate. The Mid-Ulster seat, with its Catholic majority, was winnable by a nationalist candidate if the vote were not split and, as the only non-unionist member at Westminster, Fitt recognised that having someone there with him to reinforce his campaigning would be a great boost. He favoured Austin Currie as candidate because he thought he would make the most formidable ally, but as Fitt was marooned in San Francisco he was unable to campaign for Currie and after intense machinations on the Catholic side, the young university student Bernadette Devlin, who had become a vociferous civil rights leader, emerged as the agreed candidate when nominations closed.

Fitt arrived back from the USA a few days before the election and was persuaded reluctantly to endorse Devlin's candidature at an eve of poll rally. Two barristers took him down to Carrickmore and on the way he expressed serious misgivings about Devlin. 'She'll be a disaster,' he said, but in public he said nothing, all too aware that if he should say anything about this 'cheeky, arrogant, miniskirted young lady', it would have been dismissed as sour grapes. 'Everybody who was anybody in nationalist politics was on her platform that night, which showed how the Catholic and nationalist establishment had united and taken her to their hearts as an Irish Joan of Arc.' Lord Longford, the well-intentioned but eccentric Irish peer, was there and Fitt often recalled how, the next day, he had to save him from a piece of ruthless exploitation by Paddy Kennedy, who planned to send him to canvass in some Protestant villages in the certain knowledge that he would be attacked, thus attracting national publicity. Fitt ensured this plan didn't come to fruition.

Polling day, there was a 91.5% turnout of the 68,973 electorate. Bernadette Devlin, the unity candidate, won comfortably with 33,648 votes to the 29,437 cast for her sole opponent, a majority of 4,211. Fitt was probably the only politician on the nationalist side who did not share the excitement of her victory, but events left him little time to mull things over. That Saturday night Derry had its worst night of trouble since the first march, and a cornered policeman was forced to fire a warning shot in the air – the first gunshot of the Troubles. On Sunday a water-mains serving Belfast was sabotaged and it was announced that British soldiers were to mount guard on vital installations.

By now the civil rights association had virtually disintegrated for the liberal, moderate Protestants, who had given it much of its credibility, all resigned their membership. In any case, as Devlin had made it clear in her campaign speeches, she intended to be her own woman, causing Fitt to dread what she would say and do when she got to Westminster. On Tuesday, 22 April Paul Rose, by deft use of the rules, secured a three-hour debate on the situation in Northern Ireland, to be held the following day. Because of the growing crisis, and despite his concerns, Fitt felt it was important Devlin should take her seat immediately and make her maiden speech in what was a crucial debate and exceedingly favourable circumstances. With British troops guarding key points around the province, there was a new situation of direct Whitehall involvement to be explored in further testing the boundaries of the 'convention'.

The night before the debate Fitt spent hours on the telephone, ringing everybody he could think of, trying to track down Bernadette Devlin. Eventually, late that night, he traced her to the Stormont Hotel in Belfast. Fitt later recalled,

'At first she was resentful that I was telling her what to do, then she put Loudon Seth, her agent and Svengali at the time, on the line and he eventually took my point.' Next morning there was great excitement at the Irish Club in London – Fitt's longstanding base in the capital – where the best china and silverware had been laid out for coffee on her arrival. She was delayed by a hoax bomb threat concerning her aircraft, and by the time she arrived the Club was buzzing with reporters and photographers. One newspaper proposed photographing her hula-hooping in a mini-skirt, which Fitt discouraged as being far too trivial, but another, which had secured exclusive access to her, then took her away to buy clothes for a set of pictures. John Silkin, the Labour Chief Whip, later entertained her at lunch in the members dining room and afterwards, in his office, presided at a rehearsal of the procedure for taking her seat. At first there was talk of her being sponsored by one of the Welsh nationalists, but in the end she was introduced to the House of Commons by Paul Rose and Fitt.

That day marked Devlin's twenty-second birthday, and she was the youngest woman ever to enter the House, as well as the youngest MP for some fifty years. She described her election as 'the arrival of a peasant in the halls of the great', but Fitt kept his reservations to himself as she recited the oath, bowed to the Speaker and took her place beside him on the government benches.

Devlin made her maiden speech within an hour of taking her seat. The house was electrified by her oratory, for which she received a rapturous reception and fulsome praise from both sides of the Commons – much more than the convention dictated. After the debate, the central lobby outside was seething with people: all the television programmes were bidding for her to appear and Lord Longford was inviting her to dinner. In the mêlée, Paul Rose and Fitt were attempting to restore order and seeking to advise this inexperienced young woman what to do for the best, but they realised it was already a lost cause and did not intervene when her crowd of hangers-on managed to propel her away. Later, when he was in bed at the Irish Club, Devlin rang to invite Fitt to her birthday celebrations. He made an excuse and thereafter did not have any close contact with her.

Back in Belfast, Fitt had a foretaste of the sinister forces with whom his colleague, Paddy Kennedy, was now aligning himself. Invited to a tenants association meeting in Victoria Barracks to discuss forthcoming rent increases, Kennedy said 'the OC' wanted to speak with him. 'The OC?' Fitt asked. 'Who's he when he's at home?' 'The OC – officer commanding,' Kennedy replied. 'He wants to talk to you about the rents.'

Fitt told Kennedy, in what he called 'no uncertain terms', that he was not talking to any OC nor any member of the IRA for that matter. 'I wanted nothing to do with them. It was the first indication I had of the bad company he had begun to keep,' said Fitt. The rift helped draw him into closer contact with the other Catholic MPs and as a result in discussions at Stormont a more co-operative relationship began to develop between them.

Soon there was further turmoil. Two water-mains explosions cut off Belfast's water supply, leading to rationing and stand-pipes appearing in the streets. Five hundred more British troops were flown into the province and Major James Chichester-Clark, Minister of Agriculture, resigned, followed, finally, by O'Neill. At the time it was believed the IRA had caused the explosions, but it later transpired – as Fitt had quickly claimed in Stormont – that O'Neill's downfall had been engineered by members of the outlawed UVF, who had bombed the utilities to force O'Neill out. His resignation triggered off another power struggle in the Unionist party, but Chichester-Clark pipped the favourite, Brian Faulkner, by one vote and became Prime Minister on 1 May. He faced an impossible task, one akin to putting a lid on a dangerously rumbling volcano.

Fitt benefited directly from an early goodwill gesture made by Chichester-Clark in an attempt to improve the situation when, on 6 May, all charges and convictions arising from the civil rights disturbances were made the subject of an amnesty. Paisley and Bunting were immediately released from prison, and Fitt and several other MPs benefited from pending charges being dropped, along with the likelihood of custodial sentences for their participation in various marches. Imprisonment though proved to be the final ruin of Fitt's old acquaintance, Bunting. After being convicted of unlawful assembly on 29 January 1969 for his part in the November 1968 Armagh demonstration, Bunting stood alongside Paisley at an appeal hearing there on 25 March and spurned an offer from the judge, Rory Conaghan, to waive their three-month prison sentences if both entered into substantial recognizances to be of good behaviour for two years. As a result, Conaghan – a Catholic who would be assassinated by the IRA in September 1974 – affirmed their prison terms, but increased the recognizances from £100 to £250 and ordered that, in default, they serve an additional three months. Two days later, at Bangor Magistrates Court, Bunting was convicted on three counts of assaulting and obstructing the police and given a one-month concurrent sentence for each offence, to be served at the end of the sentence imposed in Armagh. This penalty was upheld on appeal on 26 March.

Three days later, Bunting's wife, Marie, wrote from the family home at Dundonald in East Belfast to Sir Martin Gilliat, the secretary to the Queen Mother, stating that 'Ronnie's imprisonment has caused much anguish, spiritual and material, in his home' and requesting him to 'ask either the Queen Mother or the Queen to intervene decisively to end the anomalous and wicked treatment of a man whose only crime was sincerity and painstaking dedication to the cause he believes is just'. Gilliat, who was approached because he had once served alongside Major Bunting at the Tidworth Army base, was told:

> Ronnie faces two charges. The first involves 'illegal assembly' in Armagh.

Many Ulster loyalists went to Armagh in order to prevent the looting and destruction taking place there, which had characterized the ostensibly 'Civil Rights' but in reality IRA-infiltrated republican marches in Derry and elsewhere. The aim was secured and no damage occurred in Armagh for which Ronnie's reward is six months imprisonment. The second charge is 'resisting arrest'. The police arrived at our house at the unearthly hour of 6.00am and loudly clamoured for access. Ronnie, who had been under a considerable strain due to two death threats from the IRA, thought in fact that these people were not the police and the threats were about to be implemented. Within this context is it surprising that arrest was resisted? Ronnie, a man with a serious heart complaint, had an extra month added for what at worst could be termed an understandable mistake.

Replying from Clarence House on 1 April, Gilliat rejoined that the 'matter in question is completely outside the province of Queen Elizabeth, the Queen Mother, who is not in a position to intervene in any way'.

By this point, and with a scheduled release date of 25 September 1969, Bunting and his family were completely disillusioned by their plight. According to Ministry of Home Affairs records, explicit promises of financial support from Paisley's Protestant Unionist party failed to materialise and furthermore the party withdrew its support for Bunting as a candidate at the forthcoming by-election in Mid-Ulster. Marie Bunting was therefore forced to pay the mortgage on the family home and provide for their three children from their fast-dwindling savings. By mid-April those savings were exhausted and Marie Bunting applied to the Ministry of Social Security for assistance. At the same time her husband, now overcome with remorse, submitted a hand-written petition, on the prescribed Form 16, to Lord Grey, the Governor of Northern Ireland:

> Having served one calendar month and one week of aforementioned imprisonment of seven calendar months, I, Councillor (Major) Ronald Bunting (Rtd), C Eng, MIMechE, Her Majesty's devoted and loyal subject, most humbly and abjectly beg for the Queen's pardon in respect of the remaining period. I, who believed that the Union Jack should be ceremonially flown in Armagh City on 30 November 1968 and the emblems of Irish republicanism denied display, now fully recognise my grave error and have been made aware that both actions would be anathema to the vast majority of Her Majesty's Roman Catholic subjects here in Ulster …

Bunting went on to outline his 'previously unblemished record', including service in the Second World War, the Suez campaign and the Malaysian Emergency, in the course of which he was wounded and suffered permanent loss of health. His release, he continued, would enable him to obtain medical treatment at the King Edward VII hospital for officers in London and would afford him the opportunity to act as breadwinner for his family, who were currently dependent on public assistance. Alongside the petition, the prison doctor stated his health was 'fair', but noted he was 'under observation for his heart'. A supplementary police report said they would raise no objection to some remission of the prison sentence as, prior to his imprisonment, Bunting had been a man of 'very good character'. (An earlier police report, on 8 January 1969, had described how he recited scripture to the crowds from a Bible he always carried and expressed frustration at his 'cunning approach' to staying within the law and said that whether or not he was 'naïve or a knave' he was 'anyway in part an enigma'.)

As a gesture of his reformed attitude, Bunting also entered into the required recognizance to be of good behaviour, thus bringing his scheduled release date forward from September to 18 June. In the event, the amnesty meant he got out well before that. His political antics cost him a very good teaching job and in 1980 he suffered even greater anguish when his eldest son, Ronnie, who had become a notorious member of the outlawed Irish National Liberation Army (INLA), was shot dead, apparently by loyalist terrorists. His lasting political distinction is only that he was the first of many Paisley lieutenants to be trampled underfoot, one of the reasons Fitt always had a soft spot for him, despite his mercurial behaviour.

Soon after the amnesty was declared, over a drink in the bar in Stormont, Fitt was discussing the charges he had faced with one of the law officers in the former O'Neill Cabinet and was shocked to learn just how far the Unionists had been prepared to go to discredit him. Speculating that the charge on Derry would not stick, he was answered with a nodding head: 'No. The evidence that would have come out in court would have badly damaged you. When you were arrested you were taken to the police station and there were police statements that while you were there you cursed the Pope and condemned the Catholic Church with very bad language,' his acquaintance said knowingly.

'That's untrue, totally and absolutely untrue,' Fitt protested.

'Well, that's the evidence that was going to be given,' his acquaintance repeated.

On the afternoon of 4 June, in the midst of a marathon sixty-five-hour consideration of the Public Order (Amendment) Bill, Fitt collapsed at Stormont and was treated by Dr Robert Simpson, the MP for mid-Antrim, until an ambulance arrived. He was taken to the Royal Victoria Hospital where, after a night in the intensive care unit and a few more days of observation and tests, he was discharged. The doctors concluded he was suffering from extreme exhaustion and ordered him to rest. For once, he heeded them and took the family off to Cushendun, where he had rented a house for the rest of the summer, but events cut short his convalescence and after only a fortnight or so, he was once more back in an increasingly turbulent Belfast.

All that spring and early summer there was rising tension and worsening trouble at the traditional sectarian flashpoints. That July was the worst Fitt could ever recall, with trouble all over Northern Ireland. 'B' Specials fired shots over the heads of crowds, there were mounting allegations of police misconduct and brutality and, the first evictions took place from mixed housing areas while inevitable marches and counter-marches took place over the seemingly interminable Twelfth of July period. It was with growing apprehension, therefore, that he awaited the Apprentice Boys' march in Derry on 12 August. Meanwhile, the relationship between the minority MPs had been developing steadily and they had reached an informal arrangement for individuals to shadow the various ministries. As a group, they also enjoyed regular contact with Chichester-Clark and used these meetings to plead with him to find a way around what was universally regarded as an inevitable disaster should the Derry march be allowed to go ahead.

By now the Unionist hardliners were also putting pressure on Chichester-Clark, every bit as vigorously as they had done with O'Neill, and he would not have survived any interference with a march of such symbolic importance. The unionists insisted the march was traditional, just a carnival day for the city and traders. With his usual wry wit, Fitt observed privately that the traders who would benefit most would be the suppliers of hardboard and glaziers. Whilst sympathetic to Chichester-Clark's problem, the nationalist MPs left him in no doubt that the mood of the Derry Catholics was that of a 'risen people, up off their knees', who were unlikely to tolerate the racist atmosphere of the march. The same worries were transmitted to Home Secretary James Callaghan in London on 29 July, when he received a deputation of MPs, including Fitt. One particular concern raised was what might happen in Belfast should the already overstretched RUC be forced to commit all their resources to maintaining order in Derry.

The following weekend there was ample justification for Fitt's compounding fears when major clashes erupted at Unity Flats, a Catholic enclave at the city end of the Protestant Shankill Road in Belfast. On the morning of Saturday, 2 August, Fitt was at home holding a constituency surgery when a woman telephoned him to say trouble had broken out after an incident at the flats complex. In those days, the police radio transmissions could be picked up with an ordinary transistor radio and, although they used colours and other ciphers to describe their activities, the details could easily be decoded by assiduous listeners. Because of the situation, Fitt turned on his own radio and tuned to the police wavelength, and let it play in the background as he continued to deal with his callers.

Later in the afternoon Billy Napier called to see Fitt. From the radio they heard the RUC calling for reinforcements, and Fitt asked Napier to go assess what was happening while he dealt with the remaining queue of constituents. Napier called him at 5.30pm and said he had just witnessed a violent baton charge against the residents of the flats, who were entirely blameless. An hour later, Napier returned to Fitt's house and told him that an injured man had been taken to hospital and the residents were furious about what they regarded as the biased attitude of the police. Fitt decided to ring the Home Office in London to ask that pressure be brought to bear on the Northern Ireland authorities to withdraw the police from the area. Almost immediately, however, they heard a transmission from the police on the ground advising their commander that they were about to mount a 'short sharp baton-charge' to clear the area. Fitt lifted the phone again and this time called the police headquarters in the city to protest. As he continued to make calls about the situation, Napier returned there and by late evening reported to Fitt that, although there were people milling around, the situation was quiet. Fitt visited the area himself about 10.00pm and tried to reassure the people that the rest of the city was calm.

The next morning, after attending Mass at St Patrick's, Fitt returned to the flats where he found the people in 'a state of hysteria', as he described it to the Scarman Tribunal, because of rumours that Paisleyites and the UVF were planning a major attack to take the flats apart 'brick by brick'. Fitt arranged for a taxi to pick him up and, with Paddy Devlin and Paddy Wilson, he travelled across to police headquarters at Castlereagh where he demanded to see the Belfast City Commissioner. The officer was not available, he was told, but Fitt demanded a meeting because of the urgency of the situation. He was invited to wait, and the commissioner turned up thirty minutes later. Over the next hour, Fitt learned that the police were under such pressure that reinforcements were being brought in from rural areas to go to several flashpoints where there was tension between rival crowds. He offered to go to Ardoyne to see what he could do to prevent the situation there worsening, and set off by taxi, returning home in late afternoon after another visit to Unity Flats.

Overnight the level of threatening calls to the Fitt house rose steadily, and during Sunday it reached intolerable levels. By now, Fitt was seriously concerned about the safety of Ann and the children. 'By a stroke of good fortune, the next morning I noticed an advertisement for a cottage at Waterfoot, in the Glens of Antrim, rented it and, with great relief, packed them off out of the city with a friendly taxi-driver.' The confrontations were occurring every night now and although they were overwhelmingly manifestations of political and sectarian hatred there was often a flash of humour at the height of all the tension. Fitt recalled one night when three local Protestant leaders in Crumlin Road would not accept the peacemaking overtures of the Rev Robert Bradford, later murdered by the IRA when he was MP for South Belfast. The most obstinate of the three was a man with a very pronounced stammer. After a time the other two adopted the more reasonable line being urged on them, and agreed to help cool the situation, but their colleague persisted. 'Let me tell you this, let me tell you this,' he stammered repeatedly. His oratory was ended prematurely when the other two grabbed him mid-stammer and said, 'For fuck's sake come on home, Sammy.

There'll be a united Ireland by the time you tell them anything.'

Disturbances continued sporadically and sectarian tension continued to surge in the final rundown to the day of the Derry march. On 12 August, as the disputed, noisy parade with its colourful banners and shrill flute bands meandered its way through the city, the expected trouble erupted. Within a few hours the police were laying siege to the Bogside area and being kept at bay by an endless hail of petrol bombs, stones and broken paving stones. Next day the riots spread right across the province and into Belfast. Out and about in the city, Fitt witnessed some of the trouble at first-hand. There was looting on a considerable scale for the first time – the pubs being a particularly popular target – and widespread arson:

> I saw people staggering along the rubble strewn streets with cases of whiskey and a woman sitting in the broken windows of a shoe shop trying on pair after pair to get her size. Some people even stripped the tailors' dummies. The vast amount of looted alcohol flowing around freely further inflamed passions on both sides.

Protestants were whipped up to full fury on the evening of 13 August when Jack Lynch, the Irish Prime Minister, made what became known erroneously as his 'we won't stand idly by' speech. Announcing that Irish soldiers were setting up field hospitals on the southern side of the border, what Lynch actually said was:

> It is evident that the Stormont Government is no longer in control of the situation. Indeed, the present situation is the inevitable outcome of the policies pursued for decades by successive Stormont Governments. It is clear, also, that the Irish Government can no longer stand by and see innocent people injured and perhaps worse.

As the rioting continued in Derry and elsewhere, the Stormont parliament met in an atmosphere of crisis. After a vote to adjourn until 14 October, Chichester-Clark, the Prime Minister proposed:

> That this House deplores the acts of violence and hooliganism which have occurred since its last meeting, assures the government of its full support for all necessary measures to bring the situation under control, expresses its intense admiration for the courage and discipline of the police forces in the face of dastardly attacks launched upon them, and calls upon all responsible persons in the community to exercise their influence for the earliest possible restoration of that public order upon which our hopes of future prosperity depend.
>
> … This debate will test to the full our ability to rise to the level of events. Are we in this house prepared to lead the community back to peace? That is the issue. Or are we simply going to re-echo for the benefit of a watching and critical world all the fears, hatreds and animosities which have been running riot in our streets? The people of Ulster, weary of strife, yearning for peace, fearful for their future, await our answer. For myself I will seek to be factual. I must apportion blame where I believe it to lie but

I will not seek to inflame feeling or to inflict any needless wounds. I would ask all honourable members who follow me to be moderate, tolerant and positive.

Fitt then addressed the house in a powerful, emotional thirteen-minute speech that was brimming with anger and frustration:

The Prime Minister concluded his remarks by saying that he would listen to positive suggestions put forward in this House. I believe that one of the reasons why we are finding ourselves in such a troubled situation at the moment is that the government have refused to do just that. For years and years I, with other members of the opposition, have attempted to use this House to put forward expressions of the hopes and ideals of the constituents in the areas which we represent. And as we stood at this dispatch box and put forward our point of view we were treated well-nigh 100 per cent. of the time with total arrogance and contempt by the Unionist government and those who support them.

That was the reason why we found ourselves last year leading people on to the streets in an attempt to bring about in Northern Ireland a situation where social justice and fundamental freedom would be made freely available to each and every individual. One looks back to what happened on 5 October last year, when people were demanding equal citizenship with other parts of the United Kingdom, when they were demanding a parliamentary comissioner, a free form of franchise, the fair drawing of local boundaries and other matters. I do not believe that these were outlandish demands to make upon the government. But on that occasion, in that march, we were – and I say it with all the emphasis at my command – brutally batoned into the ground by members of the RUC.

Fitt then referred to the Prime Minister's stated request to 'put forward positive suggestions' and complained that all requests for an inquiry into what had happened during various incidents over the preceding months had 'been met by a stony silence from the government. Therefore, how can the government expect those who are opposed to unionism to have confidence in the RUC?'

In remarks that would have extreme long-term significance regarding the intractable difficulties surrounding policing, Fitt then outlined his own standpoint on the issue:

I am not standing at this dispatch box and condemning every individual member of the RUC. I know many of them and they are decent, respectable, honest men trying to do a very difficult job. But there are thugs within the ranks of the RUC, the thugs who attacked innocent people in the Bogside. If the Government had been acting responsibly they would have sought out those individuals who exceeded their duties and, in fact, committed criminal acts, and those people would have been removed from the force. That would have done an awful lot to re-establish confidence in the police force.

He then referred to his distaste for sitting by the television, watching the riotous scenes taking place when the RUC came under attack:

> Only last evening, just after the [late evening] news on Ulster Television, a policeman's wife rang me up – a girl who was absolutely heart-broken because she thought she recognised her husband on the screen when he was under attack by stones and petrol bombs. She told me she had a little kiddy of fifteen months and another kiddy of three months and that she was worried about her husband being in Derry on that occasion. I sympathised with her. I do not believe that she should have been put into that position. I believe the RUC has been used as a political force, not as a force which is intent on keeping law and order within this country. I believe that if the government want to instil or resurrect confidence in the RUC they must get rid, and get rid as quickly as they possibly can, of those members of the RUC who have been found guilty in the conscience of the people of this country of brutality against individual people. That is one of the positive suggestions which we have made over this number of years.

Fitt went on to recount a series of telephone calls he had received from responsible people, such as doctors, nurses, school teachers and professional people, about the recent indiscriminate use of thousands of tear-gas cartridges in Derry. In conclusion he said:

> The divisions which have existed for so long in this community over so many years have been deeply widened over the past 72 hours. I have tried to use this parliament for many years. We have been treated with contempt. Now that we have reached the situation in which gas bombs are hurtled indiscriminately at defenceless people in Derry, when old men and women and children, even babies in arms, are choking and gasping their lungs out because of the activities of the police, I intend to treat this parliament with the contempt it has showered upon members of the opposition for so many years. The [Unionist] party, the government and this parliament no longer have any relevance in the affairs of the Irish people. And I intend to make that clear in my actions from now.

Over the next two hours a series of MPs made acerbic speeches that were interrupted constantly by a string of disparaging heckles – many by Fitt. By far the most incendiary remark of the entire debate came from John Taylor, Unionist and junior minister at the Ministry of Home Affairs. Referring to the Lynch speech the previous evening, he said the movement of Irish soldiers to the border to establish first-aid posts was 'particularly provocative, but when one recalls that the military experience of the [Irish Army] is limited to action in the Congo against natives with bows and arrows, then Ulster need not be unduly alarmed'. For the strongly nationalist John Hume, who represented Derry, this was the last straw. When he was called to speak, at 4.41pm, he said:

> Probably more than any other member of this House I know what the last

few days have meant to people. I had hoped that perhaps crisis could bring out the best in some people in this House but I regret to say that the sterility of this House was never more in evidence than it is today. I do not wish to engage in any verbal battles with anyone to add to the bitterness that already exists, but after listening to Taylor's speech, which was a jack-boot speech in the present crisis, I can only say this in reply: we are quite firm; we shall not be moved. My colleagues and I, Mr Speaker, will say goodbye.

At this point, as the Official Report records, The Honourable Member for South Fermanagh (Mr Carron), the Honourable Member for Mid Londonderry (Mr Cooper), the Honourable Member for East Tyrone (Mr Currie), the Honourable Member for Dock (Mr Fitt), the Honourable Member for Foyle (Mr Hume), the Honourable Member for South Down (Mr Keogh) and the Honourable Member for Mourne (Mr O'Reilly) withdrew from the House.

As he did most evenings when in Belfast, Fitt went from Stormont directly to McGlade's bar in Donegall Street, where politicians and journalists gathered to drink and exchange gossip. After several gins there, he went around to Ulster Television to take part in the *This Week* current affairs programme. After that, around 11.30pm, he went home, where he found two of his daughters, Joan and Patsy, in a distressed state with furniture piled up against the downstairs windows, fearful of coming under attack from rocks, bottles and petrol bombs. They were alone in the Belfast house as Ann and the other three girls were still in the cottage at Waterfoot. The girls' fears had been exacerbated by a constant stream of ever more abusive and threatening calls from angry loyalists, which had been gathering pace all evening. Fitt listened to a few of them himself before taking the phone off the hook and going to bed about midnight, but he got little rest.

At 5.00am he was wakened by a loud banging on the front door. Joan, whose bedroom was closest, ran downstairs and opened the door to find three men and a woman on the doorstep. Insisting that they must see Fitt urgently, they pushed past her and went upstairs, where a groggy Fitt was still in the process of waking up. Waving a morning newspaper at him, they told him five people had died overnight in serious disturbances on the Falls Road, in the heart of his parliamentary constituency. A quick telephone call to the police confirmed the tragic news and the fact that there was now 'absolute pandemonium' in the area. By breakfast time, Fitt's phone was ringing so continuously with calls from worried constituents that he had trouble getting the line clear to ring the Home Office in London to make contact with Callaghan and make him aware of the seriousness of the situation, which was still escalating. Later in the morning, together with Paddy Wilson, he headed for the scene of the trouble to make a first-hand assessment of the situation:

> The devastation I saw struck me as forcefully as anything I had seen in
> Europe at the end of the war. As we walked amidst the rubble and the still

burning buildings, people were reporting the latest rumours to us. I discovered how the police in armoured vehicles had raked the heavily built-up area of the Lower Falls with heavy machine-gun fire and how Protestant arson mobs had burned whole terraces of Catholic-occupied houses while snipers fired at the refugees. People surrounded me, pulling at me with fear, demanding that something be done. There was an emotion and hysteria I had never experienced before that is almost impossible to describe in its intensity. The overriding feeling though was fear – of the RUC, 'B' Specials and Protestant mobs.

Accompanied by Paddy Devlin, everywhere they went they were mobbed by people asking for soldiers to protect them. 'The more we walked and talked to people in the troubled area, the more pressure there was for troops to be called in. The people literally feared being murdered in their beds that night,' he recalled. Aware that British troops had already been sent into Derry the previous evening, Fitt wanted Callaghan to send soldiers into his own constituency, where he hoped they would have a similarly calming effect. However, amidst all the turmoil, he could not get access to a phone to call the Home Office and articulate the widespread fears to Callaghan. In the end, somebody in the crowd produced the key to a bookmakers' shop in Panton Street where there was a telephone, and about 300 or so people piled in behind Fitt, or milled around the door on the street outside, as he spelled out and dialled the number: 01-WHI-8000. Within seconds he was through to Callaghan himself. He warned him of the great fears he had encountered, about more serious loss of life and said there was a crowd listening to the conversation. 'I am going to record all their names and addresses,' Fitt told him, 'and if nothing is done and there is more trouble, I will be able to read out the list in parliament at Westminster.' As he spoke, some of those present began passing out pads of betting dockets and people wrote their names and addresses on them. Fitt did not do this because he doubted Callaghan, rather the compiling of the list was a ploy to try and soothe the anxieties of the terrified people clustered around him.

In response, Callaghan was very sympathetic, but cautious. 'Gerry,' he told him, with far more wisdom than he could ever have imagined, 'it is the easiest thing in the world to put the troops in, but it will be the devil of a job to get them out again.' He said there had already been other representations for troops from responsible leaders, including churchmen, and acknowledged that, in spite of his political reservations about committing the British Army, the likelihood of further violence far exceeded the capabilities of the exhausted and overstretched RUC. Arrangements were in hand for troops to go in as soon as possible.

At a later point that afternoon, Fitt got a call from Ann in Waterfoot to tell him she had heard a report on Radio Éireann that a young boy had been shot dead in Bombay Street. He ordered a taxi to pick him up at his home and tried to reach the area by several circuitous routes. About the same time, soldiers with fixed bayonets formed up in the city centre and began taking up positions from street corner to street corner all along the Catholic Falls Road, while others deployed into the warren of terraced-housing sidestreets, setting up barbed wire and wooden chicanes where the Catholic area ended and the streets led into the Protestant Shankill area. There was still sporadic sniper fire, many premises were still burning and other buildings had collapsed into the road. In many places local people had thrown up their own, makeshift barricades, some using cars, vans and even hijacked buses. Overhead, at intervals of a few minutes, RAF *Hercules* and *Belfast* transport aircraft – the latter, ironically, built in the city – droned in on the final stage of their journey to Aldergrove Airport, bringing yet more troops. As Fitt toured round, many people recognised him and spoke frankly to him about their apprehensions. They were, he later told the Scarman Tribunal, resentful that the army was not going into the Protestant areas, from where they feared further attacks. In Fitt's opinion, observing the situation on the ground, the army had been deployed too quickly, without specific instructions and therefore did not know what to do.

Later in the evening, satisfied that soldiers were on the streets in steadily increasing numbers, Fitt set off in a taxi for Waterfoot to take Joan and Patsy out of harm's way. He intended to return to the city, but Ann prevailed upon him to wait until the morning. Overnight there was more serious trouble and Bombay Street was burned down from end to end by a mob who went from to door to door, lobbing petrol bombs into each house. Violence also continued in the Ardoyne area, and by the time Fitt returned home from Waterfoot a crowd of about thirty people had gathered outside to wait for him. Apart from their complaints, Fitt was inundated with telephone calls from people all over his constituency asking why the army had not intervened. Later Ann also returned from Waterfoot and that night they stayed in a neighbour's house in case their own was attacked. During the next day, the soldiers moved into Ardoyne and deployed extensively elsewhere throughout Fitt's constituency. As they took up positions they received a heartfelt welcome from the Catholics and were provided with an endless stream of tea and buns.

Fitt made another tour of the troubled areas that Sunday and was relieved to find that tension and trouble had virtually subsided, but now phenomenal rumours were swirling around as if they were fact. On the Catholic side, there were stories that twenty-five 'B' Specials had been shot dead, while on the Protestant side it was being said that 200 IRA men had been shot dead; both sides, it was claimed, were working overtime, secretly burying their dead. During the day, when he was in Broadcasting House, Belfast, taking part in several programmes, Fitt complained to Waldo Maguire, the organisation's local controller, about the uncritical tone of information being broadcast about an IRA uprising, without any of the claims being made by the government and the Unionist party being factually verified. Maguire said the material was coming from the government and offered to put out Fitt's own version of events if he provided it. When he got home in the afternoon, Fitt contacted John Hume and Austin Currie, who agreed to take part in a news conference with him the next day to put their own side of the story, but he was unable to find a suitable venue. Every hotel he contacted refused to let him hire a room for such an event.

Ann and he decided to sleep in their own house that night, but with the curtains drawn and the lights doused to conceal their presence. In the early hours of the morning, around 2.00am, a newspaper reporter telephoned to say he had heard the house was going to be bombed. Fitt jumped out of bed and looked out the window, where he saw a considerable number of armed police officers, both in uniform and plain clothes, had gathered. Some were concealed behind walls and hedges in the gardens of the houses on the opposite side of the road. Unable to sleep, Ann and he watched until they departed, some time after 4.00am. Later that morning, Fitt attended the funerals of three of the people who had lost their lives a few days earlier. Walking alongside a city councillor in one of the corteges, he explained his difficulties obtaining a venue for the news conference and was told that a school at Whiterock Road could be made available. Arrangements were made hastily, but nearing the scheduled time for conference, when Fitt could not obtain a taxi, so a neighbour agreed to take him to Whiterock Road. As they had to detour through some potentially hostile Protestant areas to reach their destination, Fitt decided to travel in the back of the van where he could not be seen.

By the end of that violent August, ten people had been killed, 154 wounded by gunshots and 745 hurt in the disturbances. Jim Callaghan came to Belfast to tackle the problems underlying the violence, notably the construction of a police force that would command acceptance from all sides of the community. Fitt remained in close attendance, escorting Callaghan around the constituency as he made his own assessment of the situation.

That autumn was a 'honeymoon' for the soldiers, in the words of army commander Lt-General Sir Ian Freeland, as the full extent of the human disaster became clear. Morning and afternoon, Fitt's house was full of people who were fleeing their homes in mixed areas and needed safer homes in the traditional ghetto areas.

> I had read about the sectarian pogroms of the twenties and thirties, but this was the first time I had experienced it with its awful human consequences. It spread through the city like an infectious disease from area to area, street to street, even in my immediate Dock constituency.

The intimidation was two-way as 'wrong ones' were put out of the areas to make way for 'right ones' displaced from elsewhere. Altogether some 40,000 people were involved – the largest movement of civilian refugees ever seen in Ireland and the worst such incident in Europe since the end of the Second World War.

Catholic opinion was dominated by fear of further loyalist attacks, which led to the construction of an extensive network of barricades ringing the Catholic areas and manned by self-appointed vigilantes. An organisation called the Central Citizens Defence Committee (CCDC), which attracted wide Catholic support, sprang up to assist the refugees, but unfortunately it also attracted sinister elements.

Fitt's unease about these hidden influences was confirmed when a man called James Kelly was brought to his house one night when there was trouble nearby. It turned out Kelly was an undercover captain from Irish Army intelligence, who later figured with the future Irish Prime Minister, Charles Haughey, in the 'arms smuggling affair' when it was alleged, in a Dublin court, that they had conspired with others to import £100,000 worth of arms for the IRA. All those accused were ultimately acquitted. Fitt was relieved he had kept his distance from these people of extreme republican disposition but deeply regretted that Paddy Kennedy did not and was openly associating with them. His conduct thus created a permanent rift in their relationship.

By now, the British government had taken a much more direct role in ensuring the speedy implementation of the long-delayed reform package. Some time earlier, a senior diplomat, Oliver Wright, had been posted to Belfast as the United Kingdom Representative. He took over a suite of rooms at the Conway Hotel, set in leafy grounds on the southern outskirts of Belfast, and established an office that was a 'listening post' for the British government, independent of the Stormont administration. Fitt constantly exploited his own access as a Westminster MP and Labour supporter to alert the government to the specific dangers of the situation, as he saw them, and to make representations for more effective responses to a range of problems arising from the extensive and ongoing civil disorder. During this period he had many follow-up meetings with Callaghan after his visit to Belfast and also with Denis Healey, the Minister for Defence. There was considerable sympathy in London for the Catholics' position and after one of these encounters a junior Labour minister remarked to Fitt how strange it was that, for the first time in Anglo-Irish history, the guns of the British soldiers were pointing the right way – protecting the Catholics.

In a telephone call to the Home Secretary on 4 September 1969, Fitt protested against the highly provocative content of 'loyalist' pirate radio broadcasts, which were making unpleasant threats against Ann and the families of other Catholic politicians, as well as playing Orange songs apparently requested by British soldiers. In yet another mysterious reference, which signified that there were at least some people apparently aware of Fitt's personal history, the song 'Nobody's

Child' was played repeatedly as a special dedication to him. Five days later, the operation of this illegal station, and a similarly provocative one on the Catholic side, was among the topics raised when Fitt met Wilson in the House of Commons after Prime Minister's questions. Fitt complained that the promised jamming of the extremist outpourings of pirate stations Radio Ulster and Radio Orange was ineffective and he told Wilson that among the hysterical hardline voices on air was that of Brian McRoberts, a solicitor from Armagh, who had recently been adopted as the candidate to contest Fitt's West Belfast parliamentary seat. Fitt informed Wilson in detail about threats of violence made against several of his closest political colleagues and also about the situation in mixed Alloa Street, which had twenty-two Protestant and eighteen Catholic families, where Protestants had taken over houses vacated by the fearful Catholic families and declared the entire street 'Protestant territory'. He further complained about the apparently biased treatment of the disturbances by Ulster Television, thanks to the influence of the Henderson family (who also owned the pro-unionist *Belfast News Letter*) and the role of Captain Bill Henderson as a publicity officer for the Ulster Unionist party.

Wilson undertook to get back to Fitt about these concerns, and in the meantime encouraged him to raise such matters directly with British officials in Northern Ireland, or with the army, and not to say or do anything that would inflame the situation further. When the note of this meeting reached Oliver Wright, he replied to the Home Office in London that 'Mr Fitt's allegations are probably all too true and I fear in present circumstances there is little or nothing we can do about them'. He went on to comment that 'since Mr Fitt is fairly extreme in his views, it is not surprising that the Unionists should have put up a candidate of extremist views on the other side of the fence'.

Nonetheless, Fitt's concerns were being carefully followed up at the highest level in London. At 5.00pm on 10 September, the day after he had met Wilson, Fitt had another meeting with Callaghan, who explained to him that as the pirate radios 'were running up and down the frequencies, jamming could never be 100 per cent effective'. Fitt reported that a total of seventy-two Catholic families had now left their homes and he asked for a soldier to be posted at each end of affected streets, such as Alloa Street. Callaghan, who had been briefed in advance by the Ministry of Defence, said the army believed this would be completely inadequate and that 'there was often no practicable alternative to moving families who felt in danger'. It was precisely because of the growing number of such incidents that the army had come up with the idea of a 'peaceline' to separate and provide reassurance to Catholics and Protestants living in the most troubled flashpoint areas of Belfast. For Fitt, the main purpose of this meeting was to clear lines with Callaghan about a meeting he was to have next day with a delegation from Belfast who wanted to talk about dismantling the many barricades in place in the

Catholic areas, about their distrust of the Northern Ireland government and the adequacy or otherwise of the army's proposals to protect the barricaded areas from further sectarian violence. The previous day, at the same time as Fitt was meeting Wilson, Paddy Devlin, the Falls MP at Stormont who was actively involved with the CCDC, was in touch with Downing Street to try to arrange a similar meeting for himself. He was directed to the Home Office, where Callaghan finally agreed to see him. However, the intended inclusion of Jim Sullivan, a veteran Belfast IRA leader, in Devlin's delegation prompted significant apprehension in London, which was reflected during the Fitt – Callaghan meeting. Fitt shared Callaghan's misgivings in fact and said that, in his view, 'the IRA and the People's Democracy had been allowed their heads too much behind the barricades'. His idea was to bypass them by calling together 'the parliamentary representatives on the Catholic side with a view to making an appeal for common sense', but he was aware there were people behind the barricades with genuine fears that had to be addressed.

Callaghan encouraged Fitt to take such a stand and, pledging his support, recommended he do so in conjunction with Cardinal Conway, the senior Catholic churchman in Ireland, who had been co-operating closely with Oliver Wright in an effort to prepare the way for the removal of the barricades. In order to kick-start the initiative, Callaghan said he would therefore meet the Belfast delegation next day, provided it was led by Fitt and did not include any person with IRA connections. At that point, with Fitt still present in his office, Callaghan made a series of telephone calls. He first told Chichester-Clark what was going on, then called Father Pádraig Murphy, one of the more responsible people associated with the CCDC, to confirm the meeting for 2.45pm next day. During this conversation it was agreed that the delegation, led by Fitt, would include Devlin, Tom Conaty, a prosperous Catholic who ran a fruit-trading business, and James McSparran, a prominent Catholic Queen's Counsel. It was specifically stated there would be no one with IRA connections present. Before Fitt departed, Callaghan finally rang Sir Ian Freeland, the GOC, to appraise him of the plans.

Although Callaghan wanted to keep the meeting secret, news of it leaked quickly in Belfast – not least because several members of the delegation were already on their way to London. Later that evening, when Fitt learned they had arrived and Sullivan was among them, he rang Callaghan's office. 'His arrival is going to create very great difficulties,' Fitt warned the Home Secretary.

Next day, Fitt arranged to meet the delegation at lunchtime in the Red Lion public house in Whitehall, opposite what was then the Home Office building. He quietly told those attending the meeting to go on ahead of him and check in at the Home Office and, when the time came for him to cross the road and join them, he simply slipped out of the pub, leaving the unwelcome Sullivan and Paddy Kennedy drinking at the bar. Honour was saved all round when the discussion with Callaghan was adjourned for three-quarters of an hour and the delegation returned to the pub, whereupon the two absent emissaries were consulted about Callagahan's plan for the removal of the barricades and the despatch of additional troops to Belfast as peacekeepers.

Fitt's growing misgivings about the intervention of sinister individuals were proving to be justified. At the time, although unknown to all but those involved, highly ominous developments were taking place within the closed circles of the IRA in Belfast. Men who believed that violence and force were the only means by which to unite Ireland were involved in a bitter power struggle with those of a more pragmatic and political dispensation. Their differences became public before the end of the year when the breakaway faction of 'physical force' men formed the Provisional IRA (PIRA). It was an event unnoticed by all but the most knowledgeable observers, yet it was to have the most far-reaching consequences for the entire island of Ireland than any development since the 1916 Easter Rising fifty-three years earlier.

On the ground, meanwhile, the more immediate political problem that autumn was assuaging the fears of the Catholic community. It was not an easy task. Those who had experienced the violence were thoroughly frightened and those who had flocked into the Catholic areas after being intimidated from their homes in the mixed, but predominantly Protestant, suburbs were equally uneasy. As their elected representative, it fell to Fitt to make their case and he spent hours in discussions in Belfast and in London with ministers, priests and the army, trying to push things forward. Near Divis Flats one morning Fitt was present with Dr William Philbin, Catholic bishop of Down and Connor, to supervise the first tentative steps at barricade removal. However, the people were so angry and alienated from authority by then that they spat on the bishop – an action that had a lasting effect on him. Fitt believed it was because of this that Dr Philbin largely avoided becoming publicly involved in events between then and his retirement in 1983.

Before the year closed, two landmark reports were published: Lord Cameron's inquiry into the causes of the disorder, commissioned by O'Neill; and Lord Hunt's inquiry into the future of policing. Prompted by the barrister Tony Campbell, Fitt gave evidence to the Cameron Commission on 25 July 1969 and regaled them – in his own inimitable and anecdotal way – with stories about his time as a merchant seaman, how he got into politics, the structured unfairness he found there, the frustration it caused him and his views on the current situation. Questioned about his political beliefs, Fitt reiterated his allegiance to the principles and philosophies enunciated by James Conolly and added, 'I believe and hope I will live to see the day Ireland is united into a socialist republic, but I don't believe that unity can be brought about by violence.' He went on to say that he regarded the Stormont government as an 'Orange' government and that in the Republic as a 'Green Tory' government, but he emphasised that Ireland and

Britain must live in concord – preferably within the European Common Market – and expressed his greatest respect for the English people, particularly the working class.

Cameron was clearly unimpressed by Fitt. Referring to the Dungannon civil rights march on 24 August 1968, the Scottish judge noted that 'there was some regrettable and irresponsible abuse of the police by Mr Fitt'. In respect of this event, he concluded, 'The speeches at the meeting related exclusively to immediate social issues, and apart from the address by Mr Fitt, were generally moderate in tone.' He also singled out Fitt for criticism in relation to the 5 October march in Derry, noting that,

> The publicity-seeking activities of Mr G. Fitt MP had already ensured the presence on this march of several prominent politicians ... including Northern Ireland nationalist MPs and three Westminster Labour MPs in addition to Mr Fitt himself, as well as of mass television and press coverage.

Stopping just short of accusing Fitt of orchestrating the violence, he continued, 'Mr Fitt sought publicity for himself and his political views, and must clearly have envisaged the possibility of a violent clash with the police as providing the publicity he so ardently sought. His conduct in our judgement was reckless and wholly irresponsible in a person occupying his public positions.' Cameron, however, expressed the view, and regretted the undoubted fact, that

> both Mr Fitt and Mr [Eddie] McAteer [leader of the Nationalist party] were batoned by the police, at a time when no order to draw batons had been given and in circumstances in which the use of batons on these gentlemen was wholly without justification or excuse. Mr Fitt was at this point removed to hospital with a minor head injury which he ascribed to a blow from a baton, and Mr McAteer also sustained a minor injury.

Callaghan thought these conclusions were unfair and tipped Fitt off before publication that he was to be criticised. Fitt was unmoved by the criticism, however, and believed the other findings justified his actions as the report 'roundly condemned the denial of social justice to Catholics that had been the focus of my political endeavours'. Indeed, Fitt always took the view that Cameron was a 'tame' establishment figure who did not require much prompting to broadly support the unionist line, and who all too gullibly swallowed much of their unfounded paranoia about left-wing-inspired, IRA revolutionary intentions. When they were making arrangements for his investigation, the Stormont administration took great care to ensure that the Scottish judge was protected from unfavourable influences. While in Belfast, accommodation was provided for him at the Ulster Club in Castle Place, whose sacrosanct precincts remained unbreached by even the most moderate Catholics and where opinions expressed in support of O'Neill and his policies would have been grudging, at best.

The second report, this one by Lord Hunt, the veteran conqueror of Everest, which tackled the policing problem and suggested the winding up of the historically controversial 'B' Specials, provoked a night of rioting in the Shankill Road during which Constable Victor Arbuckle became the first police casualty of the Troubles. He was shot dead, ironically, by so-called loyalists. It was a strong indication of the depth of feeling on both sides. Throughout that autumn the acrimony on the streets was mirrored in the Stormont parliament, where proceedings were dominated by word-by-word, line-by-line battles on Bills to reform the police, disband the Specials and generally bring law and order policy in line with accountable British standards after fifty years of neglect and unionist-led repression. At Christmas 1969 there was a telling indication of the depth of hatred that had been aroused.

An eleven-year-old schoolboy wrote an essay, which was read into the Stormont Hansard, suggesting Christmas presents for politicians: William Craig should receive £50; Austin Currie, a hamper with a lighted stick of dynamite; and Gerry Fitt a H-bomb.

CHAPTER EIGHT

A VARIED AND DIVERSE BUNCH

THE NEW DECADE AND THE NEW YEAR, 1970, dawned with hope still alive that rapid progress on reform might restore some normality to Northern Ireland. Callaghan had maintained a hands-on approach and the Stormont government was under relentless pressure from Whitehall to end the festering social and political abuses that were the root cause of the trouble.

One of the most pressing problems facing the Northern Ireland government was the issue of policing and the structure of the RUC. The events of 1969 had cruelly exposed its organisational and leadership weaknesses and underlined the scale of the historic gulf between the RUC and the minority community. At the beginning of 1970, Catholics were still deeply wary of the police, despite efforts to reintroduce officers into Catholic areas in the company of red-capped British military police 'minders'. Callaghan had handpicked Sir Arthur Young, schooled in the finest traditions of the classic British 'bobby', to provide vigorous leadership and revitalise the RUC, but he was facing insurmountable obstacles in his attempts to forge the kind of relationship a police force should ideally have with its community. When Sir Arthur announced that sixteen RUC officers accused of serious misconduct in earlier incidents would also benefit from the amnesty that had cleared marchers and others, there was a nationalist outcry. Fitt had reservations about the decision, but John Hume, articulating the special antagonism Derry felt for the police, called the decision 'scandalous'. The controversy was a warning that the road to reform and normality was not going to be an easy one to traverse.

During those first eventful months of 1970 the terrorist bombings began and the citizens heard for the first time the distinctive thud of the explosions that would become as familiar a feature of daily life as the theme tune for *Coronation Street*. The rattle of gunfire became equally commonplace, along with the wail of the sirens on police and army vehicles and ambulances as they fought their way through the traffic after each incident. Politicians became prime targets, and on 7 March Austin Currie's home was badly damaged in a blast, later admitted by the UVF. Two weeks prior to that another bomb had more worrying implications. It exploded inside the Crumlin Road courthouse, on 18 February, at the climax of the trial of five militant loyalists accused of causing the utility explosions in 1969. After further intimidation and threats from the UVF, which the authorities took very seriously, for the first time Fitt's home was put under continuous police and army surveillance.

A debate on the army estimates in the Commons on 12 March allowed him to vent his worries about the deteriorating situation. 'When explosions are allowed to take place within the precincts of a court, how can we ever expect to bring law and order back into the streets of Northern Ireland?' he asked. He was increasingly being overtaken by the realisation that politics had moved from the parliaments in London and Belfast onto the streets and that the two communities were locked on a crash course that army intervention had merely postponed. The city was seething with a sense of imminent collision. One of the things Fitt struggled to overcome at this time was the fact that detailed understanding of the intricacies of Northern Ireland's affairs was not then the norm at Westminster, especially, he found out, among the shorthand writers who compiled Hansard. For example, when the official report of the proceedings reached Fitt on 13 March, he was greatly amused to find that his reference to a speech by the Taoiseach in Tralee had been recorded as a speech made 'in the tea-shop in Tralee'. On this occasion, Fitt decided not to exercise his right to correct the record and let the slip stand.

On Easter Tuesday morning, an Orange parade set off along a sensitive boundary road between Catholic and Protestant enclaves. When the marching bands returned in the early evening they were ambushed and there ensued several hours of rioting at Ballymurphy. The regiment in the area at the time, the Royal Scots, went in aggressively to stop the trouble, employing batons and gas on the rioters. Their tough tactics provoked a Catholic outcry and effectively marked the end of the honeymoon period for the British Army. From then on the troops were no longer protectors and saviours in Catholic eyes, but part of the problem.

But the 'truth' of what had transpired at Ballymurphy depended on where you were. There were conflicting allegations about how the trouble started and the 'truth' depended on the standpoint of the participants. A priest said the bands over-played and the Catholics over-reacted. Some people said that tension over a Leeds – Celtic football match had played its part. The kids, it was reported, had been taunting the Scottish soldiers that Leeds were better than Celtic and the soldiers had used the riots as an excuse to get their own back. For their part, the unionists weighed in with alarmist stories about IRA involvement. The subsequent death of a two-year-old boy, rushed to hospital with persistent vomiting, was attributed to the effects of CS gas by the instant rumour factories.

Appearing on BBC radio's *The World at One* with William Hardcastle the next day, Fitt said he thought the hard republican element – the emerging PIRA – were still a minority, and he condemned hardline statements from Lt-Gen Freeland about his men having superior firepower. His warning that people would be shot in riotous situations was seen as a threat and when the rioting was discussed in parliament later that day, Fitt repeated his warning that the seeds of further confrontation would be sown if the army over-reacted to the current situation.

The situation at Ballymurphy was tailor-made for exploitation and one man who did not shy away from that potential was Ian Paisley. At that time he was in the midst of a by-election battle for the Bannside seat in Stormont, which had been left vacant by Terence O'Neill who had abandoned politics. Paisley made allegations that Protestants in Ballymurphy were being intimidated and started an exodus of families to a new estate at Glencairn. The Unionists threw everything they could into the fight to deny Paisley the seat, but failed to prevent his election to Stormont with a substantial majority. On the morning of Wednesday, 15 April, Fitt was flicking through the pages of the *Irish News* when he noticed an account of the inaugural meeting of the Fergal O'Hanlon Republican Club. The following Saturday, when an emissary from this new political force arrived at his door to invite him to attend a protest rally, he declined. The event went ahead and afterwards, when they marched along Duncairn Gardens waving Irish tricolours, groups of young Protestants took exception to the flags and slogans. Within five minutes, they had produced union flags and waved them in a counter-flurry on the Protestant side of the road. Within a further five minutes, the entire street was a battlefield and the air was thick with what the army had come to call 'Belfast confetti' – bricks, paving stones, basically anything the rioters could get their hands on.

At this early stage of the Troubles the rioters' techniques were well ahead of the military response. One group would aim missiles at the soldiers' heads and when they raised their shields to protect themselves, another group would throw lumps of bricks and stones at their exposed legs and ankles. This tactic was so successful the soldiers were falling like tenpins in a bowling alley. Before long the running battle in Duncairn Gardens had spread along the Antrim Road to the street outside the Fitt house, and from the front window the family could see rioters, most of whom they knew, confronting soldiers. Soon large numbers of reinforcements arrived at the scene and they went into action, firing CS gas and wielding batons. The gas drifted into the Fitt house and started stinging their eyes and throats. Ann, who was asthmatic, frantically searched through her kitchen cupboard for vinegar, a recognised antidote to CS gas, but all she could come up with was a jar of beetroot in vinegar. They poured out the liquid and soaked their handkerchiefs in that. Fitt recalled how, for the rest of the day, they all looked like Red Indians with warpaint thanks to the blood-red beetroot stains marking their faces.

The trouble continued through the evening and well into the night. About 5.00am the next morning, when there was still sporadic fighting, a soldier knocked on the door of the Fitt home. He was in fact a lieutenant-colonel, and he asked Fitt to open the back door to admit his brigadier. While Ann bustled around making tea for them, the two officers said they wanted to enlist his help to stop the trouble. The brigadier said, 'Mr Fitt, I want you to do something for me. There are a lot of my soldiers being injured and we cannot put up with it any longer. You and I and the colonel will go down the road and talk to Mr O'Hanlon and ask him to take his boys off the streets. I am sure he will be a reasonable man.' Fitt was rather taken aback by their naivety, so he decided to give them a potted history lesson.

> I told them of the IRA raid on Brookeborough police barracks in 1957 when Sean South and Fergal O'Hanlon were killed in a gun battle. Then I explained that the Official IRA called their clubs after socialist heroes, such as Mellowes and Connolly, while the new Provos preferred to look to the hardliners and activists like O'Hanlon for inspiration.

By the time they slipped out into the dawn, Fitt believed they were completely at a loss as to how to contain the rioting, and even more confused about why they were in Belfast in the first place. The trouble was still rumbling on hours later when Fitt and Ann decided to brave the flying missiles in order to attend Mass. On their way home afterwards, they saw a young man from the neighbourhood – later a very prosperous solicitor – directing crowds of youngsters to throw bricks at the military. 'Isn't this terrible?' said Ann. 'All the soldiers hurt and the kids beaten up.'

'It happens in Irish history,' replied the young agitator, who carefully stayed at the rear of the mobs. 'Somebody's blood will have to be spilled before all this is settled.' Fitt said he was sick to the pit of his stomach.

A few weeks later Harold Wilson called a general election and Fitt was faced with the prospect of defending his seat in the London parliament. If it had not been for the Troubles, he was sure his re-election would have been a foregone conclusion. From early morning until late at night every Saturday, the day when Fitt's constituency work was busiest, an average of forty people from all over Northern Ireland would turn up looking for his help. He estimated that four out of every ten of them were Protestants and always maintained that each time he helped somebody to get a house or sorted out a social security or employment problem for them, he not only secured their vote but also that of other members of their family circles. Given that many Protestants had come to regard him as the man who started the Troubles, he knew that he faced a tough fight to retain this support. In order to maximise it, his election address concentrated on spelling out his record at tackling common problems such as malpractice by landlords and illegal money-lending.

On Monday, 8 June 1970 Fitt took his nomination papers to the Crumlin Road courthouse. They were required to be signed by a proposer, seconder and eight assenters – in theory the most important people in the constituency. 'I asked myself who I would get to sign, who were my most important constituents? Then I got the answer. For the first time my own mother, Mary Ann, then aged seventy, was one of my constituents and eligible. So I asked her to propose me, which she did.' (Mrs Fitt and her eldest daughter, Betty, also a widow, had recently moved from their flat above a public house in York Street into 87 Antrim Road, the house next door to the Fitt residence, which Gerry had bought for them.) It was an indication of his longstanding devotion to her that he described Mary Ann Fitt as his own mother. Fitt's principal opponent was the Armagh solicitor Brian McRoberts, who had been the UVF Captain Craig, the man who had made bloodcurdling anti-Catholic threats over the loyalist pirate radio the previous summer.

Fitt's election agent was Senator Paddy Wilson, who had become Fitt's closest political ally and assistant, but the problems they had to overcome to secure votes were daunting, to say the least. In a bid to reassure both sides after the terrible events of August 1969, the army had since built a Berlin-style 'peaceline' along the entire interface between the Falls and the Shankill. This meant many thousands of voters faced the ordeal of crossing through the military checkpoints along its route to reach polling stations, which were located in what was now regarded as openly hostile territory. Given his high dependence on securing Protestant votes to hold the seat, Fitt was very worried that this factor could lead to his defeat.

Thanks to the vigilance with which his daughters monitored death notices in the newspapers and marked up the electoral register, Fitt quickly spotted that ten postal votes had been claimed by the Unionists in the names of people who were deceased. By now an adept self-publicist, he ensured the matter earned him good coverage in the local newspapers. Soon afterwards, a postman delivering his election leaflets on the Shankill Road was roughed up and the Post Office had to request police protection to complete their statutory duty of delivering the election communications. Again, this was fully exploited for its publicity value. Shortly before polling day, a battalion of Royal Marines was flown in to boost security, but the campaign passed off surprisingly peacefully. When the votes cast in West Belfast were counted, Fitt had handsomely beaten McRoberts, raising his vote to 30,649 and his majority to 3,198. (This was, incidentally, the last election he fought while designated Republican Labour.) Away from Belfast, Bernadette Devlin had been returned again and there was a minority gain in Fermanagh-South Tyrone, where Frank McManus, a solicitor with republican leanings, had been elected but neither Devlin nor McManus were great soul-mates for Fitt. What caused most interest on the national stage, however, was the election of the Rev Ian Paisley as MP for North Antrim, a victory that raised incredible curiousity at Westminster as to how this notorious product of street disorders would adapt his oratory and confrontational skills to the mother of parliaments.

In a story that lost nothing in its retelling around the bars at Westminster, Fitt regaled his companions with an account of how he had ended up sitting beside Paisley on the flight to London to take their seats after the election. When the drinks trolley came down the aisle, Fitt ordered his usual G&T and Paisley, who had a well-known aversion to the 'devil's buttermilk', declined the offer of a soft drink. When it came to paying for the beverage, Fitt discovered he had no cash and, as the story went, had to ask Paisley to 'lend him a fiver'.

It was around this time that Fitt conceived a highly mischievous scheme to persuade people at Westminster that Paisley was a secret drinker. In those days the BBC had what was called a remote studio in Westminster so that interviews could be conducted easily with MPs from other parts of the radio network. This facility was used frequently by the BBC in Belfast and, to soothe the MPs' nerves as they waited to say their piece, a small cocktail cabinet was provided along with an 'honour' book to record what beverages they had consumed. For a while, every time he visited the studio, Fitt entered Paisley's name in the book as the imbiber of several large drinks. He then began to spread the rumour that Paisley was a secret drinker. 'If you don't believe me,' he would tell his more gullible parliamentary colleagues, 'take a look at the BBC honour book the next time you're in there.'

Wilson's Labour government suffered a notable defeat in that 1970 general election and Edward Heath, the Conservative leader, became Prime Minister. Fitt was most displeased and described the outcome as 'an absolute tragedy for Northern Ireland'. His apprehension about how the Tories would handle Northern Ireland proved justified all too quickly. Barely a week after Heath had taken office and appointed Reginald Maudling Home Secretary, with responsibility for Northern Ireland affairs, there was a most significant escalation of violence. The weekend of trouble began on Friday evening when Bernadette Devlin was arrested to commence a six-month prison sentence for her part in the Bogside riots in August 1969. Within moments of her being taken into custody, disorder erupted in the Bogside and quickly spread to several areas of Belfast, where it was aggravated by the usual seasonal meanderings of Orange bands and marchers. Altogether seven people died that weekend, two of them in what became known as 'the Battle of Seaforde Street'. Provisional IRA gunmen concealed themselves in the tower of St Matthew's Church and carried out what is counted as the organisation's first armed operation – allegedly against snipers amongst rioting Protestant crowds.

The following Tuesday, Maudling arrived in Belfast to assess the situation for himself. The opposition MPs were invited to Stormont to meet him, but the temper of Paddy Devlin had not been improved by what he took to be inspired stories in many of that mornings' newspapers predicting the introduction of internment without trial to contain the drastically deteriorating situation. Devlin was specifically angry about the story in the *Daily Express* for having once been interned himself, he felt very strongly about the unfairness of it. So when the MPs filed in to see Maudling at Stormont, Devlin immediately referred to the story. 'Will you deny it?' he asked. Maudling remained non-committal as Devlin's fury increased. Finally, Devlin threw the newspaper at him and stormed out. 'Who is that chappie?' asked the bewildered Home Secretary. The incident perhaps helps explain why, on his return flight to London, Maudling told the steward to bring him a large scotch and famously sighed, 'What a bloody awful country.'

It was during Maudling's visit that Fitt was advised of a very worrying development. Shop stewards in the Belfast shipyard had advised Catholic workers – 500 among the 10,000 employees – to go home for their own safety because of the tension over the earlier 'Battle of Seaforde Street'. Fitt contacted Downing Street at once, all too aware of the yard's volatile history – in the 1920s sectarian trouble in the yard had escalated throughout the city. In this case, however, management intervened quickly and threatened instant dismissal for intimidators and, with the active help of moderate trade unionists, a potentially ugly development was safely contained.

On Thursday of that tense week, 2 July, Fitt was at Westminster to sign on for the new session. The following day the Northern Ireland situation was debated in proceedings only notable because Paisley made his maiden speech and the government and opposition affirmed a bilateral policy for handling Northern Ireland affairs. Fitt flew back to Belfast late that evening in the company of newly elected MP Frank McManus, who agreed to give him a lift into Belfast. In those days the main route into the city was round the Horseshoe Bend and down the Crumlin Road. From the bend there was a marvellous panoramic view of the city, with its chimneys, cranes and office blocks, surrounded by the green hills on three sides and the blue expanse of Belfast Lough on the other stretching out beyond Bangor, the seaside town at its mouth, to the open sea. But that evening as they rounded the Bend and travelled down towards Ardoyne, Fitt sensed an atmosphere he had never experienced before.

> There was nothing to see, nobody around, just a smell of trouble in the air.
> I said to McManus, 'There's something wrong here.' When he dropped me
> off at the house a few minutes later I quickly discovered what it was. The
> events that were to become known as the Falls Road curfew had begun.

Earlier in the day, about 4.30pm, a small party of police and soldiers had stopped outside 24 Balkan Street, a small terrace house in what was then a maze of narrow side-streets off the Falls Road. Acting on a tip-off that arms had been concealed in the house, the security force, captured twelve handguns, a sub-machine gun and an assortment of explosives and ammunition, the largest and most significant arms haul made to date. While the search was taking place an angry crowd gathered outside, and when the army and police vehicles tried to leave the area they were hemmed in. More people gathered, reinforcements were called in by the army, stones started to fly, a man was crushed to death by a heavy armoured car trying to manoeuvre its way out and large quantities of CS gas were fired. The scene was set for yet another night of trouble, but this one would be a crucial watershed because of the way it was handled.

Unknown to everyone at the time, the Unionist government, through the Stormont joint security committee comprising the army, police and Belfast and London government representatives, had successfully exploited its traditional connections with the Conservatives. During the previous week, when Maudling and junior defence minister Lord Balniel had been in Belfast, Chichester-Clark and his ministers, hard-pressed by unionist hardliners, had secured agreement that next time there was trouble, the army would go in and go in hard. In the early evening, as the trouble flared, it seemed at first as if the army were withdrawing. They were in fact regrouping and soon afterwards, with massive reinforcements, they swept into the area in their hundreds, pushing aside makeshift barricades erected during the lull. Gunfights broke out and four people died during the course of the evening. About 10.00pm a helicopter flew overhead with an officer on board using a loud-hailer to announce a curfew and order people off the streets and into their homes. At the same time a statement from army headquarters in Lisburn defined the precise area to be curfewed until further notice, ordered people into their homes and warned that anyone found on the streets after the military occupation would be arrested.

The area quietened down during the night although the army carried out house-to-house searches and at dawn more loudspeaker announcements from helicopters ordered the people to remain indoors indefinitely. On the ground, men coming to their door to leave for work were ordered back inside and at the perimeter of the sealed-off area bread and milk deliveries were turned away. Fitt recalled:

> As soon as I knew what was happening, I attempted to gain access to the area but was turned back repeatedly at the barbed wire cordons, in no uncertain terms, by very cheeky young soldiers. Representations to officers that as the MP for the area I was entitled to access were just as curtly dismissed. I went back home and made repeated efforts throughout the night to get someone in authority at the army HQ, Stormont, the Home Office and Downing Street. But unlike the recent days of the Labour government, nobody was available to me and I realised then that things had changed for the worse. Eventually I was allowed in next morning and in the late afternoon, when the curfew was lifted for two hours to enable families to purchase food for the weekend, I managed to reach the police station at

Springfield Road, where Paddy Devlin, the Stormont MP for the area, who
had spent the night inside the cordoned area, had been taken after soldiers
tried to prevent him talking to people about what was happening.

Devlin had horrifying evidence of military excess and on Sunday, when the curfew
was finally lifted at 9.00am, he and Fitt were so concerned about the well-
documented misconduct of the soldiers that they flew to London that evening to
complain.

> The tale we pieced together was one of looting, beating and assault by the
> army. Houses were turned inside-out in the search for arms and explosives,
> fireplaces ripped out, floorboards ripped up, walls knocked down and doors
> beaten down. Of the many people arrested there was persuasive evidence of
> ill-treatment by soldiers while they were in custody.

There was much human suffering, too. Old people and young babies were badly
affected by the prolonged effects of the CS gas poured into the area for many
hours. There was hardship because of the lack of food and milk in many homes,
financial loss from people being prevented from going to work and a certain
amount of resentment that people were not able to go to confession on Saturday
evening, an unbroken tradition for many older people, in particular. Two
weddings arranged for St Peter's Church that morning were also interrupted,
although one was permitted to take place several hours late.

In all, Fitt had the details of 100 complaints recorded in a school exercise book
when they met Maudling early next morning. Fitt told him the situation in Belfast
was incendiary because the Catholics felt defenceless as the British Army seemed
to be carrying out the worst excesses of unionist repression. It was a far from
satisfactory meeting, and the next day in the Commons the gravity of the step-
change in security policy that had taken place was still not appreciated by the new
government. Lord Balniel stonewalled about the legal justification for the search
and robustly defended the actions of the troops.

Almost at the same time as Balniel was speaking, Dr Paddy Hillery, the Irish
Minister of Foreign Affairs, was conducting a secret fact-finding mission in the
Falls. His stunt broke every rule of diplomacy and was more intended to impress
Fianna Fáil hardliners in Dublin than anyone else but Fitt still regarded it as an
unhelpful distraction from the enormity of the change in British government
policy, which had so suddenly taken place. Ten months earlier his constituents had
welcomed these same soldiers with open arms as their saviours. Now all that
goodwill had evaporated. It was an action that hardened opinion irrevocably and
created a permanent divide between the Catholics and the soldiers. It enabled the
PIRA to increase its profile as defenders of the Catholic community and paved the
way for the tragedies that were to follow. Fitt long remained angry at the stupidity
of the British politicians and soldiers who made such a grave miscalculation:

> The new situation effectively extinguished my hopes that reform within

Northern Ireland could contain the situation. The worst sort of tribal politics had taken over.

Despite widespread apprehension, the traditional Twelfth of July marches passed off peacefully. The government ordered all the pubs to shut, which may have helped. However the following Thursday saw the first indiscriminate bombing in the city centre. In a foretaste of much worse to come, thirty people escaped death when the no-warning bomb went off in the front hall of a bank in High Street.

Exactly one week later Fitt was in a corridor in Westminster when he noticed Dame Irene Ward, an elderly lady who usually walked slowly with the aid of a stick, coming towards him 'faster than any greyhound I had ever seen at Dunmore Park or the White City'. She pointed back at the Commons chamber and said to him, 'They've let off stink bombs in there.' Hard on her heels came Paisley. 'It's not stink bombs,' he roared expertly. 'We from Northern Ireland know only too well what it is. CS gas.' One of the policemen told Fitt what had happened. About 4.30pm, as Anthony Barber, chancellor of the Duchy of Lancaster, was making a statement about the Common Market negotiations, a man in the public gallery suddenly threw a canister onto the floor of the House. It landed near Fred Peart and Robert Mellish, but before attendants in the gallery could grab him, the man threw down a second canister shouting, 'How do you like that, you bastards? Now you know what it's like in Belfast.' Tom Swain MP and two members of the Commons staff had to be taken to hospital for treatment and even when the house resumed, after two hours' adjournment, the stinging effects of the gas were still in the air. Fitt said that while he could not condone the attack, MPs would at least now have personal experience of the dreadful effects of the widely used gas, the effects of which had so distressed those young children and elderly people subjected to it in Northern Ireland. The man who carried out the incident was James Anthony Roche, who was later sentenced to eighteen months' imprisonment for his action. He belonged to one of the militant left-wing factions that had now subverted the civil rights cause in Northern Ireland.

Tragedy struck very much closer to the Fitt home on 31 July during riots in the New Lodge Road area. What actually happened is still disputed – like so much else in modern Northern Ireland history. According to local people, when troops raided the Starry Plough Inn and made arrests, rioting ensued. The security forces, on the other hand, claimed that the trouble began when one of their vehicles was lured to the area by a hoax bomb call. Either way, the accounts agree on the fact that stoning and petrol bombing went on for some hours but then diverge again. The army claimed a group of youths were warned three times that they would be shot if they did not disperse; local accounts hold that the soldiers opened fire without warning. Whatever the truth of the matter, nineteen-year-old Danny O'Hagan fell dead with, the army said, a petrol bomb by his side. An apprentice electrician, O'Hagan lived in the block of flats on Antrim Road where the Fitts had lived previously. His father, John, was an ex-merchant seaman and the family was well-known to Fitt, Ann and their daughters. Fitt could hardly credit that young O'Hagan would be out petrol bombing, but as he ruefully recalled, 'it was not the last time I would be perplexed about the involvement of unlikely people in acts of violence, or wonder how they had become victims of terrorists themselves'.

The death of the young man provoked further rioting and increased Catholic alienation from the army. The PIRA claimed O'Hagan as a 'martyr' for the cause of Ireland, mourned him with black flags hung from every window and accorded him a republican-style funeral complete with solitary piper playing laments. As the O'Hagan funeral crossed Belfast's sectarian boundaries on its way to the cemetery, there were clashes between Protestant and Catholic crowds. In continued clashes at the New Lodge Road, troops used water cannon and, for the first time ever, fired rubber bullets at the stone-throwing crowds. Fitt watched the entire spectacle in total dismay:

> The only way forward, I now felt with increasing conviction, was political. But the increasingly uncompromising stance of the hardliners in the Unionist party against Chichester-Clark, was halting the necessary pace of reform, that would have been valuable in heading off the increasingly dangerous influence in the Catholic community of the IRA and other extreme elements. Confrontation not compromise was in fact the inevitable order of the day on both sides and I was desperate, because I knew that the eleventh hour was running out, to try and put a stop it.

Ever since the 1969 general election, all the opposition members at Stormont had been trying to establish their own individual importance. The Nationalist party had been reduced to a rump of four, all elderly except for Austin Currie, and the real running was being made by the likes of John Hume, Ivan Cooper, Paddy Devlin and Paddy O'Hanlon, all graduates of the civil rights campaign on the streets who were only just beginning to get to grips with parliamentary protocol. Soon after the election these five and Fitt had formed an informal alliance and parcelled out shadow responsibilities for the various ministries. Fitt was the spokesman on home affairs, which took in all legal and security matters. Devlin shadowed health and social services; Hume, education; Currie, housing; Cooper, community relations; and O'Hanlon, agriculture. The nationalist veterans wanted nothing to do with this set-up and as a result Currie began to drift away from them. Similarly, Paddy Kennedy and Fitt were starting to go their separate ways. Fitt was disgusted that Kennedy was becoming ever more closely identified with prominent members of the emerging PIRA alignment. The turbulent events of the summer of 1970 propelled the Stormont six closer together and slowly a formal alliance was developed through their common respect for non-violent means to achieve political progress and reform and a deep-rooted opposition to the Unionist party.

   Despite their shared values, these men were a varied and diverse bunch. Hume
had initially studied for the priesthood, then taken up teaching in his native Derry
and, through his involvement in the credit union movement, had drifted into the
civil rights struggle and full-time politics. Currie had a degree in political science
from Queen's University, Belfast, and when first elected in 1964 was the youngest
ever MP at Stormont. He tried, in vain, to encourage the Nationalist party to
adopt a more positive role in making Stormont work better for the Catholic
minority and it was he, more than any other single person, who started the civil
rights bandwagon rolling. Ivan Cooper was a Protestant with a business
background. His first foray into politics was with the Young Unionists, then the
Orange Order. Like many moderate Protestants he eventually drifted into the
NILP, and from there became a prominent figure in the civil rights movement
before winning a seat at Stormont. Paddy Devlin, another NILP man, became
involved in politics because of his passionate, non-sectarian socialist beliefs, and he
ruffled the feathers of many in the party with his strong, belligerent approach to
politics. Paddy O'Hanlon, a graduate of University College Dublin, came from a
strongly republican area of South Armagh and had also reached Stormont as a
result of his active work in the civil rights movement.
   As the violence escalated steadily throughout 1970, this group found more and
more that they were speaking with a single voice: urging the Unionists to press
ahead with reforms, complaining about the growing excesses of the army and
highlighting the apparent return to one-sided and repressive security policies, even
though both sides of the community were equally involved in violence. Their ideas
were explored and teased out over long, rambling discussions in Stormont, at the
nearby Stormont hotel, the Wellington Park hotel and at McGlade's Old Vic
lounge in Donegall Street, a haunt they shared with the ever-growing band of
pressmen posted to the city from the big national newspapers. While there was
much common ground in their viewpoints, Fitt recalled his reservations about
moving beyond an informal alliance:

> We increasingly became strong friends and every time there was a crisis the
> consensus between us grew stronger. Before long we had moved from
> simple agreement to co-operate to a conviction that the most effective
> representation we could give the Catholic community was to form a new
> party to work within the existing Stormont system. But the whole concept
> was giving me many sleepless nights. As the most politically experienced of
> the group, I had deep reservations about the different ideological strands we
> were trying to weave together. There was never much sympathy for the
> Nationalist party in Belfast, its strength was in the rural, conservative areas,
> particularly along the border. The people there had little in common with
> the working-class of Belfast for whom the question of a united Ireland had
> little or no urgency. By contrast Derry, which should have been a
> stronghold for socialist, labour policies was a nationalist city, a political

contradiction I believed, because of its close proximity to the border. Indeed, the country people thought that 'socialist' meant we would take their farms away. I feared too that there would be personality, as well as political, differences. I quite expected that my frequent absences at Westminster might lead to new alignments between the others.

A measure of the difficulties they had to overcome in order to found a new party came one Sunday in Toomebridge, where there had been an quarrelsome meeting over a long lunch. Devlin was sitting in a chair snoozing while the rest debated possible names for the new party. Hume wanted to call it the Social Democratic Party. Fitt favoured the Labour and Social Democratic party and argued at length that the word 'labour' had to be in the title, something he considered mandatory. 'I was actually ready to call the whole thing off because of Hume's opposition to the word "labour", although privately I was glad to be rid of the need to call it something "republican" because the Provos had so thoroughly discredited that term.' In the middle of this argument, Devlin woke up and said gruffly, 'You can't call it the Labour and Social Democratic party. That would be abbreviated to the LSD party and people would think we were only in it for the money, or else they would say we were political junkies.' After further discussion and debate, it was finally agreed that if they went ahead and formed a new political party, it would be called the Social Democratic and Labour party, or SDLP.

Some of the group had sounded out Conor Cruise O'Brien and Brendan Halligan of the Irish Labour party in Dublin and Michael McInerney, an eminent *Irish Times* political writer, and all were enthusiastic about their ideas, as were others who were approached quietly. Almost inevitably, however, word of the joint discussions leaked out and Austin Currie was put on the spot when asked about them on Radio Éireann in August 1970. Thinking aloud, he said that Fitt would have to be the leader of the new grouping because he was the only man who could wear the 'crown of thorns'. Fitt was in Cushendun when this interview took place and on his return to Belfast, as anointed leader, the group gathered in his house for a final brainstorming session before finally committing themselves:

> As I walked in and out of the kitchen making and pouring tea we rehearsed, once again, all the arguments for and against. Deep down I was still very worried about this unprecedented nationalist and socialist coalition. In the end the fear of the more immediate consequences of doing nothing persuaded me. Finally we all put our names to a formal document forming the Social Democratic and Labour party. At my insistence, Senator Paddy Wilson came in as the seventh founding member.

The new party was launched formally at a news conference in the Grand Central Hotel in Belfast on 21 August 1970. Its first statement of policy said that the committed aims of the party were:

> To secure an adequate distribution of wealth; to uphold and support the

democratic rights and principles of organised labour; to promote the spread of financial, consumer, industrial and consumer co-operatives; to work for the provision of minimum living wage for all workers; and to support the principle of equal pay for equal work. ... [to] secure civil rights for all citizens irrespective of race, creed or political outlook; to support the re-introduction of proportional representation for elections; to promote and encourage the development of all aspects of the nation's culture; to ensure public ownership of fishing rights of all inland waters; to formulate radical policies for the agricultural, social and economic development of the rural areas; and to work for the establishment of state industries, particularly in areas of high unemployment.

In answering questions from the press, Fitt made it clear the party would be radical, left of centre, and would have no connections with any secret or sectarian organisations. He said the party would promote the fullest co-operation between northern and southern Ireland in all fields, and that they firmly believed that Irish unity, which he said was the eventual aim of the party, could be achieved only with the consent of the majority of the people.

The initiative was received very coolly in Northern Ireland. The Alliance party, which saw itself as the middle-of-the-road, non-sectarian deliverer of peace, dismissed the move as serving only to widen the religious divide. The *Belfast Telegraph* took the same line that evening in its editorial:

> No one will blame the opposition MPs for trying to achieve greater efficiency through greater unity, particularly if the new alliance is to have a radical left-of-centre basis. But there is a great danger that the attempt to form a united opposition will be regarded as merely a new twist to an old theme and that it will inevitably lead to a hardening or orange-green divisions. At the present time any further hardening of attitudes is a development which Northern Ireland can well do without.

The *London Times* was equally discouraging in an editorial the next day headed, 'Mr Fitt's Six':

> ... the present initiative does nothing to remedy a deeper defect in Ulster politics: the coincidence of politics and religion. The need is for parties that are capable of attracting support from within both religious communities. Mr Fitt spoke, sincerely we may be sure, of the non-sectarian character of his new party. But its position in relation to the constitution and still more the political standing of its founder members make it most unlikely that it will win adherents in any number from the Protestant community.

Some have claimed that the SDLP was a creation of the media, or the Catholic Church. Fitt never accepted that. As far as he was concerned, while there may have been background influences on some of the six, the initiative and its impetus arose jointly between the founding members. Nonetheless, the Republican Labour and nationalist parties decided not to join, so the six MPs and one Senator, who made up a central executive, set about forming the new party organisation. Although Fitt and Devlin had ensured that the new party at least paid lip service to their socialist convictions, the NILP also refused to join – no doubt discouraged by the green hue that Hume, in particular, painted over the new grouping. The defection of Devlin from the NILP also sparked off rivalry, and when the British Labour party gathered in Blackpool for its annual conference in September his former party tried to use the occasion to enhance their comradely relationship at the expense of the new SDLP. A ferocious row broke out at a fringe meeting organised by the CDU and Lord Longford was appointed to referee the contest. In the end, he came down on the side of the SDLP, swayed by NILP hostility towards Fitt. 'This labour movement will not stand for this sort of an attack on people like Gerry Fitt. It is just not on,' said Longford.

The fledgling SDLP's most pressing need was for a party headquarters and a piece of good fortune secured one for them. A supporter rang Fitt to say he had premises in College Square North, in the city centre, and offered them for use. Fitt and Devlin went to take a look. There were a couple of rooms downstairs and a larger one upstairs, which was ideal for meetings. They came away with an agreement to use the premises for a nominal rent and, after having them spruced up with a few coats of paint and some carpets, Fitt declared them open on 23 October. At the event he turned to Brian Garrett, who was there as a fraternal delegate from the NILP, and said he hoped that one day there would be a united socialist movement. At this time, Fitt liked to visualise the working-classes in both parts of Ireland uniting to bring an end to the fault-line between them created by partition.

Within a month of its formation the SDLP was able to report that it had received 1,300 applications for membership, at 50p per member, and had established fourteen constituency branches. Fitt addressed several of the inaugural branch meetings and one in Dungiven, for example, attracted almost 700 people. In fact, the NDP was wound up to leave its members free to join the SDLP. The new party was ambitious, placing advertisements in both the Catholic and Protestant newspapers explaining its non-sectarian philosophy and inviting anyone who shared its principles to join. When he gave his first major interview as party leader, towards the end of September, Fitt said that although they all recognised there was a long, hard slog ahead, they were strongly encouraged by the increasingly favourable reaction to what they were attempting to achieve.

The Unionist party, for its part, was still convulsed by internal strife and all that autumn extremist pressure on Chichester-Clark was becoming more and more evident. With Paisley making loud noises off-stage, the hardliners within the Unionist party were steadily seeking to undermine him and reassert their own dominance over the political process. In August the Prime Minister deflected a determined challenge to his leadership after a lengthy meeting of the parliamentary party at Stormont, but in September he was put under further pressure when Harry West, one of the most influential hardliners, proposed abandoning the new central housing authority and called for the formation of armed reserve police units, a demand that amounted to the resurrection of the 'B' Specials. More evidence of backsliding came at the beginning of October, when Brian Faulkner, who was responsible for local government reorganisation, announced that elections under the long-overdue 'one man, one vote' franchise would probably be postponed from the proposed October 1971 date to some time in 1972.

The SDLP was so seriously concerned by these developments that it delivered a formal warning of its position on 15 October. Speaking at Dungiven, Austin Currie said that in the event of a right-wing unionist takeover and the loss of the hard-won gains of the last two years, his party was prepared to leave parliament, go out onto the streets and fight again for those objectives: 'As far as we are concerned, if the day arises when we consider there is nothing to be gained by parliamentary activity, then the SDLP is prepared to leave parliament and engage in extra-parliamentary activity.' Fully aware of the violent atmosphere prevailing, none of the MPs had consented lightly to that ominous warning, and it was a measure of their concern that they felt it necessary to make such a statement. Their sentiments were reinforced when a party deputation met Richard Sharples, a minister of state from the Home Office in London in early November. 'We repeated our fears that the unionist right-wingers might stage a putsch to prevent any further action by the British government, which they saw as interference,' said Fitt.

The year closed with the death toll standing at five – two policemen and three civilians killed in explosions – of which there had been 153, as well as 213 shooting incidents. At this point, Austin Currie was predicting the early demise of Chichester-Clark and his replacement as Prime Minister by Brian Faulkner. In a bid to placate his critics Chichester-Clark refused to rule out the introduction of internment without trial: 'I reserve the right to do whatever may be necessary to protect the security of Northern Ireland.'

The first four weeks of the New Year, 1971, were marked by more rioting. Both sides were involved in the clashes, which often lasted for hours. Moderates pleaded in vain for an end to them, but the unionist right-wingers seized on the disturbances as further evidence of the need for even tougher security policies, including internment. Chichester-Clark again threatened using it to curb the trouble, and the air of crisis heightened when he cancelled a trip to the USA and instead went to London for talks with Maudling. A few days after that meeting Fitt met Maudling to impress on him the very strong reaction there would be to any use of the Special Powers to intern people. The ordinary processes of law, he insisted, were adequate to weed out the troublemakers. Maudling politely agreed to take account of his views.

At the end of the month Richard Sharples returned to Northern Ireland to review the situation, this time accompanied by Lord Carrington, the Minister for Defence. Within a few days it became clear they had again permitted the army to increase its profile as massive arms searches began in the Clonard area of Fitt's constituency, provoking further trouble. At a news conference, a senior British officer publicly named five men as leaders of the Provisional IRA and claimed the organisation was responsible for the rioting. The Provisionals interpreted that piece of foolhardiness as a gauntlet being thrown down and the very next night, 6 February, a sniper in the New Lodge Road, firing from the cover of rioting crowds, murdered Gunner Robert Curtis of the Royal Artillery – the first military casualty of the violence. Fitt was at home, just a few hundred yards away, and heard the shots that killed him. His daughter, Patsy, remembers the moment vividly: 'In those days there was always an incredible amount of noise and shouting, bangs and explosions, but after the shots there was this awful silence and all you could hear was the sound of a dog barking.'

The killing triggered off an even more violent phase: over the next few days a child died after being knocked down by an army vehicle, the body of a young man with gunshot wounds was dumped on the airport road, five BBC engineers died when a bomb exploded under their vehicle on its way to a remote transmitter post in Co. Tyrone, twelve explosions rocked Belfast in a single night and there were ugly sectarian clashes during the military-style funerals of PIRA men killed in nightly gunfights. Fitt was shocked by the escalation:

> I had been on the streets night after night, trying in vain to cool tempers. On behalf of the party I issued a statement calling on all those engaged in armed conflict to desist now before bringing further untold tragedy to this island. 'The deaths of three Irishmen and a young British soldier in Belfast must surely testify to the futility of violence in the attainment of political or national objectives,' I said. To the death toll must be added the total sum of misery, fear and distress in every home in the city.

Over the previous ten days the SDLP had become ever more concerned about what they regarded as the counter-productive conduct of the soldiers. They were also frustrated by the difficulty of raising their apprehensions with the home and defence secretaries – the ministers in London ultimately responsible for security policy. The issue had previously been raised on 28 January, during a visit to Belfast by Lord Carrington and Richard Sharples, when the SDLP had been informed that such access would be possible if the Stormont MPs visited London. In response, on 8 February, John Hume – stepping into a role previously played by Fitt alone – put in a request for the Home Secretary to meet with a delegation from the SDLP. Despite the encouragement they had received so recently, the request caused unease in Whitehall. A submission to ministers pointed out that while they were happy to see Westminster MPs from Northern Ireland under what was a well-established precedent, widening that precedent to include Stormont MPs – especially as they would publicise the visit to show those back home that they were taking action – was stepping into uncharted territory. In the end, due to the gravity of the situation in Belfast and fears that the rioting might spread to Derry, it was decided that Richard Sharples and Ian Gilmour, his counterpart at the Ministry of Defence, would receive an SDLP delegation, provided it was led by Gerry Fitt as a Westminster MP and he was accompanied only by Stormont MPs.

The get-together took place at 11.00am on 12 February when Sharples and Gilmour met the entire founding group of the SDLP for a discussion with two main themes: security policy and the need for comprehensive political and economic measures. Fitt opened for the SDLP by calling into question military behaviour and tactics. He said he understood the difficulties faced by the army but that the soldiers nevertheless tended to overreact, often on misleading information, and that they were in fact being manipulated by extremists to cause further trouble. There could, he added, be no going back to the old ways, specifically internment without trial, to which the SDLP was firmly opposed. Instead, what was needed was a political solution and an acceptance of the SDLP by the Stormont government. He pointed out that the party had not, for instance, been consulted about the recent composition of Boards set up under the reforms.

The other members of the delegation spoke in turn, describing their own concerns about security policy and the ongoing violence, but the main thrust of their pleading was for political action. Austin Currie stated that there could be no future for Northern Ireland unless changes were made to ensure minority participation in government and he suggested the introduction of proportional representation at elections to undermine extremism and help draw the parties towards consensus politics. John Hume said the minority wanted to have a real stake in the institutions of their society. Ivan Cooper said reform was meaningless, with male unemployment rates in Ballymurphy standing at 50% and at 33% in the Bogside. Hume added that in these areas a man, his father and probably his grandfather had never worked in their lives, a situation that led to a marked deterioration in moral fibre and social responsibility. Paddy O'Hanlon said money was being spent in areas of high development rather than in poorer areas, which were occupied predominantly by Catholics. The government was able to make great play of offering incentives to industrialists, but without sound infrastructure, such as roads, industry preferred to stay in the already prosperous areas. The two ministers summed up at the end. Gilmour defended the army and said that there had been no shift of policy – if there was more shooting, this was only in response to the increasing violence used against the army. Sharples offered nothing positive, only an assurance that what the SDLP had said would be carefully considered.

When they left the Home Office the SDLP team went on to see their great ally Paul Rose and Harold Wilson. 'James Callaghan was in the doghouse as far as we were concerned, for during a recent visit to Belfast he had attempted to boost the NILP at our expense, an annoyance we communicated to Wilson,' Fitt said afterwards. That Friday morning meeting in London was significant in that, for the first time, the British government listened in depth and at a high level to the views of the elected representatives of the Catholic minority. It marked the emergence of the SDLP as a powerful political force and reflected the growing cohesion between the six founders, despite their disparate personal backgrounds and political standpoints.

The following Monday in London, during a debate on the Consolidated Fund Bill, Fitt talked publicly of the SDLP's anxieties about the surging violence and the very serious situation developing in Northern Ireland. He complained bitterly that the one-sided arms searches by the army in the Catholic ghettoes were raising tension and provoking trouble. He told the House:

> Much of the shooting in Ulster has been blamed on the IRA and there is no doubt much of it is the IRA's responsibility. But there have been a lot of incidents recently in Northern Ireland in which IRA involvement has not been proved... No attempt seems to be being made to disarm the other warring side of the community.

Fitt informed the House that during a recent search in the Clonard area, which had sparked off rioting, ten homes had been searched, but the only firearm recovered was a legally held shotgun. On another day, while he was in the same area, he had watched as the army and police suddenly surrounded several streets, but after a while they left, having found nothing. He told them that he believed the indiscriminate way in which the army was acting drove many more people into the arms of the Provos, and that he had good grounds for believing that the Provos were deliberately ringing up and giving false information about weapons and explosives, knowing full well the army would blunder in and upset the people: 'Often they used to give the address of a house where elderly or disabled people or even families with lots of young kids lived to ensure that maximum support would be generated.' (Fitt was still able to keep abreast of developments in Belfast when he was at home via the police radio. Every night he was glued to his VHF transistor radio to keep updated on the nightly troubles. He used to joke that, 'The police radio by this time had become required listening for all in the city and I often told the BBC bosses there were more people listened to the RUC than BBC Northern Ireland.')

When the SDLP next met Maudling, in March at Stormont, they reiterated their opposition to the repressive security policies, which the ring-wing unionists were demanding incessantly. They told Maudling they suspected extreme factions within the RUC who were sympathetic to hard-line unionism were leaking sensitive and confidential police security information to Ian Paisley and William Craig. They believed this because both men had read out information in Stormont that could only have been obtained from police sources. Fitt recalled:

> What worried us most about the meeting was the negative and helpless attitude Maudling presented. We were bitterly disappointed that there was no talk of a political initiative. It would be no exaggeration to say our reaction bordered on despair that Maudling did not understand what was happening or appreciate the gravity of the situation.

If Maudling had failed to grasp the seriousness of the situation, it was brought home to him very forcible scarcely a week later. In the early evening of 10 March, the bodies of three soldiers, in plain clothes, were discovered in the hills above Belfast, but it was the unusually brutal manner of their murders that provoked the subsequent reaction. That afternoon the three soldiers, aged seventeen, eighteen and twenty-three, decided to spend their day off drinking in Belfast city centre, an area that was not out of bounds to them at the time. After an afternoon touring pubs they were lured away with the promise of a party and girls but instead their abductors took them to the hills above the city and, as they urinated against a hedge, all three were shot dead.

By Friday morning emotions were running so high that 4,000 shipyard workers downed tools and marched on the city centre, demanding internment of known IRA leaders forthwith. Behind the scenes, the same demands were being made to Chichester-Clark even more stridently by people who could have been counted as moderates up to that point. Over the weekend the pressure mounted and unnerved Chichester-Clark. On the Tuesday morning he flew to London with a shopping list of tough security measures, including a massive troop reinforcement and the power to send them into Catholic areas on punitive raids. The list was too much for London, however, and he returned that same evening with a promise of only half the number of troops he had requested. On Thursday another big march to Stormont increased the pressure on him and the rank-and-file party members were far from happy at the outcome of his trip. All next day his Cabinet remained in session amid rumours that he was on the point of resigning. Heath prevailed on him by telephone to hang on and sent Lord Carrington to Belfast to see him on the Saturday morning. But London would not agree to a get-tough security policy and the Prime Minister resigned at 10.00pm that night because he saw 'no other way of bringing home ... the realities of the present constitutional, political and security situation'.

The Unionist parliamentary party wasted no time in calling a meeting to elect a new leader and Prime Minister. On Tuesday, Faulkner won decisively by 26 votes to 4. It was a resounding personal triumph for the 'little shirt-maker', as he was derisively known by the landed gentry, who were the real powerbrokers in the Unionist Establishment. The SDLP welcomed Faulkner's appointment as the lesser of a number of evils. Certainly, unlike O'Neill or Chichester-Clark, he was strong enough to stand up to the right-wing elements. Fitt's personal view of Faulkner had not changed since their first positive encounter in 1962 and privately he was optimistic that they could do business with him to cut off the ever-worsening spiral of death and destruction that menaced every citizen, regardless of politics or creed. In public, Fitt said Faulkner's priority must be to forge ahead with the reform programme and indeed enlarge it to make social justice freely available to everyone in Northern Ireland. 'Otherwise,' he warned, 'Mr Faulkner will find that he will go down in history as the last Prime Minister of Northern Ireland.'

Faulkner met Edward Heath in London on 1 April for the first prime ministerial summit, and Northern Ireland was again debated in the London Commons on 6 April when Harold Wilson revealed that, as a contingency measure, his government had prepared a Bill to abolish Stormont and rule Northern Ireland directly from London. Fitt interpreted this as a supporting shot for Faulkner from both opposition and government because at that time both parties maintained a bilateral united front in the handling of the Northern Ireland crisis. The next day Fitt met Sharples, this time alone, and expressed himself 'fairly satisfied' with the present position. Fitt said the new Prime Minister in Belfast was 'an exceptionally capable politician' who had 'confused everybody' by the composition of his Cabinet – a reference to Faulkner's effort to re-assert party unity. (Faulkner had made a typically bold gesture when appointing his Cabinet by inviting David Bleakley, a prominent member of the NILP, to become his Minister for Community Relations, making him the first non-unionist ever to sit in a Stormont Cabinet although the move did not impress many Catholics. As a balancing act, he also restored Harry West, a fiercely reactionary critic of reform, to his Cabinet as the Minister for Agriculture.) Fitt also told Sharples that Faulkner's biggest problem would be keeping his Cabinet together, then moved on to the real purpose of his meeting, which was to once more register complaints about the army's conduct during a recent search operation that had lasted a day-and-a-half, interrupted families sleeping and yielded nothing. Reminding Sharples that difficult marches were looming at Easter and in July, he repeated his concerns that the army should not provoke people and provide subversive elements with an excuse for further violence.

All the while the violence continued on the streets and hardly a night went by without several explosions, destroying a customs post, or a pub, or a factory. There was a steady flow of people through the courts for riot-associated offences, and their custodial sentences were swelling the once small prison population. Several lawyers approached Fitt with details of the selectivity involved in bringing charges against people and of the inconsistent sentences imposed on those convicted, with a discernible bias in favour of people from Protestant backgrounds. The lawyers also provided a breakdown of the judiciary, which showed there was a disproportionately small number of Catholics. Although they made up one-third of the community, there was only one clerk of petty sessions who was a Catholic and of the six clerks of crown and peace, not one was a Catholic. The tally did improve slightly on the bench, however, with four out of thirteen magistrates, one out of five county court judges and one out of seven high court judges coming from Catholic backgrounds.

The lawyers gave Fitt examples of documented inconsistencies. They pointed out that Bernadette Devlin and Frank McManus had both served six-month prison terms for offences arising from the civil rights campaign. In stark contrast the Rev Ivan Foster, a minister in Paisley's Free Presbyterian Church, who had advertised and led a march 'in defiance' of the government's ban on parades, was not even prosecuted. Another example occurred on 14 July 1969, when, according to the evidence heard by the Scarman Tribunal, a former 'B' Special brought a Sterling sub-machine gun and ammunition into Dungiven Orange Hall, in clear breach of the Firearms Act. The man was never prosecuted. Another remarkable case concerned David Kane, a nineteen-year-old member of the 'B' Specials who was issued with a gun dealer's licence from the RUC. Although he was prosecuted, no action was taken against members of both the RUC and 'B' Specials who illegally bought twenty-five firearms from him. The decision whether to prosecute him had been taken by the Attorney-General, a Unionist member of the Cabinet. On the basis of this explicit dossier, Fitt complained about alleged political partiality on 27 April when he met Lord Hailsham, the Lord Chancellor, in London:

> What I asked him to do as a matter of urgency was to act on a report, which the Attorney-General had been sitting on for several months, outlining the need for an impartial Department of Public Prosecutions to be set up. I am glad to say this was acted upon soon afterwards and ultimately this area of worry was removed.

By now Brian Faulkner's style of government was becoming clear. Harold Wilson said that he could 'dance on the head of a pin', which was precisely the sort of delicate balancing necessary to promote his reputation as a reformer, while not allowing the hardliners to become a drag on him the way they had been on O'Neill and Chichester-Clark. His most far-reaching political gesture came on 22 June when he outlined proposals for a number of powerful parliamentary scrutiny committees, which he proposed would be established at Stormont by the end of the year. The chairmanships of these committees would be full-time, salaried positions, and he promised two of the posts would go to members of the opposition. A few days later he gave further details, announcing that on top of the existing public accounts committee, there would be three new committees to consider government policy and performance on environmental affairs, social services and industrial development. Paddy Devlin described it as Faulkner's 'finest hour' and Fitt was equally enthusiastic:

> This was the sort of thing which encouraged us. For the first time in the fifty years of Stormont we were being offered a whiff of power. It was still a

long way from the participation in government we were after, but given half
a century of nothing, it was a potentially worthwhile start.

That weekend there were eleven explosions in Belfast, underlining the urgent
need, as Fitt saw it, to prevent the political process being dictated by violent
events. There had been thirty-seven explosions in April, forty-seven in May and
fifty in June and riots were still taking place almost nightly. On Tuesday, 6 July the
SDLP group met Faulkner at Stormont and the following day took part in further
talks with unionists, the NILP and nationalists – the first time in the history of
Stormont that such inter-party talks had taken place. Later that same evening, in
Derry, the army shot dead Seamus Cusack during rioting in the Bogside and
subsequently claimed that he was a gunman. Vicious rioting erupted and another
man, Desmond Beattie, was shot dead by soldiers the next afternoon. The deaths
of Cusack and Beattie marked a watershed in the history of the SDLP and
Northern Ireland. Immediately afterwards IRA supporters began marching up and
down outside John Hume's home in the Bogside to protest about the shootings
and all his constituents and associates in Derry insisted that neither man had been
armed nor throwing petrol bombs when they were killed.

In an attempt to respond to this pressure and to back up his demands for an
inquiry into the mens' deaths, Hume called an SDLP meeting at his home the
following Sunday. Fitt rang Currie from a callbox in the Glens of Antrim, where
he was spending the weekend, and was told of the scale of the Provo protests, but
he saw no pressing reason to go to Derry and stayed in the Glens. He was therefore
surprised and concerned when he heard reports on the radio and television news
on 12 July of Hume's announcement that the SDLP would withdraw from
Stormont three days later and set up its own assembly if an impartial inquiry into
the two shootings were not set up immediately:

> I was appalled for I knew that the party was backing itself into a corner with
> no room for movement. I did not accept that the two shootings were
> serious enough grounds for a step of that magnitude. If they were there had
> been many previous incidents in Belfast which should have been the trigger,
> the shooting of my young neighbour Danny O'Hagan, some time earlier,
> being but one case in point.

Outnumbered by the rest of the party, Fitt booked a seat on the first flight to
London on Tuesday, 13 July and arranged meetings with Reginald Maudling and
Lord Balniel: 'Privately, I recognised there was no way they could or would accede
to any sort of inquiry, but what I hoped I could persuade them to do was expedite
the public inquests, which normally took many months to convene. That way the
truth, whatever it was, would come out.' When they heard of the depth of feeling
in Derry and Fitt's desire not to sever the promising possibilities opening up with
Faulkner, the ministers agreed to co-operate. Later that day, however, in radio

interviews, Austin Currie ruled out early inquests as a suitable expression of outrage. It had to be an inquiry, or nothing, he maintained. On Thursday, despite his total opposition to the tactic, Fitt decided not to break ranks but instead to lead the SDLP withdrawal from Stormont. It was a purely symbolic gesture, however, as the House was then in summer recess.

> Although I chaired a press conference announcing the move, I was far from satisfied with the hook upon which we had now impaled ourselves. However, I took the expected hard line, saying we would never go back to Stormont in its present form because it was only the shrine of unionism. My colleagues were so angry and disillusioned, however, that when a bomb scare was telephoned to the hotel, Paddy Devlin refused to leave. 'Let it go off,' he said. 'We're fed up with fuckin' bomb scares.'

Before the issue could seriously test the internal cohesion of the SDLP, it was eclipsed by a far more compelling reason for boycotting Stormont, and one on which they were in solid agreement – the introduction of internment without trial.

CHAPTER NINE

A MAJOR TURNING POINT

THE INTERNMENT SWOOPS by the security forces began at 4.30am on Monday, 9 August. Fitt realised what was happening when he was awakened by the clattering of tin dustbin lids on the pavement – the traditional warning that the police and soldiers were on their way. The raids at the nearby New Lodge Road ignited rioting and before long columns of thick, black smoke drifted into the clear blue summer morning sky as hijacked vehicles burned and smouldered. In front of his house, Fitt could see continual convoys of army vehicles moving in and out of Girdwood Barracks, which, he later discovered, was the holding centre for those arrested in Belfast.

The telephone began to ring constantly and the early morning radio reports confirmed that internment had been introduced. It came as little surprise. Despite everything the army and police had tried to do, the level of disorder and violence had been increasing steadily. In July, there were ninety-one explosions – twenty in one night alone. No outrage was too daring for the terrorists. An armed gang, disguised as doctors in white medical coats, had freed a wounded comrade from the Royal Victoria Hospital in Belfast where he was under police guard. In the London Commons the previous Friday, where they had debated Northern Ireland, Jim Callaghan recognised the true seriousness of the situation. Opening the debate he said, 'I don't think I have ever approached the Irish situation with as deep a sense of foreboding and impending tragedy as I do today.' Fitt warned again that political action and reform was needed, not retaliatory violence and repression:

> The present situation in Northern Ireland can be traced back directly to the August troubles of 1969 when the right-wing of the Unionist party created a vicious backlash against the reforms which were then demanded by the British Labour government. It was not the IRA who created the backlash. It was the stubborn intransigence of right-wing extremists who believed that to bring about any reforms in Northern Ireland would endanger their

superiority. I have never condoned violence and I deeply deplore the lives, soldiers and civilians, that have been lost in the present trouble. Such deeds have been brought about by the inaction of the British government in seeking a political solution. I do not believe that the unity of Ireland can be advanced by one second by the killing of a British soldier or the indiscriminate explosions taking place. But they serve as an indication of all that has gone wrong in Northern Ireland over the past fifty years. Since the advent of the Tory government it appears there had been a decided change in army attitude towards the minority in Northern Ireland. Searches have taken place in Catholic areas by an openly belligerent and hostile British Army. In 96% of the houses that have been searched nothing incriminating had been found. It appears to me these searches have taken place to placate the right-wing extremists in Northern Ireland and indeed those who sit in this house. I know there is one section of the community in Northern Ireland who believe that the present troubles can be brought to an end by the introduction of internment, the recall of the 'B' Specials, the re-arming of the police force and the heaping of further repression on the Catholic minority. Another section of the community believes that the problem can be solved by the abolition of Stormont, the disbanding of the Orange Order and getting the British Army out of Northern Ireland tomorrow. I have no hesitation in saying that both these courses would lead to ultimate disaster with the terrible cost of human life.

With Stormont no longer available to him to sound the alarm bells, Fitt said this was the most passionate and important speech he had made to the House in a long time, because he recognised they were fast approaching a major turning-point. His words were already redundant, however. At precisely the same time as he was speaking, Faulkner and the army commander from Ulster were in secret conclave in London with Edward Heath and Reginald Maudling, putting the final touches to the internment operation. It was a decision that would have lasting and significant repercussions, leading ultimately to the prorogation of Stormont and the final alienation of the Catholic community from the six-county state.

More immediately, the introduction of internment enabled the PIRA to exploit it as the justification for accelerating its murderous activities because the operation was directed exclusively at the minority. Not one suspected loyalist, unionist or Protestant was on the list of 450 names drawn up by the RUC and army for arrest; only those suspected of IRA affiliation were taken into custody. The decision was all the more controversial because it overlooked the fact that it was the loyalists who had first resorted to violence: committing murder in Malvern Street in 1966; bringing down O'Neill with bombs in 1969; shooting the first police officer to die in the Troubles the same year. Internment without trial had always been a sore point with the minority community because of its consistently one-sided application. It was the most visibly unfair symptom of unionist repression for, until that time, not one member of the majority community had ever been interned. Internment also offended the soul of any democrat as it allowed the Executive to detain an individual indefinitely, without charge, with minimum safeguards and without the protection of the courts and judiciary. Now, in 1971, it plunged Catholic attitudes to the British Army to a new low. As far as they were concerned, the army was now doing the unionist's dirty work.

Whatever kudos Faulkner earned from his own hardliners for cracking down so ruthlessly on the IRA were far outweighed by the massive surge in violence and the alienation of the entire Catholic community. The extent of it was well illustrated by an exchange between Fitt and a very eminent Catholic lawyer; on the Friday before the swoops the lawyer had been on the phone to Fitt, telling him what a bad lot the Provos were and how they were betraying all the ideals of the nationalist cause; on Monday morning his ire was directed at Faulkner. Michael McInerney, the distinguished *Irish Times* political correspondent, was in Belfast on internment day and when he called to see Fitt he reported that the Provos were delirious with excitement because they recognised immediately just how far internment had pushed the Catholic community from the six-county state. The few Catholics who had joined the UDR resigned in protest. In Derry thirty prominent Catholics withdrew from public positions. Stephen McGonigal relinquished his post on the Londonderry Development Commission, the body set up to replace the corrupt council and modernise the city. A one day strike in Derry city attracted 8,000 supporters, while similar protests were held in Catholic towns like Newry and Strabane. More than 300 professional and business people signed a newspaper advertisement condemning internment. Against this backdrop and despite Fitt's overwhelmingly pragmatic instincts, the SDLP had no choice but to reflect this hardening line, so it endorsed a campaign of civil disobedience, asking people to withhold payment of rent and rates until internment was ended.

This course of events had been decided upon at a meeting in a Belfast hotel. Shortly before it ended, the hotel was surrounded by troops and some of them actually pointed guns into the room where the party members were talking. As they left in two cars, they were flagged down by the soldiers, searched and questioned for about twenty minutes. The officer in charge refused to consider their position as elected members of parliament, insisting he was acting on orders. It was harassment like this that compounded the difficulties of the situation and drove the wedge of disenchantment ever more deeply into the SDLP attitude. If the SDLP had not already pulled out of Stormont, they would now have done so anyway. For his own part, Fitt was deeply uneasy that the minority community was now standing on shared ground with the IRA, and it was with deep, deep reluctance that he shifted there himself:

> It is my belief that if the operation had been planned and conducted in an even handed fashion Faulkner might well have been able to soldier on. I

personally would have been able to live with it, holding no brief for the men of violence on either side. It would probably have forced the SDLP back into Stormont in due course, particularly if it had been accompanied by a continuation of Faulkner's conciliatory political programme. I regard the one-sided introduction of internment in retrospect as the most serious political miscalculation of the Troubles. I could feel the hook digging deeper and deeper into my back that morning as I considered the implications. There was no way back to Stormont now and the ground for our withdrawal shifted quickly from the comparatively lame issue of Cusack and Beattie's shooting to internment itself. Whatever about the rest of them changing their minds, which was unlikely, there was no way Paddy Devlin ever would, having been interned himself. For the next few years the cry of 'What about the internees?' was to haunt both my waking and sleeping hours.

As ever, even the gravest of situations was not without humour. In the midst of the turmoil an irate constituent called to Fitt's house. Her neighbour's door had been kicked in by the troops at 4.30am in the search for a suspect who was subsequently carted off to Girdwood. As the soldiers were leaving, they heard the sound of a radio tuned into their network: 'Come in Charlie Two. Come in Charlie Two.'

'Where is the radio, then?' said the soldier turning on her menacingly.

'What radio?' said the constituent. 'There's no radio here,' she said truthfully.

The soldiers refused to accept her assurance and set about a search – furniture was moved and examined, cushions were probed, beds were upended. In the middle of all this, the constituent suddenly realised that the noise they had heard was probably her parrot, who had become so used to listening to the police radio that he sometimes repeated what he had heard. Naturally, the parrot would not oblige when most required to, so the sceptical troops continued their rummaging. Eventually they concluded there was no radio present, and made to leave for the second time, having made a fair shambles of her house. Suddenly, the parrot squawked into life: 'Uniform to Echo Delta. Uniform to Echo Delta.' She did not see the funny side of it, understandably enough, and wanted Fitt to make a complaint about the damage the soldiers had caused to her property.

A week or so after the introduction of internment, Fitt was sitting quietly at home on his own, listening to a radio news bulletin from Dublin, when he heard that the British government was sending Geoffrey Johnston-Smith, a highly accomplished British television interviewer turned politician, to explain their side of the story in the USA. On the spur of the moment, he decided to fly out and counter his propaganda. By now there were authoritative indications from impeccable legal and clerical sources that not only had the internment operation been one-sided but had been conducted with a degree of brutality and ill-treatment that exceeded all civilised limits.

Fitt departed from Dublin Airport on 24 August and visited New York,

Boston, Chicago and Washington, spoke on eighteen radio stations and appeared on the influential, coast-to-coast NBC *Today* show. In New York, the Irish ambassador arranged for him to meet U Thant, the secretary-general of the United Nations. Although he listened politely to Fitt's submission that the documented excesses of British soldiers contravened international human rights standards, Fitt formed the clear impression that, as far as the UN was concerned, Northern Ireland was, and always would be, merely a troublesome minor blemish on the tapestry of international affairs. Whatever the anguish Fitt portrayed about the situation at home, it was as nothing compared to his personal discomfort throughout the visit. On the outward flight, he was assigned a window seat beside a priest whose enthusiasm for Bernadette Devlin, which Fitt did not share, was articulated at some length:

> To make matters worse, he was wearing a pioneer pin, the symbol of total abstinence from alcohol, on his well-cut lapel so, in a bid to find a more congenial seat and have a few drinks in peace, I excused myself. However, as I was climbing over him to reach the aisle I felt a searing pain shoot through my back. By the time I reached New York I was in great pain, unable to sit down and scarcely able to walk. Most of my appointments I fulfilled with difficulty. One Italian-American driver in New York offered me an unusual solution as he took me to a radio studio. Having hailed his taxi with some difficulty and explained I could only travel by winding down the window and lying back on the seat with my foot out, he insisted on opening the sun roof so that I could travel standing up. When I got back home I was in a sorry state. The painkillers I had been given for my slipped disc upset my duodenal ulcer and so I was rushed into hospital in Dublin.

In his absence, the violence in the North had reached critical levels and Heath and his government were shocked by the bloody avalanche that had been unleashed. Far from reducing the level of violence, as was intended, internment had provoked the most concentrated spate of killing, even by the bloody standards set since 1969. Thirty people died between January and 8 August, the eve of the swoops. The same number died between 9 and 31 August. By the year's end, 113 in total lost their lives in the post-internment violence. As the number of shootings and bombings reached new highs, it became abundantly clear that internment had been an epic miscalculation and had failed in its prime objective to crush the IRA. The need for a radical and urgent political initiative had never been more urgent, but Fitt was more exasperated than ever because the SDLP was caught on the internment hook and he had to toe the party line that there could be no talks until the last internee was released.

So, far from enjoying the period of rest and relaxation in hospital prescribed for him, Fitt played host to the Irish Prime Minister, opposition leaders, officials and SDLP colleagues, who were practically queuing up to see him at times.

Among his most important visitors was the British ambassador, Sir John Peck who carried a note from Maudling containing a remarkable carrot: the British government was prepared to seek a solution that would give the SDLP a full, permanent and guaranteed place in any governmental structures created in Northern Ireland. Maudling had first made the offer in a thirty-minute telephone call to Fitt, urging him to get the SDLP involved in round-table talks with the other Northern Ireland parties at once. Fitt recalled, 'My overwhelming private instinct was to find a way of getting movement, and John Hume and Austin Currie sympathised at first, but the depth of alienation among the Catholic community was so strong that I realised it would be suicidal to try anything at that precise time.' The SDLP was impaled firmly on what Fitt called 'the internment hook' but his own view was significantly less inflexible than that of his colleagues, or the majority of his co-religionists:

> My own view of internment was a mixed one. I certainly deplored the British Army's excesses and the torture but I knew that many of those interned were dangerous individuals. Many of my constituents knew that too. 'Thanks be to God we can sleep in our beds at night,' said one woman. 'They've got most of them out of the way.' And there were plenty of vivid reminders that despite the injustice of internment sympathy for the Provisional IRA was misplaced. Their recklessness and callousness were amply demonstrated by two particular incidents. A woman who was very badly injured in a explosion turned out to be the mother of the leader of the New Lodge Provos, who had organised the bombing attack so indiscriminately he could well have killed her. But the most harrowing of all my memories is the photograph I saw in early September of a man carrying in his arms the little white coffin of his 17 month old daughter, Angela Gallagher, who was shot dead outside her home in my constituency as IRA gunmen fired on soldiers. The president of Provisional Sinn Féin, Ruairi Ó Bradaigh, one of the armchair generals who directed the destruction in the North from the safety of the South, said that the death was 'one of the hazards or urban guerrilla warfare'. I attacked the unreality of the Provisionals in a statement from my hospital bed on 15 September. That they can ignore the political opposition to a united Ireland on the part of one million fellow Irishmen must be beyond the comprehension of all sane minds.

The other members of the SDLP had been far from inactive while Fitt was laid low. They had been tearing around the countryside, promoting their alternative forum, the Assembly of the Northern Irish people. John Hume was elected president and they arranged to have their first meeting in Derry on 5 October, the anniversary of the civil rights march, reflecting what was to become an obsession with symbolic dates. But behind the scenes the first hairline crack had become visible in the practical consensus that had led to the formation of the SDLP and survived its first turbulent year. In line with the general boycott initiated by

Catholics in protest at internment, some of his SDLP colleagues began pressuring Fitt to withdraw from the Westminster parliament when it resumed after the summer recess. Ever the pragmatist, Fitt believed politicians should never back themselves into absolute positions, so he resisted the pressure and, strapped up in a surgical corset, he travelled to Westminster on 22 September when parliament was recalled to debate the situation in Northern Ireland.

Fitt was strongly attracted to Maudling's proposition and used his time in London to advance the idea of putting the internees on trial as a means of clearing the way for negotiations. Heath and Maudling were not in favour, however, and his initiative collapsed. His sympathy with the Maudling overtures had nonetheless become so widely known that there was public speculation about a split in the party, and even some talk that he was planning to resign as leader. With the proposition in tatters, Fitt moved to kill the speculation by putting his position firmly on the record in an interview with the *Irish Independent*. He said there could be no discussions about the future unless and until the internees were either released or put on trial. The Maudling offer was a definite sign of a change in political thinking at Westminster, but it was not enough. He also felt it timely to point out to southern people that, much as they wanted to be involved in any political settlement, there would be a price to pay:

> When it comes time for the border to go, as it must, the government of the Republic, will have to make concessions to enable almost one million non-Catholics to live in peace on this island. A lot of people in the Republic believe that Protestants don't want to come into a united Ireland because they would not be able to read dirty books and use contraceptives. To judge it on that basis is to believe that northern Protestants are a crowd of sex maniacs, which is not the case at all. The Ulster Protestant will be a very strong force in a united Ireland.

After the damage his reputation had sustained as a result of internment, Brian Faulkner tried to retrieve the initiative by offering reform of the upper house of the Stormont parliament, an increase in the size of the Commons and a debate on the use of proportional representation for elections. The latter was potentially of benefit to the minority as the fact that they accounted for one in three of the population would be reflected more clearly in the outcome of future elections. During an hour-long speech in the London Commons, Fitt sounded an encouraging note:

> We must take steps to make quite certain a political solution will evolve that will prevent any other innocent person losing his life. There has to be a new system of government that will allow both majority and minority communities to participate at all levels of administration and this involvement should be written into the constitution. I recognise that you cannot shoot or bomb one million Protestants into the Republic of Ireland

tomorrow. What sort of Ireland would it be if the gunmen were successful in bringing about the abolition of the border overnight? The humiliation and coercion we have suffered for fifty years would be transferred to another section of the population and I would not want that.

Fitt was aware his words were falling on fertile ground because in corridor talk with many members of the House, including some on the government front bench, he had been told that Heath had taken the strands of the Northern Irish conflict very firmly in hand. After the debate the House was adjourned and most members set off to resume their interrupted holidays. Fitt was on his way to ring Ann when he collapsed with severe back pain. Jimmy Johnston, the Labour MP, drove him to Westminster hospital, where he was to spend the next month:

> My political lifeline was the coinbox telephone at the side of my hospital bed and every morning I had the logistical problem of getting somebody to obtain £5 worth of small change for me. Another problem I had concerned my supply of cigarettes. At that time I was an eighty-a-day man, smoking a brand known as Gallaher Blues, which were only available in Northern Ireland. I rang the Ulster Office in Mayfair, which acts as a shop window for industry, to see if they could help and, sure enough, within a few days a lifeline had been organised to supply me. But there was an odd little aside from this. When I phoned [Mayfair], by coincidence Brian Faulkner was there and he came on the line for a chat. Word leaked and I had to tell several journalists that although I had indeed been talking to him, it was not about politics but cigarettes.

That autumn the remaining members of the SDLP backed themselves further into a corner in relation to internment and established what Fitt regarded as 'the self-important irrelevancy' of an alternative assembly, which met a couple of times in Dungiven before fizzling out. More importantly, the British government fundamentally re-opened the 'Irish question' after some fifty years and began thinking how to solve it. A green paper was published in October – 'The future development of the parliament and government of Northern Ireland' – and Fitt found it stimulating because it recognised the weakness in the permanent majority – minority situation in Northern Ireland and discussed ways in which the demands and needs of the minority could be met. This was, of course, one of the primary sources of his own political dissatisfaction. Although Heath and Maudling were clearly forcing the pace, the document showed the radical pragmatism of which Faulkner was capable. He had already been involved in tripartite talks at Chequers with Heath and Jack Lynch, which were aimed at creating political movement, and although he maintained the traditional unionist hard-line, Fitt was sure he would yield ground come serious negotiations.

Fitt was still deeply troubled by the SDLP's unyielding position on internment, but he was also worried that calling for the release of the internees would be interpreted as condoning, if not supporting, the increasingly horrific crimes of the PIRA: 'From what I knew of the activities of certain people in my own constituency, I was afraid that opposition to internment might lead to the guilty going free with the innocent, or prevent the authorities locking up someone who was genuinely a danger to innocent citizens, although they did not have evidence to bring them to court.' In addition to the ongoing threats and intimidation from loyalist elements, Fitt and his family were also coming under pressure from constituents with Provo sympathies, who made forceful efforts to persuade him to lend enthusiastic public support to their activities. Fitt refused.

Against this growing unwillingness to co-operate, more than 200 delegates attended the SDLP's first annual conference at Dungiven on 23 October and heard Fitt, in his first conference speech as party leader, spell out the policy of the 'three Rs' as the cornerstone of the SDLP's beliefs: 'reform, reconciliation and re-unification'. He demanded reform within Northern Ireland, reconciliation between Catholic and Protestant and, in the long term, re-unification of Ireland by co-operation, not confrontation. He specifically asked for Protestant support for the SDLP as a socialist party, in the high hope that it might prove to be the instrument for the emergence of conventional, left-wing, non-sectarian politics. During the conference a motion to leave the negotiating door open was literally howled down, such was the strength of feeling about internment.

Fitt's abiding memory of that autumn, however, was the violence, one sickening atrocity after another, and ever more optimistic but premature statements from the army that the IRA was beaten. A Catholic UDR man was gunned down as he watched television with his children in his living room. The wife of a popular pub singer was shot dead by soldiers in a car in very controversial circumstances. There were also two spectacular IRA escapes from Belfast's Crumlin Road prison, one involving seven members of a football team, who went over the wall with makeshift ropes and grappling irons. Bombs were an almost hourly event and everyone became obsessed with radio news and the police radio as they listened for details of the latest trouble, of traffic disruption caused by bomb scares and of areas to avoid because of sniper fire. People were living on their nerves and the use of tranquillisers widely replaced the traditional cup of tea as a 'calmer'. Even when he was in London, Fitt was never out of touch with events for long: 'I would ring Ann, who would hold the phone by the radio so that I could hear the Northern Ireland news bulletins and keep up-to-date.'

Whenever he was in Belfast, the procession of people through the non-stop constituency surgery was greater than ever and a whole new range of problems were added to the traditional ones: many people who had been intimidated out of their homes faced problems of ownership and debt; others were squatting in vacant homes from desperation and needed security; those who had been injured in the violence needed advice about claiming compensation; the dependants of internees and internees themselves faced a variety of problems in relation to the retention of their jobs, hostility from workmates in mixed workplaces, entitlement to benefits to replace lost wages and other such complications. Most common of all were the early morning calls, which started about 5.00am, from the parents or wives of men lifted in the now routine dawn swoops or from the victims of the simultaneous, and none too gentle, army searches. Fitt was especially concerned about the conduct of soldiers, as it appeared the British Army behaved with routine excess towards anyone they encountered:

> Almost daily I had consistent and credible complaints about the behaviour of the soldiers. Now I was well aware of the tremendous provocation they had to face. After all they were mostly young working-class lads from the big British cities confused by the complexity of what they faced in Belfast where even Union-flag-waving mobs stoned and shot at them. But it has to be said that if the authorities abandon the concept of enforcing the law strictly within the law then the only result is the law of the jungle. That is why I could not condone the overwhelming evidence of casual and gratuitous army ill-treatment.

He came face to face with the unreasonable side of the soldiery one night early in December. It had been a routine Saturday, with the usual long queues of people in the hall and upstairs sitting room waiting to see him in the small room he used as a constituency office. Later, he went out to a meeting and when he got home late that evening settled down at the table to check his football pools. Suddenly there was a loud bang, which he recognised instantly as an explosion:

> I grabbed the telephone and within moments was told by the police that McGurk's, one of the local pubs in North Queen Street, had been blown up. I threw on my overcoat and rushed the few hundred yards from the house down to the pub. I will never forget the sight that met my eyes. The whole building was flattened into a pile of rubble. There was smoke coming from it, water pouring everywhere from broken pipes and shots of flame from the fractured gas pipes. The whole area was lit with an eerie blue from the flashing lights of the ambulances and fire engines that converged on the scene. A large crowd gathered and there was a mixture of hysteria and anger among them. I pushed my way to the front thinking of Patsy McGurk, the publican, the customers and his wife and daughter who went to the same school as my own children. I joined the people at the front who were helping firemen, soldiers and ambulance men to claw brick by brick through the rubble to find the victims. As I was digging, with my bare hands, I came across what I realised was the legs of a body. I let go as nausea threatened to overcome me. Then I felt a gun being pushed against me and I turned round to see a soldier. "Get the hell out of here," he said nastily. I explained I was the local MP trying to rescue my friends and constituents. "Move," he said even more aggressively, pushing the gun against me harder. I protested again. The gun pushed harder against my body. His tone

became more menacing. Some of the onlookers had noticed what was happening by now. A voice came out of the darkness. 'Stand back, Gerry. Stand back. Move out of the road.' I realised it was likely they would shoot him, so I reluctantly backed off in the hope that no further violence would take place.

By now the scene was bathed with floodlights and Fitt watched a sorry procession of stretchers, their contents concealed beneath grey blankets, being carried to the waiting ambulances and driven away. By dawn the full extent of the tragedy became clear: fifteen people were dead and eight were injured, while another seven, including policemen and soldiers, had been wounded in the gun battles that broke out between the angry, milling crowds that gathered after the explosion. On the Sunday morning, when he went back to the scene with Michael Sullivan and a BBC news crew to record an interview, he saw the same soldier who had been so aggressive towards him. He tipped off Sullivan and the soldier was filmed. The next day Fitt complained to the army and said the offending soldier was on camera. For once, he was not subjected to the usual stonewalling or outright denial of misconduct, and instead received an unusually contrite, handwritten letter from Lt. General Sir Harry Tuzo, the General Officer Commanding the British Army in Northern Ireland, which read:

> I feel that you are the best person to write to in these tragic circumstances. The army cannot expect to be other than unpopular in present conditions but it is, let me assure you, granted its full share of human emotions. Last night's outrage had attracted the deep sympathy of every one of us. Whether we shall ever discover where the true responsibility lies I do not know; but this is of small account beside the horrifying lessons of an outrage like this. If you can find some way of telling relatives and friends that we feel for them deeply, I would be most grateful.

When he read the letter, Fitt considered the contrast in attitude between the General and his soldier. Later in the week the General wrote again, saying he was angry to hear of the boorish behaviour of the soldier, which was 'totally inexcusable. You may rest assured that very firm action is being taken against the soldier concerned, who has been identified and who has admitted that what you say is entirely true.' The McGurk explosion became one of the great controversies of the Troubles. In his television interviews the next day Fitt had no hesitation in laying the blame on loyalists as it was a Catholic-owned and frequented pub, serving a Catholic area. The most probable motive seemed to be sectarian.

Then, a day or so later, a very senior police officer asked to see Fitt, told him the loyalist theory was 'cock and bull' and discounted the anonymous telephone call to a news organisation claiming that the previously unheard of 'League of Empire Loyalists' had carried out the attack. Instead, he claimed the bomb had been taken inside the building by an IRA man with the intention of it being picked up by a colleague, who was supposed to use it to bomb the Midland Hotel beside the York Street railway station. The device had been primed, and it exploded because the second man was late to collect it. Shortly afterwards this same version of events was embellished further by the same police officer, who told Fitt that a young man whose body was found in a street in the Markets area of Belfast a few days later had been court-martialled and executed by the IRA for failing to collect the bomb, thus causing the tragedy. This version was strengthened by subsequent official leaks that bomb and forensic experts had concluded from examination of the scene that the bomb had gone off inside the building, not at the door. This explanation was generally accepted for years, but it turned out to be officially inspired disinformation. In 1978 the truth was finally established when Robert Campbell, a UVF member, was given sixteen life sentences by Sir Robert Lowry, Lord Chief Justice of Northern Ireland, for his part in the sectarian outrage.

As 1971 was drawing to a close, and despite incontrovertible evidence that it had failed in its aim, Brian Faulkner, with the support of Heath and Maudling, was still refusing to budge on internment. The SDLP clung equally resolutely to its position, even after Faulkner and his ministers offered an increase in the size of the Stormont commons from 50 to 75 seats, which would be filled by elections run on proportional representation to guarantee more minority representation. Fitt, whose doubts about the SDLP's stand had not diminished, countered with a suggestion that the British government should take back the law and order powers originally devolved in 1921, which he judged could be presented to Catholics as presaging a more impartial security regime. As a sign of this, there could then be an independent review of the cases of all those interned. Although his colleagues were far from enthusiastic, the idea was stillborn. Fitt believed that both the London and Stormont administrations underestimated the strength of Catholic feeling regarding the unfairness of internment, interpreting it as intimidation by the IRA, or indeed fear of the IRA on the part of the SDLP. The army did not help matters by insisting the IRA was on the verge of being beaten decisively. London was also distracted at this time by their impending entry into the European Common Market, which was foremost on the agenda. Brian Faulkner was obviously feeling very secure in his position: he easily beat off a challenge from his right-wingers and followed up with a call for the SDLP to talk unconditionally as there would be no political change in the status of Northern Ireland 'as far as the political eye could see'.

By Christmas 1971 the people of Belfast were living under a self-imposed curfew. Buses, pubs, cinemas, all shut up early. The lights on the Christmas tree outside City Hall seemed entirely inappropriate given what many families had suffered during the preceding months, and underneath it was a tableau of nursery rhyme characters rather than a manger scene. It appeared that the nativity was too controversial for a city that was a battleground between Christians who exhibited little Christianity. Although the guns and the bombs stayed silent on Christmas and Boxing days, as Fitt sat down for Christmas lunch with his family he could not help thinking of the 211 people who had died since 1969 and the empty places they had left at family tables throughout Northern Ireland and Britain. His sense of gloom deepened on 2 January when he saw Austin Currie on television, taking part in an anti-internment rally in West Belfast. Dealing what seemed to be a knock-out blow to his hopes of moderating the SDLP's preconditions for talks, Fitt winced when Currie said the SDLP would not be doing any talking until the very last internee was released. On the telephone to his close friend, he complained that he had impaled them even more firmly on the internment hook. Currie explained that he had been saying 'no talks until internment ends' when a woman in the front row shouted, 'not till the last man is out' and the crowd cheered. Currie said he had agreed with her on the spur of the moment. 'Thinking back on some of my own impetuous oratorical excesses over the years,' said Fitt, 'there was little I could complain about.'

At the end of January 1972 Fitt was faced with yet another potential conflict between the SDLP abstentionist line and his own position. The rule was that any elected member of a council who failed to attend for a six-month period was disqualified, his seat was declared vacant and a by-election was called. By this regulation, if Fitt failed to attend at least one committee meeting at City Hall before the end of the month, he would be expelled. Paddy Kennedy had already been disqualified and other Catholic councillors throughout Northern Ireland would soon follow. Fitt discussed with Paddy Wilson the possibility and implications of making a swift appearance, just to get his presence recorded:

> In the end, charged by the memory of the hungry days, the hard days and all the heartbreak that I had known in driving the Unionist representatives from Dock area, I could not stomach letting them in again, most of all by default. So we went into the City Hall one morning, signed on at two committee meetings and walked out again, much to the chagrin of the Unionists, who had already their eyes on our seats. There was little reaction and some SDLP members even told us we had done the right thing. At any rate we had protected our seats from the Unionists for another six months.

During the month the Provos – who had hijacked the remnants of the civil rights movement – announced a civil rights march on 30 January in Derry in defiance of the ban on marches and parades announced earlier by the Faulkner government. The SDLP was unsure how to react, so a meeting was called in the Belfast headquarters for 28 January. The discussion revolved around whether all, or even one of them, would attend the march in defiance of the ban, and the possibility of arrest and imprisonment was considered. Fitt's martyrdom was quickly ruled out because he was still encumbered in a surgical corset and, more

Fitt's Merchant Navy record with false birth date (National Archives)

Gerry and Ann after their wedding in 1947

Left: Gerry Fitt and Harry Diamond

Above: Campaigning in Dock

Below: Fitt is served with summonses for public order offences in 1968; Paddy Wilson looks on

Opposite: Fitt and supporters

With the 'Miss Fitts

With Joan

With Mary Ann Fi

Fitt and Ann leaving their polling station in Belfast

The five founders of the SDLP after Paddy Devlin's funeral in 1999.
Left to right: Fitt, Hume, O'Hanlon, Currie, Cooper

Hume, Fitt, Currie and Devlin explaining SDLP policy

Fitt on the terrace at Westminster

Confronting his critics

*Meeting Pope
John Paul II*

*At the funeral
of Mary Ann
Fitt*

importantly, because it was more valuable for him to be available to raise ructions at Westminster about any arrests. During the course of that meeting, Fitt scribbled snatches of crude doggerel:

> The members sat down,
> they all wore a frown
> to consider if marches were lawful,
> but Gerry turned pale,
> when the talk turn to jail
> says he, my back's effing awful.

Hume was reluctant to go to the march or to support it in any way and conveyed the clear impression to Fitt that the Provos had taken it over and he was concerned they were going to use guns. Certainly, the Provos in the city had powerful weapons. Only the previous Tuesday a machine gun had been used to murder two policemen. Weighing up the likelihood of further violence, it was eventually decided none of the key SDLP figures would attend although, in the event, Ivan Cooper did so. The question of whether or not there would be gunfire assumed a far greater significance than any of them could possibly have realised that monotonous Friday afternoon in Belfast.

Fitt was at home in Belfast late on the Sunday afternoon of 30 January 1972, when devastating news began to come in, first by phone, then in the radio news. The first death count he heard was four, but then the casualty count climbed steadily to thirteen. Later that evening John Hume said the events in Derry were 'our Sharpeville. Now it is a united Ireland or nothing.' The day was promptly dubbed 'Bloody Sunday', and the question of whether or not the IRA opened fire before soldiers of the Parachute Regiment shot dead thirteen of the marchers became a matter of enduring controversy. Fitt took the view that even if the IRA had opened fire first, which was far from certain, it would not have provided justification for the indiscriminate over-reaction by the soldiers. The next morning he met Bernadette Devlin at Belfast Airport and, unusually, they travelled together all the way to Westminster. Although Fitt was well aware of her anger about what had occurred, he was shocked at the manner in which she acted:

> I watched as she took a seat in the chamber, below the gangway in a place
> normally occupied by Jeremy Thorpe. Her own regular seat in the middle
> of a backbench would not have afforded such easy access across the floor of
> the house to the government front bench. Thorpe came in, but he was too
> much of a gentleman to ask her to move so he repositioned himself. When
> the business of the day began and Maudling was making a statement about
> the shootings, Devlin flew at him, pulling his hair until she was restrained
> by two members and escorted from the house by Bob Mellish, the Labour
> Chief Whip.

That evening, back in the Irish Club, Fitt watched the reports on television of the widespread burning and rioting in Belfast and Derry and heard of the crowds massing at the British Embassy in Dublin, who eventually burned down the building. The Irish ambassador was recalled to Dublin from London and the Lynch government called for an end to harassment of the minority, for the troops to be pulled out and talks to resolve the Irish problem. Even Irish people who had lived in England for years were angry. The next day at the funerals in Derry, gazing along the line of coffins, Fitt could still barely take in the enormity of what had happened: 'I knew that the final alienation from Stormont and unionist dominance had been reached.'

The protests reverberated worldwide, so there was unprecedented international attention on a march in Newry the following Sunday. At first there was much sabre-rattling from the British side about stopping the march, but in the end it went ahead, with thousands of people marching in dignified silence as a telling protest against what had taken place and the failed political system that had allowed it to happen. Nevertheless, the authorities went ahead and prosecuted twenty-six people who had taken part in the march, including nine MPs. When his case came to court in Newry on 26 April, Fitt was given the mandatory sentence of six months' imprisonment, although it was suspended after he pleaded guilty to breaking the ban on marching.

Predictably, the terrible events in Derry provoked yet more violence. There was a reprisal attack within days when five kitchen workers and a Catholic padre died in a bomb at the Parachute Regiment's headquarters at Aldershot. Later, John Taylor, the hardline Home Affairs junior minister, was gravely wounded in an assassination attempt, but survived. Fitt's confidantes in London informed him that Heath was now firmly in personal command of the situation and wanted to the SDLP to talk to him without pre-conditions. Apart from the standing resentment over internment, Fitt said that, given the upsurge of nationalist feeling, he could not even suggest the idea to his party. The IRA kept the pressure up with a no-warning bomb in a Belfast restaurant, the Abercorn, at the height of the shopping rush one Saturday afternoon, killing two people and injuring 130 more. During the same period, six more died in Donegall Street and more than 100 were hurt when another bomb exploded without warning. Another night a bomb exploded outside The Dunowen in Dungannon, a restaurant where Fitt and his colleagues were enjoying a meal after one of their regular meetings in the venue. Adding cynicism to their callousness, the Provos then called a seventy-two-hour truce in March.

Around the same time Billy Napier's seat on the council came up for grabs at a by-election as he had resigned following the introduction of internment. Again not wanting to surrender the seat to the Unionists, Fitt and Paddy Wilson tried unsuccessfully to persuade several people to fight the election, but the Provos had put the word about that they would attack any candidate and the polling stations.

Fitt approached the authorities at Westminster to ask whether, in these violent circumstances, the election could be postponed. 'Somebody might get killed,' he told them. But it was decided that democracy must take its course. 'So I walked around for days with a set of nomination papers in my pocket, fully filled in, except for the most important entry, the name of the candidate.' On the morning of nomination day, when he was in City Hall, Fitt lost his self-control when he discovered the Unionists were going to decide, on the toss of a coin, which of them would get the seat, so confident were they that there would be no contest. 'On the spur of the moment, I went to the Members' Room, filled in my wife Ann as the candidate, and lodged the completed papers, with the deposit, at one minute to the deadline. Then I rang her. I got a candidate at the last minute,' he said.

'Oh, that's great, love,' she said.

'And it's a woman, too,' he replied.

'Oh, that's even better. We've never had a woman fight an election before. Who is it?' she asked.

'Susan Gertrude Fitt,' he said, holding his breath.

It was a measure of her equanimity that, despite the Provo threat, Ann Fitt did not object. 'We'll fight it together,' she said and, within days, according to her husband,

> she was campaigning like a veteran. Most of the people in Dock knew her already for, when I was away from home, she always managed to sort out their most pressing problems with her great streak of common sense or deft use of the telephone. Her manifesto, which she insisted on writing herself, was so well done, I did not have to change a word. It said: "When I am elected I will not be attending the City Hall, but I will be preventing a bigoted unionist from doing so in your name." On 8 March she won the seat convincingly, trouncing the Unionist by a margin of ten to one. The victory was hailed within the SDLP after initial reservations about fighting the seat and the Provos stayed well away.

Towards the end of March 1972 Heath called Brian Faulkner to London to advise him of his plans and proposed a package that included transferring security powers back to London from Belfast, as Fitt had earlier suggested. Mindful of the gathering forces of Protestant rebellion, Faulkner decided it was a step too far and, after consulting his Cabinet, returned to Heath warning they would all resign if the proposal were implemented. Heath called his bluff – very courageously in Fitt's view – and announced the indefinite prorogation of Stormont. Northern Ireland was to be ruled directly from Westminster.

The end of Stormont was a major watershed in Irish history. In the Irish Club there was euphoria that night as everyone drank in celebration. About 2.30am Fitt was called to take a telephone call from a very emotional Belfastman, who had helped found the PIRA, and was on the line from Dublin. 'What do you think we should do now?' he asked. 'Tell any IRA men you know to pack up their guns and bombs and go away,' Fitt said emphatically. In the IRA's interpretation of events, however, the British were on the run and one more push would get them out of Ireland altogether. It was as rash a miscalculation as it was ill-informed, and would lead to further misery but Fitt was relieved when the extremists on the unionist side reacted much more peacefully than he had feared. To Catholics, Stormont was a symbol of repression, discrimination and privilege, but to Protestants it was the bulwark of defence against a united Ireland, and now it was gone. But the worst reaction was a two-day general strike and the interruption of electricity power supplies. A large number of the strikers gathered at the front of Stormont to listen to belligerent speeches, but that was as far as their immediate reaction went.

Once Stormont was gone, William Whitelaw, then leader of the Commons, was appointed the minister responsible for running Northern Ireland. Fitt already knew him slightly, regarded him as a man with acutely sensitive political instincts and welcomed his appointment. 'With his help,' he told the Commons in London, 'I hope we can soon eliminate from the political vocabulary in Northern Ireland the words "majority" and "minority" and act fully in concert for all the people of Northern Ireland.' When accepting the appointment, Whitelaw had become quite emotional at the despatch box, and afterwards he talked informally with Fitt in the lobby:

> I told him that internment was the main obstacle to making progress with the Catholic community now that Stormont was gone. I said that every internee released would help to de-escalate the tension and would be seen as a positive gesture. I also made representations about a senior civil servant at Stormont, who had been an adviser to Brian Faulkner. His removal, I intimated, would show that things had really changed for the better.

A few days later Fitt received a message from Hillsborough – where Whitelaw had set up temporary headquarters in the governor's residence – advising that this mission had been accomplished. 'Later I heard the civil servant had been transferred. It was, in my judgement, a good start,' said Fitt. The release of seventy-three internees soon thereafter was an even more important gesture, one Fitt used as justification to resurrect his efforts to get the SDLP into the business of talking and seeking reconciliation. On 5 April he publicly urged an end to all violence because that was the overwhelming demand of the people in his constituency and other areas, Catholic and Protestant, who were in touch with him daily. All of these people, he said, wanted the Westminster initiative to be given a decent chance.

Ever since the Troubles had begun, the successive political crises had been played out in and around Stormont under the gaze of television cameras, but now the focus shifted to a closely guarded, secret location that was to play a pivotal role in the British governance of Northern Ireland over the next five or six years. Some time previously the British government had acquired a large, secluded detached, villa at Craigavad, near Belfast, called Laneside. It was a 6,500 square foot house with five bedrooms and extensive conversion work was carried out to make it fit for purpose, including the construction of a blast-proof 'panic room' where the occupants could take refuge in the event of a terrorist attack. At first it served as the office of the Whitehall liaison man with the Stormont government, but under Whitelaw, and later Merlyn Rees, it became the venue for secret talks with a wide range of Northern Ireland opinion. In diplomatic parlance, this was a 'listening post', and after direct rule its lavish cocktail parties and dinners soon became legendary among those in public and official life. Although any excuse, such as a birthday, or the arrival or farewell of staff, was used to host a party, they were not entirely frivolous occasions. The guest lists were drawn up meticulously to throw together people who were officially not speaking to one other, or for civil servants to sound out a range of opinions. When the invitees arrived at Laneside the military guards took the licensed firearms from those who 'carried', as it was put, and they were entertained in a large, comfortable sitting room, soundproofed to prevent eavesdropping and complete with bullet-proof windows. The small talk of the politicians and influential opinion-formers from many walks of life was memorised skilfully and the guests subtly interrogated by the civil servants. Afterwards, the proceedings were analysed avidly for what information and advice Whitelaw should be given about the way in which to proceed.

The SDLP was drawn into this clandestine web soon after the introduction of direct rule and for the first few months of Whitelaw's administration, while they were officially refusing to participate in talks, they met civil servants secretly at Laneside on a regular basis. On occasion they were invited to functions individually, but more often they came as a group. 'Some of us were wary of being dubbed traitors for trying to get round the internment issue, but we all recognised the importance of asserting political processes so we went to the talks and kept quiet about them,' said Fitt. The meetings frequently became heated when they protested about the behaviour of the troops, or allegations of partisan behaviour. At other times there was a good deal of thinking aloud by both sides and the SDLP would sometimes retreat to another room to consider some point among themselves before returning to continue a discussion.

The meetings often lasted an entire day and a buffet lunch would be laid on, then in the afternoon or evening they would be offered drinks. Despite the antagonisms, obfuscation and pipe-dreaming that often took place during these sessions with the civil servants, they covered much positive ground which, in retrospect, Fitt believed helped to lay sturdy foundations for the political moves Whitelaw later sponsored. The occasions did not always go according to plan, however. Once, early in 1972, the delegation turned up before lunch, as planned, ready to dine and then spend an afternoon in discussion with Whitelaw. Due to bad weather and a technical hitch with his aircraft, it was 6.00pm before Heath eventually reached Laneside. By then, having been plied generously with refreshments while they waited, the members of the SDLP team who had stayed on were in no fit state for serious talking. Some were arguing among themselves, Fitt was asleep on a sofa and Whitelaw, who had sunk a few himself to while away the journey, promptly suggested they adjourn until the following morning.

Three months into this exploratory process, Fitt decided to signal that while there was, as yet, no compromise on internment, the SDLP's political vision was evolving steadily. He explained their position fully in a major interview with the *Belfast Telegraph* at the end of May:

> The Provisional IRA can only use violence. I don't believe they have any political thinkers within their ranks. They can only say: 'If you do not agree with us, we will bomb you, we will kill you, we will murder you.' They have deliberately escalated the bombing campaign. We know that in face of all attempts we have made to bring internment to an end that there are still violent men in Northern Ireland, particularly within the ranks of the Provisional IRA, who are desperately trying to maintain internment, who would be lost but for the fact that internment continues. We are opposed to the men of violence and will fight them at each and every opportunity that is given to us.

The interview – interrupted by the sound of the third explosion that particular day – was a conscious effort to shift the ground away from internment alone and onto the new territory being ploughed in the talks with the British civil servants. It was also marking the revulsion people felt at the continuation of the violence and its increasing death toll. Individual acts of violence stand out because of their unique horror, or because they represent another sickening twist in the spiral, but virtually every day, in a shooting or an explosion, somebody lost their life.

The Irish government was deeply perturbed at the turn of events and was apparently unaware that the SDLP was engaged in informal dialogue with British officials, who, quite properly, did not enlighten them when the SDLP had chosen not to do so. On the afternoon of 7 June, Dr Paddy Hillery, the Irish Foreign Minister, told Peck, the British ambassador in Dublin, that he thought 'the time had come when the SDLP should be induced to get off their high horse about internment and get down to talks, if not with Whitelaw, at least with his officials.' Hillery went on to say the Dublin government had no form of control over the SDLP – Paddy Devlin, for example, detested Jack Lynch – but if they could usefully bring any pressure on John Hume and the others, they would readily do so.

The offer was discussed in London the next day between Lord Windlesham, one of Whitelaw's ministers, and Kelvin White, the head of the Republic of Ireland desk at the Foreign Office. They identified the issues of violence and civil disobedience as those for which progress would have the most impact on Protestant views. In respect of violence, they accepted the SDLP was publicly opposed to it but could not do anything more to halt it. They were keen, however, that the party should make a straight call for the end to the withholding of rent and rates by their supporters, and disappointed that the recent releases of internees had not persuaded them to do so. This was the matter on which they hoped Dublin might be able to help and the method was spelled out in instructions telexed to the Dublin Embassy on 8 June:

> We doubt whether direct pressure by the Irish government would be useful. It would, rather, be a matter of seeking to bring the SDLP along by creating the right climate of thought in the course of the discussions which members of the Irish government have with them from time to time. Those with whom the Irish government have most contact are those who take the most forward looking attitude towards these questions. What they need is a little more courage in dealing with their less enlightened colleagues and in leading public opinion rather than following it.

Fitt remembers this as a very depressing spell but an encouraging sign that the Provisionals might be prepared to consider a ceasefire came on 13 June 1972 when the IRA leader Sean MacStiofain held a press conference behind the barricades in so-called 'Free Derry'. He offered Whitelaw 'safe conduct' to meet them there and hold talks. Behind the arrogance of the Provisionals' offer, Fitt discerned the outline of a potentially deliverable peace plan. MacStiofain demanded the withdrawal of troops from nationalist areas, an amnesty and release for all internees and prisoners and a declaration granting the Irish people, north and south, the right to decide their own future.

Unknown to Fitt and the SDLP, in January 1972 the Provos had already sent private signals of their readiness to engage in some sort of peace process by participating in talks with a small cadre of academics, one of whom was General (Retd) Sir John Hackett, a distinguished soldier who had since joined the academic staff at Kings College, London. Another was Nottingham University research fellow Richard Hauser, an Austrian Jew whom the British Foreign Office described as 'an international do-gooder'. Towards the end of January 1972, Hackett wrote to Sir John Peck, the British ambassador in Dublin, confiding that he was to meet the Fianna Fáil politician Charles Haughey and Ruairi Ó Bradaigh of the Provisional movement during an imminent visit to Dublin and seeking a meeting with the diplomat because he 'might possibly learn something of interest'. Sir John Peck thought 'the phrasing of the letter was a little unhappy', feared the succession of visits was bound to attract press attention and be exaggerated out of all proportion and therefore asked the Foreign Office in London to contact General Hackett and put him off.

The old soldier was not for turning, however and argued that people were interested to learn about IRA thinking. He also dismissed fears that he might create the impression he was sent from Westminster to negotiate. A few days later, after the meeting had taken place, at which Joe Cahill, a senior IRA figure, was also present, Hauser, who had accompanied Hackett and listened while he did most of the talking, contacted the Foreign Office and insisted he come and tell them what had been said. Ó Bradaigh and Cahill, he estimated, were both 'absolutely honest and straightforward'. They said they had avoided armed action in the Republic so as not to antagonise Jack Lynch, whom they hated, and that the IRA was in good shape – unlike the British Army. As evidence for this, they quoted a newspaper interview with a squaddie who wanted 'a return ticket to Leicester' from his posting in Northern Ireland. Hauser said Hackett put them right on army morale but that he was far from clear as to what the IRA's political demands actually amounted to. There was talk of a British Army withdrawal and the creation of a nine-county Ulster Provincial Parliament, but nothing concrete on which to base peace talks. The Foreign Office was distinctly unimpressed by the account, especially when it became clear that it did not concur with the debriefing provided to the Ministry of Defence by Hackett himself. They concluded that all the episode revealed was the IRA's desire to talk with someone at Westminster.

One day in June 1972 Fitt was on the terrace at Westminster when another MP, Maurice Foley, came to tell him news was coming over the tapes about McStiofain's latest remarks in Derry. He immediately telephoned Paddy Devlin and John Hume and all three agreed there was nothing new in the Provos' points as stated, but felt the pressure for peace was getting to them and they should therefore be kept on the hook. 'Although Whitelaw had publicly rejected the proposals as an "ultimatum from terrorists", he took our point when I saw him later that day in London.'

In Belfast, the party issued a statement calling on the Provos to call a forty-eight-hour ceasefire to back up their offer, and Devlin and Hume requested a meeting with Whitelaw. Fitt had already arranged this, and briefed Whitelaw that Devlin and Hume had made contact with the Provos and were trying to mediate on a set of arrangements that would lead to the campaign of violence being stopped. Over the next twenty-four hours, Fitt met Whitelaw a number of times in the tea room and on the terrace in the Commons. One of his worries was how to handle Devlin, whose volatility was well known among British politicians after his verbal attack on Maudling. Fitt warned Whitelaw that Devlin was no respecter of protocol and would undoubtedly be very outspoken.

Meanwhile, officials in London and Dublin were involved in unpublicised exchanges to try to foster the most helpful political environment possible. After Whitelaw stated in the House of Commons that it was important for everyone to understand that the British government was not seeking to impose anything in

Northern Ireland, Dublin provided the Embassy there with an advance text of a speech to be delivered on 16 June by the Irish Prime Minister. In the light of Whitelaw's remark, Lynch indicated his speech about 'the new Irish society' would be toned down to echo Whitelaw by pledging that the majority in the South had no desire to impose anything on anyone either. Lynch also indicated that he would deliberately not use the emotive word 'reunification'.

The immediate and most pressing obstacle to achieving progress was an ongoing hunger strike by IRA prisoners at Belfast prison. One or two of them were considerably weakened as they had been refusing food for about four or five weeks, and the IRA propaganda machine was whipping up fears about their survival and demanding that the eighty republican and forty loyalist prisoners should enjoy political status. They resented being classed as common criminals and being forced to share cells with the thieves, burglars, rapists and robbers that made up the prison population. Fitt urged Whitelaw to respond positively and said that would do much to lower tension, it would be an even-handed gesture and, if it stopped the violence, it would save lives. Fitt was extremely anxious to trap the Provisionals into some form of political dialogue that would free the SDLP from the internment hook once and for all.

Devlin and Hume met Whitelaw on the afternoon of Thursday, 15 June. A short time earlier he had announced in the Commons that elections for the reformed local councils would take place in the autumn using proportional representation. It was a concession to one of the SDLP's major demands, created the right atmosphere for the meeting and enabled real progress to be made. Later, as Hume and Devlin spoke to journalists, Fitt had a quiet word with Whitelaw, who was also very pleased that dialogue with the SDLP had at last begun. Despite their fundamental differences with republicans regarding methods – politics as opposed to violence – the two SDLP negotiators had urged Whitelaw to personally meet representatives of the IRA. At that point he was not prepared to do so or negotiate with them, but he authorised Devlin and Hume to go to the IRA and explain his position in relation to the two matters with which they were most concerned. Apart from the prison issue, they wanted an assurance that, in the event they called a ceasefire, the army and police would not take advantage of it by rounding up people they had not been able to apprehend previously.

Armed with this understanding, the SDLP trio travelled to Dublin later that evening and over the weekend Devlin and Hume had contact with the Provos prior to another meeting with Whitelaw in Belfast on Monday. Although they did talk with their friends in the Irish Labour party, they did not 'condescend', as Lynch later put it with some annoyance, to keep the Irish government informed of the proceedings. However, Hume did ring to advise him that important developments were imminent and that it was therefore important for IRA leader David O'Connell to be allowed slip through the arms dragnet being enforced by the Gardaí in Donegal. Lynch agreed and issued appropriate instructions to them through Des O'Malley, then Minister of Justice.

The Dublin Embassy, as instructed by London, provided Lynch with a more detailed briefing as to what was taking place. Whitelaw was prepared to give an assurance that there would be no post-ceasefire 'lift' unless people committed criminal offences and said that, while stopping short of creating a category of 'political prisoner' – a proposal to which Dublin was vigorously opposed – he was prepared to look sympathetically at easements of the prison rules. Lynch replied that in such 'rapidly changing situations we must hold by our principles and allow a little elasticity in applying them'.

Over the weekend, Whitelaw had already made one concession to the Provos by releasing from internment, at their request, a young activist called Gerry Adams so that he could participate in the IRA's internal deliberations. He also issued Devlin with a personally signed, safe-passage note instructing any security patrols he encountered not to interfere with him or any of his passengers. Devlin did a fair bit of driving throughout Northern Ireland that weekend, with a carload of the most wanted men, while delicate understandings were articulated. After the Monday meeting in Belfast, and in a decision that Whitelaw and Fitt would later regret publicly, it was announced that republican and loyalist prisoners would be entitled to wear their own clothes instead of prison uniform, to receive extra visits and food parcels and to refuse prison work. But the arrangements were not fully implemented until after Devlin had a midnight slanging match over the telephone with one of Whitelaw's junior ministers about the delay in passing the details to the prison to get the hunger-striking prisoners to take nourishment again, especially Billy McKee, the lead hunger striker, whose deteriorating health was a cause of concern.

After more toing and froing between Belfast, Derry and Dublin, the Provisionals finally announced, on Thursday, 22 June, that a ceasefire would operate from midnight the following Monday if the 'armed forces of the British Crown' reciprocated. Whitelaw made a response in language of sufficient ambiguity to satisfy them, while at the same time not dignifying them with the status of democratic politicians. The imminent ceasefire triggered off an orgy of attacks and bombings to demonstrate the Provos' strength and there was also a spate of lucrative armed robberies before the ceasefire came into effect, as arranged, but not before two soldiers died, one in Belfast, the other in Derry, just minutes before the midnight deadline. Fitt saw these as particularly cynical acts of murder.

While Whitelaw's initiative, in which the SDLP had played a crucial role, had dramatically lowered the temperature within the Catholic community, it sent fears and tempers soaring on the majority Protestant side. Speaking in the USA, Faulkner deplored the 'tragic precedent' set by the IRA, which he said had shot its way into a negotiating position with the British government. Most sinister of all, however, had been the rise of the Ulster Defence Association (UDA), a Protestant militia, who in the past few weeks had begun to blockade their areas with barricades, replicating the IRA's 'no-go' areas. Fitt watched from a window in City Hall one Saturday morning as more than 20,000 UDA men, clad in army surplus uniforms and with their faces masked by scarves, balaclava helmets or sunglasses, marched unimpeded through the main streets of the city centre.

As part of his political tightrope-walking between the two sides in Ulster, Whitelaw had found it necessary to publicly receive the masked leaders of this 'army' at Stormont Castle, but in spite of this and the ebb of IRA violence, the militancy of the Protestants escalated. There were sectarian assassinations of innocent Catholics, further barricading operations designed to create 'no-go' areas and one night about 8,000 masked men confronted troops for five hours in West Belfast, while senior British soldiers negotiated with their masked leaders in the front room of a nearby house.

But the Provisional IRA had quickly decided in their own secret councils that there was no future in peace and were looking around for an issue to get off the ceasefire hook without the blame attaching to them. Their chosen pretext became an ongoing dispute over housing at Horn Drive in West Belfast. The Provos wanted sixteen empty houses on the interface with a neighbouring Protestant area to be filled by displaced Catholic families, but the authorities insisted normal procedures for the allocation of houses should be followed. The Provos caused a confrontation in the area at teatime on Friday, 7 July and agreed to withdraw for a time, but deadlock persisted despite a weekend of intensive talks between them, the housing authorities and senior civil servants.

Fitt was at home in Belfast at this time keeping in close touch with events as the army and housing authorities rang continually to keep him updated. He was convinced the Provos were actively seeking a confrontation, and sure enough it came on the Sunday afternoon. In a commandeered quarry lorry piled high with furniture, they attempted to force their way through an army cordon to occupy the vacant houses. The army turned a water cannon on the crowd and within minutes stoning started, which the army answered with rubber bullets. Then real bullets began to fly and a major gun battle broke out. The ceasefire was called off immediately and in ugly clashes which quickly spread throughout the city, ten people died, including a Catholic priest:

> It was the closest we were so far to the brink of all-out sectarian conflict. Protestant murder gangs were roaming the city at night, halting traffic to abduct Catholic victims, who would be found at dawn, shot or stabbed to death. One morning at 7 o'clock on her way to get the newspapers Ann had to step through a pool of blood, fifty yards from our front door, where the body of one young victim had been dumped during the night.

The Provisionals were bombing and shooting with renewed ferocity and within days of the end of the ceasefire they had killed the one hundredth British soldier to die in the Troubles. The SDLP had a meeting with Whitelaw on Friday, 14 July to express their concern about the activities of the UDA, and they were no longer so sensitive about these meetings being revealed now that the Provisionals had opened the door for them to talk. Although internment was still in existence, as long as Whitelaw continued to release internees regularly, they judged their position to be defensible. As far as Fitt was concerned, that was the real gain during this period. Nonetheless, this new-found ability to engage in purposeful talking was a long way from reaching an agreement. The SDLP still harboured deep reservations about security policy and tactics, were opposed to the proposal for a referendum to test opinion on the existence of the border and wanted to know much more about Whitelaw's plans for an all-party conference to discuss political progress. Above all, they were angered by, suspicious of and felt undermined by Whitelaw's recent admission that IRA leaders had been flown to London by the RAF for secret talks with him and some of his ministers.

Fitt and Hume were at Laneside on the morning of Friday, 21 July discussing these worries and later, as Hume was driving Fitt back into Belfast, they heard a succession of explosions. The traffic snarled up quickly and the police, who were none too friendly when they recognised them, diverted their car into the side-streets, forcing them to make lengthy detours to reach 85 Antrim Road. Just as Fitt reached the house there was a telephone call from Ulster Television, asking him to appear on the evening news programme to discuss the bombings on what had become known as 'Bloody Friday'. In the space of seventy-five minutes, twenty-two bombs had exploded across inner Belfast, all without warning. At that point the police could not tell how many people had been killed or injured because the bodies were so badly dismembered. Fitt set off by taxi for the television studio, through a city in chaos, stunned by the bloodshed:

> It was the first time I had seen panic on such a scale throughout all the city had suffered in the previous few months and, at the studio, I sat in stunned silence watching the details of the destruction on a monitor set. Nine people had died and at least 130 were injured. That did not take account of the people affected by shock and panic. The Provisionals brazenly admitted responsibility and blamed the authorities for not responding to their warnings. I felt sick at the news pictures of police and firemen shovelling the remains of the victims at a bus station into plastic bags.
>
> 'How do you justify that, Mr Fitt?' asked the interviewer.
>
> 'Justify it? There is absolutely no justification for it.'

He went to call the perpetrators of this atrocity by every word he could think of: scum, dregs of humanity, psychopaths. 'I was so enraged, my anger defeated my vocabulary and it was all I could do not to use far stronger language.'

The following Sunday there was a statement in the Dublin *Sunday Independent* attributed to an unnamed SDLP spokesman in Derry, who had said he did not agree with the remarks made by the leader of the party on television. The bombers, he said, were misguided nationalists, not bloodthirsty murderers or psychopaths. Fitt enquired high and low about the identity of this spokesman, without success. Some five years later, at a meeting in Dungannon, after the person concerned had an argument with another prominent member of the party, Fitt discovered the identity of the secret interviewee. Such was his anger towards SDLP members who were ambivalent about violence, he immediately challenged the individual, who replied with deep embarrassment, 'I know now you were right.'

The unprecedented atrocity of Bloody Friday underscored for Fitt just how necessary it was that elected politicians drove events, not unaccountable terrorists. Over the following weekend Whitelaw ordered his officials into action to persuade the SDLP to engage more fully in talks with him. Two of the key figures, Devlin and Hume, were incommunicado, but in separate talks with Fitt, Cooper and Currie, the officials stressed the government's commitment to finding a political solution and urged the SDLP to come on board and help. The British were well aware of Fitt's exasperation at his party's stand on internment and he reiterated his view that, irrespective of the ending of internment, the party ought to get back into the political arena and talk. Cooper and Currie broadly shared this view, but Currie was worried about how they could sell such a move given their position on internment. There was also agreement that the principal obstacle to progress was Devlin, whose unyielding views on internment were influenced heavily by his own experience of the practice. At this time, Fitt was very fed up with his colleague's inflexibility, a feeling aggravated by what he considered to be persistent attempts to undermine and even replace him as leader, especially when he was away at Westminster.

He was also uneasy about 'the constant running to Dublin', not least because of the great suspicion it aroused in the eyes of the unionist community, who were hostile towards any political approach that appeared to open the door to a dreaded united Ireland. While nominally committed to this final objective, the arch-pragmatist in Fitt reasoned that all the emphasis needed to be on the more easily attainable goal of some sort of accommodation in the North, especially now that the British government was directly involved and had stressed there could be no going back to institutions operated by majority, one-party rule.

In order to re-assess their position, the SDLP decided to hold an intensive two-day think-in and headed for Dungloe, on the Atlantic coast of Co. Donegal, which had become their favourite spot for brain-storming and policy-making. Fitt was so convinced of the urgent need to engage in talks, regardless of internment, he had already decided – as he confided to British officials in advance – that he would resign if the party did not agree. They urged him not to do so and counselled that if anyone had to resign, it should not be the majority of the group who were in favour of talking, but those who were not, Devlin and possibly Paddy O'Hanlon.

Fitt was sufficiently assuaged by this advice and the outcome of the Dungloe talks to once more suppress his concerns and sign up to a joint statement on 26 July. The party concluded that the agenda Whitelaw had put forward for talks was too limited and wanted a more wide-ranging discussion, so they committed themselves to seeking talks with him immediately and also with representatives of unionist opinion, the leadership of the British Labour party and the government of the Irish Republic.

Soon afterwards, Fitt's lingering doubts about joining the SDLP were tempered slightly when Paddy Kennedy, who had taken over stewardship of the Republican Labour party after Fitt's departure, announced he would be inviting the IRA to be advisers to his party delegation at Whitelaw's forthcoming conference. For Fitt, this was the final confirmation that his old friend had indeed fallen under sinister influences and had truly expelled himself from mainstream politics.

The SDLP's more positive strategy was welcomed at the Northern Ireland Office (NIO) in Belfast, but even more so in Dublin, where recent events had caused the Irish Foreign Minister, Dr Patrick Hillery, to privately express fears, strongly shared by Fitt, that in the absence of a British initiative to involve the SDLP, 'the IRA propagandists would fill the [political] vacuum in the Catholic areas' in the North. He was therefore keen to encourage the SDLP and, according to the official British note of the situation, through Sir John Peck he offered to use what he believed was his 'considerable influence' with 'the moderate SDLP, the principal exception being Paddy Devlin'. Whitelaw accepted the offer of help in applying pressure and the ambassador was instructed to inform Hillery to do so.

Stemming from previous discussions between the Irish government and the SDLP, there was already a strategic understanding between them about the way ahead. In parallel with bilateral consultations between the two governments, the aim was to promote talks between the unionist and nationalist groups with the aim of reaching an 'interim' solution by setting up a regional assembly at Stormont in which the minority politicians would play a fair part. The ultimate aim was for a quadripartite conference to reach a 'permanent [all-Ireland] accommodation', but no timescale was placed on that, not least because the Irish government was unwilling to rekindle volatile emotions about partition, the Irish constitutional claim over the North and the sort of internal reforms that would be necessary in the Republic to accommodate unionists in any arrangements for all-Ireland governance.

While these exchanges were taking place, thousands of British troops were pouring into Northern Ireland from Britain and the NATO frontlines in West Germany in preparation for what would be the biggest land operation mounted by the British Army since the end of the Second World War. On Sunday, 30 July Whitelaw rang Fitt to say he might hear a lot of activity as the troops were going into the no-go areas. Later that evening, in a special television address, Whitelaw asked the people of Northern Ireland to stay off the streets because there was going to be substantial military activity. During the hours of darkness that evening, Fitt watched the troops move out from Girdwood Barracks, opposite his home, to take part in the operation. By dawn the army had moved into every troubled area in force. The operation, known as 'Motorman', was an impartial one as the Protestant areas dominated by the UDA were 'invaded' too and their barricades removed. Given the scale of recent violent events and the proven capacity of the gunmen and bombers on both sides to cause even more destruction and murder, there was great apprehension as the soldiers went in, but it went off without major incident although two civilians died in sporadic shooting and eight others perished later in the day when an IRA car bomb exploded without warning in the Co. Derry village of Claudy.

No sooner had the operation taken place than Fitt's phone began to ring with a barrage of complaints from the newly invaded Catholic areas. Why had the army taken over the schools? What were they doing in Casement Park football stadium? With a number of intensive talking sessions with Whitelaw already pencilled in for the weeks ahead, the reaction to events reminded Fitt forcefully of the inherent danger of getting too far in front of public opinion among constituents. For much the same reason, and despite Hillery's earlier encouragement, the Irish government adopted a highly guarded public approach to encouraging the SDLP into talks given surging anti-army feelings in the Catholic areas in the wake of what was tantamount to an invasion by armed soldiers. On 1 August the SDLP had in fact run to Dublin again to discuss the immediate aftermath of both Bloody Friday and Operation Motorman. The delegation, which did not include Fitt, conceded the need to see Whitelaw without delay, but sought Irish help in securing some status for themselves as the elected representatives of the minority rather than being classed alongside 'priests and other do-gooders'.

Thus, when Hillery accepted an invitation to lunch with Whitelaw in London on 4 August, it was portrayed publicly as a general exchange of views rather than a get-together for Hillery to 'give advice' and to co-ordinate ideas for getting the SDLP into face-to-face talks. When the SDLP learned of the lunch, however, they contacted the NIO and insisted on an immediate advance meeting with a British official to discuss the implications. A get-together was hastily arranged in Derry for 6.00pm on 3 August, at which the party members expressed resentment at the impression being given that they had been driven into talks by the Irish government. They stressed they were quite capable of making such important decisions for themselves.

Nevertheless, Whitelaw used the London lunch the next day to drive home two important points from his own perspective. First, it was quite out of the question to bring internment to a complete and early end because of the touchiness of the situation, and he added that it was utterly self-defeating for the SDLP to insist on this as a condition for meeting. He assured them he would not have the slightest objection to the SDLP using the meeting to press their case and saying so publicly afterwards, and even hinted that he would be prepared to make some releases as a token to help the party establish its credentials within the Catholic community. Secondly, the British government did not see any role for the Irish in his forthcoming conference. Its main aim, he explained, was to bring together the Northern Ireland representatives who were not talking to each other so they could hear at first-hand the views of the other groups.

At the first meeting in Laneside, on the evening of 7 August, Fitt opened for the SDLP with a lengthy outline of the party's stance. Reiterating that their attitude had been not to talk until internment ended, he said that the campaign of terror by the IRA, particularly Bloody Friday, had convinced them they should not allow themselves to be held hostage to the IRA and internment, despite the fact that they had been criticised for providing the army with a blank cheque to go into the Catholic areas in strength and would be further criticised for talking before internment ended. Others joined in the discussion for the next two hours, reinforcing the opposition to internment and criticising Whitelaw for recently meeting with the IRA, which had given the impression that violence had succeeded. Before adjourning for dinner, the Secretary of State parried these criticisms and others about the army. The most important thing, he suggested, was that the SDLP attend his conference to disabuse unionists of the view that the majority of Catholics were content with the old Stormont regime and that everything had been satisfactory until the IRA and other troublemakers had intervened. 'The presence of the SDLP at the conference was essential to demonstrate that this was not so,' said Whitelaw, according to the official note of the meeting. The talking resumed at 10.20pm, after the meal, and went on until 11.00pm with neither side budging from its basic position.

When they resumed at 5.35pm the following evening, 8 August, Whitelaw opened by revealing that during the day he had signed release orders for forty-seven internees as a sign of his good intentions. The SDLP members were not impressed, saying the case for releasing forty-seven internees applied equally to all internees. They spoke at length about a whole series of specific concerns, including army behaviour and tactics, the wearing of paramilitary uniform, the number of licensed firearms and the requirement for all public employees to take an oath of allegiance to the British Crown – a requirement deeply resented by most Catholics. Whitelaw undertook to explore these matters and to investigate the possibility of organising a meeting between the SDLP and Lord Carrington, the Defence Secretary, before their next discussion with him, which was fixed for 11 August.

The official note of that encounter shows that both sides went over much of the same ground, with the only movement coming from Whitelaw, who said that 'as an earnest of his good intentions', he had that very day signed release orders for another eighteen internees. The fact that Whitelaw had released 700 internees and less than 300 remained in custody did not impress Paddy Devlin, and his forceful opposition was particularly instrumental in the party's continued rejection of Whitelaw's invitation to his conference. After some seventy-five minutes the exchanges were adjourned for the SDLP to consider in private what had been said. When the two sides came face-to-face again, Devlin led off by saying that they were 'desperate for more time and that they needed the help of the Secretary of State to retain their credibility until such time as he released more internees'. Hume echoed him. He said they must come out of the meeting with something to maintain their credibility. Devlin then suggested they could buy time by requesting a meeting to put their case directly to the Prime Minister, Edward Heath. Whitelaw ruled out an immediate meeting, but said he was prepared 'to assist the SDLP in keeping credibility' by exploring the proposition.

What Fitt and the SDLP did not know was that the British were far from enthusiastic about the request for a meeting. According to the official records, Whitelaw hoped the 'proposal could be quietly forgotten'. The SDLP did not oblige him, however, and by the end of August had applied such sustained pressure that Whitelaw was forced to send a message to Heath 'recommending' that the Prime Minister should see them. Whitelaw judged that if the party did not get an early meeting, they might use that as an excuse to drop out of the conference planned for the end of September, although privately he thought they might drop out anyway.

In response to Whitelaw's request, officials identified a potential gap in Heath's diary on 12 September after a lunch he was scheduled to host for Sheikh Zaid, the recently appointed ruler of the United Arab Emirates. Whitelaw suggested a ninety-minute meeting at Chequers, the Prime Minister's country retreat in Buckinghamshire, would suffice and said, 'You could ask the SDLP for 3pm or 3.30pm and offer them tea. Alternatively they could be asked for 5pm and drinks, but they are a very talkative bunch and you might then have them on your hands for longer.' Heath opted for tea at 3.30pm and instructed his officials to arrange an appropriate meeting for him at 5.00pm 'to help in persuading the SDLP that they should not outstay their welcome'.

On 4 September, eight days before the meeting, IRA bombers damaged the SDLP party headquarters at College Square North in what Fitt reckoned was 'a clear attempt to intimidate us' from attending Whitelaw's conference. The attack added to the depression he was feeling after a party meeting to prepare for the Heath encounter, at which:

> all the old rivalries and individual jealousies within the SDLP erupted. It
> seemed that all wanted to make an impression on Heath and there was

much argument about who would say what. At one stage on the day before we left there was an actual fist-fight in our headquarters between two party members. The rest of us had a terrible job cooling them down. That incident and the bickering knocked the heart out of me.

An RAF aircraft was offered to transport them to Chequers, and Fitt was greatly annoyed when his colleagues decided instead, for symbolic reasons, to travel to London from Dublin. 'Why they could not have gone the direct route from Belfast Aldergrove was beyond me,' he said. The evening before their departure the team gathered in the Royal Dublin Hotel on O'Connell Street for a final meeting. Fearing that Fitt's pro-Labour stance in the House of Commons might not have endeared him to Heath and conscious he would have been most unwilling to stand aside and let Hume lead off for the SDLP, Devlin, Cooper and O'Hanlon press-ganged Currie into taking on the assignment. After the meeting, Fitt went off to confess his frustrations to Brendan Halligan and Dr Conor Cruise O'Brien, his longstanding friends in the Irish Labour party. 'Would I be accused of being a traitor or not being concerned about Ireland if I resigned?' he asked them. He said it would in fact take very little for him to resign and that he was almost decided to do so after the Chequers meeting.

Upon their arrival in London, the SDLP team was picked up at Heathrow and conveyed to Chequers in 'limousines that Mafia chiefs would have been proud to occupy', as Devlin later put it in his memoir, *Straight Left*. According to Fitt's recollection, Devlin stole the show by turning up in an old jumper, just to show Heath he did not stand in awe of him. Fitt admired the Prime Minister's approach: 'We were very impressed by Ted Heath. He just sat and listened to the litany of complaints, ideas and hopes. He had no notes or papers and it was clear he was the master of his brief and very knowledgeable. Indeed of the four Prime Ministers I have dealt with, I never met another who was so well up on his subject.' Later, Cooper and Hume told British officials how impressed they were by 'the warmth and relaxed nature of their reception' and the understanding of their problems demonstrated by Heath and Whitelaw. The meeting and the attendant publicity were ultimately very useful for the SDLP's standing and influence.

In fact, despite his guests' favourable impression, Heath had not been extensively briefed before the meeting. A letter from the NIO to 10 Downing Street on 5 September forecast the SDLP's 'main and over-riding concern' would be the ending of internment, but 'apart from this, the SDLP will, no doubt, come along with their normal rag-bag of complaints and it is seldom possible to forecast what these will be'. In a memorandum setting out the likely main points the day before the meeting, a document that provided the substance for a discussion between Heath and Whitelaw in the thirty minutes before the SDLP arrived, the Northern Ireland Secretary again warned that, apart from internment, 'there was no limit to the number of points which can be raised, large and small ... and we shall have to deal with them as they arise.' He also said that with Cabinet discussions about ending internment and abolishing the Special Powers Act still ongoing, 'we cannot have, even at the back of our minds, a clear idea of the kind of package' that 'could be foreshadowed (however guardedly)'.

The SDLP team lined up along one side of a long table and the British politicians and officials sat opposite, and as arranged Currie, opened for the SDLP, pointing out the historic fact that a British Prime Minister was meeting a Northern Ireland opposition party for the first time. After that the discussion became what Fitt described as 'a clash, in a firm but quiet way, between the Heath view that we should participate in the forthcoming conference and our view, which I most unhappily endorsed, that we could not attend until a date had been set to end internment'. According to the official note of the meeting, Heath summed up by telling the SDLP that it was unrealistic to demand the fulfilment of all their objectives before attending the conference and that this was the impression they were in danger of giving.

> The force of the SDLP arguments for the ending of internment would not be reduced by their attendance at the conference. The fact was that those still in internment were violent extremists and the government had to have regard to a number of issues, including army morale, in considering their possible release.

Afternoon tea was served during the talks and Paddy Devlin took the last scone off the plate, growling, 'Well, if we're getting nothing else, I may as well have the last bun.' Fitt recalls that there was more inter-SDLP strife and rivalry when they got back to their base in London. The television news people were there en masse, but only wanted to interview him and John Hume, an attitude that caused such trouble with the others that the reporters finally relented and interviewed them as well. But there was further trouble that evening when the programmes were broadcast, as only Hume, Currie and Fitt appeared on screen. The other contributions had been edited out.

On 18 September, as expected, Whitelaw announced details of his conference, which would be held at a newly built hotel, the Europa Lodge, at Darlington in the north-east of England. Shortly afterwards Heath wrote asking that the party should attend, and against all his political instincts Fitt was forced to reply that, as no date had been announced for the ending of internment, SDLP participation was not possible. Whitelaw had asked for written submissions from all the parties by 8 September and the SDLP once again adjourned to Donegal to flesh out earlier discussions into a major policy document. By now these meetings had moved beyond discussions among the six founders. Fitt remembered:

> We had a parliamentary party, (the six of us) a party executive and a policy committee. What we came up with was a plan for joint rule of Northern

Ireland by Britain and Ireland. There would be equal status for the tricolour and union flag, people could choose whether to have a British or Irish passport and there would be financial support from both London and Dublin. The party felt this would be an acceptable way to persuade the northern majority that they had nothing to fear in a united Ireland and that ultimately that is what could emerge.

The SDLP ideas were articulated in a document entitled 'Towards a new Ireland', which was unveiled two days later at simultaneous press conferences in Belfast and Dublin. Apart from the joint sovereignty plan, they called for greater safeguards for individual rights in the North, an all-Ireland senate comprising members from both traditions in the North and the South, and demanded that the British government declare its intent to foster eventual Irish reunification by agreement. 'We were by now trying to widen the agenda of Whitelaw's developing initiative to get the basic Irish question itself on the table, not just tinkering about with Northern Ireland,' Fitt said.

Whitelaw's conference went ahead on 24 September with only the Unionist party, the Alliance and Northern Ireland Labour parties in attendance, spending four days in discussions. The extreme republican and loyalist groupings were absent, as was the SDLP. Hardline unionists, who were also unrepresented, made their position clear the following Saturday at a rally on the steps of the Stormont parliament building. 'Today we are knocking on the door and asking for our rights. Tomorrow, if they are not given, we will storm that door and set up our own parliament and government,' declared the ever more irascible William Craig.

The SDLP was at ease with its decision not to travel to Darlington on the grounds that they would probably have had to walk out early on because they could not have gone along with the proposition that a political solution should be sought entirely within the Northern Ireland context – they had identified the 'Irish dimension' as a critical element in moving events ahead.

As part of their effort to clarify and mobilise support for their proposals, Fitt led an SDLP group to Dublin on 28 September for a round of talks with each of the main political groupings there. The first encounter was with Lynch, followed by a meeting with the leaders of the main opposition party, Fine Gael, led by Liam Cosgrave. There followed from both factions warm public endorsement of the SDLP document and strong support for the concept of quadripartite talks, involving the two sovereign governments and both sides to the Northern Ireland conflict in the search for a durable political solution. This public enthusiasm masked reservations about some of the more detailed SDLP proposals, especially the suggestion that the Irish Republic contribute to a social benefit scheme in the North, which was already very much more advantageous to its beneficiaries than anything operated in the South.

There was much more serious division, however, within the nominally fraternal Irish Labour party, whose opinion of the SDLP proposals, as formulated by Dr Conor Cruise O'Brien, was startling: they were a formula for civil war and to seek any support for them would lead to an uncontrollable escalation of violence. Although they had been long been mutual admirers, these conflicting judgments provoked an enduring hostility between Devlin and O'Brien, which would have a complicating influence on moves on several fronts in the eventful period ahead. There was, moreover, friction between Irish Labour and their supposed comrades in the British Labour party, notably Harold Wilson and Merlyn Rees, who were regarded as behaving duplicitously by giving strong public support to the SDLP while at the same time seeking to build closer ties with its Irish counterpart, regardless of the widely diverging views both held about Northern Ireland.

In the meantime the SDLP was forging ahead as a political organisation. In early October formal invitations were issued to the other parties for bilateral talks and the first edition of a monthly newspaper, *SDLP News*, was published, reflecting the progress that had been made in setting up a network of support groups to develop its power base and make it an effective electoral force. For all his bonhomie and conviviality, however, Fitt was ever the strong individualist and was in an unhappy minority of one over many key issues. Indeed, at times his relationship with the party was what he himself described as 'very uneasy'. Some of this unhappiness was attributable to the strong personalities who were now sharing the spotlight with him and internal rivalries within the group. There was little love lost between Hume and Devlin, the principal intellectual driving forces, who were constantly trying to outdo one other. Relations between Fitt and Devlin, who should have been Fitt's strongest running mate, were often strained, not least because of the mercurial Devlin's antipathy towards Paddy Wilson, who was Fitt's right-hand man. On the other hand, Fitt's relationship with Austin Currie remained close and mutually supportive. The most uneasy association of all was that with the fiercely ambitious Hume, who lost no opportunity to promote his own standing, even if it meant advancing onto what Fitt hitherto regarded as his exclusive territory, notably Whitehall and Westminster.

Hume's apparent readiness to go behind not only Fitt's back but that of his other SDLP colleagues (albeit incited by British officials) is evidenced by the official account of a lengthy, wide-ranging, 'friendly and relaxed' discussion he had with Frank Steele at Laneside on 4 October 1972. During the evening, there was some discussion arising from remarks at a recent private dinner in the Dublin Embassy at which Bill Deedes, a long-serving Conservative MP and soon-to-be the editor of the *Daily Telegraph*, reported Whitelaw as being 'despondent about Northern Ireland and the hopelessness of his task there'. He was in fact keen on a transfer to another Cabinet post, according to Deedes. Hume reacted to that possibility as a potential disaster for Northern Ireland and said that, in such an eventuality, he 'would probably throw up politics'. Going on to express his admiration for Whitelaw, he said it was unfortunate that the SDLP's meetings with him had 'of necessity been hard-bargaining meetings'. Steele replied it was 'presumably impossible for Hume to have a relaxed, informal, private meeting' with him, 'as this would put him in difficulties with his SDLP colleagues'. Hume replied that if such a meeting could be arranged discreetly and in London, he would welcome it. The note records that such arrangements were indeed made.

The volatility of the internal relationships was again evident one weekend, when Fitt had returned to Belfast from Westminster and taken Ann off with him when he went to speak at a meeting of the Irish Labour party in Ballinasloe, Co. Galway. In widely reported remarks, delivered as usual off-the-cuff and not from a written script, he compared the governing Fianna Fáil party, led by Jack Lynch, to the Unionist party in the North, describing them as 'Siamese twins'. Later in the week, after returning home, he found himself under attack when he arrived for a meeting at the party headquarters in College Square North. By then there had been a shoal of letters from Fianna Fáil supporters in Dublin threatening to cancel subscriptions to the SDLP unless he publicly withdrew the remarks, and he was put under considerable pressure to do so, notably by Paddy Duffy, a wealthy Dungannon solicitor who was also the party treasurer. Duffy's task was an especially difficult one as the party depended entirely on such subscriptions, and was often in such dire financial straits that it could not even pay the couple of staff who ran the office. On such occasions, Hume would head off to the Republic and speak at fund-raising dinners, which could raise as much as £2,500 on a good night, to refill the party coffers. Despite the financial pressure, Fitt insisted nobody was going to change or challenge his beliefs – least of all Fianna Fáil supporters. If the SDLP did not like it, he would walk out of the door. The matter was dropped, but the resentments remained and would not be forgotten easily.

At the end of October 1972 the government finally published a lengthy discussion paper on the future of Northern Ireland. When it was debated in the Commons on 13 November, Fitt said

> the party which I lead agrees with the paragraph which strives to spell out the Irish dimension. The inclusion of this paragraph tells us for the first time that a Conservative government, with the support of the Labour opposition, recognise that Ulster is in Ireland, that Ulster people are Irish people, and that, sooner or later, the Irish people will have to be given the opportunity to determine their own destiny.

A couple of days later, as a sign of his priority interest in Northern Ireland, Heath visited Belfast. The party decided, very wrongly and rudely in Fitt's view, not to accept invitations to a lunch at City Hall, where he was paying a call on the Lord Mayor. Fitt did go along and chatted briefly to the Prime Minister, whom he found very friendly. That same night Austin Currie was away from home when a

group of thugs broke into his house and terrorised his wife, Anita, and their young
children. The initials 'UVF' were carved on her breast by the attackers, who also
beat her severely. The attack was a reaction to strong Protestant feelings about the
outcome of the political shake-up, which was increasingly gathering force. The
British government believed the SDLP proposals were well ahead of the current
state of Protestant thinking. Steele had recently urged Hume to make an effort to
convince Protestants they had nothing to fear from them, but Hume believed that
a declaration of intent about a united Ireland from the British government would
bring them down to earth and a realistic solution would then emerge from
quadripartite discussions. 'The northern Irish Protestants should be made to face
reality instead of continuing to indulge in wishful thinking about some form of
continuing Protestant ascendancy which in fact had gone for ever,' he told Steele.
Hume was no doubt influenced in his belief that Protestants were thinking more
radically about their future by a conversation he had with extreme unionist John
Taylor in the studios at Ulster Television who told him that extremist Protestants
were so convinced they would end up pushed into union with the South that they
were already considering their bargaining position.

On 25 November the SDLP held its second annual conference at Dungiven,
where the party made a remarkable U-turn. After heated debate a motion was
carried clearing the way for talks with Whitelaw. Armed at last with a conference
mandate, the leadership's private talks continued intermittently throughout
December but they were heavily overshadowed by grave concerns about the
continued sectarian assassinations being carried out by loyalists. One of the worst
incidents took place that month, when five people drinking in a bar in Derry died
in a hail of machine-gun fire. The bar was Catholic-owned and four of the victims
were Catholics. Altogether 120 people were assassinated during the year – eighty
Catholics and forty Protestants – out of a total death toll for the year of 467. There
was little hope of any respite. In a grim New Year message the IRA said it would
fight on as long as there was British control in Ireland.

In the first weeks of 1973 the SDLP was also preoccupied with the associated
problem of intimidation. Austin Currie had to deal with seventy families, 350
people, who had been driven out of their houses near Portadown. Virtually every
day Fitt had people calling him after suffering intimidation in work or home. 'I
was told about a poster displayed in one of the major industrial establishments –
"Any Roman Catholic who doesn't do what he's told must be threatened first and
then shot".' The situation was causing huge financial hardship. He met a
deputation of young girls who fled in fear from their jobs in the clothing factories
on Donegall Road, were not entitled to redundancy money and had difficulty
convincing the authorities they were entitled to the dole. He also had to deal with
people facing crippling financial difficulties, paying mortgages on homes they had
been forced to abandon.

Politically, this was also a very busy period. The Commons was pushing through the Emergency Provisions Act, setting up courts in which a single judge would sit, without a jury, to try terrorist cases. Fitt was consistently opposed to emergency legislation and often found himself on the same side as Paisley in contesting what they agreed was a draconian piece of law. On the positive side, from his standpoint, the need to take the oath of allegiance to the Crown was abolished, finally bringing Northern Ireland into line with the rest of the United Kingdom: 'I always thought it was patently stupid that a council labourer or a dustbinman had to swear his loyalty before digging up the road or emptying a bin, but it was obviously there as a deterrent to Catholics to take jobs which would otherwise go to unionist supporters.'

The most significant development at this time was the announcement that there would be a border poll. Fitt had opposed plans for it as it passed through the Commons, and when it was fixed for 8 March the SDLP told their supporters not to vote because the result was a foregone conclusion. In the event, 591,820 persons (57.5% of the total electorate) voted for Northern Ireland to remain part of the United Kingdom; 6,463 (0.6%) said they wanted to join with the Irish Republic; four in ten voters of the one-million-strong electorate abstained, thereby corroding the credibility of the result. The PIRA did not let the day pass without incident. Four car bombs, shipped over from Belfast, were planted outside buildings in central London: two exploded, injuring 180 people; two were discovered and defused; and one man died from a heart attack outside the Old Bailey. Fitt was at the House of Commons waiting to meet Brendan Halligan of the Irish Labour party, who was late because his taxi driver had put him out of the cab because of his Dublin accent.

The White Paper setting out the Heath/Whitelaw proposals for Northern Ireland was published on 20 March. It proposed an Assembly elected by proportional representation, an executive of committee chairmen, and a Council of Ireland. Security would remain the responsibility of the Northern Ireland secretary, who would remain in office. The party adjourned to the Altmore House hotel in the wilds of Co. Tyrone to study the document and called a press conference there two days later to discuss the verdict. The journalists who attended were very amused by the pre-Troubles hotel brochure, which commended the 'rough shooting in the countryside around'. Back in the House of Commons, Fitt summed up the party's feelings about the document:

> I cannot support its provisions relating to internment and detention. But I can support the fact that it goes a considerable way towards meeting the arguments which have been put forward from this side of the House since 1966 in relation to bringing about a society in which social justice is readily available to all the people.

The situation on the ground continued to throw up a variety of testing problems.

Locals from the New Lodge Road came to see Fitt to get ramps – 'sleeping policemen' as they are called – laid on the road to stop cars with drive-by gunmen speeding through the area. Fitt went to see the army officer responsible for such things but found him reluctant to meet the demand in case it would slow his own vehicles and make his soldiers more vulnerable to sniper fire:

> I talked to him at length about the local fears of the roaming assassins. Finally, he agreed to get the ramps put down. A team of soldiers was brought in with equipment and they were just completing the work when one of them was shot dead by a sniper. An angry colonel came up to my house and said, 'There you are.' I could say nothing. Indeed, I have lived with the thought ever since that I may have contributed to his death.

Another morning a young porter from the Europa Hotel came to see Fitt. He was scared out of his wits after he had been arrested by the army, questioned, photographed and then made to sign a statement saying he had been having an affair with the wife of an IRA man who was interned in Long Kesh. Before he was released, the soldiers told the young porter that he would have to provide them with information about people in his locality or they would give the statement to the IRA:

> I invited Simon Hoggart from the *Guardian* as a witness and then rigged up a tape recorder on the telephone before carrying out the instructions the young fellow was given to pass information. I dialled the number then said, 'Hallo, Number 28 here.'
>
> 'Have you got anything for us,' said an English voice.
>
> 'No, I have not. This is Gerry Fitt MP here and I am going to report you,' I said. The line went dead. In due course I had a meeting with Lord Carrington, Defence Minister, about this sort of army operation and he assured me publicly it would not happen again and that the soldiers concerned had been disciplined.

However, other military reports of the incident show that no action was taken and that Fitt was considered tiresome for having raised the matter in such a public fashion.

The first major political hurdle of 1973 came on 30 May in the form of the elections to the twenty-six new local councils. For the first time since 1925 proportional representation was being employed. It was the first tangible reform and the much-expanded SDLP organisation was bubbling with enthusiasm, even though there were some pretty fundamental differences and internal rivalries between various factions and individuals within the party. The old Dock constituency had been abolished during the re-drawing of the boundaries and in its place was the uninspiring 'Area G'. The election outcome was crucial for the party because it would act as a very important indicator of how it would fare in the more vital Assembly elections, which had been fixed for 28 June.

When the council polling stations closed, Ann and Fitt waited around the City Hall count with Paddy Wilson. Fitt topped the poll in his own area, Wilson got elected to Belfast City Council and Fitt was glad to see that the SDLP secured eighty-two seats in all, giving it a strong bridgehead in the reformed network of district councils right across Northern Ireland. Nevertheless, Fitt's nostalgia for the old days and his fundamental discomfort with some of the people working for his own party was all too easily provoked:

> I regretted the hostility to Wilson shown by some SDLP people and the way the party had been taken over by teachers and lawyers and academics made me feel out of step. They were running round with their clipboards and calculators doing sums, working out trends and percentages and turnouts. I regretted the passing of the days of the quick tot on the back of an envelope. What made me feel most uncomfortable was the predominance of people with a mainly nationalist outlook. There was little labour or socialist involvement.

Fitt was made to feel even more uneasy at the first council meeting when he walked into the party room to find several of the newly elected SDLP councillors putting on the red robes:

> Now I had never approved of such trappings or worn them. They symbolised the worst of the all the old days of unionist ascendancy. I made my feeling clear but I was told in no uncertain terms that things had changed. It was the first real indication that I was going to have my hands full with this party. But for a tragic event my involvement with SDLP could well have ended there and then.

Immediately the council elections were over there was a big push for the Assembly elections and Fitt was very annoyed with the people in the Falls branch, who blocked Paddy Wilson from getting a nomination, despite his claims as a councillor:

> Ever since the day Paddy and I had talked in the café in Donegall Street after Mass, we had become close personal and political friends. Indeed, apart from Ann and the family, there was nobody closer to me. The night he was rejected for a nomination he was very upset and although I had gone to bed he came into our house late at night to talk to me. He sat on the edge of the bed saying he would work to get me elected, then we would both pull out of the SDLP, where he saw no future. I did not disagree.

Towards the end of the election campaign the assistant chief constable for Belfast rang Fitt one morning to pass on a security warning. The police were so concerned that Fitt might be attacked, they insisted that he should carry a gun for his personal protection. A detective was immediately sent up with the appropriate forms, Fitt signed them and handed over £30 – the price of a suitable gun. The detective came back later with a Browning automatic pistol and a box of bullets.

'It may not save your life,' said the officer, 'but it will stop you being kidnapped if you fire it and make noise.'

On the morning of Friday, 22 June, Fitt was in party headquarters waiting for Paddy Wilson when he got a phone call from a policeman known to him who informed him that the PIRA had kidnapped David Walker, a sixteen-year-old Protestant youth and the son of a prison officer, and that the police feared for his life. 'Gerry, if you know anybody in the IRA, tell them he is mentally retarded. He knows nothing,' said the policeman. Fitt did not know anybody directly in the IRA, but he rang two priests and asked them to see if they could make contact. When Wilson arrived, he was aghast at the news: 'Those people will stop at nothing,' he said. Later that day Fitt and he were absolutely horrified when they heard the youth had been found shot dead.

The following Sunday, Wilson drove Fitt to North Antrim to canvass on behalf of two candidates there. Their first call was on Joe Campbell, the police sergeant in Cushendall, an old friend, who would later be shot dead outside the gates of his own station in long disputed circumstances. Neither politician could get the bullets into Fitt's pistol, so they sought Campbell's advice. The sergeant spotted instantly that the box of bullets were of the wrong calibre, so he gave them some of the proper size. Then he took them to a disused quarry and gave Fitt a crash course in the use of an automatic pistol. Later, Wilson accompanied Fitt through a hectic political day, with eleven meetings and hundreds of handshakes, before ending up in Carnlough at 1.00am.

Next day, Monday, the two of them attended a function at City Hall, where they were photographed with the High Sheriff, Alfie Shaw. Back at Fitt's home afterwards, Ann made them ham sandwiches and tea, but before Wilson had a chance to tuck in, Fitt insisted they go to the *Irish News* to pick up the last lot of posters and election cards for his election contest to the new Stormont Assembly. On the way back home, Fitt asked Wilson to detour around to Smithfield to collect his lucky half-crown from Joe Gunning, the jeweller, but they found his shop was closed down. Fitt was peering through the window, thinking what a bad omen it was, when a woman appeared beside him. 'Mr Fitt, you're here for your half-crown. Bobby said you would be down,' she said, leading him to her house in the next street. There, beneath a religious statue on the mantelpiece, was the customary good-luck gesture from Gunning, who had recently closed down his shop and retired. Being well aware of Fitt's perpetual superstitions, Wilson said to him, 'Well, your luck's definitely in now.'

After that they parted, having arranged to link up again later at a council meeting. It was planned that Fitt would nominate Wilson for a seat on the Health and Social Services Board, and the unionists would support him. However, Fitt was delayed in his house by constituents and, in his absence, other SDLP members said they would not be nominating Wilson. When the allocation of seats took place, they kept to their word and Wilson was left out in the cold.

> He rang me from City Hall immediately afterwards, very disappointed and depressed. 'Gerry, I'm fed up. I'm going over to the International for a drink,' he said. A bit later he rang again from the hotel. He was with a few councillors and had bumped into a girl called Irene Andrews, a council education official who was waiting for her boyfriend, so the group was adjourning to McGlade's. I said I would catch them up there. Eventually I got away from the house by taxi and went to the *Irish News* to place some election advertisements, but just as I was leaving to join Paddy in McGlade's across the road, the phone rang. It was Paddy Devlin at the party office with lots of election forms he needed to fill out urgently. I said I would go round and help him. A couple of hours later, when I had finished, I was in a taxi heading down Royal Avenue fully intending to go to McGlade's when I decided it was too late. 'Paddy will probably have gone home by now,' I said to myself. So I told the taxi driver to take me home and I went to bed, but soon after 1.00am the telephone rang and I answered it.
>
> 'Gerry, is Paddy Wilson with you?' asked Cowan Watson, editor of the *Belfast News Letter*.
>
> 'I think he was in McGlade's,' said Fitt.
>
> 'Was there a girl with him?' asked Watson.
>
> 'There could have been,' said Fitt non-committedly.
>
> 'Gerry, I think it's worse than that. We've had a call from the Ulster Freedom Fighters. They say they have murdered him and his girlfriend in retaliation for the killing of the young boy, Walker. The bodies are to be found on the Hightown Road.'

When he rang off, Fitt immediately dialled Wilson's home. His wife answered. He was not there; she thought he was with Fitt. Ann was awake by now and Fitt always remembered how the blood drained from her face. 'It's Paddy Wilson,' she said. 'He's dead, isn't he?' Fitt went down into the kitchen and the first thing he saw was the plate of ham sandwiches he had left earlier. Ann was behind him. 'And you never even let him eat his sandwiches,' she said.

A few minutes later the police arrived at the door and Fitt brought them into the room he used as an office. 'We have had a look from the helicopter. There are two bodies. Is it a red mini?' the officer said. Fitt nodded in agreement. They wanted to check out the other person and, as Fitt had mislaid his glasses, he asked them to look up the name Andrews, Crumlin Road, in the telephone book and dial the number for him.

'Could I speak to Irene, please?' Fitt asked the woman who answered the phone.

'It's very late. She's in bed.'

'It's rather important. Could I speak to her?' replied Fitt.

There was a long pause. 'Irene's not in.' Then panic. 'Who is this? Where is she?' said the voice. Fitt had to put the phone down.

'That seems to be it,' he said to the policeman.

'We can't go up there till daylight. It could be an ambush. We'll come back for you,' they said and left.

By now Paddy O'Flaherty from the *Irish News* had arrived at the house and Fitt decided to go to the scene with him. There were journalists and photographers there and a television reporter was doing a piece to camera about the murder in 'lovers' lane'. The innuendo deeply annoyed Fitt. 'If you broadcast that out, there will be an awful row,' he said menacingly. The reporter filmed an amended version. Fitt told the detectives at the scene he did not wish to go up to see the bodies. 'Just as well,' said one. 'His head is nearly slashed off. He must have put up a hell of a fight.' Fitt left the scene to go see Wilson's wife, Bridget, and their son, Paul. 'I was numb, shocked. When I got home the news was on the radio and the phone was ringing. "He always was a loser, wasn't he?" said Paddy Kennedy, unsympathetically.'

A few weeks later, Fitt received a letter from a man called Johnny White who said the police had questioned him about the murder. He did not do it, he insisted, and asked Fitt to tell the police to get off his back. Five years later, White was convicted of the murders. The judge, who heard that Wilson had been stabbed thirty-two times and Irene Andrews nineteen times, said the killings were 'horrifying in their brutality' and gave White two life sentences. In response, saying that words could not express his regret, White told the court that 'A lot of Protestants were being killed. I could see the IRA trying to take over Ulster and I was against this. I thought that if I killed any Roman Catholics it would stop them. Any Roman Catholic would do.'

Fitt always believed the motive began as robbery. Wilson was giving Andrews a lift home when they were flagged down and pulled out of the car on the lonely Hightown Road. They showed their driving licences, but the gang wanted to take the car radio and look in the boot. There they found Fitt's election posters, recognised who Paddy was and viciously stabbed him to death. The girl was a Protestant, but she had seen too much and was killed too. Other accounts of the incident suggest that the pair were targeted in McGlade's pub and followed when they left. Whatever the truth of the matter, the grim statistics of the violence now included not a constituent or an acquaintance, but Fitt's closest friend.

> I was never as sure as I was then that my lifelong abhorrence of violence was justified. More than that, I feared another life would be taken in revenge. [On radio later that morning I said], 'In God's name, don't. There has been enough, more than enough, of killing.'

CHAPTER TEN

A ROVING COMMISSION

PADDY WILSON'S FUNERAL TOOK PLACE on Thursday, 28 June – polling day for the Assembly elections. He was buried in Milltown Cemetery in Belfast after a concelebrated requiem mass led by Dr William Philbin, the Bishop of Down and Connor. Fitt received what he called 'a torrent of phone calls, telegrams and personally delivered expressions of sympathy from people of all religious persuasions and political affiliations'. A few days later, at a special meeting of the City Council, a resolution was passed regretting the brutal murders and recording Paddy's 'reputation as an impartial and vociferous advocate on behalf of those in need' for which he 'sought only to be rewarded by the success of his efforts'. After the murders, Fitt pleaded repeatedly that there should be no reprisals. He said that 'as a lifelong democrat and man of peace, Paddy would have wanted the continuation of peaceful political activity'.

For the same reason, and despite his great sense of loss and shock, Fitt decided to go ahead with his bid for an Assembly seat. It was a measure of just how turbulent and divisive politics had become that 210 candidates from twenty-two different parties or groups contested the seventy-eight seats. The PIRA called for a vote-spoiling campaign and attacked one Belfast polling station with a mortar bomb to underline their opposition. The six founder members of the SDLP – Hume, Devlin, Currie, Cooper, O'Hanlon and Fitt – were all elected on the first count. The party took nineteen seats in all, making it the second largest grouping in the Assembly, a result that was very satisfactory. Only Brian Faulkner's Official Unionist party, with twenty-two seats, outnumbered the SDLP at the table. The Alliance party secured eight seats. The third main power block in the Assembly were the factions led by Bill Craig and Ian Paisley, who could potentially muster up to twenty-eight seats if they were able to bury their individual rivalries and work together.

Whitelaw and Frank Cooper, the most senior civil servant at the NIO, visited

Heath at Chequers to digest the results and discuss the next moves. They were encouraged by the fact that extremists had 'on the whole fared badly' in the poll, but still uncomfortable that dissident loyalists of one kind or another had enough support to secure seats. The outcome they most favoured was for Faulkner and his supporters to coalesce with the SDLP and Alliance to form a power-sharing administration, but they recognised that 'this would not be easy for some of Mr Faulkner's friends to stomach and it might be that [some of them] would transfer their loyalties to Mr Craig and Mr Paisley. If so, they would then be in a position to form a coalition and a more difficult situation would be created.' Whitelaw was confident, however, that this was most unlikely.

Whitelaw and Cooper flew to Belfast the next day, 2 July, and lost no time in getting down to business by calling in the party leaders for individual talks. Initially Fitt had, in Whitelaw's words to Heath, been playing 'hard to get' on the grounds that he did not know whether he would still be the leader of the party and therefore needed the authority of his colleagues to attend. This was slightly inaccurate. In actual fact, Fitt was still shell-shocked by Wilson's death and experiencing a crisis of conscience about remaining in the SDLP. The choice was his alone. Despite their frequent grumbling about his solo style, the other members of the leadership had no intention of censuring or deposing him.

Also on 2 July, Heath met the Irish Prime Minister, Liam Cosgrave, in London, setting the scene for the most far-reaching effort since the 1921 Treaty negotiations to deal with 'the Irish question'. The objective was to create a new, mutually agreed political framework that would give what the British described as 'a square deal for Catholics' without driving the majority of Protestants into the arms of uncompromising extremists. As underlined by the all-too-predictable outcome of the earlier border poll, a united Ireland was a non-starter. The best the SDLP could hope for was an influential stake in the governance of Northern Ireland and some form of 'Irish dimension' to mollify the nationalist sentiments of their supporters. In his talks with Whitelaw prior to the Cosgrave meeting, Heath had suggested they were in a 'dealing situation', which in effect meant that in exchange for Irish constitutional recognition of the North, there would have to be a *quid pro quo*. Whitelaw and Cooper demurred. They thought it might not be in British interests to look to the Irish government for constitutional changes which it might not be strong enough to effect. Better, they said, to settle for a sustained public change of attitude, but no constitutional change.

In the months prior to and and after the publication of the much-anticipated White Paper in March 1973, there had been widespread private and informal discussions between the main political figures, many of them initiated on the periphery of radio and television programmes at BBC's Broadcasting House or UTV's Havelock House, then continued over drinks at private houses or, more often, in the first-floor bar of the Europa Hotel. The content of these discussions

was invariably reported to the two governments. The British continued to
entertain lavishly at Laneside, where, as Paddy Devlin said, copious amounts of
alcohol were used to loosen tongues and gather political intelligence. The Irish
were also active in this field. Officials from the Department of Foreign Affairs at
Iveagh House in Dublin – nicknamed 'the travellers' – trekked extensively
incognito across Northern Ireland, making their own, often colourful assessments
of events by drawing on a wide range of contacts, including many on the
Protestant side. The SDLP continued to 'run to Dublin' (albeit not as frequently),
where they were also entertained lavishly. Official Irish government files show
that, on occasion, the menus for five-course lunches and dinners, with wines, were
agreed in advance with the assurance that the chefs at Leinster House would meet
the exact requirements and tastes of the SDLP if the choice proved unacceptable.
Once, Austin Currie let slip that they were also receiving expenses for their
trouble, and the fact was reported inside the NIO by James Allan. 'I suppose this
is what is meant by liquid resources,' scrawled one of the recipients on his copy of
Allan's note.

Not surprisingly, in advance of the critical elections scheduled for mid-1973,
some pretty hardline opening positions were articulated by individuals and parties,
but all sides exhibited a promising willingness to engage in negotiations, however
much shared pessimism there was about the possibility of a successful outcome. As
Fitt recalled, 'With elections to fight and negotiations to come, whatever
compromising was to go on would certainly not take place at that early stage.'
During a New Year encounter at UTV, for instance, the ever-apocalyptic John
Taylor, who had recently been predicting all-out civil war, told Hume he wanted
an independent Northern Ireland, with its borders guaranteed by London and
Dublin. He said William Craig, the ultra-hardline Vanguard leader, was also
interested in this idea. Taylor and others were later involved in exploratory talks
with Devlin and Cooper, which the SDLP conducted with the aim of engaging
more fully with the leaders of unionist and Protestant opinion, who remained
highly suspicious of their oft-stated 'all-Ireland' ambitions. The talks explored
radical options, such as independence for Northern Ireland, a federal reunification
of Ireland and joint sovereignty by Ireland and Britain over Northern Ireland. The
meetings took place in the private houses of the parties involved and both sides
consciously kept them low-key. Nonetheless, encouraging evidence of radical
thinking emerged from their discussions. Desmond Boal, who was a major
influence on Ian Paisley, flirted publicly with the concept of a federal Ireland.
Craig spoke about a dominion solution that would recognise the aspirations of
both sections of the community. Although the SDLP responded positively to such
ideas, the apparent generosity in unionist thinking was never matched later when
it came to action.

At the same time there was another highly significant effort, led by the Alliance party, to break the traditional political mould by forming a new 'centre' party. The proposition was first mooted at a meeting in the home of party member Tom Caldwell on 21 January 1973, which was attended by members of his own party, representatives of the NILP and several prominent defectors from the Unionist party, including Stratton Mills, Robin Baillie and Basil McIvor. The Northern Ireland Liberal party also registered its interest but did not attend. As a sign of their seriousness, the Alliance team, which included the Catholic solicitor Oliver Napier, said they would dissolve and put their 18,500 fully paid-up membership, ample funds and organisation at the disposal of a new centre party. The Labour delegates were reluctant to join because of ideological reservations about preserving their socialist principles in order to attract working-class support. Napier argued that Northern Ireland was not ready for ideological-type politics and would not be for some years to come. In the present situation of sectarian and extremist politics, he said, it was the duty of the Labour party to side with the moderates to defeat the extremists. The party indicated that it would support any centre party or coalition, but insisted on maintaining its own existence. This notion was based on a vainglorious judgment that, with the help of the 'working class', they might be able to bridge the sectarian divide and thus potentially enjoy an influential role, if not a king-making one, in the coalition-making that would become necessary if power-sharing became a reality.

Prior to this meeting, Napier had sounded out Fitt about the possibility of his joining up and giving the proposed party real cross-community credibility. The SDLP was riven by factions and had virtually no party machinery, and Napier later told British officials that Fitt 'made no bones about the fact he was fed up with the SDLP and would like a chance of leaving it, particularly to join a moderate centre party.' However, he felt he could not get away with such a move unless there was a guarantee of an effective power-sharing executive, security was controlled from Westminster and there would be a Council of Ireland. Fitt also held out the possibility that Currie might support such a move. Napier was not convinced that Fitt was serious: 'The trouble with Gerry is that he loves discussion and his political view is bounded by the Belfast ghettoes – both Protestant and Catholic – and the chances of keeping his Westminster seat.' There were several more of these Sunday get-togethers – to which the SDLP members were not invited – before the idea finally foundered, but these preliminary discussions did ultimately bear some fruit in that they created understandings between disparate individuals and groups who would later co-operate successfully.

The SDLP founders were notable absentees from this initial process and, apart from Fitt and possibly Currie, were anyway unwelcome. This applied to Hume, in particular, as he was generally regarded as an irredeemable nationalist. Moreover, the putative centre group was all too well aware that Hume did not always act in concert with or with the knowledge of his SDLP colleagues. Indeed, the British actively encouraged his solo runs and continued to arrange periodic, discreet, one-to-one meetings between him and Whitelaw, at which Hume promoted his ideas, including that for a condominium solution, some form of joint rule by the British and Irish governments. Whitelaw did not express his own misgivings about its viability and listened attentively to him but privately he doubted both the extent of internal SDLP support for the concept and the practicalities of the proposals, at least well into the foreseeable future. Because he did not debate them with him, thus giving Hume the impression the proposals were being taken seriously, the SDLP man became alarmed by the lack of an adverse response, which he somewhat naively interpreted as enthusiasm. In a move that amused both the British Foreign Office and Whitelaw's own officials, he enlisted the help of Dr Garret FitzGerald to clarify the position. On 5 February 1973 FitzGerald delivered a written memorandum, which had been agreed with Hume, to Sir John Peck to illuminate 'a question of style and technique which Hume thought lay at the heart of much Anglo-Irish misunderstanding'. FitzGerald explained:

> The British never seemed to realise that the Irish, whatever their political or religious persuasion, invariably embarked on a negotiation by making an opening bid or adopting a position which was not intended to be taken seriously. The purpose was to have a serious discussion out of which an agreed, or at any rate a greatly modified, position could emerge. [The British], on the other hand, invariably refused to do more than listen and would not show [their] hand at all unless it was to say that the Irish opening bid was totally unacceptable without giving any indication of what would be. Thus, the SDLP had been horrified when their proposal for a condominium had been taken seriously.

FitzGerald added that he personally regarded this Irish habit as deplorable, but it had to be recognised as a fact of life. When the ambassador's report reached Belfast, NIO officials insisted they were indeed all too well aware that 'the Irish always in a negotiating situation overstate their opening bid which they do not expect to be taken seriously'. Frank Steele commented: 'I suppose we shall never be rid of this particular Irish myth although the British have coped with wily Orientals who have the same negotiating habits.' He went on to point out that Paddy Devlin 'from time to time reminds me that not only is he a politician, he is also an ex-trade unionist and therefore his opening bid in any matter is always about twice as much as he hopes to get in the end'. Paddy O'Hanlon coined the word 'ginking' to describe the SDLP's negotiating technique and defined it as 'acting furtively with intent to deceive'.

Steele later raised the FitzGerald contact with Hume, who said he was 'horrified' that the matter had been communicated to the British ambassador. The British did not believe him and instead concluded that Hume wanted to distance himself from the condominium concept because he was isolated and deserted within the SDLP, none of whom were keen on the idea, and from the Irish government, which had also disowned it. In March 1973, with the elections imminent, the SDLP placed an advertisement in both the *Irish News* and *Belfast News Letter* to set out its stall. Using the latter paper to make its pitch directly to Protestant readers was a ground-breaking move for what was perceived to be a 'Catholic' party, but lack of money prevented them from putting the advertisement into the more costly *Belfast Telegraph*, which was read by people from both sides.

By early summer, with the Assembly elections resolved and despite the imminence of the traditional holiday break, Whitelaw allowed the local politicians no respite by insisting the Assembly meet before the end of July so the real talking could begin. In the meantime, the emphasis shifted back to Westminster where parliament was rushing through the Northern Ireland Constitution Bill, the legal authorisation for the new institutions at Stormont. During the debate on the Bill, Fitt said:

> I have been a second-class citizen for too long under unionism to want to inflict that upon anyone. I know what it feels like to be a member of a minority that is trampled on and oppressed by one-party government. That is the last thing I want to inflict on my Protestant fellow countrymen. We must co-operate and allay these fears and we can do so only by talking and negotiation.

However, he warned Whitelaw not to push forward too quickly, saying it would take time to discuss and resolve the problems.

Despite the signs of political movement, there was no let-up in the violence and the authorities decided Fitt needed far greater personal security protection. Some of the windows in his house were fitted with bullet-proof glass and wire-mesh screens were constructed back and front to give protection from the stones and other missiles constantly being rained down on it. Thereafter, 85 Antrim Road became known as 'Fortress Fitt'. The dreadful sequence of tit-for-tat sectarian killings was still causing tremendous fear in Catholic areas. Although they were called 'tit-for-tat killings', about three times as many Catholics as Protestants were victims. The area immediately around the Fitt home was very much in the frontline and one night, outside their front door, a young man was gunned down from a passing car, which did a U-turn and sped away along the Antrim Road. Fitt's daughter, Joan, who was a nurse, rushed out and gave prompt medical attention to his serious chest wounds while further assistance, including a blood transfusion, was provided by a Royal Marines doctor. Together they prevented one lucky young Catholic from joining the growing litany of the dead.

At a post-election strategy meeting in July, the party agreed to adopt a three-pronged approach. Although now talking to Whitelaw, spurred on primarily by Devlin, they made it clear that positive moves to end internment were necessary to keep them locked into the negotiating process. At the same time, in order to placate the strong nationalist element in the new Assembly party, they opened up a high-level dialogue with Dublin, and within a month Hume and Devlin had twice led SDLP delegations there for meetings with Prime Minister, Liam Cosgrave. The third prong of the strategy was shrouded in secrecy. Calculating that they would have to do a deal with either Faulkner or the Craig – Paisley group in order to achieve majority command of the Assembly, and unsure whether Faulkner could finally deliver, they kept every option open by resuming the private talks that had taken place earlier in the year with unionist hardliners such as Craig and Taylor. However, the prospects of any progress with this faction promptly diminished and the SDLP was forced to rely on a deal with Faulkner as being their best option.

The inaugural meeting of the Assembly took place on 31 July and the first item of business was the appointment of a presiding officer – the equivalent to Speaker. The day before the meeting the SDLP had indicated it would not be making a nomination for the vacancy. When the parties arrived at Stormont, there was dissatisfaction among the newly elected representatives regarding the venue and the seating arrangements. Instead of gathering in the Commons or Senate chambers, seats had been set out classroom-style in the central hall of the building. The largest parties had been assigned places at the front, with the smallest parties being seated at the back. According to Fitt, this meant the 'speakers had to shout at the members of the larger parties in front and turn round to shout at the members of the smaller parties behind, a feat at which only Paisley, who was in the third row from the back, excelled, as many strained eardrums in Westminster and elsewhere can testify'.

Whitelaw's advisers had already soured the mood of the hardliners by issuing a set of directives, including an instruction to limit speeches to five minutes. Paisley declared the time limit 'a gag and a muzzle' on elected representatives. Nat Minford, the first nominee for presiding officer, was proposed by his party leader, Brian Faulkner but then William Beattie, one of Paisley's political clergymen, was also put forward. When a vote was taken, Minford received 31 votes, five more than Beattie and was declared elected. The SDLP abstained. It was a sign that, although the hardliners might make the most noise, they were not invincible. The signing of the roll came next and passed off without serious disruption, but as soon as Minford moved to propose the drawing up of standing orders, there was an immediate uproar. Minford refused to accept a motion of censure against himself and amidst pandemonium adjourned the Assembly to a date of his deciding.

As Faulkner's people and the Alliance and SDLP groups filed out, the hardliners sought to continue the proceedings by installing Beattie in the chair and voting him in to preside over a protest meeting, which eventually ended with the singing of 'God Save the Queen'. Johnny McQuade, a Paisleyite from the Shankill Road, actually invited Ivan Cooper onto the floor of the Assembly to have a fight. Fitt said afterwards: 'I was glad that two senior Conservative backbenchers were present as observers to see this mockery and the true Jekyll and Hyde character of Paisley coming out, for he was careful to conceal the rabble-rousing side of his nature at Westminster.' A few days later Fitt nominated Currie and Cooper as the SDLP delegates to a committee to draw up standing orders. Minford accepted them. Paisley and Craig were entitled to participate as well, but only Paisley did so.

August was yet another violent month, with the terrorists on both sides killing another twenty-two people in an ever more futile bid to prove their relevance in the face of the democratic process. In the deluge of shooting and bombing, Belfast lost, in Fitt's estimation, one of its most colourful characters:

> Edward 'Boxie' Drummond was a fixture outside the Central Library in Royal Avenue. I used to bump into him regularly on my way in or out of the Brown Horse or McGlade's nearby. He sold shirt studs, matches and razor blades in sufficient quantities to keep himself always at least three-quarters drunk on cheap wine and pay for a bed at the Morning Star hostel. But no matter how drunk he was, he was never aggressive or offensive.

Previously, Boxie had survived a bomb blast in Simon Murphy's pub at Great Patrick Street. Fitt heard the bang and rushed to the scene: 'Suddenly the debris started to move and out of the rubble staggered Boxie, bottle still in hand. 'Hiya, Gerry,' he said. 'Did you hear they bombed Simon Murphy's?' None of us could believe anyone had survived the blast.' Just a few months later, however, on 15 August, Boxie's luck ran out when a no-warning car bomb exploded outside Devenney's Bar in Dock. Boxie died and nine others were injured. 'How the death of a harmless old character like Boxie Drummond could advance any cause is beyond my understanding,' Fitt said, and it was to prevent more pointless deaths like this that he suppressed his own reservations about remaining in the SDLP and pressed ahead that autumn to make the most of the opportunity offered by the Assembly. The urgent necessity to make actual progress was underlined by Heath, who visited Belfast at the end of August and held talks with the main parties, although Craig alone refused to meet him. The day after that, Fitt led an SDLP delegation to Dublin for a meeting with Cosgrave, where the emphasis was on the possible structure and functions of the proposed Council of Ireland.

The question of a Council of Ireland had become an extraordinarily sensitive issue for the British government because of Paisley's persistent scaremongering and misrepresentation of what was actually being proposed and considered. The distortion had become so worrying that Sir Harold Black and Ken Bloomfield, Northern Ireland civil servants with longstanding unionist mindsets, drafted a speech they wanted Whitelaw to deliver to put the true position on record. The draft was considered at the highest level before it was decided that, while it was persuasive, it was 'couched in the phraseology of political combat'. Rather than provide further material for distortion and controversy, the British view was that Whitelaw should not become embroiled in what would undoubtedly be an unedifying slanging match with the unionist hardliners.

The Council was also an increasingly problematical topic for the Irish government. Under Cosgrave's leadership, the dominant policy-maker for Northern Ireland was the dynamic foreign minister, Dr Garret FitzGerald, although Dr Conor Cruise O'Brien, a former diplomat and now the Minister for Posts and Telegraph, separately promoted his own, often controversial views on the way ahead. Unlike their Fianna Fáil predecessors, this Irish government took a far more even-handed view of Northern Ireland and went to great trouble to establish and maintain relationships with both communities there. This stance offended the nationalist element in the SDLP, whose view was that they alone should enjoy Dublin's support. As a result relations between them were poor, eventually reaching rock-bottom after a Sunday newspaper published a story about the deteriorating relationship, which Paddy Devlin was accused of planting. The inference that the government was 'soft' about 'the North' concerned FitzGerald, who feared it would make it even harder for Jack Lynch to contain the hardline republican element within Fianna Fáil, and thereby maintain bipartisanship, at a time when a major political shift was occurring.

Given this background, when Fitt arrived to meet Cosgrave for the first time, the atmosphere was poisonous as the Irish were in confrontational mood and determined to isolate Devlin, who shared a mutual loathing with Cruise O'Brien. The situation compounded Fitt's own reservations about the way in which Hume was making all the running, especially with Dublin. Arising from whispers he had heard at Westminster, he was also fearful that the two governments were conducting their own discussions about the future of Northern Ireland without the SDLP being involved. This suspicion was enhanced when the Irish side exchanged their ideas with London and arranged for Heath to come to Dublin in mid-September – the first visit by a British Prime Minister since the foundation of the Irish Republic. Heath piled on the pressure by announcing that he would recall the London parliament to devolve powers to the Belfast Assembly if agreement was reached between the parties on an executive, and also by undertaking to call a tripartite London – Dublin – Belfast conference within a month of the executive being agreed. This was a powerful incentive for the SDLP because it showed he meant business in terms of conceding an Irish dimension through a Council of Ireland, which the SDLP needed in exchange for working a devolved government in Belfast.

Heath's undertakings helped clear the air all round and after a three-hour evening meeting at Laneside on 10 September between Fitt, Hume, Devlin,

Currie and Eddie McGrady, a newly elected SDLP Assembly man, Frank Cooper noted 'this was the most relaxed meeting held for some time with the SDLP. They reiterated their desire to see early movement on policing, detention without trial and the Council of Ireland.' Hume led the discussion on the Council by outlining a plan for a secretariat, a committee of Cabinet ministers and an Assembly of elected representatives drawn equally from the North and South. Fitt remained behind after the meeting and scorned Hume's plan as being based too much on 'Jesuit logic', but he was pleased to learn that both the Paisley and Craig factions had conclusively ruled themselves out of any participation in a power-sharing executive.

By this stage there was not only progressively more constructive dialogue with British officials but intensive party-to-party contact between the Alliance, the SDLP and the Faulkner-led Unionists. Nonetheless, in yet another manifestation of the division and distrust within the SDLP, the British government record of a meeting with Napier on 13 September noted that Hume was having talks with Bob Cooper of the Alliance party 'almost certainly without Mr Fitt's knowledge'. A few days later, on 21 September, Hume and O'Hanlon had a meeting with Frank Cooper at Laneside. At that meeting Hume suggested the Council of Ireland should be financed from each part of Ireland by an agreed portion of GNP, or indeed from the proceeds of VAT, as the Irish government had proposed.

Exploring these sorts of new ideas was now critical for the SDLP, which was already putting together a series of position papers to set out party policies on key issues and shape its stance at the inter-party talks to create the executive, which were now looming ever closer. Given that the stakes were so high for all concerned, it was inevitable that political infighting and distrust would intrude. Despite their relaxed meeting with Cooper just a couple of weeks earlier, James Allan received a severe dressing-down during a ninety-minute session with Fitt and Devlin at 85 Antrim Road on the morning of 25 September. Both men were angry and accused the British of misrepresenting their position to the Dublin government, especially with regard to the Council of Ireland. That same evening Fitt led a five-strong delegation to another meeting with Cooper, at which Allan was also present. Austin Currie led a pre-planned attack on what they regarded as 'foot dragging' by the British on the Council of Ireland. The SDLP was in turn accused of 'dragging their feet' about entering into the all-party discussions, but that accusation was contested and countered with the fact that SDLP members could not participate for at least another week because they would be attending the Labour party conference. The note of this meeting records that Fitt made little contribution 'and showed some personal shakiness. His colleagues appeared to be somewhat overconfident and were clearly looking for further negotiation advantage *vis-a-vis* HMG.'

Fitt's 'shakiness' may have been attributable to the mood of the party's grassroots. When the SDLP was formed, the six founders were able to get round a table and take decisions without reference to others. Now, they had a team of elected Assembly members, district councillors (among whom were some politically ambitious individuals) as well as a number of ever more active constituency branches. As became evident at a five-hour party meeting in Dungannon on 26 September, there was opposition to the way the leadership was proceeding and concern about the usual issues: policing, detention and security force conduct in the Catholic areas. Fitt was heavily discomforted by this mechanism. He was a natural loner, impetuous and instinctive, and liked to have helpers rather than thinkers around him. When their theorising became too much for him to bear, he would go the bar and expound his frustration about 'fucking teachers' or 'fucking lawyers', professions he had long reviled, telling him what to do.

Furthermore, Fitt was now also caught up in inter-governmental and inter-party talks with grave historical implications, requiring much more structured activity than the off-the-cuff style of politics at which he was so adept. His shakiness may have also been attributable to the reason for the earlier row with James Allan, the origins of which dated back to 7 September when Fitt and Hume had attended an Irish government banquet in Dublin Castle in honour of François-Xavier Ortoli, a French politician and businessman who had recently become President of the European Commission. During the evening, according to the British, Hume sought out their ambassador, Sir Arthur Galsworthy, and in conversation with him and Fitt, Hume allegedly said that the SDLP would be content with a guarantee that a tripartite conference on a Council of Ireland would meet within a month of an executive being formed. The ambassador wanted to be sure that he would report them correctly, so he asked them to repeat their position. It chimed with what James Allan later wrote was his 'distinct impression for a number of weeks that the Council of Ireland had lost its position at the top of the charts in the SDLP hit parade'. However, when Prime Minister Edward Heath met his counterpart, Cosgrave, at the Baldonnel airbase, just south of Dublin, on 17 September 1973 and this interpretation of the SDLP's position was transmitted to the Irish during the discussions, it caused such serious surprise that Sean Donlon, a senior diplomat and the most experienced Northern Ireland 'traveller', was quickly despatched north by Cosgrave himself to ascertain the SDLP's true position. Donlon later said that while the Irish were prepared to believe that 'Gerry Fitt could have said anything at the banquet', they were amazed to hear that Hume was so relaxed about the Council.

Donlon's first call was to see Hume in Derry in the early evening of 24 September. He reported that Hume was 'taken aback' at the suggestion the SDLP had changed tack. He could recall speaking to the ambassador for only five or ten minutes, and in the company of the German and French envoys. There had been no discussion of substance about Northern Ireland affairs and all he could recall was that Galsworthy had invited him to spend a weekend at Glencairn, his official residence outside Dublin. Hume was adamant no suggestion of a policy change had been made and he reiterated that the SDLP was still committed to a package linking the formation of an executive to the creation of a Council of Ireland.

After two hours in Derry, Donlon headed directly to Belfast, where he met Fitt and Devlin at 85 Antrim Road about 10.00pm. They, too, were astounded that anyone could think they had abandoned their position and put the suggestion down to an effort by the British government to drive a wedge between the SDLP and Dublin. Despite Donlon's protestations, they insisted on instantly ringing the British to clarify the position. With Donlon present in the room, Devlin then phoned James Allan and afterwards Fitt rang Cooper, who offered to come immediately to see him and sort things out. Fitt, who had described the seasoned diplomat Galsworthy as 'new to the game and not very bright', dissuaded him and agreed instead to meet the next morning. Donlon concluded that Cooper was prepared not only 'to take an earful' from them but to come over to Antrim Road 'at a very late hour on a very dark and wet Monday evening' because the SDLP had been 'playing hard-to-get' about talking to officials in recent weeks. Before returning to Dublin the following day, Donlon also visited Paddy Duffy and Austin Currie in Dungannon. They confirmed that the party line remained unchanged, which Donlon duly reported to Cosgrave.

On 29 September, a few days after his return to Dublin, Donlon met Allan in the home of a member of staff of the Dublin embassy 'to make sure there was no misunderstandings'. The conversation led Allan to wonder 'who is making the running, the SDLP with Dublin or vice-versa?' The British ambassador judged that it was Dublin, but Allan took the view that 'it is a two-way process, no doubt lubricated by injection of disinformation when necessary'.

Despite such squalls, round-table talks on the creation of an executive began in Stormont Castle on 5 October in the very room where the unionist-dominated Cabinet used to meet. Fitt claimed to have engineered the date to mark the fifth anniversary of the civil rights march in Derry, which was now generally accepted as being the starting point of what were called 'the Troubles'. According to his memoirs, Whitelaw was not optimistic about the prospects for success and told his staff to be ready for an early lunch adjournment in the hope that the break would ease the inevitable tensions and improve personal relations. Decoded, this meant that large measures of drinks were to be served to lubricate the process. He need not have worried. From the outset the representatives of the UUP, the Alliance party and the SDLP acknowledged their great differences, but then moved on to map out the substantial common ground between them.

In his opening statement Faulkner said his party hoped earnestly that the talks would be successful and promised that they would not harp back to past disagreements. He called for the other two parties to assure him they supported the Constitution Act, stressed the need to operate on the principle of collective responsibility and, while noting that all parties had frequently repudiated violence, said it was now essential that they should declare support for the security forces and unequivocally accept the RUC as the police force of Northern Ireland.

Speaking for the SDLP, Fitt declared his hope that the meeting would be productive and memorable for the whole of Ireland. He said his party wished to discuss a new approach, both in terms of broad policy and details of all aspects of life in the province. The SDLP believed that a just and democratic government could only be achieved on the basis of the involvement of representatives from all parts of the community, and they hoped an Executive would be constituted on this basis. In response to Faulkner, Fitt said his party was prepared to accept the oath and the Constitution Act and stressed the SDLP's belief that political action alone could bring an end to the violence. With regard to security, policing and detention, he pointed out they were matters reserved to the British government, with whom the SDLP was prepared to discuss them.

Currie and Hume then interjected, both making the point that initially the talks should concentrate on areas of agreement and only tackle the more difficult issues once some progress had been made. Fitt agreed that this approach would negate the effect of 'wreckers' in both communities. Whitelaw supported the SDLP strategy and said that once the non-contentious issues had been dealt with and an atmosphere of mutual confidence established, it would then be far easier to take a constructive attitude to the subjects that were going to cause disagreement.

Faulkner remained confrontational, insisting that SDLP recognition of the RUC was essential to winning public confidence and therefore non-negotiable. Devlin conceded that it would not be possible to oppose the security forces if one were a member of a power-sharing executive. Attention then turned to the draft standing orders and, in particular, a Paisley amendment requiring a prayer for the head of state [the Queen]. This obviously created a dilemma for both the Unionists and the SDLP. Faulkner said while he could not oppose the amendment, there was understanding of the SDLP position. Bob Cooper of the Alliance party suggested a compromise in the form of the Lord's Prayer, which was universally acceptable to all creeds. Whitelaw encouraged the notion of compromise and urged the parties to tackle the issue between themselves.

Oliver Napier also favoured the SDLP approach and urged the others to define an agenda, starting with the non-contentious issues. This viewpoint was finally accepted and before breaking for lunch the parties agreed they would look at the social and economic issues in the afternoon session.

When they resumed, Hume initiated the discussion and suggested they should agree on a programme to be completed in their first term of office, based on the common objectives of achieving a rising standard of living, full employment and social justice. With his business background and previous ministerial experience, Faulkner responded enthusiastically and listed a series of specific sectors where progress was possible: an expanded house-building programme with mortgage assistance and aid for railway, harbour and shipyard developments. He was also keen on educational integration, although he recognised the difficulty from Catholic insistence on running their own schools. Napier joined in, consenting to what had been said already and agreeing with Faulkner's insistence on social services parity with the rest of the United Kingdom. Whitelaw edged them onwards when he noted that the Treasury would be prepared to do more for a devolved administration in Northern Ireland than it would otherwise, and he endorsed proposals from several of the negotiators to form sub-committees to examine in more detail the strands of a social and economic programme for the Executive.

Following this remarkable meeting of minds on social and economic issues, the parties then moved on to look at the contentious issues: policing; detention; the role of the army; the Council of Ireland; and the standing orders for the Assembly. Once again there was a notable lack of acrimony as the divergent views were rehearsed, and it was agreed they would examine the issues further at a future meeting. The final item of the day was listed as 'publicity'. The parties agreed a joint statement and affirmed that none of them would make any further comment to the press, radio or television about the proceedings, which ended at 5.30pm. Fitt was exhilarated that the talks had got off to such an encouraging start, but the PIRA made sure the politicians had great trouble getting home by gumming up the city's traffic with about sixty elaborate hoax bombs.

Whitelaw and a cadre of his ministers and advisers met the SDLP negotiators at Stormont Castle on 9 October to review with them alone their standpoint on the contentious issues. He struck a notably conciliatory note at the beginning of the meeting when he thanked the SDLP for their moderate attitude at the opening session of the all-party talks, but there was nothing pragmatic about their demands for wholesale police reform and a Council of Ireland with extensive powers and responsibilities.

By the time the full Assembly held its second meeting, on 15 October, there had been two important areas of agreement. The all-party standing orders committee had travelled to London, inspected the House of Lords and Commons, the Lewisham Borough Council chamber and that of the City of Westminster, as well as the Dutch and Belgian parliamentary chambers, and then agreed a report. (According to Fitt, Paisley was on the Amsterdam delegation and during the trip he caught other members browsing through 'pin-up books' and called down the wrath of God upon them.) The report proposed that the Assembly meet in the old Commons chamber at Stormont, with the seating re-arranged into a horseshoe shape, and that the Executive occupy the front bench to the right-hand of the presiding officer. This was intended to contrast with the confrontational government – opposition approach and to reflect the more collegiate administration implicit in power-sharing. More importantly, the inter-party talks had finalised a social and economic programme very much in line with the SDLP blueprint, although not without some difficulty as Bradford and Devlin had clashed fiercely, both on policy and personality terms. In the end, the SDLP version had been toned down because it was deemed too 'left-wing' for the unionists.

In the midst of all this high politicking, Fitt was still a very active member of Belfast District Council and, other commitments permitting, continued to attend meetings at City Hall as he had done for the fifteen years since his first election victory. By the yardstick of his political achievements since then, including being on first-name terms with the Prime Minister of Britain and senior members of the British government, his unopposed appointment as chairman of the Council's Gas Committee would appear, at first glance, to be small beer. But as this was the first time for as long as anyone could remember that a Catholic had held such a prominent position in City Hall, Fitt interpreted the gesture, which had cross-party support, as one of goodwill that augured well for the ultimate success of the all-important inter-party talks. As emotion and superstition were such dominant influences in his character, he had a tendency to invest such incidents with far more significance than they deserved.

The talks continued throughout October and into November, with the focus switching to the more controversial areas, such as law and order, after detailed party position papers were submitted to Whitelaw. The process of consultation with Dublin continued simultaneously with the Belfast talks and there were also further meetings of the full Assembly, which were characterised by increasing acrimony and decidedly unparliamentary behaviour. At one meeting, Paisley held the floor for more than three hours complaining about the moves towards a sell-out. Paddy Devlin provided some background insight into the intensive political infighting that was going on behind the scenes when he arrived at Laneside for a lunch with Frank Cooper on 23 October. Hume was also due to attend, but was delayed for two hours by a security alert in Derry. In his absence, Devlin expressed optimism about the potential for power-sharing. During the talks to date, he said, the SDLP's suspicions about Faulkner had been allayed and they had become increasingly convinced of the sincerity of his desire to do a deal. He revealed that both Bradford and Taylor had made overtures to the SDLP about the possibility of doing a deal without Faulkner, but both had been rebuffed. He and Hume had also met Paisley recently and he had been exceptionally friendly to him, so he felt it was only a matter of time before some approach was made for a deal.

When Hume arrived his attitude highlighted the divisions within the SDLP.

He was pessimistic about the possibility of power-sharing as a workable mechanism. The SDLP-dominated district councils had adopted it already, but those run by unionists had not. In any case, it would be underpinned by an act of the Westminster parliament, whose attitude to Ireland had always been based on British pragmatism. He went on to express fears that Northern Ireland civil servants might refuse to take orders from power-sharing ministers, and stressed the need to correct the sectarian imbalance within the organisation. Both SDLP leaders were insistent that the planned executive should consist of five unionists, five SDLP and two Alliance ministers. They could not accept the unionist majority for which Faulkner was holding out. Shortly before this encounter, Devlin had deliberately raised the negotiating stakes by publicly stating that the SDLP should provide the Chief Executive as a really tangible sign that things had changed for the better but the remark was quickly and privately disowned by Dublin at diplomatic level. It was 'stupid', the Irish said, and they accepted Faulkner had to head any executive.

From Faulkner's increasingly precarious standpoint, Devlin's suggestion could not have come at a more inopportune moment. After weeks of sniping from those in his party opposed to power-sharing, the very same day Faulkner was seeking a mandate from his bitterly and fundamentally divided party's Standing Committee to enable his elected Assembly group to participate in a power-sharing administration, a proposition that was all the more objectionable as it became ever more apparent that it would also be coupled with an as yet undefined Irish dimension. He won the vote 132 – 105, but with the party so divided, the narrowness of the margin encouraged his opponents to push for an early meeting of the ruling Ulster Unionist Council (UUC) in a further bid to thwart him.

Fitt, Devlin, Hume, Currie and Michael Canavan of the SDLP met Irish government ministers Dr Garret FitzGerald, Dr Conor Cruise O'Brien and Declan Costello on 2 November to take stock of the situation. The two sides had been meeting every three weeks or so for this purpose, a series of high-level encounters that were disclosed publicly by the SDLP to convince their nationalist-minded supporters that they were dealing in an all-Ireland context. While not intending to let Faulkner off the hook, some SDLP members were already fearful that he had over-committed himself by agreeing to enter into power-sharing, and this time there was a sharp appreciation of the need for SDLP discretion to avoid embarrassing Faulkner, whose standing as Unionist leader was coming under increasing pressure from his uncompromising hardliners as the negotiating process continued. Conscious of unionist susceptibilities, the Irish urged the SDLP to play down their Dublin visits.

Back in Belfast, the inter-party talks were stalling dangerously on two critical issues: policing and the make-up of the Executive. These issues were addressed when Frank Cooper met the SDLP on 6 November to help head them off from what he called 'a collision course' with the Unionists. The SDLP accused the British of constantly propping up the Unionists in the main talks and complained they had won nothing for their own moderation. Hume reiterated their demand for equal representation on the Executive and, despite pressure from Cooper, refused to sign up to the concept of collective responsibility within the Executive, a doctrine of supreme importance to Faulkner. The SDLP again pushed for a tripartite conference to be held before the Executive was actually formed in order to consider the Council of Ireland.

The question of whether or not the party should support the RUC was probably the most difficult to address. SDLP support for the police force was seen by many Protestant people as an indication of their 'loyalty' to the Northern Ireland Executive and they could not understand the SDLP's reservations about the RUC although this was an area where the party itself was fundamentally divided. Fitt and Devlin did not share Hume's dogmatic hostility towards the RUC and his uncritical views on the subject. They did have deep reservations, but they were much more pragmatic in their response to reform. Fitt, in particular, had a long history of constructive relations with the police. He told the Scarman Tribunal that in fighting elections over the years he had got to know 300 or 400 of the police very well, amounting to about one-sixth of the force. (He did not tell Scarman that on one occasion during a campaign, he had agreed with the police escorting his election lorry that at a certain time he would park it close to a public house so they could keep an eye on him and at the same time watch an important football match on the pub's television. When his loud hailer failed, the police loaned him theirs and then listened with great amusement as he used it to raise some cheap cheers from the crowd by roundly denouncing them as the tool of the Unionist party.)

Hume, however, was suspicious of the RUC. At this time, without consulting Fitt or Devlin, he had drawn up a 'blacklist' of some forty officers he wanted sacked for various reasons. He gave the list to Whitelaw at one of his solo meetings and subsequently told the Department of Foreign Affairs that when Whitelaw read it, he nodded and said, 'some of these names are on my list, too'. Nevertheless, Fitt and Devlin acquiesced as Hume went on to emphasise to Cooper their enthusiasm for a common law enforcement area throughout the island of Ireland and the need for the RUC and the Irish police, the Garda Síochána, to be placed under the control of the proposed Council of Ireland. The British were sceptical that the Irish government would take this idea seriously at all and concerned about the effect of the SDLP's uncompromising demands on the two-thirds majority unionist community whom, Cooper said with masterly understatement, hold 'strong views'. The SDLP was in danger of 'over-calling its hand' and 'account must be taken of the real situation and not a theoretical one,' warned Cooper. In him, the SDLP had more than met its match. Some years earlier, he had earned a reputation as a formidably tough negotiator during a long series of talks with the intractable Archbishop Makarios in Cyprus which brought about an end to violence there and created a lengthy period of stability. Devlin, in particular, was in some awe of this and enjoyed pitting his negotiating wits against someone he regarded as a seasoned operator.

The hard negotiating line taken by the SDLP leadership reflected not only their own position but also that of the growing organisation to which they now had to account. The mood, especially among those from the country areas outside Belfast, was significantly uncompromising and nationalistic, exacerbated by fears arising from a great surge in violence by loyalist elements. In their own constituencies the SDLP were inundated with complaints about police and military conduct and tactics, and there were almost daily instances of sectarian murder and gun and bomb attacks on Catholic property, yet they increasingly felt they were complaining in vain about inaction against the perpetrators.

This frustration had first come to the fore in August 1973 when Paddy Duffy, a wealthy solicitor and Assemblyman for Mid-Ulster, took the initiative in seeking a meeting with Whitelaw to raise their concerns. The substance of their case was backed by a well-researched dossier entitled, 'Loyalist violence and the result of it – the failure of the security forces to deal with it'. This document asserted that of the 218 assassinations since 1 January 1972, republican extremists had been responsible for thirty. In spite of this, there were only twenty members of extreme loyalist organisations being held at the Long Kesh internment centre, compared with over 600 members of the republican movement. It went on to cite a sequence of recent anti-Catholic incidents within an area five miles in radius along the Tyrone – Armagh border: three persons murdered; one very seriously injured; six drive-by shootings at dwelling houses; three bomb attacks on licensed premises, destroying two of them; a blast bomb attack at a house; the kidnapping and wounding of three youths; the destruction of a Catholic church in a bomb attack; and five arson attacks on haysheds and greenhouses. Not a single person had been charged for these 'loyalist' crimes in this small area. The dossier concluded:

> It is in this background that the security forces under the control of the Secretary of State continues to intern members of the republican movement, carry out raids in Catholic areas and ignores completely the activities of the UDA and its kindred organisations. The SDLP is now reaching the end of the road in its toleration of this situation and is no longer prepared to accept pious platitudes and unfulfilled promises from the Secretary of State.

Repeated requests from Duffy for a meeting with Whitelaw were turned down until early October, when it was agreed that William Van Straubenzee, the next most senior minister, would meet them. The encounter did not go well. Van Straubenzee insisted that the number of people being charged with serious offences showed clearly that the government was taking firm action against all terrorists. He went on to point out that if, as the deputation wanted, all those interned were released, many murderers would be returned to the streets, which was not in the interest of the Catholic community. At that, Duffy led a walkout of his five colleagues.

During their meeting with Whitelaw on 12 November, Fitt and Devlin, clearly having to echo their colleagues' attitudes, said the army was paying too much attention to Catholics in West Belfast and not enough to loyalist elements. In particular, they wanted the minister to proscribe the UDA, to which they attributed responsibility for most of the anti-Catholic violence. In spite of the convincing evidence – of which the government was all too aware – Whitelaw was unsympathetic to their case. He felt such a move would not help achieve his primary object of dividing the violent from the non-violent men because it was 'an emotive rather than a practical act'.

With the unresolved issues of security policy and internment simmering away in the background, the crunch-point in the inter-party talks came on Monday, 19 November. The previous day, in a bid to crystallise what had been agreed and what was still outstanding, a government document entitled 'Inter-party discussions' had been circulated to all the parties. The SDLP was very unhappy that a good deal of what that document contained found its way into the London *Times* the next morning. They expressed their displeasure to Whitelaw during a face-to-face meeting later that day. Fitt said the proposed share-out of ministries was 'not acceptable at all', the proposals on policing too vague and those on the Council of Ireland only partly satisfactory. Whitelaw and Cooper were highly conciliatory and, when the SDLP turned the conversation to the lack of movement on internment, assured them they were trying to go as far as they could, 'but it would be disastrous to be committed to a specific date for releases' because once it was announced, 'if the men of violence stepped up their efforts, the result would be to wreck the Executive'.

The SDLP posture had more to do with brinkmanship and point-scoring than anything else. Fitt said that assenting to Faulkner becoming Chief Executive had been a major concession because (given the activities of Craig, Paisley and hardliners in his own party) Faulkner would be hard put even to match the nineteen votes the SDLP commanded in the Assembly. It was not surprising, then, that after six hours of negotiations there was still no agreement on the number of Executive members and the allocation of portfolios among the parties. For his part, Faulkner was unyielding that the division must be 6-4-1 to give him control of the Executive.

After these inconclusive exchanges, Faulkner rang Fitt at home and asked to see him urgently. Fitt invited him up to 'Fortress Fitt', where even more elaborate security measures had recently been put in place. This work followed an IRA rocket attack aimed at the sentry post for the army's Girdwood Barracks, which was directly opposite the Fitt house. The missile overshot and exploded in the attic of a nearby house where a seven-year-old boy suffered a serious shrapnel wound to the head. The youngest Fitt daughter, Geraldine, who had just left the family house, was also caught in the blast and suffered minor cuts as well as shock. Ann found her lying outside on the street: 'I rushed out and carried her into the house. I thought she was dead but, thank God, she quickly recovered.' The blast also shocked Gerry's frail mother, Mary Ann, who had recently been hospitalised with heart trouble.

When Faulkner arrived he was ushered into the house and they discussed the deadlock over tea and biscuits served by Patsy, one of the now famous Miss Fitts. It was an indication of just how much things had changed that negotiations about such a momentous political development were taking place between the former Unionist Prime Minister sitting in the home of a minority community leader. Fitt later recalled:

> We talked at length and frankly about the jobs and the people eligible for them. I said there were intense rivalries between the strong men in the SDLP and explained the pressure I was under to allocate particular ministries. Faulkner, who had his own dissidents to contend with, said he expected I would want the commerce portfolio for the SDLP. He said he did not want Roy Bradford, one of his own men to get it. As an ex-commerce minister nobody knew better than Faulkner the headline-hitting possibilities and the travel round the world the job entailed, trying to get investment and new industry.

There was, though, a more pertinent political reason for this animosity towards his colleague. For months Bradford had been at the forefront of those working to undermine Faulkner because he wanted to succeed him as party leader. He had secretly been courting the leadership of the loyalist UDA to buttress his hold on his constituency in East Belfast and had been blamed for leaking the details of party meetings to help discredit Faulkner. He had also played such a malign role in the recent negotiations that Faulkner was persuaded from dropping him only because it was feared he would do more damage from without. Instead, Faulkner wanted Fitt to take the commerce role but he declined, ostensibly because of his 'commitments as an MP at Westminster'. The reality was that, both by inclination and aptitude, the last thing Fitt wanted was to be tied to a ministerial desk and all the commitments that went with it. He was therefore more than happy to accept Faulkner's suggestion that neither of them should have a specific portfolio, but rather a 'roving commission'.

That settled, Faulkner responded positively to Fitt's suggestion that a Catholic minister urging investment in Ulster would be a revolutionary development, and they agreed on John Hume as the candidate, despite Fitt's deep misgivings about him. Fitt was not aware that Hume had already been told that the NIO would swing it for him to get the finance post, but, as Hume later confessed to Donlon, he had told them to 'stuff it' because he felt it would not give him enough scope to be seen by his own supporters to be 'delivering' for them. It was suggested within the SDLP that, with his academic and teaching background, he was a natural for the education portfolio, but Hume side-stepped that proposition too because he feared pressure for integrated education could bring him into conflict with the Catholic Church. 'I deplored Hume's dishonesty over taking the post. He was a natural, but he made it clear that he would not entertain it and he preferred to sit on the fence.' Fitt then made a strong bid to get the finance portfolio for the SDLP so he could give it to Austin Currie, his closest political collaborator within the party, but the NIO did not intervene and Faulkner would not budge from having it for his own party. Unlike Hume, Faulkner understood the power that flowed from controlling the purse strings.

Fitt and Faulkner reached an understanding that the deadlock on the division of ministerial posts could be resolved by creating four extra, non-voting posts. That would create an executive of eleven inside a total administration of fifteen ministers. However buoyed Faulkner was by this real advance, he suffered a serious blow the next day when the UUC approved the proposal to go for power-sharing by a margin of just ten votes, 379 – 369.

Whitelaw had set a deadline of the following day for the parties to agree the plan for the Executive, but when he heard of the strength of opposition to Faulkner, he rang Heath expressing little optimism that it would be met. Whitelaw's pessimism was also based on information about the tensions within the SDLP. At a meeting in Toome, some days beforehand, Fitt had encountered grave discontent among some of his backbenchers, who were still balking at the lack of movement on internment. (Fitt's personal ambivalence about ending internment had been somewhat diluted because Whitelaw had recently told him, in confidence, that among the loyalists in custody was the man the police believed was the ringleader of the gang that murdered Paddy Wilson.) As there would not be jobs for all the contenders in the new administration, Fitt feared that some of them might adopt 'conscience of the party' roles and make trouble for him. Discussing these fears with Donlon after the Toome meeting, he said they would have to learn the art of compromise now that they were real politicians, not street politicians.

By this time Whitelaw was privately aware that Heath was going to recall him to another post in London, but his brief was to conclude a deal before departing. On Wednesday, 21 November, with Whitelaw and Cooper piling on the pressure, a settlement was finally hammered out after ten hours of negotiation. The breakthrough came in a face-to-face session between Whitelaw, Fitt and Hume when they were persuaded that Faulkner would not survive if the SDLP did not back down on their demand for a new name for the RUC. Whitelaw then endorsed the Faulkner – Fitt formula for the structure of the Executive and, at 8.30pm, when everything was finally in place, they were all, in Fitt's later words,

> ...very emotional, indeed close to tears as the historic importance of what we had achieved began to sink in. I went to the head of the table and shook hands with Whitelaw, followed by Faulkner and Napier. But it was not a moment for bursting open the champagne. It was more sombre than that for in every sense the real task was only beginning and many areas of great difficulty remained.

Forty-eight hours later the House of Commons in London enthusiastically welcomed Whitelaw's news and he was praised by representatives from all parties. Fitt said they had reached the greatest watershed since the dark days of the outbreak of violence in 1969:

> I believe that the three political parties in Northern Ireland which have engaged in these discussions have opened up a new era in Northern Irish politics. For the first time we have people of different political allegiances beginning to say, in the interests of this whole community, let us think not of party but of people.

The allocation of ministries followed. John Hume was appointed Minister for Commerce and Fitt remarked, 'Let him take the onus upon himself to see whether he can direct industry to Newry, Strabane and all the other areas which have suffered grievous unemployment.' Regarding Currie, who would take charge of development, housing and local government, Fitt said, 'He will not want to see more houses built purely and exclusively for Catholics; he will want to see them built for people who need them. I know of no man of greater humanity and compassion in the Northern Ireland political arena.' Devlin was allocated Health and Social Services, while the extra two posts, with non-voting membership of the Executive, were given to Ivan Cooper, as Minister of Community Relations, and the SDLP chairman Eddie McGrady, as Minister of Planning and Co-ordination.

That night the *Belfast Telegraph*, in a front-page splash, hailed the members of the new Executive as 'Ulster's men of destiny'. Next morning the London *Times*, in a leader that sounded necessary notes of caution about the Council of Ireland, described this 'instalment of success' as 'a great achievement'. The PIRA, predictably enough, did not share this assessment of events. That evening shots were fired at the home of Austin Currie, narrowly missing two police officers on guard duty there. Currie had forecast just such an event at a meeting with Whitelaw as recently as 12 November. The IRA was convinced that the inter-party talks had arrived at an agreement on extradition, which put the SDLP members at risk. Fitt, Hume and Devlin, who were also present, were all increasingly nervous, fearing they were at risk of immediate assassination by either the IRA or extreme loyalists as a means of stopping the talks. While in their homes they were vulnerable to an IRA attack; while travelling on their own they were vulnerable to a loyalist attack. Whitelaw accepted that their concerns about their personal safety were well-founded – he was aware of the high-grade intelligence that the PIRA intended to kill one of them and make it look like the work of loyalists. From then on the ministers-in-waiting were provided with official cars and, despite their reservations about the RUC, police bodyguards. Soon afterwards, soldiers arrived to erect blast walls as part of a protection package at the Currie home, but Currie expressed great concerns about them being attacked and killed. Devlin was also worried about the safety of his police escorts as they travelled back and forward to his home in the IRA heartland of Andersonstown.

With the first part of the new political dispensation in place and the promised tripartite conference imminent, the SDLP's third annual party conference went ahead at the Europa Hotel in Belfast on 1 December. It endorsed a major social and economic programme, tasking the incoming Executive to create the infrastructure needed to attract new industry by instigating a crash building programme of roads, factories and 20,000 houses. In his scene-setting leader's speech, delivered without any prepared text, Fitt was careful to set a constructive tone and not provide any ammunition for Faulkner's enemies. It was not a victory to be participating in government, no community could have a total victory over the other, he said. Looking ahead, he predicted that the coming negotiations could bring about a system of government acceptable to all and they could forget the years of misery and divisiveness:

> I never believed that I would see a day such as this when there is such hope,
> when unionist and republicans, Protestants and Catholics, representatives
> of orange and green are prepared to sit down and discuss their differences.

He called for an end to violence, but told the conference the 'obscenity of internment' could prejudice such co-operation if it were not ended. For Fitt, it was very much a ritual statement, something he had to say to placate his own hardliners. They then flexed their muscles by tabling a motion seeking to censure the party negotiators for failing to reflect the mandate given to them and calling for an urgent review of the methods used in selecting party delegations. The leadership was defended by Paddy O'Donoghue, who said the party had picked their best team and as they were doing quite well at half-time and had the promise of a favourable wind in the second half, they should stick with them. The motion was roundly defeated and an emergency motion endorsing their action to date and giving the leadership a mandate to continue received equally overwhelming support.

The Irish government was particularly interested in the mood of the conference and Donlon provided an insightful report. The party was 'very healthy', he concluded, with a card-carrying membership of about 5,000 and 500 delegates turning up for the conference. In the previous year the number of branches had expanded from twenty to sixty-eight, there were five constituency councils and plans to create one in each of the seven other Westminster constituencies. As a result of the elections during the year, one in six of all the district councillors in Northern Ireland were SDLP members and they also held one-quarter of the seats in the Stormont Assembly. Their financial position, Donlon noted, was 'reasonably' healthy, too, not least because of the £13,000 raised on their behalf in the South by a Dublin academic. He concluded:

> The six founder members so dominate that there seemed to be a general reluctance, even on the part of the thirteen new Assemblymen, to challenge their views in any serious way.

He went on to note the widespread feeling within the party that it was political activity by the original civil rights campaigners – now heavily integrated within the SDLP – and not the ongoing violence by the IRA that had the secured gains in the new political situation that now existed. Nevertheless, there was an equally widespread feeling that internment must be ended and, although it was not said so bluntly in open session, many feared the party leadership was going too far without a cast-iron guarantee that that would soon happen. Donlon described 'Fitt's position as leader of the party is firm', but he went on to say:

> He rarely answers letters, does not even open some addressed to him from SDLP headquarters or branches, attends almost no party meetings ... and, in general, operates on his own. Despite this, there is no obvious hint of dissatisfaction from the grass-roots and any grumbling within the Assembly party appeared to be forgotten both in the general air of euphoria following the inter-party talks and in the atmosphere created by Fitt's stirring, emotional and witty keynote address.

As a measure of Fitt's remoteness from his party, Donlon pointed to the fact that he had attended only two of the seventeen party executive committee meetings in the previous year. For his own part, Fitt was obviously ill-at-ease after the conference:

> There were those in the party, as events would show, who were prepared to compromise the potential of what had been achieved on the single issue of internment. I met many of them that weekend and I knew they would ultimately cause me trouble. What annoyed me about most of them was their ambivalence to IRA violence. Many never condemned it or called for peace but some speakers did make the point that a genuine ceasefire would have removed the need and justification for internment at a stroke. I bitterly resented the fact that internment put us and the IRA on the same side. It meant we were making the same demands, and looked like we had something in common, when of course we did not.

Over that same weekend London announced that Heath had reshuffled his

Cabinet, replacing Whitelaw with Francis Pym, a wealthy, old-Etonian businessman and landowner who was being promoted from government chief whip. Fitt was highly dismayed that the sensitive and experienced Whitelaw, who had infallibly grasped the subtleties of Northern Ireland's complex politics, was leaving at such a critical moment, the eleventh hour before the Council of Ireland discussions fixed for later in the week. But as politicians, they fully understood why Heath needed his conciliatory talents at the Department of Employment, where a protracted dispute with Britain's coal miners was having ever more serious consequences for the economy and public order in Britain and shaping up into an all-out 'who rules the country' confrontation.

The deal to form an Executive and the looming tripartite talks had driven extreme unionists to renewed fury. Twice the Assembly was in uproar. On the first occasion, Johnny McQuade had to be ejected from the chamber by order of the presiding officer. The session was then adjourned amidst shouting, jeering and scuffling between the pro-Executive and opposing unionists. The hardliners met Pym on his first trip to Belfast to press their demand that they should be represented at the coming conference, and were driven to even more anger by his refusal. On Wednesday, 5 December, the eve of the conference, the Assembly session degenerated into actual fisticuffs between the unionist groupings, and several unionist members of the Executive-designate were kicked, spat upon and punched before the RUC was called in to eject the troublemakers. The same day five of the seven Westminster Unionist MPs transferred their allegiance from Faulkner. One of the two who remained loyal said it was 'a stab in the back'. As they prepared for the tripartite talks, Fitt knew the defections would not make it any easier for the SDLP to sign up to new arrangements for policing, or for Faulkner to strike a deal on the Council of Ireland.

CHAPTER ELEVEN

A TOAST TO PEACE

EVER SINCE THE PARTIES HAD SIGNED UP TO form the Executive on 21 November 1973, British officials had worked round the clock to organise the complementary tripartite conference. The venue was a difficulty. Security considerations ruled out Northern Ireland, while the Republic was unacceptable because unionists would not attend. The Turnberry hotel complex on the Ayrshire coast, within sightt of Northern Ireland, was favoured by the security advisers, but as both the British and Irish Prime Ministers preferred somewhere convenient to London, the Civil Service Staff College at Sunningdale in Berkshire was finally selected. Security fears about the thick rhododendron bushes surrounding it were dismissed; the police could put in dogs to patrol them. So too were anxieties about the standard of catering, but given the hard-drinking reputation of many of the Irish delegates, arrangements were made to provide a well-stocked cash bar for them.

Heath's heavy diary commitments pointed to the conference being held on Thursday and Friday, 6–7 December. That weekend he was scheduled to entertain the Italian Prime Minister, Mariano Rumor, before going to his Broadstairs constituency in Kent on Sunday evening to rehearse for the Christmas carol service he traditionally conducted. Before the dates were finalised, however, the Foreign Office was asked to research if either of these days had any emotive connotations in terms of Irish history. 'The Irish have an elephantine memory and most days commemorate something or other,' wrote Kelvin White, who ran the Republic of Ireland desk. He reported that on the days in question, in 1921, the Anglo-Irish Treaty partitioning Ireland had been signed at Downing Street. On a more ominous note, he recalled that it was on 8 December 1922 that the newly established Free State government had shot four IRA prisoners without trial as a reprisal for the shooting of one of their parliamentary deputies. That reprisal was justified by William T Cosgrave – himself a future Prime Minister and the father of the current Prime Minister – to 'show [the IRA] that terror would be struck into them'. None of these events was considered sufficiently problematical to change the proposed dates and official invitations were issued swiftly. The British game-plan was that the conference would open on the Thursday morning and conclude on the Friday evening, leaving Heath free to entertain his Italian counterpart. On his instructions, it was stressed to the Irish that the conference must end on Friday evening to avoid compromising his other commitments.

After much debate, it was decided that the hardline unionist leaders, Craig and Paisley, would also have to be invited to the conference, but that they would be confined to making opening statements about their opposition and excluded from any further participation. Fearing that Paisley might attempt to filibuster and disrupt the conference, contingency plans were made to have him ejected by force, if necessary. In the event both men declined their invitations and did not attend.

For their part, the Irish approached the negotiation with much trepidation. There was an awareness that these were unarguably the most fundamental Anglo-Irish talks in the fifty years since partition and, with the stakes so high, they wanted to protect the integrity of their position and walk away with dignity intact, if necessary. As a result, three Special Branch men from Dublin were included in their delegation to 'protect their offices in the conference building', and they arranged for an Aer Lingus aircraft to remain on standby at Heathrow for the duration of the negotiations. In the run-up to the talks the security-conscious Irish used Aer Lingus pilots as couriers for diplomatic messages between London and Dublin to guard against the possibility of the British security service eavesdropping on the details of their negotiating position.

In advance of the talks, the British prepared comprehensive briefings for Heath, the new Secretary of State, Pym, and others on their team. These included papers on border security, the record, strength and capabilities of the RUC, the role of the parliamentary ombudsman, the extent of discrimination in employment and housing, the implications of EEC membership and internment. They also assembled biographical dossiers on each member of the various delegations from Ireland, sometimes adding waspish character assessments to flesh them out. Cosgrave, for instance, was said to have entered politics out of a sense of family duty rather than choice. He is 'not an exciting man; he is quiet, stubborn and tough but can be cantankerous. Above all, he is honest and courageous and firmly opposed to compromising with violence.' The assessment ended by noting his considerable political acumen, wry sense of humour and that he was 'very religious'.

In other preparatory material the British also noted remarks by Sean Donlon about Cosgrave's conviction that radical police reform was possible. This was based on the fact that his father had been instrumental in setting up An Garda Síochána, which remained an unarmed force and survived the turbulent early history of the Republic. Cosgrave, it was reported, believed that just as the first two Gardaí into Cork were regarded as heroes, so too would be the first men into the Creggan. Although he recognised the importance of the northern police being linked to the Council of Ireland to help the Catholic community to identify with them, Cosgrave was reluctant for the Irish government to give up full control of the Gardaí, as the SDLP wanted.

According to the British pre-Sunningdale brief, Dr Garret FitzGerald, the Irish Foreign Minister, was a moderate socialist, a convinced European, a prolific writer on political/economic affairs and 'one of the best informed, most intelligent and articulate members of the Irish parliament, who speaks well (and quickly and at great length) and commands respect. A section of his party [Fine Gael] would like to see him as leader but he has made no challenge to Mr Cosgrave and seems unaware of political intrigues and takes no part in them.' The brief did not record that he was often fondly referred to as Dr Garrulous FitzGerald by his colleagues.

By far the lengthiest in the series of confidential portraits was devoted to Dr Conor Cruise O'Brien, a former Irish diplomat, UN envoy to the Congo and current minister for posts and telegraphs: 'Although he is a very capable deputy on the socialist left of the Irish Labour Party, he enjoys little popularity in rural Ireland and among the pious because of his divorce and the circumstances surrounding it.' (While serving at the UN in New York, he got to know the daughter of the Irish Deputy Prime Minister, whom he married after his wife divorced him.) As his party's spokesman on Northern Ireland, Cruise O'Brien was widely unpopular for a perceived sympathy with unionism, a perception that had also seriously strained his relationship with the SDLP. Described as an outstanding writer, critic and speaker, the British assessment was that he displayed 'considerable intellectual arrogance', handled people badly and made enemies because of his 'gift for cutting ridicule'.

While the brief contained biographical details of the leading Northern Ireland politicians, it was largely free of such biting personal analysis, but some individuals were singled out for comment. As Bradford, it was noted, had been involved in a number of manoeuvres to take over leadership of the Unionist party from Faulkner, his appointment to environment rather than finance must be regarded as something of a snub. John Hume was described as 'the party's theoretician, introspective and with a tendency to Jesuitical dispute'. Paddy Devlin was noted to be agnostic and described as the party's 'leading political tactician'. Ivan Cooper, 'the one Protestant in his party', was said to have dabbled in a number of small businesses and to be something of an oddball. Interestingly, with regard to both Faulkner and Fitt, the civil service biographers confined themselves to merely recording their career details and the fact that both were married.

Several days before the delegations arrived, a carefully planned security cordon was thrown around the venue. All but domestic and catering staff were evicted for the duration and the security services went in to sweep the building for listening devices and set up equipment to jam any such eavesdropping. A police command post was established at the main gate and officers were posted to guard the conference and sleeping accommodation in the complex. The SDLP team travelled from RAF Aldergrove on the eve of the conference, as did the Irish contingent from Dublin. On the morning of the conference all gathered for coffee at 10.00am to await the formal arrival of the Prime Ministers, who would inaugurate the negotiations with opening speeches. The agenda prescribed that the morning session would be completed by three further opening statements, one from each of the Northern Ireland parties. All the delegates attended that first session, forty-two each from the British and Irish governments and twenty-three from the Executive parties, including advisers. According to Fitt, Heath dominated this opening session, speaking – without notes or papers – about the objectives and agenda of the conference. In his contribution, Fitt reflected on the historical importance of the occasion and set out the SDLP's position:

> The hopes and aspirations of many people who long for lasting peace in Ireland are with us at this conference today. The talks which were recently completed in Belfast and which led to the formation of an Executive-designate for Northern Ireland, opened on a much less hopeful atmosphere. Yet they were successful. They were conducted by the parties participating in a genuine spirit of goodwill and mutual respect. It would be our wish that this Conference should be conducted in a similar spirit. Already a large measure of agreement exists on the issues which will form the major part of our agenda. The following propositions have already been agreed between HMG and the parties which form the Executive-designate:
>
> • that there shall be a Council of Ireland
>
> • that the Council should be confined to the North and South of Ireland
>
> • that the Council shall consist, not only of representatives of the Government of the Republic and the Northern Ireland Executive, but also on a separate advisory and consultative level, of representatives of the parties in Dáil Éireann and the Northern Ireland Assembly
>
> • that the Council shall have its own secretariat
>
> • that the Council shall have executive and harmonisation functions, as well as a consultative role
>
> • that the Council at Government level should operate on the basis of unanimity.
>
> If these principles are acceptable to the Government of the Republic of Ireland then it would be for this Conference to work out the detailed implementation of them. There are some other questions. It is also broadly accepted that the two parts of Ireland are to a considerable extent interdependent in the whole field of security and it is clearly evident that the problem of political violence in Northern Ireland cannot be solved without the active involvement of the Republic of Ireland. The whole field

of law and order, including policing arrangements and common law enforcement, is an area where, as the parties to the Belfast Conference agreed, the Council of Ireland might play a useful role. We have consistently argued that a solution to the problem of policing is essential to any settlement of the problems of Northern Ireland not only with regard to the immediate problem of having effective policy throughout Northern Ireland but also to ensure the permanent ending of political motivated violence. We are also insistent that if we enter a Northern Ireland executive that we must be able to give full support to the enforcement of law and order. This can only be done if the police service is acceptable throughout Northern Ireland and if all sections can identify with it. We feel these aims can best be achieved if the Council of Ireland has a positive role in policy, common law enforcement and the defence of human rights in both parts of Ireland. These are matters which we should discuss in detail as part of our agenda. No institution of this nature can be static or rigid. It will obviously evolve with time and changing circumstances and the means of such evolution should be explicit in any arrangements that are made. Finally might I say that the problems which have divided the people of Ireland at great cost for centuries and which have seriously disturbed Anglo-Irish relations are no greater or no more bitter than those which have divided the peoples of Europe. Yet we meet at a time when those same peoples of Europe are forging institutions which will develop their common interests, which will develop mutual understanding and respect and will progressively and by agreement eliminate the differences between them. It should not be beyond us, at this conference to do likewise for the people of Ireland.

By lunchtime there was full agreement that it was essential to agree on a 'package' of measures and that the main issues for discussion, as agreed by all the participants, were the structure, function and role of the Council of Ireland, a common law enforcement area, extradition, human rights and policing. Good progress was made during the afternoon plenary session. The principle of unanimity among the members of the Council of Ireland – five from each side – was settled and it was agreed the proposed secretariat would be structured to avoid duplication of existing administrative services. A sub-group, headed by the Attorneys-General, was formed to consider how extradition could be made effective, while another, led by Pym and Patrick Cooney, the Irish Justice Minister, was set up to deal with policing. After the Irish stated they could not deliver on constitutional reform, which would involve winning a referendum to remove the sovereignty claim over the entire island, it was agreed to return to that subject.

The first day adjourned at 6.00pm and appeared to have ended on an entirely upbeat note – until, that is, the Northern Ireland parties discovered that the press had been briefed by the Irish delegation about the Council of Ireland discussions. Heath had been advised of this during the afternoon break and was far from pleased that the understanding to maintain a media silence had been broken, but it was Faulkner who, understandably, was most annoyed, given the scale of criticism he was facing at home from Craig, Paisley and a growing element within his own party. Conor Cruise O'Brien issued a fulsome apology on behalf of the Irish government for what he said was a misunderstanding, and pledged there would be no repetition. This was accepted and the clash did not overshadow the carefully planned dinner Heath laid on for them all that evening at 10 Downing Street. In line with advice from the NIO, Heath had ruled that guests could wear 'day clothes' rather than black-tie. He had also asked Martin Neary, the organist and choral conductor, and a small choir to provide 'a programme of carefully selected Irish songs', but on being warned of the sensitivities surrounding the choice of items and the 'risk of some of your guests joining in', he at first decreed that one Irish song would be sufficient before bowing to further advice that the Irish would probably want to sing all night.

Most of the fifty-eight guests were driven into central London along the M4 motorway in coaches escorted by police motorcycle outriders. At what Fitt described as the 'lavish' meal that followed, he was seated beside Sir Alec Douglas-Home, the former Prime Minister, who was disparaging about the trouble caused by old-style unionism, and recalled an official encounter with Lord Brookeborough soon after the Second World War that had shocked him.

'There are strange stories about discrimination in Northern Ireland,' he said to Brookeborough, with some incredulity. 'They tell me you Unionists have a deliberate policy of discrimination to keep the nationalists in subjection.'

'Exactly,' replied Brookeborough.

After the meal, the customary toasts presented another minefield that had to be traversed carefully. According to Robin Butler, Heath's private secretary:

> ... at the end of dinner the Prime Minister proposed a toast to 'The President' to which everyone rose; and then, quickly, before anyone could sit down, he proposed 'The Queen'. The programme of music then started with 'If you're Irish, come into the parlour', which made the guests laugh; continued with a hummed version of the Londonderry air, which made them thoughtful; and concluded with 'When Irish eyes are smiling', which made them sentimental. Calls from the guests for further songs of a less formal nature from Mr Paddy Devlin were quickly forestalled by the Prime Minister rising to welcome his guests to 10 Downing Street, which he did in a few words which were as simple as they were effective. He reminded them that it was an historic occasion for him to be able to offer hospitality to the representatives of both parts of Ireland and both communities of Northern Ireland within the walls of 10 Downing Street; and he told them how impressed he had been by the atmosphere of reconciliation which had so obviously inspired the Conference. When he ended by saying, 'So I want quite simply tonight to propose a toast to the peace and prosperity of both

parts of Ireland', there was hardly a dry eye in the room. The Taoiseach replied equally simply, there was much signing of menus and, by the time that the Taoiseach and his party left and all delegates were eventually collected again into the coaches, it was apparent that Anglo-Irish relations had entered a new era.

By then the formality had truly broken down and before leaving Downing Street, the SDLP, no great respecters of dignity at the best of times, were running riot. Ivan Cooper went up to Sir Alec Douglas-Home and, slapping him vigorously on the back, asked, 'How's the grouse shooting this year, old boy?' Meanwhile Fitt, who could play a tune or two by ear on his own battered piano back in Antrim Road, was inspecting Heath's Steinway Grand and enquiring if he could play 'The Sash my father wore'. 'No', replied the musically accomplished Prime Minister, who promised stiffly to learn it before Fitt came back again. The revelry continued on the coaches during the return journey to Berkshire, with Paddy Devlin singing his party-piece, 'Carrickfergus', the first of a number of unscheduled turns. Even Brian Faulkner, who had always had a reputation for being stiff and formal, joined in, giving a much applauded rendering of 'Galway Bay'. Ken Bloomfield, soon to be secretary to the Executive, recalls the dinner as 'an extraordinary occasion'. In his memoir, *Stormont in Crisis*, he wrote:

> The tradition represented by the SDLP is the more easily convivial on an occasion such as this but I admired the way in which Faulkner, not a person of much bonhomie, went out of his way to share the spirit of the occasion. In the right circumstances, and particularly after a few drinks, members of the two traditions find a great deal of common ground, and sing the songs of the rival traditions with as much relish as their own. I thought the evening of 6 December represented a psychologically important 'bonding' exercise.

This 'bonding' continued at the cash bar well into the small hours for many of the delegates and it was not until 11.30am the next morning that the talks resumed with a brief plenary session before they broke into what were now five sub-committees to consider: finance; the functions of the Council of Ireland; the common law enforcement area; policing; and the status of Northern Ireland as between Britain and Ireland. Fitt recalled:

> Each committee met in separate rooms and I moved from room to room, helping to keep up progress. The emphasis was on defining principles rather than settling detail because that was the best way to get the major breakthrough everyone expected. Faulkner faced the loneliest role. He had ranged against him the combined weight of the Alliance party, SDLP and Dublin government and could only rely on scant support from Heath, with whom he enjoyed the frostiest of personal relations since their confrontation over the abolition of Stormont in 1972.

Work continued throughout the day, but by 6.00pm, when the first draft of a communiqué was presented to a plenary session, it was clear there were still substantial gaps to be bridged in virtually every area, but particularly on the core issues of status, law enforcement and policing. It was agreed that the groups should meet again after dinner, which they did but, as a stocktaking by the full conference at 11.15pm revealed, there had been no serious breakthrough on the most contentious matters and the conference adjourned overnight although the groups on status and law enforcement continued working. Meanwhile, the policing group resumed its work at 9.15am on Saturday. Hopeful that this last push would enable agreement to be reached by noon, Heath put off his journey to Chequers to greet his Italian visitor and stayed at the Bursar's home in the college.

By mid-morning Saturday significant progress had indeed been made, thanks to practical pragmatism rather than theoretical considerations. This was nowhere clearer than in the sub-committee dealing with the status of Northern Ireland. According to the official British note, 'there was a conventional amount of niggling, with John Hume wrestling with his soul and causing most of the problems', but, by contrast, Conor Cruise O'Brien 'was throughout skilful and helpful, quick to seize the needs of the situation and play the hand on behalf of the unionists so that confrontations were averted and John Hume coaxed back to realities'.

A serious difficulty arose, principally between FitzGerald and Faulkner, about whether the term 'the Irish Government', a colloquialism acceptable to the UK government, or the term 'the Government of Ireland' should appear in the first paragraph of the communiqué. At one point it was suggested that separate communiqués be prepared for the two governments, differing only in this single respect. The UK government had to say that it would insist on being described as 'the Government of the United Kingdom of Great Britain and Northern Ireland' before the Irish would surrender their claim to being described as 'the Government of Ireland'. However, thanks to private exchanges outside the meeting, the dispute was promptly resolved by agreeing that two declarations, one from each government, would appear side by side in the final communiqué. The Irish accepted this formula on condition their declaration was on the left-hand side of the page.

There was equally encouraging progress on the concept of a common law enforcement area, although extradition was a problematic area. The stumbling block was that the Unionists and Alliance were adamant that those responsible for murders and other crimes in the North could not continue to claim they had committed a 'political offence' and thereby benefit from the Irish courts' refusal to extradite. However, the group on policing, was completely deadlocked, with the SDLP and Unionists unable to agree a compromise. Faced with the need to intervene personally, Heath postponed his revised departure for Chequers and deputed Lord Carrington, his defence secretary, to greet the Italian Prime Minister and host his welcome lunch. Heath instead lunched with the leaders of the various Irish delegations, Cosgrave, Fitt, Faulkner and Napier, urging them on to consensus. After lunch he held a meeting with Hume and Currie to plead with them for greater understanding of Faulkner's difficulties regarding the emotive issues of the RUC and the Council of Ireland, and also to stress the need for compromise in the light of what was being achieved elsewhere in the negotiations.

By this time, the Italian Prime Minister had retired for a *siesta* and Heath's helicopter pilot was threatening to leave without him because of failing light. In the end, Heath took off at 3.45pm to link up belatedly with his guest and host a dinner in his honour. Meanwhile, thanks to the discovery that the 1861 Explosives Act, passed by the British before partition, was still in force and could be used to try people for explosives offences in any part of Ireland, the Unionists and Alliance dropped their demand for immediate extradition and agreed that the question should be remitted to a joint law commission to rapidly come up with a more legally durable solution.

There was still, however, no sign of agreement on policing and during the evening function at Chequers, Heath was advised that a final push was required to fracture the stalemate. He therefore decided to fly back to Sunningdale after dinner, which he did, arriving at 10.45pm. An immediate plenary was called for 11.00pm and when the latest version of the communiqué – still minus a draft passage on policing – was laid before the conference, Paddy Devlin engaged in good-natured banter with Heath about 'bringing advice from Rome'. The Unionists were not at all amused, and with Heath's original Friday evening and Saturday noon deadlines already hopelessly missed they were beginning to mutter about their reluctance to work on the Sabbath to bridge the last impasse to a settlement. They were soon persuaded that it would be an infringement of the Sabbath only if they went to bed and started again, but not if they worked on. This formula spurred Heath into action and he began a long night of pressure tactics, moving from delegation room to delegation room in a bid to clinch a deal. Fitt always reckoned that he ordered the bars to be closed and the heating to be turned down as an aid to concentration.

The task was made all the more difficult because Faulkner, under pressure from Bradford, had hardened rather than softened his position and was insistent that within twelve months control of the RUC should be transferred to the Executive alone, and that the Council of Ireland should have no role whatsoever in policing. This was clearly one of the key concessions the SDLP needed if they were to sign up to a public endorsement of the RUC, and during that long night Faulkner was told so in no uncertain terms by Heath and Frank Cooper, who was constantly at his elbow during this phase of the talks. In his memoir, *All Hell Will Break Loose*,

Currie recalls the two of them arriving into the SDLP room after a long encounter with Faulkner. 'Brian is still hankering after what he lost in 1972 and he is not getting it back,' Heath said.

Those not immediately involved in these exchanges were trying to get some sleep, sprawled out in chairs and on sofas around the Georgian manor house, Northcote House, which was the main conference building and the centrepiece of the civil service college. In his autobiography, *All In A Life*, Dr Garret FitzGerald recounted how Gerry Fitt 'was unambiguously asleep on a couch; indeed, I seem to recall him performing the impressively athletic feat of sleeping perched along the top edge of a couch but my memory of this may have been enhanced by time.'

At 7.00am, after a long and fruitless night of negotiation, Heath called two representatives of each delegation to the room he was using as an office. It was apparent that sheer exhaustion had become a further obstacle to progress, so Heath accepted Hume's suggestion that the policing question be left on hold until 3.00pm Sunday afternoon to enable everyone to get some sleep. All, except the unionists, agreed at once, but their renewed doubts about working on the Sabbath – a practice they rightly feared might be heavily criticised at home, not least by Paisley – were again overcome when they were persuaded that 'working for peace' could hardly count as a breach of the Lord's Day. There was, however, little respite for Heath. He left by road for Chequers, where he managed a seventy-five-minute nap before resuming his talks with Romero and hosting a farewell lunch.

Back at Sunningdale, while some slept, others got down to business, recognising that failure to crack the policing question could wreck the entire outcome of the conference and compromise the great progress that had been made. Fitt had breakfast with Heath and Faulkner and listened with some sympathy as Faulkner explained again why he was finding it so difficult to agree with the proposals on policing and the Council of Ireland. Fitt remembered:

> Heath was frustrated and impatient and showing it, tapping the table, laying down the law. It was clear he did not share Brian's analysis and had little sympathy for his difficulties. I took Brian away from the table and calmed him down. I can still see his face as the difficulty of the Herculean task he had taken on sank in. 'I cannot see myself in any circumstances being able to sell the Council of Ireland,' he said. But he knew the conference would have failed if less had been settled for and I was able to assure him we would not go overboard about it to help him.

Amidst growing concerns that Faulkner was ready to walk out and go home, FitzGerald and Cruise O'Brien suggested to Paddy Devlin that he intervene and use his old trade union negotiating skills to see if he could effect the necessary compromise. Devlin immediately tracked down Faulkner and went for a walk with him in the garden outside. After that he took part in a meeting of the entire SDLP group, during which, as his autobiography *Straight Left* recalls, 'there were fierce and emotional exchanges before we agreed to an accommodating stance'.

By the time Heath had seen off his Italian visitor and flown back to Sunningdale at 3.30pm, Faulkner and the SDLP were now in direct contact and the shape of a deal was emerging steadily as they exchanged various drafts of positions. With optimism rising all round, Heath sent for Fitt to warn him that the SDLP must close the deal rapidly and not prolong the negotiations until exhaustion set in again. At that point the SDLP was arguing that, as the name of the RUC was not being changed, it was vital that it should in some way be identified with the Council of Ireland to win support from the minority community. By 6.30pm, when Heath chaired a meeting of two delegates from each group, agreement had been reached on all but two subsidiary points. Heath then suggested an amalgamation of the conflicting SDLP and Unionist drafts, and both sides asked for a short adjournment to consider the plan, during which time the Dublin government leaned heavily on the SDLP. When they returned to the full meeting soon afterwards, Faulkner said: 'Yes, Prime Minister, we can accept that.' Hume simply nodded assent. It was a moment of huge emotion and they all went round the room, shaking hands with each other.

There was just one more understanding to be credited into the SDLP's account and they got it in a short face-to-face meeting with Heath. He confirmed that releases of internees would start as soon as possible and that he would give a public commitment to this effect. So, with the final version of the communiqué at last drafted after some fifty hours of almost continuous negotiation, the plenary session was reconvened at 8.30pm to ratify it. The leaders' speeches were graceful and expressed great mutual appreciation at the historic steps that had been taken. Fitt summed up the mood when he said:

> A hundred years ago, Prime Minister, Mr Gladstone said that his mission
> was to pacify Ireland. He failed, but by what you have achieved at this
> conference, I believe that you have succeeded.

The news conference and subsequent interviews lasted well past midnight as the details of what became known as the Sunningdale Agreement were disseminated across the islands of Ireland and Great Britain and further afield. In what was, by any standards, an historic communiqué, the status of Northern Ireland was guaranteed by the two governments, unless there was a willing move to change it by the people themselves, and that guarantee was to be registered at the UN. The framework for a Council of Ireland with powers to co-ordinate social and economic measures was drawn up and studies were commissioned to work out the detail. There was also to be further contact on policing and law and order. Measures to combat terrorists seeking sanctuary in one part of Ireland for crimes committed in the North or Britain were to be considered urgently by a joint law commission.

The unprecedented agreement cleared the way for the Executive-designate to take power and usher in a new era for the people of Northern Ireland, but as the signing ceremony was taking place a very amused Ivan Cooper whispered to Fitt, 'We're all traitors now.' Until then Cooper had been called a traitor by his former Protestant associates; now he was happy because the entire SDLP was joining him in breaking the political mould. Although committed to the settlement with all his considerable integrity, Faulkner was, as ever, the political realist and at the height of the euphoria he again said quietly to Fitt that while he could sell power-sharing, he did not think he could sell the Council of Ireland. Fitt replied that the SDLP could not have gone back without an Irish dimension, but he knew in his heart that Faulkner had been pushed out too far on a limb. It was an unfortunate necessity from Fitt's point of view: 'Although the men of violence on our side, and their fellow travellers, predictably condemned the settlement, the people I represented in Belfast would have been satisfied with power-sharing alone, but the SDLP nationalists in the rural and border areas would have revolted.' Faulkner's opponents criticised him publicly. The UDA said that like Michael Collins in the 1920s, 'he had been conned'. There were more unruly scenes in the Assembly, which had to be adjourned as a result. On 14 December Paisley spoke for three hours during an eighteen-hour debate on the Sunningdale Agreement, during which a motion to repudiate the Agreement was defeated by 43 votes to 27.

At Westminster the reaction was considerably more positive as the final stages of the legislation to devolve power to the Executive and Assembly were processed. Fitt hailed the breakthrough that had been made:

> It must not be forgotten that for the first time in three centuries of Irish history Catholic and Protestant representatives – those people believing in a United Ireland and those who wanted to retain a United Kingdom Ulster – voluntarily discussed where they disagreed and on what issues they could agree. They asked themselves, 'What cogent steps can be taken that will bring to an end of the massacre of the innocents that has been taking place here since 1969?'

He told the Commons that Faulkner had admitted hearing more constructive talk about the Northern Ireland community during the negotiations than in twenty-five years as a minister in Unionist governments.

Within the SDLP the post-Sunningdale euphoria was tempered by the unresolved matter of internment, or detention, as the NIO now preferred to describe it. As well as Devlin, whose strong views remained undiminished, the discontent focused principally on the three Assembly members – Paddy Duffy, Seamus Mallon and Michael Canavan – who wanted actual releases rather than the assurances given by Heath. Fitt had to go along with their unhappiness, despite his own reservations, which were based on the fact that he knew well that the people interned from his own constituency were steeped in militant republicanism and that many were of an extremely violent disposition.

In a secret annex to one of the Sunningdale briefing documents it was recorded that the NIO was keeping the security situation under review, with a view to releasing between fifty and seventy-five detainees after mid-December; at the time, there were 665 internees in custody. Whatever the political plight of the SDLP, who believed the IRA continued to benefit at their expense in terms of Catholic support as long as internment continued, the government had to take account of other implications. Army and police morale would be damaged if cadres of people known to be gunmen and bombers were freed to be able to repeat their crimes. Government anxiety was exacerbated by a security force analysis, which showed a correlation between the release of internees and a surge of violence after direct rule was introduced in March 1972.

When Pym met with Fitt, Devlin and Hume on 19 December, SDLP frustration at the lack of releases was the main topic, but they came away with nothing specific other than another assurance that some releases were in the pipeline – even though the IRA had exploded bombs in London the previous day. Three car bombs had injured sixty-three people, while a letter-bomb had injured a Brigadier who was an *aide-de-campe* to the Queen. The promised releases came on 20 December, when sixty-five internees were freed – sixty-three republicans and two loyalists. Some of the republicans had been in custody since internment had been first introduced by Faulkner in August 1971. Those chosen for release had been selected on a number of factors: whether they were a security risk; how they had behaved while in custody; their age and family circumstances; and whether they undergone a change of heart about violence while detained.

Far from assuaging the SDLP, the episode caused serious rancour, as was demonstrated at a hastily convened party meeting in Dungannon as soon as news of the releases was made public. Later, at an equally hastily arranged meeting with Lord Belstead, at which Fitt was notably absent, the Security Minister had to endure a tirade of dissatisfaction from Hume, Devlin, O'Hanlon and Frank Feely, who said they had just come from a party meeting where there was serious division as a result of the releases.

The SDLP was highly dissatisfied that only sixty-five people had been freed, a number so small that it had weakened the party's influence and credibility in Catholic areas and strengthened that of the IRA. Hume said he was shocked by the names of the men released: they were all from the Belfast area and included 'some very hard men'. From this the party had come to the conclusion that an arrangement had been made with 'another body' – meaning the PIRA – in order to obtain a ceasefire. Hume wanted more releases at once, including some men from Derry; O'Hanlon complained that no one from South Armagh had been freed. The SDLP went on to reveal that it had pulled a planned statement on ending the rents and rates strike in case it appeared to be a response to this inadequate release. Devlin complained that at Sunningdale they had been promised seventy-five releases and warned of the possibility of a split in the party, which raised the possibility that he and his colleagues would be unable to serve on the Executive. They were particularly critical that none of those held in Compound 8 had been freed. These inmates, who were either not connected with or had severed their links with the IRA, were enduring considerable hardship because of the bitter atmosphere between them and the other internees, and the SDLP strongly believed they could be released without any risk of them becoming re-involved in violent activity. What the party ultimately demanded was more releases before Christmas and evidence that releases would continue throughout the New Year.

In the face of this brinkmanship, Belstead was uncompromising. The release of detainees was an ongoing process and was dependent on the security situation, which could not be judged in a few days. Accordingly, further releases before Christmas were out of the question. Later that evening, Hume, Devlin, O'Hanlon and Duffy went to Laneside, where they subjected James Allan to a similar critical barrage. He also took a tough line with them, insisting there was no secret deal with the IRA about the releases and warning them that, while HMG certainly wanted to get the Executive off the ground, it could be very resolute where matters of principle were concerned and would not be deflected from what it thought was right, even if there were threats.

The government did not reveal to the SDLP the extent of the balancing act it had to perform to put the package of releases together. While the sift was taking place to decide which individuals should be freed, Judge Leonard, who was in charge of the judicial review process for holding and freeing detainees, announced that he was deeply disturbed that the process of selective political release undermined the credibility of his own, much-criticized, quasi-judicial role. However, he would not 'rock the boat' by resigning at this critical stage, particularly as he knew others would follow if he led the way. The army was also exercised about the undertaking to release any of the 'well-motivated, highly-trained terrorists' being held in the Maze while such a high level of terrorist violence continued. In a hard-hitting letter to Pym at the beginning of December, the GOC, Lieutenant General Sir Frank King, cited a list of recent atrocities, including the deaths of three soldiers, a policeman and five civilians, as evidence for his advice. He also pointed out that, judging from past experience, six out of ten of those released would resume terrorist activity as soon as they were freed.

The IRA had already announced that there would be no Christmas ceasefire and responded to the releases by an attack on four bank clerks walking to the pub for a Christmas drink. One of them, a part-time police officer, was wounded when a gunman walked up behind him and opened fire. Another of the group, Rodney Fenton, a twenty-two-year-old Protestant, was shot dead. The killing, one of fifteen that month, took place along the Antrim Road, a few hundred yards from

Fitt's home, and it deeply saddened him: 'That Christmas I remembered the families of the 250 people who had died violently during the year but I thought, for the first time in many years, there was at last cause to believe that the worst might be behind us.'

So it was with a spirit of considerable optimism that Fitt turned up to the ceremonial oath-taking event on 31 December. The protocol for what was an unprecedented occurrence had been the source of some angst among officials in preceding days because they were all too aware of the minefield that conflicting symbols could become in Northern Ireland. Too much emphasis on British trappings would alienate the nationalist sentiments of the SDLP; too little and the unionists would interpret it as a dilution of their much-cherished Britishness. Plans were therefore drawn up for Sir Robert Lowry, the Lord Chief Justice of Northern Ireland, to preside with Secretary of State Francis Pym at a function in Stormont Castle, where the new ministers would take their oaths of office, receive their warrants of appointment and say a few suitable words to mark the importance of the occasion. After that there would be a buffet lunch in another room, followed by the first meeting of the new power-sharing Executive. Frank Cooper, the most senior civil servant at the NIO, set a low-key, businesslike tone for the proceedings with the order that 'there should be no church leaders, no wives and no champagne'. Lowry, who had initially been reluctant to participate when invited by Cooper, changed his mind and, in a telex on 20 December, said he would be 'pleased and honoured to act', but his suggestion that he should wear his 'judicial robes (scarlet and ermine) … to indicate my recognition of the importance of the occasion' was turned down diplomatically. 'The Secretary of State would like everyone to wear lounge suits,' Cooper replied crisply.

A few minutes before noon on 31 December, Fitt and his colleagues took their seats in the old Cabinet room, the power base from which, for so many years, non-unionist politicians had been excluded. Pym and Lowry entered soon afterwards, and one by one the ministers of the new administration came forward to be sworn into office. Faulkner was first, followed by Fitt, as Deputy Chief Executive. In a land of Catholics and Protestants, Paddy Devlin did his own brave thing by affirming, instead of taking the oath as all the others did. In his own irreverent way he hoped his gesture might persuade some Protestants that the minority community was not entirely priest-ridden. They then received their warrants of appointment from Pym. While every other minister preserved his warrant carefully, and many were ultimately framed as keepsakes, Fitt folded his and put it in his inside pocket. Over the next few weeks, as was his habit when a note of a phone number or something had to be made, the first piece of paper that came to hand was used. Thus the back of the warrant survived a time, until all the available space was used. Eventually the document, creased and annotated, ended up in an envelope among all his other souvenirs.

At the buffet afterwards, Lowry made a jocular remark to Fitt about his Belfast Corporation investigation years earlier and then congratulated him on his new appointment. 'I'm absolutely delighted. Things have changed, haven't they,' he said, shaking Fitt's hand warmly. That afternoon, the Executive held its first meeting and issued a statement afterwards:

> We have undertaken to serve in the interests of Northern Ireland and all its people. This is the spirit in which we shall always act, both individually and collectively. We want the New Year to see the beginning, not just of a new system of Government, but of a new spirit. Let 1974 be The Year of Reconciliation.

When Fitt got to Stormont the following Tuesday morning to take up his appointment, he found he had been allocated a large room on the first floor of the Stormont Parliament building, just along the corridor from the Chief Executive, Brian Faulkner, and conveniently close to the Members' Bar, with which he had long been so familiar. The first visitor he had was the head of the civil service, who asked him to pick a private secretary and told him the civil service had a formula for doing these things: he should interview ten likely candidates, then choose the candidate he wanted. Fitt told him he was not very keen on this course of action because nine people would be offended that he had not chosen them. Instead, he suggested they pick somebody, and not necessarily a Catholic – a 'half-liberal Protestant' would do. A short time later the senior official came back, saying that he thought he had got the right man: Alec Ireland, who was originally from the Shankill Road. He came to see Fitt later that day.

'Do you object to the odd swear word?' he was asked.

'No,' he answered.

'Do you take a gin and tonic?' asked Fitt.

'Yes,' came the reply.

'Well, in that case it seems to me you are well qualified for the job,' said Fitt.

Indeed he was. During the five months they worked together, he learned how to steer Fitt along gently and to ensure that he fulfilled all his obligations, looked at critical papers and always had a gin when it was wanted, or needed. As the Executive settled down to consider the social and economic master plan for Northern Ireland, strenuous efforts were made to settle the outstanding details of the Sunningdale Agreement, so that it could be ratified formally by early February 1974. One of the first measures taken was the appointment of the members of the Anglo-Irish Law Enforcement Commission, who were tasked to find legal ways of dealing with fugitive terrorists. At the same time the RUC Chief Constable, Jamie Flanagan (later Sir Jamie), the first Catholic ever to head the force, met his counterpart from the Irish police force, An Garda Síochána Commissioner, Patrick Malone. It was the first time the two police chiefs from both parts of the island had ever met officially, although the SDLP told the Department of Foreign

Affairs in Dublin they thought the encounter was far too premature given that the policing aspects of Sunningdale remained in the melting pot.

The first week in power ended with a major blow for Brian Faulkner when the UUC – the real powerbrokers in his party – voted 454 – 374 against the proposal for a Council of Ireland. Within days the party had split into Official Unionists, led by Harry West, and Faulkner Unionists. Eighteen Assembly members stayed loyal to him and Fitt said the Executive supported him wholeheartedly as he boldly reaffirmed his support for the Sunningdale process. Despite the previous chill between them, Heath offered Faulkner support a few days later in a modestly censorious letter to Cosgrave:

> I have no doubt that, as Faulkner has himself said publicly, the help which will really make the difference must come from you. If I may in this situation be perfectly frank, some of the remarks attributed by the press to you and some of your colleagues have been interpreted as meaning that the Republic is maintaining its claim that Northern Ireland is now part of the Republic and that there is no prospect of a change in the law on extradition which is still a burning issue in the North. This has seriously reduced the value to Faulkner of the Sunningdale Agreement.

Although he had become a pretty experienced politician and parliamentarian, Fitt's position as a member of the Northern Ireland Executive and of the Westminster Parliament was unique. There had been a number of people, including Fitt himself, who had been members of both parliaments, but this was the first time anyone had been in government simultaneously. Ken Bloomfield was concerned about the potential for conflicts of interest, which he outlined in a minute to Fitt on 10 January:

> There is, however, a rather sensitive area when it comes to the making of speeches in the House about 'transferred' matters in Northern Ireland. As ministers in the Northern Ireland administration you and your colleagues have the right of direct and easy access to your United Kingdom counterparts. Thus it is possible for our Minister of Agriculture to go and see at very short notice the Minister of Agriculture, Fisheries and Food or for Mr Hume to go to DTI ministers or to other ministers concerned with the counterpart of his functions. These contacts are of the greatest possible advantage to us.
>
> There is of course another means of bringing pressure on ministers across the water to take decisions to our advantage – and that is by open political activities in the House of Commons, through speeches or otherwise. What I am a bit concerned about is whether it is really possible to pursue both lines simultaneously. I would have some concern that if we take the course of openly asking for things on the floor of the House of Commons and thereby to some extent embarrassing United Kingdom ministers, we may find them less receptive to the ministerial approaches which you and your colleagues will be making from time to time. None of

these comments applies of course to a very broad range of topics which are not concerned with matters 'transferred' to the Executive here. For example, the general economic environment, taxation, foreign affairs, etc, are all outside our remit.

This was, of course, Fitt's first experience of office and it took him some time to get used to the way the machinery worked: 'I had a police bodyguard and a driver to take me everywhere and wait for me and a private secretary to keep me right. I soon learned everything was governed by "the diary" and my commitments were quickly piled up weeks ahead.' However, as his civil servants quickly found out, Fitt was not easily organised or deflected from his often impetuous instincts to do what seemed most important to him at any given moment. They also learned that his gin had to be served with tonic water, but no ice or lemon.

Nevertheless, he was diplomatically steered into the customary obligations of a minister and in February 1974 the *Belfast Telegraph* editorial noted that 'a new era really has arrived when Mr Brian Faulkner and Mr Gerry Fitt can preside together at a reception in London for leading industrialists, financiers and businessmen'. On 18 March, he hosted a lunch at Stormont for the visiting Lord Mayor of Nottingham, and nine days later, when he hosted a reception in Birmingham for leading civic and industrial figures, the Executive's 'office of information services' prepared carefully researched and dutifully written texts for him to memorise and deliver, but in true Fitt fashion he performed his ambassadorial role in his own off-the-cuff way, although the official texts were published for the record.

One Catholic official was not too happy with his role in this brave new world. During a dinner with Sean Donlon, from the Department of Foreign Affairs in Dublin, Maurice Hayes, an assistant secretary in the Executive secretariat, complained about having less responsibility than he had expected when offered the post and said he resented what he saw as an effort to confine him, as the only senior civil servant from the minority community, to 'looking after' Gerry Fitt and 'advising' Faulkner how to pronounce 'Taoiseach' and 'Oireachtas'.

Paddy Devlin was another who was determined not to be snowed under by the well-drilled bureaucracy and he caused much consternation to his civil servants in the Department of Health and Social Services by insisting they call him Paddy, not 'Minister' as the protocol dictated. They were also bewildered by the sight of his his gun and holster hanging on the coat-rack along with his jacket and by his unorthodox habit of wandering around various offices in his shirt sleeves, files in hand, seeking out relatively junior officials. They soon saw an example of his toughness, however. A list of 'suitable' candidates for vacancies on the Supplementary Benefits Commission was presented to him. He rejected the list and announced that he was appointing Betty Sinclair. 'But, minister, she is a communist,' they cried in protest. Eventually their complaint reached Faulkner, who backed Devlin's decision.

In his portfolio Austin Currie inherited a situation of acute housing crisis: 27% of houses had no bath; 21% no water; 27% no inside flush toilet; 10% were not connected to the public water supply; and 15% were not connected to a sewer. On 21 January the SDLP published an outline programme to tackle this hardship, entitled 'Steps To A Better Tomorrow'. It was a broad programme for action on industrial development, agriculture, the eradication of poverty, better housing and a community relations drive to heal the divisions of recent years, especially among the young, on whom the future depended. The detailed action plans were to be drawn up by the departments and, in some cases, in eventual co-ordination with the Council of Ireland. The development of agricultural and tourist potential were two areas specifically identified as being suitable for an all-Ireland approach.

These ideas were hammered out at a series of Executive meetings throughout January. At the opening meeting, Fitt sat between Herbie Kirk and Roy Bradford and opposite Paddy Devlin, who was a vision in shirtsleeves and brightly coloured braces. When Faulkner came in the buzz of conversation died down and he turned up his nose at the haze of cigarette smoke, to which Fitt was contributing vigorously. Although he did not like smoking, he pressed on in his usual businesslike way. 'Good morning, gentlemen,' he said, opening a file. 'What we have to discuss today are matters to be referred to the Council of Ireland. They are in alphabetical order. First is the control and eradication of episodic disease. Now, I have no hesitation in saying I do not know what that is,' he said, looking over to the civil servants for enlightenment. Before any of them had a chance to speak, Fitt intervened, 'I got a dose of that in Hamburg when I was a merchant seaman. It's very painful and you have to get injections.' With such flashes of irreverence, the Executive developed a stimulating, constructive attitude. Faulkner and Fitt spoke almost daily to review progress. Faulkner tried to confine Fitt to apple juice during these sessions, while Fitt endeavoured to wean his colleague onto gin.

> Our personal relations and respect were closer than anyone could ever have imagined if they had seen us exchanging unpleasantries in the old Stormont. He often said how pleased he was with the air of solidarity generated between the different parties and personalities in the Executive and he contrasted it favourably with the lacklustre way the unionist cabinets had run the country in the past. Although he was a humourless man, I think he enjoyed the irreverence, mainly stimulated by the SDLP members.

Fitt's unfamiliarity with matters agricultural once caused great consternation to a delegation of pig farmers. In the absence of the agriculture minister, he was asked to meet them and was immediately ill at ease and quite mystified as they put their complaints to him in the most irate and belligerent way:

> When I replied that after all we had agreed to pay them £1 a ton to solve their problem, it was their turn to be confused. I had misheard the message whispered to me by the expert civil servant sitting in on the meeting. But

when he whispered a second time, '£1 a head,' their mood understandably changed and when they left they were all smiles and handshakes.

Meanwhile the PIRA continued its efforts to halt political progress. On Saturday, 19 January armed men planted a 20lb bomb at the Dunowen restaurant in Dungannon, where the SDLP Executive was attending a party meeting. All members were evacuated hastily, and forced to jump over a duffle bag containing the bomb on their way out the door. Outside, in his shirt sleeves, Fitt suddenly realised he had left behind his gun and jacket, with important papers in the pocket. Before anyone could stop him, Seamus Mallon gallantly dashed back and retrieved them – just minutes before the blast seriously damaged the building.

The hardline loyalists also continued their disruptive protests when the Assembly met for its first meeting since the Exectuive had assumed power. The police were deployed in strength around the building, but the proceedings had barely started when the loyalists occupied the front benches, which were designated for ministers. For more than an hour there were scenes of disorder and during the fracas they climbed on the seats, removed the mace and danced on the Speaker's table. One of the more eccentric loyalists, Professor Kennedy Lindsay, spat on Brian Faulkner. Five policemen were injured whilst removing members from the chamber. Brigadier Ronnie Broadhurst, the Deputy Speaker and an expert on the Middle East with some experience of dealing with political turbulence, said later that 'the disgraceful scenes could not have occurred in a Bedouin encampment or a Patan camp without being instantly avenged with a dagger'.

The administration did not choose to resort to such extreme measures, but later in the week passed a standing order enabling the Speaker to suspend unruly members for up to fourteen days. That threat allowed the Assembly to get down to its proper business and, well into February, a debate on a confidence motion in the new Executive filled its three weekly sessions. That over-lapped with a motion, proposed by Billy Morgan, that the Council of Ireland should not be established. Fitt told Morgan how Unionist fears of the Council were being hammered home to him everyday in every contact he had with people throughout Northern Ireland:

> I was stopped at Belfast and London airports, talked to in flight and even when I was out for a quiet drink. There was no opposition to power-sharing. It was strongly supported and there was much admiration for the enthusiastic way the SDLP ministers were seen to be working for the good of everyone in Northern Ireland. But the goodwill was being fatally eroded by constant running up and down to Dublin by some SDLP members of the Executive. I accept we had to have the Council of Ireland for presentational purposes but we should not have been rubbing the unionists' noses in it and we scored several 'own goals' with this behaviour.

One night in January, Hugh Logue, who in Fitt's view had got 'carried away with his own importance', issued a press release in which he declared the Council of

Ireland was 'the vehicle to trundle the unionists into a United Ireland'. Although Hume, who recognised the provocation inherent in the statement, stepped in and persuaded Logue to delete the remark from his speech in Dublin, the text had already been circulated to news organisations and the damage was done. That remark, widely publicised, was one of the most crucial factors in hardening opinion against the Council. The other major factor was a court action in Dublin by Kevin Boland, a former Irish minister and a man of extreme republican views, who claimed that the recognition of the status of Northern Ireland contained in the Sunningdale communiqué, and so crucial for Faulkner, was unconstitutional and therefore no Irish government could be party to it. He won his point in the lower court, but the government won the eventual appeal, but again it was too late and the harm was done.

Alone in the SDLP, Fitt agreed with Brian Faulkner that they should keep the Executive door open for the hardline loyalists to join in sharing power, and they even discussed co-opting some of them into administration at an opportune time. Fitt tried to reassure any of them he met that there would be a meaningful unionist veto over the Irish dimension:

> We always used the words 'consent' and 'agreement' in talking about a united Ireland and anyway, as I had said often enough before, there would have to be changes made in the South to remove objectionable legislation to accommodate Protestant feelings. But the fear and the historical perception was so hostile I came to realise insistence on the Irish dimension could only prejudice the power-sharing experiment. The two had become inseparable in the mind of the average Protestant.

Fitt's sympathetic rapport with Faulkner was all too cosy in the eyes of Devlin and Currie, who told Sean Donlon soon after taking office that they were trying to 'pull him back'. Devlin said that since 'he had no executive responsibilities', simply his 'room, a secretary and a cabinet full of liquor', there was plenty of time for him to develop a relationship with Faulkner that would work mainly to Faulkner's advantage. They wanted Faulkner pushed hard to fully ratify Sunningdale without delay and, if necessary, confronted to do so.

Faulkner's doubts about being able to advance the Irish dimension were confirmed on 1 February when the parties to the Sunningdale Agreement gathered at Hillsborough to progress work on the powers and structure of the Council; formal ratification was still planned to take place in February. The Irish government delegation, led by Liam Cosgrave, flew in from Dublin in three helicopters. Fearing a blockade by Paisley supporters and being aware of renewed intelligence reports about assassination bids, the Northern Ireland ministers travelled to Hillsborough by circuitous routes. At the conclusion of the talks, Fitt was every bit as worried as Faulkner:

> The proceedings that day frightened the life out of me. As I listened to the

Irish delegation I thought they had lost touch with the political realities. James Tully, an Irish minister, was so excited outlining the functions to be delegated to the Council of Ireland that it seemed he wanted everything transferred. Dublin frightened the unionists by demanding too much. They seemed to have no idea of the vulnerability of Faulkner's position. It was even worse than Sunningdale from his point of view, but he had a new willingness not to be pushed around by Dublin and after the meeting he spelled out in public what he had wisely secured in private.

In fact, Faulkner managed to secure a halt to the Sunningdale process to enable civil servants to do more work on the actual mechanisms and the power of the Council. He also clinched a halt on movement until the Law Commission report on extradition, which had run into difficulty, although that was not admitted at the time. More importantly, to divert pressure from the doubters within his own ranks, he won more time by insisting the Irish government resolve its post-Sunningdale ambiguity about Northern Ireland's status as part of the United Kingdom, which had arisen from the Boland case. As the official photographs were taken that Friday afternoon, behind Fitt's public smile lay a private and deepening sense of foreboding.

Given their anxieties about policing and security policy at this point, the SDLP would have been infuriated had they known their participation in the Executive was being used by the British government to help persuade the USA to lift a ban on supplying equipment to the British Army for use in Northern Ireland. This saga began early in 1973 when the British applied to purchase hundreds of 'unattended ground sensors' – devices about the size of a boot-polish tin that were buried around police and military bases, and other targets, to help detect the approach of terrorists, especially in sensitive rural and border areas. In asking for the sensors the Foreign Office said, 'it seems probable that their use in Northern Ireland would relieve manpower and save lives among the security forces', but US Secretary of State William Rogers personally refused the request. British diplomats in Washington reported that Rogers feared 'possible criticism from Irish-American lobbies if the transaction became public'. Another letter, from the Foreign Military Sales section at the Pentagon to the British Embassy in Washington, stated that the sale had been disallowed because of 'the US government policy of neutrality in Northern Ireland'.

On 'a point of principle', the British government decided to make another attempt to buy the sensors early in 1974 and diplomats were instructed to protest to officials at the State Department that it was 'both ridiculous and indefensible to imply a policy of neutrality as between Her Majesty's Government and the IRA – a terrorist organisation outlawed on both sides of the border'. A letter to the Washington Embassy from the Republic of Ireland Department at the Foreign Office stated: 'We would not be neutral as between the Mafia and the forces of law and order in the US.' But there was little confidence on the British side that the request would succeed. A diplomat reporting to London stated: 'A significant number of Congressmen still feel that the Catholic minority in Northern Ireland are oppressed and need a protector and that in their eyes such a role is played by the IRA. For the present, as far as sensors are concerned, I think we face a second rebuff.'

In May 1974, the new Secretary of State, Dr Henry Kissinger, took a different view from his predecessor and approved the purchase. In its report to the Foreign Secretary James Callaghan, the Republic of Ireland Department suggested that

> ... this is a first and undoubtedly important sign that the US administration are now prepared to set aside their usual fears of provoking the important Irish-American lobbies in Congress and take practical steps to support the British government in their efforts to frustrate the terror tactics of the IRA ... It may well be that the successful visit of Mr John Hume has not only secured the sympathy of some influential Congressmen who were hitherto disposed to favour the IRA but has also come to the attention of Dr Kissinger.

The beginning of the end for the brave power-sharing experiment had already taken place, however. It sprang from a most unpredictable source: a strike by Britain's coalminers for increased pay. By the beginning of 1974, Britain was plunged into a formal state of emergency because the pay dispute had widened out into a trial of strength between the miners and Heath over 'Who governs Britain?' Heath decided that the only way to resolve the question was to hold a general election, and throughout January the bars in Westminster were seething with rumours about the date. Realising that an election would be disastrous for the fragile Executive, Fitt sought a meeting with Heath:

> I told him that the election would bring the Executive down. The poll in Northern Ireland would be regarded as a referendum and with all the opposition to the Council of Ireland the Executive could be undermined before it had a proper chance to prove itself. Heath was clearly concerned that after all the effort he put in the process could well founder. But after considering the implications he stated clearly that, however unfortunate the consequences in Northern Ireland, his priorities had to be national ones.

The election was announced on 7 February, with polling day fixed for 28 February. The declaration overshadowed the impact of morale-boosting support for the Executive when the Assembly carried a vote of confidence in the Executive by 42 – 3 and voted 41 – 3 to press on with the Council of Ireland, both votes being supported by a clear majority of the seventy-eight Assembly members. The SDLP had no time to enjoy the outcome because it was gripped by gloom about its electoral prospects. Fitt was not at all confident of holding his own seat, and his mood was not improved by being forced to take part in an SDLP selection convention. Two party members, Paschal O'Hare, a Belfast solicitor, and Gerry Campbell, a former internee who had become a city councillor, both nominated themselves to become the official party candidate for West Belfast instead of Fitt. He was furious at the move, although it was quite legitimate under party rules, and refused to take part in the formal selection process that nominations had triggered. Hume and Devlin, who feared the convention would go ahead and select one of the two nominees in Fitt's absence, persuaded him to participate to head off the enormous difficulties that would then arise. When the selection meeting took place, Fitt had to endure a barrage of criticism for being soft on internment and not campaigning vigorously enough for the then hunger-striking sisters, Dolours and Marian Price, his constituents and the leaders of the Belfast IRA gang who had planted bombs outside public buildings in London in 1973. Despite these noisy recriminations, Fitt secured the nomination and began preparations for what would be his fourteenth election fight as a candidate.

The first problem was whether the Executive parties should run as a coalition. Faulkner ruled that out immediately and, on the advice of Frank Cooper, decided not to contest a seat himself because he could not identify one in which he would have 'a 100% certainty of winning'. That left the SDLP with some careful calculations to make to ensure they did not damage Faulkner unionists and thus give seats to the anti-Sunningdale forces, who had combined under the banner of the United Ulster Unionist Coalition (UUUC). The SDLP finally decided to fight all twelve seats, but found great difficulty in finding strong candidates because of the climate of intimidation. Hume thought he had persuaded a popular local doctor to stand in Derry, but the man withdrew 'for personal reasons' just a few hours before nominations closed.

It was traditionally said of the West Belfast constituency that it was the cockpit of politics in Northern Ireland and the general election of February 1974 proved that to be an accurate appellation. Fitt's main threat came from Johnny McQuade, one of the principal disrupters of the Assembly. In the old Stormont, Fitt had once memorably interrupted McQuade's reminiscences about serving as a paratrooper in the Second World War by shouting '…and landing on your head'. Now, Fitt's potential majority over McQuade was seriously threatened by the nomination of the father of the Price sisters, Albert, himself an old-time IRA man who it was hoped might damage Fitt by cashing in on the undoubted emotional support for his imprisoned daughters. Looking back, Fitt said:

> This was, without doubt, the dirtiest, most violent election I have ever been involved in. During the election more shots were fired at Austin Currie's house, Tom Donnelly, the North Belfast candidate had his house bombed and I got more than the usual threats and abuse. The dirty tricks began even before nomination day. I can only speculate where the money came from but for most of the campaign large advertisements were published in the

Irish News attacking me, sometimes by inference, other times by name. Typical was an eve-of-poll half-page in the paper containing a challenge from Price for me to defend my record at a public meeting to be held after a Torchlight Freedom March.

'If you require it, I will offer to come personally and escort you into the area,' said Price's advertisement. 'I would ask however that in decency and respect for the people of West Belfast you leave behind your Special Branch bodyguards. I can also assure you that you will not need your gun.'

Fitt was not so sure. Only a few nights earlier he was canvassing at a house in Turf Lodge when a man asked about the Price sisters, to which Fitt replied that he had no sympathy for them because they had been found guilty after a fair trial:

He turned very nasty and threatened to shoot me. Although I did not see a gun, I had no doubt in that area at that time one was not very far away. I stuck my ground for a time arguing. He threatened not to let me out of the house. I bluffed that if I did not come out, the bodyguards would come in looking for me. The bluff worked and I managed to get out, with some relief, I must say. In fact I was alone. I never would risk the lives of policemen or soldiers in those areas.

The dirtiest, and potentially most damaging, trick of all began in the early hours of polling day. A group of journalists was drinking in the Europa Hotel lounge when a prominent Dublin journalist joined them. Did they know that Gerry Fitt had been disqualified from contesting the election because he was Deputy Chief Executive? he asked. Had they heard of the 1957 House of Commons Disqualification Act? The journalist then quoted a prominent lawyer, who had links to Paisley, as the authoritative source for his 'exclusive'. By breakfast time, when the polling stations had opened, the journalist had pushed the story around widely: Fitt and two other Faulkner Unionist Executive members were 'disqualified'.

Whoever was responsible for dreaming it up, the Price camp was well prepared to make use of the story. By mid-morning they were out with fake newspaper placards and loudspeaker vans touring the constituency: 'A vote for Fitt is a wasted vote.' When news of this development reached Fitt, he instantly realised the damage it could do and contacted Frank Cooper, the Permanent Secretary at NIO. Within a few minutes his legal experts had checked the position and were able to report that the 1957 Act was specifically superseded by the Northern Ireland legislation setting up the Executive. A statement was promptly issued from Stormont Castle, but it was lunchtime before Fitt was able to go on BBC Northern Ireland and Radio Éireann to correct the position. In the meantime, he fretted about the number of votes he might have lost in what was already an exceedingly fraught contest. A later report to Dublin by Sean Donlon provided a more objective perspective on the way the election had been conducted:

There was a general feeling … that Gerry Fitt would retain his seat not least because of the SDLP label which apparently now makes it possible for many who are not attracted to Fitt's personal political style to vote for him. While there was little sign of an effective SDLP campaign in West Belfast there was massive evidence (posters, cars, meetings, stickers, etc.) of a well organised campaign for Albert Price. It was generally felt locally that this was Provo organised and it bore many of the Provo hallmarks. Some of the cars used to bring Price supporters to the booths were 'borrowed' for the day and door-to-door collectors to support the Price campaign were 'difficult to refuse'. For security reasons, Gerry Fitt scarcely left his constituency office to campaign in the days before or during the election and Paddy Devlin seemed to spend most of his campaign time in the rural areas of Northern Ireland. Late on the afternoon of election day, John Hume arrived in the constituency and showed considerable courage in doing a number of walkabouts in strongly Provo areas of Andersonstown and the Upper Falls. By coincidence I was in the area and saw the remarkable spectacle of people of all ages emerging from houses bedecked with Price stickers and rents and rates strike notices and according him a wildly enthusiastic reception. I met Hume for some hours after the polls had closed and he was pessimistic both about the SDLP performance and the performance [of Fitt]. He felt that Fitt would not retain his seat, that the SDLP vote would overall be reduced.

Fitt had never so anxiously awaited any election result. Next morning in Belfast City Hall, he was pretty relieved to hold the seat, albeit with a reduced majority. He had polled 19,554 votes, a 2,180 majority over McQuade, but down about 1,000 from the 1970 contest. He published his appreciation to the electors in a large advertisement in the *Irish News* on 12 March:

> I would like to express my sincere thanks to the electors of West Belfast for once again returning me as their spokesman to Westminster. Since 1966, when the people in this constituency first reposed their confidence in me, I have always tried to give expression to the hopes, ideals and aspirations of the ordinary people of this historic constituency. When the result of this election was declared in the City Hall, I was overcome with many emotions, the greatest of all being gratitude to the thousands of people, particularly the old and infirm who, overcoming many obstacles, had made their way to the polls once again to vote for me. On polling day throughout the constituency I saw the enthusiasm and integrity of West Belfast and its people as they stood beside me and faced the combined challenge of all my opponents who were determined to give this seat to reactionary unionism. I have no hesitation in saying that this was the most bitterly-fought contest in which I have ever been engaged and there were times when I found it heartbreaking to see such personal animosity and hostility being vented against me by my opponents and particularly by those whom I once would have claimed as supporters. I have always believed that, in the final analysis, one must have the confidence of the people before one can hope for success in any election, and I cast my mind back to that historic day in 1966 when West Belfast first returned me as the lone anti-unionist voice to

Westminster. Since then we have lived through a terrible tragedy and I am confident that throughout this time I have always given true expression to the best interests of the people who first elected me. Today I am once again the only anti-unionist voice at Westminster but I am as determined as ever to fight tenaciously until we finally have brought peace and social justice not only to West Belfast but to all of Northern Ireland. The party which I now have the honour to lead, the SDLP, is dedicated to creating a society in Northern Ireland where all can live in peace and amity. West Belfast has many problems – bad housing, high unemployment – which affect the every-day lives of its people and it is against this distress that my party and I will wage an unrelenting struggle. I am once again sitting on the benches with a Labour government at Westminster and it is my intention to support them in their attempts to right the wrongs of Tory misrule over these past years. Finally, may I say a heartfelt thanks to all those workers, young and old, who voluntarily gave of their utmost to ensure my re-election. I can only promise today to continue with my efforts to make West Belfast a constituency of which each and every one of its people can be justly proud.

Fitt's result provided the only crumb of comfort for the pro-Sunningdale parties. The UUUC had made a clean sweep of the remaining eleven seats and although they had received just half the total vote, they immediately interpreted the outcome as a decisive rejection of Sunningdale and the Council of Ireland. In the usual round of television and radio interviews, Fitt could not conceal his disappointment: 'It was too early to write off the Executive. It did not even have time to establish a track record to judge it by. But I knew in my heart then our days in office were numbered.'

A few days later, Fitt flew to London to sign on at Westminster, but when he got out of the taxi at the entrance, the policeman on duty stopped him and said he was not entitled to use that entrance as he was no longer an MP. A brief, one-sided conversation followed before the officer stepped back and waved him on his way. Later, Fitt discovered that the policeman had read a report in one of the London papers predicting his political demise. Faulkner shared Fitt's pessimism about the doubtful longevity of the Executive. After a meeting with him on 4 March 1974 to discuss the implications of the election result, British officials noted he was:

> somewhat shaken and somewhat fearful ... everyone was shattered by the extent of the feeling against a Council of Ireland ... Faulkner ended by saying that 'he was no quitter'. He is clearly, however, a worried man and will need a good deal of comfort during the next few weeks.

The election result in Britain was far from clear-cut. Heath had not improved his position and the Labour party had not made enough gains to command a majority in parliament. Heath eventually conceded to Harold Wilson, who took office as the leader of a minority government. As a lifelong labour man, Fitt pledged his parliamentary vote to them. Merlyn Rees was appointed to the Northern Ireland post along with Stan Orme, who had long been involved with the CDU. There was an interesting sidebar to the appointment of Rees as it reunited him with his old comrade, Frank Cooper. During the Second World War, when Cooper served as a RAF Spitfire pilot in Italy, his administrative officer was Squadron Leader Merlyn Rees. When Cooper was shot down in combat and held prisoner for twenty-four hours before managing to escape, it was Rees who welcomed him back to base. Now, Cooper welcomed Rees to Belfast, but painted a gloomy political picture for him:

> The general election in Northern Ireland had caused a deterioration in the political situation. Prior to it, the opposition to power-sharing was on the wane and the Northern Ireland Executive were beginning to make their mark. Time was needed; but the [British] general election came at a period when it was only too easy for the 'loyalists' to focus on the potent and emotive issue of the Council of Ireland as a first step towards unification. This issue brought together both moderates and extremists in the Protestant community. The consequences were: the UUUC won 11 out of 12 seats (or 422,000 votes as compared with 246,000 votes for pro-Sunningdale candidates); a sharp drop in the morale and credibility of the Executive; and increasing criticism of the South particularly by Unionists of all persuasions.

The brief defined the critical issues as being the outcome of the Law Enforcement Commission, progress or otherwise on the Council of Ireland (where the Faulknerites were looking for some downgrading of Sunningdale), together with more action by the South on matters of security. The new loyalist MPs lost no time in pressing their mandate for, as they saw it, an end to the Sunningdale process and the removal of 'republicans' – as the SDLP were called – from government and fresh elections to the Assembly. Both Wilson and Rees told Fitt and repeated publicly that they were behind the Sunningdale process and it was too early to write it off as a failure. But the UUUC victory had unsettled some of Faulkner's men, although not him, and the jitters took hold. From that point on the Executive began to crumble because it was being undermined and betrayed on several critical fronts.

One of the most serious betrayals, which greatly undermined the spirit of the Sunningdale Agreement, came from the Irish side. The four senior jurists, including two Supreme Court judges, who comprised the Law Commission came out against extradition from the Republic to Northern Ireland on political as opposed to legal grounds. The issue was of grave concern to the Unionists and to the British government because in the previous two years, twenty-two warrants issued for people wanted for serious crimes in Northern Ireland, including murder, had been thrown out. According to a British diplomat in Dublin in a report to the Foreign Office in London, 'The Irish courts found a multitude of reasons for rejecting warrants, largely on technical or procedural grounds, including such absurdities as papers being stapled together rather than pinned.' He added that the Irish judicial attitude was in effect giving the IRA a licence to murder. This issue was also a cause of concern to the beleaguered Faulkner, who was being heavily criticised for leading unionists into the power-sharing executive and giving a commitment to take part in a Council of Ireland at a time when fugitive IRA terrorists could plead in the Irish courts that their offence was 'political' and thereby escape extradition to Northern Ireland. At a summit meeting in Hillsborough in February 1973, Faulkner told Cosgrave that it was 'a matter of life and death' and that Sunningdale could be ratified and sold to hostile Unionists only if there were clear progress in countering the impression that the IRA had a safe haven in the Republic.

When the issue could not be agreed during the Sunningdale negotiations, it had been remitted to the jointly appointed Law Enforcement Commission, set up in December 1973 to decide the 'most effective' means to bring to justice fugitive IRA terrorists who had committed crimes in Northern Ireland and fled south. The four Republic of Ireland jurists were Mr Justices Walsh and Henchey, who sat in the Supreme Court, D Quigley from the Attorney-General's Office and TA Doyle, Senior Counsel. The other members of the Commission were Sir Robert Lowry, Lord Chief Justice of Northern Ireland, Lord Justice Scarman, who had conducted the judicial inquiry into the 1969 disturbances, Sir Kenneth Jones, legal adviser to the Home Office, and Brian Hutton QC, Senior Crown Counsel for Northern Ireland. The British note of their first meeting at Hillsborough Castle on 16 January 1974 records that during the morning the Irish did not seem to be 'generally inclined to the extreme urgency of producing a report', but as a result of encouragement by British officials and 'possibly the consumption of food and wine ... the atmosphere of the meeting improved perceptibly after lunch.'

During these discussions, Lowry reported on a close study he had made of the Irish extradition legislation and stated his view that there were no constitutional, international or legal difficulties in handing over what the Irish regarded as 'political' offenders. The note of the meeting records that Lowry requested and received 'an unqualified assurance from Mr Justice Walsh that this was indeed the case'. Less than a month later, however, on 7 February, when the Commission held a two-day meeting in Dublin, Walsh took Lowry aside after a dinner at Kings Inns and said 'there was no point in continuing to discuss extradition because he could assure him that it was politically quite unacceptable and would never be implemented by the Irish government'. Lowry replied that he would not be party to a report that said there were legal difficulties about extradition when this was not the case. He would insist on a report outlining the correct legal position.

The Commission met for the third time in London at the end of February, and

British exasperation was reflected in the official note, which read: 'the Irish were content to stonewall and showed little interest in making noticeable progress.' When it came to drafting the report at the fifth meeting in London, on 21 – 22 March 1974, the British forced the Irish to include an explanation as to why they considered extradition an impossibility. 'Clearly the Irish are embarrassed by this legal argument and want either to lose it altogether or make it so long and boring that nobody reads it or gets the point.' In the end the Commission suggested a system of extra-territorial courts, enabling offenders to be tried in one Irish jurisdiction for specified offences committed in another.

When this draft report reached Ken Bloomfield, secretary to the Stormont power-sharing Executive, he prepared a *precis* for the ministers: 'The central political problem is that the report says extradition is the most effective means of dealing with the problem. How are we to accept a means which, in the view of all but the Southern Irish members, is a second best?' Any Irish law, he continued, has to be interpreted by judges in the South and 'the fact that British jurists consider their colleagues to be bad lawyers doesn't make them more likely to reach favourable decisions – rather the reverse.' A note from the Dublin Embassy to the Foreign Office remarked that 'the myth of British injustice still weighs very heavily in the political balance in the South'. It is abundantly clear from the official records that the Irish refusal to move on extradition helped to disintegrate the Sunningdale consensus, but by the time the deeply unhelpful report was completed and studied in May 1974, other fatally corrosive issues were also at work.

Before it left office, the Heath – Pym regime failed to satisfy the SDLP's insistence on ending internment, despite repeated and forceful pressure on the matter. At a meeting on 23 January 1974, the party returned to the question of its dissatisfaction with the identity of those released before Christmas and, reflecting the grave disquiet in his ranks, Fitt went so far as to allege the government had chosen to free such 'dangerous men' in the knowledge that they would return to violence, thus enabling the government to withstand pressure for further releases. At the same meeting the SDLP also pressed for an extension of compassionate parole schemes, the provision of special transport for relatives to visit prisoners, the payment of benefits to the families of those in custody and that the families be allowed to provide clothes for the prisoners. Sustained pressure from the party grassroots was openly referred to at another meeting on 6 February when a six-strong party delegation, which did not include Fitt or Hume, made a further plea to Pym for urgent action on detention. There was to be a meeting of the party's central council in ten days, at which all branches would be represented. It was intimated that without a major release – a figure of 150 detainees was mentioned – the party leadership might be forced to change tactics and withdraw their co-operation in running the new political institutions. The issue remained in abeyance over the period of the general election, but their position was summed up in the political brief prepared for the incoming Secretary of State, Merlyn Rees:

> They are holding together well but are looking for movement on detention and a Council of Ireland in its full sense (including executive responsibilities, a consultative 'chamber' and a full-time secretariat). They are seeking to bargain support for the RUC in return for a full Sunningdale Council of Ireland.

This was precisely the hand that was played when a group of SDLP Assemblymen met the newly arrived Rees soon afterwards, on 19 March. They argued that the only effective way of dealing with violence was political advance, which was essential to restoring normality. As the most important political matter was Sunningdale, it was vital to have it ratified and the Council of Ireland formed. Furthermore, by being seen to 'deliver' on this, the SDLP's credibility would be reinforced. Challenging the implication that it was the British side that was delaying the process, Cooper intervened to point out that, despite its undertaking to do so, the Irish government had not yet even drafted a Bill to create its own Police Authority.

The appalling human cost of the civil disorder and violence in a community as small as Northern Ireland was highlighted on 11 April 1974 when the *Belfast Telegraph* listed the names of each of the 1,000 people who had lost their lives since 1969. One day earlier, Rees had reported to the British Cabinet in London

> ... that the security situation in Northern Ireland was cause for great concern and the political situation, which was already bad, could deteriorate dangerously. The pattern of violence had changed and consisted largely of attacks with fire bombs prepared and placed by women, and the placing of car bombs by civilians who were not themselves terrorists but who were acting under extreme duress.

By the time Harold Wilson, the recently elected Prime Minister, arrived in Belfast for an eight-hour visit on Thursday, 18 April 1974, another six people had been killed. After visits to both the police and army headquarters and calls into two frontline security bases in Belfast, Wilson went to Stormont Castle where, accompanied by Rees, other ministers and advisers, he conducted a major audit of the situation with Faulkner, Fitt, the other members of the Executive and their officials. Hume was absent. Faulkner told Wilson that 'what was required now above all else was peace' and 'it needed to be said again and again that violence would not pay'. In his view, Sunningdale had been 'going sour' since before the recent election because of the lack of Irish security co-operation and the unfavourable glosses put on the declaration on the status of Northern Ireland by Cosgrave after a court ruling in Dublin on 1 March. Although the Irish government upheld the Sunningdale position, it did so with a legal subtlety that was not at all widely understood, especially in the north of the island. As a result, Sunningdale had become such 'a focus of conflicting emotions' within the Northern Ireland (unionist) community and while he wanted to maintain its 'spirit and essence', full ratification was impossible for now.

Fitt took the view that it was impracticable to expect full implementation overnight; there would have to be a sensible approach to this given the realities of the situation. However, he warned that Sunningdale was the only hope and the longer it took to ratify, the greater would be the gain to the IRA, which believed it could break Sunningdale by violence. Similarly, the Protestant extremists thought they could force a reversion to the *status quo ante*. Fitt wanted Wilson to make it perfectly clear, in public, that the extremists on both sides could not force the issue by violence and that there could be no return to the old system. On internment, Fitt said it was the 'raw nerve' of the Catholic community, who accepted the conviction of terrorist offenders through due process of law but 'abhorred' their detention without trial. He urged continuing movement on releases.

Both leaders went on to tell Wilson that the Executive members had been engaged in their own deliberations to find a way forward and there had been some progress towards reaching a united viewpoint. Wilson affirmed his support for the people of Northern Ireland deciding their own future and his absolute determination that there would be no question of bombing the government or the army out of the province, regardless of public opinion in Britain. He concluded by saying that it was vital for the Executive and power-sharing to be a success and sounded a warning by saying that in discussions about its possible failure, that words like 'civil war' had been used 'with reason'.

While that assessment of failure may have been something of an apocalyptic exaggeration, the Executive was in fact steadily imploding, not least because of the escalating tensions within the SDLP, which were aggravating the already well-established differences between Fitt and the rest of the party, which he led ever more nominally. These differences were all too evident at a meeting in Dublin on 22 April when Fitt and Devlin talked to the Prime Minister and the five most senior members of his government about a suitable timetable for the ratification and implementation of Sunningdale. The official Irish note of the meeting records that the discussion was quite inconclusive and that 'to, a considerable extent, Mr Fitt seemed to act as an advocate for Mr Faulkner. He was at pains to stress Mr Faulkner's difficulties and, in general, seemed to have considerable sympathy for Mr Faulkner's approach at this stage.' Fitt took an optimistic view and told the Irish that Faulkner was 'personally ready to go along with the full [Sunningdale] package but he was afraid that he couldn't carry his troops with him' unless they proceeded gradually. Devlin was far more pessimistic, revealing that Roy Bradford was plotting with hardliners John Laird John Taylor and Harry West with a view to deposing Faulkner and reuniting the unionist group with Bradford as leader and chief executive. In this, Devlin said, Bradford was assuming the SDLP would accept him in this role, but that was not on: they had some understanding with Faulkner, but never knew where they stood with Bradford.

Fitt was frank about all his difficulties when he lunched with Rees and Faulkner in the flat at Stormont Castle on 30 April 1974. The SDLP grassroots were unhappy that, even though the policy of internment was continuing, Executive ministers Austin Currie and Paddy Devlin were behind moves to bring an end to the rent and rates strike and to recover arrears by docking social security benefits. The 'civil disobedience' protest had been initiated after the first swoops in August 1971 and still had wide support. There was also serious party discontent, especially among the elected SDLP Assemblymen, about the lack of progress on internment and the evident stalling on the full ratification of Sunningdale. The turbulence had become so serious that at least two councillors were threatening to resign their seats in Derry, while others were known to be of like mind. More damaging still, the disgruntlement was reaching right into the Executive itself. Although he was enjoying a heyday as a popular and effective minister, Devlin was under such pressure in his Andersonstown neighbourhood that he was preparing to resign his post.

Fitt told Rees and Faulkner that the SDLP Executive had held two meetings the previous evening at which there had been unanimous agreement that Sunningdale had to be ratified in its entirety and at once; at the same time, it could be implemented 'this year, next year, some time, never'. He said that he had not attended the meeting because he did not agree with the resolution but knew it would be passed, and as party leader he had not wanted to be in a minority of one. According to the official note of the meeting, Faulkner, 'looking rather grim', asked whether the SDLP realised that if they pressed ahead with this line, it would break power-sharing and hand everything on a plate to Ian Paisley. Faulkner countered that if he were pressed to establish a Council of Ireland now, with executive functions, everything would fail. Fitt replied that while he recognised the present position, there was the distinct possibility of a direct clash between Faulkner's Unionists and the SDLP, with all the consequences that would flow from that, although his colleagues did not see this so clearly. It was not the Belfast Catholics who were the cause of the trouble, rather it was the Catholics from the border areas, for whom the link with the Council of Ireland was so emotive.

Despite the cumulative importance of all these issues in destabilising the ground-breaking Sunningdale consensus, the killer blow would come in an unprecedented and completely unforeseen manner. At this time only the keenest observer of the subterranean strands of loyalist politics would have been aware of the Ulster Workers Council (UWC), which had first flexed its muscles by organising two short loyalist strikes shortly after the introduction of Direct Rule in March 1972. It had not escaped the organisers that if electricity supplies were cut off, workers in virtually every industry and the entire community, willing or not, would become party to what these loyalists termed 'constitutional stoppages'. In what amounted to a clear and serious intelligence failure on behalf of the government and security forces, throughout late 1973 and early 1974 this small group plotted secretly to 'bring Northern Ireland to its knees if all else failed to stop the Council of Ireland'. Early in 1974, their plans ready for activation, they took William Craig, Ian Paisley and Harry West – the leaders of the UUUC – into their confidence. The politicians would get one chance to kill off the Council of Ireland and the Executive. If they failed, the plan would be activated.

The political battle took place both on the floor of the Assembly and in the Commons at Westminster. In Belfast Brian Faulkner fought tenaciously to get the assurances he needed from Dublin about the status of Northern Ireland and extradition, but all the while never flinched from his full commitment to the 'spirit and essence' of the Sunningdale process. Wilson and Rees remained publicly in full support of the process and repeated their stance in meetings in London with Cosgrave, Faulkner and Fitt. Nevertheless, the ratification deadline slipped steadily to sometime in May, largely due to the disagreement within the Law Commission regarding extradition. Meanwhile, the Irish authorities, bound by the attitudes of history, were still being difficult about handing over terrorists on the run from the North, a situation that was highly provocative as IRA and loyalist extremists continued to batter the community with their guns and bombs.

During this period there were more heated debates in the Assembly, but the death knell sounded on 14 May after a motion was tabled calling for a renegotiation of the 1973 Constitution Act because of the result of the general election. Faulkner countered with an amendment supporting the Sunningdale Agreement, if it were concluded in 'the letter and spirit' already entered into by the British and Irish governments. This amendment was carried by 44 votes to 28 in the Assembly, thanks to the combined votes of the Executive parties. That was the last straw for the UWC observer watching in the gallery. Before leaving Stormont, he announced a general strike, saying that power cuts would begin that night.

At 7.00am on Wednesday, 15 May the strikes began and before lunchtime their effect, together with widespread intimidation, had initiated what would ultimately become a complete shutdown of industry right across the province. That evening, at Stormont Castle, Stanley Orme, the Minister of State at the NIO, met Ian Paisley, leader of the DUP, William Craig, MP for East Belfast, and John Laird, a member of the Northern Ireland Assembly. They were accompanied by three members of the UWC and three, allegedly armed, members of loyalist paramilitary organisations, who were introduced as 'observers' so that Orme would not be seen to be negotiating with representatives of paramilitaries. Orme told them they would not get what they wanted by attempting to intimidate the government with a political strike and that, if it continued, there would be no alternative but to have essential services maintained by the army.

Hume had already been directly affected by the strike. That morning, his East Belfast Protestant driver, Charlie, had joined the protest and was therefore not available. The minister was bemused. Although he had been given the option of recruiting his own driver, Hume had opted for the driver assigned to him from the Stormont car pool. Over the months he had tried to befriend him, giving him a bed in his own home three or four nights a week so that he could pocket his subsistence expenses and paying him generously when he drove him to Dublin and elsewhere on unofficial trips.

Meanwhile, the powerlessness of the government in Whitehall to match its tough talk with action became evident very quickly. Harold Wilson suggested that a nuclear submarine might be deployed to Belfast to provide an emergency power supply, but officials at the Ministry of Defence promptly advised him that, while a fleet could be ready to leave for Belfast within forty-eight hours of the order being given, 'the difficulty is that electricity generated by a nuclear submarine is not compatible with the national grid'. A few days later, at a meeting of ministers, the army expressed its reluctance to become involved. The Chief of General Staff, General Sir Peter Hunt, expressed concern about bringing in troops and warned that

> if the army intervened to break the strike and appeared to be succeeding, confrontation and violence would probably follow. The army would be sucked into an endless situation and greatly increased numbers of soldiers would be required to run the territory.

On day three of the strike, civil servants interrupted an early evening meeting of Executive members to tell them of car bombings in Monaghan and Dublin, which claimed thirty-three lives and caused hundreds of injuries. The attacks, which were attributed to loyalist paramilitaries, seriously increased tensions. By Saturday morning, day four, the power had been reduced to one-third of its normal load and supplies were being rotated around Northern Ireland on a four-hour on-off basis. Belfast city had been virtually blocked off by hijacked vehicles parked across the main roads, as had the ferry port at Larne. Factories and shops had been forced to close by gangs of patrolling intimidators and a system of passes had been established by the strike organisers to enable essential workers, like doctors and nurses, to move around and vital supplies, like bread, milk and animal feedstuff, to be distributed. Armed and masked thugs manned the roadblocks and Executive ministers were told of the experience of one man who was stopped. Asked what he was, he replied, 'Consultant in the Royal Victoria Hospital.' 'Well you can't go through then,' came the reply. 'Only doctors and nurses.'

That Saturday evening at Stormont, Merlyn Rees told the Executive that he would not be talking to or negotiating with the strikers. Fitt recalled:

> We were comforted by his tough line with the loyalist politicians, but dismayed that he would not give the order to the army and police to go in and open up the roads by removing the barricades. It was the unanimous view among all of us in the Executive, during what were almost continuous meetings, that such tough action could stop the increasingly firm hold the strikers were gaining. The city was paralysed by then, the Stormont car pool had run out of petrol and there were thugs manning barricades on every major road so army helicopters had to be used to ferry several of us between our homes and Stormont.

Rees and Orme were pinning their faith on the mainstream trade union movement, with a plan to bring over to Belfast the General Secretary of the TUC, Len Murray, to lead back-to-work marches. 'I knew that was doomed the moment I heard about it,' said Fitt. The back-to-work exercise took place on the seventh day of the stoppage and, as Fitt had expected, it proved to be a humiliating flop. Only two hundred marchers turned up and although many police and troops were present, there were ugly scuffles with supporters of the strike. Losses in agriculture and industry were now piling up as an increasingly confident UWC enforced its putsch more effectively with each passing hour. Fitt recalled how:

> We in the Executive could only watch with dismay as control seemed to shift inexorably from our offices in Stormont to the detached house at Hawthornden Road, less than a mile away, where the UWC had its headquarters. Their credibility was enhanced to a major extent by the BBC, which broadcast strike bulletins reporting the decisions and attitudes of the UWC as if they were being handed down by a government-in-waiting. The BBC, quite wrongly in my view, treated the Executive and UWC as equal rivals, failing to recognise we were an elected legal body, while they were self-appointed with no mandate or democratic credentials.

Late that night, Sean Donlon, who was in the North to monitor events for his government, reported to Dublin:

> The overall situation in Belfast and in the areas of Northern Ireland through which I travelled is completely chaotic. The power situation is very bad and even essential food supplies are scarce. What is most dramatic and obvious, however, is the UWC control of the situation. Any part of 'normal life' which is continuing is doing so only by licence from the UWC.

On day eight, Wednesday, 22 May, the Executive moved to try and regain the initiative. For some weeks, as Faulkner had told Wilson during his visit the previous month, an all-party executive sub-committee had been examining the ways in which Sunningdale would be ratified and had come up with a range of ideas for phasing the process. That morning the Executive decided phasing was now inevitable and, before they were announced, the proposals for deferring ratification of the Agreement and postponing the formation of a Council of Ireland were put to the Assembly party of the SDLP. As Fitt recalled:

> Some of them did not want the news that we were even considering phasing to leak out in case it would further encourage the UWC but the majority would countenance no watering down of the Agreement. Over lunch time they voted 11 – 8 not to accept phasing. Details of the vote were quickly passed to Stormont Castle and Faulkner. He busied himself drafting a resignation letter, having made an appointment to see Rees in early afternoon. But I went to Stan Orme in a last-ditch bid to save the Executive. He asked me to get our party members together to speak to them himself.

Faulkner was already on his way to the chamber to announce his resignation when Fitt intercepted him: 'Hold on, Brian. Stan Orme is talking to our boys.' Over the next tense ninety minutes, while Faulkner waited with his letter in hand, Orme succeeded in persuading the Assembly group to pass the plan for phasing by a narrow, but sufficient, majority. New assurances about the run-down of internment were the clincher, but there was also a realisation that if the power-sharing experiment collapsed, so too would the prospect of any Irish dimension – a point Orme emphasised more than once.

After this step back from the brink, opinion within the Executive hardened considerably that decisive and swift action must be taken to enforce its dwindling authority. The SDLP position was that the government should put military experts into the power stations to restore normal electricity supplies and that troops should take on and break the UWC's stranglehold on the daily life of Northern Ireland. They firmly, but wrongly, believed that this was not already happening because of an argument between Rees and Roy Mason, Minister for Defence, over the deployment of the army. The Executive had drawn up a plan with its civil servants to take over petrol stations and tankers and set up an emergency fuel distribution system. The work would be undertaken by civil servants, while the army would provide protection for them and the garages they would commandeer at key points throughout Northern Ireland. In Fitt's view, 'We felt this plan would meet the clear sensitivities already exhibited by Rees, Orme and Roy Mason, the Defence Minister, about involving the army in "strike-breaking."'

During the next day, the ninth of the stoppage, they pressed their demands even more vigorously and it was decided they should meet Wilson at Chequers, together with Roy Mason and Attorney-General Sam Silkin. Early the following morning Faulkner and Alliance leader Oliver Napier were flown to England by the RAF, where Fitt joined them having travelled to London the previous day to speak in the Commons. There he had warned that Northern Ireland was being held to ransom and insisted the army must go into the power stations and take over the supply of petrol and oil 'within a very few hours, or there will be total economic chaos'.

At Chequers, all three ministers left Wilson and his entourage in no doubt as to their determination to resign, whatever the consequences, if the Executive fuel supply plan was not implemented and further decisive action taken to back the writ of the Executive. Faulkner warned the PM that

> the issue was now not whether the Sunningdale Agreement would or would
> not survive. The outcome which the Protestant extremists sought was
> without question an independent, neo-fascist Northern Ireland.

The Chequers meeting broke up at 4.30pm after five hours of talks. While Wilson was careful not to give firm assurances, the ministers came away believing their demands would be met and that, as well as implementing the fuel plan, military technicians competent to run the power stations would be sent in if the UWC went ahead with its threat to shut down the power system completely. Fitt recalled: 'We all left Chequers to return to Belfast, confident that, after the Cabinet meeting called for that evening, we would get action.' Indeed, all three were telephoned after 11.00pm to say the Cabinet had endorsed the proposals. 'I went to bed in Belfast that night, happier than for many days, sure that when we woke up next morning the action would have begun. But that Saturday morning we telephoned each other in some puzzlement. Nothing had happened.'

What the Executive had not been told was that the British government had now decided that the entire Sunningdale process was irretrievable. On 24 May a minute circulated to the British Cabinet by its secretary, John Hunt, stated:

> If we do nothing, the Executive will collapse over the weekend. On the
> other hand an attempt by the British Army in effect to run the country
> would require the commitment of unacceptable forces and would probably
> fail.

It was the powerlessness of the army's position that was the final clincher: even if military personnel could get the power stations running again, which the generals felt was highly doubtful, they would still need to post guards at every distribution pylon in Northern Ireland to prevent sabotage and 'even if we put in the entire British Army, there still wouldn't be enough soldiers'. More worryingly from the Executive's standpoint, Rees was preparing a memorandum for Wilson examining 'The Short-term Possibilities for Northern Ireland and the Executive':

> While the Northern Ireland Executive remain in being, there can be no real
> movement. But the situation changes if they go. From our point of view the
> most desirable situation now is that they should go of their accord. In view
> of the intervention, they cannot make any plausible complaints that they
> have not received full support from HMG.

The intervention to which Rees was referring was a much scaled-down version of the Executive fuel plan. Before it was rolled out, Wilson decided to make a major statement live on national television. The broadcast went out that evening and during it Wilson said:

> As this holiday weekend begins, Northern Ireland faces the gravest crisis in her history. It is a crisis equally for all of us who live on this side of the water. What we are seeing in Northern Ireland is not just an industrial strike. It has nothing to do with wages. It has nothing to do with jobs – except to imperil jobs. It is a deliberate and calculated attempt to use every undemocratic and unparliamentary means for the purpose of bringing down the whole constitution of Northern Ireland so as to set up there a sectarian and undemocratic state, from which one third of the people of Northern Ireland will be excluded. This is not – this has not been at any time over these past few difficult years – a party matter in the House of Commons or in this country at all. Where the political wildcats of Northern Ireland seek to divide and embitter, all the major parties in Britain have sought to heal and to unite.
>
> We stand by, as our predecessors stood by – and still stand by the decision taken last year that the Northern Ireland Assembly and the Northern Ireland Executive provide the only basis for peace, the only basis for order and good government in Northern Ireland.
>
> The people on this side of the water – British parents – have seen their sons vilified and spat upon and murdered. British taxpayers have seen the taxes they have poured out, almost without regard to cost – over £300 million a year this year, with the cost of the Army operation on top of that – going into Northern Ireland. They see property destroyed by evil violence and are asked to pick up the bill for rebuilding it. Yet people who benefit from all this now viciously defy Westminster, purporting to act as though they were an elected government; people who spend their lives sponging on Westminster and British democracy and then systematically assault democratic methods. Who do these people think they are?
>
> The people of Northern Ireland and their democratically elected Assembly and Executive have the joint duty of seeing this thing through on the only basis on which true unity can be achieved – democratic elections, constitutional government and the spirit of tolerance and reconciliation. And in doing that they will have the support of the British Government, with our responsibilities within the United Kingdom and our responsibilities in world affairs, for law and order in Northern Ireland. We intend to see it through with them.

Throughout the day, Fitt and his ministerial colleagues were told nothing officially other than that Wilson would appear on television. Most significantly they were kept entirely ignorant of the dramatic policy change that had taken place. When it came, Wilson's broadcast was therefore a bitter disappointment to them. 'There was no talk of decisive action to back us, only condemnation of ritual kind of the

UWC and a reference to the loyalist people as "spongers", which only infuriated them even more,' was Fitt's opinion. He too would have been entirely furious if he had known that at that point, in light of the political judgement that had already been made, Wilson's undertaking to see the crisis through with the 'democratically elected Assembly and Executive' was an entirely dishonest one.

Fitt's Antrim Road house stood opposite the street leading to the main entrance into Girdwood Barracks, one of the army's key operational bases in Belfast. Overnight he leapt from bed several times after hearing the rumble of military vehicles, to see if any of the comings and goings heralded the activation of the fuel plan. But next morning, Sunday, day twelve of the strike, there was still no sign of action and Fitt went to Stormont Castle early to see Rees: 'I was alone, for Paddy Devlin was so disgusted he would not go. I got no reassurance. Rees was actually rushing off to meet Wilson in Cornwall.' That Sunday lunchtime Fitt's increasingly angry SDLP colleagues gathered at his house to review their options:

> We drafted an ultimatum saying we would all resign unless the petrol plan was put into action by 6.00am next morning, the thirteenth day of the strike. Paddy Devlin and Ivan Cooper went to Dublin to tell Liam Cosgrave what was going on.

At 5.00am on Monday morning, Fitt was wakened by the distinctive whine of the Saracen armoured personnel carriers leading the long military convoys that were finally leaving Girdwood Barracks. Despite the belated deployment to twenty-one petrol stations, the Executive members were in a mood of total despair when they gathered at Stormont later in the morning. As Fitt recalled:

> We had reports saying the UWC had gone ahead with its threat to impose a total shutdown of power, which would permanently damage the system. We all realised the game was over, but we did not know by who or how the final whistle was going to be blown.

There were those around the table who believed the only course of action left open to them was to negotiate with the strike leaders. Roy Bradford had been of this view all along and had become increasingly vocal about it. Fitt recalled that 'in the weeks leading up to the strike, he was foremost among Faulkner's ministers having the jitters and, when the strike began, we all wondered how long Faulkner could hold him because of an action that bordered on betrayal of the Executive.' That action had occurred on Friday, 17 May, day three of the strike, when Bradford had met two of the UWC committee at his home, a contact he maintained as the strike progressed. He claimed they were constituents of his, which they were, but that he would talk to them at that time and leak information from the Executive caused profound hurt, according to Fitt.

Meanwhile throughout Monday as the discussions wore on, Fitt was shown maps and technical data by civil servants pointing out which areas would flood first when the power stations closed, the electricity supply halted and the pumps failed, causing Belfast's untreated sewage to flow back into the streets, spreading disease. Brian Faulkner was at home when a civil servant rang him to graphically describe the nightmare.

Earlier that day, returning from their trip to Dublin, Devlin, Cooper and Eileen Fitt – second eldest of Fitt's five daughters, who had decided to hitch a lift home for a break from her studies at Trinity College – were involved in an incident that vividly demonstrated the state of almost total anarchy that had come to prevail. After their car crossed the border, heading north, by prior arrangement it rendezvoused with an unmarked police car carrying a number of ministerial close protection officers. Although they had been informed that the road ahead to Belfast was clear, the two cars were stopped by a flag-waving crowd of about one hundred people, including men armed with cudgels and other implements, near Dromore, Co. Down. The police car, which was travelling in front, was waved through, but farm tractors and other pieces of machinery were then drawn across the road to block the second car, while other vehicles closed in from behind. The quick-thinking driver, from the Stormont car pool, managed to evade them by crossing the central reservation of the dual-carriageway road and sped off southbound in the direction from which it had come. The five-strong crew of a police Land Rover watched the incident, but declined to intervene when approached by the close protection officers. Noticing that they were being followed, the minister's car took to side roads as Devlin and Cooper sat with their personal protection weapons on their laps. An official report of the incident records that 'the ministers were first taken to Newry police station where the Superintendent was most helpful but other RUC men in the station were openly hostile'. Devlin and Cooper, together with Fitt's terrified daughter, later reached Belfast safely by an alternative route.

Early the next day, the fourteenth day of the strike, following more talks with officials, Faulkner met his Assembly party and Executive members at Stormont and announced that, in view of the grave consequences flowing from the rundown of the power stations, he had changed his mind and now supported mediation with the strikers. Oliver Napier and Bob Cooper of Alliance backed him; the SDLP did not. He left the Cabinet room in Parliament Buildings and as he went down to nearby Stormont Castle to see Rees, the other members of the Executive watched from the windows as a massive protest convoy of tractors and farm machinery, all with Ulster flags flying, trundled up the long drive towards them. Faulkner returned to the Cabinet room at 1.20pm to announce that Rees was not prepared to talk to the UWC, which gave him no alternative but to resign. 'We all walked around the green cloth-covered table shaking hands warmly with each other. There was no recrimination or bitterness, only emotion, respect and a sense of friendship,' said Fitt. The Alliance and SDLP ministers decided they would not resign, but wait to be sacked. Fitt realised his unique position: 'With Faulkner gone, I was effectively Prime Minister of Northern Ireland, a post I held until nineteen hours later when Merlyn Rees called me in and withdrew my warrant of appointment.'

Before being sacked, Fitt held court in his office, reviewing the course of events with a stream of callers, including other politicians, civil servants and journalists. All were urged to drink up from the contents of his cocktail cabinet, and when the supply was exhausted he instructed one of his private office staff to raid Faulkner's stock to replenish it: 'There'll be plenty there. Wee Brian is virtually teetotal and he never gave anybody a drink when they call to see him.' Despite the brave front he was maintaining, Fitt was deeply, deeply annoyed at the extent of the hard-won gains that had been lost:

> At the time I was puzzled why Rees seemed so reluctant to defend the Executive as vigorously as we had a right to expect. But looking back, and having talked the matter over with those involved, I believe Rees and those close to him made their minds up at a very early stage of the strike that the Executive was fatally flawed, and was not worth saving. From the very beginning Rees and Orme were sensitive about the name of the strike-leading organisation because it contained the word 'workers', an emotive one in the political vocabulary of any socialist. So the precedent of turning British troops against 'workers' was one they were reluctant to create, despite the fact that both Rees and Orme knew well there was no similarity between the self-appointed UWC and any proper workers' representative group.

Fitt came to believe that the NIO also doubted the fibre of two members of the Executive, namely Bradford and Devlin. Roy Bradford was suspect because of his thinly veiled disloyalty to Faulkner and eagerness to do business with the strikers. Rees, Orme and Cooper all doubted how long Paddy Devlin would stay in the Executive: he was still highly critical of internment and consistently took the view that mass releases would put irresistible pressure on the IRA to end violence. He frequently became very angry when Pym, Rees or Cooper would produce reports, presumably from the army, saying that some released detainee had promptly gone back into the IRA.

Judging by Devlin's behaviour on day three of the strike, they were right to be suspicious. That day he had announced his resignation at a meeting between the British ministers and Executive, saying he was doing so because of Rees's inertia in phasing out internment. Fitt heard of his decision when he got back from London and was accosted in the corridors at Stormont by a succession of colleagues who were very critical of Devlin and his action at that highly inappropriate time. Before he had to deal with the fall-out from the resignation, Devlin heard of the Monaghan and Dublin bombings and telephoned Fitt at home: 'Could you talk to Faulkner about my resignation and freeze it until this is settled?' he asked. Fitt said he had never heard of a 'frozen resignation', but he did talk to both Faulkner and Orme, repeating Devlin's assurance of his complete co-operation in dealing with the UWC strike.

> With hindsight I believe the Northern Ireland Office, especially Frank Cooper, was of the opinion that the Sunningdale process was imperfect because a major faction was absent, the men of violence. Our suspicions that a bit of two-timing might have been going on were first aroused in the final stages of the Sunningdale conference. A list of 130 names of detainees was being shown around by officials. People like Paddy Devlin, Ivan Cooper and myself were asked about those who came from our constituencies. The object was not to select for release those who would get involved in violence or who would be a destabilising influence in the community. All of us had regularly, and sometimes successfully, lobbied Whitelaw about individual cases, so being consulted was no surprise. What did surprise us all was that none of the sixty-three people released on 20 December were on the Sunningdale list and many of the individuals released caused us all to raise our eyebrows because of their track records. It seemed as if the actual release list was a carefully designed sop to the doves in the Provisional IRA, designed to strengthen their hands against the hawks. There was further, and more persuasive, evidence that encouraging the terrorist doves into politics was indeed a basic strand of policy. Merlyn Rees was barely a month in office when he announced the removal of both Provisional Sinn Féin and the Ulster Volunteer Force from the list of banned organisations and future events would show this was indeed a priority.

Above all, however, Fitt blamed the ultra-nationalists in the SDLP for the loss of the great political advance that was the Sunningdale Agreement:

> Blind to everything but their precious Irish dimension, they stoked up the anger of the hardline loyalists by pressing uncompromisingly for the Council of Ireland. My view, if I had been in absolute control, was that we should have agreed to take matters in two stages, consolidating the very real prize of power-sharing and the effectiveness of the Executive before tackling the Irish dimension over a longer period of time. That was the real concern of the loyalist hardliners, not power-sharing. As it turned out, the SDLP had finally to accept this two-stage approach, but only when it was too late and the initiative had been seized by the Ulster Workers Council. As a result they lost everything, not only the prospect of a Council of Ireland but power-sharing as well.

CHAPTER TWELVE

ULSTER NATIONALISM

WITHIN A FEW DAYS OF THE END OF THE STRIKE, Merlyn Rees prorogued the Assembly and held a news conference at which he announced the emergence of a new political phenomenon among the Protestants. He called it 'Ulster nationalism', but at the time more attention was paid to the truly awful impersonation he did of Paisley during the exchanges with journalists. His formula for taking account of it was to call an election to appoint a constitutional convention. The thinking behind his policy was outlined in a 'personal and confidential' minute he prepared for Harold Wilson after a round of talks with the entire range of parties:

> The mood of the discussions throughout was quiet and sombre. There was no bombast. There was a greater sense of the need to face up to reality than even the older hands here can remember. The main theme that is beginning to emerge (though the SDLP has still a good way to go) was that of 'let Ulstermen try to work it out between themselves'.

He thought the British government – within specified criteria – should indeed 'let them have a shot at it themselves' by agreeing a form of government and a constitution during the Convention and putting it forward for approval. He also stated that, at the end of the day, Northern Ireland should deal directly with the South on all-Ireland matters, without the British as intermediaries. Rees further believed a new 'Ulster' identity should be created rather than continuing on the basis of allowing 'aspirations' to both Dublin and London to exist but most interestingly his submission confirmed that he had always doubted the durability of the entire Sunningdale process:

> As I indicated to you from the start of our taking office and, regrettable though it may be, the probability has always been that it was only a matter of time before the Executive fell. The 'strike' brought it all to a head. The Westminster elections [in February 1974] started this process. The effect on popular opinion of the IRA bombing campaign (particularly the big bombs

in the cities) fuelled it. The dwindling support for the Faulknerites has grown apace. This is not to say that power-sharing is wrong in principle or that it would not work. But it will not work against this background (including some of elements of the Sunningdale Agreement).

Finally, he also noted a sense of 'tit-for-tat': the republicans toppled Stormont; the loyalists brought down the Executive.

A White Paper setting out the framework for the Convention was published on 4 July. After fresh elections, on a date to be confirmed, the politicians would be set the task of considering 'what provisions for the government of Northern Ireland would be likely to command the most widespread acceptance thoughout the entire community'. Fitt recalled: 'The Unionists correctly interpreted this as a "blank cheque" to write their own constitution and, triumphant at the collapse of the Executive, they set their face firmly against any further power-sharing or Irish dimension.' With all its gains from the Sunningdale process wiped away, the SDLP was far from enthusiastic about the plan and, for a number of reasons, considerably uncertain about how it should proceed.

After the expectations raised by Sunningdale, Catholic opinion in general was described as 'shell-shocked' after the UWC strike, with people disillusioned, or frightened or both. In an assessment of their mood, prepared for Frank Cooper in July 1974, Maurice Hayes judged that 'the middle-class will return to an abstentionist variety of nationalism which will survive by nursing its wrath and collective sense of injustice'. Younger people, he forecast, would 'turn towards violence as they attempt to wreck a society which they feel has nothing to offer them'. In considering the prospects for the SDLP, he said they were:

> standing on a very thin plank indeed and that plank is narrowing. Recent events have in Catholic eyes seriously questioned the validity of the SDLP approach. This has left them with diminished credibility. They have held together publicly as a party better than might have been expected. Nevertheless there are rumblings. John Hume seems to have taken a more positive lead than Gerry Fitt. Nevertheless the former ministers seem all to be very despondent. A British general election will put them under considerable strain.

Cooper was not entirely persuaded by Hayes. In a minute to Rees he wrote: 'This is too gloomy. The [SDLP] certainly have had to contend with a difficult situation but we have no evidence that their electoral support is likely to wither away.'

The party was in turmoil on several fronts, however. It was seared with an interlocking and overlapping series of personal antagonisms and fundamental differences on policy. On policing, for instance, Hume remained utterly opposed to any notion of reforming the RUC, while the infinitely more pragmatic Devlin was encouraging the NIO to begin a process of 'seepage' to gradually re-establish normal policing in the most troublesome Catholic areas of Belfast. Like Devlin,

Fitt was on highly cordial, but not uncritical, terms with police officers of all ranks and shared the belief that steady modernisation – dating from Callaghan's day and the introduction of Direct Rule – had met many of their concerns about impartiality and accountability. There had been, for instance, 2,000 police officers recruited since 1970, bringing much-needed new blood into the RUC. An NIO political assessment at this time noted within the SDLP the continuation of 'the traditional rift between Belfast and Londonderry' as well as 'a strong spirit of independence in the rural areas of the southern parts of Northern Ireland'.

After a three-day visit to various individuals in the days immediately after the end of the UWC strike, a Department of Foreign Affairs 'traveller' told Iveagh House that 'the mood of the SDLP is generally one of considerable depression, frustration and despair. As might be expected a serious and potentially divisive debate is going on within the party as to what its future policy should be and there is much bickering between the leaders, bad feeling between many of the backbenchers and the leadership, and internal disputes over media leaks and counter-leaks.' All nineteen Assemblymen reported a massive swing of support away from the party. The 'traveller's' report continued:

> Devlin and Fitt said they now had no support in Belfast. The personal abuse about which they were complaining so bitterly up to last week had stopped but had been replaced by an even more hurtful political, and in some cases, personal ostracisation. Many of the leaders, particularly Hume and Currie, seem to feel that the SDLP is finished as a political force. They had pinned their colours firmly on power-sharing within Northern Ireland and partnership between north and south and neither of these was now possible. Hume made it clear that he believes any hope of Irish unity was gone forever, that the prospects for a minimal Irish dimension to the Northern Ireland solution in the next 200 years were virtually non-existent and that there was no brand of unionism present or on the horizon which would be prepared to share power with the SDLP.'

The party was also struggling to cope in extremely straitened financial circumstances. Now that the Executive and Assembly had been disbanded, most of its former elected representatives, its main activists, were without income or jobs. (Fitt was the exception as, for the time being at least, he had his Westminster salary.) The party had recently paid £17,500 for a substantial house at Derryvolgie Avenue in South Belfast to use as a party headquarters, but could not raise the £3,000 it had been quoted to provide suitable security protection for the building and its occupants. It was also finding it hard to make ends meet on its operating expenses. The Joseph Rowntree Social Service Trust, one of its most substantial benefactors, had awarded them only £6,000 out of a bid for £25,000, and the planned appointments of a £3,000-a-year fund-raiser and a £2,000-a-year research officer were currently in question. Fitt and Devlin were anxious lest Hume would exploit this financial weakness by bringing in money from Fianna Fáil circles in the Republic, thus tilting the SDLP away from the strictly neutral relations they had hitherto maintained with all the main political parties in the South. That standpoint was severely strained in the aftermath of Sunningdale, with Fitt and Devlin being particularly critical of the Dublin government for not implementing its side of the bargain far more rigorously and for not stepping in to help defend the Executive during the days of crisis in May and help to salvage something from the wreckage.

A wide cross-section of the party's policy-makers converged on Bunbeg, in Co. Donegal, on 24 – 25 August to take stock of where the party was headed and to set out a new strategy. It would not be an exaggeration to say there was still an acute sense of shock, and in some cases rationality seemed to have evaporated completely. Many of those present were convinced that the British were on the verge of announcing a withdrawal from Northern Ireland and that they were facing a 'Doomsday scenario'. Hume told the observer from the Department of Foreign Affairs that the party would do all in its power to provide the British with a face-saving rationale for withdrawal with honour. According to the same source, another party Assembly member, Aidan Larkin, one of Fitt's fabled 'teachers', was even more apocalyptic. He foresaw, in the violent aftermath of withdrawal, 'the Irish Army operating in minority areas while the British Army took on the loyalists'. Regarding an Irish military involvement, he thought the most important preparation the Irish Army should make was to 'acquire 1,000 lorries, a stock of rifles and such things as gas stoves and provisions'. In a reference to the 1969 deployment, he said 'field hospitals would not meet the case'.

Such wild assessments apart, lingering resentment and fear of losing further credibility and support introduced a shriller tone into the long-standing criticism of internment and security policy. It also prompted more threatening noises that the party might go completely 'green', boycott the planned Convention and campaign for a united Ireland but having tasted power, however briefly, the party was united in hankering for it and eventually that sentiment won the day. As Fitt described it:

> Despite all the emotion and disappointment, we pulled ourselves together and maintained our commitment to the Sunningdale process as being the best way to fairly meet the conflicting aspirations of all the people. The phrase 'agreed Ireland' became a key one in our political vocabulary as we sought to impress on the Unionists that we accepted any move towards an Irish dimension had to be with their full 'consent'. But the continuation of internment and the frustrations that the political deadlock renewed gave me many headaches in keeping the party together and my frequent absences at Westminster provided plenty of opportunity for SDLP internal strife.

Faulkner, who was licking his own political wounds and plotting his renaissance, commented that the SDLP's machinations made the party look less like one with which they could contemplate renewed co-operation. The British took a far more critical view. A report classified as 'Secret' spelled out in stark terms the new political reality:

> The minority will not co-operate in the institutions of the province until those institutions are reformed to their liking; the majority are unprepared to make concessions to a minority whose attitudes they regard as treasonable. The province is now moving ineluctably to demands for a Protestant administration based on majority rule. HMG can restrain the Protestant majority but cannot coerce it beyond a certain point simply because it is the majority. The question is therefore no longer what can be done to satisfy the minority but rather what the minority, and this really means the SDLP, are prepared to do to strengthen the hand of HMG in consolidating the political gains won for the minority since 1968. A continued adherence to Utopian policies by the SDLP, with or without the support of the Irish Government, strengthens the hand of extreme Protestants and ultimately threatens to leave the SDLP in a posture of permanent and impotent opposition. Is this what they want?

For his part, Cooper refused to be deterred by the historic intractability of the situation. 'Political solutions: I've got a drawer full of them,' he would say, sliding open his desk. 'The real trouble is getting one of them accepted.' He also knew that finally settling the 'Irish question' would be a long, drawn-out process. 'This is only round two or three of a long fight and I wouldn't care to speculate on just how many rounds there will be.'

Unknown to Fitt and Devlin, at that point other senior British government officials were pre-occupied with the question of how they should be treated in an entirely different political context. Their dilemma was grounded in what had become known as 'the Irish state case' – proceedings instituted in December 1971 by the Irish government alleging breaches of eight Articles of the European Convention on Human Rights (ECHR) by the British government in Northern Ireland. The most serious complaints asserted that the security forces had unlawfully deprived people of their liberty and used torture and ill-treatment, that fair, prompt and public trials had not taken place and that there was institutionalised discrimination against Catholics. The case further soured what was a traditionally uneasy relationship between the two governments when it came to security matters. The level of British resentment was articulated in a letter from the NIO to the Irish Foreign Office in April 1973, which suggested making an approach to the Irish Prime Minister, Liam Cosgrave, to withdraw the proceedings:

> It is possible ... that Mr Cosgrave does not apppreciate what sort of beastliness is going to take place if the Irish state case comes to a hearing ... it may be also that Dr Garret Fitzgerald [Foreign Minister] and Declan

Costello [the Irish Attorney-General] are too starry-eyed to appreciate this.'

The letter went to on to say that 'if the case did come to a hearing that it would be a massive blow to Anglo-Irish relations and to our hopes of co-operation between the two countries in many fields.' It concluded by suggesting that if the argument about damage to relations was of no avail with the Irish, then 'we should perhaps be considering other cards of persuasion'.

The European legal process was tortuously slow, as well as embarrassing for the British, therefore when Heath met Cosgrave at the Baldonnel airbase, just south of Dublin, on 17 September 1973, he made the suggested plea and successfully persuaded the Irish to invoke the 'friendly settlement' procedures of the Convention to settle the matter and thus avoid forthcoming hearings at which a number of witnesses for the Irish state, including Fitt and Devlin, would have to give evidence.

However, before this proposition was formally considered, another scheduled preliminary hearing of the main case took place the following month at which Costello, according to the British version of events, 'reneged on the Baldonnel understanding. He did not simply conduct a lawyer's case; his manner was acid and hostile,' an official later recorded. The British also believed that before the hearing he had resiled from private undertakings given to their Attorney-General, Sir Peter Rawlinson. These were that he would respond to the court's proposals for a friendly settlement hearing and publicly absolve United Kingdom ministers of any responsibility for ill-treatment. The fact that Costello pressed for an early hearing of the witnesses was interpreted as a sign that he was not serious about seeking a friendly settlement. When this possibility was discussed at a meeting in Paris on 15 November 1973, there was little surprise in Whitehall when it failed.

During the early months of 1974, while Fitt and Devlin were serving as members of the power-sharing Executive, the Irish continued to pursue the case and in April the ECHR indicated it would hear six Irish witnesses in camera at Strasbourg between 22 and 25 July. Apart from Fitt and Devlin, the other witnesses called were Andrew Boyd, Tom Conaty, Father Brian Brady and Paschal O'Hare. When he learned the date, Fitt said in the House of Commons on 4 April that he would not be withdrawing the allegations he had made in two lengthy sworn affidavits made on 27 May 1972 and 5 September 1973. In the first, he described how the Orange Order's and Apprentice Boys' marches frequently culminated in rioting. He made reference to the water supply explosions in the spring of 1969, which had resulted in the proscription of the loyalist UVF, and said that much of the subsequent civil disorder in August 1969, which led to the British Army being deployed, was directed against Catholics. Between 1 January 1969 and 31 December 1970, he stated, forty-two licensed premises in Belfast owned by Catholics were maliciously destroyed and in the majority of instances no charges were ever brought. Recalling that the Catholic population became estranged from the army because of repressive operations and legislation and the selective and partial administration of justice, Fitt went on to say that internment, which was not necessary for the preservation of the peace and the maintenance of order, was applied only to that section of the community which did not actively support the (unionist) government.

In his second affidavit he referred to 'extremist loyalist organisations', numbering many tens of thousands of members, which had been established, regulated and trained on a military basis, possessed large quantities of arms, ammunition and explosives, and carried out the most extreme forms of violence against members of the minority community and against the security forces of the UK government in Northern Ireland. Despite this, he averred, the powers of internment and detention had been used against only ten members of these extreme organisations, although some 2,000 members of the minority community have been interned or detained without trial. He then cited statistics to underline the manner in which the weight of security policy was directed against the minority community, despite the violent activities of these groups. Between 30 November 1972 and 20 June 1973, 436 'loyalist' houses had been searched, as compared with 3,708 houses of the minority community. In the eighteen months from January 1971, over 4,000 cases of intimidation – 83% against Catholics – had been reported to the police, but only forty-one persons had been detected and just twelve of those convicted. In support of his various allegations, Fitt initialled and submitted a file of newspaper cuttings, photographs and other documents. The affidavit concluded:

> It is my belief and conviction that internment and detention without trial
> in Northern Ireland has been carried out by the government of the United
> Kingdom with discrimination on the grounds of political opinion.

In his affidavit of 23 November 1972, Paddy Devlin made the same claim, pointing out that this was the case 'even though the commission or attempted commission of acts of terrorism spring at least equally from the side of the majority community'.

He went on to criticise the use of both written and oral evidence, which would not be admissible in a court of law, by the Commissioner, who determined whether detaines should be freed or not, and condemned the discriminatory behaviour of the security forces 'whose provocative behaviour and coarse and insulting language' is now accepted by the minority community as commonplace and routine. He accused them of failing in their duty to protect members of the minority community from threats, direct and indirect intimidation and attack.

The prospect of Fitt and Devlin giving evidence, in these terms, against the former administration, which had been headed by Brian Faulkner, with whom they were now serving in the power-sharing Executive, was addressed in a confidential NIO minute circulated on 24 April which stated there was 'a double problem' and asked, 'Should we acquiesce in these two members of the Executive giving evidence; and if they do appear, how strongly should they be attacked?' The considerations to be taken into account were outlined as follows:

> Responsibility for the alleged acts of discrimination which Messrs Fitt and Devlin quote attaches at least in part to Mr Faulkner. While the actual proceedings at Strasbourg are in camera the fact that the affidavits have been lodged is public and if, as can be expected, they go to Strasbourg as required by the Commission it will soon become known that Messrs Fitt and Devlin gave evidence at this international tribunal at the behest of the Government of the Republic against the actions of the Security Forces, HMG and Mr Faulkner's previous administration. This would no doubt be the cause of some strong reaction in the Protestant community in Northeri Ireland (whether pro- or anti-Sunningdale); it would also amount to two members of the Executive attacking their own Chief Minister, and – to put it no higher – these two factors could place considerable extra strain on the Executive.
>
> If they are not attacked and handled roughly and doubt cast on their testimony, there is a strong possibility that the Commission will accept as true what they allege as members of the present 'government' of Northern Ireland. We shall have the usual difficulty of proving a negative and our whole case about the necessity for detention may be jeopardised and there could be an eventual finding against HMG on this count, which while perhaps not as serious as a finding against the UK under Article 3 (about the use of ill-treatment and torture) will not enhance HMG's international reputation.
>
> On the other hand if they are handled roughly in cross examination they may harbour some resentment and this could have repercussions in the Executive. It seems unlikely that this would cause them to resign from the power-sharing set-up (which would be cutting off their own noses) but they must be made to realise that their activities at Strasbourg could disrupt the Executive, and that Strasbourg cannot be kept in a water tight compartment. It is perhaps a matter of political judgement on how hard Messrs Fitt and Devlin should be handled in cross examination; while the international aspect seems to demand that every step should be taken to secure a favourable outcome for HMG, it may be that what is paramount in the next few months is to avoid placing the Executive under unnecessary strain.
>
> In the light of what Mr Fitt said on 4 April it is unlikely that he and Mr Devlin could be persuaded to withdraw their affidavits, but some of the possible reaction in Northern Ireland might be avoided if the two could be persuaded not to appear at Strasbourg. If necessary it might then be possible to make it appear that while the affidavits were in their view true at the

time, the advent of 'power sharing' and the new regime had made it
unnecessary to pursue the matter further.

The minute concluded by recommending that the most serious efforts should be
made at the highest level to persuade Fitt and Devlin not to go to Strasbourg, on
the grounds that their action would amount to an attack on their Chief Minister
and on the British government and would therefore have serious divisive effects on
the Executive and on Northern Ireland society generally.

> While it is desirable to cast the maximum doubt on the accuracy of their
> testimony, should they appear at Strasbourg the question of the tactics to be
> followed in cross examination there (whether to play it rough or gently) will
> need to be agreed in the light of any approach as above.

At the same time, the NIO asked the press office and James Allan to come up with
examples of any 'inconsistencies' that could be used to challenge Fitt in cross-
examination. Allan was on leave, so it was not until 6 May that he replied:

> Gerry Fitt has frequently said in private that he understands the need for
> detention (and the fact that he now believes that the murderers of his friend
> Senator Wilson were detained no doubt reinforces him in this view).
> Nevertheless these private remarks would be difficult to substantiate. Gerry,
> like many politicians, is all things to all men and is particularly loquacious.
> Nevertheless, when pressed he, like Paddy Devlin, would assert that it is the
> Catholics who have had to suffer the brunt of security force activity and
> this, in their book, is discrimination even if in private they acknowledge the
> villainy of the IRA.

In response to 'the highly delicate question of how rough Counsel should be with
'Messrs Fitt and Devlin', Allan said:

> You probably know better than I whether it is essential for signatories of
> affidavits to appear at the proceedings. If it is not I would think that
> attendance by Fitt and Devlin would depend upon the situation here. If the
> current difficulties of the SDLP (lack of movement by the British on release
> of detainees, and lack of movement by the Unionists on ratification of the
> Sunningdale Agreement) have been at least partly solved by the date of the
> bearings, I would guess that Fitt and Devlin would not be there. (Gerry Fitt
> has refined the art of diplomatic absence to a considerable art form – when
> there is a tricky SDLP party meeting in Northern Ireland he is usually
> firmly ensconced at Westminster!) Should, however, there be a near
> breakdown situation with the SDLP ranged against HMG and the
> Unionists then no doubt Messrs Fitt and Devlin might see no disadvantage
> in putting their oar in at the proceedings. (I realise that Strasbourg can be
> regarded as a negotiating ploy both by the Irish Government and the SDLP,
> and there could be an element of brinkmanship come the end of July.) My
> own view is that should Fitt and Devlin appear then we should certainly
> give them as good as we get while seeking not to overplay our antipathy to

'Ministers' who insist on giving aid to those who are proceeding against us. This is however a matter of global tactics and political judgement which can only be met at the time.

Nine days after this was written, the UWC called its general strike and by the end of May the Executive had been brought down, prompting renewed anxiety in London about the Strasbourg hearing. The NIO took the view that, 'in the light of the current situation', any pressure on Fitt and Devlin to withdraw their affidavits or not to attend at Strasbourg might well be counter-productive and could misfire badly. The NIO anticipated that the two would, in fact, be keen to go and would be encouraged by Dublin to do so, in which circumstances 'they should be attacked and handled as roughly as possible'. However, the assessment continued, 'as regards attacking Messrs Fitt and Devlin, so far we have been singularly unsuccessful in finding any material that counsel might use [for cross-examination]. Neither Mr Allan, from the Laneside records, nor press section, has come up with anything to contradict or discredit what Mr Fitt, for example, may say.'

On 10 June the lawyers at the NIO came up with a new idea. In a letter to Allan at Laneside they asked:

> … are there, for example, any Special Branch dossiers on these two? … It would be helpful to know what these contain in case they open up any line of cross-examination. I have heard Gerry Fitt was closely connected with the Civil Rights movement in its early days and that during the last war, Paddy Devlin was interned as being a member of the IRA. Are these stories true? If there is anything in the Special Branch dossiers then I think we must arrange … to see them.

The trawl for damaging information proved inconclusive, however, and eleven days later a senior official suggested another new strategy:

> We could play it rough, although much of the evidence of their highly ambivalent attitudes cannot be used (since it arose in discussion with us). There is, however, a penalty to be paid. Both men are likely to resent rough treatment and since both are important public figures in Northern Ireland, it is open to question whether it would be wise to sour our relations with them. There is, however, a more important point. We want to bring home to Dublin that their behaviour is not universally admired … There is, therefore, something to be said for HMG refusing to cross-examine Mr Fitt and Mr Devlin. At the conclusion of their evidence in chief, a statement would be made by our representatives that, while we did not accept their evidence, we considered that it would not advance our over-riding aim to bring peace and harmony to Northern Ireland – an aim which, if it were not for this case, we would have assumed that we shared with Dublin – to enter into controversy before the Commission with two leading figures in Northern Ireland public life. We had the recent White Paper set out our

plans for the future and in particular expressed our admiration for the work
of the Northern Ireland Executive, of which Mr Fitt and Mr Devlin played
a distinguished part; it served no useful purpose to endanger future political
developments by entering into old, unhappy controversies with them at
Strasbourg. A good deal could be made of this approach. It goes without
saying that we would not disclose in advance to Dublin, or anyone else, that
we proposed to adopt this approach.

In spite of all efforts to the contrary, the Strasbourg hearings went ahead as
scheduled and Fitt and Devlin both gave evidence and were cross-examined.
During August, the transcripts were circulated within the NIO and analysed in
detail. The lawyer who was co-ordinating the case concluded:

> My general impression on reading through the Fitt and Devlin evidence is that
> it is so biased and one-sided that it is difficult to know where to start to put
> the general picture right. The majority of people in this country will, I think,
> automatically discount a lot of what they said, but I doubt whether the
> Continental academics who make up the Commission would do so without
> counterbalancing evidence. On the whole therefore it seems to me that Messrs
> Fitt and Devlin have damaged the UK standing in this case at Strasbourg.

Whatever the British unease, the Strasbourg appearance, as an NIO political
assessment noted soon afterwards, 'added to the irritation of loyalists but evoked
goodwill among most Roman Catholics'. There were further evidence-taking
sessions, including one in Norway, and it was not until September 1976 that the
ECHR delivered its verdict on the Irish state case, finding that the interrogation
techniques used in Northern Ireland did constitute a breach of the Convention on
Human Rights because they not only involved inhuman and degrading treatment,
but also torture. The ECHR made its final ruling on the case on 18 January 1978,
holding that the Commission was wrong to use the word 'torture', but agreeing
that the internees had been subjected to 'inhuman and degrading treatment'.

Meanwhile, in mid-1974 the burning political question was when would
Harold Wilson go back to the country and try to win an overall parliamentary
majority for his government? Many thought he would not get as far as the summer
recess, but he finally settled on 10 October as polling day. Again, the issues in
Northern Ireland were different from elsewhere and the main point of interest was
whether or not the UUUC could repeat its clean sweep of February and win a
renewed mandate for its uncompromising policies. The SDLP initially decided to
fight all twelve seats again, but later pulled out of East Belfast and North Down
and became involved in efforts to stop splitting the Catholic vote in the highly
winnable seats of Mid-Ulster and Fermanagh-South Tyrone. Fitt wanted Austin
Currie to stand in Fermanagh, but Frank McManus, who had been defeated in
February, disliked Currie and said there were no circumstances in which he would
stand down. The deadlock triggered intense manoeuvres to find an agreed 'unity'

candidate, and Fitt spent a great deal of time trying to arrange for a former Stormont MP, John Carron, to stand. Shortly before nominations closed, Carron complained he was being intimidated to withdraw, and did so. Fitt never did get to the bottom of how the agreed candidate emerged or muscled in, but it was Carron's nephew, a publican from Lisnaskea named Frank Maguire, who finally secured the nomination. 'I wondered what sort of character he would turn out to be when in his only interview of the campaign he said, "'I haven't got a policy, I'm a publican. I'll get a policy when I get there.'''

Fitt's own campaign in West Belfast was uneventful, and he more than comfortably held the seat with a majority up from 2,180 to 5,556. The overall SDLP share of the vote throughout Northern Ireland again hovered at the 22% mark, the same as in February. Nevertheless, thanks to republican clubs splitting the Mid-Ulster vote, Ivan Cooper was prevented from taking that seat. But, reflecting the electoral arithmetic, Maguire topped the poll in Fermanagh and was elected MP. Although they had lost another seat, the hardline unionist vote increased from a 50% share to 58%, while Faulknerites could manage to attract only a 3% share, representing a loss of 10% support since February. Nationally, Wilson led the Labour party to a slightly stronger position, with an overall majority of three. By virtue of having his vote to bargain with, Fitt's influence at Wesminster was therefore potentially valuable in the uncertain political conditions that lay ahead.

Unlike Fitt, Maguire proved to be an infrequent attender at Westminster, but one morning not long after the election, Maguire sat down beside Fitt on a plane bound for London. It was only the second time they had met, and although Fitt had already told Wilson that Maguire was 'half a Provo' at a private meeting on 15 October 1974, he changed his mind now that he found him to be 'one of the most generous, friendly men you could meet, but absolutely without any sense of politics'. During the flight, Fitt chided Maguire about his refusal to condemn the brutal murders by the IRA, which were taking place regularly in his constituency. 'I'm a publican. If I say anything about those things, my pub will be blown up,' replied Maguire. Fitt told him he should choose between being a publican and an MP; an MP should not let himself be frightened or intimidated by the IRA. Behind his back, in the bars at Westminster, Fitt promoted a whole series of Frank Maguire jokes, exploiting the concept of the simple Irishman let loose in London. Mystified by the complexities of the underground as he tried to find his way from Heathrow to Westminster, Fitt told his drinking companions, Maguire had listened to the passenger in front of him at the ticket office. 'Maida Vale single,' said the passenger. So when his turn came he said: 'Frank Maguire – married.'

In November 1974 there was little funny about being Irish in England. Fitt said it was actually shaming and embarrassing because since 1972, when the

Officers' Mess at Aldershot had been bombed, Irish terrorists had regularly carried out attacks in Britain, killing and maiming many people. Their previous callousness was surpassed on the evening of 21 November 1974 when two no-warning bombs exploded in pubs in Birmingham. In the blasts 162 people were injured and twenty-one others blown to pieces or burnt to death. Fitt said:

> Of all the atrocities that had taken place throughout the Troubles the Birmingham bombs made my blood run coldest. The reputation of the English for being the most tolerant race on earth was amply justified after that outrage. In many countries the compatriots of the bombers would have been lynched for less. I had become frustrated at the inadequacy of existing words of condemnation to keep pace with the increasing savagery of the bombers, whether at home or elsewhere. Saying once more that no cause was justified by the use of violence, that I deplored it, seemed a less than adequate response.

(It is worth recording that, despite his abhorrence of terrorism and those who perpetrated it, Fitt was strongly opposed to capital punishment and sided with the abolitionists, who rejected a motion to hang terrorists who caused death by a margin of 369 – – 271 in a free vote on the issue in the Commons soon after the Birmingham bombings.)

That autumn there was no respite from violence for the people back at home. A vicious spiral of tit-for-tat killings started up again and the savagery from both communities knew no bounds. Many of the victims, Catholic and Protestant, were Fitt's constituents, murdered indiscriminately while in their workplaces, out shopping, or enjoying a drink. Others were singled out for no other reason than they were of the opposite religion to the killers, while some died whilst carrying out violent activity, shot by the security forces or executed by the malfunctioning of their own bombs. When he could, and it was appropriate, Fitt attended their funerals. By 1974 he calculated he had been to sixty-two in the previous couple of years. On the occasions when he could not attend, he would send a wreath and so regular was the occurrence that he maintained an account with a florist in Belfast for the purpose. Fitt asked Harold Wilson to impose far tighter security measures because of the fear, within his constituency, and in Belfast generally, expressed to him by Catholic and Protestant citizens who called at the house, stopped him in the street or came up to him in pubs when he was in Belfast. Such were the tensions of the time, Fitt quipped that he now sat in his favourite bars with his gin in one hand and the other on the gun inside his jacket pocket.

He and Devlin now entered into public dialogue with the RUC, breaking significant new ground by formally meeting the chief constable, Sir Jamie Flanagan, the first Catholic ever to hold the job. In order to reassure them that the RUC was doing all in its power to pursue the killers, whether republican or loyalist, Flanagan introduced them to detective chief superintendent Billy

Mooney, the charismatic officer who was leading the investigation teams. Fitt and Devlin were extremely impressed by him, and after these meetings Fitt went on radio and television to ask people to give information about the killers to the security forces:

> For every murderer there is a mother or a wife, a relative or friends who knows who is responsible. These are the only people who can stop the assassinations. I don't need to spell out what these people should do. They have got to examine their own consciences and then they will know what I am getting at.

Fitt was not merely asking people to give information about the IRA. The loyalist assassins struck as much fear into Catholic hearts as the Provos into Protestant ones. Nevertheless, in making this plea he was demonstrating his own personal courage by laying himself open to the cry of 'informer' from the PIRA and criticism from the 'hard green' element within the SDLP. Hume and his many allies were predictably opposed to the initiative, and Hume laid bare the very wide differences within the party on the policing question and the future of the RUC in a forceful speech at the end of October:

> The past days have seen one of the most despicable campaigns that I have witnessed in an attempt to pressure the SDLP into changing its views on the crucial question of policing. The weapon that is being used is the brutal and murderous series of sectarian assassinations. It is particularly disgusting that the Secretary of State and the supposedly impartial Police Authority have lent themselves to this campaign.

In private, Hume was intensely critical of Fitt and accused him of compromising the SDLP's negotiating position at the worst possible time by allowing the British to use him in a major exercise to seek minority support for the RUC. During a conversation with Sean Donlon, he said that 'the logic of Fitt's position would be for the British to organise [sectarian] assassinations all over the place so that the minority would be driven in desperation to a "come back RUC, all is forgiven" position'. Donlon noted that Hume had remained deeply embittered about the RUC largely because of the incidents in the Bogside in 1968 and 1969.

By now the SDLP had come to conclusion that its best tactic for the forthcoming Convention elections and subsequent negotiations was to be as uncompromising on other issues as they were on policing – a stance they maintained rigidly during their ongoing contacts with Rees and officials from the NIO. Despite his long identification with the British Labour party, Fitt felt betrayed and was exasperated by Rees and 'the absolutely disastrous' way he had handled events. The entire SDLP leadership was also at loggerheads with Rees and confused by his demeanour. At one meeting, as Fitt later told ministers in Dublin, Rees was incoherent and gave the impression of being close to a nervous breakdown. Of the same encounter, Hume was convinced that Rees did not appear to be in control of himself.

At one of their regular, and calmer, sessions with British officials on 27 November, Austin Currie talked of a 'drift to civil war' because no British government had been prepared to stand up to the Protestant extremists, who comprised only 1% of the total population of the UK. What was needed, he insisted, was a firm statement, prior to the Convention elections, of the consequences of the loyalists rejecting power-sharing. The SDLP was concerned that the unionists would have everything their own way and that there were no contingency plans for the almost certain collapse of the Convention. Currie suggested that in such circumstances, the British should announce an intention to withdraw and to remain only as long as it took for an Ireland-wide solution to be achieved. In order to back up their demands, the party's leaders constantly threatened to boycott the Convention if their demands were not conceded.

Although Cooper and Allan said that such a scenario was out of the question, the government was secretly examining in depth all sorts of radical, and hitherto unthinkable, options for the future of Northern Ireland, along with what were widely called 'Doomsday' plans. A lengthy paper studying the potential for international involvement in the Northern Ireland problem, for example, recommended that British missions abroad should assess likely attitudes to international intervention in the Irish Republic, in Northern Ireland and in the UN. The conclusions continued:

> Then it might be worth drawing up a list of prominent individuals who might be suitable as mediators and considering in each case whether they would be likely to accept. Similar consideration should be given to the choice of other governments. Then, as British plans for the convention/referendum approach begin to take more detailed shape, it may be possible to identify more precisely the various stages at which a breakdown might occur and might conceivably be remedied by resort to international involvement. The main argument for this kind of contingency-planning stems from the probably critical character of the time-factor. It could easily happen that a situation calling for international involvement will arise at very short notice and that, if we are to have any success with a proposal of this kind, it will have to be put forward promptly and in reasonable detail. Insofar as we can obtain the necessary information now and draw up contingency plans without allowing news of our intentions to leak out, it seems desirable that this should be attempted. If we wait till the contingency arises, it may be too late.

The Foreign Office in London conducted a major piece of research into a negotiated independence for Northern Ireland, the assumptions in the resulting comprehensive paper based on the fact that Britain 'would regard [it] with ... due safeguards on the defence and security side and on terms which would preserve our relations with the Republic, as a not unwelcome development'.

In October 1974 an even more sobering assessment – especially from the SDLP's unyielding standpoint – came in yet another paper from a senior political adviser in the NIO. A covering minute to his document, which was graded 'Secret/UK Eyes' (meaning it was not to be circulated to the police, or any officials of Northern Ireland origin), stated:

> I conclude that we shall have confrontation with the majority (which we shall lose) unless HMG in effect changes its policy toward the constitutional convention by watering down the requirement of power-sharing and the Irish dimension to accommodate Protestant views about how these requirements should be met.
>
> I do not think we can or should evade the issue by calling off the Convention. 'Can' because we have nothing to put in its place and pressure for provincial elections is probably irresistible. 'Should' because the convention may give a last opportunity for the feeble voice of moderation to be heard.
>
> Our objectives in relation to the Catholics must be redefined. We need to protect them. But seeking to give them parity in political terms is no longer possible, produced no response from them when we tried it and, in the present climate, is positively harmful to their interests. I think we have got to do something for the Catholics in practical rather than political terms. (Security guarantees; no army harassment; ease or end detention.)

The Irish government was not, of course, privy to the full and radical nature of British thinking at this time, but it had divined enough from its own wet fingers in the political wind to be seriously alarmed by what was being considered. Its response was to create an Inter-Departmental Unit to discuss the implications of British withdrawal, taking account of all the social, economic and security factors. Clearly influenced by SDLP fears that, in the wake of the UWC strike, the British would never stand up to the loyalists, Garret FitzGerald formally warned the government, on 18 November 1975, of the 'very grave danger' arising should the British pull out in circumstances that could provoke a civil war:

> Our own ability to act effectively in these circumstances is clearly extremely limited and might not even be sufficient to prevent the emergence of a de facto independent Protestant state in east Ulster or a de facto independent state controlled by the Provisional IRA in west Ulster.

Against this fear-provoking background, where longstanding constants had been jettisoned and the previously unthinkable had become plausibly possible, Rees made a wide-ranging statement to the House of Commons during a debate on Northern Ireland on 5 December 1974. He said the troops would be withdrawn in an orderly fashion once the violence ceased, stressed that internees were not being held for their political views and stated that in a society split by religion, origin, social customs and history, any form of government must take account of these differences.

Although the details had been kept secret, there was growing speculation that the root-and-branch reconsideration of every political and security doctrine relevant to Northern Ireland was preparatory to a British disengagement from its last and most troublesome colony. The way that the convention was to be conducted at arms-length from the two governments reinforced this perception, especially in Dublin where the government was concerned about the consequences of such a move and experiencing great difficulty in forging a coherent post-Sunningdale policy. Irish anxieties about the political fluidity were expressed when officials from both sides met in Dublin on 12 December. They took the view that, at Sunningdale, both governments had irrevocably committed themselves to the linkage of power-sharing and an Irish dimension, and that could not now be dissolved. The Irish were specifically concerned about the effect of this on the SDLP and mentioned the 'wide divergencies becoming apparent' between Fitt and Devlin in Belfast, who had virtually disowned the Irish dimension, and those in Derry and elsewhere, for whom it was essential. They were troubled that if the SDLP as a whole were to publicly abandon that aspiration in the run-up to the constitutional convention elections, Catholic support might well switch to the IRA.

None of these elements was on public display at the party's fourth annual conference, held over the weekend of 17 – 19 January 1975, when an appearance of cohesion was skilfully maintained. An NIO assessment of the conference said the party remained sectarian, with a tendency to dwell on the past, and the debates did not produce any results of startling novelty. 'The impression is of a party marching resolutely sideways into the future,' the NIO official commented. By contrast, Sean Donlon found that the 'hopelessness and depression' which dominated at Bunbeg a few months previously had lifted and been replaced by a more positive mood. 'The biggest change that has taken place in the last year is the opening out of discussion within the party', he noted, contrasting this with the reluctance to challenge the founders that had been so evident the year before. As an indicator of this, he pointed to the outcome of the debate on policing, where a Hume-inspired policy document was attacked so 'forcibly, constructively and logically' that it was rejected 62 – 53 and referred back to the party executive for further consideration.

Donlon also noted the growing influence of Derry on the party – the word 'Derry', of course, being synonymous with Hume. Only one of the five elected party officers and one of the fifteen party executive members was from the Belfast. At that time there were just seven branches of the party in the city, compared with twenty in Derry and the surrounding county. Donlon further commented that it was very much a middle-class, white-collar party, with six teachers, an engineer, a solicitor, a pharmacist and an accountant on the party executive. He calculated that twenty of the thirty-four office-holders had third-level education. A clear majority of the party hierarchy were now regarded as 'Hume-men', but the Hume – Devlin axis and their mutual respect for and friendship with both Currie and O'Hanlon were still major factors in steering the party.

These developments considerably weakened Fitt's position and influence, especially the glaring lack of any working-class involvement in the party. There were only two branches in his entire West Belfast heartland, for instance, compared with twenty in the Derry constituency. During the past year his attendance record at party executive meetings had improved slightly – six out of seventeen – and he had, for the first time and after four years as leader, completed the necessary formalities to make him a fully paid-up member of the party, but all the while he was actually becoming more and more detached from it. He did not get openly involved in the controversy about policing, and the original reservations he had harboured about joining and forming the SDLP in the first place, which had temporarily evaporated with the formation of the Executive, were once again uppermost in his mind: 'I could sense an ever-widening gap opening up.' In retrospect, this can be seen as the crucial turning point that ushered in, what were for Fitt, years of disillusionment and led, inevitably, to his final break with the party – although the final sunder was still some way off.

Towards the end of 1974, after five years of unremitting violence, there was an inexorable pressure for peace in Northern Ireland. For years the government and politicians had been plagued by professional peacemakers, many of them American, who did the rounds and produced what Fitt disparaged as 'ten-inch-thick dossiers' pinpointing what give and take there could be. Privately and secretly, a series of far more credible efforts had been made to persuade the British government to engage more purposefully with the IRA, and also with loyalists, in order to bring about an end to violence. The British were adamant they would not talk. Harold Wilson himself had assured the Executive members, during his April 1974 visit, that

> there could be no solution through violence and the British government
> had not talked and would not talk to people, whoever they might be, who
> looked to violence.

Although it had so actively discouraged General Hackett's earlier manoeuvres, the British government was nevertheless not averse to keeping itself informed as to the evolution of the IRA's thinking and the 'order of battle' of its various personalities. For this purpose it maintained links with a former priest and a businessman in Derry, a 'back-channel' that would still be in use twenty years later and would prove critical in igniting the peace process in the 1990s. What was also treated with the utmost secrecy was the intelligence product gleaned by the long-term undercover 'agents' inside the organisation, carefully nurtured by the police and the security services. Ever since their role in the abortive 1972 ceasefire, Hume, Devlin and also Paddy O'Hanlon – who could read the mind of the exceptionally ruthless South Armagh cadres better than anyone – monitored IRA activity carefully and, from time to time, used their information to promote a response from the government that might help to bring about an end to violence. Of course, such approaches were rooted equally in a desire to see off the IRA and secure a political advantage for themselves but despite raising hopes, they inevitably proved to be a false dawn.

This was the case in September 1973, at precisely the same time as the SDLP were engaged in the talks to agree power-sharing. That month Hume and O'Hanlon, in an initiative confided only to Fitt and Devlin, met a leading IRA figure one Sunday night, within hours of being summoned by telephone. The man, introduced by the *nom de guerre* John Murphy, intimated that, with the imminent arrival of Heath in Dublin and the ongoing talks about a Council of Ireland, the IRA might be amenable to calling a unilateral ceasefire. Hume said the IRA would have to put its proposition in writing, before rushing off to the NIO to reveal to Cooper what had been going on. It had been arranged that the two SDLP men would see the IRA again forty-eight hours later, but when the get-together took place they were told that, as a result of the IRA's unfavourable interpretation of what Heath had said at the end of his meeting in Dublin, the idea of a ceasefire was off. Hume told Cooper this was a tragedy: 'Monday could have been a great day for peace in Ireland.' Fitt had little sympathy with the operation and, although he did not make an issue of it at that time, Hume's apparent readiness to bring the IRA along compounded his antipathy towards him. Around this time, in another ultimately fruitless initiative of which Fitt does not seem to have been made aware, Hume was advising Bishop Edward Daly – the priest who gained worldwide exposure when he was pictured on Bloody Sunday, waving a white handkerchief as he escorted the body of one of the victims – in his efforts to persuade Martin McGuinness to halt the campaign in Derry alone.

But Fitt was aware that, contemporaneously, Devlin was promoting his own peace plan to Cooper, which was predicated on the belief that an end to internment would expose the hollowness of the IRA's case for war and clear the way for serious political talks. Cooper responded favourably to what he flatteringly called 'the PD formula', but never took the contents as seriously as Devlin believed they deserved. Fitt was more sympathetic to Devlin because he supported his passion for ending internment and knew well that Devlin was most certainly not a tribune for the IRA.

During these episodes Cooper had been adamant that he was strictly observing Wilson's assurances about not talking to the men of violence, but while they could not prove it at the time, the SDLP strongly suspected that after the fall of the Executive, the terrorist organisations on both sides were getting the Laneside treatment from British civil servants. Their suspicions, which ultimately turned out to be accurate, were nourished from hints dropped during exploratory conversations Paddy Devlin was conducting with UDA leaders and Glenn Barr, one of the loyalist strike-leaders, who was acting as the UDA's political adviser. Fitt recalled:

> This development was a source of great anger to me and many others in the party for the British government seemed to be moving to a position where the ballot box and the gun barrel were of equal status when it came to political recognition. It was also a gross betrayal of the unambiguous assurances we had been given by Wilson and repeatedly by Rees and Cooper.

However, he well understood why it was necessary for these backstage moves to be kept under wraps by the Wilson government. With its wafer-thin parliamentary majority, his government could not afford to antagonise him and risk losing his vote in the Commons. Equally, if there had been confirmation of any flirting with the IRA, instead of abstaining in most divisions, the ten UUUC MPs would have turned hostile.

However, the veil over these machinations was dramatically swept aside on 10 December when the Irish Special Branch swooped on a small hotel in Feakle, County Clare. Inside they found a group of Protestant clergymen from Northern Ireland having lunch. Their real quarry, virtually the entire leadership of the IRA, had fled just moments earlier, having been tipped off about the impending raid. The operation reflected the Dublin government's determination to deny the IRA any scintilla of political credibility. Immediately after the Birmingham bombs an official statement had repudiated 'any claim of the IRA to act or speak on behalf of the Irish people'. Upon their return to Belfast, the clergymen, who had informally briefed Cooper in advance of their secret misson, went to see him again. A few days later, clearly endorsing the Feakle initiative, the leaders of the four main churches, Catholic and Protestant, inserted full-page advertisements in all the Irish daily newspapers exhorting their congregations to pray together the following Sunday for peace. On 18 December, after a meeting between Rees and five of the Feakle clergy, he said he would 'naturally respond' to a 'genuine sustained cessation of violence' over a period of time. A day later, one of the Feakle group travelled to Dublin for another meeting with the IRA, but ten minutes after he arrived at a north city hotel the Special Branch swooped again and his IRA contact fled. The Irish government then issued another statement, insisting it was up to elected representatives in Britain and Ireland to work for peace, reconciliation and justice in Northern Ireland.

Despite these obstructions, in messages exchanged through the Protestant clergy, the IRA was prompted to declare a unilateral ceasefire that would last from 22 December until 2 January. Rees repeated what he had said previously, but it was clear from decoding the conflicting statements that both sides were obliquely signalling an intent to engage. The violence halted on cue and the entire community, which had been imprisoned under a self-imposed curfew for half a decade, suddenly rediscovered normality. The shops were thronged, restaurants and cinemas thrived again and the pubs were packed. Behind all of the euphoria, as 1974 passed into Irish history as a year that would never be forgotten, Fitt could not help feeling pessimistic:

> The year had begun with more promise for permanent peace than any since the 1920s. But it turned out to be far from the year of reconciliation the Executive had called for. Instead, we were back to square one politically. I was among very few that Christmas who did not see the very welcome ceasefire as a new beginning. To me, it was a false dawn.

There were two principal reasons for his pessimism: the political immaturity of the Provisionals and their destruction of the social fabric where they operated, in what were now called the ghetto areas. Fitt wondered what the Provos would do when the violence stopped because the first attempt they had recently made to define a political programme, a pamphlet entitled 'Eire Nua', he considered to be 'a pie-in-the-sky scheme for a united Ireland':

> I also felt strongly that official dealings with these self-appointed terrorists was undermining the democratic process and the status of elected representatives like myself. They would prove that people could bomb their way to the conference table. Another reason I was sure that the ceasefire was only a false dawn was because too many Provos and their hangers-on now had a vested interest in lawlessness and violence. There were individuals I had known all my life who had never worked and after five years of violence were spending their days propping up the bar counters in drinking clubs, paying for rounds from rolls of banknotes.
>
> I knew of respectable businessmen who were being soaked dry by racketeers demanding protection money. Post Offices were robbed of money intended to pay out pensions and family allowances; bookmakers were cleared out, especially on Derby and Grand National days; postmen were held up when Giro cheques for benefits were due and the cheques fraudulently cashed. Housing contracts, to get people into badly needed homes with modern facilities, were delayed and costing more because of extortion.
>
> The moral fabric of the close-knit, extended family, with married daughter, mothers and grandmothers living close to each other and supporting each other had broken down. I knew this from my constituency work. Before the troubles there would have been very few unmarried mothers; now there were lots of young girls, often with a couple of kids, who described themselves as a 'common-law wife'. Their partners were

invariably on the run, imprisoned or interned.

This threat to the family unit, for generations the core of working-class life in Belfast, was hardly surprising in a community where people were prepared to kill others in cold blood, or kneecap, or tar and feather members of the community who had broken unwritten rules. The same crowd who had stimulated this social breakdown had a vested interest in the continuation of violence and lawlessness, and I could not see them observing any lengthy ceasefire.

During revelries in Stormont Castle just before Christmas, Fitt and Devlin cornered one of the senior officials involved in the ceasefire process. His assessment confirmed their own of the worthlessness of dealing with the IRA. The 'troglodytes', as he referred to the 'hawks' or hard men, were firmly in control and although he expected them to flirt with the political process for a time, he predicted that, in the end, they would go back to the gun and bomb as the most effective instruments for achieving change.

Because of Fitt's continued importance in helping the Labour government to remain in power, Rees was careful to nurture his support during this period. The two met in London on 8 January for an exchange of views and two days later he saw him again, this time in Belfast with Hume and Devlin. All three pressed for the release of the internees to help decisively turn Catholics away from the IRA. Hume made the point that of all the Derry detainees released, only two had become re-involved and many of them had come to him to express resentment at the restrictions placed on them in the Maze by the IRA. There was now a real war weariness, he said. Fitt suggested one hundred internees should be freed at once because the more releases there were, the more pressure would be imposed on the IRA to maintain the ceasefire.

On 2 January the first ceasefire was extended until 17 January, but it quickly collapsed because of mutual distrust. That same morning Fitt and Devlin had breakfast at Stormont with Rees and Cooper, where they found Rees exasperated because the IRA leadership had failed to properly decode his statement in the Commons three days previously, when he had promised to end internment and reduce the army presence to peacetime levels. The IRA was in a state of confusion. The leadership had voted by only four votes to three to prolong the ceasefire, and the organisation was coming under great pressure from the Irish Special Branch – a reflection of the Dublin government's deep hostility to anything that would even indirectly boost the IRA's profile. Devlin again encouraged Rees to release internees in order to put more pressure on the IRA and, while he urged him to use officials to explore channels with the IRA, he recommended Rees should keep his distance and state publicly that there would be no negotiation with the IRA, or Sinn Féin, about the constitutional position of Northern Ireland, which was a matter for elected representatives alone. After exchanges between officials and

Sinn Féin frontmen, an open-ended ceasefire came into force on 10 February, underpinned by written understandings and monitoring arrangements.

As it became clear to the SDLP that, despite its public obfuscation, the government was indeed heavily engaged in direct negotiations with the IRA, they, and Devlin in particular, were convinced that Rees and Cooper were striving to lure the IRA and loyalists into mainstream politics and engineer, through the Convention, a comprehensive political settlement that would finally allow the British to get out of Ireland. 'Increasingly to British eyes, Northern Ireland amounted to nothing more than a painful, and costly, boil on John Bull's backside,' Devlin recorded in his autobiography, *Straight Left*.

In February, Fitt temporarily left the problems of divided Belfast behind and visited another divided city, West Berlin, for a meeting of the Socialist International. There he met many renowned international figures, such as Golda Meir from Israel, Olaf Palme from Sweden, François Mitterand from France and Bruno Kreisky of Austria. Willy Brandt, the former German Chancellor, introduced him at the main press conference, where questions about problems in Northern Ireland were posed. 'I found a great deal of sympathy and interest in our plight among the international socialist community, but I was told that because they all had their own terrorist problems, there was little they could do,' he said afterwards. He ensured the visit was not downplayed at home by ringing the *Irish News* to regurgitate, for publication, the points he had made at the conference. Next day the paper did him proud, with a front-page splash headed: 'Fitt puts NI facts to World's Socialists.' The detailed story began:

> History was made in West Berlin City Hall at the weekend when SDLP leader, Mr Gerry Fitt MP, presented the facts of the political situation in the North and the reasons for the present conflict before a distinguished audience of leaders of the Socialist International at a two-day meeting.

On his return from these heady circles to the more mundane realities of life in embattled Belfast, he found there had been a very worrying development in the ongoing flirtation between the government and the IRA. In exchange for the open-ended ceasefire, the government had set up incident centres designed to prevent the minor incidents threatening the truce from developing into major problems.

> I knew well the Provos would soon turn these centres into local community contact points, in a bid to undermine the SDLP. People would be too afraid to go anywhere else with their problems. I was the only MP to recognise the dangers and I said so vehemently to Merlyn Rees in parliament and privately.

At the end of March, when he again visited Belfast, Harold Wilson announced that 1 May would be the date for the Convention elections. 'There is no overnight solution to deep-rooted problems, no magic formula,' he said. 'Patience, tolerance and goodwill are needed from all sides of the community.' There was little sign of of them, however. Although the IRA had stopped their bombing and shooting at soldiers, they had instead become involved in bitter feuding with other groups in the Catholic areas and people had been killed by both sides. More seriously, there was another upsurge in sectarian killings, which enabled the IRA to adopt a new role as 'community policemen', operating out of the incident centres in direct competition with the RUC. They meted out brutal beatings, with concrete blocks being used to break the arms and legs of so-called offenders. The practice of 'kneecapping' or 'elbowing' transgressors by shooting them in the joints of their limbs also became more common at this time. The word 'nutting' was coined as a cruel euphemism for murdering people by shooting them in the head.

Before Christmas 1974 the SDLP had reserved its position regarding whether it would contest the election to appoint members to the Convention. Hume argued strongly for a complete boycott, but others thought they should use the threat of non-participation to extract as many advance concessions from the government as they could. Devlin did not rule out fighting the elections, but suggested they could boycott the actual convention if its final terms of reference were not to their liking. Reflecting his own attitude, Fitt's North Belfast branch of the party put forward a motion for the annual conference in January calling for less emphasis on the Irish dimension and more on local political co-operation.

Hume was once again conducting parallel solo discourses with the NIO whenever the opportunity arose. On 9 April he had a two-hour meeting with James Allan, who spent a day away from Laneside and travelled to Derry. Hume, whom Allan judged to be in a moderate and thoughtful mood, said he believed every effort should be made to destroy the PIRA and pressed again his oft-repeated view that ending detention would help to completely destroy the organisation. He professed himself to be against absentionism in the imminent election and, in an aside that was breathtakingly ill-informed, suggested to Allan that Wilson would soon be gone from power and Heath returned to office. Entirely oblivious of Heath's sophisticated aloofness towards the Irish problem and the fact that he had no kinship whatsoever with the SDLP, Hume added: 'He feels at home with the SDLP ... because coming from a modest background, he does not have to keep up to any high Tory pretence with us.'

In the event, the SDLP decided to run the physical and political risks involved, fight the election and participate in the Convention because they judged that stepping aside from the democratic process would only enable the self-appointed IRA to emerge as the leading influence on the minority community. The party manifesto spelled out criteria for political stability and social and economic progress, the need for a powerful and representative Northern Ireland Assembly, an administration in which both sections of the community participated to the full, and a recognition and acceptance of both the Irish and British dimensions. At a breakfast meeting with Rees on 15 April as the election campaign got under way, Fitt was confident the Convention would not fold within days, not least because the local politicians of all parties felt incensed that they had lost their Assembly incomes and for this reason they would want to stay on what he called the 'Convention gravy train' for the full six months at least. During the final run-up to polling day, Fitt stressed time and time again the crucial choice facing the Catholic community between the ballot box and the gun. He said it was 'the last chance for sanity'. His call was influenced partly by the IRA's call to boycott the poll and fears that Catholics would feel intimidated as a result and not come out to vote.

The SDLP won seventeen of the seventy-eight seats at the election, the seventh poll in the province in little over two years. Fitt topped the list in North Belfast, with 6,454 first-preference votes, and the SDLP's 23.7% share of the overall vote showed that its standing had not been eroded by recent events. There was, however, some residual bad feeling within the party that the highly ambitious Seamus Mallon failed to accept party direction and had run a strong personal campaign in Armagh, which helped cost Paddy O'Hanlon a seat. (O'Hanlon, one of the SDLP's founding six, abandoned politics soon afterwards, studied law and subsequently carved out a successful career as a barrister.)

Their election victories came as a great relief to the party's main activists because they could now draw a salary of £2,500 a year, plus expenses. Fitt interpreted the results as a clear rejection of the IRA and, above all, of violence. This unambiguous stand would, he hoped, pave the way for talks with the UUUC, which had attracted more than half the total vote cast, and enabled it to dominate the Convention with forty-seven seats. The Convention was to be chaired by Sir Robert Lowry with two advisers, John Oliver and Maurice Hayes, both experienced civil servants, one Protestant, the other Catholic. Hume was wary of Lowry's appointment initially, but came round. However, as he told Allan in a late-night chat at Laneside on 22 May, he was gloomy about the possibility of loyalists showing any signs of compromise, believing they would push forward with their own plans and suppress all Catholic aspirations. Allan asked him what he would do. Hume replied that the British could well indicate that they were going to leave Northern Ireland and to prevent a breakdown in law and order, the party should enter into agreements with the Irish Republic to ensure the transition was as peaceful as possible. In his note on the encounter, Allan dismissed the answer as yet another of Hume's 'pretty naive' ideas.

Hume's apparent naivety was, in truth, a reflection of the paralysis that had gripped SDLP policy-making after the election. A committee chaired by Seamus Mallon had produced a document that met with no favour and fuelled a demand that the party should back negotiated independence for Northern Ireland as its favoured option. This radical idea was debated seriously, however, before being abandoned and the party fell back on a re-statement of its basic Sunningdale objectives: power-sharing and an Irish dimension.

By the end of June, the Convention was well under way even though the dominant UUUC was both suspicious and angry about the ongoing government – IRA talks and convinced that British withdrawal was being negotiated behind their backs. While there quickly emerged broad agreement among the elected representatives that the way forward was by form of devolved government, that was as far as the consensus stretched. The unionists wanted majority rule and an exclusive Cabinet. The SDLP countered that would only open the way to the abuses and unfairness that had characterised the period before the civil rights campaign. Some years later Fitt reflected:

> The unionists could never understand the frustration of having to live in a situation where you would never have an effective say in government. That was the essential contrast between Westminster and Stormont. Indeed, it was one of the strengths of the British democratic system, and one of the things I envied most, that the people could change their government. In the House of Commons the leader of the opposition can look across the despatch box at the Prime Minister and say to himself, 'Come the next election, that's me.' And the Prime Minister thinks: 'If I don't change my ways and fall in with public opinion, then come the next election I may be over there.'

Fitt believed that the main reason conventional politics, class politics, right-left politics had never thrived in Northern Ireland was because of the border question:

> The Unionists always feared we were disloyal, working hand-in-hand with the IRA to suck them into a united Ireland. They chided us for carrying Irish passports, for recognising our Irish nationality. If we ever got our hands on the levers of power, they believed we would only use them to do away with Northern Ireland. It was a fundamental misreading of our position and the problem was persuading them of our sincerity.

They did try. One evening Fitt arrived at Stormont to attend the Convention and bumped into Bill Craig. He told him that in discussion with John Hume, he had asked what the SDLP's attitude to the IRA would be in the event of a coalition government being formed. Hume replied by reminding Craig that a previous Irish government had executed seventy-two IRA men for threatening the stability of the state. Fitt said: 'As far as we were concerned, there was nothing new or radical in what Hume had said. In our think-ins over the previous few years we had frequently discussed the possibility that we might end up in office having to intern or even execute IRA or UVF men.'

Impressed by his chat with Hume, Craig then put forward the idea of a 'voluntary coalition' to pursue an agreed emergency programme, as a British national government would do in time of war. The envisaged programme would have involved the SDLP in the formulation and operation of security policy. Fitt said:

> We were very interested in this approach. We were sure that once we had got into a situation where we shared in the fight against republican and loyalist terrorists, we could have proved to them our commitment to working within the Northern Ireland context, without threat to the British dimension they valued so highly. From that position of confidence, we were sure that eventually we could persuade them they equally had nothing to fear by allowing us to slowly develop a corresponding Irish dimension.

Towards the end of August it became clear the talks were breaking down and the SDLP suggested exchanging papers to clarify where both sides actually stood. The UUUC document, passed over during a meeting on 26 August, opted for majority rule on the British model, but nevertheless contained the observation that 'where an emergency or crisis situation exists and parties by agreement come together in the national interest for the duration of the crisis', they could accept coalition.

Fitt was extremely wary of the proposition, convinced, as he was, that the Convention was on course for an early collapse. Because the likely course of events thereafter was entirely unpredictable, he was also consumed by a combination of dread and pessimism. He had spelled out his anxieties during a private meeting with Lowry at Stormont on 25 August, expressing a belief that both the British Labour and Conservative parties were gearing up for disengagement as a method of 'solving the Irish question'. He was convinced, he went on, that the loyalists were now preparing for independence, a step that would be disastrous economically and would result in the slaughter of many Catholics. In a further baring of his soul, he referred to Desmond Boal, the eminent QC with close links to Paisley, as 'a sinister influence, consumed by a hatred of all things English, who held court at his [Co. Down] home and entertained Paisley, Devlin and others' while he promoted the idea of some kind of independence. Of his SDLP colleague, Paddy Devlin, he said he was 'a good man, susceptible to flattery'. Austin Currie he described as 'very intelligent, able and sincere', while Hume was 'an inflexible fanatic who saw everything in terms of Derry and could not take a wider view'. Hume had his own audience with Lowry the next day, during which he complained that Rees was wilfully undermining the Convention and the elected politicians and preparing the public mind for negotiations with paramilitary leaders.

Nevertheless, the SDLP affirmed its interest in Craig's proposal and on 28 August, when the parties saw Lowry, separately and together, they asked him to see if he could create further movement on the voluntary coalition idea. The UUUC policy committee discussed the concept, and on September 3 their three negotiators took the situation significantly further by asking Lowry to prepare a paper on voluntary coalition but, before he had time to produce anything, the UUUC called a meeting of its full Convention line-up and the hardliners, manipulated by Paisley, forced through a motion refusing to share power with the SDLP in any circumstances. Only Craig voted against. Among the supporters of the motion were two of the three UUUC negotiators, and one of them then promptly compounded his irrationality by making a television appearance, deploring the grave security situation and advocating land-mining the border.

The SDLP was deeply upset. The voluntary coalition proposal had not been a casual one. It had been articulated in a formal document, drawn up after lengthy private talks with the express purpose of avoiding misunderstandings about progress and the position of the parties. The hardliners, it was now clear, were not prepared to share power in any way and wanted Northern Ireland to continue only as a Protestant ascendancy state. The breakdown of the talks on this fundamental issue effectively meant the Convention had failed to find a form of government that would command widespread acceptance, and the SDLP formally withdrew to underline its dissatisfaction. Undaunted, the UUUC drafted a final report that amounted to a call for the restoration, unchanged, of the old Stormont regime. In November, after a total of thirty-one plenary sessions, this report was completed and presented to Merlyn Rees.

In a bid to ensure their views were fully understood, the SDLP had already produced a pamphlet enunciating in detail its own political requirements. Their key demands were: for all sections of the community to be represented in an Assembly and government; devolved policing; agreed north – south institutions; a standing cross-border agreement on security and policing; and socio-economic co-operation on matters of common concern. The party said all this should be underpinned by referenda in both parts of Ireland to ensure widespread support. Dublin was supplied with an advance draft of the document, and this latter suggestion found great disfavour with the Prime Minister, who said in a letter to Donlon on 23 October that 'the question of a referendum involving the whole island of Ireland bristles with difficulties'.

Fearing that the suggestion could re-open the scars of the civil war, Cosgrave was especially incensed at the SDLP argument, running right through the document, he said, that 'the problem is the problem of the legitimacy of all institutions in Ireland, north and south' and that 'they somehow need legitimisation by way of a referendum over the whole island'. Scorning the idea as 'an anachronism', he said that 'while the subject may have been live fifty years ago, it has no relevance today'.

In public, Fitt retained his usual cheerful bonhomie and continued to promote the party line with his customary fluency, but the latest events had stimulated SDLP in-fighting to such an extent that it had exacerbated his own frustrations with the party. His true feelings came bubbling up to the surface with more than his usual frankness when he met Cooper on 25 September, in what the mandarin observed was 'a somewhat inebriated state'. After waxing eloquent about the iniquities of the incident centres, Fitt said, according to Cooper's note, that he wanted to play no active role whatsoever in any future government of Northern Ireland. The SDLP was split to an extent it had never been before, and Hume now appeared to be acceptable to the loyalists when compared with their new *bête noire*, Seamus Mallon, a former headmaster from Markethill, County Armagh, who was typical of 'the fuckin' teachers' in the SDLP Fitt so despised. According to Cooper, Fitt went on to be 'vitriolic about Paddy Devlin to a degree far in excess of anything I had heard from him before'. Referring to Devlin's efforts to engage the IRA, hold dialogue with the UDA and engage Craig and Paisley in negotiations, Fitt complained 'he was playing about with everyone under the sun'. There was undoubtedly an element of *in vino veritas* about the conversation, but it provides a frank insight into the way in which Fitt's disillusionment was steadily driving him away from the SDLP.

Despite what had been said during this unbuttoned moment, Fitt and Devlin arrived together to see Cooper on 8 October while everyone waited for Rees to give his verdict on the Convention report. After pressing him to ensure Convention members remained on the payroll for as long as possible, Devlin let slip the hope that Craig might be able to regroup sufficient support within the UUUC to resuscitate the coalition proposal, but minus Paisley's faction. He believed that, after his talks with the SDLP, Craig had realised for the first time in his whole life that the SDLP was as much against the IRA as he was himself. The trio then discussed the IRA ceasefire. Fitt said that he thought the government had now discovered that they could not talk the IRA into switching off the violence without making concessions they were not prepared to make. He said he would never criticise the government for talking, 'it was worth a try', but he always knew what the outcome would be because the Provos were too 'thick' to benefit from the political opportunity on offer.

A month earlier, on 10 September, Cooper had said much the same himself at a 'secret' seminar for the 'UK/Eyes only' category of officials at Laneside. The Provos had been able to acquire a political image in Derry, but they had tried and failed to do so in Belfast because they had not been able to deliver the goods, he said. At the seminar Cooper also revealed that, despite Craig's 'appearance of moderation', his real aim was to achieve a return to one-party government after using the SDLP in an emergency coalition just long enough to crush republican violence. Cooper predicted the Convention would not succeed and warned they would soon be in the midst of another constitutional, and perhaps security, crisis when the problem returned to British hands, a crisis that would be even more intense than before. As a result, he added, it might no longer be possible to govern Northern Ireland in the accepted sense of the word.

A week before that, on 3 September, similarly grave opinions were expressed by both Faulkner and Fitt at a meeting with Rees and Cooper requested by all the party leaders in the Convention. In the event, Craig, West and Paisley failed to attend. Faulkner said the situation was the worst he had known since 1969 and he 'feared the impending outbreak of civil war and a pogrom of Roman Catholics'. Fitt declared that the sectarian murderers were trying to further polarise the two communities. He feared an attack on a Catholic chapel or school and said that if that happened, there might be no middle way left. Oliver Napier, who was also present, agreed with Faulkner and Fitt in condemning the credulity that had been lent to the paramilitaries at the expense of elected representatives. People believed they now had leverage, he said, which created fear in both communities. Rees sought to reassure them that nothing untoward was taking place: 'There was no deal, no agreement, no immunity [from arrest]. '

These sombre attitudes were clearly grounded in the fact that, as Fitt had forecast, the PIRA ceasefire progressively imploded from July onwards, and serious violence resumed in both Ireland and Britain. There followed some of the most notorious outrages of the entire Troubles. One of the most horrendous acts was the IRA killing of five Protestants in a South Armagh Orange Hall. The UVF went on the rampage, too, killing three members of a Dublin-based showband in an ambush that went badly wrong when a bomb exploded prematurely, killing two of the terrorists involved. The SDLP's green wing were especially outraged by this, and other atrocities perpetrated around the time, because there was incontrovertible evidence that members of the UDR were either directly involved in the attacks or conspiring with the killers. The party made a series of detailed complaints, including the names of individuals they claimed were involved, to Rees and Orme and were assured the army command was conducting a special investigation, but they were never given clear outcomes to their allegations, although time proved them to be both well-informed and accurate. The IRA's political front, Sinn Féin, had already failed to respond to legalisation by not participating in the Convention elections and the legalised UVF had similarly put itself beyond the political pale in October after a day of violence in Belfast in which twelve people died, leading Merlyn Rees to re-proscribe the organisation.

It was against this violent backdrop that the SDLP's fifth annual conference took place at the beginning of December, again in Belfast's Europa hotel. Fitt's tone in the leader's speech was optimistic because he had been privately forewarned by Rees that the release of the last internees would take place within days but it was swiftly eclipsed for the divisions that were steadily eating away at Fitt's ever more tenuous position within the SDLP opened even wider at that conference. The issue was policing and the acceptability of the RUC. At the previous year's conference, a policy document entitled 'The Northern Ireland Police Force', largely written by Hume to reflect his own hardline view of the

RUC, had been returned to the party executive for further consideration. Fitt favoured a distinctly more pragmatic approach. In his view, the 'black sheep' within the RUC were being weeded out steadily and he was prepared to give the others the benefit of the doubt when they claimed to be acting impartially:

> Certainly many of the individual officers I knew were men of integrity and I had no qualms whatever about their impartiality. I knew very many of them personally, as many as 300 or 400, from the years when they escorted me around Dock during the various elections. Underpinning my position was a conviction that the party could not champion lawlessness for the benefit of the murderers, gunmen, bombers, robbers, kneecappers and intimidators who were then running rampant.

Pushed by the SDLP hardliners, the conference adopted the policy document, which did not make it any easier for Fitt or those in the UUUC the SDLP still regarded as harbouring hopes of progress on a voluntary coalition. A few days later, on 5 December, as he had promised Fitt and despite the resurgent violence, Rees stuck to his word and released the last fifty-seven 'hard-core' internees, effectively bringing the policy of internment to an end. A short time previously he had signed the order to release the loyalist who had been involved in a plot to assassinate him near the Stormont estate in East Belfast. Fitt's praise was fulsome in a lengthy statement dictated to the *Irish News* for publication next day:

> I am thankful that the evil scourge of internment has been brought to an end. From the very second of its inception, we recognised the political disaster that it would be, antagonising as it did the entire Catholic community. Thousands and thousands of the minority were alienated by the imposition of this scourge on their fellow co-religionists. People who, in normal circumstances, would give no support whatsoever to any men of violence, felt themselves alienated from every political institution in Northern Ireland.

He went on to give full credit to Rees and his old friend, Stan Orme, clearly excising much of the bitterness that had accumulated through their failure to defend sufficiently, as Fitt saw it, the hard-won gains of Sunningdale. The year may have ended on an encouraging note with this development, but as the ceasefires collapsed and optimism evaporated, 1975 had proved to be yet another appalling year, with 247 deaths attributable to the violence, 635 bombs planted, of which more than half had exploded, 1,803 shooting incidents and 1,197 people charged with serious criminal offences.

Merlyn Rees finally responded to the Convention report in January 1976 by asking the parties to gather and reconsider the fundamental issues. They did so, but in vain. After a series of meetings during February, at the final sitting on 3 March the unionists pushed through a report calling exclusively for their own demands. Forty-eight hours later, Rees dissolved the Convention and made the politicians redundant. Confirming his long-held, private expectations, the local politicians had proved they were indeed unable to make a deal. Inside the NIO, Cooper and his officials were already considering how best to engineer the emergence of a new generation of more pragmatic and realistic politicians, and calculating how long it was likely to be before the intransigent old guard could be swept aside.

With the passing of the Convention, the last vestiges of hope that the IRA could be drawn into the political process were also extinguished. As had been widely predicted, the 'hawks' had gained absolute control of the organisation and everyone braced themselves for more violence. In a sign of the change of policy, the Belfast Sinn Féin man who had been fronting the ceasefire negotiations announced he was resigning for health reasons. One of the newly dominant 'hawks' interpreted the shift to a more militant policy by saying, 'It's nothing to do with his present health, it's his future health.'

Fitt believed the government should have taken a stronger line against the intransigents in the UUUC. In early January some of them were actually threatening the British government about what they would do if the report were not accepted. One even threatened the 'final conflict'. As always, the PIRA did their bit to stoke up loyalist unease. On January 4, five Catholics were brutally killed in two separate incidents in South Armagh. The following day a group of armed and masked men stopped a mill workers' minibus at Kingsmills. The gunmen told the single Catholic on board to run off. As he took to his heels in the darkness they opened fire, killing all ten Protestant passengers. Even by the vicious standards set by the IRA in South Armagh, this incident was unique, and in some eyes comparable only with the way Hitler had massacred Jews.

Fitt pleaded privately with Rees to recall the Convention to see if any agreement could be reached, but while Rees agreed, he neither took on the UUUC nor helped the SDLP. He said their attitude on the issue of policing was an obstacle to progress and their insistence on an Irish dimension unrealistic. As party leader, Fitt knew that some recognition of the Irish dimension was necessary to carry the party, but his own view remained that there should be a two-stage process, as had eventually been mooted to ratify Sunningdale. As it happened, progress never reached the point where the internal conflict in the SDLP became an obstacle. The chairman presided over inter-party talks for three weeks in February, but the crucial encounter lasted barely an hour. Fitt asked Harry West, a backward-looking politician, about power-sharing and elicited the reply that the UUUC would not in any circumstances be prepared to sit in a Cabinet with the SDLP. Paddy Devlin asked for an adjournment so they could consider the position. After twenty-five minutes the SDLP returned to announce they considered the talks were not serious.

The Convention was wound up on 9 March amidst disorder caused by disgruntled unionists. That spring, Northern Ireland drifted into another political vacuum when Harold Wilson was replaced by Jim Callaghan as Prime Minister and Airey Neave was appointed by the new opposition leader, Margaret Thatcher, as the Northern Ireland shadow minister. The SDLP judged that they should stick firmly to their well-thought-out demands and wait for more favourable political circumstances to pursue them. The Official Unionists, having taken stock of the situation, wanted SDLP help to create renewed political momentum and over May and June six unpublicised meetings took place between John Hume, Paddy Devlin, Martin Smyth and Austin Ardill, at his home in Carrickfergus. These talks pre-empted an initiative by Bill Craig, who had plans to explore the coalition ground further, but that initiative was successfully torpedoed by Paisley in mid-June when he leaked details to the newspapers before they had even come close to reaching the point where proposals could have been made to Rees. That summer, as the politicians settled more deeply into the political doldrums, there was a heavy traffic of students and academics writing theses and dissertations about the problem and about the inability of the politicians to settle it. One researcher cost Fitt much more than the time he spent with him:

> From time to time I enjoy a flutter on the horses. So one morning on the plane returning to Belfast I chose four horses to make up an £11 'Yankee' bet. My intention was to telephone the bet to my London bookie when I arrived home. But when I got there, the place was crowded as usual with people wanting to see me. Among them was a crowd of hysterical women, relatives of a lorry driver, who had been arrested the day before after his lorry was used to convey a bomb into a police station. My own phone was out of order so I went next door to make representations about him. Back in my own house I had a run of customers and got so caught-up with them until early afternoon I forgot about the telephone bet. My detective arrived to escort me out and I had every intention then of placing the bet in a city-centre bookmaking shop. But as I was leaving, another caller, a professor, stopped me on the doorstep and was so insistent on chatting to me I went back inside, organised tea and sat listening to him ramble on about federalism in the South Tyrol of Austria and the comparisons with our political situation. One eye on the clock reluctantly forced me to abandon thoughts of placing my bet. However the true cost of my time that afternoon only became clear later that evening when I checked the horse racing results. My four selections had all won at 8/1, 10/1, 11/1, and 12/1. I banged the wall with my fist and my frustration was not helped next morning when the highly relieved bookmaker in London calculated my £11 would have won £27,000.

Ever since August 1972 it had been the habit of IRA supporters to commemorate the anniversary of the introduction of internment, which included holding a noisy demonstration outside the Fitt house. The clatter of dustbin lids would normally begin at midnight and reach a crescendo at 4.00am, but the higher netting wire erected after Paddy Wilson's murder was usually sufficient to stop the accompanying barrage of stones, petrol bombs and even paint tins. The family dreaded the event, but felt reasonably confident that the mobs would not get into the house as there was also a two-way radio linking them with the RUC, plus an army sentry in the guard post for Girdwood Barracks, directly opposite. The authorities had often suggested a guard be placed on the house itself, but Fitt had always declined: 'I did not want the life of a soldier or policeman exposed to the possibility of an IRA sniper attack on my account.' As it happened, Fitt was talking to Merlyn Rees a few days before the 1976 anniversary and mentioned the likelihood of attacks on his house. Rees said he would arrange for discreet cover by the security forces, so that if the demonstration got out of hand they could move in and disperse it. On the evening of 8 August Fitt returned home late in the evening and settled down to await the inevitable onslaught. Rees telephoned him from Stormont Castle to confirm that his offer had been followed up and shortly after 11.00pm an inspector rang from the local RUC station to confirm this. 'We have been told to keep an eye,' he said. Reassured that they were under active guard Ann, Geraldine and and Fitt himself went to bed.

On the stoke of midnight they heard the usual whistle-blowing and bin-lid bashing, and could not sleep as they awaited the inevitable 4.00am crescendo. What happened next was clearly planned, not spontaneous. Peering through the curtains of their bedroom at the front of the house, Fitt and his wife saw a concerted attack by a crowd of roaring demonstrators, who threw a barrage of stones, paint and petrol bombs at the house.

> At first we were not worried, thinking the promised cover was nearby and would soon move in to disperse the troublemakers. But as the attack continued with more intensity, and there was no sign of assistance, we began to realise, with fright, that this was unlike the others. What was undoubtedly the longest twenty-five minutes of our lives began.

Almost as soon as the attack started he contacted the police, both by landline and over the special radio linked to their headquarters in East Belfast. As the assault continued, he made further calls. In all, he communicated with them eleven times:

> I could tell Ann was really frightened because she took an asthmatic attack. I was reassuring her and telling her not to worry, the police and soldiers would arrive soon. Then Geraldine ran into the bedroom and said, 'Daddy, I heard a bang. They're coming up the stairs.' Because of the ferocity of the attack, the front door had come off its hinges and was flat on the floor in our hallway. Some of the mob were running over it and coming up the stairs. I put on the hall lights to see them, lifted my gun from the side of the bed and clad in singlet and underpants, went onto the landing to confront a crowd that to me seemed like over 200 strong. I feared they were going to rush me and I remember thinking to myself, 'Well, this is it.' I

pointed the gun straight at the man in front of the mob. I recalled reading somewhere that if you stopped the ringleader, you stopped the mob. My language was not very polite, but was calculated to be clearly understood by him. As I stood there, staring at him, pointing the gun, shouting at him to back off down the stairs, I really thought I was going to be killed. Ann and Geraldine had come out behind me onto the landing. 'Gerry, don't shoot, don't shoot,' I heard her say. I kept telling the ringleader at the front to get down the stairs. I stared at him and repeated it over and over again. Eventually I saw him crack. He turned and jumped over the banisters shouting, 'He's got a gun, he's got a gun.' The rest of the mob turned tail and all I could feel was a sense of great relief. I called an ambulance for Ann and, using my gun for cover, went downstairs, past the open door, to get her inhaler. The crowd were standing outside on the street shouting, 'We'll be back.' There was still no sign of the police and army, but just as we were ready to leave in the ambulance for hospital an RUC inspector arrived. We had a nasty exchange. I was extremely angry. 'Don't say you're protecting me. Stay away.' As I left with Ann for the nearby Mater hospital, soldiers arrived as well. I complained about them leaving us uncovered to the major who was in command.

When they got to hospital, the doctors found Fitt's heart was beating too fast and admitted him too, but before being confined to bed he asked to make a telephone call. Having no money, he persuaded the hospital operator to put through a call to Merlyn Rees, who couldn't believe what had taken place and said he would get somebody up to see him. Later, armed with flowers, his wife Colleen and David Gilliland, one of his closest advisers, arrived. Ann and Fitt were discharged later in the morning and when they got home found the press and television of the world waiting on their 'boarded-up doorstep'. Fitt had already been branded the 'fastest gun in a vest' and a picture they took of him, gun in hand, re-enacting what had taken place, went around the world. (The following December a man from the local New Lodge area, who had been at the head of the gang, pleaded guilty to riotous assembly and riotous damage and was jailed for twelve months.)

That evening Ann and Fitt departed for London, to stay with their daughter, Joan. Fitt was acutely worried about the effect of the attack on Ann's health. But almost as soon as they arrived, they heard of a tragedy. PIRA gunmen in a car being pursued by soldiers lost control of the vehicle after one of the occupants was shot dead. The car then ploughed into the railings of a West Belfast church, killing three young toddlers and seriously injuring their mother, Anne Maguire. It was the latest in a series of tragedies in Fitt's constituency, but it roused in the people a previously unseen revulsion. Ordinary men and women, spurred on by the dead children's aunt, Mairead Corrigan, and by another local woman, Betty Williams, took to the streets demanding peace. They rang and asked Fitt to attend a peace rally in Andersonstown, but as Ann was still ill he apologised and explained why he could not attend. However, he issued a statement strongly supporting them and watched with great interest as, on successive Saturdays, in both Catholic and Protestant areas, women of both religions turned out in staggering numbers to lead marches for peace.

> It was clear there was a major political opportunity here to be exploited, not by the established politicians like myself, but by the ordinary people whose gut frustrations and anger at the continued violence had driven them out onto the streets.

Shortly afterwards, restored to good health and back at home, Ann rang Betty Williams to enquire about arrangements for a rally in Derry, saying she and Fitt wanted to be identified with the demand for peace. But Williams, who had achieved instant popularity, did not seem pleased with their interest this time. 'If Gerry wants to come, he can be an ordinary supporter,' she said. 'Tell him to stay well back from the platform.'

'That's me finished with them,' Ann said, slamming down the telephone. 'Neither of us need to cling to the peace people.'

Although the two 'peace women', as they became known, won the Nobel Peace Prize at the end of 1978, by then they were already a spent force. Fitt reckoned that their failure to capitalise on what was an unprecedented cross-community phenomenon and build a broad-based, Catholic – Protestant leadership was their first error. The second, he believed, was in taking their campaign to the cities of Britain and Europe, as well as to America: 'The problem was in Northern Ireland, not abroad, and the failure to build on the feelings unleashed by the tragedy must rank among the most serious political failures of the entire Troubles period.'

In September 1976 the ongoing violence struck once more into the very heart of Fitt's personal circle. One evening that month Danny Walsh, one of his closest friends, was driving home after visiting his wife Eileen, who was recovering from surgery in the City hospital. At 8.15pm, as he passed the junction of Union Street and Little Donegall Street, a device concealed in his car, consisting of four ounces of high explosive, a battery and a wristwatch timer, suddenly exploded. Walsh was flung from the vehicle onto the street and sustained extensive injuries, including the loss of a leg:

> I was still conscious and remember crawling around the street shouting for help. A policeman with a gun appeared and I thought he might shoot me, thinking I was planting a bomb or something. Then a soldier began to tend to me. He shouted I was bleeding to death and I heard the policeman say he had called an ambulance. I asked the soldier to get me a priest and to get in touch with Gerry Fitt. The priest arrived quickly and gave me the last rites and when I got to the hospital, Gerry was already there, crying his eyes out. I asked him to make sure the news was kept out of the papers because I didn't want my wife to know what had happened. He said he would do what he could.

The following morning, having kept vigil at the Mater hospital for much of the night while Walsh was undergoing emergency surgery, Fitt arrived at the City hospital to visit Eileen Walsh. He enlisted the help of a nurse to tidy up the ward by removing all newspapers so that she would not see any report of the incident, then told her that Danny had asked him to call because he had gone off urgently to Glasgow to chase some money after a big cheque paid to his scrap business had bounced. Still recovering from her own treatment, Eileen accepted the explanation, but a few day later when Fitt had to tell her the truth, she immediately discharged herself and rushed to her husband's bedside. Why Walsh was targeted remains one of the many mysteries of the Troubles. The bomb yielded no clues as to its origins and no group ever claimed responsibility for maiming Walsh, whom the police cleared of any suspicious activity or associations.

That same month, Callaghan moved Merlyn Rees back to London as Home Secretary and sent Roy Mason, formerly Defence Minister, to Belfast. When he heard the news from parliamentary journalists in the St. Stephen's Tavern at Westminster, Fitt was not surprised; he had been observing Mason's blunt Yorkshire ways closely since his name was first mooted for the job. He did not like what he saw: 'Mason cultivated an abrasive, hard-man personality and had all the arrogance you often find in small men. I was sure these qualities were the last thing needed by a Northern Ireland secretary at that particular time so when asked for my reaction to his appointment, I was far from enthusiastic.' Callaghan, who heard Fitt's remarks broadcast on BBC, was sufficiently concerned to ring him next morning at the Irish Club. The Prime Minister told him not to worry, that he would still be in overall command of Northern Ireland policy. Fitt realised that the real purpose of the call was to keep him on side:

> The Callaghan government was permanently on a knife-edge, depending on votes from a medley of minority parties and individuals, like myself, to carry forthcoming crucial divisions on Scottish and Welsh devolution as well as nationalising shipyards and the aerospace industry to stay in power.

Soon afterwards, Mason asked Fitt to come in for a chat, but their first meeting did little to counter Fitt's unfavourable impression: 'He sat back in his chair, puffing at his pipe, like a pale imitation of Harold Wilson. He confessed he was not going to get involved in any attempts at political reform, which were sure to founder. Instead he was going to concentrate on the economy and security, areas where he could see room for improvement.' Quite independently, the British Army shared Fitt's doubts about Mason. After explaining his reasoning to them, senior officers promptly christened the ex-miner 'pit-prop', on the grounds that his policies were liable to sudden collapse.

Mason was, of course, correct in his political assessment, but it was Fitt's view, and that of the SDLP, that it was not good enough to sit back and do nothing. Fitt did not fully realise it then, but Mason's primary concern – under Callaghan's explicit direction – was not to upset the unionists. Although they would be unlikely to vote for his precarious government, Callaghan wanted them sufficiently neutralised so that they would not, at least, vote against it.

It was one of Fitt's constant gripes that 'there was never much socialism in the SDLP' and the hard nationalists in the party were far from happy that he always supported a Labour government. But as Mason quickly antagonised other influential SDLP figures, such as Hume and Mallon, there was soon open resentment of Fitt, and when he subsequently voted for the government in a couple of tight divisions, he was accused of keeping them in power. Fitt believed that, apart from making life even more difficult for him within the SDLP, Mason's posturing played into the hands of the ultra-nationalists and helped to push the SDLP into an even greener position than it had ever adopted before. The hairline fracture that had hitherto defined Fitt's relationship with the SDLP now became a very visible crack, and all his doubts and unease about being associated with the party were again perplexing him: 'I genuinely began to worry where my real loyalty should lie; to my socialist ideals, or the SDLP.' One of the greatest irritations for him was the tendency of many SDLP members either to fail to condemn IRA atrocities outright or, in some cases, even to find excuses for them. He was particularly exercised at times of difficulty, when John Hume would always say: 'Keep your head down.' Fitt was most certainly not accusing Hume, or indeed anyone else in the party, of condoning violence, but he deplored the frequent ambivalence about it, especially from those who were afraid to condemn it outright:

> The atmosphere at party meetings in the latter part of 1976 became greener and greener. In fact, some members only stopped short of ending every meeting with singing the Irish national anthem.

The annual conference that December provided an authentic first measurement of just how nationalist-minded the party had become when a motion calling on the British government to declare its intention of leaving Northern Ireland was defeated narrowly, by just 42 votes (153–111). Fitt said that attitude was tantamount to saying to Britain: 'Get to hell out of Northern Ireland, but on the way, leave your purse on the mantelpiece.'

Whatever the political disenchantment there had been for him in 1976, the year ended in something of a personal triumph for Fitt – he gave up cigarette-smoking, a habit that had started with the 'Royal Avenue butts club' some thirty-eight years earlier. The breakthrough came one morning in December when he started coughing so badly during a phone call, he was forced to end the conversation abruptly. 'I had a fag in my hand at the time, so I stubbed it out and said, "That's it. No more."' When he rang Ann to tell her that he had stopped,

she suggested perhaps he should not come home for several weeks. He had no
adverse reaction to the change at all, however, which pleased his doctor who had
been pleading with him to cut down smoking, if not stop altogether. 'I found all
the talk about going up the walls, kicking the cat or beating the wife was all
bunkum.' Reflecting on the money he would now save from kicking the twenty-
to sixty-a-day habit, he calculated that he must have smoked at least 300,000
Gallaher's Blues over the years. He was still mightily impressed when he met a
seventy-eight-year-old who had been smoking since the age of four and reckoned
he had puffed his way through something like 2.5 million cigarettes.

During 1977 Mason's unacceptability to the SDLP and his policy of 'skirting
the political whirlpool' progressively forced the internal tensions within the party
into public view. Typical of the outbursts Fitt had to face was a public letter from
a Belfast councillor, who declared that Callaghan and Mason might do more for
Northern Ireland if they were to 'waken up some morning and discover that [Fitt]
was no longer a puppet on a string dashing off to Westminster at every crack of
the Labour party whip.' Whatever about their ultra-nationalism, which he
deplored, such attacks served only to regenerate Fitt's antipathy to the 'fucking
teachers and lawyers' who now dominated the SDLP:

> Until 1973 they were just plain 'Mr', then, in the space of a very short time,
> some of them became both councillors and members of the Assembly.
> Several of them aspired to be members of parliament, standing at the two
> general elections in 1974. In quick succession then a number of them
> became Convention members. With only a handful of exceptions, the
> majority had a meteoric rise to political prominence. Unfortunately such an
> accelerated political apprenticeship exposed their lack of political skills. I
> will never forget the attitude of some of them at Sunningdale. As the cut
> and thrust of inter-party negotiation developed they got carried away with
> collective hallucinations about being Henry Kissinger and started getting
> on the telephone to their constituency organisations seeking mandates for
> this, that and the other. What we had were too many inexperienced
> politicians, wrestling with one of the most intractable constitutional and
> political problems anywhere in the world.

Paddy Devlin was also increasingly ill at ease within the SDLP at this point. One
afternoon in September, when Fitt was attending a funeral, a number of people
approached to tell him that Devlin had resigned as chairman of the constituency
representatives. Disenchantment had set in after the collapse of the Convention
early in 1976, as Hume and his cronies autocratically rebalanced the party in a
fashion that Devlin said was 'alien to his [socialist] values'. He resented the way
Catholic nationalists with conservative economic principles had come to
dominate the party and was also appalled at how closely they had swung the party
towards Fianna Fáil. In his memoir, *Straight Left*, he noted how 'some of the SDLP
people were far too cosy with Charlie Haughey's hardline wing of the party for my

liking. At meeting after meeting, I would cringe when some of them would intervene with, "Charlie said this", or "Charlie said that".' Devlin was also critical of their 'vicious opposition to the RUC in every shape and form' and 'the silences in the aftermath of some dreadful [IRA] outrages'. He had also long been antagonised by Hume's naked political ambition, especially his masterly efforts at building relationships with people who could advance his personal position. Hume was never content with cultivating the reporters and political writers, he wanted to influence the leader writers and editors, so that his own ideas and ambitions would be fully promoted. To the great annoyance of everyone, except Hume's closest disciples, and especially to Devlin's annoyance, an article in this vein was published in the *Irish Times*, pressing Hume's claim to be the SDLP candidate for the first direct elections to the European Parliament, which were due in 1979. The article lauded his intellect and ability to speak fluent French as qualities that put him ahead of any party rival. As if to press his suitability, he went off that summer to Brussels to join the Cabinet of Dick Burke, the Irish Commissioner to the EEC.

Hume was, of course, rearing a young family, without a regular job or income, but that was not fully understood by everyone in the party and his approach to politics stimulated unwelcome rivalries, not least with Devlin, who was in fact nourishing his own legitimate ambitions of becoming the candidate. The final straw came when Hume announced that he would be the SDLP candidate for the inaugural elections to the European Parliament. Devlin, who was anti-European, was furious that there had been no party selection procedure to allow his own candidature to be considered. At a meeting soon after Hume's announcement, Devlin declared he was standing down from party office. Fitt and Ivan Cooper both struggled to keep the door open for him to come back and explain himself, but he refused and quickly terminated his party membership as well. Fitt knew that even if he had been able to calm him down, any compromise to keep him on board would have been simply papering over the cracks because in reality the party was now hopelessly divided. With Devlin gone, Fitt was ideologically isolated and knew that, for as long he remained within the party, he would have to go along with an increasingly nationalist policy of which he did not entirely approve: 'It did cross my mind to sever my own links, but on reflection, I felt, for the time being anyway, it was better to stay.'

He won temporary bonus points with the ultras in August, during the Queen's Jubilee visit to Northern Ireland, by sticking to the party line and declining to attend any of the official functions. It was no sacrifice for Fitt, who had no intention of attending anyway because he did share the wider SDLP reservations about the way Mason escorted the Queen around in 'a manner more akin to a Viceroy than a cabinet minister', as he put it. 'It was the high spot of his cockiness.'

In spite of Callaghan's urging not to upset the unionist community, Mason's popularity with them was as low as it was with the SDLP. Early in 1977 the PIRA murdered a number of businessmen in another twist of what they said was 'economic warfare', designed to ruin business confidence in Northern Ireland. These and other outrages prompted Paisley to attempt to stage another strike on the 1974 pattern. Ostensibly it was a demand for tougher security measures, but Fitt and many others took the view that it was a thinly disguised bid to seize power, and was rooted in the lingering belief among the 1974 strike leaders that they had settled for half-a-loaf at the point of no return.

Despite Fitt's great reservations about Mason, he watched in admiration as he vigorously confronted the unionist threat. The leaders of the power-station workers were personally flattered by him and persuaded not to give their support to the stoppage. He courted the trade union leaders with equal compulsion and thwarted industrial stoppages. Extra troops were flown in to prevent intimidation on the streets by the loyalist paramilitaries and in Belfast the RUC charged rioting Protestant crowds. Paisley himself was arrested after a lengthy confrontation at a barricade in Ballymena, and his putsch collapsed in ignominy.

For Fitt, there was a most unexpected sting from the anti-Paisley backlash. The Official Unionists were so delighted to see Paisley humiliated that they entered into a deal with Callaghan and Mason. In exchange for an understanding that they would acquiesce in keeping the government in power, Callaghan would put the wheels in motion to increase the number of Northern Ireland MPs returned to Westminster. The first Fitt heard of the plan was when he received a letter from Callaghan saying he had decided to set up a special Speaker's conference to consider the issue. Northern Ireland had long been under-represented at Westminster, with twelve members for a population of 1.5 million, but the existence of the Stormont parliament had meant this imbalance was never a matter of concern. Now, however, the Unionists were pushing for an increase in the number of seats to between seventeen and twenty, which reflected their wish for the British government to more fully integrate Northern Ireland into the UK, along the same lines as Scotland and Wales, rather than continue to look for agreement on restoring power to Stormont. Allowing the district councils to run the area had the twin attraction for them: it would bring to an end any attempts to make them share power with nationalists or create an Irish dimension.

Fitt was utterly disgusted that a Labour government, above all, would be party to such an endeavour. Apart from being a ploy to keep the Unionists from bringing down the Callaghan government, the move effectively extinguished hopes of achieving the objectives Fitt had been campaigning for over the previous ten years:

> I vowed then that at the right moment I would make my opposition known. Michael Foot, then Leader of the House, came to me almost shamefacedly I suspect, to tell me I had been selected to serve on the Speaker's Conference. But when I looked at its composition I saw there was

no way I could win. It had been rigged by Mason. None of the MPs from the left or the old campaign for democracy in Ulster, who would have given me support, had been nominated. I was on my own.

Although he fought all the way through the proceedings, the conference ultimately settled on seventeen seats for Northern Ireland. Fitt's was the only dissenting vote.

By the autumn of 1977 Fitt was thoroughly disillusioned with both Mason and the SDLP, and even a letter from Mason to the party leaders launching what he described as a limited political initiative failed to re-ignite his old fire. In the invitation, setting out an agenda for a round of talks with his officials, Mason proposed: 'There are two options open to us. One is to continue with direct rule. The other is to try to find an interim system of devolved government which will help to make progress towards the aim of a fully devolved administration and in the meantime will bring a larger measure of local participation back into the government of Northern Ireland.'

Fitt thought the initiative was an entirely inadequate response to the damage his 'no politics' was causing and, convinced it was nothing more than an empty gesture, he decided to concentrate his energies on another political problem: to ensure there would be a minority voice from Northern Ireland in the European Parliament. At that point, with the election due in 1979, the draft of the enabling legislation proposed that all Northern Ireland's Westminster constituencies would be grouped together to form a Euro-constituency, and that two people would be elected using the traditional first-past-the-post system. Fitt believed that this formula would allow the Unionists to dominate the vote and win the two seats allocated to Northern Ireland. What Fitt wanted was a third seat for the Euro-constituency and for the method of election to be proportional representation. This way, he believed, there would be two Unionists and one minority candidate returned, which would constitute a proper reflection of the majority – minority balance in the Northern Ireland community.

The Callaghan government, prompted heavily by the Irish government, had accepted this formula at an EEC summit in 1976, but their own party members, who were totally opposed to any form of proportional representation in the UK, would not support its use in Northern Ireland because it would be regarded as the thin end of the wedge. So Rees told Fitt it was up to him to persuade them that Northern Ireland was a special case.

> The campaign lasted night and day for months and was one of the biggest parliamentary battles I ever fought. I was therefore delighted in January 1978 when the House of Commons approved the plan. Although I felt justice had been done, I was disappointed that it had been such a half-hearted concession on the part of a Labour administration, who should not have needed to be reminded of the need for it.

For Fitt, one of the most satisfying dimensions of the battle was the bettering of Enoch Powell on the floor of the Commons: 'During the exchanges we clashed on the unfairness and bigotry of the unionist tradition, but I turned his arguments back on him with sufficient force to win a round of applause from Frank Maguire and carry the house with what one Northern Ireland Office civil servant described to the *Irish Times* as the "speech of my life".' It was the last significant political advance Fitt was to make in his career. At the beginning of 1978 the talks between Mason's officials and the Northern Ireland parties foundered, as predicted, accelerating the final unravelling of Fitt's relationship with the SDLP.

Earlier in 1977, however, Fitt's great oratorical and fixing instincts had been successfully deployed to help the Alliance councillor, David Cook, become Lord Mayor of Belfast. From 1842 until 1889 every mayor of the city, and thereafter every Lord Mayor, had been a unionist, but the outcome of the 1977 local government elections terminated the party's traditional dominance in City Hall. With the unionist – others breakdown now standing at 26 – 25, Cook was encouraged to challenge for the position of First Citizen when the annual election for the post fell due in May. The incumbent, James Stewart, was confident he would be voted in again, but on the eve of the crucial council meeting at the beginning of May, two of the Unionists announced their defection. Josh Cardwell, who was just completing a year as deputy mayor, decided to withdraw his support because of his dissatisfaction with the number of times during the year Stewart had allowed him to make use of the mayoral Rolls Royce limousine. His close colleague, Victor Brennan, like Cardwell a pro-Faulkner Unionist, shared his sense of grievance and decided to back his protest. But rather than merely abstaining in the coming contest and allowing Stewart into office, for other, private reasons they were prepared to cast their votes for Cook. Cardwell was a long-standing client of Cook's legal practice, while Brennan, a teacher, was a colleague of Cook's father, who had been the headmaster of the prestigious Belfast public school, Campbell College. With their help, Cook was comfortably elected, albeit by a single vote.

The unionists reacted with fury at the historical reverse and indicated that they would seek to re-run the vote when the council met again at the beginning of June. Such an action was without precedent, and Cook remembers that with 'the arithmetic so tight there was nail-biting tension' in the final hours before the meeting; one unionist councillor was taken from his hospital bed and brought into the council chamber on a wheelchair so that he could vote. In order to cast his vote for Cook, Paddy Devlin had returned from a trade union conference in Sligo. Meanwhile, Cardwell and Brennan were being put under intense pressure to withdraw their support for Cook, but neither flinched. As the meeting got underway, at 6.00pm, there was a message from the independent councillor, Seamus Lynch, to say he had been unavoidably delayed by a family problem and would get to City Hall as quickly as possible. For Cook, the situation was now unbearable. Unless Lynch turned up, the vote would be tied 25 – 25 and, with his casting vote, Stewart was quite entitled to vote himself into office for another year. Having worked hard to ensure that every one of the eight SDLP councillors was present and wishing to press defeat on the unionists, Fitt immediately began a filibuster, raising spurious points of order and asking all manner of procedural questions. 'After what seemed like a lifetime, but was in reality more like ten minutes,' recalls Cook, Lynch slipped in and took his seat. Fitt then sat down and allowed the roll-call vote to proceed. As each member declared his or her preference, the outcome was not clear until the very last vote, when Cook clinched victory 26 – 25. He attributes the credit to Fitt:

> It would not have been possible without Fitt. He had both the presence of mind and the parliamentary skills and experience to prevent the vote being taken until Lynch arrived, and I am sure he would have been able to keep going much longer if it had been necessary.

CHAPTER THIRTEEN

THE FINAL INSULT

ONE AFTERNOON WHEN FITT WAS RESTING AT HOME, he went out to answer yet another caller to the front door. As he opened it, a young man pushed past him, slammed the door shut, ran into the adjacent front room and began looking out the window. 'Aye, Aye,' said Fitt. 'What the fuck do you think you're playing at?'

The man ignored him and said, 'Mr Fitt, I'm in prison in England. Would you be able to get me back to do my time in Northern Ireland?'

Fitt was taken aback. 'But if you're in prison in England, how come you're here now?'

All the time, the man was peering anxiously out of the window, as if watching for someone. 'I've escaped and I'm on the run, but I would go back if you could promise to get me a transfer to serve my sentence here,' he explained.

It transpired that he had been imprisoned in England for robbery, but wanted to be closer to his girlfriend. They both came from the New Lodge area, and Fitt actually knew the man's grandmother. He let him slip out the back door, but before going in to lobby for his transfer, he decided to ask the granny about him. 'Och, he's a great fella, Gerry,' she said. 'He just went off the rails a bit because of this girl. He spent every penny he got on a ring for her and he just wants to be back home.'

Another prisoner whose plight Fitt championed was that of his constituent Patrick 'Giuseppe' Conlon, who was sentenced to twelve years in 1976 for his alleged role in an IRA conspiracy to plant bombs in Britain. Conlon arrived in London in December 1974, shortly after his son, Gerry, had been arrested for questioning in connection with the Guildford pub bombing earlier in the year, when four soldiers and a civilian died and over 100 people were injured. Police followed Conlon from the airport to his solicitor's office and then to the home of the Maguire family in Willesden, relatives by marriage, with whom he had arranged to stay. After a six-week trial at the Old Bailey in 1976, Conlon, Annie Maguire, four other members of her family, and a close friend were all found guilty of making bombs and imprisoned despite protesting their innocence.

Soon after the trial, Conlon extracted a deathbed promise from Fitt that he would continue the fight to clear his name. About the same time, three of the most senior detectives at Scotland Yard took Fitt for drinks and a meal at Jack's Place in Battersea, where they confided that the case against the 'Maguire Seven' had been trumped up for political reasons, to assuage public feeling about the IRA. This private revelation, and his pledge to Conlon, prompted Fitt to lead a campaign to have the convictions quashed, but Conlon, who had a history of heart trouble, died in prison in January 1980 before the verdict could be overturned. It was not until June 1991 that the Court of Appeal finally declared a miscarriage of justice, by which time the others had been freed from prison.

Throughout the years of violence and political turmoil, these were just two examples of the many people Fitt assisted with a vast range of problems. His Belfast home remained a magnet for those in need of help and they continued to call in considerable numbers, regardless of the security situation in the city. Wherever he was out and about, he was soon surrounded and inundated with pleas for aid but he had a particular compassion for those laid low by illness, handicap or disability, and was always keenly interested in their welfare – 'the forgotten people of Northern Ireland,' he called them. The Troubles had increased the number of people with mental and physical handicaps who had special needs and Fitt was all too aware that attention and provision for them had long been inadequate.

As a result, early in 1975, while events around the Convention were occupying much of his time, Fitt took more than a passing interest when he heard that deaf people were at a disadvantage because the 1968 Hearing Aid Council Act, which provided for the establishment of a Hearing Aid Council to register and control persons engaged in the supply of hearing aids and to advise on their training, contained a clause specifically excluding its application to Northern Ireland. As he had been successful in the ballot to introduce a Private Members Bill, Fitt decided to use the parliamentary slot to promote an Act to extend the Act to Northern Ireland. His Bill was introduced at the beginning of April and, thanks to a fair wind from the government, earned sufficient support from MPs on both sides of the Commons to become law the following July, as the Hearing Aid Council (Extension) Act 1975. Apart from regulating the supply of hearing aids, the new legislation also entitled people requiring them to reclaim the VAT.

Emboldened by this success, and after gaining another slot in the ballot for private bills two years later, Fitt decided that this time he would campaign for the 1970 Chronically Sick and Disabled Act to be extended to cover Northern Ireland:

> I got my chance to do something about it early in the 1977/78 parliamentary session through using again the special procedure whereby

parliament provides time for a Bill proposed by an individual member. As a preliminary to tabling my Bill, I bombarded the Northern Ireland Office with about 150 parliamentary questions. Some of the answers were quite horrific. The authorities had not carried out a survey to establish just how many disabled people there were and we were away behind the mainland in provision of facilities, such as wheelchair ramps and telephones, for disabled persons. I am glad to say my Bill was successful and went on the official list of statutes as the Chronically Sick and Disabled Persons (Northern Ireland) Act 1978, an achievement I regard as one of the most satisfying of my parliamentary career.

By 1978, with the world recession biting hard in Britain, Northern Ireland was considerably worse off. As one local trade union leader put it, 'When the mainland gets a chill, we get pneumonia.' The resulting poverty, and the lawlessness now deeply embedded in Northern Ireland's social fabric, was all too apparent from the levels of debt that had accumulated. In the three years since 1975, rent, rates, gas and electricity arrears had doubled to £28 million. Out of this sum, rent arrears alone amounted to £16 million. There was one street in Belfast where twenty-nine out of the thirty-four houses owed gas arrears of over £7,500, while thirty-three were in debt to the electricity board for over £10,500. Fitt said the figures showed that the vast majority of the debtors simply could not make ends meet because wages and earnings in Northern Ireland were only about three-quarters of those elsewhere in the UK, and energy prices were higher than in any other region:

> The situation in my constituency was so bad I had no hesitation in claiming it as the most underprivileged and socially deprived part of the UK, or Western Europe, in terms of housing and unemployment.

A BBC survey showed unemployment varied from 25% to as much as 35% in some areas. Of 6,214 people signing the register at the Falls Road social security office, only 2,015 qualified for unemployment assistance. The others had been unemployed for so long, they were entitled only to supplementary benefit. Many were not even required to sign on weekly because their chances of obtaining work were regarded as so remote. To save administrative effort, they were only required to attend once every three months. Some were people consigned to the scrapheap as young as fifty years of age, a situation certain to demoralise and knock the heart out of the even the most resilient.

Fitt was assured that every effort was being made to attract inward investment and create jobs 'by scouring the world', as a minister put it to him. One day in 1978, Fitt was tipped off about a piece of good employment news, which he promptly passed on to Des McCartan of the *Belfast Telegraph*. A US car manufacturer, John De Lorean, was to locate a major factory in Fitt's West Belfast constituency, which would manufacture luxury sports cars for the American market. Mason was furious that the news had leaked because it meant he was unable to claim the full personal credit for the announcement. Fitt recalled:

> The £35m project was beyond my wildest dreams. There were to be 600 jobs, which would progressively rise to 2,000 in five years. In the short-term hundreds of other people would get employment building and fitting out the factory. But as things turned out the project was indeed beyond my wildest dreams. De Lorean was not a visionary entrepreneur bringing hope to a hopeless community but a flamboyant conman.

In July 1984, when the House of Commons Committee on Public Accounts reported on the De Lorean scandal, they described the affair as:

> one of the gravest cases of the misuse of public money to come before us for many years. The evidence discloses a shocking misappropriation of public and private money and shows also that Mr De Lorean's automobile companies received about £77m of United Kingdom taxpayers' money and lost most of it within four years. We have concluded from the evidence received that there was misplaced optimism by government and its advisers when the original investment decision was taken and when additional investments were made, and that there was ineffective supervision of the project as it proceeded.

'In all my experience, I have never heard a more scathing indictment of any public project,' said Fitt, who took the view that those most betrayed by the fiasco were not taxpayers but the poor people of West Belfast, who were supposed to be the beneficiaries but despite his disdain for Mason, Fitt did give him credit for 'a genuinely honest attempt to help an area of special hardship'.

Meanwhile, Fitt's ever more semi-detached and unhappy relationship with the SDLP continued to deteriorate. The reasons Devlin quoted for resigning in August 1977 could equally have been cited by Fitt, who was now completely isolated in the party ranks. He continued to maintain a discreet silence, however, and largely nursed his own discontents in private. The party's eighth annual conference, in November 1978, demonstrated how wide the rift had become, and there was more ritual than passion as Fitt made his usual rousing leader's speech, outlining yet again the message that the only way forward was by political agreement and that Ireland could not be unified at the point of a gun. His speech did not chime with the most notable outcome of the conference – a landslide vote in favour of a motion calling for British withdrawal. Just two of the 600 delegates opposed it. Gone was any commitment to the proposition that unionist consent was an essential condition for any all-Ireland settlement. Fitt took the view that such an approach was as futile as Mason's, who was doing nothing to discourage unionists from their increasing enthusiasm for integrating Northern Ireland with the rest of the UK in line with the constitutional arrangements for Wales and Scotland. Although they would not have another Stormont under such an arrangement, they believed it would strengthen the union and also offered the bonus, for them, that there would be no requirement to share power with Catholics. As far as Fitt could see, both sides were moving further and further away from seeking to re-establish the Sunningdale consensus, the most fruitful basis he could see for political progress. Neither side, he judged, was anywhere near ready to make the necessary compromises to energise new negotiations.

As 1978 melted into 1979, the major political question facing Britain was how long the Callaghan government could continue to stagger along. The country was crippled by a seemingly endless series of strikes, the economy was in a dire state and Callaghan could not muster a majority in parliament to allow him to get a grip on the situation. Given these pressing problems, Callaghan and Mason were indifferent about giving the Northern Ireland political process the kick-start Fitt believed it needed. He was therefore outraged to hear Mason, in a radio interview in early February 1979, categorise the SDLP as extremist and the unionists as moderate. Although Fitt had much private sympathy with the notion that the SDLP was far too green, he let fly, accusing Mason of being in the pockets of the unionists, who had been managed carefully by the Callaghan government for some months now to ensure they did not help to bring down the government. What Fitt interpreted as the government's unsympathetic *ennui* with Northern Ireland's intractable problems would soon exact a heavy price.

On 1 March the people of Scotland and Wales decisively rejected government proposals for devolution and thus further weakened Callaghan's position. The leader of the opposition, Margaret Thatcher – the first woman ever to lead the Conservative party, saw her chance and moved in for the kill with a motion of no confidence. The vote was fixed for 28 March 1979 and from the outset of the crisis, Fitt knew the parliamentary arithmetic was so tight that his vote would be vital, essential even, to the survival of the Callaghan administration. In his frequent contact with government ministers and backbenchers in the bars and corridors at Westminster, Fitt had been making no secret of his disillusionment and, after the row with Mason, had already indicated he would be unlikely to vote with Labour in the event of a confidence motion. With so much at stake, he braced himself for the arm-twisting that would inevitably follow in an attempt to persuade him to go through the government lobby.

Throughout his political career, Fitt had demonstrated repeatedly that he was entirely his own man and in all his years as an MP had never allowed anyone to instruct him what to say, or how to vote. This independence continued to bring him into conflict with the nationalist hardliners in the SDLP, who increasingly remonstrated with him about his public comments, or criticised him for supporting Labour policies. He had quite recently come under heavy fire from them for voting in favour of public money to prop up the ailing Belfast shipbuilding and aircraft industries, which they regarded as funding work for Protestant extremists.

A few days before the confidence vote, Fitt got the message he had been expecting: Callaghan wanted to see him. They met across the Cabinet table in Downing Street where, Callaghan told him, the Israeli Prime Minister Menachem Begin had been sitting just a few days earlier. Callaghan then recalled the days of Lloyd George and Churchill, who had also sat at the same polished table. 'I could tell he enjoyed being Prime Minister,' said Fitt, 'reliving the happenings throughout the centuries in that historic room, carrying on what he saw as a very worthy tradition.' Their relaxed and friendly conversation moved onto the general topic of Northern Ireland and how Fitt viewed matters: 'I reminded him of our meeting the day after Mason's appointment and my warning that he would be a disaster.' Callaghan listened intently, then came to the point. From his pocket he produced a piece of paper with his latest calculations for the forthcoming vote. 'How are you going to vote?' he asked.

'I told him my mind was made up. I could not support his government because of Roy Mason. He did not argue or try to persuade me,' said Fitt. Whatever slim chance there might have been that Fitt would change his mind was totally lost when one of Callaghan's aides slipped in and set down on the table beside Fitt a bottle of gin, a bottle of tonic and a glass. He did not regard it as hospitable gesture and was deeply offended at the inference that he could be turned for a few gins. 'That really, really got me. I said, "Take it away out of the road." No, no. You don't do that. That was the final insult.'

When Walter Harrison, an old friend of Fitt's and the deputy chief whip, whose job it was to maximise Callaghan's support, stopped him in the corridor outside Annie's Bar an evening or so later, their encounter was polite and understanding.

'We know each other well. What are you doing?' he asked Fitt in his blunt, northern way. 'Are you voting for the government?'

'No,' Fitt replied.

'That's fine. I can make up my figures,' said Harrison without rancour.

In the days before the vote, as the government sought to call in every favour, Fitt was telephoned and lobbied by several of his friends in the trade union movement, but they understood well the reasons for his disenchantment and accepted his decision as final. However, one run-in, with NIO junior minister Tom Pendry, rankled: 'He asked me to support the government. I said, why should I listen to him when I had rejected representations from other people. "Because I'm a Catholic, too," said Pendry. "In the name of God, how could you stoop to that level?" Fitt asked.'

On the day of the vote, Westminster was seething with rumour and excitement. 'In all my time there I had never seen anything like it. My daughter, Eileen, who was then working at the BBC in London, came to share it,' he recalled. The Callaghan government was fighting to the bitter end and looked like it had even managed to split the Unionists. John Carson, the North Belfast MP whom Fitt regarded as having socialist leanings, said he was going to vote for the government because he thought they had done a good job for the people of Northern Ireland. As he was shortly giving up his seat for health reasons, he could defy the party whip with impunity. More significantly, Fitt heard that Harold McCusker, MP for Upper Bann and Carson's close friend, had begun to waver. McCusker was a thinking Unionist MP, who liked to make up his own mind and did not like being ordered about by Enoch Powell, who had joined the Unionists in 1974 after losing his seat in Britain. After talks with Don Concannon, a member of Mason's ministerial team, Carson and McCusker went to Downing Street to see the chief whip and Roy Hattersley.

The vote was such a close run thing that a stroke, or a piece of bluff could decide it. Therefore, Fitt pricked up his ears when a Labour member tipped him off that Frank Maguire had come over for one of his rare visits and was carefully quarantined in the building with Labour ministers until he cast his vote. The story made sense because Fitt knew Callaghan had been counting on Maguire's vote in his calculations. 'The story in the corridors was that they were getting Maguire drunk to keep him happy, but whatever else I had said about him, I knew he was a drinker and could have drunk any of the Englishmen under the table,' said Fitt. Later he learned that earlier in the day, Don Concannon, 'just by accident', had an engagement in Fermanagh, so he 'called into' Maguire's pub at Lisnaskea 'for a drink'. Maguire was surprised to see him, and even more surprised to hear about the vote. After a few drinks, he agreed to go to Westminster and accepted Concannon's offer of a lift. When they arrived, Maguire was indeed quarantined, mainly, his Labour friends told Fitt, so that he could not get to him.

The debate in the House of Commons began about 3.30pm, with Mrs Thatcher opening. Outside the chamber an unprecedented phalanx of members' guests were milling around in the lobbies and corridors, but in an ironic symbol of what had become known as Callaghan's 'winter of [industrial] discontent', a sudden strike had shut all the bars. It was 6.27pm, according to Hansard, when Fitt was called to speak and over the next twenty-one minutes he delivered what he described as 'the unhappiest speech I have ever made in this house':

> When I was elected in 1966, I sat on the Labour Benches. I was under no compulsion to do so, but I had been a committed Socialist all my life. Therefore, when I came to this House I felt proud and honoured to associate myself with the Labour cause. When the Labour Government were defeated, I took my place among Labour Members on the Opposition Benches. Throughout a fourteen-year period in Parliament I have never once voted in the Conservative Lobby. I have at all times committed myself to support the policies which I honestly believed were for the good of the United Kingdom. Even in the years when we were in opposition and when the Conservative Government were courageously trying to grapple – and,

to some extent, succeeding – with the problems of Northern Ireland, I voted on every other issue with the then Labour Opposition. I repeat that the Conservative Government of 1970-74 tried courageously to reach a settlement in Northern Ireland. However, all that we had built up so laboriously was wrecked by the election in February 1974. We then, in May of that year, experienced the UWC strike. That strike terrified the Labour government. Since then the Labour government have been running away. They have not stood up to unionist and loyalist extremists as they should have done. When we look back in history, we see clearly that Labour governments are not the best governments to grapple with the Irish problem. That does not apply to Labour Oppositions. When Labour is in Opposition, one sees the real conscience of the Labour Party. Labour Members are not then restricted by the reins of office. But I believe that the policy on Northern Ireland adopted by the Labour government since 1974 has been disastrous for the communities in. Northern Ireland. The Conservatives tried to bring people in Northern Ireland together, but the communities are now more divided than they have been since the onset of the present troubles in 1969-70.

Fitt said he did not blame Mason personally because he 'is only implementing Labour Government policies ... consolidating Unionist supremacy in Northern Ireland', but he did condemn Mason's unwillingness to tackle the political question and willingness to seek a military solution instead:

> Every Monday morning at 10 o'clock he sees the Chief Constable. Every Monday at 1pm, we hear on the news that so many IRA men have been caught and so many have been sent to jail. Every Monday the Secretary of State looks for a military solution. But there will be Mondays and Mondays and more Mondays when there will be no military solution and there will be no solution at all until we start to grapple with the political problem of Northern Ireland.

Fitt told the House that the single greatest cause of his discontent was the Bennett Report, published two weeks earlier, which 'clearly states that men were brutalised and ill-treated in the holding-centres in Northern Ireland'. (The report was commissioned by the government after an investigation by Amnesty International suggested that IRA and other suspects being questioned by the RUC had been subjected to beatings and assaults to force them to sign statements incriminating themselves in terrorist actions. Fitt regarded this issue as the worst manifestation of Mason's security policy and had clashed angrily with him as the affair developed.) To the House, Fitt said: 'I hope that even now the government will say that there was something wrong in the interrogation centres in Northern Ireland and that the Bennett Report may be debated on the floor of the House. I hope that they will establish a sworn inquiry on this matter.' During his speech, Fitt ensured it would be impossible for Maguire to vote with the government by pointing out that the people who had elected him had not sent him to Westminster to support a government that did deals with the unionists and acquiesced in the wrongdoings exposed by Bennett. In concluding, Fitt said:

> In all conscience, and understanding the real needs of Northern Ireland, I would be a liar and a traitor to the people who sent me here if I were to go into the lobby tonight with the Labour Government to express confidence in their running of the affairs of Northern Ireland. I want to see an election as soon as possible. I want to see the Labour Government win with such a majority that never again will they have to rely on the votes of the unionists in Northern Ireland.
>
> I have a loyalty to this Government, to my own working-class and trade union background, and to the whole working-class movement in the United Kingdom and further afield. But I have a greater loyalty to the people of Northern Ireland who have suffered so tragically over the past 10 years. I am speaking with their voice tonight. It is their voice saying that because of what the Government have done in the past five years – disregarded the minority and appeased the blackmailers of the Northern Ireland unionist majority – I cannot go into the Lobby with them tonight.

When Fitt finished speaking and resumed his seat, Stan Orme, came up to the backbench and whispered to him that Michael Foot, who had been listening carefully to his speech, wanted a word. Fitt moved across the chamber and slipped onto the bench beside him. Foot said he could understand Fitt's feelings and that, whatever way the vote went, he would harbour no ill-will. Towards 10.00pm, as the winding up speeches got underway, the House filled up. There are, in fact, not enough seats for all the members and on great occasions like this, people sit on the steps of the aisles or crowd in at both ends of the chamber to watch and listen. That night, Fitt was perched on one of the gangways as Foot began to sum up for the government:

> Opposite me I noticed one of the Conservative members, howling for him to resign. He was the epitome of all that I hated about them; the sort of fat, well-fed, cigar-smoking, pin-striped, public-school twit that haunted the bars and smoke rooms. I remember thinking that, if I stayed and watched him, he would force me into the Labour lobby, so I left the chamber and went across to my office.

At the time Fitt was accommodated in what was known as the Norman Shaw Building, situated on the Victoria Embankment overlooking the River Thames, close to the Houses of Parliament. From 1890 until 1967 the building had been occupied by the Metropolitan Police and was recognised all over the world as Scotland Yard. After that it was converted into offices for MPs. There, looking out over the night skyline of London and watching the traffic snaking across Westminster Bridge, Fitt listened to the fall of the Callaghan government on a radio (parliamentary proceedings were not televised at that time):

> I had no qualms about my stand when the outcome was declared and the
> government fell by a single vote, 311 to 310. It was a unique parliamentary
> experience to speak that night. Everybody knew how I was feeling but, as
> the division bells had not then rung, they listened to every word with rapt
> attention to see if I had changed my mind, or been bought off. There was
> no heckling from either side; the Conservatives did not want to annoy me
> in case I would vote against them; Labour did not want to antagonise me
> any further in case I would go into the opposition lobby. In fact, I was heard
> in complete silence.

McCusker and Carson voted with Labour. Maguire, in his now-celebrated phrase,
'abstained in person'. Having failed to go into the voting lobby with Labour, Fitt
knew he was not going to be the most popular man at Westminster that evening,
but he walked back to the main building because he was determined to be seen
around in case anyone should think he was ashamed or frightened. In the
corridors, only two or three people refused to speak to him. For most of his fellow
MPs, many of them long-standing friends, the vote was already water under the
bridge. They were now facing into an uncertain election and survival instincts
took over as they had began appraising their chances of holding their seats. On his
way out of the building, one of the messengers handed Fitt a sheaf of messages.
When he read them later, they were mostly supportive, although he was amused
to see that many of them had come from SDLP people in Northern Ireland he
would have regarded as his critics.

The next day, as election fever took over, Fitt was shuttling around London
from one radio or television studio to another well into the evening, discussing the
prospects and issues for the election on programmes beamed throughout the
British Isles. On several occasions during the day he found himself, for the first
time, in close company with Airey Neave, the opposition spokesman on Northern
Ireland, who had famously escaped from Colditz, the supposedly escape-proof
castle used by the Germans to confine troublesome prisoners during the Second
World War. More recently, Neave had masterminded Margaret Thatcher's triumph
in the conservative leadership election. Fitt found him

> ... an interesting character and obviously very tough and brave. That day I
> came to respect him. We talked about my reasons for voting against the
> government and my reservations about the ill-treatment of suspects. 'Gerry,
> I give you the assurance that if I am Secretary of State for Northern Ireland
> after the election, I will have a most searching enquiry into those allegations
> and if it is found they were taking place, then, they will meet with the full
> brunt of my wrath, because I myself was subjected to interrogation at the
> hands of the Gestapo and, Gerry, it leaves its mark on you.'

The next day, Friday, the House was due to debate a Credit Unions Bill and, at lunchtime, while waiting for the Bill to come up, Fitt was talking to Des McCartan about the prospects for the election:

> About 2.40pm we were making our way upstairs to the Commons chamber when we met Neave on the stairs. We talked briefly together for a few moments then he went on his way. McCartan and I parted in the central lobby and a few minutes later, just before 3.00pm, as I was sitting in the chamber, trying to catch the eye of the Speaker, I heard the all too familiar crack of an explosion. I knew it was close by. But I had hardly time to dwell on it for I was called to speak. Ten minutes later, my speech completed, I ran out to the members' entrance. I met one of the policemen I knew putting up white tape to seal the area off. 'It looks like Airey Neave,' the policeman said grimly. 'He's still alive but there's not much of him left.' We ran over to the car park ramp where his car had stopped. Ambulancemen and police officers were working to try and free him from the smoking wreckage of his car, but he died from his injuries on the way to hospital. When the enormity of what had happened, only minutes after he left us, sank in, the killing was a great shock to McCartan and I. Words were once more inadequate to describe the actual outrage and anger I felt. Another life had been taken in the cause of Irish freedom, but it would not, could not and did not contribute in the slightest way to solving the problem.

The assassination dominated the election campaign and Fitt returned to Belfast in a mood of utter depression, once more far from confident of holding his seat. Soon, he was embroiled in the SDLP squabbling that had come to characterise every election campaign. As ever, the Fermanagh-South Tyrone seat was the first point of controversy. Fitt wanted the SDLP to fight the seat and thought that, as Maguire had not been a particularly attentive MP, Austin Currie had a good chance of taking it and becoming for the SDLP a very able elected representative at Westminster. However, Hume and his chain of command had their eyes set solely on the forthcoming elections to the European Parliament and feared that if the SDLP split the vote in the general election and allowed the unionists to retake the seat, a valuable block of votes would be denied him in the wider European contest. The party was therefore prevailed upon not to contest the poll.

Fitt encouraged Currie to go ahead nonetheless, so he resigned as chief whip and stood as 'Independent SDLP'. Although he failed to oust Maguire, he came third and won a respectable 10,785 votes. The episode is significant in that it illustrates the extent of the division that had developed within the Hume-dominated SDLP. Of the six founders, Cooper and O'Hanlon had drifted away, Devlin had been driven out, Currie was now openly at odds with the hierarchy, and Fitt was more alienated than ever from the party. In West Belfast, where rival unionists fought for the non-Catholic vote, Fitt confounded his own fears and successfully defended the seat with an increased majority, up from 5,556 in 1974 to 8,235. Although they fielded nine candidates, Fitt was the only SDLP member returned to Westminster after polling on 3 May. For the election workers, there was barely time to recover from the travails of the general election campaign before facing it all again, this time for the elections to the European Parliament, which would take place on 7 June.

Despite the barely concealed contempt Fitt now felt for Hume, he put it aside and threw his weight behind his campaign, canvassing in his own constituency to help turn out the pro-Hume vote. One Saturday morning he toured around the hardline Divis Flats area, with its over-crowded dwellings, endemic unemployment and poverty, which, he mused, 'was not sympathetic territory for the Common Market'. One resident had told him they would just as readily shoot farmers as British soldiers; farmers were regarded as being treated with outstanding largesse by Europe. Shortly before 1.00pm, as Fitt was being driven home by three female party members who had helped in the canvass, the driver turned on the radio news. The first item was the details of yet another brutal murder of a member of the UDR. 'My God! What a terrible murder,' said Fitt. There was no reaction. 'Jesus Christ. Isn't that awful?' he asked. Again, no response. 'My God,' he said again, 'isn't that a terrible murder?' Silence. By now they had reached the front door of his house and he got out of the car, but before the women drove off, he said to them: 'I have an idea that you're half in support of what happened, that way down deep in your bellies you can find some justification for murders like that.'

'Yes, Gerry,' one of them said before driving off. 'We don't feel as bad as you obviously do.'

> I stood on the footpath in amazement. I was feeling more and more a stranger in my own tribe, but most of all I was beginning to feel I must divorce myself from people who were as ambivalent about violence as those SDLP women. What worried me most is that I knew they were typical of so many people in the party.

Hume was elected to the European Parliament with a 24.6% share of the vote. Paisley topped the poll with 29.8% support and John Taylor took the third seat with 11.9%. Fitt's loathing of the developing trends within the SDLP increased dramatically at the end of August. In the early afternoon of the August bank holiday, he turned on Downtown Radio to catch the news. Reports were just coming in of an explosion in County Sligo. Fitt knew straight away who had been targeted – Earl Mountbatten of Burma - who always spent part of his summer holidays there. It was later confirmed that he had indeed been killed, together with his fourteen-year-old grandson and a crew boy the same age, when a radio-controlled bomb in his boat was detonated a short distance offshore. The Dowager Lady Brabourne died later from injuries sustained in the explosion.

Before anyone had time to come to terms with the enormity of that atrocity, another, of even grimmer proportions, took place at Narrow Water Castle, near

Warrenpoint. Eighteen soldiers died in two explosions – the second timed to kill and maim rescuers as they came to the aid of the casualties from the first. It was the worst single incident of the Troubles to date, and the worst single day for casualties. 'I walked up and down and up and down the sitting room in Belfast. I was frustrated, angry, powerless, in the face of such ruthlessness,' Fitt said of that tragic day.

The morning after the double atrocity, the *Daily Mirror* had the single word 'bastards' in big, black letters on its front page. Fitt approved. 'The Provisionals were the worst thing that had ever happened to Ireland, including Cromwell and the Famine,' he said. When he discovered that the Irish Prime Minister, Jack Lynch, had remained on holiday in Portugal, he was incredulous and issued a public statement calling for his return. The SDLP called an emergency meeting in Dungannon to discuss the political implications of the major crisis that had blown up. Before the meeting got under way, Paddy Duffy said he wanted to express his dissatisfaction that Fitt had joined in the chorus of criticism of Jack Lynch. Fitt stopped him and defiantly told him he had not joined it, but started it. According to Fitt's recollection, Denis Haughey then produced a folder of newspaper cuttings and quoted extracts from them to criticise Fitt, saying he should be concerned with defending what he called 'the national interest'. Fitt shouted back that it was 'the so-called national interest and nationalism that gave the killers some sort of half-justification, excuse for their savagery'. He went on to 'angrily and bitterly disassociate myself from those who would justify or condone such violence'. This was the first open confrontation between Fitt and those within the SDLP whom he now regarded as political enemies, primarily because of what he regarded as their ambivalence to violence.

Fitt did not have any doubts about the stand he was taking, but one month later, on 30 September, when he was among the 250,000 who gathered at Drogheda during the papal visit, he felt especially vindicated by what Pope John Paul II said that day:

> To all of you who are listening, I say: do not believe in violence; do not support violence. It is not the Christian way. It is not the way of the Catholic Church. Believe in peace and forgiveness and love, for they are of Christ. On my knees I beg of you to turn away from the paths of violence and to return to the ways of peace. You may claim to seek justice. I too believe in justice and seek justice. But violence only delays the day of justice. Violence destroys the work of justice ... do not follow any leaders who train you in the ways of inflicting death. Those who resort to violence always claim that only violence brings about change. You must know that there is a political, peaceful way to justice.

'I never forgot the impact of his words on me,' said Fitt, who had listened with tears welling in his eyes. 'I knew then there could be no turning back for me. The

SDLP and I were now most certainly going in different directions.'

Throughout that violent and depressing summer of 1979, as the toll of death and destruction climbed steadily higher, Fitt talked regularly to Humphrey Atkins, whom Prime Minister Margaret Thatcher had appointed to the Belfast hot-seat. They got on very well, and Fitt told him frankly that the SDLP was making impossible demands and adopting unrealistic attitudes. 'I made it completely clear that I was out of step with the party,' he said. 'The marriage was over, all that remained was for the formal divorce to take place.'

The trigger for what would be the final confrontation between Fitt and the SDLP came on 20 November when Atkins formally unveiled his plans for a political initiative, proposing a round-table conference at Stormont for the four main parties to discuss ways of again putting a devolved government for Northern Ireland into place as 'direct rule' from Westminster was not a satisfactory basis for the government of Northern Ireland. In line with Thatcher's belief that Northern Ireland was 'as British as Finchley', her own north London constituency, Atkins ruled out any discussion about constitutional status and also stated that the ideas of British withdrawal, a united Ireland, confederation or independence – concepts which had been so actively promoted by Rees and Cooper – were all ruled out. It had been agreed with Hume, who had a more 'pressing' engagement in Europe to attend, that Fitt would handle the reaction, so he went on radio and television to say, without specific commitment, that the proposals were worth examining and no suggestion should be ruled out. When he reached Dungannon later that evening for a party meeting, it was clear he had not been saying what the hardliners wanted to hear:

> What I encountered was open hostility. It was made very clear to me that the party would not consider any solution within Northern Ireland, including power-sharing with the unionists, unless there was an Irish dimension. I argued strongly, but they remained deaf to my belief that a deal should first be reached on power-sharing. They decided to reject the invitation to take part in Atkins' round table conference.

For Fitt, one of the most striking exchanges during that meeting was with Seamus Mallon, who talked of holding 'our people' together. Fitt replied that they must no longer be talking about the same people. The remark was still running through his head when he reached home that evening and found Ann, staring at the television:

> Obviously she had been crying. 'What's the matter?' I asked her. 'Gerry, they're all going mad. You can't lead that party anymore. Mallon was on the television saying you don't speak for them and that you had annoyed the grass roots,' she said. I put my arm round her and said, 'I've been thinking that all evening. I'm going to resign. We're not talking the same language anymore.'

The following morning Fitt left for London where, that evening, he heard that the the party executive had formally confirmed the rejection of the Atkins document. As far as he was concerned, that clinched the issue. Early the next morning, Thursday, 22 November, he telephoned Des McCartan and told him of his decision to resign from the SDLP. He wanted the full story in the *Belfast Telegraph* that afternoon. He then called a press conference at the Irish Club to announce he was giving up the leadership of the SDLP and resigning from the party. 'I have a feeling of unutterable sadness to see at this time the party which I helped to create turning so violently on the concepts on which it was founded. We have come to the end of a very hard road,' he said, but he felt only relief, not regret. Fitt's resignation generated extensive news coverage, recalling the highlights of his career and analysing the background to his departure. For years, Ann had shared his, and suffered her own, frustrations, largely in silence, but now she decided the time had come to speak out. In an interview with the *Belfast Telegraph* she said:

> Gerry has been unsettled for a considerable time and last night's meeting was the straw which broke the camel's back. We had a heart-to-heart talk, one of the most serious we've ever had, and he decided that if his party refused to go to those talks he would get out. And I'm right behind him – 100 per cent. He was dealing with a very hardline body of people. Personally I'm very, sorry for them, but good luck to them. My feelings are entirely in agreement with Gerry's views. He is a sensible man and knew what he was about. He decided that if people were going to start pushing republican views, then he would cut his ties with the SDLP. He has had his ups and downs, but never once since the Troubles started has he given a crumb of support to the men of violence. He never will. Of course, we have our Irish aspirations but why couldn't the SDLP have got round the table first and tried to make some reasonable political progress? We didn't make this decision lightly. He gave it a lot of thought. I'm in no doubt that if Gerry stands for parliament again, he'll get back in. There will be no problem.

The years of living under siege and her round-the-clock role as her husband's amanuensis had profoundly affected Ann Fitt. She had come to call her house 'Fort Knox' because of the extensive security paraphernalia that was necessary to protect the family. She still suffered from acute asthma and had been taken to hospital several times for treatment. By now the Miss Fitts had grown up and were pursuing their own lives. Joan, a trained nurse, was living in London with her husband, Vincent Hanna, a Belfast-born solicitor, who was earning great recognition for his role as an acerbic political analyst and pundit on the BBC. Eileen had graduated from Trinity College Dublin, then moved from a job with a trade union in London to become a researcher in the BBC's current affairs department. Patsy started working in a bank in Belfast, but later moved to London and qualified as a teacher. Betty was working as a nurse. Only Geraldine had remained at home in Belfast to complete her schooling. As Ann told the *Belfast News Letter* in October 1979:

> They left because they are healthy-minded, lively girls and this place has little to offer. I'm heartbroken they've gone away. My girls are my whole life. All I could visualise for the future was my girls growing up and having grandchildren I could visit and who could visit me. I have one grandchild, but what do I see of her. 'Hello, granny', that's all I hear [on the telephone from London]. They like me to visit them. But they don't like coming here. All I have now is Geraldine, my youngest girl who is studying A levels. All I ever wanted was my children living convenient to me with loads and loads of grandchildren swarming around. And I've been denied that. Yes, it's making me more and more discontented with my life because I can't go on indefinitely like this.
>
> This time last year I would have said I'd learned to live with this house. But in the last few months I've been so very unhappy and I just wish there was some place else. But where can a man like Gerry, who has been so outspoken about the Troubles, go? If we moved somewhere quiet in a different area, we could be jumping from the frying pan into the fire. Look at our house. It's barricaded up completely. What would a bungalow be like with all that round it? And wouldn't it make our neighbours very nervous? Come to that, not many people would welcome us near them. I know they'd think, 'with the reputation they have, someone might have a go at them and mistaking our house for theirs'. This is an endless worry to me. What do we do? Where do we go? Our social life is in tatters. I couldn't bring anyone back to our house looking like it does. I can't have proper friendships, can't entertain people here. I suppose if I were to push Gerry he would look for somewhere else because I know he considers me first. But his life is my greatest concern. A miracle may happen. But I don't really think there's much hope of that. The constant verbal abuse gets me now.

Within days of Fitt resigning from the SDLP, John Hume succeeded him as leader of the party. Within a month, and despite what had gone on between Fitt and the party, Hume took the decision that they would, after all, attend the Atkins conference. By this point a series of landmark events were already underway, the culmination of which would not only bring an effective end to Fitt's political career but would fundamentally transform the political landscape in Northern Ireland.

The starting point came in September 1976 when Ciaran Nugent was convicted of hijacking a van in the Cullingtree Road area of Fitt's constituency and imprisoned in the Maze. As the first prisoner to be convicted of an offence committed after 1 March 1976, the authorities denied him 'special category' status and he was put into the first of the new H-shaped cellblocks, issued with prison uniform and told he would be expected to conform to a regime more in line with that operated in Britain. To the IRA this was 'criminalisation' and they were very prickly indeed about being classified as 'ordinary decent criminals', as the prison authorities called them. The IRA insisted their imprisoned members were 'political prisoners' and they wanted 'special category' status and privileges maintained – the concession Fitt and Devlin had helped secure for them from Whitelaw in 1972. (Whitelaw later admitted publicly this was a mistake, and Fitt had come to support him.) The political prisoners lived in compounds, organised their own lives, wore their own clothes and really lacked for nothing but their freedom. However, early in 1975, after the publication of a study by Lord Gardiner 'to consider, in the context of civil liberties and human rights, measures to deal with terrorism in Northern Ireland', the government moved to abolish 'special category' status. Privately, the authorities had dubbed the compounds as a 'university of terrorism' because lectures were given in everything from weapons training to political philosophy. As had been threatened by the IRA, Nugent refused to conform and instead of prison uniform wore a blanket. The 'blanket protest' was born, and the stage was set for an all-out confrontation between the prisoners and the authorities.

Outside the prison, in recent times the young, street-hardened IRA hardliners from Belfast and Derry had ousted the older 'armchair generals' from Dublin and taken control of the organisation, shifting its centre of gravity northwards. They were all graduates from the Maze 'university' and were inspired as much by Marx as by the more traditional heroes of the Irish struggle. They set about whipping up support for the 'blanket men' with marches and rallies but when they signally failed, the prisoners escalated their protest in early 1978. As well as refusing to wear prison clothing, they now urinated and excreted on their cell floors and daubed the resulting mixture on the walls. As most people were revolted by this disgusting development, the 'dirty protest', as it was called, did not catch the imagination and sympathy of the general Catholic population.

But then came what proved to be a highly significant intervention. Onto centre-stage strode Archbishop (later Cardinal) Tomás Ó Fiaich, the recently appointed Catholic primate of all-Ireland. Fitt was no fan of the bluff, blunt, pipe-smoking countryman from the border town of Crossmaglen, not least because he was a publicly committed nationalist. In Fitt's estimation, Ó Fiaich's predecessor, Cardinal Conway, born in the Falls Road area, had been a surer-footed leader, but Fitt felt that Ó Faich's republican roots and his move from the cloistered tranquility of the Maynooth seminary were no qualifications for coping with the swirling allegiances of Catholics in Northern Ireland. At the beginning of August 1978 the authorities allowed the archbishop into the prison and after his pastoral visit he issued a statement, part of which read:

> Having spent the whole of Sunday in the prison I was shocked by the inhuman conditions prevailing in H Block 3, 4 and 5 and where over 300 prisoners are incarcerated. One would hardly allow an animal to remain in

such conditions, let alone a human being. The nearest to it that I have seen was the spectacle of hundreds of homeless people living in sewer-pipes in the slums of Calcutta. The stench and filth in some of the cells, with the remains of rotten food and human excreta scattered around the walls, was almost unbearable. In two of them I was unable to speak for fear of vomiting. The prisoners' cells are without beds, chairs or tables. They sleep on mattresses on the floor and in some cases I noticed that these are quite wet. They have no covering except a towel or blanket, no books, newspapers or reading material except the Bible (even religious magazines have been banned since my last visit); no pens or writing material, no TV or radio, no hobbies or handicrafts, no exercise or recreation. They are locked in their cells for almost the whole of every day and some of them have been in this condition for more than a year and a half.

In these circumstances I was surprised that the morale of the prisoners was high. From talking to them it is evident that they intend to continue their protest indefinitely and it seems they prefer to face death rather than submit to being classed as criminals. Anyone with the least knowledge of Irish history knows how deeply rooted this attitude is in our country's past. In isolation and perpetual boredom they maintain their sanity by studying Irish. It was an indication of the triumph of the human spirit over adverse material surroundings to notice Irish words, phrases and songs being shouted from cell to cell and then written on each cell wall with the remnants of toothpaste tubes.

Fitt was in London when he first heard what Ó Fiaich had to say and he later described it as 'one of those unforgettable moments that just sickened me to the heart'. During a disturbed and sleepless night, he reasoned that 'I could no longer stand up to the IRA and its violence while senior churchmen cut the feet from under me', so he took the difficult decision to resign the West Belfast seat:

> Next morning I was sitting at a table, in the area by the members' entrance, writing and rewriting a suitable resignation letter, when I happened to answer a ringing telephone. It was my daughter, Joan, who said she had been frantically trying to contact me everywhere she could think of. She asked me not to resign for ten minutes, then she would ring me back. I waited for her call. When it came she told me she had just been speaking to Archbishop Ó Fiaich about his statement and he had asked to see me and urged me not to resign. I rang Ann and said I was having second thoughts about resigning, but I never did meet him because of my deep, hostile feelings to his attitudes.

What horrified Fitt most was the archbishop's failure to point out anywhere in his remarks that the conditions he described were entirely self-inflicted by the prisoners themselves, and that instant improvement could have been achieved if they had begun to wash, use the lavatories and behave like civilised people. He was also critical that the statement contained what he described as 'the code-words and the qualifications, sentiments that stopped diplomatically short of outright encouragement for the prisoners'. The archbishop had called them 'boys' in follow-up broadcast interviews – these 'boys' are determined not to have criminal status; the 'boys' could be out playing football – and in Fitt's judgement the archbishop fuelled the flames of future confrontation with his subtle, ambiguous language:

> Words in Northern Ireland can be as lethal as bullets. His intervention set my political alarm bells ringing. The Catholic Church in Ireland had a long tradition of political ambivalence to republican violence and I believed in the developing crisis over prison conditions such an attitude by the church could only be dangerous. Ordinary people fail to discern the difference between Christian or humanitarian concern, which is what the churchmen use to justify their interest and often outright support. This is not only bewildering for Catholics but sows the seed of confusion in Protestant minds and causes both fear and anger. Getting onto this slippery slope therefore tends to encourage the gunmen and bombers and then before we know where we are, violence begets more violence.

Some years later, Fitt heard from the Irish author Dervla Murphy just how important the Ó Fiaich visit had been in the eyes of the Provos. At that time, she told Fitt, she had been researching a book and found them to be rather despondent, almost on the point of calling off the 'dirty protest'. When she returned the following day to their dingy headquarters on the Falls Road, however, she found a totally different atmosphere, a change of mood to renewed enthusiasm. Asked to account for it, one of the Sinn Féin people pointed to the newspaper reports of the Ó Fiaich statement: 'That's why. He's on our side.' The gathering storm on the issue finally erupted at the end of October 1980 when, to force the authorities' hands, seven of the prisoners went on hunger strike to the death. Fitt felt strongly on this issue:

> I was strongly opposed to any concession because that would imply justification of the terrible violence of the previous thirteen years. In my firm belief there was no justification for blowing the leg off Danny Walsh, one of my closest friends; for stabbing Paddy Wilson to death; for planting a bomb without warning in the Abercorn restaurant; for killing countless British soldiers; for repeatedly ambushing policemen and women, on and off duty; for murdering UDR men, Protestant or Catholic; for cutting a man's throat because he was a Catholic or planting a bomb in a pub to kill people as revenge. No cause is so worthy that it justifies violence.

Fitt was well aware of the emotional potential a hunger strike offered and of the ruthlessness with which the IRA would exploit it. He already had first-hand experience of that when, a few years earlier, a Belfast priest had asked him to intervene in the case Frank Stagg, who was fasting to death in Wakefield prison to secure political status. Home Secretary Roy Jenkins told Fitt there could be no question of granting such status, but suggested a formula to save Stagg's face: if he came off his fast, they would allow him to take full-time lessons instead of prison work. Fitt communicated this to the priest, who seemed so well pleased he offered to say a Mass for him. Back in Belfast, a woman with a strong southern Irish accent telephoned. 'Is that Fitt?' she asked gruffly. 'What have you got to offer? I'm Frank Stagg's sister.' Fitt explained, but her only response was a string of filthy language. 'Keep your nose out,' she concluded. 'If my brother wants to die, keep your nose out.' Fitt was aghast: 'I had been trying to save a life, but the Provisionals clearly seemed prepared to ruthlessly sentence one of their own men to death, knowing that the effect would be greater than a boatload of rifles and gelignite.'

Towards the end of 1980, as the hunger strike escalated, the potential for disaster on a major scale was causing Fitt huge anxiety. Early in November, he called Ann and his five daughters together for an important family conference. 'If I was a shrewd politician,' he told them, 'I would keep my head down and say nothing. If I was a dishonest politician, I would support the prisoners and lead the inevitable protest marches through my West Belfast constituency to ensure my permanent popularity.' But he told them he could not live with himself, or his conscience, if he followed either of those dishonourable courses:

> I said I had decided to make an honest speech in the House of Commons in London condemning the Provisional IRA and the hunger strike and advising the British government to make no concessions whatever to the prisoners. I had walked behind the coffins of far too many victims of the Provisional IRA and other terrorists to do anything else. I impressed upon the family the consequences of what I was doing. I predicted it would lead to more attacks on our house in Belfast. I told Geraldine, our youngest daughter, who was then still at school in Belfast, that it could make life even more difficult for her. I speculated that it might even provoke the IRA into trying to shoot me. I realised that it could lead to my political defeat at the ballot box, when I was required to submit myself for re-election. But, despite all these potential consequences, the family unanimously and wholeheartedly supported what I intended to do.

Fitt felt so strongly about the situation that he went to the Deputy Speaker and tipped him off that he proposed to bend the rules and say something important about the hunger strike in a debate about Northern Ireland: 'I knew the time had come to break the straitjacket of Catholic tribal politics.'

Fitt made his speech and was still in London when the inevitable hostile reaction began. By telephone Ann told him that, almost as soon as he had finished speaking, stones and paint had been thrown at their house. A few nights later, as the condition of the hunger strikers began to deteriorate and doctors said they would soon die, the sound of the stones glancing off the brickwork and the paint tins squelching on the front door was overlaid with a different sound. As Fitt listened, with Ann and Geraldine, they heard the steady thump of tramping feet, shouts and the beating of a drum. Eventually there was silence, except for the drum. Every five seconds or so, one booming note rang out in the night. Fitt put out the lights in the front room and slipped open the curtain. Outside in the darkness was a large crowd, some holding flaming torches. In the flickering light he could pick out some familiar faces, neighbours and local people who had until then been among his staunchest political supporters:

> As I looked at this eerie vigil I was reminded of the Ku-Klux-Klan and it would be less than honest to say it did not have its intended effect on me. It was meant to intimidate and frighten. My entire political life, everything I had fought for, the injustices and hardship I had campaigned against, all ran vividly through my mind. That demonstration was a decisive turning point in my life as a politician and I knew then my opposition to the hunger strike marked the beginning of the end of my career in the House of Commons.

One of the faces in that torchlight vigil in December 1980 was a lady well-known to Fitt, a neighbour for many years and an enthusiastic election worker. The Sunday after the vigil he met her coming out of Mass in St Patrick's Church. She said she had taken part that night because her two grandsons were in prison, having been caught up in the terrorist net. 'I knew then,' said Fitt, 'that blood was indeed the strongest human bond and I felt relieved. I realised then it was the community that had changed, not me.'

With strong feelings being stimulated there was the usual surge of anonymous hate mail in Fitt's postbag as those promoting the hunger strike actively worked to stir up hatred and hostility towards him. An elaborate piece of graffiti was painted on a wall in the constituency: 'The Germans had Lord Haw-Haw. The Brits have Gerry Fitt.' He did not know whether to laugh or cry when a reporter from the *Sunday Times* told him she had encountered a toddler in Divis Flats rattling the bars of his cot and chanting, 'Gerry Fitt is a Brit.' The reaction to his bold stand was not entirely unfriendly, however. Of the 1,000-plus letters that poured into his home in Belfast and office in London, the overwhelming majority supported him. A common theme in many of the letters, some of which were anonymous, was fear of the IRA. No one felt they could disagree with the hunger strike in public.

One note struck Fitt particularly hard. The brother of a young Catholic who was a victim of the 'Shankill Butchers', the notorious Protestant murder gang who terrorised North Belfast in the late 1970s, said he would be appalled if the killers were granted political status. This letter reminded Fitt of a situation that had caused much heartache in his own family. About this time Betty was in her final year of nursing training and she had become very friendly with one of her patients, a woman who was suffering a total nervous breakdown. As the relationship developed, she would often ask Betty to sit and talk. During one conversation, Betty asked why she was so distressed. 'Sit there and I'll tell you,' said the patient. She had one daughter, 'the apple of my eye the way you are the apple of your parents' eyes'. One night her daughter had come home and announced she had found a boyfriend. Later, she said they wanted to marry. Her mother was very upset, but despite her opposition to the marriage she agreed to meet the boyfriend. Before long she fell for him and withdrew her objections to the wedding. Soon after they married the husband bought his wife a little dog as a present. It was entered in a dog show and won first prize. At this point in the story the woman dissolved into uncontrollable tears again. She told Betty how the couple had gone to the prize-giving for the dog show at the La Mon restaurant, where they had been burnt to death. The whole Fitt family eventually became friendly with this woman. Fitt often talked to her on the telephone and was very sensitive to the fact that the plight of such victims of the Troubles was being overshadowed and forgotten amidst the concern about the prisoners on hunger strike.

The atmosphere of crisis heightened throughout the following weeks as the physical conditions of the hunger strikers deteriorated. Then, on 18 December, when one of the hunger strikers was on the point of death, the fast ended abruptly on its fifty-third day. The Provisionals announced the 'blanket' and 'dirty' protests would be phased out in response to changes in the prison regime outlined in a new government policy document. The principal change was that the prison uniform would be replaced by civilian-type clothes for all prisoners in Northern Ireland. Welcoming the end of the hunger strike and the step back from the brink, Fitt said in Parliament that 'we had emerged from a period of crisis and it was not a time to be claiming victory or defeat'. The relief was not to last long, however. The settlement terms proved to be riddled with ambiguity, and before the end of January the prisoners were accusing the government of 'reneging'. On 27 January 1981 furniture and cells were smashed in a riot that involved ninety-six prisoners, and on 5 February a new hunger strike was announced. Commencing on 1 March, it would be led by Bobby Sands, who was serving fourteen years for possessing firearms and ammunition. It was around this time that Fitt had another sharp reminder of the way traditional allegiances were changing:

> A man and his wife, whom I remembered calling at my house previously, arrived on the doorstep. Their demands were in direct contrast with their views the first time they called. Then they had come seeking my help in getting information about a son who had been arrested by the police. I was able to tell them he was being questioned. The parents were insistent he had nothing to do with the IRA, that his arrest was a mistake. Indeed, they believed the IRA were a crowd of murdering thugs who had dragged the

name of Ireland in the gutter. Now their tune had changed. He had been convicted of offences and was in the Maze demanding political status. What was I going to do? After all, they insisted with some belligerence, he did what he did for his country and was entitled to be treated as a patriot. It was further evidence for me of the changes in the community, where previously opposed people were being drawn into the IRA's web by involvement of their children.

Fitt again feared the consequences should any of the prisoners starve themselves to death, as they were threatening to do. That, he knew, would create an even more dangerous situation and he was more anxious that usual to keep in touch with every development, particularly when he was in London. So, from there on 5 March, as he frequently did, he rang Ann just before the hour to hear one of the regular news broadcasts on Downtown, the local radio station. The main development was that Frank Maguire had collapsed and been taken to hospital. Less than an hour later Ann rang to say he had died. Fitt was devastated: 'I remember sitting at my desk in London, putting my hands over my head and saying, "Jesus Christ, what is this going to let us in for?"'

The by-election to fill Maguire's seat was set for 9 April and, as Fitt had feared, Bobby Sands was put up as a candidate for election, with his supporters resorting to skulduggery to ensure he was the sole candidate on the nationalist side. The SDLP nearly tore itself asunder deciding whether to put up a candidate or not, but in the end accepted Frank's brother, Noel Maguire, as the agreed candidate. Currie and Fitt were watching the situation very closely and Currie had completed nomination papers with the intention of slipping them in at the last minute if Maguire backed out, thus preventing Sands from having a clear run. Splitting the vote would mean handing the seat to the unionists, but at that stage, they agreed, even that unthinkable option was preferable to having a dying hunger striker as MP.

When nominations closed, Maguire and Sands were the candidates, standing in opposition to Harry West. But as soon as the deadline passed, the Provos immediately cornered Maguire in the upstairs room of a public house. There, by threatening to smear him as a homosexual, they forced him to withdraw his nomination papers, which was perfectly legal up to an hour after the close of nominations but by forcing Maguire's hand then, it was not possible for Currie, or anyone else, to nominate. In the subsequent straight fight between the two candidates, Sands beat West by 30,492 to 29,046 – a majority of 1,446. It was a 'disgusting' result in Fitt's opinion and, like many Protestants, he could not believe that so many Catholics would vote for a convicted gunman.

Community tensions soared sky-high as the the Provos fully exploited the countdown to the expected death of Bobby Sands. On 20 April three members of the European Parliament, all from the Irish Republic, were permitted to visit him in the Maze to try to seek a way out of the impasse. The Red Cross and other interested groups became involved, too. The Newry-born private secretary to the Pope, Father John Magee, flew from Rome and shuttled between the prison, where Sands was now in the infirmary, Stormont Castle, where he met with Atkins, and Cardinal Ó Fiaich's house in Armagh. Fitt watched what he called this 'bizarre pantomime' with mounting horror, wondering what had happened to the sentiments expressed so recently by the Pope. The entire situation was equally bewildering to Protestants, who saw the Church and Southern Irish politicians lined up solidly with the IRA. In early May, as the entire community waited for Sands to die, the tension was unbearable. Ann Fitt had been taken ill again and admitted to hospital, and Fitt blamed her condition on the months of threats and tensions over the hunger strikes:

> Hardly an hour went by, when I was in Belfast, without a nasty telephone call or a tin of paint of some other missile hitting the front or back of the house. The walls all over West Belfast were daubed with slogans and graffiti in support of the 'Rt Hon Bobby Sands MP'. It struck me as ironic that the Provos, with their hatred of Britain, should revel in glorifying him as a British MP.

Finally, in the early hours of 5 May, Sands died after sixty-six days without food. Fitt had sent Ann to England, so he was alone in the house when the news arrived, in a tip-off from a friend at Stormont Castle. Soon afterwards, as news of the death spread, the threatening calls began. 'Gerry, I'm an ex-internee from the New Lodge and I'm going to get you for Bobby,' said one of the first callers. 'Join the queue,' said Fitt, throwing the phone off the hook so he could get some sleep. By now he could hear the sound of rioting and other commotion outside, so he kept all the lights turned off. At dawn the road outside the house was littered with glass and bricks, the routine debris of a night's rioting, and the remains of a milk lorry were twisted around a lamp-post. He later heard that when rioters lobbed a concrete block at it, the lorry had run out of control, killing the milkman and his son. At the end of the road the police were lined up behind riot shields. As ever, there was gallows humour. Having run out of stones and other ammunition, the rioters looted a shop and the police then came under a fierce hail of bottles of brown sauce and tomato sauce. 'I think they're preparing to eat us,' said one of the beleaguered policemen. Not far away the rioters had broken into Cummings' shop. Buckets of stewed apples and trays of pastry were upended and urinated on, while stock in the shop was swept from the shelves and destroyed. There was no doubt the Cummings had been singled out because of their close friendship with the Fitts.

Inevitably, Sands' death overshadowed the local council elections on 20 May. Against the current background it was quite impossible for Fitt to fight the election in the customary way. Canvassing was out of the question because hostility to him was running so high. A friend warned him to stay away from a meeting in Clonard about housing, for example, because the Provos intended to abduct him, strip him and parade him through the area in a blanket. Another afternoon he was in a city-centre pub when a crowd gathered and began haranguing him about the hunger strike. 'They were in a nasty mood. My police bodyguard was very concerned, but after a few minutes we managed to talk our way out, helped by one of the crowd, a young fellow I knew, who cooled down a few of the hotter heads.' Determined not to allow the intimidators to claim total victory, Fitt stood in the election, content to fight on his record and accept the decision of the ballot box:

> At least that way the IRA could not call me a coward, but I was so sure I would lose I did not even attend the count in the City Hall. Instead I heard over the radio that I only got 514 votes and lost my city council seat, my first election defeat in seventeen contests over twenty-three years. Ann took the defeat very badly and although I tried to keep her in London, in a flat we had just rented as a bolthole, she insisted on coming back and staying with me in Belfast through what was an exceptionally turbulent summer. 'We've always been in this together,' she insisted.

By now, Fitt and his wife had almost decided to settle full-time in London and were spending less and less time in Belfast. 'It was the only way I could get her peace and preserve her health,' he said. All through the summer of 1981, as the house came under renewed siege and attack with the death of each successive hunger striker, they began to stealthily remove some of their most cherished possessions to the flat in London. 'We both feared the whole place would go up in smoke one night, but we could not be seen to be moving out for that would have provoked the very attack we feared.'

Sands had planned that there would be a succession of prisoners reaching death at progressive intervals and, on average, every fortnight through June, July and August the death of a hunger striker was announced, amounting to ten deaths in all. Sands' election agent, Owen Carron, held the Fermanagh seat at the subsequent by-election and two other hunger strikers were elected to the Dublin parliament during the general election in the South in June. All the time the two communities in the North were retreating behind ever more solid tribal walls. Thatcher's government had remained firm on its basic position throughout the summer – that there could be no special status – but the first cracks in the deadlock came in September when the relatives of the prisoners, prompted by Father Denis Faul, began to authorise medical help as soon as their loved ones lapsed into terminal comas. A face-saving formula was then cobbled together that gave all prisoners better conditions, including the right to wear their own clothes, and thus an uneasy truce came into force. Fitt noted with dismay that the prisoners had gained nothing more than what had been on offer long before Sands or the other prisoners died. Outside the prisons the community was in a state of angry turmoil, which reached virtual breaking point on Saturday, 14 November.

That morning Fitt was in his London office, writing letters and making phone calls, when his daughter Joan rang: "Daddy, Daddy, isn't that terrible news. They've shot Robert Bradford.' Bradford, the Official Unionist MP for South Belfast, had been holding a constituency surgery in Belfast when he was gunned down. His London office was just two doors along the corridor, so Fitt immediately walked there.

> The door was open and I found his desk was tidy, as he had left it only the previous Thursday afternoon. I sat down and looked over at the empty chair where he had been sitting then, talking to me, gossiping about Paisley and his other colleagues and telling me the sort of outrageous jokes you would not expect to hear from a clergyman. I could scarcely take in what had happened.

Back in Northern Ireland the Protestant community, whose tolerance had been stretched to extremes by the hunger strike, finally snapped. Protests about the killing took place all over Northern Ireland and, at the funeral, the new Ulster minister James Prior was hissed and booed and his security men had to push hard to get him away through the angry demonstrators:

> I had a lot of sympathy for Protestant feelings at that time. If the Catholic community had seen Protestant clergymen and politicians walking behind the coffins of a succession of UVF terrorists there would have been uproar and protest. It was hypocritical of Catholics to criticise the Protestants for their reaction to the hunger strikes, for the way the Church and community closed tribal ranks behind the hunger strike must have been deeply offensive and frightening. I was relieved to see the end of 1981, a bad year that could have been much worse. But despite the drawback from the brink the year left a terrible political legacy, for it was from that point on that the IRA also became a political force.

It was Prior who had to struggle with that legacy in the opening months of 1982. The SDLP's green wing was now moderate by comparison with the sort of people who had become prominent during the hunger strike, but the party took a pretty tough line as Prior outlined his plans for what he called 'rolling devolution'. This involved setting up an Assembly at Stormont that initially would have only advisory and scrutiny powers. As it proved its efficiency and the two sides demonstrated they could work together, then progressively real power would be devolved to it.

The unionists went through the motions of opposing it, but there was never any real possibility of them refusing to work the scheme. The SDLP, on the other hand, seemed to step back and let Sinn Féin make the running. They took an old-fashioned abstentionist position: they would fight for seats, but not take them, just as Sinn Féin had already committed themselves to doing. And in the same way that he conceived the idea of an alternative assembly in 1971, this time John Hume conjured up the idea of a New Ireland Forum in which Dublin would effectively say what was on offer in a united Ireland and all the other parties, ideally including the unionists and others from the North, would put forward their own views. Fitt responded by saying the forum would only provide a platform for a replay of the divisions of the civil war sixty years earlier. He told this to Prior and also said he feared there could be little movement within Northern Ireland. Prior pressed on with his initiative, nonetheless, and set 20 October as polling day. As the election for the latest Assembly drew nearer, Fitt was debating with himself the arguments for standing and not standing:

> I did not want the Provos to be able to claim they had frightened me out, but I was deeply concerned about Ann and frustrated at the political deadlock and community polarisation. I obtained a set of nomination papers and filled them out. On balance, at this stage, I planned to stand. But on the day before nominations closed Ann and I were listening to the early news on BBC when it was reported from Belfast that a young soldier had been killed in my constituency. Ann was terribly distressed. 'Gerry, you can't stop them doing things like that, you can't change them. They've all gone mad,' she said. That death and her views had a big effect on me but my mind was not fully made up. I left the flat and headed for my office. There I telephoned a few people in Northern Ireland and sought advice. In mid-morning I called Ann back and told her I had made my mind up not to stand. Then I rang Billy Flackes at the BBC in Belfast to tell him my decision. It would have been the same, I said, if it had been soldier, policeman, UDR member or innocent civilian. Politics would not work while there was violence. I felt powerless.

The election adequately demonstrated the new polarisation. Sinn Féin won five seats in the Assembly, and Fitt admitted to himself, for the first time, that he would have a hell of a struggle holding onto the West Belfast parliamentary seat when Margaret Thatcher eventually called the next general election:

> It was clear I had committed the unforgivable sin in Irish politics of breaking away from the tribal mould. However I had no regrets about the political plight I was in. It was a matter of conscience to me. All my life I had regarded violence as wrong. At this late hour of my career I was not going to change that conviction to save my political life. So through the early months of 1983 I waited patiently for the election to be called.

Ann and Fitt mainly stayed in London during this period, but every time they arrived back in Belfast and put the lights on in the house the local hooligans attacked. One evening in April they had just flown in and Fitt left Ann at the house before heading to the Europa Hotel to meet some journalists. 'But I was no sooner there when Ann phoned. I rushed home and found her gasping for breath after an unusually severe attack of asthma, triggered off by paint with strong fumes, being thrown at the front door.' Another evening he was in a pub when pictures appeared on the television showing an army bomb-disposal robot tackling a suspect device on the doorstep of his house.

It was with some relief, therefore, that he welcomed the announcement that the general election would take place on 9 June 1983. He was now fairly convinced that he would not be able to hold the seat and was resigned to moving to London so that Ann could be closer to their daughters and grandchildren. His last contribution in the Commons took place on the evening of 12 May, the eve of dissolution. The day had been given over to clearing up Northern Ireland business and although he did not admit it publicly, Fitt well knew that his remarks on the renewal of the Emergency Provisions Act amounted to his valedictory speech. He described an incident in his constituency only the previous week when, as a result of police vigilance, two vans were detected, one of which carried detonating equipment and the other a bomb, although the four people who were in the vans got away. The IRA subsequently issued a statement charging a priest in the constituency with informing the police that the bomb was in transit and warned that the priest should have considered what would have happened if the security forces had shot and killed the four men. Fitt said the priest was morally justified in taking that action to prevent the bomb being taken through the heavily populated area of West Belfast:

> The IRA did not consider for a moment what would have happened had that bomb reached its destination, or how many other people would have been killed. If IRA men are killed, the security forces are regarded as murderers. If the IRA carries out its continuing number of ruthless murders, that is regarded as a continuation of the armed struggle.

He went on to condemn those who gave 'support and succour to the most bloodthirsty murderers who have ever lived in Ireland' and said there was little difference between Provisional Sinn Féin and the IRA, whose membership was of a dual type and therefore would be soliciting votes for democratic election within the next few weeks. Fitt stressed that he did not have 'one second's sympathy' for terrorists and their awful practices in Northern Ireland and in Britain, but said he also opposed repressive legislation and had voted consistently against it: 'I am not too sure that any Honourable Member will accompany me into the lobby, but I shall attempt to divide the House. Whenever this legislation has come before the House I have voiced my objections, for many reasons. Today is the last chance I have to object and I shall be consistent. Even if I cannot gather support, I shall lodge my objection.'

When the division for the Emergency Provisions Act took place, together with Jock Stallard, another of his oldest Labour friends, Fitt acted as teller for the noes. The division went resoundingly against them, 62-0. Downstairs in the Strangers

Bar afterwards, the conversation was all about who would win and hold their seats and who was vulnerable. Fitt went out to the terrace, undoubtedly his favourite spot in the entire palace of Westminster, a place where he often stood watching the riverboats and the Thames itself. As he looked out over the water, he wondered what the future held for him.

For the first time the election in Northern Ireland was being fought on the seventeen-seat basis conceded by the Callaghan government. Although his West Belfast constituency seat was virtually unchanged, save for a few minor boundary alterations, Fitt was now thoroughly resigned to defeat. He knew that Gerry Adams, the Provisional Sinn Féin candidate, was riding on the crest of the political wave triggered off by the election of Sands and the emotional impact of the hunger strikes. Since then Sinn Féin – the political front for the IRA – had begun campaigning for power in Ireland with an Armalite in one hand and a ballot paper in the other. Fitt said the ballot paper he agreed with, but the Armalite was for those who didn't agree with them. To his intense disgust, Sinn Féin won five Assembly seats in 1982 and secured a 10% share of the overall vote, compared with some 18% support for the SDLP. Fitt could not fathom the rationale of voting for them, he could not understand why anyone would cast a vote for them given their republican pedigree and all the terrible acts that had been carried out in the name of that cause over recent years.

Whatever slim chance Fitt had of successfully defending the seat was fatally diminished by the SDLP's decision to put up a candidate against him. Dr Joe Hendron was a popular medical practitioner who was widely known in the area and would clearly attract significant support – which would otherwise have gone to Fitt. The intervention of his former party was a particularly hurtful act. Fitt believed that, as the sitting MP and with his long record of service, in the circumstances then prevailing the SDLP should not have nominated against him. Above all, he believed that by doing so, they were handing the seat to the IRA. As far as Fitt was concerned, Sinn Féin and the IRA were inextricably the same organisation. He regarded the party's decision as full justification for his view that the SDLP was indeed ambivalent when it came to condemning IRA violence, and that affirmed in his own mind that he was absolutely right to have left the party.

On previous occasions, Fitt had always feared losing his election contests, but his inner confidence always spurred him on. This time there was no real fight in him. Although he had little time for Enoch Powell, he did agree with him when he said that all political careers end in failure. Fitt was too shrewd a politician to fool himself that he could win again. He knew that the ever-changing political imperatives that had swung him into power in 1966 were now gathering to sweep him out again in 1983. For him the actual election contest thus became a combination of farewell parade and a defiant last-stand. Every time he ventured out in the city centre, he was surrounded by well-wishers. 'How I wished they had all lived in West Belfast,' he quipped.

> My days of fighting elections ended in a bizarre contrast to the way they had
> begun. Then I could never have ventured into Protestant areas. But in the
> days before the 1983 election, encouraged by messages of support from
> many Protestant constituents, I decided to demonstrate that I stood, as I
> always did, for peaceful, non-sectarian politics. The Provisional IRA had
> shot a man dead and wounded his wife in a Protestant area of Bangor. Then
> they issued an 'apology' for killing the wrong person. I was so disgusted I
> attended the funeral and outside the church I was surrounded by people
> who were pleased at my condemnation of violence. The people in the bars
> in the Shankill gave me a warm welcome and I had a job resisting the drinks
> they wanted to press on me. On the Falls, the scene of my previous
> triumphs, there was nothing but unremitting hostility. My posters were
> torn down as soon as they were put up and there were endless threats about
> what would happen to me if I went 'up the road'. Nevertheless a small band
> of loyal supporters stood by me throughout the campaign.

As had been the case with the council elections in 1981, these friends warned Fitt
not to expose himself to danger by going into the IRA-supporting parts of his
constituency. 'Whatever the risk to my own life, I did not want to take my police
bodyguards into situations where they would also be targets,' he said.

Fitt decided that, apart from posters, the centrepiece of his campaign would be
a full-page newspaper advertisement reproducing the entire contents page from
Hansard, which listed every parliamentary debate in which Fitt had spoken, all the
questions he had asked of ministers and detailed each of the motions and issues he
had raised or supported. (Before leaving Westminster, the librarians had helped
him compile the list.) 'My opponents make promises – my record stands', was the
heading. The other strand of his campaign was the customary election leaflet, but
there were serious doubts about the feasibility of delivering one to every house
after a contact told Fitt that the IRA had warned the postmen not to handle them.
Hearing of this difficulty, one of Fitt's closest supporters allowed his enthusiasm to
get the better of him. One evening, in the run-up to polling day, he arrived
breathlessly into the Europa hotel where Fitt was having a few gins. He had hired
a small plane, he told him, and early the next morning it would fly over West
Belfast, dropping the leaflets over the hostile areas. Fitt gently vetoed the idea.

The count took place in Belfast City Hall on 10 June 1983, the day after
polling:

> The place was buzzing with rumours when I got there with Ann in mid-
> morning. She had been up at dawn to go on the breakfast television shows
> with Eileen Paisley. The first rumour was that I had lost my deposit and
> Adams had won by a landslide. It was impossible to tell the position as the
> black metal ballot boxes were tipped open into basket trays and the votes
> were elastic-banded into bundles after being counted. So I wandered out

around the City Hall, chatting to friends and journalists, as the count went on. Eventually at lunchtime we were warned to stand by for the result and one of the officials pulled me to the side to tell me quietly I had been beaten.

The result was declared formally live on national television at 1.30pm. Adams topped the poll with 16,379 votes, a majority of 5,445 over Hendron, who came second. Fitt, standing as an Independent, got 10,326. As the combined total number of votes cast for the UUP (2,435) and DUP (2,399) was 4,834, Fitt concluded that something like half his vote must have come from his former Protestant constituents. Proving his non-sectarian credentials was, for Fitt, the most positive outcome and as he analysed the figures he said that if the SDLP had stayed out, as they should have done if their supposed contempt for Sinn Féin and what it represents as the Siamese twin of the IRA were genuine, then it would have been a different story. As if to underline Fitt's point, during his acceptance remarks Adams defended the murder of a British soldier, in what was now his constituency, earlier that very morning. For Fitt, this was the most revolting aspect of that disappointing day.

Just as Fitt had been in 1966 when he first won the seat, Adams was surrounded by police who pushed a path for him and his supporters through crowds of angry loyalists to get him out of City Hall. Fitt left quietly with his regular bodyguard and Ann, and went round to the Europa hotel where he did another series of radio and television interviews. It was not the landslide that had been predicted for Adams, and as Fitt heard from people involved in the count that his votes had indeed come half from Catholic West Belfast and half from Protestant areas, he considered that to be a moral victory and a more than satisfying political epitaph:

> I remembered what an old man on a bicycle had said to me at the front
> door one morning shortly before polling day. 'The Irish are a violent people
> and you turned too fast for them.'

Fitt and Ann stayed on in Belfast for a few days after the election to pay the bills and sort out the last of the constituency affairs, but there was still a constant stream of people coming to the door looking for his help. 'Look, Gerry's not an MP anymore,' said an exasperated Ann one morning. 'Go away over to Sinn Féin and see what they will do for you.' They returned to London on Saturday, July 2, looking forward to a restful summer break and time to take stock of the rest of their lives. For a man who listed full-time politics as his recreation, there was a lot to come to terms with:

> I had recently bought a little boat and moored it on the Thames and I was
> intending to sail up country along the rivers and canals, my favourite form
> of relaxation. But late on the Sunday night I got a call from the police in

Belfast telling me the house had been attacked again and this time, severely damaged by fire. I caught the first flight to Belfast the next morning. What I saw when I got there sickened and disgusted me. The wreckers had broken in at the back, opening a window above the security grille to get access. Then they systematically went through the house, smashing furniture, ripping out fittings and breaking up our family possessions. Some things were dragged out into the back yard and burned in a bonfire, the rest were burned in the flames started inside the house. As I walked from blackened room to room, inspecting the damage, I realised the house would never be home for us again. The damage was too bad. I was only glad Ann and the kids did not see it. I flew back to London that night utterly depressed. 'Terror will never drive me out of politics. I will never be intimidated into silence. This may be the end of my house, but it is not the end of Gerry Fitt,' I told the reporters before leaving.

The destruction of 85 Antrim Road and their family possessions hurt him and his family far more than was ever admitted in public. One of the most distressing features for Fitt was the sight of irreplaceable family photographs torn in pieces and thrown all over the floor. Virtually the only item left undamaged was the poster of Che Guevara on the wall in what had been Eileen's bedroom. Back in the mid-1970s Fitt had strenuously contested a vesting order to take over the house so that 350 old dwellings could be demolished and replaced by 200 modern homes. He had opposed the scheme and said he would go to any court in the land to protect his ownership of his home. In the end, after protracted litigation, he won the argument and it was proposed that the distinctive terrace should be preserved as one of architectural value. Not long after the July 1983 attack, however, the entire terrace was demolished and the planned redevelopment went ahead. Today the house number is assigned to one of the dwellings in a standard, Housing Executive, red-brick terrace; all traces of 'Fortress Fitt' have been removed.

Three weeks after his violent and traumatic expulsion from his home and heartland, Prime Minister Margaret Thatcher, who had been returned to power, with the agreement of the Labour opposition leader, Michael Foot, awarded Fitt a life peerage in the dissolution honours list. Foot had originally included Fitt on his list, but Thatcher insisted he should go on hers. Foot had in fact signalled the offer of a life peerage to Fitt shortly before the election. It was customary then for long-serving and distinguished back-benchers to be elevated to the House of Lords, or 'the other place', as it was described by parliamentarians. There, they could continue their political career until old age rendered them incapable. If Fitt had come from anywhere else other than Northern Ireland, the offer would have been unremarkable and been seen simply as due recognition of a career of public and political service. But among Catholics in Northern Ireland, British honours were taboo because of their perceived association with 'British Imperialism'. The SDLP's official position was that such awards endorsed the British state and the Royal family.

This left Fitt impaled on the horns of a dilemma when he was officially offered the life peerage after his election defeat. If he accepted, he knew he was laying himself open to criticism and even ridicule by his former political allies. On the other hand, what was he to do with the rest of his life? The only proper job he had ever had was as a merchant seaman and that was clearly out of the question for him now. He had no business experience so was unlikely to pick up the sort of lucrative directorships doled out to many ex-politicians. In any case, he knew he had neither the aptitude or skills for such work. He was a born politician, that was all he ever had done and it was the only thing at which he excelled. His family and closest friends advised him to accept the peerage and damn his critics, and that is exactly what he did. The moment he finally made up his mind was while standing in the ruins of Antrim Road, looking at the shreds of his wedding pictures. 'Bastard. Bastards. I'm going to the Lords,' he said to himself. His sense of humour had not deserted him, however. When he walked into one of the Westminster bars on his return to London, his first words were, 'I've just come from a house-warming.'

Once he had decided to accept the life peerage, he then had to choose a suitable title. He most wanted to be known as 'Lord Fitt of Dock in the city of Belfast', but the House of Lords authorities, whose interpretation of the Byzantine regulations is final, ruled out that suggestion. But they registered no objection to the title Lord Fitt of Bell's Hill in the County of Down, chosen because that is where the Fitt family was evacuated from Belfast during the war, and also where he and Ann had lived for a short period after they were first married.

When it was announced, the locals were somewhat mystified by the chosen title. It was unclear to them whether the proper spelling was Bellshill or Bell's Hill, as there was no townland of that name, only a Bellshill House, which had been first settled by the Hutton family who arrived in the area in 1690, about the same time as William of Orange. The neighbouring house where the Fitts actually lived was known as Toughlee, which by then was derelict and crumbling and fenced-off to keep the cows out. Mrs Fitt was remembered affectionately by the older locals, but her son less so because he lived there only for short periods between the various voyages he made as a merchant seaman. They did, however, recall him going to borrow books from and have a chat with Master Rea at Inch school during his brief spells at home. Ann Fitt also achieved public recognition in her own right when *Woman's Own* magazine commended her as one of their 'Women of the Year' at a lunch attended by Princess Anne. By then the couple had received some 7,000 letters of sympathy after the election defeat and the burning of the house.

Fitt was formally introduced into the House of Lords at the end of October 1983. His sponsors were Lord Scanlon and Lord Brockway, two longstanding socialist friends: Lord (Hugh) Scanlon of Davyhulme was a former British trade union leader; Lord (Fenner) Brockway was a life-long pacifist and campaigner for the cause of conscientious objection to warfare. Mindful of his antipathy to ceremonial and the ridicule his opponents would generate, he took great care that there were no pictures taken of him in the ermine-trimmed robes which were *de rigueur* for the occasion.

CHAPTER FOURTEEN

WHEN GOD SEES FITT

DURING THE SUMMER OF 1983, with their home in ruins, the Fitts decided to cut their lifelong links with Belfast and buy the modest basement flat they had been renting at 25 Vincent Square in London. The property, overlooking the playing fields of nearby Westminster school, was a ten-minute walk from the Houses of Parliament and a similar distance from the shops on Victoria Street and the mainline railway station. From there frequent trains ran to Ashford, in Kent, where Joan, Patsy and Betty had all settled after their marriages. At long last, Ann was able to be closer to the grandchildren she so cherished and she soon spent as much time in Ashford as she ever did in London. Eileen still worked at the BBC and lived in London, while Geraldine, the youngest, moved from Belfast to finish her college course. At that time she was going through what she now calls her 'punk phase' and one day, during the final months in Belfast, she was swollen with pride when she bumped into her father in the Europa and he insisted on buying drinks for all her exotically attired friends. 'Most dads would have disapproved and got offside, but not mine,' she recalled proudly.

Fitt made the occasional trip back to Belfast that summer to settle outstanding affairs and because he could not get his favourite 'brown (smoked) cod' in London, he brought back a supply each time. One morning in late September, while he was steaming a portion for breakfast, he heard a person moving about in the flat above his own. He knew that the person concerned was Harold McCusker, the Unionist MP for Upper Bann, but McCusker did not know that during his absence from London over the long parliamentary recess, Fitt had become his new neighbour. So when he went upstairs and knocked at the door, McCusker invited him in and immediately apologised for 'the awful fish smell. Somebody's moved in below me during the summer and they're steaming fish,' he said. He was quite embarrassed when Fitt told him he was the fish lover! Despite their political differences, they had been and remained on sociable terms and frequently walked together to and from parliament.

By now, Fitt had become something of an institution at Westminster and recent events had only served to enhance his popularity, reminding his colleagues that he was more than just a gregarious character but also a man of convincing courage. Everyone recognised him as he walked the corridors with his distinctive rolling gait and all he encountered were greeted with a broad smile and his unique 'Ah-ha', the all-purpose adage he also used to introduce himself in person or on the telephone. He was no respecter of rank or title and once said 'Ah-ha, Margaret' when introduced to the Queen's sister. The one time he was impressed was an evening when Margaret Thatcher, with whom he got on well personally but not politically, greeted him warmly and kissed him on the cheek. 'He was chuffed for days after that,' recalled Mick Skelton, then Principal Doorkeeper at the House of Lords.

Fitt had always prided himself on his socialism, but at Westminster he was more regarded as the most social of men. When he went into the bars to drink with his closest cronies, he would soon become the centre of attention and other groups would eavesdrop openly as he rattled off jokes, wisecracks, political gossip and ventilated his ideas about the events of the day. Not for him the fickleness of political correctness. He swore frequently, still called all the women he met 'love' and talked of 'darkies' and 'niggers' without prejudice, but in a way that had long since become impolite. His regular drinking partners were an eclectic bunch and included Des McCartan, the *Belfast Telegraph*'s man in London, Barry Porter, a Liverpool Conservative MP, and Anthony Beaumont-Darke, another Conservative and wealthy stockbroker who was well known for his willingness to give pithy quotes to newsmen about every conceivable topic under the sun. Fitt never had to order a drink for himself, merely gesture, as every member of the catering staff knew that he invariably drank a gin and tonic, without ice and lemon, and always insisted on a large one because the English measure, one-sixth of a gill, was notably shy of the quarter-gill customarily served in Northern Ireland. When Michael Jones, the *Sunday Times*' political correspondent, bumped into Fitt in any of the bars, he would always run away in mock horror crying, 'Irish measures, Irish measures', before downing one or two English ones himself.

With some justification, Fitt enjoyed a reputation as an epic drinker. He often said that the glass of gin that tipped him from sober to drunk was somewhere between the fifth and the fifteenth, but no matter how many times he tried he could not work out which one. He was emphatically not an alcoholic; he was a social drinker and indeed rarely drank at home. He was also something of a legend in his own lifetime and featured in many stories, usually exaggerated from a grain of truth, which were affectionately told and retold about him. There was the one about the New Scotland Yard bodyguard who had been warned by his predecessor that he would have to match Fitt gin for gin if he was to get on with him. The officer quailed at the prospect and arranged with various barmen that every time

a gin was ordered for Fitt, he would just get a straight tonic. When he went off
sick after a few weeks, his replacement told Fitt that the poor man was down with
quinine poisoning because of the excessive amount of tonic he had consumed.

On one occasion, when there were no seats left on the last flight of the day
from London to Belfast, his bodyguards persuaded the British Airways pilot to
take Fitt in the only available space: the jump-seat in the cockpit. When he
emerged through the cockpit door mid-flight to visit the lavatory, there, in the
front row, was an astonished Ian Paisley. 'Don't worry. I've left it on automatic
pilot,' he told his great political rival as he pushed past. Because of the affection in
which he was so widely held at Westminster, Fitt got away with things no one else
would have. For a time, he kept his modest cabin-cruiser alongside the
Metropolitan Police riverboats at their Westminster mooring. One day, just as he
set out on a trip along the Thames with a friend from Belfast and his police
bodyguard, Fitt discovered that, while there was plenty of gin on board, there was
no tonic. He promptly sailed under Westminster Bridge and pulled alongside the
terrace where the Lords and MPs socialised and asked somebody to get the barman
from the Strangers Bar to come out to the wall. When he did, Fitt ordered a dozen
tonic. A few moments later, when the order, in a brown paper bag, was being
reached down to him, the security alarms protecting parliament went off and
armed police came running from every direction. 'We've just run out of tonic,'
said Fitt, nonchalantly. 'Nothing to worry about.'

Fitt was also an inveterate gambler with a series of 'lucky' lottery numbers and
a penchant for interlocking bets, which involved a selection of three or four horses
and were often so complicated they were beyond the calculations of his son-in-law,
Benny Hall, who was a bookmaker. On one memorable occasion, after one of his
selections triumphed, the calculation was even beyond Fitt himself. After
struggling with the figures for several hours during the night, he finally rang his
friend, John Carmichael, at 6.00am and said, 'You're an accountant. You're good
with figures. Tell me how much I've won.' No day was complete without a flutter,
the horses he backed frequently tipped on the Westminster grapevine.

He was also exceedingly generous. In company he was not only the centre of
attention but the first to buy a round not only for his own company but others in
the bar with whom he was acquainted. This extended to the staff, too. In the Peer's
Guest Room there was a walk-in storage cupboard by the bar. Whenever Fitt was
present, he would arrange for a large scotch to be placed in the cupboard for the
doorkeepers to enjoy when they came in to deliver telephone messages, and he
would direct them to the cupboard on the pretext of carrying out a security check.
When other peers saw what was going on they followed suit, and Mick Skelton
recalls that after one such 'security check' a member of his staff, who had downed
four large drams, was 'rolling along the corridor like a snooker ball'. When Fitt
showed people around the Lords, the tour always ended in one, or frequently

more, of the bars and nobody was allowed to put their hand in their pocket. He was a generous tipper and when he encountered anyone who was down on their luck, he would surreptitiously slip them some money. On one occasion, when a family with young children got caught up in one of the most notorious incidents of the Troubles, Fitt flew to Belfast, drew £2,000 out of his bank account and quietly pressed it on the mother of the family when he called to sympathise.

After all his years in the Commons, Fitt was instantly at ease with the move from the green benches of the Commons to the red benches of the Lords. Ann sounded the only note of caution: 'Now that you're a Lord, it doesn't mean you have to get as drunk as one.' Many of his former political colleagues were already there, so he was not short of good company and, as an ex-MP, he was entitled to use the drinking places reserved for the members of the Commons, with which he was already familiar. His favourite and most frequented watering holes were the Staff Sports and Social Club and Norah's bar, another staff facility named after Norah Connor, its Irish-born manager. William Whitelaw found him an office close by the Lord Chancellor's Gate, which soon became known as 'Fitt's shebeen' because of the frequent revelry he hosted there. It was an exception for a peer to have an office, and Fitt took great delight in showing visitors the diminutive lockers assigned to Lords, with a lineage of hundreds of years, by contrast with his own accommodation complete with a desk, filing cabinet, bureau – which served as a cocktail cabinet – and comfortable three-seater sofa. The most important facility was the telephone, which he used extensively to maintain his network of friends and to deal with the problems that continued to be referred to him from people all over Northern Ireland.

In his own uniquely convivial way, Fitt quickly made a cadre of colourful new friends in the Lords. Among them was the seventh Earl of Munster, Tony Munster, who described himself, to Fitt's great amusement, as 'the last of the royal bastards', because King William IV had originally conferred the title on his eldest illegitimate son in 1831. Another associate was Patrick, the 9th Earl of Courtown, an Irish peer whose title was created in 1762 for James Stopford, who had represented Wexford and Fethard in the Irish House of Commons. Lord Rod Calverley was another regular companion. His title had originally been awarded to his grandfather, George Muff, in 1945 when he stepped down as Labour MP for Hull East after fourteen years. Rod Muff, then aged twenty-five, became the Third Baron Calverley of Bradford when his own father, an insurance executive and the Second Lord Calverley, died in 1971. By then Rod was serving as a West Yorkshire police officer and continued to do so until 1997, when he retired after thirty-three years with the force. He and Fitt hit it off because, from 1979, Muff had served a two-year secondment as a detective with the RUC, based at North Queen Street, Fitt's local station in Belfast. The Irish peer, Lord Kilbracken of Killegar, County Leitrim, who had been educated at Eton and Oxford, was another frequent companion and their conversations usually centred on matching memories of the Murmansk convoys. While Fitt was on board ship, squadron commander Kilbracken was a daring Swordfish fighter pilot with the British Fleet Air Arm, who was awarded the Distinguished Service Cross for his exploits.

One person always absent from the company was Fitt's old Stormont friend, Phelim O'Neill, who had now succeeded to his father's title and was the 2nd Lord Rathcavan. He had retired from active politics and farming in Co. Antrim some years earlier, moved to Co. Mayo and made a new home there with his second wife, Bridget. He and Fitt kept in touch by telephone, but he could never be persuaded to come over to London to the House of Lords:

> You know what would happen, Fitt. You and I would go round the bars and have a few G&Ts and then you would persuade me to make a rousing speech and I would, and by the time I got back home to Mayo again the place would have been burned down by rebels.

Later, after Phelim died in 1994, his son, Hugh O'Neill, inherited the title and became the third Baron Rathcavan. A former Irish Guards officer, financial journalist and later London restaurateur, he did attend the Lords and became another fixture in the Fitt circle until 1999, when all but ninety-two of the hundreds of hereditary peers were expelled from the House of Lords.

After the trials and tribulations of their years in Belfast, 1983 marked the beginning of what could be called the most contented years of Fitt's personal life. For the first time he enjoyed real financial well-being with his parliamentary pension and attendance fees from the Lords. He relished the new sense of security his peerage gave him. 'I will never have to fight another election,' he said with glee. Ann and he frequently went to the cinema together and he became surprisingly knowledgeable about the latest movies. They also enjoyed walking around the city together, especially on a Sunday. In his boat, and often with Ann, he began to explore the rivers and the canals along the Thames Valley, getting to know the lock-keepers and the regulars in many of the riverside pubs. One summer they made a long trip along the waterways, right up to the north of England and back. Whereas before they mainly confined their holidays to the Glens of Antrim, now they went further afield. For one summer break they travelled down to Cornwall, while another time they visited northern France. Fitt had become friendly with the Irish Guards because of the association with his brother, George, and he had been invited to their St Patrick's Day shamrock parades. The regiment was able to provide him with the location of George's grave and during their visit, for the first time, Fitt and Ann visited his final resting place in the St Charles de Percy Military Cemetery in Normandy.

There was another unforgettable holiday in Rome, during which they attended a Papal audience, this time with Angus Montagu, the twelfth Duke of Manchester, and his wife. Montagu inherited the title in 1985 when his brother died but the family estates and money, including once-prosperous holdings in Northern Ireland, had long since gone and the colourful twelfth Duke had been forced to work for a living, with spells as a Texas oilfield hand and a crocodile wrestler in Sydney on his impressive *curriculum vitae*. Ann Fitt was somewhat bemused to find out he had two previous wives, and Fitt himself was highly intrigued that he had recently been acquitted at the Old Bailey after the judge ruled that he was so 'absurdly stupid' he could not have played any part in a conspiracy to defraud the National Westminster Bank of £38,000 by using forged US bonds as security. They were very surprised when they heard, some years later, that the Duke had been imprisoned in the US for two-and-a-half years, after being convicted for his part in a fraudulent plot to take over a struggling Florida ice-hockey team.

Despite these activities and distractions, Fitt maintained an avid interest in Northern Ireland affairs and politics. Most days when the Lords was in session, he would visit the library and conceal copies of the *Irish Times* and *Belfast Telegraph*, under his jacket, to be taken home and read later. He would also obtain copies of *Hansard*, which he scrutinised closely for accounts of Northern Ireland debates. During the recess periods he would amble along the Vauxhall Bridge Road to Victoria, where he could obtain the Irish papers from a vendor who originally came from the Ardoyne area of Belfast. He found out that by ringing 8060, he could listen to the latest hourly Downtown Radio news bulletins, which he did when there were major incidents or political controversies engulfing Northern Ireland. Later he had cable television installed in the flat and, a confirmed insomniac, he revelled in the growth of the twenty-four-hour news channels and the continuous broadcasting of Parliament. He was also very keen on catching up with local Northern Ireland current affairs programmes, so his daughter, Eileen, who was now a senior member of the team running the BBC's flagship evening news bulletin, or friends in Belfast were prevailed upon to record programmes and send him the videotapes.

Fitt made his maiden speech in the House of Lords on 21 November 1983. The previous evening three church elders had been killed and seven members of the congregation wounded when gunmen burst into a Sunday service at the Pentecostal Church at Darkley, County Armagh, and opened fire indiscriminately with automatic weapons. The attack was claimed by the previously unknown Catholic Reaction Force (CRF), but there was no doubt that it was nothing more than a convenient *nom de guerre* for republican gunmen motivated not by patriotism but by sectarian hatred. Next afternoon, although the Lords was debating the Access to the Countryside (Northern Ireland) Order, when Fitt was called to speak at 3.14pm, he immediately turned his attention to the atrocity:

> I had hoped that, on the occasion of my maiden intervention in the House,
> I should have been able to exude some confidence or express some hope for

Northern Ireland in the future. However, the events of yesterday afternoon in County Armagh have determined otherwise. The happenings yesterday afternoon in a little church not far from the border in Northern Ireland will, I believe, have shocked and appalled every Member of this House. I myself, who have spent my lifetime in Northern Ireland, cannot yet fully understand what was the motivation of those who carried out such a brutal and callous murder of innocent people in a place of worship.

I had hoped last week that this Order could have been moved and debated in a non-controversial manner. It deals with access to the countryside. Northern Ireland has a beautiful countryside, but the actions of those men yesterday have desecrated and defiled the very soil of the island of Ireland both North and South and have brought nothing but shame and degradation to the name of Ireland. I know that I shall have the support of the whole House in expressing my sympathy to the relatives of those who were so cruelly cut adrift from their loved ones in Northern Ireland.

I remember most vividly my maiden intervention in another place in 1966. Again, it 'was to highlight the awful state of society as it then was in Northern Ireland.' Sadly, every day and every year has only led to an exacerbation of the awful situation as it then was. The events of yesterday, I believe, were deliberately calculated to provoke a religious civil war in Northern Ireland. I believe that that was the deliberate and calculated intention. I can only make an appeal to those who are the target of that provocation not to fall into the trap that has been set for them.

Focusing briefly on the subject of the debate, he said that 'on looking at the 56 articles, I personally, having been a city representative, cannot see anything dreadfully controversial, but it may be that some of the rural members from Northern Ireland will see something in this proposed legislation which I do not see'. He concluded:

I have risen to my feet this afternoon to speak on this Bill, but my real intention is to put on the record of this House the appalling tragedy which befell the people in Armagh last night and to emphasise the need for us, everyone in this House, to say to those who were responsible that, however devilish their deeds may be, they will not succeed in attaining their political aims.

Seven minutes later, Lord Underhill took the floor:

My Lords, I am certain that the whole House will have been pleased to hear the maiden speech of my noble friend Lord Fitt, and will be pleased that he is with us in this House. I am certain that he will bring to the House added sincerity and conviction on the issues of Northern Ireland. I am sure that the whole House will pay tribute to his courage and to his conviction. Knowing his views on political and social matters I feel certain that the House will wish to hear my noble friend not only on Northern Ireland issues but on other matters as well. We thank him for his contribution this afternoon.

Over the years thereafter, Fitt proved to be an assiduous attender and played a full part in the proceedings of the House. During the 2001 – 02 parliamentary session, for instance, he attended for 132 days and signed on for 159 and 164 days respectively in the following two sessions. He took a predictable interest in Northern Ireland legislation, but often voted on other issues. As always, he satirised the voting procedure. 'With all the old Lords hobbling in on their sticks, crutches and wheelchairs, it was like the geriatric Olympics,' he would say.

His political career was effectively ended when he lost the West Belfast seat in 1983 and thereafter he became an observer rather than a player in the landmark events that followed. In fact, from the outset of his time in the Lords, where he sat on the crossbenches, and as the tone of his maiden speech reflected, Fitt's political views became steadily more influenced by emotion, nostalgia and abiding pessimism. These values were reflected in his impassioned and consistent criticism of the continuing violence, as he condemned successive atrocities and expounded the weaknesses of the political reactions to them. Would there ever be peace in Ireland? a German television interviewer asked him one day. 'Only when God sees fit,' he replied with unconscious ambiguity.

Not surprisingly, Fitt greatly disapproved of the 1985 Anglo-Irish Agreement (AIA), which he believed was flawed because it was pushed through and implemented without any unionist involvement or consent. The Remembrance Sunday bombing at Enniskillen, when eleven people were murdered by the IRA, had shocked him deeply, but he was just as upset when, soon afterwards, John Hume initiated a series of discussions with Gerry Adams of Sinn Féin, aimed at persuading the IRA to call off its campaign of violence. Fitt shared this objective, of course, but he found it repugnant that the talks appeared to be giving credibility to people and organisations whose political standpoints were unmistakably rooted in violence. Undoubtedly there was at least some element of dented pride in the ferocity of his opposition. He had long been critical of Hume's strong nationalism and, apart from the links between Adams and the IRA, there was clearly a sense of hurt and resentment of the fact that both had played such a clear part in his own political downfall. Adams, in line with the republican policy of abstention, did not take his seat at Westminster, but Hume did, as MP for the new Foyle seat in 1983. When his and Fitt's paths crossed at Westminster, there was only a cordial greeting, although that did not occur too often as Hume was ill at ease in the London Parliament and much preferred the international buzz at the European Parliament.

As what became known as the 'peace process' unfolded ever more tortuously over the following years and resulted in unilateral republican and loyalist ceasefires in 1994, Fitt was plunged into almost permanent personal turmoil from a political point of view. On the one hand, he most certainly wanted an end to violence and the endless cycle of murder and destruction that had blighted life and politics in

Northern Ireland for as long as he had been an elected representative, but on the other hand he found it hard to accept the *bona fides* of notorious republicans, like Adams and Martin McGuiness, who came to increasing political prominence. The fact that many West Belfast people and others in Northern Ireland continued to write and telephone seeking Fitt's help with their problems compounded his sense of injustice. Adams, he believed, was failing many of his constituents by not taking his seat. He was almost equally outraged by what he saw as Hume giving Sinn Féin a helping hand at the expense of the SDLP, a feeling that gnawed away inside him for years and offended his concept of democracy. Indeed, he never could come to terms with the fact that the Catholic people seemed so easily to have forgotten the IRA's excesses and were prepared to vote for them in ever increasing numbers after their 1983 electoral breakthrough.

Fitt was no more forgiving when former loyalists stepped into the political arena and were rewarded with political legitimacy by becoming involved in the expansion of the protracted inter-party and inter-government talks begun on the instigation of Peter Brooke at the end of April 1991. When John Major and Tony Blair, who had replaced Major as Prime Minister after the 1997 general election, began to deal directly with Sinn Féin and they regularly trooped in and out of Downing Street for talks, Fitt was deeply perturbed on each occasion. 'Look at that, look at that,' he would say, pointing to the television with gushing disapproval. It tipped over into rage on 22 July 1996 when Major agreed to meet, for the first time, a joint delegation from the PUP and the UDP – the political fronts for the loyalist paramilitary groupings, the UVF and UDA. The overwhelming focus of Fitt's rage was that the deputation included John White, Paddy Wilson's murderer, who had finally confessed to the crime in 1978, and been sentenced to life imprisonment. He emerged as a political adviser for the UDA after his release in 1992. Fitt grew more angry by the hour as the time for the Major meeting approached, and friends had to physically restrain him from going to Downing Street to confront White and make his strong feelings known in person. That would have been an undignified spectacle and it would probably have backfired on Fitt.

As the moves to consolidate the ceasefires, secure the decommissioning of terrorist weapons and forge a lasting political settlement gathered pace throughout 1996 and 1997, Fitt remained gloomy about the prospects. At the beginning of November 1996, Ronnie Flanagan, soon to be chief constable of the RUC, chanced to meet Fitt and two Conservative politicians on a flight to London. Unlike Fitt, the two Conservatives were great admirers of Enoch Powell, the controversial British politician who had served for a time as Unionist MP for South Down, and enthused about how be brought his peerless powers of intellect and impeccable logic to bear on trying to solve the great problems of the day, like Northern Ireland. 'Logic. Logic?' spluttered Fitt. 'Sure tell me – what's the use of impeccable logic when you're dealing with two sets of illogical politicians in Northern Ireland?'

Fitt's scepticism was widely shared, but nonetheless the long drawn out political talks at Stormont finally concluded successfully on Good Friday 1998 when the far-reaching Belfast Agreement was concluded. Fitt had little time for Seamus Mallon, one of the SDLP MPs at Westminster, but he did appreciate his wry assessment that the deal was 'Sunningdale for slow learners'. A quarter of a century after the original agreement and some 2,350 violent deaths and countless other acts of terrorism later, both sides settled for a framework embodying the same basic principles – power-sharing and an Irish dimension – that Fitt had fought tenaciously to achieve and to defend. Although the deal received decisive endorsement in simultaneous referenda on both sides of the border and Fitt himself desperately wanted to see the process succeed, he feared in his heart that the tribal divisions in Northern Ireland, as he liked to describe them, were now even more deeply embedded than in his political heyday. His reservations were compounded by the early release of hundreds of terrorist prisoners from the Maze in a deal Fitt judged to be tantamount to an amnesty.

On 15 August 1998 twenty-eight people, including nine children, died in a no-warning car bomb explosion at Omagh. Fitt was so distressed he travelled to the town to sympathise with the bereaved and spent several days the following week attending many of the victims' funerals, Catholic and Protestant. He saw the bombing, carried out by a breakaway faction from the IRA, as a sign that the much-heralded Agreement was no more than yet another false dawn. When its implementation, in key respects, became entangled in distrust and prolonged difference between the parties, he became more and more negative. One provision to which he took serious public exception was the policing legislation arising from the Patten Commission report, which was established to study how the RUC could adapt from an era of conflict to meet the fresh challenges of a more conventional policing environment. In 1999 the Commission decided that, with the legacy of distrust among Catholics and a growing alienation from and hostility towards the force among many sections of the Protestant majority, a new beginning was necessary. The report made 175 recommendations for reform, including the renaming of the RUC to symbolise the fresh start.

Fitt spoke on the topic in the Lords on 8 November 2000 in a contribution that showed how wide the divergence had become between his views and prevailing nationalist opinion in Northern Ireland:

> I am a Catholic, as I keep repeating. But even my intervention in this debate will be grossly misconstrued by nationalist politicians in Northern Ireland. I recently made a speech on this Bill and the next morning I was the subject of nasty cartoons in the press. I was classified as a unionist. I was almost classified as anti-Catholic, because I supported the retention of the

name of the RUC. Perhaps my reason for supporting the retention of the name is a heart-over-mind matter. I am prepared to admit that that may be so. But I have carried the coffins of so many RUC men who were killed by terrorists, both loyalist and so-called IRA. I met their wives and children, and I know how deeply they feel that they are being humiliated and demonised by Sinn Féin/IRA ... I repeat – and, again, I received a headline in a nationalist newspaper for stating this – that, if it had not been for the RUC, Northern Ireland would have sunk into a pit of anarchy. However much I may be abused for repeating it, I shall do so. Who is to deny that, without the courage and resolution of the Northern Ireland police force throughout these terrible thirty years, civilisation as we know it in Northern Ireland would have gone by the board?

Fitt continued by pointing out that 'by removing the alienation of one community, we alienate the other', and he then referred back to letters published in nationalist newspapers after a previous speech on the subject:

'Does he forget that the RUC hit him over the head with a baton when he was leading a civil rights march on 5th October 1968?' I do not forget that at all. I thought it very wrong of the RUC to attack me and others when I was engaged in demanding civil rights for everyone in Northern Ireland, Catholics and Protestants. But it is thirty years since that happened. Many changes have taken place in the RUC over that period. I believe that the RUC, as presently constructed, together with these reforms when they are implemented, will turn out to be a totally different force from what it was under unionist domination over many years. By rejecting the name, we shall offend many, many people in Northern Ireland [but] it will not bring support from that section of the community which has been so opposed to it over the past thirty years.

In the Lords, as recently as May 2004, Fitt continued to paint a picture of Northern Ireland in anarchic terms: 'The people of Northern Ireland are living in a maelstrom of paramilitary activity, with the resulting murders, executions and knee-cappings that are taking place.' There was, of course, complete justification for this remark, which mirrored the continuing dark side of life in his native land. However, it also reflected his remoteness from his roots and his unwillingness to recognise the great social and economic resurgence that had flowed from the peace process. It was as if all of his perceptions had been frozen in the late 1980s and he did not want them to thaw.

Virtually all of his speeches in the Lords over the years had been sparked by the consideration of Northern Ireland-related legislation and concentrated on security and political matters, but he did continue to take an interest in other humanitarian issues brought to his attention and, from time to time, when he thought it would help, he would raise them in the House. One such instance was in June 2001, when he received a letter from a parent in Belfast who explained that her small daughter was suffering from juvenile arthritis:

> What she said in the letter really affected me. I jumped on a plane next morning and met the parent. Having spoken to her, I became personally and passionately involved in an issue – post-code medicine – that had never affected me throughout the whole of my political life. What I found out is in total contradiction to every idea of the National Health Service as we know it.

Through contacting the hospital where she was being treated, Fitt quickly learned that they had some seventy-five other patients in the same condition of pain and distress and that the consultants treating them were dismayed that they were unable to prescribe two new drugs, Etanercept and Infliximab. These drugs had absolutely no side-effects, were available freely in England and the Republic of Ireland, and had already been in use in the USA for five years. Fitt argued:

> The reason this drug has not been used in Northern Ireland as in other parts of the United Kingdom is that it is expensive: the cost per year is between £6,000 and £7,000. If one sees, as I have, the terrible consequences of this disease, that would be a very small price to pay to alleviate the suffering.

He described how the family of one female patient, who felt she could no longer bear the immense pain of the condition, were clubbing together to see if they could raise the finance to enable her to get the new drug. 'The consultant, to whom I have spoken, says that undoubtedly if this patient is given the drug it will help deal with the complaint.' Fitt also told of a young man, aged about twenty-one, who was unable to work with computers after developing arthritis: 'He was put on a waiting list and was told that it would be a year before he could receive any treatment. His family went around and collected £6,000 among themselves. The drug was given to the young man and there was a great improvement. I shall not try to say that it was a miraculous cure, but he is back working now because he received that drug.'

Fitt hit out at the government for not prescribing the drug simply because of its cost and said that money should not be the determining factor where people are suffering from a grievous illness:

> Since speaking to the mother I have become involved. I rushed out to phone the Minister of Health in the Northern Ireland Parliament who is a member of Sinn Féin. It is well known from the years that I have been in your Lordships' House that politically I do not have anything to do with Sinn Féin. However, I let my misgivings go because I wanted to speak to the Minister about the terrible case about which I had just heard. She was on and off the phone or somewhere else. Perhaps she did not want to speak to me as I am an opponent of her political party. My attitude in this case was determined by humanity, not politics.

For some time afterwards Fitt persisted with this cause and his efforts helped kick-start a campaign, but it would be two years more before the drugs were made generally available, and then only for patients with severe rheumatoid arthritis who had failed to respond to existing drug therapies.

The episode was entirely typical of Fitt, whose own health had long troubled him. Indeed, the long-suffered effects of his ulcer and heart problems frequently landed him in hospital, such interludes usually being brought on by the strain of the relentless pace he set himself and the highly animated way in which he reacted to events. Although he maintained an air of indifference, he was an incorrigibly superstitious, emotional man and a worrier. When there was any sort of calamity, big or small, he would usually respond by putting his hands on his head and crying out, 'Jesus Christ, Jesus Christ, that's it', or by groaning, 'What's going to happen now?' On one occasion, before setting out to meet Ted Heath in London, he said he could not go because the little pouch of talismans he always carried, in what he invariably called 'my arse pocket', was missing. His wife and daughters searched the entire Antrim Road house and he agreed to depart only after they discovered the pouch, which had fallen inside one of his shoes in his bedroom. Naturally enough, he refused to accept the conventional medical wisdom that smoking and drinking also took their toll on his health. In 1986, three years after his elevation to the Lords, his heart reached crisis point and he had to undergo a quadruple bypass, which was performed by the world-renowned cardiac specilist Magdi Yacoub. The operation gave Fitt a completely new lease of life and did not curb his enjoyment of gin and tonic.

He suffered a heavy emotional blow on 13 August 1989 when eighty-eight-year-old Mary Ann Fitt, the woman he uncompromisingly regarded as his real mother, died and was buried at Loughinisland, Co. Down. As he helped carry her coffin from the church after the requiem mass, he was visibly emotional. For some years previously, after enduring the stressful collateral effects of living next door to 'Fortress Fitt', Mary Ann had lived with Betty in nearby Downpatrick. She was intensely proud of all that her adopted son had achieved and disapproved of only one thing: his tendency to use what she called 'sailor talk'. Whenever he was on radio or television, she sat with her Rosary beads and prayed he would not swear.

By far the greatest personal and emotional blow he ever endured came on 23 January 1996, when his beloved Ann died at the age of seventy-four. The previous June, Fitt had accompanied her on what both thought would be a routine visit to her doctor. She was generally in good health for her age, although still plagued by periodic asthma attacks, as she had been for many years. After examining her, the doctor suggested changing her medication from cortisone to one with fewer side effects and said he wanted her to go into hospital for a few days to make the transition. She looked at Fitt and he nodded approval. A few days later he took her by taxi to the Chelsea & Westminster Hospital, where she was admitted to the Nell Gwynne ward. As he later recalled:

> That evening my wife was walking up and down the ward and talking to all our daughters on the telephone. She was in the same good form the next day, but when I went to see her for the third time, there was a big commotion going on at the far end of the ward where they had put screens around a lady. Ann told me she had heard something about a bug called MRSA. I had never heard of it and did not know what it meant, but I put my hands to my head when she told me and said, 'Jesus, Ann, if there's a bug in this hospital you're going to get it.' The next morning when I went to the hospital I was given rubber gloves and a rubber apron to wear because Ann had got MRSA and was in a side ward. After that when any members of the family visited they were also given aprons and gloves to wear in the ward. When hospital staff brought food, they pushed it in on to the bedside table and left as quickly as possible. It was the way you imagined lepers would be treated. I could see Ann wasn't going to survive and she knew it as well.

When the end came, Ann was surrounded by Fitt and the rest of her family. Her eleven grandchildren (a twelfth had born a few days earlier), of whom she was so proud, played a prominent role in the requiem mass at St Teresa of Avila Church in Ashford. Afterwards she was buried in nearby Godmersham, at the parish church of St Laurence, which dates back to the twelfth century. The churchyard is bordered by the River Great Stour and overlooks the Ashford to Canterbury road. A regular worshipper there in the late 1700s was the novelist Jane Austen, whose family lived in the vicinity.

Fitt was utterly devastated by Ann's death. He had recorded the depth of his regard for her in a will he had dictated in hospital just before his own bypass operation in August 1986. Bequeathing his estate to 'my dear wife Ann' he said:

> In making this [provision] I am conscious of how inadequate any material gesture could be in the face of her constant love, devotion and loyalty in our life together. Words can never express adequately my love and devotion for her.

His grief knew no bounds. When one of her uncancelled premium bonds yielded a £100 prize soon after her death, he bought £100 worth of red roses and laid them on her grave. The cheque was never cashed. It went instead into his little pouch of keepsakes and talismans alongside some of her earliest love letters to him when he was at sea. Barely a month after her death he went back to the spot at Hyde Park Corner where they had met on their first date in February 1947. For many years afterwards they had re-enacted that first date, and each time he again bought chocolates and nylons for her. This time, for the first time, he was alone, and the gifts were given to his daughters. The following Easter, when the Lords was in recess, he travelled over to Belfast and asked a friend to take him on a sentimental journey to the Glens of Antrim, where he had shared so many happy times with Ann. During the trip he went to Murlough Bay and along the steep, narrow lane that winds down through the wooded slopes to the remote, rocky shore. Halfway there was a house they had rented for holidays and, at the bottom, close to a white-painted former fisherman's cottage, he located the tree where, many years earlier, they had carved their initials into the trunk. Later, in Ballycastle, Fitt discovered that the cottage was owned by the National Trust and was available to rent. By the time the Lords rose for the long summer recess, he had negotiated a tenancy and at every opportunity thereafter he would retreat to Murlough where, in the final, lonely years of his life, he found both great contentment and consolation as his long romance with north Antrim and the sea was rekindled. Even in winter he relished the rugged natural beauty of the spot, with its views across the water to the Scottish coast.

Much as he enjoyed the isolation, he ensured there was a regular lifeline should he need it. Every day while he was in residence, he had instructed Geraldine to post him a card from London to ensure the postman would come all the way down to the cottage. Back along this link, he would pass his bets for the bookie in Ballycastle, receive his (frequent) winnings and often hitch a lift into the town for a drink and to stock up with food and newspapers. He would get a taxi back again. Most Sundays, one of the McCarry family, whose farm was at the top of the hill, would come down and fetch him for Mass at Ballyvoy. Davy Patterson, his police bodyguard, also acted well beyond the call of duty, for the ninety-minute journey to and from the airport would often take much longer. On a visit he made, Mick Skelton remembers it taking them seven hours to travel from the airport to Murlough because Fitt insisted on calling to visit pubs and see a series of friends along the way.

Fitt's yearning for Ann never ceased and every time he went to or passed Ballyvoy church, he threatened to have her exhumed and reburied there in a spot he favoured. He confessed to close friends that, before she died, they had made a pact never to be apart and promised one another that whichever of them died first would come back and comfort the other. Sometimes in the still of the night at Murlough, when his grief became unbearable, he would call out to her to keep her promise and come back to him. The inevitable silence sorely tested his deep Catholic faith and he would suffer doubt and distress that he would never again see Ann, but then as the dawn of the new day rose spectacularly up over the Mull of Kintyre, he would brighten up and re-affirm his customary faith and total confidence that one day they would indeed be reunited in Heaven.

Soon after Ann's death, Fitt learned that the super-bug that had killed her was known as methicillin resistant staphylococcus aureus (MRSA), that it was the result of cross-infection and that it was rampant in many hospitals. Such was the general concern about its life-threatening capability that it came up for debate in the Lords on 4 November 1996. Of the many speeches he made during his parliamentary career, none was as heartfelt or heavy with emotion as Fitt's contribution to that debate, made soon after 6.30pm that evening:

> MRSA is a real danger to people in this country and all over the world. It has been said that the problem is out of control because antibiotics have been so freely available. They have been used in an indiscriminate way so that the bacteria themselves have become used to them and the infection cannot be treated. I believe that it is the duty of the Government to use all means in their power to find a way to remedy the awful effects of MRSA.

He went on to describe, in graphic detail, the course of events that followed after Ann was first admitted to hospital and taken seriously ill. After deciding that 'MRSA was killing [his] wife', he said he had taken her to Kent by private ambulance:

> On the day I took my wife out of the hospital, the consultant said to me: 'By the way, your wife is very weak.' He did not have to tell me. I could see it at every second. He said that MRSA had created such devastation that she would never again be able to deal with an attack of 'flu. He said that if she ever caught 'flu, she would not be able to combat it. However, in Kent I and my daughters stayed with her every second of every day. We began to build her up. She still had MRSA when she left hospital. She was still taking vancomycin. On 4 January this year she had to go back to the Brompton hospital for a test. There they said that she had made remarkable progress and that she should return to the hospital in June. When I took her back to Kent, she asked me for the loan of my handkerchief and said, 'Gerry, I've got the flu.' That was exactly what had been predicted by the consultant. So devastating had been the effect of MRSA that she caught flu and within a week she had died. I should say that, although I have criticisms in relation to what happened to my wife, and will have until the day I die ... there was nothing the [hospital] staff could have done to prevent the terrible onslaught of MRSA in my wife's case. I look upon this debate on MRSA as a matter that is very personal to me. I do not want the same to happen to anyone else. Had it not been for the fact that I took my wife to hospital for an attack of asthma, whereupon she contracted MRSA, I should have been celebrating my forty-ninth wedding anniversary tomorrow.

As he uttered those last words, his voice was trembling with emotion and as he sat down he was on the verge of tears. The following year he flew to Belfast for what would have been their fiftieth wedding anniversary and on that morning attended Mass in the church at Crossgar, where he and Ann had married.

Fitt and his family suffered another untimely death in July 1997. That month, Joan's husband, Vincent Hanna, had agreed to stand in as host of BBC Radio Ulster's daily 'Talkback' programme while David Dunseith, the regular presenter, was on holiday. One afternoon, after the programme, Hanna and Joan drove from Belfast to Murlough where they spent the afternoon with Fitt before returning to their temporarily rented flat in Belfast. Almost as soon as they arrived there, Hanna suffered a massive heart attack and died. Fitt never had much time for Hanna's father, Frank, who was both a solicitor and a Labour MP at Stormont, and he had been somewhat perturbed when the son came wooing his eldest daughter. Ultimately, he came to terms with the relationship, gave it his blessing and came to value Hanna as a son-in-law. Within a few hours of his death, Fitt arrived in Belfast to support Joan, but after suffering severe chest pains he was rushed to hospital where he was detained for treatment for several days. Unable to attend Hanna's funeral, Eileen's husband, Paul Gibbs, a television executive, read a tribute on Fitt's behalf.

He made a swift recovery on that occasion, but ended up in hospital in Belfast again in February 2000. This time the trouble started at Murlough, during an afternoon spent cutting logs with one of his grandsons, Jack. After feeling more and more unwell over the following few days, he finally sought medical advice and was rushed to the Royal Victoria Hospital in Belfast to be treated for an arrhythmic heartbeat. 'My heart was racing and taking off without me,' he said. It was decided that he should receive electric shock treatment to regularise his heartbeat, a prospect that caused him to send for Joan so that he could tell her what to do in the event he didn't make it through the procedure. As Ann had predeceased him and he was reluctant to make another will in case it tempted providence, Joan was instead given details of a number of bank accounts. Some hours later, Joan and his other daughters were present when he came back from the operating theatre. His hair was standing on end from the effect of the electricity and he was still slightly groggy from the anaesthetic. 'Am I through it and am I alright?' he asked.

'Fine, Daddy. You're going to be okay,' they all assured him.

'Well, see all that stuff about bank accounts. Forget it. You never heard any of it,' he said.

Almost exactly a year after that episode, Fitt celebrated his seventy-fifth birthday with a family party in London. He was again in good health and spirits and told the *Irish News* that he checked their obituary column everyday 'to make sure I'm not included'. He had also become notably more self-reliant. For some time after Ann's death, Norah Connor at the House of Lords had dragooned him into one of the canteens to make sure that he had a good hot meal every day. More recently, thanks to Geraldine's influence, he had learned to use a microwave oven and when she came up from Ashford to visit him she would lay in a supply of ready-meals for him to eat. He still travelled over to Murlough as often as possible, but while the Lords was in session he spent most weekends in Ashford with his daughters and grandchildren. They adored him and were well used to coping with his ways. Eilish

Hall recalls how he would ask: 'Would you like a cup of tea, Eilish?' and when she said yes he would say, 'Well, make one for me when you're at it.'

Accompanying his daughters to the supermarket also became something of a ceremony. All would be invited to come at the same time and he would shuttle them round, encouraging them to fill their trolleys. Then he would line them up at the checkout and pay for all three loads. Patsy thinks the gesture was important to him as a throwback to his own childhood: 'He knew only too well what it was like to be both poor and hungry, and I suppose it was his way of making sure we were not.' From time to time he would slip £50 notes to some of his older grandchildren. Geraldine Millner recalls the performance it caused whenever she used the money to go shopping. 'Big notes like that are quite rare, so when you handed it over the shop assistants would be holding it up to the light and calling for supervisors. It was really quite embarrassing.'

Despite his advancing years and inevitable bodily decline, Fitt remained physically strong and as mentally sharp, alert and articulate as ever, although he became prone to a certain hypochondria. One morning, after passing what seemed to be blood-red urine, he rang one of his two nurse daughters for an opinion. He was advised to go and see his doctor at once, but a short time later he called back to say the problem had been resolved. When he went into the kitchen he had found an empty beetroot jar and then remembered he had opened and consumed the entire contents late the previous evening when he had returned home from the Lords. He still walked from the flat to Westminster, but more slowly now and invariably took a taxi home.

His quick wit and sense of mischief remained undimmed. When he was at Murlough he was frequently recognised by other visitors to the beauty spot. Often they would boost his ego by recalling how in the past he had got their parents a house, or performed some other helpful service. Many of these people were offered his hospitality and plied with tea or gin, or sometimes both. One summer morning at 7.00am or so, as Mick Skelton recalls, they were sitting outside when a young woman, clad only in underwear that had become transparent in the water, clambered from the sea over the rocks and approached them. Fitt rushed to get her a towel and when he noticed she was shivering, insisted she have a medicinal gin to warm her up. A short time later her friends arrived in a car to collect her, and they too were offered a gin. 'We were all merrily drunk and singing our heads off by 10.00am,' Skelton recalled.

Fitt liked to chop logs and, as Mick Skelton also remembered, one day when he was doing so a group of tourists halted at the gate. 'This is the cottage of Lord Fitt,' said one. 'You can see his manservant is busy chopping wood, ready for his return.' Fitt invited them in for tea and during conversation they asked what sort of an employer His Lordship was. 'Oh, he's a right bastard,' said Fitt. 'Works me into the ground for a pittance'. Only later did they learn who he was.

Fitt also liked to play, or more accurately scrape, his violin while in the privacy of Murlough. When another passer-by he was entertaining turned out to be a professional and accomplished player, he persuaded her to play down the telephone line while he tried to convince several of his daughters that practice had at long last made him the perfect player.

Early in 2005 came the first sign that Fitt's long and eventful seventy-nine-year-old life was drawing to a close. In December 2004 a gang removed £26 million from the vaults of the Northern Bank in Belfast and the IRA, none too convincingly as far as many were concerned, denied its involvement. Two months later, at the end of January, there was a brutal murder in Belfast. Referring to both incidents on 22 February when the Lords was discussing the renewal of the Prevention of Terrorism legislation, Fitt returned to the theme of his long-held hostility towards the IRA and expressed as depressing an opinion on the prospects of a durable political agreement as he had ever done:

> My Lords, there cannot be anyone in your Lordships' House or in the House of Commons who can feel any degree of optimism about the present situation in Northern Ireland. Let us analyse what has brought this about. It was the enormity of the money stolen from the Northern Bank coinciding with the brutal murder of the young IRA man. We have been here before. That was one murder of a young IRA man, but one must think of the scores of IRA men and others whose bodies were found just on the border area of Armagh over many years carried out by the IRA. There was not the same talk about governments wielding sanctions against it. The last time I spoke in this House, someone told me later that I was expressing the view that I did not see any hope for Northern Ireland. I have no intention of changing my opinion of what has happened over the past two or three weeks. I hear from the government in the Republic and from the Government here that the only way we can have a restored devolved government in Northern Ireland is by inclusivity. If you insist on inclusivity, meaning bringing the IRA and Sinn Féin back into Northern Ireland, you are bringing about a further exclusion of the majority of people in Northern Ireland. I cannot see the members of the Unionist party, at any time in the future, under any circumstances, in any year, being willing to sit down with Gerry Adams and Martin McGuinness, who have been quite aptly described as members of the army council of the IRA. If the Government insist on bringing Sinn Féin back into the fold ... they will be excluding at least two of the major parties in Northern Ireland. To insist on such a development will ensure that there will not be restored devolution in Northern Ireland. I put it to the Government that now is the time to take a stand against Sinn Féin and to say that under no circumstances will it be permitted to take part in a devolved government if that means the exclusion of the other political parties. The Government will have to live with the realities of the situation as it presently exists.

Later the same day he made another short speech, commenting on the Electoral Registration Bill, but some hours on, before the vote was taken at the conclusion of the day's business, Fitt rose to his feet again shortly before 10.00pm:

> My Lords, I wish to make a personal statement. Earlier today I inadvertently stated that the murder of Robert McCartney in Belfast was the murder of a young IRA man. What I had intended to say was that it was the IRA murder of a young man. I apologise to the House. I was of course talking about the IRA and the murders it has committed of innocent people.

Robert McCartney had died in hospital on 31 January, the morning after he had suffered multiple stab wounds in a fight in a crowded Belfast bar and was left unconscious on the street outside. The case became notorious because IRA members were both present and involved, but after the incident their associates prevented the police or an ambulance being called, warned witnesses to remain silent, destroyed security cameras and cleaned up the bar with bleach to destroy forensic evidence. It was entirely uncharacteristic of Fitt to make such a slip but it occurred during what turned out to be his very last speeches in parliament. A couple of weeks later he began to complain of severe pains in his back, which he attributed to injuring himself while getting into a taxi one evening outside the Lords. When the pains did not clear up, he went to his doctor and, after further tests, it was discovered he had actually suffered quite a serious heart attack. Indeed, they were amazed it had not laid him low at the time. After a short period in hospital he was allowed home.

By this point, Tony Blair had called a general election and parliament was suspended awaiting the outcome. When it resumed on 12 May and Fitt turned up to sign on again, those who had not seen him for weeks were stunned by how much he had failed. He had become painfully thin, his face was gaunt and there was only a faint glimmer of his trademark smile and sparkling eyes. He played no further part in the proceedings of the Lords. Within days he was back in hospital, in Chelsea, and by the end of June his doctors had decided that his heart had deteriorated so far that further repair surgery was impossible. Soon afterwards, knowing that the end was nigh, Fitt insisted on being discharged and went back to his flat in Vincent Square to await death. Although even more failed and weak, his mind remained completely alert and he was at ease with the imminence of his demise. 'The only thing that bothers me is that Paisley is going to outlive me,' he joked. They had been born within days of each other in 1926, causing Mary Ann Fitt to remark later that 'the divil had been busy that week'.

Fitt was, however, a demanding patient for his daughters, who came up from Ashford in turn to care for him for forty-eight-hour periods. Sleeping only fitfully and for brief spells, he listened to some of his own cassette tapes, watched television, read papers, telephoned friends and received a stream of callers. He put on a brave face for them and repeatedly said how much he yearned to get back to Murlough before the end of the summer. On 7 July two of his daughters got caught up in the turmoil following the suicide bombings that killed fifty-six people in London. Fearful of more attacks and disruption, and with no spare bed in the small London flat for them to rest, they came up with the idea of moving Fitt to Ashford, where the ordeal of looking after him could be shared more easily and where his grandchildren could come and visit. While arrangements were being made for the move, to which he consented enthusiastically, he asked to go to the Lords one last time and chose the day of the summer recess, 21 July, for what he knew would be his final visit to Westminster.

That morning, accompanied by Geradine, he struggled into a taxi for the short journey. When he got there he went out onto the terrace where he had so often held court and watched the boats on the river. He recalled how he used to wave a glass at the tourists on the sightseeing boats and shout: 'It's all free, you know.' His reminiscences were suddenly interrupted when the security alarms sounded and everybody was instructed to evacuate the terrace and go inside the building. There the police told them to stand back from the windows and that all doors in the building were being locked and sealed. Word went round that another terrorist attack on the London transport system had been detected and that a number of would-be suicide bombers had been arrested. There was renewed turmoil and the public transport system had inevitably ground to a halt. With no taxis available, Mick Skelton managed to get a wheelchair and Geraldine and Martin Shaw, who worked in the House of Lords as a researcher, were able to wheel Fitt home. Fitt joked that it was the first time he had ever been carried out of the building – drunk or sober.

He was eventually driven from Vincent Square to the flat in Ashford on 10 August, but he was very weak and although his condition deteriorated steadily after his arrival, he continued to talk to close friends on the telephone until a few hours before he died, peacefully, at 12.55pm on 26 August, with his five beloved daughters around him. His body was brought back to Westminster Cathedral in London, where Father Michael Seed celebrated a funeral Mass on 31 August. Standing on his coffin was a wreath from his five daughters inscribed: 'Dad, you taught us that all men were equal, but you were a cut above the rest.' Inside was a box of chocolates and a pair of nylons for Ann. In a eulogy, Austin Currie said that 'a hatred of injustice was the fire in Gerry's belly. It was not flags or borders or seeking after power.' As his coffin was taken from the church afterwards, it was led by Pipe Major Roy Allan of the Irish Guards, who played a traditional lament.

Later that day, in the sunny afternoon tranquility of the churchyard at Godmersham, Fitt was laid to rest alongside his beloved Ann. As his coffin was lowered into the grave, his daughters threw on top of it handfuls of soil brought in a box from Murlough by John Carmichael. Close by, in a final salute, Eleanor

McEvoy, a friend of the family, played the haunting notes of 'Danny Boy' on her violin.

Fitt's passing prompted a surge of fulsome tributes and assessments of his life and achievements poured in from prominent figures in both Ireland and Britain. Dr Sean Brady, the Catholic Primate of All-Ireland and Archbishop of Armagh, said,

> Gerry Fitt played a vital role at a critical stage in the search for justice and civil rights in our society. Always a courageous opponent of violence, he served people from all sections of the community at no small sacrifice to himself. The Catholic community, in particular, owes him a great debt of gratitude. He has left a positive and lasting mark on our history.

Dr Robin Eames, the Church of Ireland primate and Archbishop of Armagh, said: 'Gerry Fitt was the most courageous politician I have ever come across in Northern Ireland.'

Mark Durkan, who had succeeded Hume as SDLP leader, said:

> Gerry Fitt was a key figure in the civil rights movement and in the political life of the North for many years. As MP for West Belfast, he broke down the wall of indifference that British Ministers and Westminster has previously shown towards Northern Ireland. He was instrumental in founding the SDLP on the principles of non-violence, partnership and equality and in bringing about the Sunningdale Agreement, with its core features of power-sharing, a strong all-Ireland dimension and human rights. The tragedy for him and everyone else was that Sunningdale was opposed and brought down by intransigent unionism and violent republicanism. While he was a great character and good company, Gerry Fitt should be remembered, above all, as someone who cared very deeply about the people.

The SDLP's deputy leader, Dr Alasdair McDonnell, MP for South Belfast, said:

> I feel that Gerry Fitt has left those of my generation a tremendous legacy. In the politically dismal early 1960s, Gerry stood up for decency, honesty and integrity. Before the foundation of the SDLP he often had to stand alone. He lit a torch for civil rights, and the image of a battered and bloodied MP on 5 October 1968 exposed the then cesspit of Northern Ireland politics to a world stage. I believe that Gerry deserves a massive share of the credit for the advances we have made over the last thirty-five years.

By contrast, the words of his great adversary, John Hume, were clumsy and clearly disingenuous:

> Gerry was a great human being, he was a very humorous man, but also a very committed man. We always regretted when the break between himself and ourselves took place. It came to our surprise and we regretted that very much, but in his early days we strongly supported what he did because he

was very strongly in the Civil Rights Movement and strongly campaigning for Civil Rights. He was the first MP from Northern Ireland to be allowed to even raise the Northern Ireland problem in the House of Commons. Gerry's political legacy really was that he was down-to-earth, working-class, totally involved in trying to improve the living standards of his people.

Danny Kennedy, deputy leader of the UUP, said that Fitt

will always be respected and remembered for his consistent and resolute opposition to the Provisional movement and their terrorist campaign, which ultimately resulted in the loss of his Westminster seat. As a parliamentarian many unionists will always remember him for his opposition, in the House of Lords, to the changing of the RUC's name. He was a passionate defender of the socially and economically disadvantaged and made a lasting contribution to the political landscape in Northern Ireland.

Lord Kilclooney, the former John Taylor, said, 'Gerry was a wonderful character. Some politicians you cannot trust, but with Gerry you could always trust him.' Ian Paisley merely issued a message of sympathy: 'I am very sorry to hear of the passing of Gerry Fitt. I offer my sincere sympathies to his family circle and his friends at this time.' Peter Hain, the Northern Ireland Secretary, said Fitt was 'a true democrat, grounded in his working-class roots. He always championed the rights of the most vulnerable in society and often at great personal cost to himself and family.' Bertie Ahern, Prime Minister of the Irish Republic, said:

During a long and brave career in the wider labour movement and as a public representative he made a very significant contribution to constitutional politics and civil rights in Northern Ireland. Through turbulent times at the height of the Troubles, he provided leadership to constitutional nationalists and an example to people of every creed. He was a man who practised the message of moderation and tolerance that he courageously preached. He was often in the front line of the Troubles and he experienced violence at first hand from both sides of the divide in the North. He was an excellent parliamentarian and a passionate speaker and he delivered many compelling speeches in both Houses of Parliament at Westminster. He had a deep-seated commitment to equality and basic fair play, that stemmed from his strong socialist beliefs. Above all he abhorred sectarianism and violence. In the ongoing quest for a peaceful settlement and constitutional politics in the North, history will record that he played his part by word, by deed and by example. Gerry Fitt with his late wife Ann and their children, gave selfless public service to their community and to politics on these islands.

On behalf of his critics, Danny Morrison, once a prominent member of Sinn Féin who was involved in the 1981 hunger strike, said Fitt had taken Margaret

Thatcher's side against them: 'He was pro-British and was guilty of hypocrisy. He was a cheerleader for the British and he deserted his roots. He took the Queen's shilling.' Paul Butler, a former prisoner who had become the Sinn Féin leader on Lisburn City Council, said: 'He was no friend of republicanism and I think his opposition to the hunger strikers led to his political demise. His legacy was one of bitterness. He still tried to fight republicanism instead of fighting the real cause of the conflict, which was the British in Ireland and partition.'

During his political lifetime, Fitt respected the right of people to criticise or hold conflicting views about him, but when his opposition to violence was questioned he was rigorously uncompromising and strongly defended his reputation. Indeed, several libel wins handsomely contributed to the £658,321 estate he left on his death. Now, freed from the risk of further legal action, some of his detractors restated assertions they had signally failed to prove during his lifetime. The allegations were based on unverifiable recollections by individuals, remarks taken selectively out of context or highly ambiguous quotations. Fitt was an emotional man who spoke impulsively and from the heart and, by his own admission, prone to oratorical excesses on occasion. However, woven into the record of his political life is an unequivocal and consistently repeated opposition to the use of violence to achieve political ends. That was the pole star in his moral and political compass and the one issue on which he was determined never to be misrepresented.

Although a requiem mass had been celebrated in the Crossgar Church, where he was married, at the same time as his funeral in London, Fitt's daughters wanted to have his death marked at home in Belfast. After discussion, they decided that rather than having a conventional memorial service, especially in a Catholic church, which would necessarily have discouraged many from other faiths attending, they would ask to use Belfast City Hall for a celebration of his life. As a neutral venue, they hoped people from both sides of the deeply divided community would feel comfortable about coming to celebrate his life.

On 23 September the City Council determined that it would be inappropriate to accede to the request. The decision, taken by a committee of the council, was widely criticised and soon afterwards reconsidered. In a face-saving formula it was agreed that 'the criteria for the use of the City Hall be amended to include provision for the holding of a secular non-denominational service in memory of Members or ex-Members of the Council who have served on the Council for three or more terms and accordingly that the application submitted on behalf of the family of Lord Fitt be approved.' Even then the decision was only approved by a vote of 42 – 6 in favour. The event was scheduled for 25 November, but before it took place Joan Fitt took ill at her home in Kent and died suddenly on 27 October. It was found that she had been suffering from untreated heart disease. Therefore, some two months after her father's death, she too was laid to rest in

Godmersham, alongside Fitt, her mother and her husband, Vincent Hanna. With the four surviving daughters plunged further into grief, the memorial event was postponed.

The celebration of Lord Gerry Fitt's life finally took place on 10 March 2006 and was attended by over 300 people. They came from every strata and standpoint in Northern Ireland life and ranged all the way from people who had been connected with the IRA in the past to a Duke and several peers of the realm. Lord Laird, who had known Fitt for forty years, said it was a remarkable turnout: 'Nobody else but Gerry could have done it.' The choir from Hazelwood Integrated College – Fitt had cut the first sod for their building some years earlier – performed a song in his honour entitled 'Peace', but the event ended with all joining Eugene McEldowney in a rousing version of what had become his lasting political anthem: 'They're voting for Fittsie down Sandy Row way.'

INDEX